Private Law and Human Rights

Private Law and Human Rights

Bringing Rights Home in Scotland and South Africa

Edited by Elspeth Reid and Daniel Visser

EDINBURGH
University Press

Edinburgh University Press Ltd
22 George Square, Edinburgh EH8 9LF
www.euppublishing.com

Typeset in 10/12pt Goudy Old Style by
Servis Filmsetting Ltd, Stockport, Cheshire, and
printed and bound in Great Britain by
CPI Group (UK) Ltd, Croydon CR0 4YY

A CIP record for this book is available from the British Library

ISBN 978 0 7486 8417 5 (hardback)
ISBN 978 0 7486 8418 2 (webready PDF)
ISBN 978 0 7486 8419 9 (epub)

Contents

Preface

This volume had its origins in conferences hosted by the School of Law of the University of Edinburgh and the Faculty of Law of the University of Cape Town in June 2010 and June 2011 respectively. We wish to express our thanks to both institutions, as well as to the Edinburgh Legal Education Trust and the South African National Research Foundation, for their generous support of these events.

The law is stated as at 31 December 2011 but it has been possible in some instances to take account of subsequent cases and developments.

Elspeth Reid
University of Edinburgh

Daniel Visser
University of Cape Town

Contributors

Ross Gilbert Anderson is Lecturer in Corporate and Financial Law at the University of Glasgow.

Jaco Barnard-Naudé is Professor in the Department of Private Law at the University of Cape Town.

John Blackie is Emeritus Professor of Law at the University of Strathclyde.

F D J Brand is Judge of the Supreme Court of Appeal of South Africa, and Extraordinary Professor of Private Law at the University of the Free State.

Jonathan Burchell is Professor of Law at the University of Cape Town.

David Cabrelli is Senior Lecturer in Commercial Law at the University of Edinburgh.

François du Bois is Professor of Law at the University of Leicester.

Anton Fagan is W P Schreiner Professor of Law at the University of Cape Town.

Loretta Feris is Professor of Law, Institute of Marine and Environmental Law at the University of Cape Town.

Sheldon Laing is an Associate, Davis, Polk and Wardwell, New York.

Max Loubser is Professor Emeritus and Research Associate at the University of Stellenbosch.

David Carey Miller is Emeritus Professor of Property Law at the University of Aberdeen.

J M Milo is Associate Professor, Molengraaff Institute of Private Law at Utrecht University.

Hanri Mostert is Professor of Law at the University of Cape Town and Visiting Professor in the Department of Private and Notarial Law, Groningen Centre for Law and Governance, Rijksuniversiteit, Groningen.

Roderick R M Paisley is Professor of Commercial Property Law at the University of Aberdeen, Scotland.

J T Pretorius is an Attorney, Professor of Law in the Department of

Mercantile Law, College of Law, at the University of South Africa, and Life Member of Clare Hall, University of Cambridge.

Elspeth Reid is Professor of Scottish Private Law at the University of Edinburgh.

Andrew J M Steven is Senior Lecturer in Law at the University of Edinburgh, and Scottish Law Commissioner.

Elaine E Sutherland is Professor of Child and Family Law at The Law School, University of Stirling, Scotland, and Professor of Law at Lewis and Clark Law School, Portland, Oregon.

Daniel Visser is Deputy Vice-Chancellor and Professor of Law at the University of Cape Town.

Peter Webster is a Solicitor (Scotland).

The late **John Gibson**, who sadly passed away during 2012, was Professor of Marine Law at the Institute of Marine and Environmental Law at the University of Cape Town.

Table of Cases

Table of Statutes

Chapter 1

Introduction

Elspeth Reid and Daniel Visser

1.1 THE STARTING POINT

The distinctiveness of mixed legal systems has long been recognised,[1] but in the twenty-first century this 'extended family',[2] sharing the dual legacy of civil law and common law, has acquired a new self-awareness, marked by the publication of numerous volumes of comparative scholarship,[3] the formation of a World Society of Mixed Jurisdiction Jurists,[4] and the hosting of numerous international conferences.[5] A parallel development has been the emergence of various bilateral studies.[6] In particular the private laws of Scotland and South Africa have provided a fruitful basis for discussion, and their many points of similarity have already been examined at length.[7] As observed by Reinhard Zimmermann, these are jurisdictions where 'legal history and modern legal doctrine have not categorically been "thought apart" and where the "vital connection" between the past and the present is thus particularly evident'.[8] Neither system has ever codified its private law, and in both systems the jurists of the seventeenth to the early nineteenth

---

[1] For a history see K Reid 'The Idea of Mixed Legal Systems' (2003) 78 Tulane LR 5.

[2] V V Palmer (ed) *Mixed Jurisdictions Worldwide* 2e (Cambridge University Press 2012) 3. The family includes South Africa, Scotland, Louisiana, Quebec, Puerto Rico, the Philippines, Botswana, Malta, Sri Lanka, Israel and others around the world.

[3] Notably Palmer *Mixed Jurisdictions*, note 1 supra, as well as the first edition of this work, V V Palmer (ed) *Mixed Jurisdictions Worldwide* (Cambridge University Press 2001); see also E Örücü (ed) *Mixed Legal Systems at New Frontiers* (Wildy, Simmonds and Hill 2010).

[4] Founded in 2002: see *http://www.mixedjurisdiction.org/*.

[5] E.g. the World Society of Mixed Jurisdiction Jurists has held major conferences in New Orleans (2002), Edinburgh (2005), Stellenbosch (2009), Jerusalem (2011) and Valletta (2012).

[6] E.g. R Zimmermann, D Visser and K Reid (eds) *Mixed Legal Systems in Comparative Perspective: Property and Obligations in Scotland and South Africa* (Oxford University Press 2004); V Palmer and E Reid (eds) *Mixed Jurisdictions Compared: Private Law in Louisiana and Scotland* (Edinburgh University Press 2009).

[7] For a detailed comparison of historical background, see R Zimmermann, '"Double Cross": Comparing Scots and South African Law' in Zimmermann et al, *Mixed Legal Systems in Comparative Perspective*, note 6 supra, 1.

[8] Zimmermann, 'Double Cross', note 7 supra, at 4.

centuries (who are recognised as 'Institutional' and whose writings follow the civilian tradition) have been highly significant in the development of each country's private law.[9] At the same time, both have been shaped to a very considerable extent by common-law influences, Scotland since the Union of the Scots and English Parliaments in 1707, and South Africa since the Cape Colony was taken over by the British in 1806.[10] In both Scotland and South Africa, civil procedure is much closer to the English than continental European models, judicial decisions are regarded as a source of law, and the doctrine of precedent is applied. Civilian principle remains important, but to the extent that it is embedded in case law, it is increasingly developed by applying common-law forms of reasoning.

While these shared features have so far provided a fruitful basis for detailed comparative study of modern private law in Scotland and South Africa, important issues now arise as to the future direction of such projects. The enactment of the new Constitution of the Republic of South Africa and of the Scotland Act 1998[11] and the UK Human Rights Act 1998 has compelled actors within these legal systems to take account of the human-rights standards imported thereby. Human-rights values, traditionally articulated largely within the terminology of public law, must now be translated into the domain of private-law regulation. Does this new shared imperative increase the utility of bilateral comparative study, or are the differences between these respective human-rights documents so profound as to cause the paths of private law in the two systems to diverge? This book takes as its starting point earlier work presented in collections such as *Mixed Legal Systems in Comparative Perspective*, edited by Zimmermann, Visser and Reid and published in 2004,[12] but it also goes on to assess the impact of human-rights considerations upon the intricate pattern of similarity and difference traced therein. The topics chosen reflect the broad spectrum of private law. The engagement of fundamental rights in some of the areas under review, such as defamation or land law, has already received detailed consideration in the courts and academic literature. To others, little consideration has as yet been given, but as the author of the chapter on commercial law reminds us, 'private lawyers who think that fundamental rights

---

[9]   On Scotland see T D Fergus and G Maher 'Sources of law' in T B Smith et al (eds) *The Laws of Scotland: Stair Memorial Encyclopaedia* vol 22 (Butterworths 1987) paras 532–538. For South Africa see E Fagan 'Roman-Dutch Law in its South African Historical Context' in R Zimmermann and D Visser (eds) *Southern Cross: Civil Law and Common Law in South Africa* (Oxford University Press 1996) 33.

[10] See H J Erasmus 'The History of the Rule-making Power of the Supreme Court of South Africa' 1991 (108) *SALJ* 476.

[11] The Scotland Act 1998 provided for the creation in 1999 of a separate Parliament in Edinburgh with devolved competence to legislate on a wide range of subject matter including most of private law (s 29).

[12] R Zimmermann et al *Mixed Legal Systems in Comparative Perspective*, note 6 supra.

can be excluded or ignored are guilty of wilful blindness rather than wishful thinking'.[13]

1.2 'CONSTITUTIONAL MOMENTS' CONTRASTED

The differences between the 'constitutional moments' in the two jurisdictions under review are very obvious. The European Convention on Human Rights (ECHR) rose from the ashes of the Second World War, largely as a reaction to human rights abuses that had been at their most egregious beyond British shores. While British lawyers were active in the drafting process, and the British courts have exerted an important influence upon the way in which the Convention evolves,[14] there is a perception at the highest level that the European Court of Human Rights (ECtHR) remains a 'foreign court'.[15] The United Kingdom was one of the first signatories to the ECHR when it ratified the Convention on 8 March 1951.[16] However, when it finally gave effect to the Convention rights[17] in its domestic law on 2 October 2000, by means of the Human Rights Act 1998 (HRA),[18] the impetus to 'bring rights home'[19] was prosaic in nature – UK litigants would thus be enabled to enforce their Convention rights in the UK courts, rather than having to incur the delay and expense of taking their cases to Strasbourg, and there would be the added advantage of increased interchange between the UK courts and the ECtHR.[20] To the extent that the 'values' expressed by the ECHR were

---

[13] Section 14.12 infra.

[14] See N Bratza 'Britain should be Defending European Justice, Not Attacking it' *The Independent* 24 January 2012.

[15] See, e.g., the British prime minister, David Cameron, responding in Parliament to a question from the floor whether he would 'succumb to the diktat from the European Court of Human Rights in relation to prisoners voting': 'The short answer to that is yes. I have always believed that when someone is sent to prison they lose certain rights, and one of those rights is the right to vote. Crucially, I believe that it should be a matter for Parliament to decide, not a foreign court. Parliament has made its decision, and I completely agree with it': Hansard: HC Deb 23 May 2012, col 1127.

[16] The ECHR was signed on 4 November 1950. Updated text at *http://www.echr.coe.int.*.

[17] HRA, s 3. For an explanation of the term 'Convention rights' and its definition in the HRA s 1, see R Reed and J Murdoch *A Guide to Human Rights Law in Scotland* 3e (Tottel 2011) para 1.29. These are the rights and fundamental freedoms set out in (a) Articles 2 to 12 and 14 of the Convention; Articles 1 to 3 of the First Protocol; (b) Articles 1 to 3 of the First Protocol; and (c) Article 1 of the Thirteenth Protocol. (The content of ECHR Articles 1 and 13 is dealt with by the HRA itself.)

[18] Shortly before, the Scotland Act 1998 had already determined the competence of the new devolved Scottish Parliament so as to exclude legislation incompatible with the Convention (s 29(1)(d)) and from the time of its formation in May 1999 required the Scottish Government to act compatibly with the Convention (s 57).

[19] According to Lord Irvine of Lairg, the then Lord Chancellor, Hansard, HL Deb 3 November 1997, col 1228, echoing the Labour Party's 1997 manifesto pledge, and see also *Rights Brought Home: The Human Rights Bill* Cm 3782, 1997.

[20] *Rights Brought Home*, note 19 supra, para. 1.18.

regarded as having 'deep roots in our national history and culture',[21] this
initiative was not accompanied by any profound social or political reform
agenda.

As Alastair Price has observed, the HRA was largely 'a *consolidating*
rather than an aspirational instrument'.[22] By contrast, the comprehensive
Bill of Rights that lies at the heart of the Constitution of the Republic of
South Africa[23] has had a key role as an instrument of transformation in the
post-apartheid legal order. One of its perceived strengths is the inclusive and
transparent process by which it came into being, 'hammered out within the
country in the course of long and detailed negotiations between political
parties, attended by considerable public debate'.[24] This broad-based support
has made it less susceptible to controversies of the sort levelled at the application of Convention rights in terms of the UK Human Rights Act, which
some would wish to replace with a 'home-grown' British Bill of Rights.[25]

There is, moreover, a significant age gap between the ECHR and the Bill of
Rights. Although the ECHR is to be interpreted as a dynamic 'living instrument', capable of adapting to changing conditions,[26] the relative youth of
the South African Bill of Rights, half a century more recent, means that it is
considerably more comprehensive, dealing squarely with important social
and economic rights which are absent from, or only indirectly protected
by, the ECHR, including most notably free-standing rights to dignity[27] and
equality.[28] The chapters which follow demonstrate that in certain key areas,
including the rights of children,[29] the general right not to suffer unfair discrimination[30] and the right to a clean environment,[31] such express provisions
have sustained a significantly more rapid reform process, as compared with
the more guarded incremental approach adopted by the UK courts.

---

[21] Lord Hoffmann 'The Universality of Human Rights' (2009) 125 *Law Quarterly Review* 416 at 422.
[22] 'The Influence of Human Rights on Private Common Law' (2012) 129 SALJ 330 at 265.
[23] S 7. The Interim Constitution that came into force on 27 April 1994 incorporated a com-prehensive Bill of Rights, as does the Final Constitution by which it was replaced it on 4 February 1997.
[24] S Kentridge 'Parliamentary Supremacy and the Judiciary under a Bill of Rights: Some Lessons from the Commonwealth' 1997 *Public Law* 96 at 100.
[25] For discussion see H Fenwick 'The Human Rights Act or a British Bill of Rights: Creating a Down-grading Recalibration of Rights against the Counter-terror Backdrop?' 2012 *Public Law* 468; C Gearty 'The Human Rights Act – An Academic Sceptic Changes his Mind but not his Heart' (2010) *European Human Rights Law Review* 582.
[26] See *Tyrer v United Kingdom* (1979–80) 2 EHRR 1.
[27] Article 9.
[28] Article 10.
[29] See discussion in paras 4.2 and 4.7 infra.
[30] See discussion in para 9.3.4 infra.
[31] See discussion in section 20.7 infra.

1.3 CONSTITUTIONAL STRUCTURES

The HRA and the Scotland Act 1998, which provided for the establishment of a devolved Scottish Parliament in 1999, are regarded as 'essential elements of the architecture of the modern United Kingdom'.[32] The HRA requires all primary and subordinate legislation in the United Kingdom to be read and given effect in a way that is compatible with the Convention rights. The Scottish Parliament, to which legislative power on most matters of private law is devolved,[33] cannot competently enact legislation that is incompatible with Convention rights,[34] so that any new Scottish legislation found to be in this category is quite simply not law.[35] At the same time, the principle of parliamentary sovereignty is retained to the extent that legislation which emanates from the Westminster Parliament and which is found to be incompatible with these rights cannot be ruled invalid with immediate effect; a court may make a 'declaration of incompatibility' but the offending provision remains effective until amended by the legislature.[36]

While there is no doubting the profound changes achieved, there has been no 'constitutional revolution' comparable to that experienced in South Africa.[37] The South African Constitution is 'supreme law', so that 'law or conduct inconsistent with it is invalid, and the obligations imposed by it must be fulfilled'.[38] Its Bill of Rights binds the legislature, the executive, the judiciary and all organs of state,[39] and any law or conduct found to be unconstitutional must be declared invalid by a court asked to adjudicate upon it.[40] In both jurisdictions the division of powers between the legislature and the judiciary has been altered in important ways, but the shift towards the latter in South Africa has been more marked, significantly broadening the scope of judicial review, as well as introducing a wide range of positive obligations to which all actors in the legal system must now adhere.

It is further important to understand the interaction between European and national authorities. Although section 2 of the Human Rights Act 1998 provides that domestic courts determining questions arising in connection with Convention rights must 'take into account' any judgment, decision or

---

[32] *Somerville v Scottish Ministers* 2008 SC (HL) 45 per Lord Mance at para 169.
[33] See note 11 supra.
[34] Scotland Act 1998 s 29(1)-(2).
[35] For a recent (unsuccessful) attempt to have legislation declared beyond the competence of the Scottish Parliament see *AXA General Insurance Ltd and others v HM Advocate* [2011] UKSC 46; 2012 SC (UKSC) 122; [2012] 1 AC 868.
[36] HRA s 4.
[37] L Ackerman 'The Legal Nature of the South African Constitutional Revolution 2004 *New Zealand Law Review* 633.
[38] S 2.
[39] S 8(1).
[40] S 172.

declaration or advisory opinion of the ECtHR, it does not stipulate they are
bound by such decisions. While in the absence of special circumstances the
courts will almost certainly follow 'any clear and constant jurisprudence'[41]
of the ECtHR, it is also essential to consider how this jurisprudence has
been mediated through the domestic courts. Strasbourg jurisprudence is
undoubtedly a primary point of reference in interpreting Convention rights,
but at the same time, the position of the ECtHR in relation to the Scottish
legal system is hardly comparable with that of the Constitutional Court
within South Africa. The ECHR provides a set of minimum acceptable
standards for the protection of human rights, but unlike in South Africa
where the Constitutional Court is the ultimate authority, it is accepted that
there is no 'uniform European conception of morals',[42] and accordingly
the choice of mechanisms and substantive law frameworks to realise these
standards is left to national authorities.[43] As the studies contained in this
volume will demonstrate, the width of the local 'margin of appreciation' left
to national authorities in making such choices varies significantly, depending
upon the nature of the rights asserted by the parties and the social, political
and economic contexts within which they are exercised. Indeed, doubt as
to the extent of the local margin of appreciation in any given circumstances
has made the South African judiciary circumspect in following European
authority:[44]

> 'The jurisprudence of the European Court of Human Rights provides some guid-
> ance as to what may be considered necessary in a democratic society, but the
> margin of appreciation allowed to national authorities by the European Court
> must be understood as finding its place in an international agreement which has
> to accommodate the sovereignty of the member states. It is not necessarily a safe
> guide as to what would be appropriate [under section 36] of our Constitution.'

As the author of the chapter on 'Protection of Ownership and the Right
to a Home' in this volume shows,[45] such caution is not out of place. Calling
for a reminder to Europeans of the central importance of fundamental rights
in private law, he demonstrates in a detailed case study how latitude offered
to national jurisdictions in determining the content of private law can in
many areas allow traditional paradigms to dominate.[46]

---

[41] R *(Alconbury Developments Ltd and Others) v Secretary of State for the Environment* [2003] 2 AC
      295 per Lord Slynn at para 26.
[42] *Handyside v United Kingdom* (1979–80) 1 EHRR 737 at para 49.
[43] See discussion in *Hatton v United Kingdom* (2003) 37 EHRR 28.
[44] *S v Makwanyane* 1995 (3) SA 391 (CC) per Chaskalson P at para 109. (The original reference
      was to section 33 of the Interim Constitution, on limitation. This has been replaced by
      section 36 in the Final Constitution.)
[45] Chapter 19 infra.
[46] See section 19.7 infra.

1.4 HORIZONTAL EFFECT

It is uncontroversial that both the UK Human Rights Act and the South African Bill of Rights provide an important check on the powers of state or public authorities by regulating the 'vertical' relationship between them and the individuals whom their actions affect. A UK public authority may not act in a way that is incompatible with a Convention right.[47] Similarly, the South African legislature, the executive, the judiciary and all organs of state must adhere to the Bill of Rights.[48] The force of this 'vertical' effect and its impact upon the private law obligations of public authorities is discussed below in relation to areas such as nuisance[49] and contract law.[50] In both jurisdictions, however, the 'horizontal' reach of these instruments into relations between private entities is more contentious. The HRA makes no express direction to the effect that Convention rights are to be given 'direct horizontal' effect, and the interpretation of the UK courts continues to leave this question in uncertainty. In contrast the South African Constitution gives a stronger steer. Section 8(2) of the Bill of Rights allows for its direct application insofar as it 'binds a natural or a juristic person if, and to the extent that, it is applicable, taking into account the nature of the right and the nature of any duty imposed by the right'.[51] At the same time, the circumstances in which this may occur are not further specified, nor are the rights that may be susceptible to such application, and in practice, examples of such direct application of the Bill of Rights to private law relations remain to some extent contentious.[52] Much of the focus in the chapters that follow is therefore on the horizontal effect of human rights documents in Scotland and in South Africa.[53]

In the UK the ECHR cannot be directly invoked as the sole basis of a claim between private parties, but the courts are themselves public authorities for

---

[47] HRA s 6(1). The term 'public authority' is not defined in the HRA, but on the broad meaning that has been ascribed to it see R Reed and J Murdoch, *A Guide to Human Rights Law in Scotland*, 3e (Tottel 2011) paras 1.64–1.76.

[48] S 8(1).

[49] See section 11.3.2.2 infra.

[50] See section 12.2.2.2 note 23; also discussion at section 14.10.3.

[51] S 8(2).

[52] See sections 7.2 and 8.8 infra for discussion of *Khumalo v Holomisa* 2002 (5) SA 401 (CC), a defamation case involving a media defendant, in which the Constitutional Court stated that the right to freedom of expression was of such 'intensity' as to be capable of direct horizontal application as contemplated by section 8(2) (per O'Regan J at para 33) (given the reasonable publication defence had earlier been established within the common law, that right was already given appropriate recognition). For a clear summary of the present position, see A Cockrell 'Private Law and the Bill of Rights: A Threshold Issue of Horizontality' in *Bill of Rights Compendium* (Lexis Nexis, 1996 and regularly updated) paras 3A1 – 10. For discussion of the effect of the Bill of Rights upon contract law in the controversial case of *Barkhuizen v Napier* 2007 5 SA 323 see Chapters 12 and 13 infra.

[53] On the philosophical foundations for indirect horizontal effect see Chapter 2 infra.

the purposes of the Human Rights Act 1998, and are thus required to act compatibly with Convention rights, not only in deciding cases brought against public bodies but also in resolving disputes between private parties, both in cases of statutory interpretation and in the development of the common law.[54] By this means the values embodied in the Convention may have the potential to become 'as much applicable in disputes between individuals or between an individual and a non-governmental body such as a newspaper as they are in disputes between individuals and a public authority',[55] and in this way to become intermixed with 'the very content' of the common law.[56] Describing the HRA as a 'catalyst across the board'[57] Lord Rodger has assessed the impact of Convention rights as follows:[58]

> 'Although the Act is not entrenched, the Convention rights that it confers have a peculiar potency. Enforcing them may require a court to modify the common law. So far as possible, a court must read and give effect to statutory provisions in a way that is compatible with them. Rights that can produce such results are clearly of a higher order than the rights which people enjoy at common law or under most other statutes.'

The South African Bill of Rights is more explicit as to its effect, a stronger commitment to horizontality perhaps explained, at least in part, by the perception that the key rights of human dignity, equality and freedom have in the past been compromised not only by public bodies but also by private entities.[59] When it is applied to non-state actors, a South African court 'in order to give effect to a right in the Bill, must apply, or if necessary, develop, the common law to the extent that legislation does not give effect to that right'.[60] Moreover, section 39(2) directs that 'When interpreting any legislation, and when developing the common law or customary law, every court,

---

[54] For a more detailed introduction to the application of Convention rights in domestic law, see R Reed and J Murdoch *A Guide to Human Rights Law in Scotland*, 3e (Tottel 2011) ch 1; see also *Attorney General's Reference No 3 of 1999* [2009] UKHL 34; [2010] 1 AC 145 per Lord Hope at paras 18–19, Lord Brown at para 54. For discussion of different interpretations of 'horizontal effect' see G Phillipson and A Williams 'Horizontal Effect and the Constitutional Constraint' (2011) 74 *Modern Law Review* 878.

[55] *Campbell v MGN* [2004] 2 AC 457 at para 17 per Lord Nicholls, commenting on the nascent tort of misuse of private information. For further discussion see section 7.3 infra.

[56] *McKennitt v Ash* [2006] EWCA Civ 1714; [2008] QB 73 at para 11 per Buxton LJ, citing Lord Woolf CJ in *A v B plc* [2003] QB 195 at para 4.

[57] *Wilson v First County Trust Ltd* [2004] 1 AC 816 at para 182

[58] *Wilson v First County Trust Ltd* [2004] 1 AC 816 at para 180.

[59] Price 'The Influence of Human Rights on Private Common Law', note 22 supra, 369.

[60] S 8(3). It is important to note that the common law need only be developed where it is inconsistent with the Constitution: See Cockrell 'Private law and the Bill of Rights', note 52 supra, para 3A10; and *Khumalo v Holomisa* 2002 5 SA 401 (CC) paras 32–45; *Brisley v Drotsky* 2002 4 SA 1 (SCA) paras 93–95; *Afrox Healthcare Bpk v Strydom* 2002 6 SA 21 (SCA) paras 19–24.

tribunal or forum must promote the spirit, purport and objects of the Bill of Rights'. The Bill of Rights has thereby exercised a 'radiating influence'[61] on the content of private law, not only where a common law rule is in conflict with one of its provisions, but also where a common law has deviated from its spirit, purport and objects.[62] It has 'humanised' private law, 'ensuring that interpersonal justice not merely makes everyone count, but makes everyone count as a human, a normative agent with concrete needs and aspirations'.[63]

It may be said therefore that in essence 'South African law requires, whereas English law merely permits, human-rights norms to influence judicial development of the private common law'.[64] Considerable controversy may prevail in both jurisdictions as to which rights may be enforced between private parties, but the contributions to this volume indicate that the transformative potential of the Bill of Rights and that of the HRA cannot be compared in a straightforward way.

1.5 LIMITING OF RIGHTS AND PROPORTIONALITY

The principle of proportionality is accepted in both Scotland and South Africa. Where fundamental rights require to be limited in order to achieve a fair balance between the interests of individuals and those of the community more generally, there must be 'a reasonable relationship of proportionality between the means employed and the legitimate objectives pursued by the contested limitation'.[65] The term 'proportionality' is not defined in the ECHR or the HRA, but the South African Bill of Rights stipulates that such limitation is permissible only to the extent 'reasonable and justifiable in an open and democratic society based on human dignity, equality and freedom'.[66] The factors to be considered must include: (a) the nature of the right; (b) the importance of the purpose of the limitation; (c) the nature and extent of the limitation; (d) the relation between the limitation and its purpose; and (e) whether there are less restrictive means to achieve the purpose. This formulation bears clear similarities to the criteria that have emerged in the UK case law, namely that (i) the objective of the limitation is

[61] M du Plessis and J Ford 'Developing the Common Law Progressively – Horizontality, the Human Rights Act and the South African Experience' 2004 *European Human Rights Law Review* 286 at 292. (The metaphor is in fact borrowed from the rhetoric of the German Constitutional Court.)

[62] See e.g. *Carmichele v Minister of Safety and Security* 2001 (4) SA 938 (CC), and see discussion at section 12.2.2.1 infra.

[63] See section 2.5 infra.

[64] Price 'The Influence of Human Rights on Private Common Law', note 22 supra, 331.

[65] *Fayed v United Kingdom* (1994) 18 EHRR 393 at para 71. See also *R (Razgar) v Secretary of State for the Home Department* [2004] 2 AC 368 per Lord Bingham at para 20.

[66] S 36(1). See generally *S v Makwanyane* 1995 6 BCLR 665 (CC), 1995 (3) SA 391 (CC) paras 104–9 and I M Rautenbach 'Introduction to the Bill of Rights' in *Bill of Rights Compendium* (LexisNexis 1996, updated regularly) para 1A46 et seq.

sufficiently important to justify limiting a fundamental right – and the more severe the limitation, the more important that objective must be; (ii) the measures proposed to realise the objective are connected to it in a rational way – they should not be arbitrary or unfair; and (iii) the means applied to limit the right or freedom should be no greater than is necessary to achieve the objective in question.[67]

But while the mechanisms applied in this balancing exercise are broadly similar as between the two jurisdictions,[68] the weight actually attributed to competing factors is in certain areas strikingly different. A conspicuous example is found in the chapter on land law in this volume, which considers the limiting of ownership rights by reference to a land reform imperative in South Africa that has no parallel in Scotland. Its author concludes that the 'position regarding private law and the protection of the human right of property in South Africa and Scotland is too different for any comparative exercise to have primary utility'.[69]

1.6 HUMAN RIGHTS AND PRIVATE LAW

Notwithstanding a shared heritage as mixed jurisdictions, Scotland and South Africa plainly started from a very different private-law base in the late twentieth century. In the area of contract, for example, legislation was already in place in Scotland, as in the rest of the UK, to address the issue of inequality of bargaining power between parties.[70] And in land law the broad principle of 'stewardship' in Scots law – the notion that land is held 'subject to the "common weal"' – was already being discussed, without direct prompting by human-rights considerations.[71] Indeed, the chapter on child law in this volume concludes that most of the more radical legislative developments in that area 'would almost certainly have come about had there been no Human Rights Act and, indeed, no European Convention, since they were prompted by public opinion, the lobbying efforts of special interest groups and academics and the UN Convention on the Rights of the Child'.[72] In South Africa, on the other hand, legislation of this nature had

---

[67] See R *(Daly) v Secretary of State for the Home Department* [2001] 2 AC 532 per Lord Steyn at para 27; see also A Lester et al (eds) *Human Rights Law and Practice* 3e (2009) para 3.10.

[68] For a detailed study see G van der Schyff *Limitation of Rights: A Study of the European Convention and the South African Bill of Rights* (Wolf 2005).

[69] See section 18.7.

[70] Unfair Contract Terms Act 1975; Unfair Terms in Consumer Contracts Regulations 1999; and see the discussion in section 12.3.2.1 infra. Note also the Sex Discrimination Act 1975 and the Race Relations Act 1976, now consolidated in the Equality Act 2010.

[71] See, e.g., D W McKenzie Skene 'Stewardship: From Rhetoric to Reality' (1999) 3 *Edinburgh Law Review* 151; T Guthrie 'Access Rights' in R Rennie, (ed) *The Promised Land: Property Law Reform* (W Green 2008) 125. These discussions were to lead ultimately to the Land Reform (Scotland) Act 2003.

[72] Section 4.7 infra.

made far fewer inroads by the time apartheid was dismantled,[73] and it was left to the new constitutional considerations to effect a series of urgent and radical shifts which, in some cases at least, go well beyond what has been achieved in Scotland.[74] Thus the chapter on labour law reflects that the impact of the HRA upon UK law has been 'modest to negligible at best', but it looks to recent South African experience as demonstrating that 'casting labour rights as human rights has the potential to reclaim territory lost in recent decades to the neo-liberal imperatives of economic competitiveness, efficiency and flexibility'.[75]

Despite the close affinities in the underlying private-law structures, therefore, a study of the impact of human rights in Scotland and South Africa is essentially a study in difference. The chapters that follow trace that difference in respect of a number of key topics and offer an assessment of its significance. And in doing so they suggest paths for the future development of the law in both jurisdictions.

---

[73] See Price 'The Influence of Human Rights on Private Common Law', note 22 supra, 372.
[74] See, e.g., sections 12.3.2.1; 18.3.2 and 4.7 infra.
[75] Section 15.5 infra.

Chapter 2

Private Law in the Age of Rights

François du Bois*

2.1 INTRODUCTION

We live in 'the age of rights'.[1] Ours is an era marked by the widespread legal positivisation of human rights in national constitutions, as in South Africa, as well as in judicially enforceable supra-national charters such as the European Convention of Human Rights that obtains in Scotland. Since their first appearance in the political thought of seventeenth and eighteenth-century Europe and North America, the influence of human rights has expanded not only across the globe but also well beyond their original field of application, the relationship between political authorities and citizens. Today, human rights frequently also shape the law governing relations among citizens. Their impact has reached the heartlands of private law.[2]

Yet this crossing of the traditional boundary between public law and private law remains controversial. Three broad positions are discernible.[3] The first is a sceptical one, which would prefer private law and constitutional human rights law to continue as separate pathways, albeit following generally

* This chapter forms part of the project entitled 'Irritating Rights?' supported by a British Academy research grant. I am very grateful to all who have assisted me with this project, especially to the current and retired judges of the South African Constitutional Court and Supreme Court of Appeal who generously made time available to share their insights and experiences with me in September 2010.

1 L Henkin *The Age of Rights* (Columbia University Press 1990); N Bobbio *The Age of Rights* (Polity Press 1996).

2 See D Friedman and D Barak-Erez (eds) *Human Rights in Private Law* (Hart Publishing 2001); A Sajó and R Uitz (eds) *The Constitution in Private Relations* (Eleven International Publishing 2005); T Barkhuysen and S D Lindenbergh (eds) *Constitutionalisation of Private Law* (Martinus Nijhoff Publishers 2006); D Oliver and J Fedtke (eds) *Human Rights and the Private Sphere: A Comparative Study* (Routledge-Cavendish 2007); G Brüggemeier, A Colombi Ciacchi and G Comandé (eds) *Fundamental Rights and Private Law in the European Union* vols I and II (Cambridge University Press 2010).

3 See generally the literature cited in the preceding note. Regarding Scotland in particular, see H MacQueen and D Brodie 'Private Rights, Private Law, and the Private Domain' in A Boyle et al (eds) *Human Rights and Scots Law* (Hart Publishing 2002) 141, as well as D Hoffman (ed) *The Impact of the UK Human Rights Act on Private Law* (Cambridge University Press 2011); on South Africa, see S Woolman 'Application' in S Woolman, M Bishop and J Brickhill (eds) *Constitutional Law of South Africa* vol II 2e (Juta 2006) ch 31.

the same direction and with occasional crossings. The second position takes the opposite line, urging the displacement of private law by constitutional human rights. The space between is filled by a stance that values the distinctiveness of private law but insists that it cannot do without the direction given by constitutional human rights.[4] In the jargon of legal doctrine this third approach represents the 'indirect horizontal application' of fundamental rights, in contrast to the 'direct horizontal application' reflected in the second position and the 'purely vertical application' of the first.[5]

Indirect horizontal application appears to be the norm in Scotland and the United Kingdom as a whole,[6] and to be endorsed by the South African Constitution in its stipulation that the obligations imposed by its rights on private persons must be given effect through legislation, common law or customary law.[7] This chapter accordingly examines the philosophical foundations of that approach, exploring both why the horizontal application of such rights should respect rather than displace private law and why private law should nevertheless conform to constitutional human rights. It therefore investigates whether the maintenance of private law as a distinctive legal domain serves any valuable purpose, as well as whether recourse to constitutional human rights contributes to the achievement of that purpose.

Doing so requires a conception of the nature of that domain, that is, a definition of private law. This is an undertaking fraught with difficulty and cannot be done full justice here.[8] However, for our purposes it suffices to

[4] By 'constitutional human rights' I refer throughout also to rights that, though not enshrined in a document formally entitled a constitution, nevertheless bind the legislative and adjudicative institutions of a national jurisdiction, as do the rights in the European Convention in the case of Scotland. I employ this phrase in order to exclude the application of human rights on the international plane from my discussion.

[5] For a detailed discussion of this technical terminology, exploring nuances that cannot be captured here, see A L Young 'Mapping Horizontal Effect' in Hoffman, note 3 supra, at 16.

[6] See MacQueen and Brodie, note 3 supra; Hoffman, note 3 supra.

[7] See s 8 of the Constitution of the Republic of South Africa, 1996 and the discussion thereof in F du Bois et al (eds) *Wille's Principles of South African Law* 9e (Juta 2007) 39–43. O'Regan J has referred to this as 'direct application' (*Khumalo v Holomisa* 2002 (5) SA 401 (CC) at para 33), apparently because s 8 not merely subjects *the law* to the Bill of Rights but makes such rights directly binding on *individuals*. The distinction between direct and indirect effect can certainly be drawn in this way (see also H Cheadle 'Application' in M H Cheadle, D M Davis and N R L Haysom (eds) *South African Constitutional Law: The Bill of Rights* 2e (Juta, 2005) paras 3–4 to 3–10), but a distinction focusing on the means by which constitutional human rights are given effect when they bind individuals, which is commonly employed in the UK (see e.g. M Hunt 'The Horizontal Effect of the Human Rights Act' 1998 *Public Law* 423; G Phillipson 'The Human Rights Act, "Horizontal Effect" and the Common Law: A Bang or a Whimper?' (1999) 62 *Modern Law Review* 824), is better suited to the purposes of this chapter.

[8] See R Michaels and N Jansen 'Private Law Beyond the State? Europeanization, Globalization, Privatization' (2006) 54 *American Journal of Comparative Law* 843; N Jansen and R Michaels 'Private Law and the State: Comparative Perceptions and Historical Observations' (2007) 71 *Rabels Zeitschrift für ausländisches und internationales Privatrecht/The Rabel Journal of*

conceptualise private law in general terms that are broad enough to encompass the topics conventionally included under this heading yet able to
distinguish it from public law, the other general category long employed in
legal thought. Hence this chapter takes private law to consist of the specifically bilateral rights and duties of private persons rather than their general
normative relationship as members of the same society or the interactions
between individuals and society via its representative, the state.[9] As such, it
is the domain of interpersonal justice among normative equals. This is not
to say that its content is exclusively determined by the bilateral relations of
individuals – private law can, and should, it will be argued below, also reflect
public, social concerns. Nor is it the only legal field that attends to the interests of individuals and dealings between them; criminal law and many of the
state's public measures and regulations do so as well. But private law is distinctive in operating a system of legal claims (that is, remedies or 'secondary
rights') among persons that derive from considerations of what one person
may demand from another ('primary rights') *directly* rather than via the state
as agent of the public interest. Although the creation and development of
private law rights, as well as the limits of their reach, turn on considerations
of public interest, their application abstracts the parties from their broader
social setting, asking 'what do they owe to each other as directly interacting
persons?' rather than 'what do they owe to each other as members of the
same political community?' The latter question is at the core of public law,
which concerns itself with the conditions and institutions of social justice.

2.2 PRIVATE LAW AS THE REALM OF LIBERTY

Attempts to analyse private law at a fundamental, theoretical level offer
remarkably little support for the notion that private law has intrinsic value.
Some decry the public/private distinction and strive for the 'publicisation'
of all law.[10] Others see private law as no more than an instrument for the
pursuit of general social aims such as wealth maximisation or distributive

---

Comparative and International Private Law 345; S Hedley 'Is Private Law Meaningless' (2011)
64 *Current Legal Problems* 89.

[9] One should not be distracted by the application of private law principles, such as tort and
contract, to relations between private persons and the state. Such cases involve either the
treatment of the state as if it were a private person, or the extension of the principle beyond
the boundaries of private law so that it would no longer be correct to regard tort, for
example, as belonging in its entirety to private law. See F du Bois 'State Liability in South
Africa: A Constitutional Remix' (2010) 25 *Tulane European and Civil Law Forum* 139; F du
Bois 'Human Rights and the Tort Liability of Public Authorities' (2011) 127 *Law Quarterly
Review* 512.

[10] See e.g. D Kennedy 'Form and Substance in Private Law Adjudication' (1976) 89 *Harvard
Law Review* 1685; D Kennedy 'The Stages of the Decline of the Public/Private Distinction'
(1982) 130 *University of Pennsylvania Law Review* 1349; P S Atiyah *Accidents, Compensation
and the Law* 3e (Weidenfeld & Nicholson 1980) 627.

justice.[11] And the leading proponent of private law's distinctiveness has proclaimed that it serves no purpose other than that of being private law.[12] However, there is also a remarkably persistent association of private law with the preservation of individual freedom. On this account, private law secures the freedom of persons inter se by setting and protecting the rights that they have against each other, rights which are ultimately anchored in the equal right of all to be free from coercion by others. Yet such theories frequently end up either acknowledging that, since social (distributive) justice serves this end as much as interpersonal (corrective or commutative) justice, private law plays no special, indispensable role in this regard,[13] or restricting the claims they make to a justificatory explanation of judicial law-making in the field of private law.[14]

The most prominent exception is Robert Nozick's libertarian theory of justice.[15] Nozick's argument that the state should not pursue a 'patterned' conception of justice that seeks to bring about a socially preferred distribution of goods, but rather an 'historical' conception limited to preventing and reversing coercive transfers among persons, can be read as a defence of interpersonal justice against social justice. Individual freedom is seen as compromised by measures harnessing private law to collective ends that override private choices, while it is promoted by a private law left free of such measures. On this view, private law does have a privileged role in securing individual freedom; indeed, it is the primary means of doing so, since public measures may legitimately be employed only in support of interpersonal justice.

More recently, Arthur Ripstein has argued that private law provides a distinctive service that can co-exist with a social commitment to 'patterned' distributive justice. Drawing on the work of John Rawls, Ripstein posits a division of responsibility between society and the individual in which the responsibility of the former to 'see to it that citizens have adequate shares of primary goods' is complemented by 'a special responsibility for how his or her own life goes' on the part of each citizen.[16] By regulating individual transactions on the basis of considerations that are specific to private interactions and distinct from the considerations that govern the allocation

---

[11] R A Posner *Economic Analysis of Law* 1e (Little Brown 1973); R Dworkin *Law's Empire* (Harvard University Press 1986) at 295–309.

[12] E J Weinrib *The Idea of Private Law* (Harvard University Press 1995) 5.

[13] This is the position of Weinrib *Idea of Private Law*, which depicts private law as grounded in the Kantian conception of the person as a free and rational agent, and is endorsed by A Beever *Rediscovering the Law of Negligence* (Hart Publishing 2009) 63–68. See also R W Wright 'Substantive Corrective Justice' (1992) 77 *Iowa Law Review* 625 at 628; J L Coleman *Risks and Wrongs* (Cambridge University Press 1992) 367, 493–4.

[14] See R Stevens *Torts and Rights* (Oxford University Press 2007) 325–40.

[15] R Nozick *Anarchy, State, and Utopia* (Basic Books 1974).

[16] A Ripstein 'The Division of Responsibility and the Law of Tort' (2003–2004) 72 *Fordham Law Review* 1811 at 1812.

of goods across society as a whole, private law in Ripstein's view ensures that individuals take such special responsibility for their own lives. Thus private law secures individual freedom by protecting its counterpart – individual responsibility for individual choices – from being dissolved by the pursuit of distributive justice.

Of course, neither of these sets of ideas may in the end turn out to provide a convincing account of the distinctive value of private law. But they do provide a useful starting point for reflecting on whether the maintenance of private law as a distinctive legal domain serves any valuable purpose.

2.2.1 The libertarian account of private law

To begin the exploration of a libertarian understanding of private law, it is instructive to call to mind G A Cohen's famous example of Mr Morgan's yacht:

> 'Let us suppose that I wish to take Mr. Morgan's yacht, and go for a spin. If I try to, then it is probable that its owner, aided by law-enforcing others, will stop me. I cannot do this thing that I wish to do, because others will interfere. But liberty . . . [according to libertarians like Nozick] is 'doing what we wish without the interference of others'. It follows that I lack a liberty here.'[17]

Cohen here reminds us of what should be obvious: that it is a mistake to think that private property rights – and indeed private-law rights generally – simply protect freedom and that all governmental regulation or redistribution amounts to a restriction of freedom. Private law rights do protect the freedom of some, but they invariably do so at the cost of restricting the freedom of others. In fact, their very purpose is to restrain others. The point of the example is to demonstrate that the redistribution of wealth does not necessarily compromise freedom: Mr Morgan's freedom is undoubtedly infringed if his yacht is seized by the state and transferred to another, but, Cohen insisted, the beneficiary of the state's largesse then enjoys a corresponding increase in freedom. Thus freedom is reallocated rather than diminished. Cohen's discussion forms part of a justification of socialism, arguing that in a 'communising world' there is more freedom than in a capitalist world,[18] but one need not follow him all the way to that conclusion in order to see the basic truth highlighted by this example. This is that every private law right, in imposing a correlative duty on others, and thus licensing coercion, had better be justified by reference to something more than just the right-holder's freedom in the abstract. It must be grounded in a justification that explains why *this* freedom (exclusive control and possession of

---

[17] G A Cohen 'Capitalism, Freedom and the Proletariat' in A Ryan (ed) *The Idea of Freedom: Essays in Honour of Isaiah Berlin* (Oxford University Press 1979) 9 at 11–12.

[18] Cohen, note 17 supra, esp at 16–17.

yachts) is to be protected at the cost of sacrificing *another* freedom (access to yachts whenever one feels like sailing or needs shelter). Mr Morgan's freedom encroaches on the freedom of everyone else, and if the coercion that it licenses is to be justified, then that *allocation of* freedom to Mr Morgan must be justified. If private property, or any other private law right, is to provide a ground for the legitimate exercise of legal coercion, a thorough-going account is needed of the relative significance of different concrete freedoms.

This was (of course) already grasped by Kant, whose state-of-nature explanation of the origins of legal rights has served as a model for libertarian arguments. It is worth looking at this more closely, as Kant's philosophy of law does not, in fact, support the libertarian project. To the contrary, it demonstrates why the libertarian attempt to inject distinctive value into private law is doomed to fail. Kant's discussion of the state of nature and its displacement by what he calls 'the civil condition' is not meant as an histori-cal or sociological account of law, but as a heuristic device for showing what rights among persons are presupposed by the operation of public institu-tions that exist for the purpose of securing such rights.[19] These rights must necessarily be intelligible independently of the decisions of the institutions that exist for the sake of enforcing them,[20] and so Kant uses the device of an imagined absence of institutions to explore what rights these are. Kant calls this imagined condition the 'state of nature', as well as 'private right', and he explains what system of rights would emerge from the basic principle that everyone is to have the maximum amount of freedom that is consistent with the equal freedom of others. Through a complex chain of arguments Kant demonstrates that this simple freedom-maximising principle gives rise to the standard private law rights to bodily integrity, property and the performance of contracts, as well as the rights associated with status relationships such as marriage and parenthood, and to the central structural features of these rights, such as their range of operation (for example, the limited, *in personam* reach of contractual rights) and their modes of acquisition.[21]

If one follows him only up to this point, one might think that Kant was a libertarian *avant la lettre* who demonstrated quite clearly the distinct freedom-promoting role of private law. However, his analysis of law did not stop here. He sought to provide a philosophical account of actually

---

[19] For a superb analysis of the pertinent parts of Kant's work, see B S Byrd and J Hruschka *Kant's Doctrine of Right: A Commentary* (Cambridge University Press 2010).

[20] Kant *The Metaphysics of Morals* Part I in M J Gregor (trans and ed) *The Cambridge Edition of the Works of Immanuel Kant: Practical Philosophy* (Cambridge University Press 1996) 365 at 6:256. Page references are to the Prussian Academy edition of Kant's works (*Immanuel Kants Schriften. Ausgabe der königlich preussischen Akademie der Wissenschaften* (W de Gruyter, 1902–), on which Gregor's translation is based, and appear in the margin of the *Cambridge Edition*.

[21] See Kant *Metaphysics of Morals*, note 20 supra, at 6:258–6:303.

existing law, and was perfectly aware of the fact that this is characterised by the presence rather than the absence of public institutions. Kant therefore also explored what he termed the 'civil condition' or 'public right', which is the 'condition in which public institutions actualize and guarantee these rights',[22] and reflected on the point and consequences of the existence of such institutions. In doing so, as we are about to see, Kant demonstrated the fundamental incoherence of the libertarian approach.

The imagined state of nature also has a second purpose in Kant's legal philosophy. This is to explain the need for public institutions and thereby to illuminate the nature of law in the civil condition. Public right, Kant argued, is necessary to overcome the inadequacy of private right. Rights in the state of nature can, as he shows, be fair to both parties, respecting their reciprocal and equal entitlement to freedom, but they suffer from a fundamental weakness. Kant explains:

> 'When I declare (by word or deed), I will that something external [to myself] is to be mine, I thereby declare that everyone else is under obligation to refrain from using that object of my choice, an obligation no one would have were it not for this act of mine to establish a right ... Now, a unilateral will cannot serve as a coercive law for everyone with regard to possession that is external ..., since that would infringe upon freedom in accordance with universal laws.'[23]

In other words, the state of nature cannot, consistently with the postulate that everyone is equally entitled to freedom, generate conclusive rights to external things. This contradiction between the coercion-eliminating purpose of private rights and their coercion-justifying effect – so neatly captured in Cohen's example of Mr Morgan's yacht – is resolved by what Kant calls 'the civil condition':

> 'So it is only a will putting everyone under obligation, hence only a collective general (common) and powerful will, that can provide everyone this assurance. – But the condition of being under a general external (i.e., public) lawgiving accompanied with power is the civil condition. *So only in a civil condition can something external be mine or yours.*'[24]

It is vital to notice that the problem with the state of nature Kant identified in these passages is not merely, as it is sometimes claimed, that the interpretation and enforcement of rights is, in the absence of a public institution for doing so, ultimately subject to the unilateral will of the stronger party.[25] The

---

[22] E J Weinrib 'Private Law and Public Right' (2011) 61 *University of Toronto Law Journal* 191 at 195. See also Kant *Metaphysics of Morals*, note 20 supra, at 6:311.

[23] Kant *Metaphysics of Morals*, note 20 supra, at 6:256.

[24] Kant *Metaphysics of Morals*, note 20 supra, at 6:256. (Emphasis added.)

[25] That is the only defect in the state of nature acknowledged by Weinrib – see note 22 supra, at 195, and *The Idea of Private Law*, note 12 supra, at 105–9.

shortcomings of the state of nature run much deeper in Kant's argument, reaching all the way to the allocation of rights. It is clear that there 'is for Kant no pre-civil validation of right-claims over particular things by those whom the claims purport to exclude'.[26] In Kant's view, external things can only *provisionally* be mine or yours in a state of nature, and it 'is possible to have something external as one's own only . . . under an authority giving laws publicly, that is, in a civil condition'.[27] Kant realises only too well that the contrary view, according to which the appropriation of previously unowned things in a state of nature establishes a right of ownership, simply licenses unilateral coercion. This is obviously incompatible with a genuine commitment to freedom as an innate right of persons. And so Kant's analysis of the state of nature reveals libertarianism as incoherent: while it professes attachment to individual freedom, libertarianism allows coercion to run rampant.

As importantly, Kant fatally undermines the libertarian case for the intrinsic value of private law. Kant does not treat private law as coterminous with 'private right'.[28] Since every right to an external object is, at most, provisional until it has been established by the 'collective general (common) . . . will', it follows that the institutions of public justice, whose task it is to articulate this will by operating in a disinterested and impartial manner,[29] 'may always shift things around pursuant to a public interest, and [that] it is only the right conferred by the united will of citizen legislators that innate right will allow to be conclusive'.[30] Indeed, they have the duty to re-assess whatever private law rights might have developed, and to do so on the basis of an impartial and disinterested assessment of what array of rules and principles would accord with an 'omnilateral will' in the sense of reflecting a position that all members of society could rationally have imposed on themselves.[31] Only such a position is compatible with a commitment to the innate freedom of individuals. That position is not necessarily going to be the one reached by private law. A genuinely impartial and disinterested assessment of property rights, for example, might well in some circumstances reach the conclusion

---

[26] A Brudner 'Private Law and Kantian Right' (2011) 61 *University of Toronto Law Journal* 279 at 288.

[27] Kant *Metaphysics of Morals*, note 20 supra, at 6:255–6:256. See also 6:264.

[28] English translations of Kant sometimes use 'private law' where I and most authors cited in this chapter (following Gregor) have used 'private right' – see e.g. Byrd and Hruschka *Kant's Doctrine of Right*, note 19 supra. Gregor's translation is preferable since it is clear that Kant did not use this term or its cognate public right/law as lawyers do to refer to branches of posited law, but to distinguish between states of affairs marked by the absence or presence of posited law respectively – see Byrd and Hruschka *Kant's Doctrine of Right*, note 19 supra, at 28–32.

[29] Kant's discussion of the details of constitutional arrangements appears in Section I ('The right of a state') in the *Metaphysics of Morals*, note 20 supra, at 6:311ff.

[30] Brudner, note 26 supra, at 293.

[31] I adopt the term 'omnilateral' from Weinrib, note 22 supra, and Brudner, note 26 supra.

that freedom is compromised rather than enhanced by the adoption of a bilateral, interpersonal perspective that disregards questions of social justice – perhaps because of how property rights interact with homelessness,[32] or because of their impact on the accessibility of nature[33] or socially significant spaces.[34] Thus, depending on context, freedom may require a shrinking of the area of law governed by interpersonal justice and an extension of the area subjected to considerations of social justice. It may even on occasion require the displacement of a long-established private law regime from a significant part of its field of its application: witness the proposed replacement of the South African law of delict by a system of restricted compensation out of a public fund for personal injuries suffered in road traffic accidents, endorsed by the Constitutional Court in *Law Society of South Africa v Minister of Transport*,[35] a development that is by no means idiosyncratic.[36]

This might well lead to the conclusion that private law lacks any intrinsic value rendering it worthy of preservation as a matter of principle. True, interpersonal justice long played an indispensable role in securing individual freedom, a role recognised by the sixteenth and seventeenth-century natural lawyers as well as the creators of the great codifications of the subsequent centuries,[37] but this does not seem to be the case any longer. The state has since then developed into a vast and complex institution that is both dedicated to Kantian public right and, by virtue of the extensive administrative means at its disposal, may be much better at realising it than private law has ever been.[38] One might plausibly think that private law is at best an occasionally useful remnant from times predating the formation of the modern state. Given the central role that the state administration today plays in fostering individual freedom through measures of social justice, why not simply apply the principles which give expression to this feature of contemporary polities – that is, constitutional human rights – directly to the relations among individuals? Would this not be more effective at achieving the ends of Kantian public right than the circuitous route of doing so via private law?

---

[32] See e.g. Extension of Security of Tenure Act 62 of 1997; Prevention of Illegal Eviction from and Unlawful Occupation of Land Act 19 of 1998; *Brisley v Drotsky* 2002 (4) SA 1 (SCA); *Port Elizabeth Municipality v Various Occupiers* 2005 (1) SA 217 (CC).

[33] See the Land Reform (Scotland) Act 2003.

[34] See *Victoria & Alfred Waterfront (Pty) Ltd v Police Commissioner, Western Cape (Legal Resources Centre as Amicus Curiae)* 2004 (4) SA 444 (C).

[35] 2011 (1) SA 400 (CC).

[36] See e.g. South Africa's Compensation for Occupational Injuries and Diseases Act 130 of 1993; most dramatically, the New Zealand Accident Compensation Act 2001.

[37] See generally F Wieacker *A History of Private Law in Europe: With Particular Reference to Germany* (T Weir (trans) Clarendon Press 1995).

[38] This development and its implications for private law was an important theme in the work of Léon Duguit – see his *Le droit social, le droit individuel et la transformation de l'Etat* (1908) and *Les transformations générale du droit privé depuis le Code Napoléon* (Alcan 1912).

2.2.2 Rawlsian account of private law

We must be careful not to jump too quickly to the conclusion that private law has *no* independent value. Perhaps the truth lies somewhere between the libertarian's understanding of public law as the servant of private right, and the converse reduction of private law to an instrument of public right. Private law might yet turn out to be a necessary complement to measures dedicated to the pursuit of public, social, justice (that is, public law), playing a role which the latter cannot fulfil. Kant's legal philosophy indeed suggests as much. Taken together, his discussions of private right and public right can be understood to demonstrate that 'the enforcement of [private law] rights is justified because it alone makes it possible for a plurality of persons to realize their freedom together, but such enforcement must realize the freedom of everyone'.[39] Thus Kant appears to envisage a role for both private law and public law in the actualisation of freedom.

Ripstein has sought to develop this idea into an account of the distinctive value of private law that acknowledges the emergence of the state as the primary agent of public right. He argues that '[j]ustice requires that private law – tort, contract, property and unjust enrichment – have a certain kind of independence'.[40] Although 'these private law regimes' can legitimately be limited 'by the concerns of public justice . . ., particular transactions can be judged on their own terms, rather than being subordinated to distributive justice'.[41] The reason is that '[p]rivate rights protect an important kind of freedom' and are thus 'not simply bestowed on citizens by the state so as to increase prosperity or provide incentives'.[42] Specifically, 'private law is the form of interaction through which a plurality of separate persons can each take up . . . [their] special responsibility for their own lives, setting and pursuing their own conceptions of the good in a way consistent with the freedom of others to do the same'.[43] On this account, there is a division of labour between the 'rules of distribution' (public law) and the 'rules of transactions' (private law), which expresses a more fundamental division, a division of responsibility between society (or the state) and individuals.[44] Because individuals remain responsible for leading their own lives with the goods bestowed upon them, even as society via the state assumes responsibility for ensuring that goods are distributed justly, rules are needed to ensure that this special individual responsibility is maintained.[45] These are supplied by private law.

---

[39] A Ripstein 'Private Order and Public Justice: Kant and Rawls' (2006) 92 *Virginia Law Review* 1391 at 1437.

[40] Ripstein, note 16 supra, at 1814–15.

[41] Note 16 supra, at 1815.

[42] Note 39 supra, at 1392.

[43] Note 39 supra, at 1393.

[44] For the Rawlsian roots of these ideas, see Ripstein, note 39 supra, at 1396–402.

[45] See esp Ripstein, note 16 supra, at 1829–37.

This need for private law is generated by the demands of freedom. Freedom requires that, as among individuals interacting as such (that is, as 'a plurality', or severally), everyone is responsible for only his own life and remains so responsible, taking the consequences of his choices upon his own shoulders.[46] This is so because, as Kant already taught, the non-consensual transfer of goods is only compatible with freedom when it takes place through public institutions that act omnilaterally, on behalf of and in the interest of all affected thereby.[47] Hence, '[e]ach person has a claim against society as a whole to a just basic structure, and claims as against other citizens to justice in transactions'.[48] Through its 'dual focus on protecting what people already happen to have and allowing them to decide how their powers will be used',[49] private law secures this division of responsibility – and thus freedom itself – by supplying the rules that ensure that individuals remain responsible for their own choices when they interact severally rather than omnilaterally.[50] That is, private law brings about the necessary division of responsibility because it establishes a system of rights that demarcates mine and thine. Consequently, Ripstein insists, 'private law *must be* part of the coercive structure of . . . justice: its obligations are the protections that enable the reciprocal exercise of [what Rawls calls] the first moral power',[51] that is, the ability of an individual to set and pursue a conception of the good.

This is an attractive argument, not least because it makes sense of what we actually see all around us in contemporary legal systems: the co-existence of, on the one hand, a private law that protects what people happen to have and enables them to do with it what they want, irrespective of the distributive justice of their holdings, and, on the other hand, a vast separate array of laws and governmental programmes dedicated to redistributing what people have, often undoing or even preventing the exercise of private choice. Ripstein's argument is nevertheless ultimately unsuccessful. Closer inspection reveals that his division of labour between private law and public law follows arbitrary boundaries. Consider, for example, his discussion of an issue recently before the South African Constitutional Court in a case mentioned above.[52] This is the question whether tort liability for personal injuries arising from motor accidents should be protected against its abolition and replacement by a governmental social insurance scheme. The question is a crucial one for Ripstein's theory, as tort liability unsurprisingly occupies a central place in his explanation of how private law ensures that individuals are held responsible for the consequences of their choices. It is therefore significant

---

[46] Esp Ripstein, note 16 supra, at 1832–3, 1836; Ripstein, note 39 supra, at 1402–5.
[47] Esp Ripstein, note 39 supra, at 1427–9, 1432–3.
[48] Note 39 supra, at 1411 n 47.
[49] Note 39 supra, at 1411.
[50] Ripstein, note 39 supra, at 1402–11; Ripstein, note 16 supra, at 1836–43.
[51] Ripstein, note 39 supra, at 1411. (Emphasis supplied.)
[52] *Law Society of South Africa v Minister of Transport*, note 35 supra.

that he acknowledges that a system of social insurance for injuries sustained in accidents can be seen as an integration of three components: (1) a form of compulsory liability insurance (paid via taxation), which (2) dispenses for reasons of administrative efficiency and cost with proof of negligence, and (3) is operated by the state.[53] Provided that accident victims receive full individualised compensation (in cash and services), such a system would, as he also acknowledges, be entirely compatible with the special responsibility of individuals for their own lives. If this proviso is met, such a system would continue to reflect the basic commitment of tort law to ensuring that no one is made to bear the costs of others' choices.[54] But if this is so, then the special responsibility of individuals for their own lives *can* be secured without a system that specifies and administers rights that individuals hold directly against each other, that is, without private law.

Still, Ripstein's justification of private law does appear to have some bite, since he rejects a system, like the one approved by the South African Constitutional Court, in which private rights are displaced by a standardised schedule of payments.[55] This kind of alternative to tort would not safeguard individuals' special responsibility for their own lives, since many victims would be left to bear some of the costs (or indeed sometimes receive more than the costs) imposed on them by tortfeasors, who would, in turn, be paying less into the insurance pot collectively than is needed to cover the full costs actually flowing from their choices. So the special function of private law identified by Ripstein does appear to limit the alternatives by which it might be displaced: these, it seems, must at least mimic private law. We may not need private law in name, one might say, but we at least need it in substance.

---

[53] Ripstein, note 16 supra, at 1837 n73. See also Coleman *Risks and Wrongs*, note 13 supra, at 493. Both refer to the New Zealand accident compensation scheme. For two excellent analyses of the scheme, see S Todd 'Privatization of Accident Compensation: Policy and Politics in New Zealand' (2000) 39 *Washburn Law Journal* 404 and G McLay 'Accident Compensation – What's the Common Law Got to Do With It?' 2008 *New Zealand Law Review* 55.

[54] Fagan contends, in Chapter 6 infra 'The Right to Personal Security' at section 6.4, that such a scheme could never obviate the need for corrective justice to be done by the wrongdoer in respect of the autonomy that is lost when a person is wrongfully injured by another. The reason is that the compensation paid under a scheme of this type can annul the infringement of the financial interest the victim has in her body but not of the autonomy interest that she has therein. The underlying idea is that the wrongdoer's secondary duty to correct only disappears if the primary duty not to impose the wrongful harm is eliminated. But this argument overlooks the existence of excuses (as opposed to grounds of justification), which are reasons for not imposing secondary duties despite the breach of primary duties. So a secondary duty can disappear for reasons other than the negation of the primary duty. And a wrongdoer faced with a claim from her victim who has already been compensated by such a scheme can rightly assert that such compensation excuses her from doing so because this is what the lawmakers decided should follow. Moreover, unlike Fagan's consoling husband, a public compensation scheme is not a third party trying to right another's wrong: at least in a democracy, the state acts on behalf of the wrongdoer.

[55] Ripstein, note 16 supra, at 1837 n 73.

This conclusion would be too quick, however. As the Constitutional Court's reasoning reveals, the restriction and standardisation of benefits in such an alternative compensation scheme appear to result from considerations of social, distributive justice.[56] If it is legitimate to take account of such considerations, then they may, as the Court correctly concluded, justify the restriction of benefits. In evaluating a system of this kind, we must therefore bear in mind that it might reflect more than one legitimate purpose, and might seek to balance the protection of individuals' special responsibility with considerations of distributive justice. A libertarian may, of course, reject this as illegitimate, but this option is not open to Ripstein, who insists as strongly on the necessity and legitimacy of the pursuit of distributive justice through public institutions as he does on the need for safeguarding individuals' special responsibility for their own lives. Thus Ripstein's unqualified rejection of schemes of this kind is out of kilter with the thrust of his theory. Consistently applied, the commitments built into his theory provide no principled reason for rejecting compensation schemes that provide only limited, standardised payments.

The reason for the failure of this specific argument is instructive, for it points to the fatal flaw in his account of a division of labour between private law and public law. Ripstein's argument against standardised payments schemes fails because he wrongly assumes that such schemes have but a single purpose; once it is recognised that the scheme may serve more than one legitimate purpose simultaneously, his objection melts away. Importantly, this assumption that a legal institution can only serve a single purpose – either justice in transactions or justice in distribution – is not confined to this small corner of his argument but provides the foundation of his general division of labour between private law and public law. Most revealing in this respect is his discussion of private property and poverty. In contrast with libertarians, and following Kant, he appreciates the need for both the protection of private rights and the redistribution of wealth:

> 'Free persons can authorize enforceable property rights, because those rights are a way of enabling them to exercise their respective freedom. Yet they could not authorize rights up to the point that they made some people entirely subject to the discretion of others, because such powers would be inconsistent with the freedom of those who were dependent in this way.'[57]

So the dependency on others, which is one of the results of poverty, has to be counteracted. For Ripstein the solution is clear: 'taxation for [the sake of] those in need'.[58] In this way, public law ensures justice in distribution even as private law's protection of private property secures justice in transactions.

[56] See *Law Society of South Africa v Minister of Transport*, note 35 supra, at paras 45, 49–50.
[57] Ripstein, note 39 supra, at 1431.
[58] Ripstein, note 39 supra, at 1431.

The poor person is not allowed to shift his burden onto the shoulders of any other individual (Mr Morgan does not have to tolerate a homeless person using his yacht as a place to sleep); however, society as a whole acts through the state to shoulder that burden in accordance with the demands of distributive justice (the state uses tax revenue collected from Mr Morgan along with others to provide shelter to the homeless).

But this is not the only way in which the relationship between poverty and property can be managed. Quite apart from expropriation and redistribution of individual parcels of property, which could arguably be described as an extreme (or, perhaps, primitive) form of taxation, there is also the alternative of redefining private property rights. It is perfectly possible – and again South Africa provides an example – to combat homelessness by limiting the rights of the owners of land so that they are legally obliged to tolerate the presence of others on their property.[59] Curbing the exercise of private law rights in this manner is just as much an attempt to manage the tension between poverty and property by ameliorating relations of dependency as are tax-and-welfare schemes. Thus distributive justice and public purposes do not *have* to be pursued by public law means. Private law can be, and sometimes *is*, used to pursue such purposes, not only in respect of land ownership but across a wide field of human activity and in diverse ways.[60]

There is accordingly no neat division of labour between private law and public law that ties the former exclusively to transactional justice and the latter to distributive justice. That the law must carry out both tasks entailed by the division of responsibility does not mean that it must do so through separate legal pathways. Private law can do both jobs and so, as we saw in the discussion of the displacement of tort by a social insurance scheme, can public law. Private law and public measures can be interchangeable means for achieving the same purpose, a point also neatly brought to the fore by the UK Supreme Court when it turned down a human rights-based challenge to the Damages (Asbestos-related Conditions) (Scotland) Act 2009 in *Axa General Insurance Ltd and others v The Lord Advocate and others*.[61] As several Justices pointed out, the aim of this act of the Scottish Parliament, which ensures that persons diagnosed with pleural plaques are able to institute damages claims in the Scottish law of delict, finds its parallel in the creation of the extra-statutory Pleural Plaques Former Claimants Payment Scheme for England and Wales:[62] both seek, in the interest of social justice, to mitigate the decision of the House of Lords in *Rothwell v Chemical & Insulating*

---

[59] See the materials cited, note 32 supra, and generally, A J van der Walt *Property in the Margins* (Hart 2009).

[60] See further D Oliver *Common Values and the Public Private Divide* (Butterworths 1999).

[61] [2011] UKSC 46; 2012 SC (UKSC) 122; [2012] 1 AC 868.

[62] Ibid paras 14–15 (Lord Hope DP); 68–71(Lord Brown); 127 (Lord Reed).

Co Ltd[63] that pleural plaques did not constitute an injury capable of giving rise to a claim for damages. Here Scotland used private law to achieve an end that in England and Wales was pursued via a public measure. Hence Ripstein fails to provide convincing support for his claim that the idea of a division of responsibility between individuals and society requires 'that there be separate institutions charged with the separate tasks required by that division'.[64] He assumes rather than proves that there is a division of labour between private law and public law. We therefore still have no reason to think that anything of real value would be lost if private law were to be displaced by the direct application of constitutional human rights.

2.3 PRIVATE LAW AND CIVIL SOCIETY

Ripstein's theory has the undoubted virtue of conforming to contemporary legal reality. Despite centuries of growth in the capacity of states and in the variety of means open to them to pursue the task of public justice so clearly identified by Kant, private law still lives on as a distinct entity alongside public legal measures. Public compensation schemes have displaced private tort law only in limited respects, and the adjustment of private law rights plays a minute role in the redistribution of wealth when compared to tax-and-welfare schemes. Perhaps most tellingly, private law continues to treat as indispensable two doctrines that severely limit its use as an instrument for pursuing public purposes, and can only be explained satisfactorily on the basis that it serves to ensure interpersonal responsibility: the requirement of causation and the distinction between misfeasance (acts) and nonfeasance (omissions).[65] Is there a more successful explanation for this than the one offered by Ripstein?

There is, but in order to find it we must depart from Ripstein's Kantian orientation. Ripstein's explanation of the division of responsibility and the role of private law is, as he emphasises, rooted in the ideas of Kant. He follows Kant in seeing the function of law and the state as revolving around the protection of individual rights, all ultimately rooted in an original innate (and inviolable) right to external freedom.[66] And there lies its problem. The point of the division of responsibility between individual and society, and the accompanying division of labour between private law and public law, can only be grasped once it is appreciated that the state's task in securing individual freedom is more complex than this. The key to these divisions, as I shall

---

63 [2007] UKHL 39; [2008] AC 281.
64 Ripstein, note 16 supra, at 181516
65 See du Bois 'Human Rights', note 9 supra, at 599–600; Ripstein, note 16 supra, at 1839–43.
66 Kant expressed this by saying (*Metaphysics of Morals*, note 20 supra, at 6:306) that the 'condition of public right . . . contains no further or other duties of human beings among themselves than can be conceived in the former state [i.e. the condition of private right]'.

explain, lies in the apparently paradoxical need for the state simultaneously to adopt a more modest stance and to pursue a much richer programme than the protection of individual freedom.

The foundations for this explanation were constructed by Hegel. One of Hegel's enduring contributions to political philosophy was to highlight the dependence of freedom on what he referred to as *Sittlichkeit*, that is, social ethics. As Allen Wood explains,

> 'Hegel thinks that the greatest enemy of personal and subjective freedom is a 'mechanistic' conception of the state, which views the state solely as an instrument for the enforcement of abstract rights; for this sets the state up as an abstraction in opposition to individuals ... The only real guarantee of freedom is a well-constituted ethical life, which integrates the rights of persons and subjects into an organic system of customs and institutions providing individuals with concretely fulfilling lives.'[67]

Thus freedom is not solely the achievement of the state; equally necessary is the existence of a social order possessing such an ethical life, which Hegel called 'civil society'. Hegel is nevertheless rightly also seen as a champion of the state, for he took the view that the state plays an essential part in bringing about the kind of social integration Wood refers to. This integrative role of the state takes its functions well beyond the Kantian one of administering justice in the service of the external freedom of individuals. In Hegel's analysis the state comes to be seen as also playing a crucial role in the construction of the 'common good', that is, the rich and complex array of goals and values that constitute the particular social ethics of a given concrete community. Admittedly, these two strands in Hegel's writings can be thought to pull in different directions.[68] But it is ultimately more in keeping with Hegel's methodology to see them as identifying two elements of modern polities that are both indispensable because the interplay between them is what allows the existence of freedom.[69] On this reading, civil society is essential because it makes possible (in a variety of ways to be outlined below) the reconciliation by the state of individual goals and the public interest; and the state is necessary because it provides (again in ways to be explained below) the external regulation that enables civil society to play this freedom-securing role.

Civil society was thought of by Hegel as a specific social formation that arose along with the modern state out of the Protestant reformation and the French Revolution and was characterised by a social ethics that supported

---

[67] A W Wood 'Editor's Introduction' in G W F Hegel *Elements of the Philosophy of Right* (A W Wood (ed) H B Nisbet (trans) Cambridge University Press 1991) xvi.

[68] See C Taylor 'Hegel's Ambiguous Legacy for Modern Liberalism' (1988–1989) 10 *Cardozo Law Review* 857; R Fine *Political Investigations: Hegel, Marx, Arendt* (Routledge 2001) 5–40.

[69] Ibid. See also A Arato 'A Reconstruction of Hegel's Theory of Civil Society' (1988–1989) 10 *Cardozo Law Review* 1363; J L Cohen 'Morality or *Sittlichkeit*: Toward a Post-Hegelian Solution' (1988–1989) 10 *Cardozo Law Review* 1389.

and facilitated the pursuit of individual goals.[70] Civil society in this sense lies between 'the family, the private society based on love . . . and . . . the state, i.e. the public community based explicitly on reason and aiming at collective or universal ends'.[71] It is accordingly 'the realm in which individuals exist as persons and subjects, as owners and disposers of private property, and as choosers of their own life-activity in the light of their contingent and subjective needs and interests'.[72] In civil society individuals (and families) pursue their private projects in their own interest, including in their economic activities. However, it is also a realm in which people, acting in this individualistic way, produce genuine social relationships, 'a universal family' that makes collective demands on its members and has collective responsibilities towards them.[73] Thus Hegel endorsed the notion, made familiar through the writings of Adam Smith, that the competitive individual pursuit of economic self-interest can produce an outcome that serves the collective interest. But he understood that, left to its own devices, civil society would undermine the individual freedom of some of its members. He saw the state as the means by which to counteract this through its capacity to restrain the unbridled pursuit of individual goals and to harness resources for the promotion of collective well-being.[74] Nevertheless, Hegel considered it a crucial feature of civil society – indeed the feature through which it enables the reconciliation of individual freedom and state authority – that it is the realm where individuals develop a sense of concrete social identity, especially through membership in groupings ('estates' and 'corporations', as Hegel called them in the language of his time) through which shared interests are pursued, developed and safeguarded.[75] Being highly sceptical of the effectiveness of individual participation in political processes, Hegel saw these groupings as the means whereby individual voices could be aggregated and represented in the political system, thus directing and controlling the state's determination of the

---

[70] See Hegel *Elements of the Philosophy of Right*, note 67 supra, at § 182A. For discussion, see Wood, note 67 supra, at xvii-xix and Arato, note 69 supra. One need not be persuaded by Hegel's view that a civil society in the sense meant by him – a social formation distinct from the affective ties of familial/clan relations as well as from larger-scale all-encompassing associations such as he believed characterised ancient societies and the medieval Church – has existed only in the particular historical epoch identified as 'modern'. It seems to me that it has been present to some degree in a long line of societies, although often occupying a smaller social stage than in Europe after the Reformation and the French Revolution. But for present purposes this is of no consequence; all that is important is Hegel's insight that a civil society is indispensable for the existence of a modern/rational state.

[71] Wood, note 67 supra, at xviii.

[72] Wood, note 67 supra, at xviii.

[73] Hegel *Elements of the Philosophy of Right*, note 67 supra, at § 239.

[74] Hegel *Elements of the Philosophy of Right*, note 67 supra, at § 185 and 185A.

[75] Hegel *Elements of the Philosophy of Right*, note 67 supra, at §§ 250–6. For discussion, see Wood, note 67 supra, at xix-xx.

common good.[76] In sum, Hegel saw freedom as achievable only through the state, but believed this to require the co-existence of a vibrant civil society.

Hegel has been accused of both statism and naiveté, but it is clear that he was, at least at some points during his writing career, acutely aware of the dangers posed by both the state and civil society.[77] His work displays a concern with ensuring that each controls the other. This is evident in his views on the organisation of the state just referred to, as well as in his insistence that civil society – especially the 'system of needs', that is, the economic realm – would subvert freedom if left to operate unchecked.[78] These two aspects of Hegel's writings are pivotal to understanding the nature of constitutional human rights as well as their significance to private law. But before we turn to that, it is instructive to note that Hegel describes the administration of justice as an aspect of civil society, distinguishing it from what he calls 'the police' (*Polizei*), which he explores as the central task of the state.[79] By 'police' Hegel, in common with his contemporaries, referred to what we would today understand as public policy or the public interest: it covers not only the maintenance of order, but also, and primarily, the pursuit of social welfare.[80] Hegel can therefore be said to have drawn a distinction between private law and public law in which the former is associated with civil society and the latter with the state.[81] In his words: 'In relation to the spheres of civil law [*Privatrecht*] and private welfare, the spheres of the family and civil society, the state is . . . an *external* necessity . . .'.[82]

In doing so, Hegel supplied the key to unlocking the value of private law.[83] This lies in the fact that private law, by carving out a sphere of

---

[76] Hegel *Elements of the Philosophy of Right*, note 67 supra, at §§ 301–3, 311R.

[77] See the literature cited in note 69 supra.

[78] Hegel *Elements of the Philosophy of Right*, note 67 supra, at §§ 236, 243, 245.

[79] The paragraphs headed 'The Administration of Justice' constitute part B of 'Section 2 Civil Society' in Hegel *Elements of the Philosophy of Right*, note 67 supra. The 'police' is described as 'an external order' in § 249.

[80] See M Loughlin *Foundations of Public Law* (Oxford University Press 2010) 422–9.

[81] Note, however, that he also discusses crimes under the heading of 'Administration of Justice'.

[82] Hegel *Elements of the Philosophy of Right*, note 67 supra, at § 261.

[83] Of course, Hegel occupied himself with larger questions than the theory of private law. Nevertheless his work contains discussions of property and contract, in particular, which others have moulded into subtle and illuminating accounts of the central areas of private law. See esp P Benson 'Abstract Right and the Possibility of a Nondistributive Conception of Contract: Hegel and Contemporary Contract Theory' (1988–1989) 10 *Cardozo Law Review* 1077; M Rosenfeld 'Hegel and the Dialectics of Contract' (1988–1989) 10 *Cardozo Law Review* 1199; A Brudner *The Unity of the Common Law: Studies in Hegelian Jurisprudence* (University of California Press, 1995). For present purposes we do not have to dig as deeply as they have done. We can put aside the question of what implications Hegel's insights have for a full understanding of what the law of property or of contract, say, seeks to achieve, as our concern is only with the more general question of why there should be a private law at all.

decision-making that is governed by interpersonal justice rather than the logic of public welfare, draws a boundary around the 'police' functions of the state. The existence of private law thereby serves to secure civil society as a realm of social interaction that is distinct from the state, and in this manner makes a vital contribution to the legitimacy of a society's political institutions. To be sure, in any contemporary society – as indeed in Hegel's Prussia – the state is deeply enmeshed in the maintenance and development of all areas of private law, not only through legislation but also through supplying the primary institutions of adjudication, and, when exercising these functions, cannot do otherwise than to steer private law in accordance with its conception of the public interest. All areas of private law may, and indeed in practice do, contain a mixture of considerations of interpersonal and social justice.[84] But to the extent that conflicts of interest are resolved in terms of considerations pertaining to the participants rather than to the public as a whole, the logic of public welfare has a limited field of application even in the institutions maintained by the state in the public interest – and space is left for conducting social interactions on terms that are autonomous of the state's objectives.[85] In this way, private law helps constitute civil society. In its absence conflicts would be relentlessly subject to the objectives of the state. Indeed, without private law there can be no civil society – and, given Hegel's explanation of the indispensable role of civil society as a complement to the state, no freedom.

Hegel's own account of the value of civil society is complex, not to say obscure, partly because of the evolution of his thought over time and partly because of some ambivalence on his part.[86] Nor does every aspect of it convince in the light of subsequent historical experience: especially his assimilation of civil society and the economy is problematic in light of what we now know of the stresses to which a market economy subjects social bonds and about the interdependence of economic and political elites. However, his fundamental insight that a polity regulated by a state – that is, a specialised institution dedicated to the pursuit of social welfare – can only preserve freedom if it also contains, outside the state, a sphere of social interaction in which the social values and objectives that are to govern the state as well

---

[84] Thus Hegel observes that the state is not only an external necessity, but also 'the higher power to whose nature their laws and interests are subordinate and on which they depend': Hegel *Elements of the Philosophy of Right*, note 67 supra, at § 261.

[85] Importantly, this understanding of the function of private law does not claim that any area of private law – say, contract law or property law – serves specifically to safeguard individual autonomy so that its integrity is interfered with when the state (including the courts) injects it with considerations of public policy. On the contrary, it acknowledges that all areas of private law exhibit a mixture of interpersonal and social justice. The point is simply that the state's pursuit of public purposes is constrained to the extent that the resolution of, say, a tort claim or a contractual dispute is not *entirely* governed by public welfare aims.

[86] See the literature cited in note 69 supra (emphasis added).

as the other prerequisites for democratic participation are generated, is convincing.[87] It is for this reason that private law provides an irreplaceable social service and merits protection, despite the importance of social justice, and even in an environment where the state is able to – and does – pursue the freedom of all through its public measures.

This is not to say that private law has limitless value. As the law constituting the domain of civil society, private law is valuable only to the extent that an autonomous civil society indeed serves to promote freedom. And there are limits to this, too. When the standing risk that civil society might subvert freedom is realised, and indeed more generally whenever the state is better placed to promote freedom, private law should give way to public 'police' measures. Thus, for example, private law rights of ownership must be restricted when the resolution of a conflict over the use of a plot of land on the basis of the interpersonal consideration of who owns the land and who does not, would lead to an unacceptable restriction of freedom through the resulting homelessness of non-owners. Similarly, a public compensation system ought to displace tort liability to the extent that the state is better able through public measures to prevent and ameliorate the general loss of freedom resulting from personal injuries (suffered in the workplace, in road traffic, or generally) than a private law system of liability – especially if interpersonal considerations continue to govern other instances of harm infliction. And the protection of individuals' reputation and other personality interests through private law remedies should take account of the public value of freedom of speech and the press. Examples can be multiplied and their complexities elaborated, but the basic point is a straightforward one: because both civil society and the state, both private law and public law, play indispensable roles in safeguarding freedom, a balance must be struck which combines them in the way that best serves individual freedom. This is no simple matter, but it is unavoidable.

2.4 WHY PRIVATE LAW NEEDS FUNDAMENTAL RIGHTS

Hegel's account of the role of civil society illuminates the distinctive and irreplaceable contribution made by private law's pursuit of interpersonal justice to the promotion of freedom. This has at least one clear implication for the relationship between private law and constitutional human rights: if freedom is best served by applying such rights horizontally, this must be done in a manner that preserves the integrity of private law as a realm of interpersonal justice. That is, constitutional human rights should be given indirect rather than direct horizontal effect. But there remains a final question: why apply *constitutional human rights* in order to counteract the potential adverse effects of giving free rein to interpersonal justice? Granted that private law must

---

[87] See generally J L Cohen and A Arato *Civil Society and Political Theory* (MIT Press 1992).

not be treated as divorced from public concerns – why must constitutional human rights feature in this reasoning process, except, perhaps, as setting a limiting framework?[88] After all, courts have taken account of public policy and social values when adjudicating private law disputes since long before the current 'age of rights'. Why not continue as before?

The answer begins with noting that a particular conception of the public interest is necessitated by Kant's insights regarding the role of 'public right' in securing freedom. It is one that is public not only by virtue of its impartiality as between individuals, but also, and more profoundly, because it represents the (rational) perspective of *every* individual member of society, i.e. is 'omnilateral'. Such a conception of the public interest therefore differs fundamentally from other impartial notions of public interest, such as the median or aggregate notions that are familiar to us as forms of utilitarianism, in which individual interests are dissolved in a larger pool. Thus Kant refers to the 'concurring and united will of all'.[89] Kant himself appears to have thought that the construction of appropriately representative institutions through which individual interests can enter into the decision-making process would fashion the state into the agent of the omnilateral perspective.[90] The same idea is also present in Hegel's writings, which pay considerable attention to the manner in which civil society ought to be linked to the state as well as to the prerequisites for making this effective.[91] They do not mention anything like contemporary constitutional human rights in this context. Given the techniques of public law around at the time, this is unremarkable – neither the French Declaration of the Rights of Man, nor, it seems, the American Bill of Rights was then regarded as affording judicially enforceable subjective rights.[92] It is nevertheless easy to see how constitutional human rights can fit into, and reinforce, their ideas of how omnilaterality can be ensured in the state's decision-making. Such rights provide a further route into the decision-making process, one that can be seen as helping to counteract the threat that electoral majorities pose to genuine omnilaterality. Moreover, many such rights serve to maintain a distinction between the state and civil society as well as to support, directly and indirectly, autonomous processes of will-formation through which notions of the common good may come to be formulated and injected into state institutions. Unsurprisingly, many writers have depicted the function of constitutional human rights in just these ways.[93]

However, this understanding of constitutional human rights provides

---

[88] See e.g. *National Media Ltd v Bogoshi* 1998 (4) SA 1196 (SCA) and *Amod v Multilateral Motor Vehicle Accidents Fund (Commission for Gender Equality Intervening)* 1999 (4) SA 1319 (SCA).

[89] Kant *Metaphysics of Morals*, note 20 supra, at 6:314 (emphasis added).

[90] See Kant *Metaphysics of Morals*, note 20 supra, at 6:313–6:330, 6:339–6:342.

[91] See Hegel *Elements of the Philosophy of Right*, note 67 supra, at §§ 300–20.

[92] Loughlin *Foundations of Public Law*, note 80 supra, at 350.

[93] The best-known and most influential version is J Hart Ely *Democracy and Distrust: A Theory of Judicial Review* (Harvard University Press 1980).

only limited support for thinking them particularly valuable to private law reasoning. True, such rights are helpful in the various ways just listed when it comes to ensuring that legislation on private law matters reflects an omnilateral perspective; but much private law development is in the hands of the judiciary and here the ordinary procedures and institutions of civil justice already provide an avenue for individuals who wish to ensure that their interests enter into the decision-making process. This is true especially of jurisdictions, such as Scotland and South Africa, where the basic framework of private law principles is for the most part uncodified and therefore open to judicial alteration even in the absence of an overriding constitutional obligation. Moreover, as we saw in the preceding section, private law's focus on interpersonal justice helps in its own right to constitute and maintain civil society; it does not need constitutional human rights in order to do so.

It is again Hegel's insight that safeguarding individual freedom requires more than a state responsive to individual interests that reveals the real benefit to private law reasoning of having recourse to constitutional human rights. As he realised, individual freedom in a social setting is only possible if all individuals strive after the same goal; as long as there is disagreement about the objective to be pursued, some will unavoidably lose out when a collective decision is formulated and a genuinely omnilateral perspective will remain a vain hope. Individual freedom therefore requires the forging of a common good, representing a valued state of affairs genuinely shared by all individual members of society as a goal that each is duty-bound to pursue.[94] Hegel understood that this is particularly problematic after the emergence of civil society, the very social formation that is most closely associated with the emancipation of the individual, because of its corrosive effect on the bonds of tradition and religion that used to provide a common identity of just this kind. As already pointed out, he regarded the state as the best available agent for such integration.[95] The dire potential and actual consequences of such statism became more than obvious in the twentieth century, and it seems unarguable that Hegel was unduly optimistic about the state – even though the sting of such criticism should be tempered by awareness that all philosophers are hostage to the times in which they live. Nevertheless, his views on the role played by the state in the forging of a common good open up another perspective on what constitutional human rights do. This is that they not only serve as a bridge between civil society and the state, but, in doing so, also give direction to the state's construction of the common good of a given polity.

Such an understanding of constitutional human rights is supported by

[94] For a lucid explanation, see Wood 'Editor's Introduction' in Hegel *Elements of the Philosophy of Right*, note 67 supra, at xxii-xxvii.

[95] Thus: 'The state is the actuality of concrete freedom.' (Hegel *Elements of the Philosophy of Right*, note 67 supra, at § 260.)

their genealogy as well as their operation. The origin of these rights lies in reactions to the excesses and failures of states, and they represent an attempt to find an effective mechanism for keeping state institutions focused on the tasks from which their authority derives its legitimacy. This mechanism functions by enabling the measures adopted by state institutions to be assessed against a text which establishes certain valued states of affairs as so fundamental that these measures *must* comply with them. In doing this, con-stitutional human rights set up an ideal of social interaction in (at least) the political realm, thereby establishing a common good for the members of the society, a goal for all to pursue. Importantly, Hegel also saw that not just any valued state of affairs could count as the common good of civil society; given the centrality of individual freedom to this social formation in particular, the common good of civil society is individual autonomy, that is, a commitment to the dignity of the individual.[96] This is precisely the commitment that lies at the heart of constitutional human rights charters.[97] Moreover, such charters are always produced by specific historical experiences and contexts, result-ing in texts and interpretative practices that articulate the understandings of individual autonomy and dignity endorsed by concrete political communi-ties with their own specific characteristics. Crucially, experience everywhere has shown that these understandings are not static, locking in some founda-tional 'original intent', but dynamic: the broad and aspirational language of such documents facilitates challenges to the status quo, encouraging ongoing political debate on society's fundamental goals in legislatures, courts and beyond. In a nutshell: a constitutional human-rights charter establishes not only the 'subjective' rights of individuals, but also a commitment to the common pursuit of certain values, or, as the South African Constitutional Court put it, an 'an objective, normative value system'.[98]

Understood in this way, constitutional human rights do bring something specific to private law: they enable private law's inescapable engagement with public purposes to proceed from a public perspective that is omnilateral rather than, say, aggregative. Private law reasoning that finds the articula-tion of public policy (or, in South African legal jargon, the *boni mores*) in constitutional human rights proceeds from a conception of the common good that remains compatible with individual freedom even in a setting characterised by the diversity of civil society rather than the consensus of tradition or religion. In this way, constitutional human rights anchor the

---

[96] '[T]he end of the state is both the universal interest as such and the conservation of particu-lar interests within the universal interest as the substance of these. . .' (Hegel *Elements of the Philosophy of Right*, note 67 supra, at § 270.)

[97] This has been prominent in the judgments of the South African Constitutional Court. See generally A J Barnard-Naudé, D Cornell and F du Bois (eds) *Dignity, Freedom and the Post-Apartheid Legal Order: The Critical Jurisprudence of Laurie Ackermann* (Juta 2008).

[98] *Carmichele v Minister of Safety and Security (Centre for Applied Legal Studies Intervening)* 2001 (4) SA 938 (CC) at para 54.

legitimacy of private law reasoning in democratic societies.[99] Little wonder that the character of constitutional rights charters as catalogues of the values to which polities have committed themselves has been central in the judicial justification of the horizontal application of such rights across the globe.[100] Indeed, the diverse instances of horizontal application surveyed in the contributions to this work show that it is precisely in this way that private law is being influenced by constitutional human rights: in fields ranging from respect for private life in the UK to the safeguarding of the home in South Africa, private law is being realigned to the new sets of values introduced into Scots law and South African law by their respective charters of human rights.

2.5 CONCLUSION

As we saw, even in the interpersonal relations that are private law's concern, the protection of individual freedom requires what Kant called a 'system of public right' so that what counts as an infringement of freedom can be determined from the 'omnilateral' perspective representing all affected persons rather than the partial perspective of some. The state has come to provide that service through the development of active programmes of legislation and powerful institutions of adjudication which have combined to turn it into the prime agent for the development of private law. However, in contemporary states these features are intertwined with another dimension of state activity: the direct promotion of public welfare, cultural as well as material. Thus the state does more than Kant envisaged: it pursues not only justice but also the common good. As Hegel saw, this is essential for the actualisation of individual freedom in a context where the loose association of civil society has taken the place of the strong bonds of affective community. For that reason private law must make way for public measures when these are better able to secure freedom. Indeed, the evolution of the state's social role poses the question whether there still is any defensible purpose to a system of interpersonal justice: should private law not now be subsumed under the scheme of social welfare, functioning at most as one among several regulatory techniques serving the common good? Hegel's demonstration of the need for civil society shows that the answer to this is 'no'. In constituting the domain of civil society, private law's pursuit of interpersonal justice makes a distinctive and irreplaceable contribution to the promotion of freedom.

---

[99] For further elaboration of this point, see F du Bois 'Social Purposes, Fundamental Rights and the Judicial Development of Private Law' in D Nolan and A Robertson (eds) *Rights and Private Law* (Hart 2011) 89.

[100] This notion originated in German constitutional jurisprudence (specifically the reasoning in (1958)7 BVerfGE 198 (*Lüth*)) and is also accepted in Canada (*Retail, Wholesale & Department Store Union, Local 580 v Dolphin Delivery Ltd* [1986] 2 SCR 573; (1987) 33 DLR (4th) 174 (SCC)).

It nevertheless benefits from recourse to constitutional human rights: in a world of moral diversity, the realm of values established by charters of such rights gives concrete yet elastic shape to a conception of the common good to which private law reasoning can orientate itself when playing its discrete role in the 'system of public right'.

In this way, the indirect horizontal application of constitutional human rights provides an apt normative framework for private law reasoning, relating claims of interpersonal justice to the wider context of a society's moral commitments. It directs attention to which array of interpersonal rights and duties is best calculated to enable the sorts of lives a given polity is committed to enabling people to live.[101] The content of that commitment may vary significantly from country to country; but where it is enshrined in a constitutional charter of human rights, such a social ideal always represents a conception of human beings as ends valuable in their own right rather than means available for the purposes of others.[102] For that reason, recourse to such rights serves to 'humanise' private law, ensuring that interpersonal justice not merely makes everyone count, but makes everyone count as a human, a normative agent with concrete needs and aspirations.[103] Legal experience in both Scotland and South Africa bears this out, not least in contexts where individuals have all too often been treated as mere units of production.[104]

---

[101] For discussion of some concrete examples, see du Bois, note 99 supra, at 102–6.

[102] For a compelling argument to this effect, see J Griffin *On Human Rights* (Oxford University Press 2008).

[103] It is this idea that judges and writers seek to convey by associating constitutional human rights with the concept of human dignity.

[104] See esp Chapters 12, 13, 15 and 17 in this volume by Webster, Laing and Visser, Cabrelli, and Pretorius, respectively.

Chapter 3

The Politics of Private Law: Sexual Minority Freedom in South Africa and Scotland

Jaco Barnard-Naudé

'To be is to be queer.'[1]

3.1 INTRODUCTION

In their edited collection entitled *Human Rights in Private Law*,[2] Friedmann and Barak-Erez explore the influence of the introduction of various human rights regimes on the private law of the jurisdictions under consideration in their book. Friedmann and Barak-Erez's central premise is that private law, although not explicitly invoking the term, has always been concerned with human rights.[3] They go on to argue that the transformation triggered with the introduction of human rights into private law 'may be considered merely terminological in nature'.[4] Yet the authors immediately concede that a change in terminology may have a more profound effect than mere substitution of words, since language is not merely a tool with which we convey our thoughts, but also 'a process that affects our analysis and conceptions'.[5] In this regard, they acknowledge that the introduction of human rights brings with it 'values to which private law has hitherto attributed little weight'.[6] This fact, the authors believe, spells the likelihood of a considerable transformation.

Yet, as they continue to argue, the introduction of human rights into private law also means that human rights concepts themselves cannot remain unaltered, cannot be introduced into private law without undergoing, then, a certain transformation. This is the case, argue Friedmann and Barak-Erez, because private law is ruled by the concept of intersubjective formal equality, whereas human rights have traditionally been ruled by the notion of inequality between the state and its citizens.[7]

---

[1] J Derrida 'Justices' (2005) 31(3) *Critical Inquiry* 689 at 703.
[2] D Friedmann and D Barak-Erez 'Introduction' in D Friedmann and D Barak-Erez (eds) *Human Rights in Private Law* (Hart 2001) 1.
[3] Ibid 3.
[4] Ibid.
[5] Ibid.
[6] Ibid.
[7] Ibid.

To put the authors' argument about transformation in more Hegelian terms: we are faced with a *dialectical* notion of transformation when human rights meet private law. My recourse to Hegel here is motivated by the attempt to convey more clearly that we encounter a 'both, and' movement of transformation in this context. Friedmann and Barak-Erez argue that it is not just the case that private law will need to transform when it faces human rights law; it is also the case that human rights law faces transformation if it is to have a transformative effect in private law. The authors seem to allude to what is referred to as indirect horizontal application in South African law – briefly, the idea that human rights values should transform the substantive content of the traditional value-based, open-ended concepts of private law.[8]

Indirect horizontal application might well represent this notion of dialectical transformation, since it requires both human rights law and private law to undergo transformation. From the perspective of human rights law, the transformation that it has inevitably undergone and is arguably still undergoing under the aegis of indirect horizontal application lies in the conception of the nature of rights. Traditionally, human rights are regarded as shields with which the individual protects herself against the all-encompassing power of the state. An application of human rights in private law (as a rights regime that is by its very nature 'other-directed' in Ernest Weinrib's words)[9] mandates a paradigm shift in that a less hierarchical, relational (that is, a horizontal) understanding of rights is implied in it.[10] For present purposes, it is not necessary to dwell any further on the question of indirect horizontal application. Suffice it to say that, in the context of legal recognition and protection of sexual minority freedom through the decriminalisation of non-heterosexual sex and the adoption of marriage-like institutions in both Scotland and South Africa, indirect horizontal application has not yet been explicitly relied upon.

But this does not mean that the rhetoric and vocabulary with which indirect horizontal application is justified, is irrelevant when it comes to sexual minority freedom. On the contrary, from what follows, we will see that, in the same way as it is argued that human rights should determine the content and meaning of so-called 'open-ended' private law concepts such as 'public policy' and delictual 'wrongfulness', it is argued that human rights

---

8 See in general J van der Walt 'Progressive Indirect Horizontal Application of the Bill of Rights: Towards a Co-operative Relation between Common-Law and Constitutional Jurisprudence' (2001) 17 *SAJHR* 341.

9 E J Weinrib 'Corrective Justice' (1991–1992) 77 *Iowa LR* 403 at 406.

10 H Botha 'Democracy and Rights: Constitutional Interpretation in a Postrealist World' (2000) 63 *Tydskrif vir Hedendaagse Romeins-Hollandse Reg* 561 at 574–6 argues that the Constitution does not support a liberal conception of rights as boundaries between the individual and the collective; the rights in the Bill of Rights have a contingent and non-absolute meaning and to that extent they do not operate as a shield against government intervention or as trumps over collective interests.

values should determine the meaning and content of private law terms that for centuries were regarded as fixed; terms such as 'family', 'marriage' and '*consortium omnis vitae*'. To this extent, the dialectical transformation at issue when private law meets human rights remains highly relevant for the recognition and protection of sexual minority freedom in both Scotland and South Africa.

3.2 PRIVATE LAW AND THE POLITICS OF EQUALITY

Whilst this chapter explores Friedman and Barak-Erez's contentions against the background of the recognition and protection of sexual minority freedom in Scotland and South Africa, it is important to pause at the meaning of what will remain at issue throughout the chapter – the idea of formal equality as what Ernest Weinrib calls the 'immanent rationality' of private law.[11] For Weinrib, as for many a private lawyer, the coherence of private law relationships exists in their form – they represent instances of relationships capable of corrective justice.[12] In other words, corrective justice is for Weinrib 'the normative structure that underlies'[13] private law as a 'normative framework for claims arising out of human interaction'.[14]

In his reading of Aristotle, Weinrib argues that the rationality of private law is immanent in its form as an arithmetic (as opposed to a geometric) relation. This arithmetic form is the precondition of corrective justice. But a further precondition, prior to the arithmetic form as such, is formal equality. Aristotle is eminently lucid here:

> '[I]t makes no difference whether a good man has defrauded a bad one or vice versa, nor whether a good man or a bad one has committed adultery; all that the law considers is the difference caused by the injury; and *it treats the parties as equals*, only as asking whether one has committed and the other suffered an injustice, or whether one has inflicted and the other suffered a hurt. Accordingly the judge tries to equalize the inequality of this injustice.'[15] (Emphasis supplied.)

Weinrib argues that Aristotle's account of corrective justice '*presupposes* a formal equality that has become the object of serious reflection only in the last few centuries'[16] (emphasis supplied). He continues, with reference to Kant and Hegel's concept of right, to describe the formal equality

---

[11] E J Weinrib 'Legal Formalism: On the Immanent Rationality of Law' (1988) 97(6) *Yale LJ* 949.

[12] Weinrib, note 9 supra, at 418.

[13] Ibid 425.

[14] E J Weinrib 'Right and Advantage in Private Law' (1988–1989) 10 *Cardozo LR* 1283 at 1286.

[15] Aristotle *The Nicomachean Ethics* (H Tredennik (ed) and J A K Thomson (trans) Penguin 2004) at 121.

[16] Weinrib, note 9 supra, at 404.

of corrective justice as 'the abstract equality of free purposive beings'.[17] Weinrib is very close to Hegel's idea of abstract right here[18] – a term with which Hegel essentially indicates that a legal subject remains a rights bearer equal to other rights bearers from the perspective of Right, regardless of his or her particular and indeed, sometimes peculiar, circumstances.[19] For Weinrib it is this immanent rational form of private law that insulates it from political considerations, be they utilitarian or otherwise. Private law, he argues, under the assumption of the abstract equality of free wills, asks only whether the relationship between the parties is *capable* of corrective justice, nothing more and nothing less.[20]

In her discussion of formal equality – a term which she translates as 'liberal' equality – Robin West echoes the tones of Weinrib's description with slightly different, if illuminating terminology. West emphasises that this equality is justified with reference to human commonality. She writes: 'It is by virtue of our commonality that the state must accord all of us, without regard to race, sex, or sexuality, equal protection of the law and the dignity and respect that it entails'.[21] For West liberal legal protection, that is, the protection afforded by formal equality, is founded in 'our universally shared but radically differentiating rationality'.[22] Equality law in the era of liberalism, she argues, 'holds that we must be treated the same, unless a case can be made for the rationality of various distinctions between us'.[23] For West, formal equality in the liberal era is thus justified precisely by the fact and realisation of human commonality.

The history of the recognition and protection of sexual minority freedom in both Scotland and South Africa, however, reveals that, contrary to Weinrib's assertion,[24] private law is not immune from politics. In other words, it is not in and of itself the progressive legal realm ruled purely and

---

[17] Ibid.
[18] This is not surprising, given his clear reverence for Hegel. See Weinrib, supra note 14, at 1286: 'The treatment of abstract right at the beginning of Hegel's *Philosophy of Right* is the purest and most uncompromising account of private law from the perspective of right'.
[19] Hegel *Elements of the Philosophy of Right* (Allen W Wood (ed) H B Nisbet (trans) Cambridge University Press 1991).
[20] Weinrib, supra note 9, at 425. Here, the assumption of the abstract equality of free will should be emphasised. Private law treats minors and the mentally challenged differently from those who have attained the age of majority and are mentally capable, precisely because the assumption of free will is negated in private law relationships where one of the parties has not attained the age of majority or is mentally challenged. As Weinrib puts it elsewhere: '[T]he rights of private law are seen as expressions of the universal nature of the will's freedom': Weinrib, note 14 supra, at 1286.
[21] R West 'Universalism, Liberal Theory, and the Problem of Gay Marriage' (1997–1998) 25 *Florida State University LR* 705 at 706.
[22] Ibid.
[23] Ibid 705–6.
[24] See Weinrib 'Legal Formalism', note 11 supra.

exclusively by the notion of formal equality. In fact, it is politics (in particular, battles about the meaning of substantive equality and what consequences, if any, the law should attach to the fact of difference) that determine at what level of commonality formal equality – what Weinrib also calls the 'abstract equality of doing and suffering'[25] – operates in private law. In other words, this chapter argues that, from the perspective of sexual minorities,[26] the availability of corrective justice through the recognition and protection of private law family relationships, is not determined by the 'unpolitical' idea of formal equality at all, but rather by thoroughly political matters.

Admittedly, the Marxian undergarment of my argument is already showing itself here, but to invoke the terminology explicitly for the sake of clarity, private law as an indispensable part of a society's ideological superstructure, does not escape politics – especially when it comes to family matters. It was not for nothing that the French Marxist, Louis Althusser, described the family as an ideological state apparatus[27] – a societal institution through which state power, and, therefore, political control, is exercised. In the context of the family, then, the actuality of private law betrays its formal rationality. For, if it was the case that liberal formal equality, as West describes it, governs in modernity the recognition of relationships (as private law relationships) through and through, then there would hardly have been so severe and relentless a controversy as the one about the recognition and protection of same-sex relationships on the same basis as relationships of the opposite sex.[28]

Some will object that family law cannot and should not be considered under the narrow classical definition of private law given to it by Aristotle and later endorsed by Kant, Hegel and (in our own day) most prominently by Weinrib. Yet, existing family law is, in most part, as capable as any other settled category of private law of such an explanation. Family law is treated as part of private law precisely because the familial relationship – be it spousal or between spouses and children – is capable of satisfying the acid test for private law recognition: it is capable of corrective justice.[29]

---

[25] Weinrib, note 11 supra, at 988.

[26] That is to say, those members of society who do not exclusively engage in, or base their sexual relationships on, monogamous, heterosexual sex.

[27] L Althusser *On Ideology* (Verso 2008) at 17.

[28] Also see Weinrib, note 11 supra, at 984: 'A relationship can be construed as one of corrective justice if the justification applicable to it is an explication of the equality applicable to doing and suffering'. If this was really the case, private law would long have recognised cohabitation relationships (of whatever gender mixture) in which partners have undertaken reciprocal duties of support.

[29] In 'Savigny's Family/Patrimony Distinction and its Place in the Global Genealogy of Classical Legal Thought' (2010) 58 *Am J Comp L* 811 at 827 Duncan Kennedy formulates this capacity of family law for private law recognition in a different, but related way. For him, family law is private law because it consists of 'reciprocal rights and duties enforceable through civil process'.

This chapter continues to argue that the principle of substantive equality, which forms part and parcel of traditional human rights discourse, plays a supplemental role and, as such, in turn undermines Weinrib's argument that private law recognition depends purely upon a relationship's formal capacity for corrective justice. The encounter between private law and human rights in this context further suggests that, contrary to the idea that private law has 'always been concerned with human rights', it has actively resisted, in overtly political ways, the concerns of human rights.

At the very least, the novelty that human rights introduce into private law is the idea of substantive equality.[30] There is much controversy as regards the exact meaning of this term but at the minimum it stands for the eradication of legal obstacles in the way of an equality of opportunity.[31] This eradication does not simply involve the recognition of equality before the law – treating equally people who are, substantively speaking, the same.[32] Rather, substantive equality requires the acknowledgement of past injustices through unequal treatment. More broadly, substantive equality is about the law's recognition of difference.[33]

In the context of sexual minority freedom, it is precisely the fact of difference, as well as the acknowledgement of past injustice done to sexual minorities because of their difference, that justifies the argument for the recognition of formal legal equality between opposite-sex and same-sex relationships. Justice Albie Sachs describes this view of equality in his separate concurring judgment in what is often referred to as the first *National Coalition* case[34] – the case in which the Constitutional Court declared the common law crime of sodomy unconstitutional.[35] Referring to the equality guarantees of the 1996 Constitution, Sachs J writes as follows:

> 'Equality means equal concern and respect across difference. It does not presuppose the elimination or suppression of difference ... Equality therefore does not imply a levelling or homogenisation of behaviour but an acknowledgment and acceptance of difference ... This judgment holds that in determining the normative limits of permissible sexual conduct, homosexual erotic activity must be treated on an equal basis with heterosexual, in other words, that *the same-sex quality of the conduct must not be a consideration in determining where and how the law should intervene.*'[36]

---

[30] See R Leckey 'Family Law as Fundamental Private Law' (2007) 86 *Canadian Bar Review* 69 at 88.

[31] See M Rosenfeld 'Substantive Equality and Equal Opportunity: A Jurisprudential Appraisal' (1986) 74 (5) *California Law Review* 1687 at 1687–90.

[32] West, note 21 supra, at 711.

[33] Ibid 712.

[34] *National Coalition for Gay and Lesbian Equality and Another v Minister of Justice and Others* 1999 (1) SA 6 (CC).

[35] At para 73.

[36] At paras 132–3 (emphasis added).

The Constitutional Court's reading of substantive equality, then, affirms that the right to be different, and the fact of difference, afford the right to the same treatment.

This chapter claims that the introduction of substantive equality via human rights into the private law of both South Africa and Scotland should be read as a moment in which a politics of equality is constituted. With a 'politics of equality' I attempt to convey the idea that the law's recognition of difference in the context of conjugal relationships has produced substantive outcomes in the respective jurisdictions that are very different, but that nevertheless share (or ought to share) the same concerns from the perspective of formal equality. In Scotland and the rest of the UK, the acknowledgement of difference has (at best) led to a situation of *separate formal equality*, in that a formal separation between opposite-sex and same-sex relationships, at least still at the time of writing,[37] formed the basis of the first legislative protection of same-sex relationships, although the legal consequences of entering into a civil partnership are virtually the same as those that follow from marriage.

In South Africa, the law's acknowledgment of difference took a different and perhaps more complex direction. Against the background of the enormous influence of the mantra of the Constitutional Court that the right to be different gives me the right to be treated equally, the recognition of difference between same-sex couples and opposite-sex couples only strengthened the argument for non-separate formal equality, that is, the opening up of the institution of marriage to same-sex couples. As will be seen, my argument is not that the enactment of the gender-neutral Civil Union Act[38] represented a perfect or unproblematic opening-up of the institution of marriage. But it cannot admit of any doubt that the Act's gender-neutral definition of a civil union as including a 'marriage'[39] represents a massive leap forward in the direction of the recognition of full formal equality for same-sex couples in South Africa.

The engagement of formal equality and substantive equality at the site of private law's interaction with human rights in this context can be regarded as either destructive or productive, depending on which side of the political playing field one is on. I believe that this engagement has been, and can continue to be, a productive one in a very specific sense, namely, that it is precisely the transformative power of substantive equality that can serve to

---

[37] See, however, the Scottish Government's progressive stance on the urgent legalisation of same-sex marriage: G Campbell 'Gay marriage to be introduced in Scotland' *BBC News* 25 July 2012, available at *http://www.bbc.co.uk/news/uk-scotland-scotland-politics-18981287*, and the Catholic Church in Scotland's active resistance against it: L Davies 'Same-sex Marriage: Scotland Urged to Resist Catholic Church Campaign' *The Guardian* 26 August 2012, available at: *http://www.guardian.co.uk/society/2012/aug/26/same-sex-marriage-scotland-catholic*.

[38] Act 17 of 2006.

[39] S 1.

reinforce, rejustify and thus re-legitimate the conception of private law as a purely Aristotelian form.

It is with these cards on the table that I continue to comparatively examine the legal developments in Scotland and South Africa.

3.3 SCOTLAND AND SOUTH AFRICA: DECRIMINALISATION AND ITS DISCONTENTS

3.3.1 Introduction

It might strike many a reader as odd that I include in this chapter a discussion of the history of the decriminalisation of male homosexual sexual conduct in both the jurisdictions under investigation. Surely, such a reader would argue, decriminalisation falls to be considered squarely within the domain of public law. However, for two reasons, I regard an inclusion of this history here as crucial.

The first reason is succinctly provided by Norrie: '[D]ecriminaliza-tion removes the primary justification for treating same-sex couples less favourably than opposite-sex couples'.[40] In other words, decriminalisation is precisely what removes the primary obstacle in the way of private law recognition (that is, formal equality recognition) of same-sex relationships. Without decriminalisation, then, human rights are not only effectively blocked from irradiating private law, criminalisation also prevents private law development from within. The second reason why I include a discussion of decriminalisation here is related to one of the overarching themes of this chapter, namely to illustrate the deep connection between law and politics in this field of law.

3.3.2 Scotland

As was the case in the South African common law, Scottish common law provided that male homosexual conduct was a criminal offence. Davidson and Davis point out that in Scotland indeed the majority of offences were prosecuted under common law and not statute,[41] which was also the way things stood in South Africa. However, when compared to England and Wales, sentences imposed in Scotland were generally lighter.[42] Moreover, while the Vagrancy Laws in England and Wales were exploited to charge

---

[40] K McK Norrie 'Marriage and Civil Partnership for Same-sex Couples: The International Imperative' (2005) 1 *Journal of International Law and International Relations* 249 at 255.

[41] R Davidson and G Davis '"A Field for Private Members": The Wolfenden Committee and Scottish Homosexual Law Reform, 1950–67' (2004) 15(2) *Twentieth Century British History* 174 at 177.

[42] Ibid.

large numbers of men with soliciting, Davidson and Davis point out that the corresponding provision in Scotland (the Immoral Traffic (Scotland) Act of 1902) was never used to prosecute homosexual soliciting.[43]

Against this background, the establishment of the Wolfenden Committee in 1954, marked a significant turning point, although it would take a number of years before its recommendations were implemented.[44] Davidson and Davis argue that the Wolfenden Committee commands a strong position 'in the historiography of the sexual politics of late twentieth-century Britain, and of homosexual politics in particular'.[45] The reason lies in the fact that the Committee's report marked a critical moment in the quest for the recognition of sexual minority freedom, in that it introduced a new moral economy (by recommending decriminalisation) that was to underpin significant, if unduly dragged out, reforms.[46]

As mentioned, the Wolfenden report famously recommended the decriminalisation of all private adult male homosexual conduct in the UK. It is significant to point out that the majority of those testimonies before the Wolfenden Committee that were in favour of decriminalisation relied on a facile separation of law and morality according to which 'private morality' was not the law's business, while those opposed to decriminalisation refused the opposition.[47] Exemplary of the former was the testimony of the 'moral purity' movement who argued that the law should not interfere with the personal morals of consenting adults, as this merely created a 'police des moeurs' with duties that were 'ugly, degrading and demoralizing'.[48]

Yet the evidence of medical experts, while discouraging incarceration as punishment, still labelled homosexuality as dysfunctional, even pathological and, in any event, antisocial.[49] As Davidson and Davis put it, 'their opposition to legal coercion was that it served merely to magnify not only the homosexual's sense of isolation but also his homosexual ego'.[50] This evidence was of course anticipated by the leading thinker of sexuality and the clinic at the time, Michel Foucault, who had already argued that once homosexuality was identified as a psychiatric condition, it became susceptible to a host of corrective clinical 'treatments'.[51]

In terms of the Scottish evidence before the Committee, the opposition to

[43] Ibid 182 n 29.
[44] See Anon 'Great Britain: The Wolfenden Report' *Time Magazine* 16 September 1957 available at *http://www.time.com/time/magazine/article/0,9171,809883,00.html*.
[45] Davidson and Davis, note 41 supra, at 175.
[46] Ibid.
[47] Ibid 192 and 199.
[48] Ibid 182.
[49] Ibid 188.
[50] Ibid 184.
[51] M Foucault *The Will to Knowledge: The History of Sexuality* vol 1 (R Hurley (trans) Penguin 1998).

decriminalisation was almost unanimous. In a strange twist, it was the very fact of a low incidence of convictions for homosexual behaviour that was used to argue *against* decriminalisation. In this regard, the argument was that decriminalisation was not necessary precisely because the conviction rate was low. The Crown Agent at the time, Lionel Gordon, argued succinctly that the procedural constraints (that were in large part responsible for the low conviction rate) in no way constituted a condonation of homosexual practices.[52] He continued that decriminalisation would be a retrograde act and at odds with Scottish public opinion.[53] Here we see how the refusal to separate law from public morality hindered the recognition of sexual minority freedom. In the end, however, a disappointing aspect of the Wolfenden report was its revelation of reliance by both the separationists and the non-separationists upon arguments located in a deep commitment to the belief that homosexual conduct is a moral aberration.

The Wolfenden Committee submitted its report to Parliament in September 1957. Unfortunately, its recommendations on decriminalisation did not draw much favour from the legislature. In the Scottish context, it was the dissent of James Adair, OBE and former procurator-fiscal, that carried the most weight when it came to Scottish homosexual law reform, or rather the lack thereof. Adair argued that decriminalisation would be contrary to the interests of the community and would have very serious degenerate effects on the moral fabric of social life.[54] Decriminalisation, he argued, would be tantamount to 'condoning or licensing licentiousness'.[55] At Adair's instigation, the Church of Scotland (which had sent neither a delegation nor a submission to the Wolfenden Committee) launched an investigation into homosexuality. The investigation culminated in a report in which the Church and Nation Committee of Scotland opposed decriminalisation, arguing that '[t]he criminal law must of necessity reflect the standards of morality generally accepted by the nation' and that homosexuality is so contrary to the Christian ethic that it should not only be regarded as sinful, but also as criminal.[56] In the same fashion, if somewhat more vehemently, the Free Presbyterian Church opposed law reform from as early as 1954.

Almost a decade went by before the legislature proposed its first Sexual Offences Bill in 1965 as a response to and relying heavily on the Wolfenden report. The vast majority of Scottish MPs employed the reports of the churches to strengthen their already vehement opposition to homosexual law reform. Again, the low incidence of prosecutions was ironically used to

---

[52] Davidson and Davis, note 41 supra, at 187.
[53] Ibid.
[54] Ibid 190.
[55] Ibid.
[56] Ibid 192. This antiquated sentiment seems to have become a permanent feature of the major institutionalised religions the world over. In the contemporary Scottish context, see Davies, note 37 supra.

argue against law reform, with MPs arguing that Scotland 'never experienced the controversies surrounding certain notorious English prosecutions'.[57] It is not necessary to go into all the arguments that Scottish MPs used to oppose the Sexual Offences Bill – the intensity of the opposition can simply be gauged by its effect: '[I]n deference to the legal, cultural, and political arguments' raised by Scotland during debate on the Bill, it was excluded from the application of the Sexual Offences Act of 1967.[58] Decriminalisation came to Scotland only thirteen years later with section 80 of the Criminal Justice (Scotland) Act 1980. Davidson and Davis describe the period between 1967 and 1980 in Scotland as one riddled with 'often bitter and divisive sexual politics'.[59] If anything, this discussion illustrates that, contrary to the dominant impression, private law *is* often nothing but politics.

3.3.3 South Africa

With the advent of democracy in South Africa it became common cause that the democratisation process would have to address all measures that had been taken by the apartheid government with a view to oppressing sexual minorities. Recognising the particularly harsh fate sexual minorities suffered under this legislative dispensation during apartheid, section 8(2) of the Interim Constitution of the Republic of South Africa[60] famously became the first constitutional provision in the world expressly to prohibit unfair discrimination, directly or indirectly, on the ground of sexual orientation.[61] Carl Stychin writes that the inclusion of sexual orientation as a ground of presumed unfair discrimination in the Constitution was the result of a single-minded pursuit by a group of activists and individuals during the years leading up to the acceptance of the Interim Constitution.[62]

Gay anti-apartheid activist Simon Nkoli is an important example in this regard. In 1988 Nkoli founded an organisation called GLOW (Gays and Lesbians of the Witwatersrand). He had been a co-accused in the Delmas

---

[57] Ibid 198.

[58] Ibid 199.

[59] Ibid.

[60] Constitution of the Republic of South Africa, 1993 ('Interim Constitution').

[61] Commentators refer, somewhat carelessly, to this inclusion as a 'key challenge to the edifice of heteronormativity through the 'queering' of the Constitution'. See M Steyn and M van Zyl 'The Prize and the Price' in M Steyn and M van Zyl *The Prize and the Price: Shaping Sexualities in South Africa* (HSRC Press 2009) 3. As I see it, the mere inclusion of sexual orientation as a ground for presumed unfair discrimination does not spark any meaningful queering of the Constitution. A Constitution is read, interpreted and given effect to by the courts, the legislature, the executive and the body politic. Queering the Constitution – if there is such a thing – depends in the final instance on the collective (ethico-political) practices of these bodies.

[62] C F Stychin 'Constituting Sexuality: The Struggle for Sexual Orientation in the South African Bill of Rights' (1999) 23(4) *Journal of Law and Society* 455 at 456.

treason trial and his prominence as a freedom fighter and openly gay black man within the struggle played a key role in forging a particularly strategic alliance between the gay rights movement and the mass democratic movement.[63] This alliance contributed significantly to the inclusion in the African National Congress' (ANC's) pre-democracy constitutional proposals[64] that the 'right to be protected from unfair discrimination must specifically include those discriminated against on the grounds of ethnicity, language, race, birth, sexual orientation and disability'.[65]

The founding of the National Coalition for Gay and Lesbian Equality in 1994 represents another important moment. Although this was not the first gay activist organisation in South Africa,[66] what set the Coalition apart was the explicit inclusion in its founding aims of ensuring that sexual orientation would be retained in the final Constitution.[67] The Coalition became a national umbrella organisation for over 40 groups and garnered the support of important public figures such as then Archbishop Desmond Tutu. In addition, the Coalition managed to persuade all major political parties not to oppose the inclusion in the final text of the Constitution of sexual orientation as a ground of presumed unfair discrimination.[68]

The inclusion of sexual orientation in the equality clause (as part of a justiciable Bill of Rights) meant that the courts (and ultimately, the Constitutional Court) were tasked with the responsibility to determine what amounted to unfair discrimination on the ground of sexual orientation. Section 2 of the Constitution declares its sovereignty and goes on to state that all law and conduct which is inconsistent with the Constitution is invalid. It was thus immediately apparent that the continuous criminalisation of male homosexual practices would be questionable. But, in the face of a newly formed government that was required to deal with the vast structural inequalities of apartheid and, in addition, due to a probable lack of political will, the

---

[63] For an excellent rendition of this history see J Cock 'Engendering Gay and Lesbian Rights: The Equality Clause in the South African Constitution' (2002) 26 *Women's Studies International Forum* 35 at 36–8.

[64] ANC Policy Proposals for a Final Constitution (available at *http://www.anc.org.za/show.php?id=284*) adopted by the National Conference of the African National Congress on 31 May 2002.

[65] Ibid. For a detailed account of the way in which the sexual orientation clause found its way into the South African Constitution see E C Christiansen 'Ending the Apartheid of the Closet: Sexual Orientation in the South African Constitutional Process' (2000) 32 *New York University Journal of International Law and Politics* 997. See also M F Massoud 'The Evolution of Gay Rights in South Africa' (2003) 15(3) *Peace Review* 301; and S Croucher 'South Africa's Democratisation and the Politics of Gay Liberation' (2002) 28(2) *Journal of Southern African Studies* 315.

[66] See P de Vos 'The "Inevitability" of Same-sex Marriage in South Africa's Post-Apartheid State' (2007) 23 *SAJHR* 432 at 435.

[67] Stychin, note 62 supra, at 461.

[68] Ibid 462.

decriminalisation of sodomy (and other relevant crimes), ranked relatively low on the list of legislative priorities.

A judicial pronouncement was thus called for. Again, the National Coalition played a decisive role in this regard. At its first conference in December 1995, it resolved that the organisations under its umbrella would not embark on constitutional challenges on their own. In this way, the Coalition gained control of the 'process of deciding when and in what order to bring constitutional challenges regarding the various aspects of discrimination against gay men and lesbians'.[69] It was decided that the most obvious litigation strategy was to focus first on decriminalisation, as this was 'the most obviously obnoxious aspect of discrimination suffered by gay men and (indirectly) lesbians'.[70]

By the time the Coalition launched its challenge to criminalisation, the case of *S v Kampher*[71] had already been decided in the Cape High Court. This was the first court in South Africa to declare that the common law crime of male sodomy ceased to exist after the coming into operation of the Interim Constitution on 27 April 1994.[72] The decision, however, only applied in the geographical jurisdiction of the Cape High Court. In addition, the 'final' Constitution had not yet come into operation when the alleged offence occurred that led to the accused in *S v Kampher* being charged (although the High Court in *Kampher* held that the criminalisation of sodomy was, in any event, also inconsistent with the provisions of the 'final' Constitution that had come into effect when the accused appeared in court for the first time).[73]

The National Coalition subsequently launched its challenge to criminalisation before Mr Justice Heher in the Witwatersrand Local Division of the High Court.[74] It applied to this court for an order declaring unconstitutional the common law crimes of sodomy and the commission of 'unnatural sexual acts between men' as well as various legislative provisions in connection with such criminalisation, including the infamous 'men at a party' provisions of section 20A of the Sexual Offences Act.[75]

The High Court declared the common law crimes as well as all the related statutory provisions unconstitutional.[76] The Constitution, however, provides that where a lower court declares an Act of Parliament unconstitutional, such an order, to have force and effect, must be referred to the

---

[69] De Vos, note 66 supra, at 443.
[70] Ibid 444.
[71] 1997 (4) SA 460 (C).
[72] At paras 58–64.
[73] See *S v Kampher*, note 71 supra, at para 3.
[74] *National Coalition for Gay and Lesbian Equality v Minister of Justice* 1998 (2) SACR 102 (W).
[75] See in this regard *National Coalition*, note 34 supra, at paras 7–9 and 13.
[76] *National Coalition*, note 74 supra.

Constitutional Court for confirmation.[77] In the first *National Coalition* case the Constitutional Court held that a confirmation of the constitutional invalidity of the statutory provisions necessarily required it to pronounce on the constitutionality of the underlying common law crimes.[78] To this extent the Court carefully considered the meaning of 'sexual orientation' in section 9(3) of the Constitution and adopted a broad and generous interpretation of the phrase:

> '[S]exual orientation is defined by reference to erotic attraction: in the case of heterosexuals, to members of the opposite sex; in the case of gays and lesbians, to members of the same sex. Potentially a homosexual or gay or lesbian person can therefore be anyone who is erotically attracted to members of his or her own sex.'[79]

The court held that the phrase applied equally to bisexual and transgendered orientations as well as to those, who, on a single occasion find themselves attracted to a member of their own sex.[80]

Given that sexual orientation is included in the Constitution's equality clause, the court proceeded to lay out the relationship between equality and (sexual) difference. It linked the concept of equality in a specific way with difference stating that '[t]he desire for equality is not a hope for the elimination of all differences' and that it is 'deceptively simple and so devastatingly injurious to say that those who are handicapped or of a different race, or religion, or colour or sexual orientation are less worthy'.[81]

The court continued to evaluate the impact of the discrimination and noted that the criminal proscriptions and prohibitions in question, in addition to violating the dignity of gay men, enforce already existing prejudices and increase their negative effects which lead to psychological if not physical harm.[82] In addition, the impact of the discriminatory prohibitions is more serious precisely because they are aimed at a political minority that cannot rely on political power in order to secure favourable legislation. It is here that the court first recognises the often harsh effect of the prevailing heteronormative hegemony on sexual minorities.

The court concluded that the discrimination is unfair and therefore con-

---

[77] Section 172(2)(a) of the Constitution provides as follows: 'The Supreme Court of Appeal, a High Court or a court of similar status may make an order concerning the constitutional validity of an Act of Parliament, a provincial Act or any conduct of the President, but an order of constitutional invalidity has no force unless it is confirmed by the Constitutional Court'.

[78] *National Coalition*, note 34 supra, at para 9.

[79] At para 20, citing E Cameron 'Sexual Orientation and the Constitution: A Test Case for Human Rights' (1993) 110 *SALJ* 450.

[80] At para 21.

[81] At para 22.

[82] At para 23.

trary to the right to equality envisaged in section 9 of the Constitution.[83] It also held that the criminal proscriptions violated the right to dignity under section 10 of the Constitution: 'There can be no doubt that the existence of a law which punishes a form of sexual expression for gay men degrades and devalues gay men in our broader society. As such it is a palpable invasion of their dignity and a breach of s 10 of the Constitution'.[84]

Given that the South African Constitution introduces a legal 'culture of justification'[85] by virtue of its section 36 provisions, the court was required to visit the question whether the violation of the rights mentioned above were justifiable in 'an open and democratic society based on human dignity, equality and freedom'.[86] It held that this exercise is essentially one of balancing of different interests: 'In the balancing process and in the evaluation of proportionality one is enjoined to consider the relation between the limitation and its purpose as well as the existence of less restrictive means to achieve this purpose'.[87] Accordingly the court held that no valid purpose or justification for the limitation had been suggested. The court also placed significant emphasis on the fact that the general trend in open and democratic societies has been towards decriminalisation of sodomy – a trend which provides further support for the contention that there is no legitimate purpose served by criminalisation.[88] It therefore endorsed the order of the High Court that the common law offence of sodomy, as well as its incorporation into the relevant statutes, was unconstitutional and invalid.[89] The court went on to declare section 20A of the Sexual Offences Act unconstitutional for fundamentally the same reasons as were advanced in relation to sodomy.[90]

3.3.4 Decriminalisation in Scotland and South Africa: similarities and differences

In both South Africa and Scotland it was the decriminalisation of same-sex sexual activity that constituted 'the spark that lit the fuse'[91] for law reform based on the recognition of sexual minority freedom, because it removed

---

[83] At para 27.

[84] At para 28. The court also held that the constitutional right to privacy was violated independent of the violations of the rights to equality and dignity.

[85] The phrase was coined by Etienne Mureinik in a now seminal article, 'A Bridge to Where? Introducing the Interim Bill of Rights' (1994) 10 *South African Journal of Human Rights* 31 at 32.

[86] See s 36 of the Constitution.

[87] *National Coalition*, note 34 supra, para 35.

[88] At paras 39–57.

[89] At para 73.

[90] At para 76.

[91] Norrie, note 40 supra, at 225.

a status differentiation between homosexual and heterosexual couples – same-sex couples are no longer 'criminals'.

There are, however two important differences between Scots law and South African law when it comes to decriminalisation. As mentioned, Scotland abandoned the prohibition on same-sex sexual activity in 1980, that is, long before human rights were brought to bear on private law through the enactment and coming into effect of the Human Rights Act in the United Kingdom, but also well after liberal democratic reform in this area in the rest of the United Kingdom. We have seen in section 3.3.2. above that this situation had much to do with the conservative tactics of Scottish politicians in the legislature. In South Africa, on the other hand, the abolition of the common law crime of male sodomy only arrived with the enactment of the Interim Constitution in 1994, that is, along with the introduction of a culture of human rights, as discussed in section 3.3.3 above.

A further difference is of course that decriminalisation in Scotland was, for better or for worse, achieved through the legislative process, whereas in South Africa it was achieved through the judiciary. In Scotland, decriminalisation did not coincide with a radical change in government or constitution, whereas in South Africa it coincided with the dismantling of a totalitarian government that had been in power for over 40 years and the introduction of arguably the world's most aspirational constitution. In Scotland, decriminalisation was not depicted as part of a larger liberation struggle for recognition, whereas in South Africa decriminalisation was presented as part and parcel of the anti-apartheid struggle. The differences reflect the radically different forms of government that prevailed while sodomy was a criminal offence in these jurisdictions. In Scotland decriminalisation appears to have been a slow and gradual process, whereas in South Africa decriminalisation formed part of a more progressive and urgent process of radically transforming the social fabric.

What is interesting is that decriminalisation in both jurisdictions was marked by a human rights moment. The South African human rights moment speaks for itself, the Scottish one is less publicised. In 1979 Ian Dunn, founder of the Scottish Minority Group (which was later renamed as the Scottish Homosexual Rights Group), and two other activists approached the European Court of Human Rights, arguing that they were victims within the meaning of Article 25 of the European Convention on Human Rights (ECHR) in the sense that they suffered '"prejudice by reason of fear of prosecution for the commission of homosexual acts", that they "suffered psychological harm and distress as a result thereof" as well as "social stigma and loss of esteem", and that they were "open to blackmail, intimidation, and harassment"'.[92] They also claimed that they

---

[92] R Davidson and G Davis 'Sexuality and the State: The Campaign for Scottish Homosexual Law Reform, 1967–80' (2006) 20(4) *Contemporary British History* 533 at 547.

suffered discrimination as citizens of the United Kingdom 'by reason of Scottish national minority status'.[93] Alkarim Jivani argues that it was this appeal that finally paved the way for Scottish homosexual law reform.[94] The government realised that it was facing a long and expensive battle which could only result in defeat. As a pragmatic, perhaps more than a principled, response, it introduced section 80 into the Criminal Justice (Scotland) Act 1980.

3.4 LEGAL PROTECTION OF SAME-SEX RELATIONSHIPS – THE BEGINNINGS

3.4.1 Scotland

In Scotland legal protection of sexual minority freedom would come almost twenty years after decriminalisation and in the rest of the UK almost 30 years later. The Human Rights Act 1998, which came into force on 2 October 2000,[95] incorporated the ECHR into the domestic law of the whole of the United Kingdom. In 1999 the European Court of Human Rights held that sexual orientation was 'intolerable' to the non-discrimination requirements in Article 14 of the European Convention even though it was not explicitly mentioned in that article.[96] In anticipation of the coming into effect of the Human Rights Act, the Scotland Act 1998 prohibited the Scottish Parliament and courts from as early as July 1999 from acting in a way incompatible with the ECHR.

Lord Reed argues that the incorporation of the ECHR in Scottish Law brought about profound changes not so much immediately in legal doctrine, but more astoundingly in legal culture.[97] Immediate doctrinal changes were also slowed down (at least until July 1999) because of the Local Government Act 1988, a UK statute which prohibited the promotion of homosexuality by local authorities,[98] including the teaching of homosexuality as an acceptable 'pretended family relationship'.[99] At least until July 1999, the Act could be used to block any attempts in Scotland to have a same-sex relationship recognised as a family. It is no wonder then that homosexual

---

[93] Ibid.

[94] A Jivani *It's Not Unusual: A History of Lesbian and Gay Britain in the Twentieth Century* (Indiana University Press 1997) at 177–8.

[95] G Rose 'Rights and Wrongs: Who Benefits from the Human Rights Act?' *Scotland on Sunday* 29 May 2011, (available at *http://scotlandonsunday.scotsman.com/opinion/Rights-and-wrongs-who-benefits.6776063.jp?articlepage=2*).

[96] *Salgueiro Da Silva Mouta v Portugal* (2001) 31 EHRR 1055.

[97] Lord Reed 'The Constitutionalisation of Private Law: Scotland' (2001) 5(2) *Electronic Journal of Comparative Law*.

[98] Local Government Act 1988, s 28(1).

[99] Ibid.

activists considered decriminalisation in Scotland to have been a very limited victory indeed.[100] As late as 1992, the Scottish Law Commission still considered it necessary to exclude same-sex relationships from their recommendations for various extensions of legal protection to cohabiting couples.[101]

A significant advance in the struggle for sexual minorities in the period before the coming into effect of the Human Rights Act was achieved with the decision of the House of Lords in *Fitzpatrick v Sterling Housing Association*[102] in 1999. It recognised that, in certain cases and for certain purposes, a same-sex couple could be recognised as a family, although it was made clear that partners in a same-sex relationship could not be each other's spouses.[103] The rationale was that 'family' means different things, that its breadth or narrowness vary in accordance with the context in which the word is used and that it therefore does not have a technical meaning. Rather, the alleged family relationship should be tested against the hallmarks of a family. These include a degree of mutual interdependence, sharing of lives, caring, love, commitment and support.[104] Since the same-sex couple in this case was in a 'longstanding, close, loving and faithful, monogamous, homosexual relationship', they could be regarded as the members of a family.[105]

Norrie writes that the *Fitzpatrick* decision effectively abolished the Local Government Act's notion of same-sex relationships as 'pretended family relationships': '[t]he decision in *Fitzpatrick* completely subverts the policy behind that piece of symbolic and meaningless (but nevertheless spiteful and harmful) legislation – even before its eventual repeal'.[106] Earlier on in his reflection on the effect of *Fitzpatrick*, Norrie points out that this decision did not simply undo the many exclusions and discriminations based on homosexuality in Scots law, and that much remained to be done in order to provide for legal protection of families based on same-sex relationships. But given that the European Court of Human Rights decided two months after the decision in *Fitzpatrick* that the ECHR, and therefore the Human Rights Act, was incompatible with sexual orientation discrimination, the 'tide of equality' had become 'relentless'.[107]

---

100 Davidson and Davis, note 92 supra, at 533–58.
101 K McK Norrie 'We are Family (Sometimes): Legal Recognition of Same-sex Relationships after *Fitzpatrick*' (2000) 4 *EdinLR* 256 at 257.
102 [1999] 4 All ER 705.
103 The word 'spouse' was still exclusively reserved to denote a married person, a husband or a wife.
104 *Fitzpatrick*, note 102 supra, at para 23, per Lord Slynn of Hadley. See Norrie, note 101 supra, at 261.
105 *Fitzpatrick*, note 102 supra, at para 6, per Lord Slynn of Hadley. See Norrie, note 101 supra, at 258.
106 Norrie, note 101 supra, at 269.
107 Ibid 257–8.

3.4.2 South Africa

In South Africa decriminalisation and the first active protection of sexual minority freedom happened within less than a year of each other. The case from South Africa that is comparable to *Fitzpatrick* has become known as the second *National Coalition* case.[108] In this case the National Coalition instituted proceedings in the Cape High Court for an order declaring section 25(5) of the Aliens Control Act[109] unconstitutional in that it facilitated the immigration into South Africa of the spouses of permanent South African residents, but did not extend the same benefits to men and women in permanent same-sex life partnerships with permanent South African residents. The High Court declared the section unconstitutional, whereupon the National Coalition applied to the Constitutional Court for a confirmation of the order of constitutional invalidity. The National Coalition also sought a variation of the original full order and, to that extent, appealed against the judgment of the Cape High Court. The Minister of Home Affairs, as respondent, appealed against the entire judgment.

The Constitutional Court decided that section 25 of the Act was unconstitutional in that it unfairly discriminated against same-sex relationships on the basis of sexual orientation and marital status. The court held that the word 'spouse' in the provision complained of[110] could not in its context be construed as including a partner in a permanent same-sex life partnership.[111] Such a construction would 'distort' the meaning of the expression. Much like the court in *Fitzpatrick*, the Court relied explicitly on what it called the 'ordinary' meaning of the word spouse as denoting a husband or a wife.[112] The court also emphasised that the word 'marriage' as used in the relevant legislation did not extend 'any further than those marriages that are ordinarily recognised by our law'.[113] In short, the court's decision was that a same-sex life partnership could not be regarded as a marriage. This is not to say that the court did not recognise that the discrimination in this case was based on 'harmful and hurtful stereotypes of gays and lesbians'[114] and accordingly 'denies to gays and lesbians that which is foundational to our

---

[108] *National Coalition for Gay and Lesbian Equality v Minister of Home Affairs* 2000 (2) SA 1 (CC). For the first *National Coalition* case see note 34 supra.

[109] Act 96 of 1991.

[110] Section 25 provided that only the 'spouse' or 'dependent child' of a person who is permanently and lawfully resident in South Africa can apply for an immigration permit. The applicants contended that the section was unconstitutional because it did not allow the partners of permanently resident South Africans in permanent same-sex life partnerships to also apply for such permits.

[111] *National Coalition*, note 108 supra, para 23.

[112] At para 25.

[113] Ibid.

[114] At para 49.

Constitution . . . the concepts of equality and dignity, which at this point are closely intertwined, namely that all persons have the same inherent worth and dignity as human beings, whatever their other differences may be'.[115]

Given the court's approach to the interpretation of the words 'spouse' and 'marriage' in the contested legislation, the unconstitutionality of the relevant legislation could only be cured by reading the words 'permanent same-sex life partnership' into the statute. This remedy would afford partners in same-sex life partnerships the same statutory rights as spouses in legally recognised marriages. Although the remedy was limited to the statute only, it was clear that similar provisions in other statutes would not survive constitutional scrutiny and that the remedy would probably be the same in substance.[116] Mindful of this fact, the judgment included a list of factors[117] which would assist in the determination whether the same-sex life partnership was 'permanent' and thus worthy of protection as a form of family.[118]

3.4.3 Shared criticism

Progressive criticisms of the *Fitzpatrick* and second *National Coalition* judgments occur along the same lines. As regards *Fitzpatrick*, Norrie argues that there is an 'insidious danger in seeking legal legitimacy for a same-sex couple's relationship from the social similarity that that couple has with an opposite-sex couple'.[119] Such an approach risks denying real differences between the two types of relationship. It also suggests that the closer a same-sex relationship resembles a marriage, the easier it will be to qualify as a family and thus to access the statutory benefits available to a family.[120] As Norrie concludes, this approach has implications for equality: '[T]rue equality would require society and the law to recognise the legitimacy of a diversity of family forms. But there is nothing in *Fitzpatrick* to suggest that the law is moving in that direction'.[121]

Pierre de Vos echoes these concerns in his criticism of the second *National Coalition* case. With reference to the work of Johnson, de Vos

---

[115] At para 42.
[116] At para 82.
[117] See para 88. Such factors included the ages of the partners, duration of the partnership, nature of any partnership ceremony, perceptions of relations and friends, whether and how the partners shared a common abode and living expenses, arrangements for financial support, pension provision, and the nature of any partnership agreement or provision in the partners' wills.
[118] Ibid.
[119] Norrie, note 101 supra, at 269.
[120] Ibid 269–70.
[121] Ibid 270.

argues that when the Constitutional Court was in this case, for the first time, faced with the question of legal *protection* of same-sex partnerships (as opposed to decriminalisation of same-sex sexual activity), it lapsed into the more familiar rhetoric of heteronormativity and the politics of passing.[122] As Johnson indicates, passing involves the construction by the heteronormative hegemony of a '"good homosexual" subject . . . that still reinforces heteronormative conceptions of citizenship'.[123] With reference to the set of factors identified by the court as indicative of a permanent same-sex life partnership, de Vos surmises that the cumulative effect

> 'suggests that relationships that do not closely map that of an idealized heterosexual marriage, will not be worthy of equal concern and respect. The judgment seems to support a rather narrow conception of family, even while it professes to endorse a more open-ended view of the legal regulation of intimate relationships. It is silent, say, on a relationship in which a gay man and a lesbian make arrangements to have a child and to act as co-parents of that child but do not engage in a conjugal relationship traditionally associated with the joint parents of a child.'[124]

For de Vos as for Norrie, there is a substantive equality concern here: the second *National Coalition* case failed to consider the possible legal consequences of the right to be different.

It appears that, at least as regards the concepts 'spouse' and 'marriage', the experience in Scotland and South Africa has been that these concepts dexterously resist intrusion from the realm of human rights into their traditional private law, gender-specific definitions. The experience indicates that private law admits relationships capable of corrective justice (and therefore formal equality) on an arbitrary or contingent *political* basis and not on the basis of the relationships' immanent arithmetic rationality of form, as Weinrib and others would have it. Moreover, it admits these relationships conditionally – they should resemble, as closely as possible, the ideal (definition of) marriage, or the heterosexual family, while creating 'separate but equal' regimes, such as the 'permanent same-sex life partnership', for their legal recognition. In a country like South Africa (where the adversity as regards 'separate but equal' regimes is exacerbated by our racist history), it is no wonder that Sachs J described such regimes as 'unthinkable'.[125]

---

[122] P de Vos 'From Heteronormativity to Full Sexual Citizenship: Equality and Sexual Freedom in Laurie Ackermann's Constitutional Jurisprudence' 2008 *Acta Juridica* 254 at 266–71.

[123] C Johnson 'Heteronormative Citizenship and the Politics of Passing' (2002) 5 *Sexualities* 317 at 320.

[124] De Vos, note 66 supra, at 452.

[125] *Minister of Home Affairs v Fourie (Doctors for Life International and Others*, Amici Curiae); *Lesbian and Gay Equality Project v Minister of Home Affairs* 2006 (1) SA 524 (CC) at para 151.

3.5 DEVELOPMENTS LEADING UP TO FULL(ER) RECOGNITION

3.5.1 *Scotland*

On 29 March 2000, the Scottish Parliament became the first legislature in the United Kingdom actively and intentionally to recognise the concept of a same-sex family. It did so by including members of conjugal same-sex couples in the definition of 'nearest relative' in the Adults with Incapacity (Scotland) Act 2000, section 87, amending the definition previously applied by the Mental Health (Scotland) Act 1984, section 53.[126] Norrie argues that the 'relative obscurity' of the provision should not detract from the fact that it indicated a 'fundamental shift in social and legal attitudes towards sexual orientation'.[127] A few months later, the Human Rights Act came into force. Its incorporation of the ECHR into UK law had the effect that cases founded on the Convention could now be litigated in the domestic courts. In December 2002, Barbara Roche, Minister for Social Exclusion and Equality, announced that the UK Government would start to look at proposals for 'civil partnership rights'. This was followed by the publication in June 2003 of a consultation document on civil partnerships by the Woman and Equality Unit of the Department of Trade and Industry.[128] The timing of these developments (and the relatively quick succession of the one by the other) was no coincidence.

Against this background, it is said that the 2004 decision in the case of *Ghaidan v Godin-Mendoza*[129] made legislation recognising same-sex relationships in the UK on the same basis as marriage inevitable. In this case, the House of Lords held that the non-discrimination provisions of the ECHR compelled an interpretation of the phrase 'living together as husband and wife', used in UK statutes to denote unmarried couples, as including same-sex couples. This meant that same-sex couples could access all rights and responsibilities afforded by UK statute to unmarried heterosexual couples.[130] It was clear that the next step would be to allow same-sex couples to attach virtually the same legal consequences to their union, should they so choose.

---

[126] These provisions have now been repealed. The current definition of 'nearest relative', which is similarly inclusive, is contained in the Mental Health (Care and Treatment) (Scotland) Act 2003, s 254. See, in particular ss 254(2)(b) and 254(7)(a)(ii).

[127] K McK Norrie 'Sexual Orientation and Family Law' (2001) *Family Dynamics: Contemporary Issues in Family Law* 151.

[128] United Kingdom Department of Trade and Industry (Women and Equality Unit) (2003) *Civil Partnership: A Framework for the Legal Recognition of Same Sex Couples.*

[129] [2004] UKHL 30, [2004] 2 AC 557.

[130] Norrie, note 40 supra, at 252–3.

3.5.2 *South Africa*

A flurry of decisions which vindicated important rights for same-sex couples followed the decision in the second *National Coalition* case. These developments occurred against the background of a society in which decriminalisation and piecemeal legislative and curial protection did not do much to eradicate extreme conservatism regarding sexuality and sexual orientation. It was clear that the climate was not right for full legislative recognition of same-sex couples on the same basis as marriage. There had to be a period for the South African body politic more or less to get used to the idea of sexual minority freedom. During this period, the piecemeal relief granted in the courts would continue and significant inroads would be made into conservative traditional assumptions about homosexuality and the family.

In *Satchwell v President of the Republic of South Africa*,[131] the applicant challenged the constitutional validity of two sections of the Judges' Remuneration and Conditions of Employment Act[132] (as well as certain regulations promulgated in terms of this Act). The applicant's contention was that these sections were unconstitutional in that they failed to extend the benefits contained in them to partners in permanent same-sex life partnerships. Madala J held that the denial of these benefits to the same-sex life partners of judges constituted unfair discrimination on the grounds of sexual orientation and that there was no justification for the limitation of the right to equality.[133]

The judgment emphasised that the equality clause does not generally require benefits extended to spouses also to be extended to same-sex life partners.[134] The Constitution will only impose these benefits on same-sex partners where reciprocal duties of support have been undertaken. Whether or not such duties of support exist depends on the circumstances of each case.[135] Accordingly the Court ordered the reading-in of the words 'or partner, in a permanent same-sex life partnership in which the partners have undertaken reciprocal duties of support' after the word 'spouse' wherever it occurred in the challenged legislation and regulations.[136]

On the basis of this decision, the Supreme Court of Appeal subsequently extended statutory benefits for spouses of road accident victims to partners in permanent same-sex life partnerships.[137] The decision also had a

---

[131] 2002 (6) SA 1 (CC).
[132] Act 88 of 1989.
[133] *Satchwell*, note 131 supra, at para 26.
[134] At para 24.
[135] At para 25.
[136] At para 37. See also para 34.
[137] *Du Plessis v Road Accident Fund* 2004 (1) SA 359 (SCA).

significant impact on the extension of joint adoption rights to same-sex life partners in the case of *Du Toit*[138] where it was held as follows:

> 'The impugned provisions do not prevent lesbian or gay people from adopting children at all. They make no provision, however, for gay and lesbian couples to adopt children jointly. In this regard, they are not the only legislative provisions which do not acknowledge the legitimacy and value of same-sex permanent life partnerships. It is a matter of our history (and that of many countries) that these relationships have been the subject of unfair discrimination in the past. However, our Constitution requires that unfairly discriminatory treatment of such relationships cease.'[139]

In this case Skweyiya J also referred to the many statutes recognising permanent same-sex life partnerships that had been passed since the advent of democracy in South Africa.[140]

In J[141] the Constitutional Court similarly made use of the reading-in remedy in order to cure the unconstitutionality of section 5 of the Children's Status Act[142] precluding the partner of a permanent same-sex life partnership who did not give birth to a child, conceived by artificial insemination, from becoming a legitimate parent of that child. The Court made it clear that '[c]omprehensive legislation regularising relationships between gay and lesbian persons' had become necessary, because '[i]t is unsatisfactory for the Courts to grant piecemeal relief to members of the gay and lesbian community as and when aspects of their relationships are found to be prejudiced by unconstitutional legislation'.[143]

3.6 THE POLITICS OF RECOGNITION: 'CIVIL PARTNERSHIP' V 'MARRIAGE'

3.6.1 Introduction

Up to this point, similarities in developments as regards the recognition and protection of sexual minority freedom in Scotland and South Africa have amounted to more than the differences and divergences. Similarities in the stages of development (decriminalisation followed by limited recognition and protection granted in a piecemeal fashion) as it is tied to the arrival of human rights on the doorstep of private law have been most evident. The discussion up to this point attempts to illustrate that private law has *not*

---

[138] *Du Toit v Minister Of Welfare and Population Development (Lesbian and Gay Equality Project as* Amicus Curiae) 2003 (2) SA 198 (CC) at para 39.
[139] At para 32.
[140] At para 32 n 33.
[141] *J v Director General, Department of Home Affairs* 2003 (5) SA 621 (CC).
[142] Act 82 of 1987.
[143] *J*, note 141 supra, at para 23.

always been concerned about the right to be free from unfair discrimination based on sexual orientation. Both in Scotland and South Africa the ethico-political and later legal recognition of human rights played a significant role in opening up private law (through decriminalisation) to the recognition and protection of sexual minority rights. In Scotland this was primarily achieved through the acknowledgment by the courts and the legislature that same-sex couples can and do constitute, at least initially, only for certain purposes, a family. In South Africa the recognition and protection was achieved through the creation of the 'permanent same-sex life partnership' separate from the family.

However, it is with regard to the theme of full and equal recognition of same-sex life partnerships where the two jurisdictions part ways. And this parting of ways cannot but be considered with reference to the prevailing politics of each jurisdiction, while acknowledging that the two Acts (the Civil Union Act 2006 and the Civil Partnership Act 2004) were 'responses to the same pressure: the desire to move away from the historical discrimination suffered both socially and legally by lesbian and gay individuals and same-sex couples'.[144]

3.6.2 Scotland

The Civil Partnership Act 2004 received Royal Assent on 18 November 2004 and came into effect on 15 December 2005. The Act creates a separate institution, by way of an opt-in registration process, for legal recognition of same-sex life partnerships *only*. This institution is the civil partnership. It has been noted that the procedure for registration of the partnership bears hardly any difference, apart from the obvious changes in terminology, from that which must be followed for a civil marriage. The legal consequences of the registration are also not substantially different from that of marriage. In fact, as Norrie notes, the Civil Partnership Act constitutes an attempt to provide the opportunity for same-sex couples 'to access all the rights and liabilities traditionally available to opposite-sex couples through the ancient and ubiquitous institution that we call marriage'.[145] Norrie further points out that the Scottish part of the Civil Partnership Act virtually duplicates the wording of existing Acts and common law rules applicable to marriage.[146]

One of the main differences between 'marriage' and the 'civil partnership' (apart from the differentiation based on sex) is that the civil partnership is

---

[144] K McK Norrie 'South Africa's Civil Union Act 2006: A Scottish Perspective' (2010) 21(1) *Juridical Review* 21 at 21.

[145] Ibid.

[146] Ibid at 35.

completely secularised. Until recently,[147] no civil partnership in the UK could be concluded in a place associated with religious worship, *and* only registrars, not marriage officers, could conduct the registration ceremony. The grounds for dissolution associated with sex, which are available in marriage (such as adultery and failure to consummate), are also unavailable when it comes to dissolution of civil partnerships. It is against this background that the Scottish Government announced on 25 July 2012 that it intended to legislate for the legalisation of same-sex marriage.[148]

3.6.3 South Africa

3.6.3.1 The Fourie judgment and the legalisation of same-sex 'marriage' in South Africa

After the Constitutional Court's clear message to the legislature in the *J* case that 'comprehensive legislation regularising relationships between gay and lesbian persons' had become necessary, one would have expected the legislature to expedite the process for such regularisation. Whatever the increase in pace on the part of the legislature may have been after the *J* case, it was not quick enough to halt the Constitutional Court's declaration in the *Fourie* judgment that the common law definition of 'marriage', as well as the 1961 Marriage Act, to the extent that it relied on that definition, were unconstitutional.[149]

The court based its declaration on its earlier jurisprudence in which it stated over and over again that the family and family life of gay men and lesbians are in all significant respects indistinguishable from those of heterosexual spouses, and in human terms as important.[150] Where the law fails to recognise the relationship of same-sex couples, argued the court:

> 'The message is that gays and lesbians lack the inherent humanity to have their families and family lives in such same-sex relationships respected or protected. It serves in addition to perpetuate and reinforce existing prejudices and stereotypes. The impact constitutes a crass, blunt, cruel and serious invasion of their dignity.'[151]

Conservative arguments before the court in *Fourie* nevertheless charged that even if one recognises that absence of a comprehensive legal regime to protect same-sex couples is discriminatory, the remedy does not lie in radically altering the law of marriage, which, by its very nature and as it has

---

[147] The Marriages and Civil Partnerships (Approved Premises) (Amendment) Regulations 2011/2661, which came into force in December 2011, make provision for the conclusion of a civil partnership in a place associated with religious worship in England and Wales.
[148] See Campbell, note 37 supra.
[149] *Fourie*, note 125 supra, at para 162.
[150] *Fourie*, note 125 supra, at para 54.
[151] Ibid quoting from the judgment in *National Coalition*, note 108 supra, at para 54.

evolved historically, is concerned with heterosexual relationships.[152] The answer, they said, is to provide appropriate alternative forms of recognition to same-sex family relationships.

The court considered the age-old argument that the constitutive and definitional characteristic of marriage is its procreative potential and can therefore never include same-sex couples.[153] It found this argument to be deeply demeaning to couples (married or not) who, for whatever reason, either choose not to procreate or are incapable of procreating when they start a relationship or become so at any time thereafter. It is also demeaning for couples who start a relationship at a stage when they no longer have the capacity to conceive or to become adoptive parents.[154] Although this view might have some traction in the context of a particular religious world view, from a legal and constitutional perspective, the court found it could not hold.[155]

Another familiar argument that was rejected was the assertion that marriage is by its very nature a religious institution and that to change its definition would violate religious freedom in a most fundamental way.[156] Although the court recognised that religious bodies play a large and important part in public life and are part of the fabric of our society,[157] the open and democratic society contemplated by the Constitution requires mutual respect and co-existence between the secular and the sacred:

> '[The] acknowledgement by the state of the right of same-sex couples to enjoy the same status, entitlements and responsibilities as marriage law accords to heterosexual couples is in no way inconsistent with the rights of religious organisations to continue to refuse to celebrate same-sex marriages. The constitutional claims of same-sex couples can accordingly not be negated by invoking the rights of believers to have their religious freedom respected. The two sets of interests involved do not collide; they co-exist in a *constitutional realm* based on accommodation of diversity.'[158]

This entails, plainly, that the religious beliefs of some cannot be used to determine the constitutional rights of others.[159] In an open and democratic society there should be a capacity to accommodate and manage difference and the view of the (religious) majority on marginalised minorities should

---

[152] *Fourie*, note 125 supra, at paras 79–81.
[153] *Fourie*, note 125 supra, at paras 85–7. For a typical account of the 'procreative potential' argument see J M Finnis 'Law, Morality and "Sexual Orientation"' (1994) 69 *Notre Dame Law Review* 1049 at 1066.
[154] *Fourie*, note 125 supra, at para 86.
[155] Ibid.
[156] *Fourie*, note 125 supra, at paras 88–98.
[157] At para 92.
[158] At para 98 (emphasis added).
[159] At para 92.

not be imposed in ways that would reinforce unfair discrimination against a minority.[160] A contrary view smacks unpleasantly of the authoritarian/totalitarian tactics so characteristic of the National Party government during the apartheid era.

Having found the discrimination in the Marriage Act to be unfair, the court was obliged to consider whether justification existed under section 36 of the Constitution for the violation of the equality and dignity of same-sex couples by virtue of their exclusion from civil marriage.[161] Two inter-related grounds of justification were advanced that intricately related to the arguments for the preservation of marriage. The first argument was that the inclusion of same-sex couples would undermine the institution of marriage.[162] The second ground of justification was part and parcel of this view. It contended that the inclusion would undermine and intrude upon strong religious beliefs about marriage.[163]

Both these grounds were rejected. The court held that granting same-sex couples the right to marry would in no way impair the capacity of heterosexual couples to marry in the form they wished and in accordance with their religious beliefs. As regards the second ground, the court held that it was based on a prejudice that is at odds with the constitutional requirements of equal treatment and respect for difference.[164]

The court concluded that the common law definition of marriage and the Marriage Act, to the extent that it relies on this definition, were unconstitutional.[165] Instead of an immediate reading-in to remedy the unconstitutionality, the court suspended the reading-in for one year to give Parliament a chance to address the unconstitutional exclusion of same-sex couples from enjoying the *status and entitlements* coupled with responsibilities that are accorded to heterosexual couples by the common law and by the Marriage Act.[166] It was very clear from the decision that the confines of this mandate to Parliament were extremely narrow. The court expressly held that whatever the legislative measures Parliament took, it could not subject same-sex couples to new forms of marginalisation or exclusion by the law, either directly or indirectly.[167]

It is important to note in this regard that the court affirmed the importance of marriage in South African society. Marriage, held the court, is a

---

[160] At para 94.

[161] At para 110.

[162] At para 110.

[163] Ibid.

[164] At para 113.

[165] At para 114.

[166] At para 135. In a dissenting judgment (at paras 167–9) O'Regan J held that it was not appropriate in this case to suspend the order of invalidity, given that Parliament's choice was a narrow one that would be unaffected by providing immediate relief.

[167] At para 147.

unique institution and constitutes 'much more than a piece of paper'.[168] On the one hand, until recently marriage was the only institution from which a number of socio-economic benefits would accrue. These include the right to maintenance, medical insurance coverage, adoption, access to wrongful death claims and post-divorce rights. On the other hand, marriage also bestows a myriad of intangible benefits on those who choose to enter into it.[169] As such, marriage entitles a couple to celebrate their commitment to each other at a public event so celebrated in our culture.[170] Well aware of and affirming the centrality attributed to marriage and its consequences in our culture, the court held that to deny same-sex couples a choice in this regard 'is to negate their right to self-definition in a most profound way'.[171] As Sachs J put it:

> 'The exclusion of same-sex couples from the benefits and responsibilities of marriage, accordingly, is not a small and tangential inconvenience resulting from a few surviving relics of societal prejudice destined to evaporate like the morning dew. It represents a harsh if oblique statement by the law that same-sex couples are outsiders, and that their need for affirmation and protection of their intimate relations as human beings is somehow less than that of heterosexual couples. It reinforces the wounding notion that they are to be treated as biological oddities, as failed or lapsed human beings who do not fit into normal society and as such do not qualify for the full moral concern and respect that our Constitution seeks to secure for everyone. It signifies that their capacity for love, commitment and accepting responsibility is by definition less worthy of regard than that of heterosexual couples.'[172]

It is clear, then, that the court contemplated in its judgment that the exclusion of same-sex couples from marriage had both a *practical* and *symbolic* impact, which meant that the unconstitutionality could not be rectified through the recognition of same-sex unions outside the law of marriage. In responding to the unconstitutionality of the existing marriage regime, *both* the practical and the symbolic aspects had to be taken into account.[173]

In the light of the above, Parliament had to be 'sensitive to the need to avoid a remedy that on the face of it would provide equal protection, but

---

[168] At para 70.

[169] See L Schäfer 'Marriage and Marriage-Like Relationships: Constructing a New Hierarchy of Life Partnerships' (2006) 123(4) *SALJ* 626 at 633 on the intangible advantages of marriage, and D Wides 'Family and Equality in Post-Constitutional South Africa: An Argument for Same-sex Marriage' (2003) *Responsa Meridiana* 81 arguing that the jurisprudence developed in such a way that the only way to avoid a successful constitutional challenge would be to legislate for no other form of recognition but same-sex marriage.

[170] *Fourie*, note 125 supra, at para 72.

[171] Ibid.

[172] At para 71.

[173] At para 81.

would do so in a manner that in its context and application would be calculated to reproduce new forms of marginalisation'.[174] It would therefore be completely unacceptable for Parliament to adopt a 'separate but equal' approach because this would serve 'as a threadbare cloak for covering distaste for or repudiation by those in power of the group subjected to segregation'.[175]

In the light of the above, the Constitutional Court ordered, first, the common law definition of marriage to be inconsistent with the Constitution and invalid 'to the extent that it does not permit same-sex couples to enjoy the status and the benefits coupled with responsibilities it accords to heterosexual couples'. Second, the omission from section 30(1) of the Marriage Act after the words 'or husband' of the words 'or spouse' was declared to be inconsistent with the Constitution, with the result that the Marriage Act was declared to be invalid to the extent of this inconsistency.[176] Parliament was given one year to remedy the defect.[177]

3.6.3.2 The South African Law Reform Commission's recommendations

In March 2006, the South African Law Reform Commission (SALRC) (having in the *Fourie* matter provided the Constitutional Court with a memorandum on its project regarding domestic partnerships) published its report on domestic partnerships. This recommended that the institution of 'civil unions' without the simultaneous institution of 'marriage' for same-sex life partnerships would not, in its opinion, satisfy the Constitutional Court's judgment in *Fourie*.[178] These recommendations were based on the Commission's understanding of the requirements set out in the *Fourie* judgment for the constitutionally valid regulation of same-sex relationships. The Commission referred to the fact that Sachs J 'clearly stated that the solution lay in the correction of the Marriage Act and the common-law definition of marriage, hence the order for the amendment of the Marriage Act if Parliament fails to correct the defects in the legislation by 1 December 2006'.[179] In the Commission's opinion, civil partnerships (as the only remedy and as exclusively applying to the formalisation of same-sex unions) could be successfully challenged constitutionally. It concluded that '[s]ince the tenet of equal treatment was an important part of the motivation for permitting same-sex marriage, the creation of a separate but equal status would be discriminatory'.[180]

---

[174] At para 150.

[175] Ibid.

[176] At para 162.

[177] Ibid.

[178] South African Law Reform Commission (Project 118) *Report on Domestic Partnerships* (2006) at 292–3 para 5.3.15, 296 para 5.4.11 and 305 para 5.6.2.

[179] Ibid at 300 para 5.5.15.

[180] Ibid at 296 para 5.4.11.

The second route that the SALRC indicated was the Dual Act option. In terms of this option an Orthodox Marriage Act would be enacted together with a Reformed Marriage Act. The Orthodox Marriage Act would have the same format as the current Marriage Act with a limited definition of 'orthodox marriage' as 'the voluntary union of a man and a woman concluded in terms of this Act to the exclusion of all others'.[181] The Commission justified the need for this Act on the basis of the 'religious concerns' expressed by opponents to same-sex marriage. The Reformed Marriage Act, proposed to be enacted simultaneously with the Orthodox Marriage Act, would be the generic Act, open to everybody, and the Commission insisted specifically that the State's marriage officers had to be appointed under the generic Act.[182] The Commission also envisaged that the Orthodox Marriage Act would ultimately resort with an Islamic Marriages Act, the Recognition of Customary Marriages Act and perhaps a Hindu Marriage Act in a 'religious marriages' category of legislation.[183] Ultimately, the recommendation of the Orthodox Marriage Act would be a concession to the religious majority which, in the opinion of the Commission, would not impugn the dignity of homosexual couples, because the differential treatment of opposite-sex couples who would choose to be treated differently would not violate the dignity of same-sex couples.[184]

3.6.3.3 The first draft of the Civil Union Bill, public participation hearings and the Civil Union Act 17 of 2006

Parliament's response to *Fourie* eventually came in September 2006,[185] two months before the deadline of 30 November 2006. The first draft of the Civil Union Bill[186] did not provide same-sex couples with the choice to enter into a marriage or to conclude a civil union. The long title of the Bill made this abundantly clear: the purpose was to 'provide for the solemnisation of *civil partnerships* [and] the legal consequences of *civil partnerships*. . .'.[187] Another way of stating the long title of the Bill would simply have been: '[To] preserv[e] the traditional, historic nature and meaning of the institution of civil marriage'.[188]

---

[181] Ibid at 310 para 5.6.17.

[182] Ibid at 310 para 5.6.19

[183] Ibid at 311 para 5.6.20.

[184] Ibid at 310 para 5.6.18. For criticism of this view see P de Vos and J Barnard 'Same-sex Marriage, Civil Unions and Domestic Partnerships in South Africa: Critical Reflections on an Ongoing Saga' (2007) 124(4) *SALJ* 795.

[185] A Quintal 'Same-sex Marriages Bill Tabled in Parliament' (available at *http://www.iol.co.za/ index.php?set_id=1&click_id=13&art_id=vn20060825011114223C978307*).

[186] Civil Union Bill 26 of 2006.

[187] Ibid (emphasis added).

[188] This was in fact the long title of the Massachusetts Civil Union Bill (Senate No 2175) that was struck down as unconstitutional by the highest court of that state. See Opinions of the Justices to the Senate, 440 Mass 1201 at 1209–10.

The argument was made that although it was not called 'marriage', in substance, the 'civil partnership' provisions of the first draft complied with the Constitutional Court's directions.[189] However, it was never made clear why it would be necessary to create the separate institution of 'civil partnership' for same-sex couples exclusively, if this was in substance exactly the same as heterosexual marriage. The Bill's repeated reservation of the category of 'marriage' for relationships other than same-sex partnerships (that is, heterosexual relationships) effectively meant that the legislature's drafters denied the re-definition of 'marriage' endorsed in *Fourie*. Ultimately, the Bill purported to create precisely the separate but equal regime declared as 'absolutely unthinkable' in the *Fourie* decision.

Given the Constitutional Court's view that the concept of marriage has a profound symbolic, emotional and political power in our culture that gives it a special status, the refusal to allow same-sex couples the right to enter into an institution called 'marriage' meant that the Bill deprived them of the right to access the status associated with the term 'marriage'. Members of the lesbian, gay, bisexual, transgender and intersex (LGBTI) community throughout South Africa were outraged[190] and not unjustifiably so. These provisions of the Bill that were supposed to vindicate gay and lesbian rights instead became a source of insult and humiliation.

Ultimately, it was the pressure exerted by parliamentary legal advisors and activists at the public participation hearings as well as the support of these views by the SALRC (discussed above) that resulted – at the last moment – in a radical redrafting of the first draft of the Civil Union Bill.

The ruling ANC came out in support of a sober (if somewhat conservative) interpretation of the Constitutional Court's judgment on 7 November 2006 when it tabled before the Parliamentary Portfolio Committee on Home Affairs a proposal that would become the Civil Union Act.[191] This version of the legislation differed markedly from the first draft. Gone were the provisions relating to domestic partnerships. Gone was the proposed 'civil partnership' institution exclusively for same-sex couples. In came the right (for same-sex and opposite-sex couples) to conclude a civil union by way of either a civil partnership *or* a marriage. In came the first and only legalisation of same-sex marriage on the African continent.

---

[189] See A Quintal 'Civil Union Bill will Codify Inequality' *Cape Times* 23 October 2006 at 4.

[190] J du Plessis 'Gay Activists see Red over Civil Union Bill' *Pretoria News* 18 October 2006 at 3; W J da Costa 'Same-sex Bill will Make it Harder for Gays to be "Accepted"' *Cape Times* 17 October 2006 at 4; G Bough 'Same-sex Union Bill gets Passions Going' *Cape Times* 10 October 2006 at 4.

[191] Act 17 of 2006.

3.7 WHY SEPARATE IS SELDOM, IF EVER, EQUAL (READ 'BETTER')

Norrie contends that the marriage available in terms of the Civil Union Act (coupled with the retention of the Marriage Act of 1961) is a dishonest way of continuing to differentiate between opposite-sex and same-sex relationships.[192] The dishonesty, he believes, lies in the pretence that the Civil Union Act's marriage provisions make no distinction between that marriage and a marriage in terms of the Marriage Act of 1961. For Norrie there remains a firm distinction between the 1961 Marriage Act marriage and the Civil Union Act marriage. The latter's distinction from 'civil partnership' in the Civil Union Act, he argues, amounts to a distinction 'of name only'.[193]

Norrie believes that 'there is really no juristic point in having different categories of relationship unless the social or the legal consequences are different'.[194] He goes on to argue that the UK approach of separating marriage from civil partnerships but nevertheless making them legal equivalents of one another constitutes 'a more honest' attempt to recognise the relationships of same-sex couples.[195] Whilst conceding that in South Africa a 'separate but equal regime would clearly not be acceptable' because 'the history of that doctrine showed it to be a shoddy and transparent attempt to provide a spurious legitimacy to deeply ingrained and deliberately structure inequality', Norrie believes that 'separate cannot in principle be synonymous with "worse"'.[196] Indeed, Norrie argues that separate is sometimes better: 'same-sex couples *ought* to have a separate institution, because they are different'.[197]

Norrie perceives what he calls an 'unswerving hostility' in the South African LGBTI community 'to anything less than an institution with the name "marriage" as a means of achieving equality between same-sex couples and opposite-sex couples'.[198] He further identifies 'an unfortunate tone of superiority'[199] on the part of LGBTI activists over other countries who 'settled' for civil partnership. This tone of superiority is apparently heard in particular in an article by Pierre de Vos[200] which discusses, from an internal point of view, the history that led up to the enactment of the Civil Union Act.

It is a particular fact of *this* history that the LGBTI community in South Africa did not settle for civil partnership. There are good reasons why. Norrie refers to some of them in passing before he goes on to criticise the

---

[192] Norrie, note 144 note, at 37.
[193] Ibid.
[194] Ibid at 25.
[195] Ibid.
[196] Ibid.
[197] Ibid at 37.
[198] Ibid at 35.
[199] Ibid.
[200] De Vos, note 66 supra.

Civil Union Act and the distinction without difference it allegedly makes between a marriage and a civil partnership.

I believe that Norrie's argument pays too little attention to at least four aspects of the recognition debate in South Africa: first, the symbolic and psychosocial effect on the body politic of a separate but equal political ideology, harnessed as it was to decades of apartheid; second, the fact that the marriage in terms of the Civil Union Act is, indeed, gender-neutral; third, the view that marriage in our society, for better or for worse, has what Sachs J referred to as 'a profound symbolic, emotional and political power in our culture that gives it a special status'; and fourth, Sachs J's early and repeated emphasis on the meaning of the right to be different.

As regards the first aspect, little attention is paid to finding an explanation for Sachs J's discussion of the 'separate but equal' dispensations of apartheid South Africa in his judgment on same-sex marriage. In its discussion, the court referred to the famous case of *R v Pitje*[201] where the appellant, an African candidate attorney, occupied a place at a table in court that was reserved for 'European practitioners' and refused to take his place at a table reserved for 'non-European practitioners'. Steyn CJ upheld the appellant's conviction for contempt of court as it was 'clear [from the record] that a practitioner would in every way be as well seated at the one table as at the other, and that he could not possibly have been hampered in the slightest in the conduct of his case by having to use a particular table'.[202]

As pointed out earlier, according to Sachs J '[t]he above approach is *unthinkable* in our constitutional democracy today not simply because the law has changed dramatically, but because our society is completely different'.[203] The court warned explicitly against providing an apparently neutral remedy that could have a severe impact on the dignity and sense of self-worth of the persons affected. Although different treatment itself does not necessarily violate the dignity of those affected, as soon as 'separation implies repudiation, connotes distaste or inferiority and perpetuates a caste-like status . . . it becomes constitutionally invidious'.[204]

I think Sachs J included these instructions in his judgment because he, as someone who was deeply committed to and politically involved in the struggle and who clearly paid dearly for that involvement, remained acutely aware of the fact that the legalisation of same-sex relationships occurred in a unique social and political context that remains marked by the disastrous consequences of the apartheid government's pervasive 'separate but equal' regimes – regimes that permeated every single aspect of peoples' lives for decades, including who they could marry.

---

[201]   1960 (4) SA 709 (A).

[202]   Ibid at 710E-F.

[203]   *Fourie*, note 125 supra, at para 151 (emphasis added).

[204]   At para 152.

Sachs J was at pains to point out that, whatever the legislature's solution to the non-recognition of same-sex relationships, it would not be allowed to introduce a regime that could be perceived as second-class. Any legislative remedy had to be 'as generous and accepting towards same-sex couples as it is to heterosexual couples, both in terms of the intangibles as well as the tangibles involved'.[205]

A separate but equal regime could survive constitutional scrutiny only if it could illustrate that there was a rational basis for the distinction. A distinction solely upon the basis that one relationship is between members of the opposite sex and the other between members of the same sex does not qualify as rational, because it suggests that there is a qualitative difference (and thus the need to distinguish) between the two, whereas in fact there is none, in the same way as there is no qualitative distinction between a marriage between a sterile black man and a divorced coloured woman or one between a middle-aged black woman and a young white male. In other words, there is absolutely no rational basis upon which to base a distinction between these unions in terms of the procedure for formalisation and the legal consequences that ensue from such formalisation.

This is precisely what the formal equality inherent in private legal relationships means. In terms of recognising a legal relationship, private law does not treat the poor negligent law student who accidently crashes his car into the rich, male law professor's BMW any differently from the drunken celebrity who crashes his car into the poor law student's. Both of these scenarios result in what we call delictual or tortious relationships. Why, then, if the poor, female law student and the rich, female law professor decide that they want to 'get together', should we call their relationship a civil partnership, but if Britney Spears elopes to Pretoria with the poor male law student, should we call their relationship a marriage?

I am reminded here of one of my favourite characters in English literature – the one who ventures through a looking glass into Wonderland where she bumps into Humpty Dumpty. They have a fairly lengthy discussion about words. 'The question is' says Alice, 'whether you *can* make words mean so many different things'.[206] To which Humpty Dumpty replies 'When I make a word do a lot of work like that I always pay it extra'.[207] One need not have read Derrida or invoke the dreaded word 'deconstruction' to see the point here: a word can mean a number of different things; it can, as Humpty Dumpty says, 'do a lot of work'. In South Africa, the word 'marriage', admittedly, does a lot of work. This work emanates directly from the nature of South African society as a radically plural one, one in which there is a need

---

[205] At para 153.
[206] L Carroll *Alice's Adventures in Wonderland and Through the Looking-Glass* (H Haughton (ed) Penguin 1998) at 186.
[207] Ibid 187.

for many different forms of marriage, but one in which the word 'marriage' plays an enormously significant – many would say 'central' – social-symbolic role. More than in any other country in the world, in South Africa anyone who is 'of age and capacity' can get married to anyone else of age and capacity and even to more than one. I claim that such an opening up and re-appropriation of traditional, Western, monogamous, heterosexual marriage is part and parcel of a transformative response to our history of draconian marriage laws. Moreover, this reinvention and pluralising of marriage could be read as a profound challenge to heteronormative power or to what Butler calls the 'heterosexual matrix', signifying that it does not have the power to determine the meaning of marriage for all time into eternity. The redefinition and appropriation also confirms what de Vos refers to as the 'constructed nature of marriage'[208] – the fact that marriage is not 'an institution with certain fundamental and essential elements'.[209] Relying on Foucault, de Vos emphasises that the definition of marriage is dynamic because it is linked to other social attitudes and institutions.[210]

In its jurisprudence after the decriminalisation case, the Constitutional Court repeatedly based its arguments for recognition on the fact that same-sex couples are in every material way as capable of forming a family as opposite-sex couples. Take, for instance, the court's comments in the *Fourie* case, summing up its determinations over the years about same-sex couples:

> 'iv. [G]ays and lesbians in same-sex life partnerships are as capable as heterosexual spouses of expressing and sharing love in its manifold forms, including affection, friendship, eros and charity;
>
> v. they are likewise as capable of forming intimate, permanent, committed, monogamous, loyal and enduring relationships; of furnishing emotional and spiritual support; and of providing physical care, financial support and assistance in running the common household;
>
> vi. they are individually able to adopt children and in the case of lesbians to bear them;
>
> vii. in short, they have the same ability to establish a *consortium omnis vitae*;
>
> viii. finally . . . they are capable of constituting a family, whether nuclear or extended, and of establishing, enjoying and benefiting from family life which is not distinguishable in any significant respect from that of heterosexual spouses.'[211]

---

[208] P de Vos 'Same-sex Marriage, the Right to Equality and the South African Constitution' (1996) 11 *SAPR/PL* 355 at 371.

[209] Ibid.

[210] Ibid.

[211] *Fourie*, note 125 supra, at para 53, citing *National Coalition for Gay and Lesbian Equality v Minister of Home Affairs* 2000 (2) SA 1 (CC) at para 53.

It is true that the court here is at risk of denying important differences between same-sex and opposite sex couples and thus exposes itself to the shared criticism of Norrie and de Vos, articulated earlier. Yet it is possible to read the court here as indicating that, despite important differences, same-sex couples are as capable of forming a family as heterosexual couples. In other words, whatever the important differences may be, they are not differences that register for purposes of recognition. No wonder, then, that American commentators like Mary Shaw argue that '[h]aving a separate institution for committed same-sex couples is no more equal than were the black alternatives to the whites-only facilities of the Jim Crow era. True equality is just not possible where you have an "us" vs. "them" dichotomy'.[212]

When the Supreme Judicial Court of Massachusetts was called upon to advise the state legislature on the question whether a civil union regime would pass constitutional muster in that state, the court responded that marriage alone would meet constitutional standards. Considering the separate but equal question, it again referred to the political history of this dispensation, holding that '[t]he history of our nation has demonstrated that separate is seldom, if ever, equal'.[213] As regards the contention that it would be a distinction of name only, the court reiterated that the dissimilitude between the terms 'is not innocuous; it is a considered choice of language that reflects a demonstrable assigning of same-sex, largely homosexual, couples to second class status'.[214] It explicitly dealt with the rational basis for any such distinction and dismissed the assertion that such a basis exists: '[f]or no rational reason the marriage laws . . . discriminate against a defined class; no amount of tinkering with language will eradicate that stain'.[215] In a way very similar to the South African Constitutional Court, the Massachusetts court pointed to the fact that it is marriage that affords a status that is specially recognised in society and that has 'significant social and other advantages'.[216]

In my own view, the reason why a 'separate but equal' regime seldom, if ever, amounts to a 'better' dispensation is closely connected with the question of the pervasiveness of disciplinary, heteronormative power. Foucault reminds us that power does not fear sexuality, it is rather that sexuality is one of the means through which power is exercised.[217] Indeed, Foucault goes as far as claiming that 'sexuality is a recourse which no modern system

[212] M Shaw 'Marriage v Civil Unions: Separate is Never Equal' 10 January 2010 (available at *http://www.countercurrents.org/shaw100110.htm*).
[213] Opinions of the Justices to the Senate, 440 Mass 1201 at 1206 (Mass. 2004); A Sullivan *Same-sex Marriage: Pro & Con: A Reader* (Vintage 2004) at 119.
[214] At 1207; Sullivan, note 213 supra, at 120.
[215] At 1208; Sullivan, note 213 supra.
[216] Ibid; Sullivan, note 213 supra.
[217] B-H Levy 'Power and Sex: Interview with Michel Foucault' (from *Telos*, 1977) in J Escoffier (ed) *Sexual Revolution* (Running Press 2003) 670 at 676.

of power can do without'.[218] Let us recall Sachs J's statement that a separate but equal regime would be unacceptable if it served 'as a threadbare cloak for covering distaste for or repudiation by *those in power*'.[219] Clearly Sachs J was not unaware that heteronormative power would play the decisive role in the means by which same-sex relationships would become recognised by the law. Laws that regulate and order sexuality will always reflect, then, the exercise of the heteronormative power through which they are constituted – not *unbridled* heteronormative power, but heteronormative power nevertheless. As mentioned earlier, Judith Butler used to refer to the normative structure in which heteronormative power operates in this regulatory way, as the heterosexual matrix.[220] As Chambers explains, the heterosexual matrix turns on the fact that 'heterosexuality is the median point on the normal curve: not only that which is statistically dominant, but also that which is expected, demanded and always presupposed in society'.[221]

South Africa and the UK, in particular Scotland, are by no means immune to this exercise of power through the discourse of sexuality. In fact, it is hardly controversial to point out that the Civil Partnership Act and the Civil Union Act represent the outcome of heteronormative/homonormative power struggles which could also be described as a negotiation with heteronormativity. Norrie's argument seems to pay little attention to the fact that it is the hegemony of heteronormative power itself that determined when and on what basis same-sex relationships would be decriminalised and, finally, recognised by private law.

All of this still does not suggest that the Civil Union Act represents a 'better' negotiation within the heternonormative matrix than the Civil Partnership Act. From a critical point of view, they are more or less equally bad. For instance, the objectionable provision in the Civil Union Act that a state marriage officer can refuse on grounds of conscience to register a civil union where it is entered into between two people of the same sex[222] is not rendered any less objectionable because the Act provides for marriage as a subspecies of the civil union (civil partnership being the other).[223] Yet it is this very wording, coupled with the gender-neutral definitions of 'marriage' and 'civil partnership' in the Act, that makes the Civil Union Act open to both gender mixes. At the risk of sounding highhanded, this is something which the Civil Partnership Act does not do.

Of course the retention of the 1961 Marriage Act in South Africa remains problematic, in the same way as it remains problematic that in both Scotland

---

[218] Ibid 677.
[219] *Fourie*, note 125 supra, at 580E-F (emphasis added).
[220] J Butler *Gender Trouble: Feminism and the Subversion of Identity* (Routledge 1990) at 42–3.
[221] S A Chambers '"An Incalculable Effect": Subversions of Heteronormativity' (2007) 55 *Political Studies* 656 at 663.
[222] Civil Union Act 17 of 2006, s 6.
[223] Ibid s 1.

and the rest of the UK there are still established state churches that seem to think they hold the monopoly over the meaning and nature of marriage.[224] Once again, at the risk of sounding superior, this is not the case in South Africa, as my earlier discussion of the plurality of marriages attempts to illustrate. It is true that the Civil Union Act does not completely secularise civil unions, be they marriages or civil partnerships, as the Civil Partnership Act clearly does. Religious denominations can apply for affiliation under the Civil Union Act in order to conduct registration as part of the religious ceremony.[225] This fact makes the Civil Union Act neither better nor worse than the Civil Partnership Act, but it does allow for religious institutions that have overcome their homophobia to marry or civilly partner members of their congregations who have decided to tie the proverbial knot with a member of the same sex and who do not see such a decision as a basis for their excommunication from the church. It is thus no wonder that the ban has been lifted on the conclusion of civil partnerships in places associated with religious worship in England and Wales.[226]

3.8 RECENT DEVELOPMENTS AND STAGNATIONS

3.8.1 Scotland

The discussion above attempts to illustrate that the irrationality of the distinction that justifies the Civil Partnership Act 2004 continues to be of concern. In short, separate is only 'better' in this context when it results in the availability of a choice for an institution with the same societal *status* as that of marriage. And this is not yet the case in Scotland and the rest of the UK. But the indications are that the LGBTI community in the UK and Scotland will soon enjoy wider and more formally (and substantively) equal legal recognition than what was afforded them under the Civil Partnership Act; for the debate on extending marriage to same-sex couples has started and it is rapidly gaining ground across the UK.[227] On 17 September 2011, UK Equalities Minister Lynne Featherstone announced that the current parliament would move to legislate for same-sex marriage before the next general election and the Government engaged in a formal consultation

---

[224] See BBC News 'Church of Scotland against Gay Marriage Law Change' 1 December 2011 (available at *http://www.bbc.co.uk/news/uk-scotland-scotland-politics-15989691*).

[225] Civil Union Act, s 5.

[226] Equality Act 2010, s 202; Marriages and Civil Partnerships (Approved Premises) (Amendment) Regulations 2011.

[227] In February 2011, eight British couples filed a joint application to the European Court of Human Rights (ECtHR) seeking legalisation of same-sex marriage as well as opposite-sex civil partnership. See A Travis 'Gay Marriages and Heterosexual Civil Partnerships may soon be Welcomed' *The Guardian* 17 February 2011 (available at *http://www.guardian.co.uk/lifeandstyle/2011/feb/17/civil-partnerships-marriage*).

process to this end between March and June 2012.[228] Interestingly, this *followed* the newly elected Scottish Government's announcement (already on 6 June 2011) that it would begin consultation on same-sex marriage.[229]

Because of the fact that marriage and civil partnership are devolved matters, the proposal mentioned above – to lift the ban on the conclusion of civil partnerships on religious premises – applies to England and Wales only. However, in a recently published consultation paper, the Scottish Government has clearly indicated that it also intends to lift the ban in Scotland.[230] As regards same-sex marriage, the Scottish Government has also made it abundantly clear that it is in favour of legalising same-sex marriage. As Deputy First Minister Nicola Sturgeon writes in the foreword to the consultation paper: 'same sex marriage should be introduced so that same sex couples have the option of getting married if that is how they wish to demonstrate their commitment to each other'.[231]

The consultation paper is also at pains to emphasise that these matters are 'devolved matters for the Scottish Parliament' and that 'if Scotland were to move to allow same sex marriage, the Scottish Government would discuss the practical implications with the UK Government', since many of the rights and responsibilities that flow from marriage are reserved.[232]

When one compares the above approach with how civil partnership became a reality in Scotland (namely, through the unusual measure of a Sewel motion, now known as a legislative consent motion)[233], it is once again apparent how deeply these matters are affected by politics. When civil partnerships stood to be introduced in Scotland in 2004, the then Labour/Liberal Democratic administration opted for the Sewel motion, allowing the Westminster Parliament to legislate Scottish provisions into the Civil Partnership Act. The justification given at the time was that it would produce consistency and that many matters affecting civil partnership are, in any event, reserved.[234]

The Scottish Nationalist Party (SNP) in opposition condemned this approach as 'totally unacceptable', citing the fact that more than 80 per cent

---

[228] See E Barrett 'Government Move to Legislate Same-sex Marriage' *The Independent* 17 September 2011 (available at *http://www.independent.co.uk/news/uk/politics/government-move-to-legislate-samesex-marriage-2356475.html*).

[229] See C Brocklebank 'Scottish Government Pledge to Begin "Process of Consultation" on Gay Marriage' (available at *http://www.pinknews.co.uk/2011/06/06/scottish-government-pledge-to-begin-process-of-consultation-on-gay-marriage/*).

[230] N Sturgeon 'Foreword' in Scottish Government *The Registration of Civil Partnerships, Same Sex Marriage: A Consultation* (2011). Also see Scottish Government ibid at 4.

[231] Sturgeon 'Foreword', note 230 supra.

[232] Scottish Government, note 230 supra, at 14.

[233] For further information on such motions see *http://www.scotland.gov.uk/About/Government/Sewel*.

[234] See Scottish Executive *Sewel Motion for the Civil Partnerships Bill* (2004) at 3 (available at *http://www.scotland.gov.uk/Resource/Doc/1097/0000923.pdf*).

of legal matters affected by civil partnerships are devolved to the Scottish Parliament and accusing the Scottish Executive of attempting to 'side-step' the issue because of the social controversies it attracts.[235] Now that the SNP is in power, it is highly unlikely that, given this history, it would opt for UK legislation through a Sewel motion when it comes to the recognition of same-sex marriage.[236] The Scottish Government's bold approach in this regard appears to be supported by Scottish popular opinion. The Scottish Social Attitudes Survey for 2010 found that 61 per cent of Scots who participated in the survey are in favour of same-sex marriage.[237] Recently the Scottish Human Rights Commission also expressed support for the legalisation of same-sex marriage in Scotland.[238] In the light of the above, it is indeed likely that Scotland will be at the forefront of the recognition of same-sex marriage in the UK, provided it can withstand the pressure exerted on it by the churches.[239]

3.8.2 South Africa

One respect in which South Africa finds itself troubled on the issue of same-sex marriage is, precisely, on the matter of public opinion. The discussion above on the history of the enactment of the Civil Union Act illustrates that, by and large, the South African *demos* and even a significant portion of its government[240] remains not only opposed to same-sex marriage, but indeed finds the very idea of same-sex sexual activity abhorrent and reprehensible. Moreover, the phenomenon of 'corrective rape'[241] continues to plague the lives of many lesbians in South Africa who find themselves in social contexts in which there exists little state protection for their chosen way of life. Continuing reports of the rape and murder, particularly of lesbians who

---

[235] See *http://www2.snp.org/node/12030*; Scottish Government, note 230 supra, at 2.

[236] In this regard see also the Scottish Equality and Human Rights Commission's report on its Equal Marriage Symposium: E Folan and M Sayers *Equal Access to Marriage: Ending the Segregation of Same-Sex Couples and Transgender People in Scotland* (EHRC Scotland 2011) 46–7.

[237] The Scottish Government *Scottish Social Attitudes Survey 2010: Attitudes to Discrimination and Positive Action* (2010) at 70 (available at *http://www.scotland.gov.uk/Publications/2011/08/11112523/0*).

[238] The Scottish Human Rights Commission *Submission to the Registration of Civil Partnerships Same Sex Marriage – Scottish Government* (2011).

[239] See Davies, note 37 supra.

[240] The National House of Traditional Leaders, as recently as a few months ago, advocated a constitutional amendment to remove the reference to 'sexual orientation' in section 9(3) of the Constitution. See SAPA 'Traditional Leaders Oppose Gay Rights' *News24* 6 May 2012, available at *http://www.news24.com/SouthAfrica/News/Traditional-leaders-oppose-gay-rights-20120506*.

[241] The social phenomenon where lesbians are brutally raped and often murdered, because the offender(s) believes that the rape will cause the woman to change her sexual orientation to heterosexuality.

live in informal townships across the country, suggest that it is a widespread occurrence in South Africa, partly exacerbated by the reported tardiness in the investigation and prosecution of these crimes.[242]

In addition, the Government has failed to address the anomaly that has emerged as a result of the Constitutional Court's jurisprudence on same-sex relationships. The Court's decision in *Gory v Kolver*[243] made it clear that where it has granted piecemeal relief (in respect of same-sex life partnerships) prior to the enactment of the Civil Union Act (which led to same-sex unmarried cohabitants being in a better legal position than cohabiting heterosexual partners), it was up to Parliament to address this problem.[244] To date, Parliament has not come up with any solution to this anomaly, save for the stagnant (and rather flawed) Draft Domestic Partnerships Bill of 2008 which attempts to afford legal recognition to both same-sex and opposite-sex cohabitations.[245] Furthermore, there are currently no plans afoot to challenge the unconstitutional provisions of the Civil Union Act or the continued existence of the Marriage Act alongside it. In the meantime, conservative family law scholars continue to insist that the marriage in terms of the Civil Union Act is inferior to the marriage in terms of the Marriage Act.[246]

3.9 CONCLUSION: ARISTOTLE'S DREAM

The analysis embarked upon here suggests that marriage law as a category of private law has not since time immemorial been as concerned with human

---

[242] See Human Rights Watch 'South Africa: No Arrests in Lesbian Murder Case' (available at *http://www.hrw.org/news/2011/05/02/south-africa-no-arrests-lesbian-murder-case*); and B Khalo 'South Africa: Townships Still Not Safe for Gay, Lesbian and Transgender people' *AllAfrica* 5 October 2012, available at: *http://allafrica.com/stories/201210051578.html*.

[243] 2007 (4) SA97 (CC).

[244] At para 30.

[245] See Department of Home Affairs *Domestic Partnership Bill, 2008* (available at *http://www. info.gov.za/view/DownloadFileAction?id=76707*). On the flaws of this Bill, see P de Vos 'Still Out in the Cold? The Domestic Partnership Bill and the (Non)Protection of Marginalised Woman' in J Sloth-Nielsen and Z du Toit (eds) *Trials and Tribulations, Trends and Triumphs: Developments in International, African and South African Child and Family Law* (Juta 2008) at 129–42; P de Vos 'A Judicial Revolution? The Court-Led Achievement of Same-Sex Marriage in South Africa' in Katharina Boele-Woelki (ed) *Debates in Family Law around the Globe at the Dawn of the Twent-First Century* (Intersentia 2009) at 250. A significant curial development here was achieved in the recently decided case of *Paixão v Road Accident Fund* (RAF) Case no 640/2011 (SCA) in which it was decided that a surviving unmarried life partner (whether of the same or different sex) of a deceased breadwinner who was killed in a road accident has a claim against the RAF (as third party insurance fund) for loss of support, provided that they can prove an express or implied, written or oral contractual agreement of reciprocal support.

[246] J Heaton *South African Family Law* (3rd edition) (Lexis Nexis 2010) at 27. For an alternative position, more in step with the jurisprudence, see A Barratt (ed) *Law of Persons and the Family* (Pearson 2012).

rights as Friedmann and Barak-Erez suggest. The opposite is the case: 'marriage' and 'family' as private law categories have in fact been deeply resistant to an infiltration by relationships between people of the same sex – relationships that are, nevertheless, as formally capable of corrective justice as a union between members of the opposite sex.

The history shows that when and how private law opted to include members of same-sex couples within its ambit was not determined by purely formal questions, but rather by long and often vociferous political struggles. The existence of the formal structure of relationships capable of recognition by private law did not, in either South Africa or Scotland, change what Oliver Wendell Holmes once referred to as '[t]he felt necessities of the time'.[247] It was politics that changed it all.

In apartheid South Africa private law's resistance to legal recognition outside the white, heterosexual, monogamous marriage came in the form of the Prohibition of Mixed Marriages Act[248] read with the 1961 Marriage Act, which in turn based its definition of marriage on the common law as the union, while it lasts, between one man and one woman. Simultaneously the resources of public law were enlisted to ensure that same-sex couples would be kept outside of private law recognition through the common law criminalisation of same-sex sexual activity where it occurred between men.

All of this was changed by the human rights moment in South Africa. We have seen that it was the sexual orientation ground in the equality provision of the Constitution that sparked decriminalisation, cleared the public law obstacle to private law recognition of same-sex relationships and, finally, paved the way for a human rights analysis that would result in the declaration of the common law definition of marriage as unconstitutional and the adoption of the Civil Union Act – an Act that is, admittedly, less than perfect, but that nevertheless constitutes an enormously symbolic beginning for the full and equal legal recognition of sexual minority freedom in South Africa.

In the same way, it was the involvement of human rights that resulted in the initial decriminalisation and, finally, in the recognition for same-sex couples through the Civil Partnership Act 2004 in Scotland and the rest of the United Kingdom. It was the pressure exerted by the growing international culture of human rights on private law that led the House of Lords crucially to hold that same-sex couples could constitute a family, and it was the European Court of Human Rights' decision in the *Godin-Mendoza* case that moved the legislature to consider and adopt a recognition of same-sex partnerships on the same basis as, if separate from, marriage.

However, this chapter also shows that human rights discourse based on substantive equality and the significance of difference has not managed fully

---

[247] *The Common Law* (Little, Brown 1881) at 1.
[248] Act 55 of 1949.

to break private law's resistance to a full recognition of same-sex conjugal relationships on the basis that the right to be different affords the right to formally equal treatment. In Scotland, there is a sentiment that this fact does not represent a failure on the part of either human rights or private law: same-sex relationships are different from opposite sex relationships and therefore should be treated separately, albeit equally. However, as recent Scottish opinion and Scottish Government views illustrate, this is not a sentiment shared by the Scottish *demos*. In fact, indications are that Scotland is at the forefront of same-sex marriage recognition in the UK.

In South Africa the legal landscape remains scarred and fissured by the legacy of apartheid's separate but equal regimes. For this reason, LGBTI activism almost organically resulted in the insistence that recognition could not come in any other way than through opening up the institution of marriage. Given the plurality of marriage regimes that existed in South Africa already prior to the marriage provided in terms of the Civil Union Act, the recognition that same-sex couples could also be 'married' represented a significant moment in the ongoing deconstruction of the dominant definition of marriage as a monogamous, heterosexual union.

This is not to say that the marriage granted to same-sex as well as to opposite-sex couples in terms of the Civil Union Act is one without its problems and challenges. In this regard, the retention of the 1961 Marriage Act and the conscientious objection clause in the Civil Union Act where the marriage or civil partnership is formed between members of the same sex suggests that same-sex marriages are not yet, from a formal equality point of view, on the same footing as their heterosexual counterpart – the irrationality of the distinction remains.

At the same time, it seems to me that the two jurisdictions considered here may do well to acknowledge that as long as the irrationality of the separate but equal distinction remains and as long as this distinction results in a 'lesser' societal status, it is appropriate to wish each other luck in their different, but related struggles for Aristotle's dream of an equality that, before it can be blind, must remain ever watchful of the differences in humankind in respect of which the law should attach no sanction.

Chapter 4

Child Law: Respecting the Rights of Children

*Elaine E Sutherland**

4.1 INTRODUCTION

By virtue of their age, inexperience and traditional disempowerment, children and young people are undoubtedly amongst the most vulnerable members of any community, something recognised in all developed societies by extending special protections to them. Being the object of protection, however, is not the same thing as having enforceable rights. That is not to suggest that child protection is unimportant, and it was a failure to acknowledge the protective dimension that so undermined the position of the early child liberationists.[1] Indeed, the 'right to protection' is now regarded as one – but only one – important aspect of children's rights.[2] Whether children can be rights-holders[3] and, if so, the precise content of their rights[4] has long troubled moral and legal philosophers. In addition, enforcing children's

---

* I am immensely grateful to Professor Jacqueline Heaton of the University of South Africa for her most helpful comments on an earlier draft of this chapter. My thanks go to Amanda Tufts, JD 2013, Lewis and Clark Law School, for her research assistance. The usual disclaimer applies and responsibility for the chapter remains my own.
1. See, e.g., R Farson *Birthrights* (Macmillan 1974) (for whom children's rights included not only the more traditional rights to education and justice, but also the more controversial rights to sexual freedom and choice of living arrangements); J Holt *Escape from Childhood* (Penguin 1975) (similar, but included the right to experiment with drugs). For a more modern exposition, see B Franklin (ed) *The New Handbook of Children's Rights: Comparative Policy and Practice* (Routledge 2002).
2. Acknowledging a right to protection, alongside a range of other rights, both generates the 'rights v welfare' debate and provides some answer to it. Nonetheless, the balancing of these two elements continues to present a fundamental challenge.
3. T Campbell 'The Rights of the Minor' in P Alston, S Parker and J Seymour (eds) *Children, Rights and the Law* (Clarendon Press 1992) 15; N MacCormick 'Children's Rights: A Test Case' in N MacCormick *Legal Right and Social Democracy: Essays in Legal and Political Philosophy* (Clarendon Press 1982) 154.
4. B Dickens 'The Modern Function and Limits of Parental Rights' (1981) 97 *Law Quarterly Review* 462; J Eekelaar 'The Emergence of Children's Rights' (1986) 6 *Oxford Journal of Legal Studies* 161; M Freeman *The Rights and Wrongs of Children* (Frances Pinter, 1983); M Minow 'Rights for the Next Generation: A Feminist Approach to Children's Rights' 9 *Harvard Women's Law Journal* 1 (1986); M Wald 'Children's Rights: A Framework for Analysis' 12 *UC Davis Law Review* 225 (1979).

rights undoubtedly presents challenges.[5] Respect for family privacy, combined with a belief that parents will promote their children's best interests, has been advanced as a reason for the state to show restraint in promoting children's rights.[6] Yet, as the plethora of child abuse and neglect cases demonstrates amply, relying on parents alone is a dangerous course and an abdication of responsibility by the wider community.[7] Children and young people are not the only holders of rights in an increasingly 'rights-conscious' world, but reconciling competing rights is nothing new for legal systems. It is what legislatures and courts are frequently called upon to address.

This chapter situates children in a variety of contexts in which their rights are often at issue and analyses the comparative impact of the European Convention on Human Rights, on Scots law, with that, in South Africa, of the Constitution of the Republic of South Africa. The law does not exist in isolation, of course, and the socio-economic circumstances of an individual child will often be of far greater practical significance for the child's life than laudable expressions of rights as interpreted by the courts. Nonetheless, legal systems create the climate in which rights can be fulfilled[8] and sound fundamental principles, combined with appropriate legislation and judicial interpretation, can do much to translate theoretical rights into practical reality for children and adults alike.

4.2 CHILDREN'S RIGHTS, THE CONSTITUTION OF THE REPUBLIC OF SOUTH AFRICA AND THE EUROPEAN CONVENTION ON HUMAN RIGHTS

It is axiomatic that constitutions, conventions and the like are products of their time, and nowhere is this illustrated more clearly than in the divergent approach to children reflected in the South African Constitution and the European Convention. One manifestation of this temporal consideration is the fact that each document resulted from a very different drafting process. Fundamental to the drafting of the South African Constitution was a process that was designed to be inclusive, accessible and transparent, and considerable effort was made to involve all stakeholders, including young people.[9]

---

[5]　See section 4.3.3 infra.

[6]　BC Hafen and JO Hafen 'Abandoning Children to their Autonomy: The United Nations Convention on the Rights of the Child' (1996) 37 *Harvard International Law Journal* 449

[7]　J Eekelaar 'Personal Rights and Human Rights' in P Lødrup and E Modvar (eds) *Family Life and Human Rights* (Gyldendal 2004) at 179. See further section 4.4.1 infra.

[8]　P McG Crotty 'Legislating Equality', (1996) 10 *International Journal of Law, Policy and the Family* 317 at 318 ('law can be a starting point and basic foundation for the attainment of equal rights . . . No matter what type of law is involved or how closely it reflects a nation's culture, law can serve as a first step in transforming social realities and fostering equal rights').

[9]　H Ebrahim *The Soul of a Nation: Constitution-making in South Africa* (Oxford University

What emerged was a thoroughly modern constitution which, unlike many older equivalents, makes express mention of children. Not only do they receive the general constitutional protections, but the Bill of Rights guarantees them a number of legal, social and economic rights listed in section 28. As we shall see, this has enabled children to secure tangible benefits in the courts.

In contrast, the European Convention was drafted many years earlier by a small group of somewhat elderly, white males.[10] Public consultation was simply not part of the process and it was unsurprising at the time that the resulting text makes no mention of children.[11] Happily, this failure to acknowledge the separate existence and needs of children has not resulted in them being denied Convention rights, for the very obvious reason that, as human beings, children are within the Convention's ambit, and there is a growing body of children's rights jurisprudence emanating from the European Court of Human Rights. In addition, it is trite law that the European Convention is a 'living instrument'[12] and that the European Court takes a 'dynamic and evolutive'[13] approach to interpreting it. That said, it is worth remembering that the ethos of the European Court is very much less proactive than that of the Constitutional Court in South Africa,[14] with the former permitting states a wide 'margin of appreciation' in implementing Convention rights,[15] and often taking a cautious and incremental approach on specific issues.[16]

Press 1998) at 179–80 ('[I]t was not good enough merely to invite submissions, but it was necessary to reach out to and solicit . . . views deliberately. To this end, an elaborate media campaign was devised to reach as many South Africans as possible'). See particularly, the work of Theme Committee 4, dealing with fundamental rights, discussed at 184–5. See also GE Devenish *A Commentary on the South African Constitution* (Butterworths 1998) at 21 ('the process of drafting the text [of the final Constitution] involved thousands of South Africans in the largest public participation programme ever devised in our history').

[10] J P Grant and E E Sutherland 'International Standards and Scots Law' in A Cleland and E E Sutherland (eds) *Children's Rights in Scotland* 3e (W Green 2009) at paras 3–02–3–05.

[11] Nor did that change with subsequent additions. Even article 2 of the First Protocol to the Convention, guaranteeing the right to education, which clearly anticipates educational provision for children, refers to the parental right to ensure that education is provided in conformity with the parents' religious and philosophical convictions. No mention is made of children, far less of their convictions.

[12] See section 1.2 supra.

[13] *Stafford v United Kingdom* (2002) 35 EHRR 32, para 68.

[14] See E Bonthuys 'Realising South African Children's Socio-Economic Claims against Parents and the State: What Courts Can Achieve' (2008) 22 *International Journal of Law, Policy and the Family* 333.

[15] See, for example, *Glaser v United Kingdom* (2001) 33 EHRR 1 at para 64 ('it is not for the Court to substitute itself for the competent domestic authorities in regulating contact questions, but rather to review under the Convention the decisions that those authorities have taken in the exercise of their power of appreciation').

[16] See, e.g., its approach to the rights of non-marital fathers and on physical punishment of children, discussed at sections 4.5.3 and 4.5.4 respectively, infra.

These documents, however, tell only part of the story since no analysis of child law in either jurisdiction would be complete without noting the importance of the United Nations Convention on the Rights of the Child (the 'UN Convention').[17] Both South Africa and the United Kingdom (and, thereby, Scotland) are parties to the UN Convention and, thus, bound by its terms. While neither country has yet incorporated the UN Convention into domestic law,[18] a step taken in a number of other countries,[19] its impact on each legal system is unmistakable. In South Africa, the African Charter on the Rights and Welfare of the Child (the 'African Charter')[20] is of parallel importance.

As the language of section 28 indicates, both the UN Convention and the African Charter informed the drafters of the South African Constitution, and the courts make frequent reference to both instruments. The UN Convention post-dates the European Convention by several decades and when the Human Rights Act 1998 incorporated the European Convention into the law of the various parts of the United Kingdom, children's rights activists in Scotland were concerned that it might be 'a dormant virus waiting to attack children's rights'.[21] That fear stemmed, in part, from the way in which other 'rights' documents, like the United States Constitution, have operated to secure parental rights while doing little for the rights of children and, in part, from some of the older decisions of the European Court itself.[22] However, the European Court of Human Rights has long used the UN Convention as an aid to interpreting the European Convention,[23]

---

[17] 1577 UNTS 3; (1989) 28 ILM 1448.

[18] While the proposals for a Rights of Children and Young People (Scotland) Bill would require the Scottish Ministers to have 'due regard' to the terms of the UN Convention, this would not amount to incorporation: *A Scotland for Children: A Consultation on the Children and Young People Bill* (Scottish Government 2012), available electronically only at *http://www.scotland.gov.uk/Publications/2012/07/718 1*. Some respondents to the consultation, including the present author, have urged incorporating the Convention into Scots law in so far as that is competent under the Scotland Acts 1998 and 2012.

[19] The Convention was incorporated into Norwegian law in 2003. In other countries, like the Netherlands and Russia, a similar result is achieved since treaty obligations take precedence over domestic law. See E E Sutherland 'Imperatives and Challenges in Child and Family Law: Commonalities and Disparities' in E E Sutherland (ed) *The Future of Child and Family Law: International Predictions* (Cambridge University Press 2012) at para 1.54.

[20] 11 July 1990, OAU Doc CAB/LEG/24.9/49.

[21] E E Sutherland and A Cleland 'Children's Rights in Scotland – Where Are We Now?' in Cleland and Sutherland *Children's Rights in Scotland*, note 10 supra, at para 1–02.

[22] See, e.g., *Nielsen v Denmark* (1989) 11 EHRR 175, where the Court found a mother's decision to commit her son to a psychiatric institution, largely because he kept running away to live with his father, to be protected by her art 8 right to respect for private and family life and no violation of the boy's art 5 right to liberty.

[23] See, e.g., *Keegan v Ireland* (1994) 18 EHRR 342 (right of a non-marital father to prevent his child being adopted: art 7 of the UN Convention used by the Court in interpreting art 8 of the European Convention) and *Costello-Roberts v United Kingdom* (1995) 19 EHRR 112 (cor-

something reinforced by the Grand Chamber when it observed, in *Sahin v Germany*: 'The human rights of children and the standards to which all governments must aspire in realising these rights for all children are set out in the Convention on the Rights of the Child'.[24]

It appears, then, that the textual divergence between the South African Constitution and the European Convention, in their approach to children, may have been militated somewhat by the impact of the UN Convention and the 'living' nature of the European Convention itself, leading to the very real possibility of a degree of common ground in the way the legal systems in South Africa and Scotland approach matters involving children.[25] A good example of substantial commonality can be found in general principles of child law in each jurisdiction.

4.3 CHILD LAW: THE GENERAL PRINCIPLES

4.3.1 Equality and non-discrimination

Given its genesis and history, it is hardly surprising to find the right to equality guaranteed to children and adults alike in the South African Constitution, this guarantee encompassing equal protection before the law, an affirmative obligation on the state to promote equality and advance persons disadvantaged by discrimination and a prohibition on the state and individuals discriminating against anyone unfairly.[26] Of course, implementing this obligation requires appreciation that the rights of one person must be understood in the context of the rights of others and general, societal interests. The European Convention prohibits discrimination in respect of rights contained in it.[27] While this creates a narrower range of protection than that set out in the Constitution, European Court jurisprudence has established that the state is not only under a negative obligation to refrain from prohibited discrimination, but is also under positive obligations to secure Convention rights.[28] A number of important European Convention rights, known as 'qualified' rights, permit deviation from them where that

---

poral punishment of a child: art 16 of the UN Convention used in interpreting arts 3 and 8 of the European Convention).

[24] (2003) 36 EHRR 43, para 39.

[25] Another explanation for common ground lies in the fact that Scots law, including the Children (Scotland) Act 1995 and the Scottish Law Commission consultations and recommendations that preceded it, was one of the comparative models used by the South African Law Reform Commission in its deliberations that led to the Children's Act No 38 of 2005.

[26] Section 9.

[27] Article 14. With the entry into force of Protocol No12 to the Convention, (2000) ETS No 177, on 1 April 2005, art 14 became free-standing. Previously, discrimination had at least to implicate another Convention right before it became operative.

[28] *Belgian Linguistics Case (No 2)* (1968) 1 EHRR 252.

deviation is in pursuit of a 'legitimate aim' and there is 'reasonable relationship of proportionality between the means employed and the aim sought to be realised'.[29] Both the UN Convention and the African Charter contain prohibitions on discrimination.[30]

4.3.2 Best interests of the child

The South African Constitution is unambiguous in providing that '[a] child's best interests are of paramount importance in every matter concerning the child',[31] a principle carried through into legislation.[32] In this, it goes somewhat further than the requirements of both the UN Convention and the African Charter,[33] both of which accord the child's best interests the arguably lower status of, respectively, 'a' or 'the' 'primary consideration'. Much energy has been expended, internationally, exploring the importance of such linguistic differences[34] but, for our present purpose, it is sufficient to note that, in all cases, the child's best interests are accorded considerable importance and in none are they treated as the *sole* consideration.

Scots law accords the welfare of the child a similarly dominant position, again, treating it as 'the paramount consideration' in the legislation addressing the intra-family setting and public law decisions about children.[35] Arguably, the central position of welfare in the legislation owes more to the ratification of the UN Convention than it does to the European Convention since modern European Court jurisprudence emphasises the balancing of the child's rights with those of others, particularly those of the child's parents.[36]

---

29 *Abdulaziz, Cabales and Balkandali v United Kingdom* (1985) 7 EHRR 471. On proportionality, see further section 1.4 supra.

30 UN Convention, art 2; African Charter, art 3.

31 Section 28(2).

32 Children's Act No 38 of 2005, s 6 and Child Justice Act No 65 of 2008, s 2(a), requiring protection of the child's constitutional rights. Burman has dismissed the applicability of the standard, in the African context, as 'a Utopian doctrine that deludes the classes in power into believing that the interests of children are being taken care of' and, in respect of sections of the population that do not accept its validity, as a 'recipe for social and legal conflict': S Burman, 'The Best Interests of the South African Child' (2003) 17 *International Journal of Law, Policy and the Family* 28 at 38.

33 UN Convention, art 3; African Charter, art 4.

34 Discussions here explore the import of the use of 'a' as opposed 'the' and distinction between 'paramountcy' and 'primacy'.

35 Children (Scotland) Act 1995, ss 1(1) and 11(7)(a) and Children's Hearings (Scotland) Act 2011, s 25. In the public law context, the child's welfare may be treated as only 'a primary consideration' if such an approach is justified in order to protect the public from serious harm: 2011 Act, s 26.

36 E.g., in the child protection context, in *Johansen v Norway* (1996) 23 EHRR 33, at para 78, the Court opined that 'a fair balance must be struck in the interests of the child and those of the parent and, in striking such a balance, particular importance must be attached to the welfare of the child which, depending on their nature and seriousness, may override those

4.3.3 Right to participate in decision-making

Another of the core principles of the UN Convention and the African Charter is the child's right to particulate in the decision-making process, that right comprising two separate elements.[37] First, the child must be given the opportunity to express his or her views freely on matters affecting him or her, with due weight being accorded to these views in the light of the child's age and maturity. Secondly, the child must be heard or represented in judicial or administrative proceedings affecting him or her.

The first element finds expression in both jurisdictions through legislation requiring that, when a person exercising parental responsibilities or rights is contemplating taking a major decision in respect of a child, he or she must take account of any views the child wishes to express in the light of the child's age and maturity.[38] For the sufficiently mature South African child, there is a general right to participate in any matters affecting him or her[39] and the Constitutional Court has not been slow to emphasise the importance of this provision.[40] In Scotland, an obligation is placed on the court to give the child the opportunity to express views and to have regard to these views, in so far as practicable and in the light of the child's age and maturity.[41] As the Inner House of the Court of Session has made abundantly clear, the courts must take this obligation seriously.[42] A similar obligation is placed on other tribunals and decision-makers.[43]

When decisions are being taken in judicial or administrative proceedings, having an *effective* voice may require legal representation, something most children cannot afford to pay for themselves. Thus, the South African Constitution gives the child the right 'to have a legal practitioner assigned to the child, and at state expense, in civil proceedings affecting the child,

of the parent'. That view has been repeated in numerous subsequent cases dealing with both child protection and the private law rights of parents. See further, J Fortin, *Children's Rights and the Developing Law* 3e (Cambridge University Press 2009) at 64–72, and Grant and Sutherland, 'International Standards and Scots Law', note 10 supra, at paras 3–38–3–44.

[37] UN Convention, art 12; African Charter, art 4(2).

[38] Children's Act No 38 of 2005, s 31; Children (Scotland) Act 1995, s 6. The South African statute improves on the Scottish version by offering a definition of what constitutes a 'major decision'.

[39] Children's Act No 38 of 2005, s 10.

[40] *Christian Education South Africa v Minister of Education* 2000 (4) SA 757 at para 53 (the children's 'actual experiences and opinions would not necessarily have been decisive, but they would have enriched the dialogue, and the factual and experiential foundations for the balancing exercise in this difficult matter would have been more secure'), approved in *MEC for Education KwaZulu-Natal and Others v Pillay* 2008 (1) SA 474 (CC) at para 56.

[41] Children (Scotland) Act 1995, s 11(7).

[42] *Shields v Shields* 2002 SC 246 (lower court decision overturned because a seven-year-old boy was not given the opportunity to express his views).

[43] 2011 Act, s 27. Decision-makers are freed from the obligation to take account of the child's views in respect of granting certain protective orders and in other limited circumstances.

if substantial injustice would otherwise result',[44] and children have been provided with legal assistance in order to participate in decisions about their future care.[45] Scots law achieves a substantially similar result with a child under the age of sixteen having the capacity to instruct a solicitor provided that he or she has a general understanding of what it means to do so,[46] and legal aid being granted to enable children to participate in civil legal proceedings.[47] After years of debate in Scotland it was conceded by government that the European Convention guarantee to a 'fair hearing'[48] required that state-funded legal representation should be made available to children at children's hearings (the juvenile justice system) where representation is necessary to allow the child to participate effectively or where the child faces the possibility of being deprived of his or her liberty.[49]

4.4 STATE OBLIGATIONS TO CHILDREN

4.4.1 *The provision of services*

In addition to the rights generally available to all under the South African Constitution, children are given a host of socio-economic rights,[50] including the right 'to basic nutrition, shelter, basic health care services and social services'.[51] Does it follow, then, that the state is under a corresponding obligation to provide these benefits? That question was addressed in *Government of the Republic of South Africa and Others v Grootboom and Others*,[52] where the respondents were some 510 children and 390 adults who had been living in terrible conditions while they waited for low-cost housing to be allocated to them and who sought to enforce their right to shelter.[53] The Constitutional

---

[44] Section 28(2)(h).

[45] *Soller v G* 2003 (5) SA 430 (W) (fifteen-year-old boy provided with representation in an application he brought for variation of a care order that had been made in his parents' divorce), and *Legal Aid Board v R* 2009 (2) SA 262 (D) (twelve-year-old girl obtained representation in parental dispute over her care).

[46] Age of Legal Capacity (Scotland) Act 1991, s 2(4A). A child of twelve is presumed to have this level of understanding and it is not unusual for younger children to demonstrate it.

[47] *Henderson v Henderson* [1997] Fam LR 120 (ten-year-old girl was granted legal aid and represented separately in her parents' divorce proceedings).

[48] Article 6(1). The European Court has interpreted this as meaning that 'each party must be afforded a reasonable opportunity to present his case . . . under conditions that do not place him at a disadvantage *vis-à-vis* his opponent': *Dombo Beheer v Netherlands* (1994) 18 EHRR 213 at [33].

[49] Legal Aid (Scotland) Act 1986, s 28B et seq, as added by the Children's Hearings (Scotland) Act 2011, s 191.

[50] Section 28(1).

[51] Section 28(1)(c).

[52] 2001 (1) SA 46.

[53] That adults' claim derived from s 26 of the Constitution which gives everyone 'the right to have access to adequate housing' places the state under an obligation, 'within its available

Court examined the range of rights provided for in section 28 and concluded that, 'the Constitution contemplates that a child has a right to parental or family care in the first place, and the right to alternative appropriate care only where that is lacking'.[54] The obligation to provide shelter thus lay on the parents and 'section 28(1)(c) did not create any primary state obligation to provide shelter on demand to parents and their children if children are being cared for by their parents or families'.[55]

The necessary element of an absence of parental care was found to be present in *Minister of Health and Others v Treatment Action Campaign and Other (No 2)*[56] and the Court had no difficulty in concluding that the state was obliged to make nevirapine (an antiretroviral drug used to prevent the transmission of HIV from mother to child at birth) available to hospitals and clinics so that it could be provided to, largely indigent, women who would not be able to gain access to it otherwise.

The comparative position in Scotland is somewhat similar, at least in terms of the outcome. Numerous statutes place government agencies, usually local authorities, under statutory obligations to provide services to children. Yet the courts show a marked reluctance to translate that obligation into a right that an individual child can enforce against the local authority. So, for example, in *Crossan v South Lanarkshire Council*,[57] the local authority had fulfilled its statutory obligation to assess the special educational needs of a thirteen-year-old boy with Down's Syndrome, concluding that his needs included after-school care. However, the boy's father was unsuccessful when he sought judicial review of the local authority's refusal to pay for the requisite care. Despite the authority being under a statutory duty to 'safeguard and promote the welfare of children in need',[58] the court concluded that '[n]o inference arises, however, that a local authority are bound, once an individual child has been assessed as having a particular need, to meet that need'.[59]

Given the fact that the European Convention does not guarantee the detailed rights found in section 28(1) of the South African Constitution,[60]

---

resources, to achieve the progressive realisation of this right', and prohibits eviction without a court order.

[54] 2001 (1) SA 46 at para 77.

[55] Idem.

[56] 2002 (5) SA 721.

[57] 2006 SLT 441. See also *R(G) v Barnet London Borough Council* [2004] AC 208 (while the local authority has an obligation to a homeless child, it was no violation of art 8 for it to fulfil the obligation by housing the child without his or her parents).

[58] Children (Scotland) Act 1995, s 22(1)(a).

[59] 2006 SLT 441 at para 24.

[60] See *Andersson and Kullman v Sweden* (1986) 46 DR 251 (complaint inadmissible, the European Commission observing, at 253, 'the Convention does not as such guarantee the right to public assistance either in the form of financial support to maintain a certain standard of living or in the form of supplying day home care places').

it may be of little assistance. However, the state is not freed from all obligations. In X *(Minors) v Bedfordshire County Council,*[61] the House of Lords (now the Supreme Court) refused to hold a local authority liable in damages to a number of children who had been failed by the child protection system. The European Court disagreed and found that the failure to protect the children violated their article 3 rights as well as their right to an effective remedy under article 13.[62] While it would reflect infinitely more respect for children's rights to offer effective protection in the first place, the fact that a government agency may be held to account when it fails to do so may provide some incentive to the agency to fulfil its obligations.

Where a child protection system fails to provide timeous and appropriate intervention, the risk is that a child will suffer avoidable harm, as evidenced by the seemingly endless catalogue of children seriously injured or killed by parents and other family members. It is the magnitude of the danger that is often used to justify the extensive powers given to social workers and the courts to remove children from the home. However, while the European Court has accepted the need for child protection measures, it has been critical of legislation and practices that violate Convention rights, with the fair hearing rights of parents, under article 6, and the right to family life, under article 8, most often being at issue.[63] Undoubtedly, the numerous decisions of the European Court played their part in shaping law reform of child protection in Scotland to ensure greater compliance with the Convention's strictures.[64] Where a child is removed from his or her parents and it is discovered later that the action was unjustified, the rights of both the child and the parent may have been violated. Again, while the House of Lords was unwilling to hold the local authority liable in such circumstances,[65] the European Court disagreed, awarding damages to both the mother and the child.[66] In South Africa, the Constitutional Court addressed the issue of removing a child from parental care, concluding that aspects of the legislation were inconsistent with the Constitution to the extent that they provide for a child to be removed from family care by state officials and placed in

---

[61] [1995] 2 AC 633.
[62] *Z and others v United Kingdom* (2002) 34 EHRR 3. See also the Scottish case, *E v United Kingdom* (2003) 36 EHRR 31.
[63] See, for example, *W v United Kingdom* (1988) 10 EHRR 29 (procedure in place at the time allowed parents the opportunity to challenge the decision only after the child had been removed from their care: violation of art 8); *McMichael v United Kingdom* (1995) 20 EHRR 205 (parents and child had no access to reports on the basis of which decisions were taken: violation of arts 6 and 8); *Venema v Netherlands* (2004) 39 EHRR 5 (denial of parents' right to effective participation in decision to remove: violation of art 8);
[64] The Children (Scotland) Act 1995, Part II and, more recently, the Children's Hearings (Scotland) Act 2011.
[65] *M v Newham London Borough Council* [1995] 2 AC 633.
[66] *TP and KM v United Kingdom* (2002) 34 EHRR 2.

temporary safe care without the decision being reviewed automatically by a court.[67]

4.4.2 Respect for religion and culture

The European Court and South African Constitutional Court differ markedly in their approach to respect for religious and cultural practices in state institutions. For the European Court, the issue is one of freedom of religion. Since this is one of the qualified rights under the Convention, member states are afforded a generous margin of appreciation and the Court recently restated and clarified the balancing test applicable in such cases.[68] It is questionable that this will alter the thrust of its earlier decisions upholding prohibitions on the wearing of religious (particularly Muslim) attire in educational institutions[69] which the English courts followed.[70] It is quite likely that a Scottish court would adopt similar reasoning.[71]

For the Constitutional Court, the issue has been one of equality, since 'religious and cultural practices are protected because they are central to human identity and hence to human dignity which is in turn central to equality', leaving no room for application of any margin of appreciation.[72] Of course, these differences turn, in part, on how the cases have been argued to the courts involved and the different human rights instruments at stake, but there is no escaping the conclusion that South African young people are benefiting from greater respect for their cultural and religious freedom than are their counterparts in Europe.

---

[67] *C and Others v Department of Health and Social Development, Gauteng and Others* (CCT 55/11) [2012] ZACC 1.

[68] *Eweida and others v United Kingdom* [2013] IRLR 231.

[69] *Şahin v Turkey* (2007) 44 EHRR 5 (exclusion of a young woman from university for wearing a *hijab* in breach of a university prohibition did not violate her art 9 right to freedom of religion nor her right to education) and *Dogru v France* (2009) 49 EHRR 8 (similar finding where a young woman was expelled from school for wearing a *hijab* in physical education classes). Conversely, the margin of appreciation that enabled the Court to find the obligatory display of crucifixes in Italian state schools unobjectionable: *Lautsi v Italy* (2012) 54 EHRR 3.

[70] *R (on the application of Begum) v Denbigh High School Governors* [2007] 1 AC 100 (exclusion of a fourteen-year-old pupil from school for wearing a *jilbab* rather than the school uniform did not violate her art 9 right to freedom of religion nor her right to education).

[71] The hope was expressed, pre-*Eweida*, that they would not do so: E E Sutherland 'A Veiled Threat to Children's Rights? Religious Dress in Schools and the Rights of Young People' 2008 *Juridical Review* 143.

[72] *MEC for Education KwaZulu-Natal and Others v Pillay* 2008 (1) SA 474 (CC), at paras 80–81 (school prohibition on the wearing of a nose stud amounted to discrimination on the basis of religion and culture despite the fact that wearing the stud was not required by the fifteen-year-old Tamil Hindu student's religion).

4.5 THE CHILD IN THE FAMILY SETTING

4.5.1 *The child's right to 'family'*

The right to respect for private and family life, guaranteed by article 8 of the European Convention, pervades the family law jurisprudence of the European Court.[73] When read along with the article 14 prohibition on discrimination, it has been used to create a more inclusive and diverse approach to adult relationships.[74] Similarly, it has secured recognition of a broader range of child-adult relationships. We shall return to the issue of the non-marital father presently. For now, it should be noted that, while marriage is a strong indicator of family life, it is not a prerequisite and the European Court has long taken a functionalist approach to determining when family life has been established.[75] While numerous factors, including public opinion and the provisions of the UN Convention, contributed to a climate that resulted in domestic legislation permitting same-sex couples to adopt children[76] and recognising the mother's female partner as a donor child's second parent,[77] in certain circumstances, this inclusive approach by the European Court undoubtedly played its part.

An illustration of the impact of article 8 is found in the 'immigration cases,' reaching back to the early days of European children's rights jurisprudence. If deporting a parent would result in separating the parent from his or her child, deportation may be a violation of the rights of both parties, particularly where they have a close relationship.[78] The issue presented itself somewhat differently in *EM (Lebanon) v Secretary of State for the Home Department*,[79] where a Lebanese mother, EM, was successful in appealing

---

[73] For a discussion of the case law, see C Prest 'The Right to Respect for Family Life: Obligations of the State in Private Law Children's cases' (2005) 35 *Family Law* 124.

[74] See, most recently, *Schalk v Austria* (2011) 53 EHRR 20, discussed in E E Sutherland 'A Step Closer To Same-Sex Marriage Throughout Europe' (2011) 15 *EdinLR* 97.

[75] *Johnston v Ireland* (1985) 9 EHRR 203 (family life present where the parents of a child were in a committed relationship when the child was conceived, albeit they separated later); X, Y *and* Z *v United Kingdom* (1997) 24 EHRR 143 (while the margin of appreciation saved the UK from a finding that art 8 had been violated, the Court found family life to be present between a woman, her child conceived by donor insemination and her female-to-male transgendered partner owing to their living together and the adults fulfilling parental roles in respect of the child); *Görgülü v Germany*, App No 74969/01, 26 February 2004 (family life existed between a father who sought custody of his son who had been placed with foster parents and later adopted despite the fact that the child-father contact had been limited and supervised).

[76] Adoption (Scotland) Act 2008, s 29.

[77] Human Fertilisation and Embryology Act 2008, ss 42–7, dealing with civil and other female partners. The Act continues the approach found in earlier legislation of recognising the mother's husband or male partner as the child's second parent: 2008 Act, ss 35–41.

[78] *Berrehab v The Netherlands* (1989) 11 EHRR 322.

[79] [2009] 1 AC 1198. Following a marriage to AF's father and repeated domestic abuse, EM had

against the decision of the United Kingdom immigration authorities to deport her and AF, her twelve-year-old son, to Lebanon. Once there, Shari'a law would have required her to hand the boy over to her former husband and his male relatives, none of whom the boy had ever met, her contact with him being confined to occasional, supervised visits. Lord Bingham acknowledged the stringent test applied by United Kingdom courts, in these circumstances, in the following terms:

> 'This country has no general mandate to impose its own values on other countries who do not share them. I would therefore question whether it would avail the appellant to rely on the arbitrary and discriminatory character of the Lebanese custody regime had she not shown, as in my opinion she has, that return to Lebanon would flagrantly violate, or completely deny and nullify, her and AF's right to respect for their family life together.'[80]

The South African Constitution does not guarantee respect for family life, something explained by the Constitutional Court as being common in many African and Asian constitutions, reflecting 'the multi-cultural and multi-faith character of such societies' and a desire to avoid the invidious process of deciding which family forms are worthy of protection.[81] It does, however, give children the right 'to family care or parental care, or to appropriate alternative care when removed from the family environment'[82] and children and other family members benefit from the constitutional rights to equality,[83] human dignity[84] and privacy.[85] As Sloth-Nielsen and van Heerden explain, 'the impact of the Constitution has been to reshape the understanding of what constitutes a family, what protections families should be afforded, and the relationship between family members (including children)'.[86]

Several years before same-sex marriage became available in South Africa, the equality rights of same-sex couples gained recognition. This, combined with 'the stability, commitment, affection and support important to a child's development' offered by adoption[87] and the fact that 'the Constitution

---

divorced her husband and, ultimately, fled the country to avoid having to hand EM over to his father.

[80] Ibid, para 42.

[81] *Ex parte Chairperson of the Constitutional Assembly: In re Certification of the Constitution of the Republic of South Africa Act, 1996* 1996 (4) SA 744 (CC) at [99].

[82] Art 28(1)(b).

[83] Art 9.

[84] Art 10.

[85] Art 14.

[86] J Sloth-Nielsen and B van Heerden 'The Constitutional Family: Developments in South African Family Law Jurisprudence under the 1996 Constitution' (2003) 17 *International Journal of Law, Policy and the Family* 121 at 122.

[87] *Du Toit and Another v Minister of Welfare and Population Development and Others* 2003 (2) SA 198 (CC) at para 21.

recognises that family life is important to the well-being of all children',[88] led the Constitutional Court to conclude that preventing adoption by same-sex couples was unconstitutional. Similar reasoning was applied to legislation that made no provision for recognition of a mother's same-sex partner as a donor child's second parent.[89]

A very clear manifestation of respect for the South African child's family life is illustrated by the attention paid to the impact on a child of maternal imprisonment. This process began when the (then) President granted remission from the remainder of their sentences to 'all mothers in prison on 10 May 1994 with minor children under the age of twelve years', something that was done in order 'to serve the interests of children'.[90] Setting the scene for future developments, the Constitutional Court found that the President's generosity did not discriminate against incarcerated fathers who were not afforded the benefit, since 'mothers, as a matter of fact, bear more responsibility for child-rearing in our society than do fathers'.[91] The Constitutional Court followed this lead, in S v M,[92] when it established the general principle that, when a court is considering imposing a custodial sentence on the child's primary care-giver, it must address the effect this would have on the child. However, it was at pains to emphasise that its goal was 'not to permit errant parents unreasonably to avoid appropriate punishment. Rather, it is to protect the innocent children as much as is reasonably possible in the circumstances from avoidable harm'.[93]

That this does not amount to *carte blanche* for offending parents was made clear by the Constitutional Court itself a few years later, in S v S,[94] where it concluded that incarcerating a mother would not inappropriately compromise her children's best interests because she was not their sole care-giving parent, their father being available to care for them, albeit with some difficulty and inconvenience.[95] The Court amplified its original statement, reasserting the central role of the interests of children as an independent consideration in the sentencing process, but

---

[88]　Ibid, para 18.

[89]　*J and Another v Director General Department of Home Affairs and Others* 2003 (5) SA 621 (CC).

[90]　*President of the Republic of South Africa and Another v Hugo* 1997 (4) SA 1, at paras 2 and 37.

[91]　Ibid, para 37.

[92]　2008 (3) SA 232 (CC) (single parent exclusively responsible for the children's care was spared a prison sentence after a conviction for fraud).

[93]　Ibid, para 35. For an example of this principle being applied, see *S v Londe* 2011 (1) SACR 377 (ECG) (confirming a mother's conviction of assault with intent to do grievous bodily harm, but setting her custodial sentence aside because no investigation had been made into the effect that incarceration of the accused would have on the interests of her children; case remitted back to the lower court with an order to obtain pre-sentence and correctional supervision reports that considered the children's interests, to consider those reports, and to reconsider an appropriate sentence for their mother).

[94]　2011 (2) SACR 88 (CC).

[95]　Ibid, paras 62–3.

noting that 'it would be wrong to apply *S v M* in cases that lie beyond its ambit'.[96]

These decisions were greeted with enthusiasm by children's rights activists, in Scotland,[97] where there is no express requirement to take account of the impact of maternal incarceration on children, albeit, reference to an individual's parenting responsibilities will be made in the social enquiry report that must precede imprisonment, in certain circumstances, and mention will often be made of them in pleas in mitigation.[98] However, in the coincidentally-named Scottish case, *S v M*,[99] where a mother was sentenced to three months imprisonment for quite spectacular contempt of court,[100] the fact that she was her child's primary care-giver was insufficient to help her when she sought to appeal against the sentence.

4.5.2 *The birth status of children*

Historically, both Scots and South African law drew a distinction between 'legitimate' and 'illegitimate' children and discriminated against the latter. In both jurisdictions, legislation gradually eroded this discrimination and, for almost all purposes, children are now treated equally, irrespective of their parents' marital status.[101] In Scotland, this was a process that began in the nineteenth century,[102] but there is no mistaking the impact of the European

---

[96] Ibid at para 62. See also, *Van Der Burg and Another v National Director of Public Prosecutions (Centre for Child Law as Amicus Curiae)* (CCT75/11) [2012] ZACC 12 (while the best interests of children affected by forfeiture of their parents' property under the Prevention of Organised Crime Act 121 of 1998 must be considered by the court, that did not require the appointment of a curator to represent their interests where the lower court had taken account of these interests without appointing a curator).

[97] L Adams 'Impact of parent's jail term on children should be factor' *The Herald* 2 March 2010 at 9.

[98] In England the issue of the child's welfare has arisen over the policy of separating a child born to an incarcerated mother from the mother when the child is eighteen months old: *R (P, Q and QB) v Secretary of State for the Home Department* [2001] 1 WLR 2002.

[99] 2011 SLT 918.

[100] Over a two-year period, in the course of opposing an action by the child's father for contact, the mother went to great lengths to obstruct the court proceedings, absenting herself, feigning illness, making false allegations of abuse against the father and giving the court undertakings she had no intention of honouring.

[101] Law Reform (Parent and Child) (Scotland) Act 1986, s 1(1), as substituted by the Family Law (Scotland) Act 2006, s 21(2)(a), and Children's Act No 38 of 2005, s 2. The more recent legislation is very much a product of the work of the relevant Law Commissions. In Scotland, see *Report on Illegitimacy* (Scot Law Com No 82, 1984) and *Report on Family Law* (Scot Law Com No 35, 1992), paras 17.1–17.15. In South Africa, see South African Law Commission *Report on the Investigation into the Legal Position of Illegitimate Children* (Project 38, 1985), South African Law Reform Commission *Review of the Child Care Act* (Discussion Paper 103, 2002), and South African Law Reform Commission *Report of the Review of the Child Care Act* (Project 110, 2002) paras 6.2 ff.

[102] See further E E Sutherland *Child and Family Law* 2e (W Green 2008) paras 6–052–6–060.

Convention on it.[103] The most recent Scottish legislative amendment claims to have abolished the status of illegitimacy altogether[104] and, while the claim is substantially accurate, an exception remains for succession to titles and honours which continue to devolve through the legitimate line.[105]

In South Africa, the Constitution and, in particular, the guarantee of equality in section 9, signalled an end to the legitimacy-illegitimacy distinction, at least as far as the rights of the child are concerned and, in the deliberations that preceded the Children's Act, the word 'illegitimate' was replaced by the more neutral and objective term 'extra-marital'.[106] In addition, the focus of the Act is on the responsibilities of parents and others across the whole range of family relationships. An example of its impact of these developments is found in the decision of the Constitutional Court, declaring invalid the customary law rule of male primogeniture which discriminated against both female and non-marital children in matters of succession.[107] Equal treatment for children, however, does not necessarily mean equal treatment for parents, as the position of the non-martial father illustrates.

4.5.3 *The non-marital father*

Traditionally, Scots and South Africa law accorded the non-marital father little recognition beyond enforcing his financial obligation to his child. While his legal position has improved considerably in both countries, the non-marital father is not necessarily placed on a par with married parents and single mothers. Married parents are in a position of equality in respect of their child and gain a range of parental responsibilities and parental rights automatically, the content and operation of which is very similar in both jurisdictions.[108] Similarly, single mothers acquire these responsibilities and rights automatically.[109]

The non-marital father can secure these rights, in Scotland, by agreement with the child's mother[110] or by registering as the child's father, something he can only do with the consent of the mother or after establishing his paternity

---

103 See *Marckx v Belgium* (1979) 2 EHRR 330 and its manifold progeny.

104 Law Reform (Parent and Child) (Scotland) Act 1986, s 1(1), as substituted by the Family Law (Scotland) Act 2006, s 21(2)(a), headed 'Abolition of status of illegitimacy'.

105 Law Reform (Parent and Child) (Scotland) Act 1986, s 9.

106 South African Law Reform Commission *Review of the Child Care Act* (2002) at paras 8.5.2 ff, and *Report of the Review of the Child Care Act* (2002) at paras 6.2 ff.

107 *Bhe v Khayelitsha Magistrate (Commission for Gender Equality Intervening); Shibi v Sithole; South African Human Rights Commission v President of the Republic of South Africa* 2005 (1) SA 580 (CC).

108 Children (Scotland) Act 1995, ss 1–3, and Children's Act No 38 of 2005, ss 18–22.

109 Children (Scotland) Act 1995, s 3 and, Children's Act No 38 of 2005, s 19.

110 Children (Scotland) Act 1995, s 4. These agreements were always little used and are likely to become obsolete now that a non-marital father can acquire full responsibilities and rights simply by registering his paternity.

in court.[111] Thus far, it will be apparent that considerable power vests in the child's mother and her position is strengthened further by the fact that only she can consent to a young child providing the requisite sample to enable paternity testing to be carried out.[112] While the court can draw an 'inference' from her refusal to consent, it cannot substitute its own consent for hers.[113]

How does all of this sit alongside the European Convention guarantees to respect for private and family life and the prohibition on discrimination on the basis of, amongst other thing, sex and marital status? In *Lebbink v Netherlands*,[114] the European Court made clear that a non-marital father will only gain protection if he has done more than simply father the child: 'The Court does not agree with the applicant that a mere biological kinship, without any further legal or factual elements indicating the existence of a close personal relationship, would be regarded as sufficient to attract the protection of Article 8'.[115] Thus, in *Söderbäck v Sweden*, the Court found no violation of article 8 where a child was adopted by her mother's husband in the face of the birth father's opposition, since the child had been raised by the mother and her new partner and the father's contact with the child had been 'infrequent and limited in character'.[116] That decision can be contrasted with the situation in *Zaunegger v Germany*,[117] where the unmarried parents had lived together for the first three years of the child's life and the father had cared for his daughter for the two years following their separation, with the parents agreeing that she would spend substantial periods of time with him thereafter. The father's application for joint custody was refused by the German court since, under the German Civil Code, such an order was only available to a non-marital father where the child's mother consented, and the European Court had no difficulty in finding a violation of article 8 in these circumstances.

The developing European jurisprudence suggests that Scottish fathers who choose not to register their paternity should expect no sympathy in

---

[111] Children (Scotland) Act 1995, ss 3(1)(b)(ii) and Registration of Births, Deaths and Marriages (Scotland) Act 1965, s 18. Conversely, where the parties are not married, the mother cannot register a man as the child's father without his consent.

[112] Law Reform (Parent and Child) (Scotland) Act 1986, s 6. A child of sufficient age and understanding can consent to such testing but, usually, the child will not have reached that level of maturity: Age of Legal Capacity (Scotland) Act 1991, s 2(4).

[113] Law Reform (Miscellaneous Provisions) (Scotland) Act 1990, s.70. There is no guarantee the court will draw a contrary inference, particularly if the child's mother is married: *Smith v Greenhill* 1993 SCLR 776 (refusing a declarator of paternity to a married woman's former lover).

[114] (2005) 40 EHRR 18.

[115] Ibid at para 37.

[116] (1998) 29 EHRR 95 at para 32.

[117] (2010) 50 EHRR 38. See also, *Sahin v Germany* (2003) 36 EHRR 43 (the father had lived with his daughter for the first year of her life and continued to have contact with her thereafter for some time).

Strasbourg. However, it is certainly arguable that, by enabling mothers to block (by refusing consent to testing of the child) non-marital fathers who are seeking legal recognition, Scots law violates the spirit, and possibly the letter, of the European Convention. Domestic courts are open to persuasion that existing law should be re-evaluated in the light of European Court developments,[118] and it may be that a challenge on this issue would be successful.

It might be expected that the South African constitutional guarantees of equality and dignity would result in more generous treatment of the non-marital father. Certainly, they have resulted in an improvement in the position of such a father and he now acquires parental responsibilities and rights automatically if he lives with the child's mother in a permanent life partnership at the time of the birth of the child or, regardless of whether they have ever lived together, if he is identified as the child's father or pays damages in accordance with customary law and contributes to the child's upbringing and maintenance for a reasonable period.[119] In short, responsible, committed fathers gain this benefit. Where paternity is disputed, the court has the power to dispense with the mother's consent to testing of the child, although it will be guided by the child's best interests in deciding whether to do so.

What this means, in practice, for non-marital fathers was clarified by the Constitutional Court in *Fraser v Children's Court, Pretoria North*.[120] There, an unmarried woman placed her child for adoption in the face of opposition from the child's father from whom she had separated after a relatively short period of cohabitation. The relevant statute dispensed with the need for the non-marital father's consent to adoption and the father here challenged it on the basis that it violated the constitutional guarantee to equality. The Court accepted his reasoning and declared the statutory provision invalid. However, in order to avoid creating a *lacuna* in the law, it was left in force and Parliament was given two years to correct the offending provision. The aggrieved father continued to litigate in the attempt to have the adoption order set aside and three years after the adoption order had been granted he was refused leave to appeal on the basis that '[c]ontinued uncertainty as to the status and placing of the child cannot be in the interests of the child'.[121] Ultimately, then, the best interests of the child trumped the constitutional rights of this father.

---

[118] See, e.g., *Reporter v K* 2011 SC (UKSC) 91, where the UK Supreme Court found legal provisions that precluded an engaged, non-marital father from participating in a children's hearing in respect of his child, as interpreted to date, violated art 8. However, the Court found that it could be read in a manner that would render it compatible with art 8. The new legislation, the Children's Hearings (Scotland) Act 2011, s 200, makes compliance clearer.

[119] Children's Act No 38 of 2005, s 21(1).

[120] *Fraser v Children's Court, Pretoria North* 1997 (2) SA 261 (CC).

[121] *Fraser v Naude* 1999 (1) SA 1 at para 9.

4.5.4 *Physical punishment of children*

While physical punishment of children is no longer permitted in the context of education[122] or state care,[123] in either South Africa or Scotland, parents in each jurisdiction are permitted to hit their children. Given the emphasis in the South African Constitution on human dignity and the express right of the child to be 'protected from maltreatment, neglect, abuse or degradation', it is not surprising to find that the South African Law Reform Commission recommended that parents too should be prohibited from inflicting corporal punishment on their children.[124] However, this recommendation was dropped from the Children's Bill as it made its way through Parliament and parental physical punishment of children remains lawful. Given its previous decisions on the issue in other contexts, it may be that the Constitutional Court would find this situation to be unconstitutional. However, as Heaton has observed, '[p]ublic opinion has not yet shifted in favour of a ban on corporal punishment by parents and a complete ban . . . would be meaningless without such a shift'.[125]

In Scotland, the matter has been the subject of heated debate for the last quarter of a century. Influenced, in part, by the evolving European Court jurisprudence,[126] the Scottish Law Commission recommended reform of the law to clarify and restrict, but not to abolish, the parental right.[127] The recommendation was implemented, by statute, 'justifiable assault' replaced 'reasonable chastisement', as the statutory defence available to a parent charged with assault and the limits on what is permitted were spelt out,[128]

---

[122] In South Africa, see *Christian Education South Africa v Minister of Education* 1999 (2) SA 83 and *Christian Education South Africa v Minister of Education* 2000 (4) SA 757. See also *Tyrer v United Kingdom* (1978) 2 EHRR 1 ('judicial birching' was a breach of art 3) and *S v Williams* 1995 (3) SA 632 (finding judicially-ordered whipping of children to be unconstitutional). In Scotland, see Standards in Scotland's Schools etc. (Scotland) Act 2000, s 16, a position influenced by the European Court decision in the Scottish case *Campbell and Cosans v United Kingdom* (1982) 4 EHRR 293.

[123] In South Africa, see General Regulations Regarding Children, 2010, regs 65(1)(h) (foster parents), 69(1)(b)(iv) (cluster foster care) and 76(2)(d) (child and youth care centres). In Scotland, see Fostering of Children (Scotland) Regulations 1996, SI 1996/3263, reg 8.

[124] *Report of the Review of the Child Care Act* para. 9.7.2 and cl 142 of the draft Children's Bill.

[125] J Heaton 'South Africa: Changing the Contours of Child and Family Law' in Sutherland, *The Future of Child and Family Law*, note 19 supra, at para 13.30.

[126] *Warwick v United Kingdom* (1986) DR 60. (Commission found caning a child at school to be degrading punishment); *Costello-Roberts v United Kingdom* (1994) 19 EHRR 112 (corporal punishment could involve a breach of art 3, but minimum level of severity had not been reached in that case); *A v United Kingdom* (1999) 27 EHRR 611 (requisite level of severity reached, violation of art 3).

[127] Report on Family Law (1990), paras 2.67–2.105, rec 11 and draft Bill, cl 4.

[128] An assault will never be 'justifiable' if it involved a blow to the head, shaking or the use of an implement: Criminal Justice (Scotland) Act 2003 s 51(3). In other cases, the court is directed

sending a very clear message to parents that it is acceptable for them to hit their children, provided they stick to the rules. It will be remembered that the European Court often approaches controversial issues incrementally and, as more European jurisdictions prohibit all physical punishment of children, it may well be that the European Court will take the final step in outlawing the practice.

The UN Committee on the Rights of the Child is unequivocal that continuing to permit parental physical chastisement of children violates the UN Convention,[129] and it has criticised both the United Kingdom (including Scotland) and South Africa for their failure to bring their law into line with the Convention.[130] Why two countries that profess such a commitment to children's rights should disregard this admonition is something of a mystery, but politicians' perception of public opinion may be one explanation.[131]

4.6 CHILDREN'S RESPONSIBILITIES

Thus far, we have been concerned with children's rights and those of other family members. What of children's responsibilities in the wider community? Arguably, gaining recognition in a legal system is not simply a matter of having rights since recognising capacity carries with it the corollary of responsibilities. That point is made explicitly, in South Africa, with legislation providing that, 'Every child has responsibilities appropriate to the child's age and ability towards his or her family, community and the state'.[132] While there is no parallel provision in Scots law, the responsibilities of children are discernable from the common law and issue-specific legislation. A major issue for all developed societies is the extent to which children should be held accountable when they break the rules, with criminal responsibility and delictual liability providing key examples of the issues at stake.

---

to a checklist of factors in assessing justifiability: 2003 Act s 51(1).

[129] UN Committee on the Rights of the Child *General Comment No 13: The right of the child to freedom from all forms of violence* (2011).

[130] *Concluding Observations of the Committee on the Rights of the Child on the United Kingdom of Great Britain and Northern Ireland* (2008), CCR/C/GBR/CO/4, at paras 40–43, repeating the unequivocal criticisms expressed in previous reports, and *Concluding Observations of the Committee on the Rights of the Child on South Africa* (2000), CCR/C/15/Add.122, at para 28.

[131] Curiously, Canada, another country with a generally sound record on children's rights, is also delinquent on this matter, with the Supreme Court of Canada upholding the constitutionality of parents being allowed to use 'reasonable coercive force' in raising their children. See *Canadian Foundation for Children, Youth and the Law v Canada (Attorney-General)* [2004] 1 SCR 76.

[132] Children's Act No 38 of 2005, s 16.

4.6.1 Criminal responsibility

Until recently, South Africa and Scotland shared the dubious distinction of being amongst the jurisdictions with the lowest ages of criminal responsibility in the world, that age being seven and eight years old, respectively.[133] In neither case was the law quite as draconian as it first appeared since South African law employed a rebuttable presumption that a child under fourteen years old was *doli incapax* and Scots law permitted evidence that the child did not, in fact, have the requisite capacity. Nonetheless, the United Nations Committee on the Rights of the Child was critical of the position in each jurisdiction,[134] favouring 'the age of twelve years as the absolute minimum age' of criminal responsibility.[135] Quite separately, domestic children's rights groups called for law reform.

In 1997, the South African Law Reform Commission examined the age of criminal responsibility as part of a larger project on juvenile justice,[136] with the matter also being addressed by the Portfolio Committee on Justice and Constitutional Development. Discussion centred on whether the age of criminal responsibility should be raised to ten or twelve and whether a *doli incapax* presumption should be retained in respect of children under the age of fourteen. In the event – and owing largely to a paucity of reliable statistics of the number of children between ten and thirteen accused of committing offences – the legislation passed in 2008 raised the age of criminal responsibility to ten and retained the *doli incapax* presumption for children under the age of fourteen.[137] However, the legislation also contained a provision requiring review of the age of criminal responsibility within five years of the Act being implemented.[138] Research, paving the way for that review, has now been published and, influenced by the various international instruments

---

[133] Another common area of concern is how the legal system should deal with sixteen- and seventeen-year-old offenders. On the one hand, they are 'children' in terms of the UN Convention. On the other hand, the prospect of serious or persistent offenders in that age group being treated as such attracts criticism of undue leniency in some quarters. In Scotland, these young people are dealt with largely by the adult criminal justice system, albeit custodial sentences are served in separate institutions. The position in South Africa was clarified with the decision in *Centre for Child Law v Minister of Justice and Constitutional Development and Others* 2009 (6) SA 632 (CC) (mandatory minimum sentences for sixteen- and seventeen-year-old unconstitutional).

[134] See *Concluding Observations of the Committee on the Rights of the Child on South Africa* (2000), CCR/C/15/Add 122, at para 17, and *Concluding Observations of the Committee on the Rights of the Child on the United Kingdom of Great Britain and Northern Ireland* (2008), CCR/C/GBR/CO/4, at para 78.

[135] UN Committee on the Rights of the Child, *General Comment No 10: Juvenile Justice* (2007), CRC/C/GC/10, para 32.

[136] South African Law Reform Commission, *Report in Juvenile Justice* (Project No 106, 2000) and Child Justice Bill B49 of 2002.

[137] Child Justice Act 75 of 2008, s 7.

[138] 2008 Act, s 8.

addressing the matter, the views of the UN Committee on the Rights of the Child[139] and constitutional considerations, it supports raising the age of criminal responsibility to twelve.[140]

Meanwhile, in Scotland, children's rights groups lobbied to have the age of criminal responsibility raised and pointed to criticism of the existing law by the UN Committee on the Rights of the Child. However, government attention was focused on the need to address the issue by the decision of the European Court of Human Rights finding that the procedure adopted in England in the infamous 'Bulger case'[141] violated the rights of the accused under article 6 (right to a fair trial).[142] The matter was considered by the Scottish Law Commission[143] and legislation based on, but not replicating, its recommendations followed. The welcome extended to that legislation is tempered with a degree of disappointment. Rather than simply raising the age of criminal responsibility to twelve years old, the legislation adopted the more convoluted formulation of retaining the age of criminal responsibility at eight years old, but prohibiting the prosecution of a child under the age of twelve or any person in respect of acts committed while under that age.[144] Thus, while a ten-year-old wrongdoer cannot be prosecuted, he or she may still be referred to a children's hearing in respect of the offence.[145] The child's welfare will play a central part in what happens, thereafter, but the fact that Scots law still has one of the lowest ages of criminal responsibility in the world – an approach motivated largely by what was thought to be politically palatable – falls short of compliance with the spirit of the UN Convention.

4.6.2 Delictual liability

Actions in delict against children are something of a rarity, largely because there is little point in pursuing an action against a person who does not have the resources to pay any damages (and costs) awarded. However, a recent

---

[139] UN Committee on the Rights of the Child *General Comment No 10: Children's Rights in Juvenile Justice* (2007).

[140] A Skelton and C Badenhorst *The Criminal Capacity of Children in South Africa: International Developments and Considerations for a Review* (The Child Justice Alliance 2011).

[141] Two-year-old James Bulger had become separated from his mother at a shopping centre when Robert Thompson and Jon Venables, both ten years old, lured him away and killed him. They were convicted of his murder, in 1993, and their conviction, sentencing and subsequent privacy rights gave rise to much litigation in the English courts.

[142] The European Court found that there had been violation of rights of the accused under art 6 to a fair trial and the key issue was whether the young person could participate effectively in the proceedings: *V v United Kingdom* (2000) 30 EHRR 121, para 108. See also *SC v United Kingdom* (2005) 40 EHRR 10, para 27.

[143] *Report on the Age of Criminal Responsibility* (Scot Law Com No 185, 2001).

[144] Criminal Procedure (Scotland) Act 1995, ss 41 and 41A, the latter being added by the Criminal Justice and Licensing (Scotland) Act 2010, s 52.

[145] Children's Hearings (Scotland) Act 2011, s 67(2)(j).

South African case, *Le Roux and Others v Dey*,[146] provides insight into their liability for deliberate acts and required the courts to balance competing constitutional rights. Three school pupils, aged between fifteen and seventeen, produced a computer-generated image in which the face of their school's deputy principal, Dr Dey, and that of the principal were superimposed on a picture of two naked men sitting in a sexually suggestive pose. The image was distributed electronically and in hard copy. The three boys were subject to school discipline and the criminal charges against them were resolved through diversion and community service. In addition, Dr Dey raised an action in delict, alleging defamation and injury to his dignity, and he was successful in the lower court, with an award of R45,000 (approximately £4,000) in damages being made against the pupils.[147]

Essentially, the appeal that came before the Constitutional Court pitted the rights of the young people to freedom of expression against Dr Dey's right to dignity, with reference being made to the paramountcy of the welfare of the children involved.[148] While the Court divided and all of the judgments reward reading in their entirety, the majority affirmed the finding that Dr Dey had been defamed and, had that not been the case, would have found that there had been injury to his feelings. In the words of Brand AJ,

> 'even though it could be called a schoolboy prank, it humiliated and demeaned the victims of the prank . . . teachers are entitled to protection of their dignity and reputation; no less than to the protection of their bodily integrity. Conversely, learners are not exempted from delictual liability.'[149]

The damages awarded were reduced to R25,000, the young men were ordered to make an unconditional apology to Dr Dey and no order for costs was made in respect of the proceedings in the Constitutional Court and the Supreme Court of Appeal.[150]

How would a Scottish court approach such a case and, in particular, what impact might the European Convention have on the outcome? Certainly, the age of the school pupils would be unlikely to act as a bar to liability since Scots common law sets no minimum age for delictual liability.[151] In one of

---

[146] 2011 (3) SA 274 (CC). See also discussion at section 7.2. infra.

[147] The Court of Appeal found that to allow both causes of action to succeed would amount to an impermissible accumulation of actions.

[148] Numerous other legal and social issues were discussed in the case, including the elements required for the relevant delictual acts, the tendency of young people to engage in ill-considered action and the power imbalance inherent in the relationship between the parties.

[149] 2011 (3) SA 274 (CC) at paras 116–18.

[150] The children were ordered to pay the plaintiff's costs in the High Court.

[151] The older authorities suggest that a pupil child (girls below twelve and boys below fourteen years old) could be liable: *Davie v Wilson* (1854) 16 D 956 per Lord Robertson at 960. The Age of Legal Capacity (Scotland) Act 1991, s 1(3)(c), explicitly excludes the law of delict from its ambit.

the very few recent cases involving a child-defender, the fact that he was twelve years old did not render the action incompetent where it was alleged that he injured a classmate (negligently) in the course of after-school horse-play.[152] That no mention was made of the welfare of the child-defender in the case is unsurprising. While the concept permeates statutory child law in Scotland, raising it in the common law context is somewhat uncharted territory. What would be the impact of article 10 (right to freedom of expression) of the European Convention in a Scottish case like *Le Roux*? Since article 10 is one of the 'qualified' convention rights, lawful and proportionate infringement is permitted on a range of grounds, including respect for the rights and freedoms of other, suggesting that a result along the lines arrived at by the Constitutional Court would not be inconceivable, in Scotland.

4.7 CONCLUSIONS

We have seen very considerable convergence in many aspects of child law in each country, a fairly common phenomenon worldwide in the light of increased international communication and mobility.[153] Essentially, Scots and South African child law begin from a number of common principles and arrive at similar outcomes when applying them in terms of respecting the child's right to family and to equality. Each is prepared to qualify the rights of third parties where that can be justified as serving the best interests of the child, while holding the child responsible for breaking the rules. Where each jurisdiction fails to respect the rights of the child, as is the case on physical punishment of children by parents, they fail equally. But, to return to our central question, what has been the primary influence driving these developments?

To attribute all or even most of the developments in Scots child law to the European Convention would be to overstate its influence. Granted, the foregoing discussion demonstrates that it has been influential and much is owed to the European Court over a whole range of issues, including the liability of the state to children it has failed, the child's birth status, the right to family life and in respect of criminal prosecution. But most of these developments would almost certainly have come about had there been no Human Rights

---

[152] *Hunter v Perth and Kinross Council* 2001 SCLR 856. In the vast majority of cases relating to injury at school, the pursuer will raise the action against the education authority. In this case, the pupil responsible was called as second defender in the case against the education authority but, in the event, neither defender was found to be liable. See also the English case, *Mullin v Richards* [1998] 1 WLR 1304, where the liability, for negligence, of a fifteen-year-old for an injury caused during horseplay in the classroom was assessed on the basis of the likelihood of injury that a reasonable fifteen-year-old would have foreseeing in the circumstances, and the defendant was not found to be liable.

[153] E E Sutherland 'Imperatives and Challenges in Child and Family Law: Commonalities and Disparities' in Sutherland *The Future of Child and Family Law*, note 19 supra, at para 1.18.

Act and, indeed, no European Convention, since they were prompted by public opinion, the lobbying efforts of special-interest groups and academics, and the UN Convention on the Rights of the Child.

It is unlikely that that the enormous advances achieved in promoting the rights and interests of children through legislation and judicial decisions in South Africa would have come to pass, in the absence of the Constitution, not least because the Constitution was innately tied to the immense political and social changes taking place contemporaneously. The very clear statements of principle and specific rights elaborated in the Constitution, generally, and the Bill of Rights, in particular, permeate all that followed. There is simply no mistaking their stamp on legislation and on judicial decisions. That the child-centred provisions of the Constitution themselves were influenced by the UN Convention and the African Charter is, again, clear, and both international instruments have played their part in the content of legislation and the reasoning of the courts, with frequent reference being made to them in law reform discussion documents and in judicial decisions.

The main distinction between the jurisdictions is one of speed. It is less than two decades since the Constitution was adopted and, in that time, huge strides have been made in reforming child law in South Africa to reflect greater respect for children's rights. In contrast, the incremental approach of the European Court has taken decades to reach the same position. Similarly, the United Kingdom ratified the UN Convention over twenty years ago and while some child-friendly reforms, like the Children (Scotland) Act 1995, followed fairly quickly, the remainder are of much more recent origin. A constitution, it seems, when coupled with the requisite legislative and judicial will, can effect change more quickly than can international instruments.

Chapter 5

Property Deprivation of an Absentee in Emulation of the Laws of Succession: The Laws of Scotland and South Africa Compared

Roderick R M Paisley

5.1 INTRODUCTION

Involuntary deprivation of privately owned property is a phenomenon against which safeguards are found both in the South African Constitution[1] and in the First Protocol to the European Convention of Human Rights (ECHR)[2] as the latter applies to Scotland. Albeit the structures and technical effects of these legal instruments are very different, both serve to entrench and protect private property rights. In this area of private law there is a long consistency of provision in the sister legal systems of South Africa and Scotland. Both their domestic laws of property are built on a longstanding Civilian principle enshrined in the maxim set out by the Roman jurist Pomponius and found in the *Digest*:[3] *Id quod nostrum est sine facto nostro ad alium transferri non potest*. When paraphrased this is to the effect that an owner cannot be deprived of his property without his consent. This chapter will seek to examine the laws of South Africa and Scotland applicable to a particular deprivation of property in the context not of the operation of the laws of succession but of rules that deprive a person presumed to be alive, in emulation of the laws of succession that would apply if he were dead. In function, if not in form, one might regard these rules as the pre-emptive strike of the laws of succession.

5.2 DEPRIVATION AND LIFE'S PERSONAL CRISES

However ancient the principle of protection against non-voluntary deprivation of private property and however fundamental the newly acquired public law or constitutional protections may be, a private proprietor's right to pro-

---

[1] Section 25.
[2] Article 1 of the First Protocol ECHR referring to 'possessions'.
[3] D 50.17.11. For Scotland: Stair *Institutions* 2.1.34. For South Africa: *Kahn v Volschenk (189/84)* [1986] ZASCA 34; [1986] 2 All SA 300 (A). Of course this rule was not absolute in Roman law and some rights, for example, could be lost by non-use of the holder.

tection against deprivation suffers well recognised exceptions when it comes to some of life's major crises. In both Scotland and South Africa significant among these personal crises are the actual death of an individual, the death of a personal relationship leading to divorce, and the death of a business venture leading to bankruptcy. When they happen to a property owner, all three events involve a compulsory deprivation and an involuntary distribution of estate[4] respectively effected by the laws of succession, the laws of divorce and the laws of bankruptcy.

The policy behind the various deprivations is different. Upon divorce the assets of the parties may be redistributed between the partners to the former relationship and a continuing provision made for dependents. On bankruptcy the assets of the insolvent party are divided amongst creditors and existing obligations extinguished. In both of these processes there is no aim to strip the deprived party entirely of all his estate – the policy of the law includes a desire to leave the party deprived of assets with something, and to enable a failed businessman or woman, and a party to a failed relationship, to start afresh. There is life after divorce and bankruptcy, after all. However, on actual death, the aim of the law of succession is to take all of the estate of the deceased and distribute every bit of it to creditors and beneficiaries. The policy of the law recognises the deceased has no further use for his earthly goods. Consequently, when it comes to property rights the most radical deprivation of all occurs on actual death. This paper will examine to what extent there is a fourth personal crisis – absence – which may open the door to a complete deprivation of the absentee's property. Care requires to be taken to distinguish absence from the much more familiar situation where a presumption of death or deemed death can arise from being missing without trace. To use the vernacular, absence deals with those who have 'departed the scene' and not those who have departed life.

5.3 DEATH AND ITS EFFECTS

A good starting point for analysis is the familiar phenomenon of death itself. If we can establish what occurs here, it will facilitate the establishment of clarity by comparison with a benchmark event. However, we must accept some disappointment. Albeit death does sometimes have the effect of terminating certain rights,[5] there is no clear authority in Scots or South African law as to whether death itself effects a general deprivation of the property right of the *de cuius*.[6] In both legal systems it seems plausible to argue that it

---

[4] K Reid *The Law of Property in Scotland* (LexisNexis Butterworths 1996) paras 597, 613, 663 and 664(4) but the last reference relates to the confirmation of executors.

[5] E.g. a liferent or usufruct. Certain contracts also provide for termination of rights on death.

[6] For Roman Dutch law see Grotius *Inleidinge* 2 32 2; van der Keesel *Prael ad Gr* 2 32 2. Cf South African law *Greenberg v Estate Greenberg* 1955 (3) SA 361 (A).

does not because there is a strong Civilian tradition, shared by both Scotland and South Africa, upon which to base the proposition that the personality of the deceased subsists after death (at least until his property is distributed): the property remains vested in the *de cuius* albeit he is represented by the heir or executor as the case may be. At the heart of the law of succession, centred as it is on the fact of death, it is ironic that there is this legal fiction of the continued legal personality of a deceased.

If there were to be a human or constitutional right to die, to rest in peace and enjoy one's death unmolested (the ECHR and the South African Constitution do not expressly contain such), it is likely that this long-standing fiction not of continued life but of continued legal personality would not be regarded as infringing that right. However, even if the deceased is presumed to retain a personality after death, in both legal systems it is indisputable that the estate of the deceased is available for distribution to creditors and beneficiaries after his death. Indeed, the case may be stated higher than that: the estate of the deceased must be distributed to such parties. No testator may provide that after his death his creditors are not to be paid and his estate is to be retained and accumulated *ad infinitum* and not to be distributed. All he or she can do is vary the pattern of distribution within the limitations of testamentary freedom. Even an instruction by the testator to destroy all of his or her property after death rather than distribute it would probably be regarded as *contra bonos mores* or contrary to public policy. It is insufficient to assert that the testator could legitimately have done the same during his own lifetime. Such limitations on *mortis causa* provision are well established in both South Africa and Scotland and do not themselves amount to a deprivation of property. So, even if it does not effect the deprivation itself, in a very direct way, death does open the door to a complete, uncompensated, involuntary deprivation. A curiosity of the law of succession is that it does so by yet another legal fiction to the effect that the deceased is giving his or her own property away and making the *post mortem* gifts: the executor or heir, as the case may be, who effects the distribution is regarded as *eadem persona cum defuncto*. In short, the fiction is that the deprivation is voluntary and even intestate succession is based on the presumed will of the testator.

5.4 DEATH AND ITS VARIANTS

As indicated above, the deprivation of property rights effected on death is not only comprehensive but it is inevitable and carried out without compensation to the deceased.[7] For these reasons the deprivation effected on death must be closely controlled and confined. This is relatively straightforward

---

[7] There are rare situations in testate succession where a beneficiary is permitted to buy some estate from the estate but these sale proceeds must themselves be distributed.

when the term 'death' denotes actual death. However, as was noticed by the European Court of Human Rights:

> 'La mort est au centre du droit successoral, parce que c'est la cause normale de l'ouverture de la succession.'[8]

> 'Death is central to the law of succession because it is the normal reason for succession to occur.'[9]

Death may be the 'normal' reason for the law of succession to apply but it is not the sole reason. Civil death is another occasion for the operation of the law of succession. The particular variant of civil death that this chapter will touch upon is the deemed or presumed death of a person who is missing without trace. Legal systems must address the problem of proof of death where a person has disappeared and it is not known whether he or she is still alive. Specific laws dealing with the matter are to be found in ancient legal systems.[10] They are common throughout modern jurisdictions of many traditions including Civilian, Common Law, mixed legal systems and those based on Islamic jurisprudence. There are provisions in both Scots law and the law of South Africa.[11]

However, what is highly unusual in both the law of Scotland and the laws of South Africa is that, even whilst a person is presumed to be alive, the Courts may permit the distribution of that person's estate in emulation of the distribution of the applicable law of succession. In this context a person who is not dead, who is not even regarded as civilly dead but is still presumed to be alive, may be deprived of his or her property. Such persons are absentees and the procedures for depriving them of their property are both under-researched and somewhat surprising.

5.5 THE SECOND WORLD WAR AND CONSEQUENT DEVELOPMENTS

The era immediately following the Second World War saw a concerted move to develop a number of international legal conventions to address some of the horrors and barbarism experienced in that cataclysm. Significant amongst these was the ECHR itself. However the enthusiasm for international conventions did not stop at the general statement of lofty ideals and some considerable progress was made on the detail of rather more practical and consequential matters. One such issue was the status of missing persons

---

[8] *Affaire Marckx c Belgique* Requête No 6833/74. Arrêt Strasbourg 13 Juin 1979 opinion en partie dissidente de M Le Judge Pinheiro Farinha para 2.

[9] *Marckx v Belgium* (1979–1980) 2 EHRR 330 at 384 para 2 per Judge Pinheiro Farinha.

[10] See the varied Roman law provisions in D 7.1.56 (Gaius); 33.2.8 (Gaius); 24.2.6 (Julian); C 1.2.23(2).

[11] R A Jordaan and C J Davel *Law of Persons* 4e (Juta 2005) para 7.4.

and their property. The disappearance of millions of individuals,[12] and in some tragic cases complete families, during the Second World War and its immediate aftermath led to concerted international efforts to develop more effective laws. These culminated in the signing of the Convention on the Declaration of Death of Missing Persons at Lake Success in New York on 6 April 1950.[13]

The impetus for these improvements was found chiefly in mainland Europe where many of the disappearances had occurred and in North America where large numbers of surviving relatives had found refuge. As the United Kingdom and the Republic of South Africa were not parties to the 1950 Convention, Scots law and the law of South Africa remained largely unaffected by these international developments. Both countries had been spared the tragedy of invasion and extermination of their populations. Perhaps also it was considered that both legal systems already met the new international standards.[14] Whatever the case, at least as indicated in the various published case reports, the law of South Africa and Scots law continued to focus on individual tragedies involving persons who had gone missing in what might be regarded as the traditional range of disappearances in contexts such as emigration, transportation accidents, fires and explosions. Even within this limited compass Scots law was found to be far from adequate for modern needs. It was not until the late 1970s that Scots law was updated and improved. Despite continuous development by case law, there has been no similar comprehensive updating or improvement of the common law in South Africa, albeit there are limited statutory provisions dating from 1959[15] and 1962[16] enabling a Court to declare a presumption of death of persons who die what is termed an 'unnatural death' or who die in an aircraft accident.

---

[12] E.g. the Scottish case *Thomson's Trustee, Petitioner* 1948 SLT (Notes) 28. In the case *Mrs Isabella Hall or Maher* (1969) Edinburgh Sheriff Court Scottish National Archives reference SC39/17/1170/B2004/1969 a petition was raised by a surviving sister of the wife of a disappeared person in terms of the Presumption of Life Limitation (Scotland) Act 1891 to enable her to succeed to the estate of her sister. As part of the pleadings the petitioner had to show that her sister's child by the disappeared man had also predeceased. Evidence was presented that he was a Second World War serviceman who went missing in action in an explosion on a ship on 7 November 1944. See also the South African case *Ex parte Parker* 1947 (3) SA 285 (C).

[13] Convention on the Declaration of Death of Missing Persons UN Doc A/Conf 1/9, Lake Success 6 April 1950 extended by protocols in 1957 and 1967. See (1999) 4 *Unif L Rev* n s 989.

[14] The Convention of Death of Missing Persons at Lake Success 1950 is nowhere mentioned in Scottish Law Commission *Consultative Memorandum: Presumptions of Survivorship and Death* (Scot Law Com CM No 11, 1969) or Scottish Law Commission, *Report on Presumption of Death* (Scot Law Com No 34, 1974).

[15] Inquests Act 58 of 1959.

[16] Aviation Act 74 of 1962.

It is fair to say that both Scots and South African law now have twin-track approaches. They both have a common law and statutory procedure to deal with this area but the statutory scheme of Scotland is more comprehensive. Arguably it is this very comprehensive aspect of Scots law that requires it to take more detailed care not to infringe the protections against deprivation of property rights in the context of a declaration of death. The author would submit that the protections also exist in South Africa, albeit in a slightly different and, to an outsider, perhaps less immediately obvious form.

The law of succession is sometimes regarded as a sleepy backwater of staid principle and rather rusty mechanics. However, both as regards substance and appearance, this un-altering consistency has not always been the case. During a period of less than thirteen years in the 1930s and 1940s, the Nazi state in Germany adapted a sophisticated legal system to facilitate genocide. That regime built a wall of legal disenfranchisement denying economic livelihood to Jewish people and others regarded by the state as undesirable. In this fanatical and monstrous project, the laws of property and even the laws of succession were enthusiastically pressed into service. These laws were altered incrementally so as to deprive Jewish people and others of rights to own, acquire and inherit property.[17] It might strike one as rather odd that to achieve this end, the Nazis did not employ the *Verschollenheitsgesetz*[18] – the law on disappeared persons – which could have been altered very simply so as to deprive undesirables of their property. At a stroke such parties could have been presumed or deemed dead, not because they were missing, but because they were locked out from society. Perhaps, a one-fell stroke approach was avoided because, even in a totalitarian regime based on terror, domestic politics and social pressures required the Nazis to introduce their abhorrent measures by gradual turns of the screw. In the event, a comprehensive Nazi law of succession remained in draft form at the end of the war. However, the gradualist alteration of the property laws had already achieved its end. Jewish and other undesirable parties were so stripped of rights by the Nazis that, even before they were murdered, they were, to adopt the phraseology of the Civilian inheritance, effectively *civiliter mortuus* or, to use the modern vernacular, 'dead men walking'.

This brief and, of necessity, oversimplified narrative will perhaps assist in explaining to some extent why there appears to have been no detailed or specific consideration of the human rights aspects of the potential abuse of the laws relating to disappeared persons in the immediate post-war 'golden' era for the creation of human rights treaties. The emphasis of the immediate

---

17 E.g. *Gesetz zum Schutze des deutscher Blutes und der deutscher Ehre* and *Reichsbürgergesetz* RGBI I, 1146 1147 and the executry ordinances of November 14 1935 RGBI 1333 1334. These were repealed by Control Council Law No. 1, Art I(k) enacted at Berlin, 20 September 1945 found at (1946) 15 *Department of State Bulletin*, 859 at 860.

18 *Verschollenheitsgesetz vom 4 Juli 1939 (RGBI I S 1186).*

post-war succession lawyers appears to have been on facilitating the inheritance by the surviving relatives of disappeared persons rather than precluding the abuse of the laws of succession or rules emulating those laws to strip the deceased of property. However, it is submitted that the potentially deleterious effect of an abuse of the laws on absentees and missing persons is significant, but dealt with appropriately in the relevant parts of the South African Constitution and the European Convention on Human Rights.

A final brief postscript is needed on this point before we move on. It must be said that far more may be engaged in the legal concept of civil death than a mere deprivation of property. Albeit it may have a multiplicity of variants, the effects of the civil death comprise aspects of other rights. However, this chapter will concentrate only on deprivation of property.[19]

5.6 MISSING PERSONS AND MERE ABSENCE

One major safeguard against deprivation of property on an individual's being presumed or declared dead is that the laws of both Scotland and South Africa do not immediately leap to regard an absent person as 'missing'. Although this is clear in the reported case law and associated commentary it tends not to be emphasised: less still is the policy and consequence that the property rights of absentees are generally protected against distribution. However, that policy and its attendant consequence are important and will be examined here. In addition, an exception to that policy will be highlighted in terms of which a person may be deprived of all property even whilst he is presumed to be alive. It is of significance that such a deprivation is usually universal but it is normally made with the possibility of compensation.

5.7 ABSENT PERSONS DISTINGUISHED FROM ABSENTEES

In common parlance an 'absent person' is someone who is not where he or she should be. The term comprises an individual who may be absent in a very temporary sense. Such a person may be absent from a social event, a school lesson, church, work or another engagement.[20] It is accepted in both Scots and South African law that a temporary absence of this sort, in many if

---

[19]   The ECHR rights potentially engaged by a declarator of death of a missing person include: (a) art 6 – the right to a fair and public hearing in the determination of a person's civil rights and obligations; (b) art 8 – respect for private and family life; (c) art 9 – right to freedom of thought, conscience and religion; (d) art 12 – right to marry; (e) art 13 – a right to effective remedy for breach of rights and freedoms; and (f) art 1 of the First Protocol – right to possessions and freedom from deprivation. In the South African Constitution they potentially extend to art 10 (human dignity); art 11 (right to life); art 20 (deprivation of citizenship) and art 34 (access to courts).

[20]   M Planiol with G Ripert *Treatise on the Civil Law* 12e (Louisiana State Law Institute trans 1959, 2005 Reprint), vol 1 part 1 § 611 at 369.

not most cases, may have no impact whatever on a person's rights or obligations.[21] For example, in the context of the law of succession, the domicile of the *de cuius* does not alter just because he was on holiday or visiting friends when he died. Similarly, a beneficiary is not usually excluded because he is not actually at home when the *de cuius* dies and his estate opens for succession. So too, if the consent of a particular person is required in relation to the proper disposal of the subjects of a legacy it is inappropriate to act without that person's consent just because he is absent from home.[22]

In other cases, however, both Scots and South African law recognise that absence may have a bearing on rights and obligations arising from contract or otherwise but has no effect on a person's status. If the absence becomes more extended, there can be a greater impact on the rights and obligations of the absentee. For example, absence from work or a meeting may amount to breach of contract. Absence may lead to the removal of a trustee.[23] A number of rights both personal[24] and real[25] may be extinguished by prescription, known as 'negative' in Scotland and 'extinctive' in South Africa,[26] where not claimed, acknowledged or exercised for a certain period of time. For example, the entitlement to sums in bank accounts may negatively prescribe albeit, in Scotland, banks do not insist strictly on this and dormant bank accounts are subject to a special scheme.[27]

When the absence is of an even greater degree, where the present whereabouts of the absent person is unknown and there is doubt as to whether he or she is alive or dead, then this can have a bearing on that person's status.[28] It is this degree of uncertainty that is the badge of the person who, for present purposes, may be termed as 'an absentee'.[29] Unlike in other legal systems,[30] the word 'absentee' is not a term of art in Scots law or in the law of South Africa. However, it can usefully be adopted for purposes of

---

[21] This point has been illustrated in relation to many obligations from the earliest of time: e.g. *Kirk Session of Lauder v The Good-man of Gallowshiels* (1630) Mor 7913.

[22] *Cunningham's children v McMichael's Executors* (1624) Mor 8047.

[23] The South African cases speak of prolonged absence: *Ex parte Zive* 1934 NPD 378; *Ex parte Maronie Catholic Church* 1928 WLD 217, and correspond to a similar common law power in Scotland: *Grieve Petitioner* (1873) 10 SLR 317 (nine years). The Trusts (Scotland) Act 1921, ss 22 and 23 provide for removal of a trustee upon disappearance or absence from the UK continuously for a period of six months.

[24] Prescription and Limitation (Scotland) Act 1973, ss 6 and 7 and Sch 2.

[25] Prescription and Limitation (Scotland) Act 1973, s 8 and Sch 3.

[26] H J Fabricius 'Prescription' in *The Law of South Africa* vol 21 paras 92–7.

[27] Dormant Bank and Building Society Accounts Act 2008.

[28] J L Carriere 'The Rights of the Living Dead: Absent Persons in the Civil Law' (1989–1990) 50 *La L Rev* 901 at 901 and 902.

[29] Planiol with Ripert *Treatise on the Civil Law*, note 20 supra, vol 1 Part 1 § 611 at 369 and § 634 at 379–80; J A Rogron, *Code civil expliqué* 2e (Paris 1826) 50.

[30] E.g. Louisiana Civil Code arts 47–59; Civil Code of Québec arts 84–91; Rwanda Civil Code ch 3 arts 25–57.

analysis and to distinguish such a person from a 'missing person' who may be presumed dead under the common law of South Africa or declared dead in terms of Scottish common law or the Presumption of Death (Scotland) Act 1977.[31] The principal distinction between the two classes of person is that the absentee, whether he or she wishes or not, benefits from the common law presumption of life and cannot be declared dead in terms of common law of South Africa or Scotland or under the 1977 Act.[32] It is *a fortiori* the case that a person who is known to be alive may be an absentee but cannot be presumed or declared dead in Scotland or South Africa. Absentees might include, for example, a prisoner of war, a person who is detained abroad for legitimate business purposes but whose general whereabouts is known[33] or even someone who simply does not respond to any form of communication and wishes to live the life of a hermit or a religious or academic recluse and be dead to the world.

5.8 THE POLICY BEHIND THE LAW FOR ABSENTEES

In the Roman[34] and Roman Dutch[35] tradition shared by both Scots and South African law a parallel has been drawn between a person who is physically absent and a person who has become insane and whose mind is absent.[36] Consonant with this, in the modern law of both Scotland and

---

31 Unfortunately the terms 'absentee' (e.g. paras 9, 14) 'absent person' (e.g. para 14) 'missing person' (e.g. paras 11, 12, 15) are used interchangeably in Scottish Law Commission *Consultative Memorandum: Presumptions of Survivorship and Death* (Scot Law Com CM No 11, 1969). See also the use of 'absent person' in Presumption of Life Limitation (Scotland) Act 1881.

32 For a similar position in France: P Malaurie and L Aynès *Droit civil: les personnes les incapacités* 3e (Editions juridiques associées 2004) 20 at para 16.

33 Cf instances where a *factor loco absentis* was appointed to someone whose general whereabouts abroad was known but was difficult to contact: *Matthew Dickie writer in Edinburgh factor on estate of Colonel William Fullarton of Fullarton v Factor loco absentis for Colonel William Fullerton of Fullerton presently in East Indies: Act appointing factor loco absentis* 5 March 1782 National Archives CS224/49 (the Colonel had gone abroad to escape his creditors and the process was being used effectively as a sequestration to supersede a voluntary trust deed); *Act and Factory of Captain Donald Fraser of Bruiach as factor loco absentis for James Fraser of Belldrum then in Berbice [Guyana] in the West Indies* 16 June 1808 and extracted 25 June 1808 Scottish National Archives GD23/10/663. The urgent business was the administration of his recently dead father's estate and the fact that instructions from the absent person would take five or six months to be received. Similarly in *Ex parte Kuhr* 1940 CPD 227 a *curator bonis* was appointed to a German national who had gone to Nazi Germany and remained there during the war.

34 D 50.17.124(1) (Paul citing Pomponius) and 50.16.246 (Pomponius); 47.10.17(11) (Ulpian); 27.7.2(3) (Julian).

35 Voet *Pandects* 22.5.2 and 27.10.3 translated in Gane 3 762 referring to D 50.16.246 (under-age regarded as not present) 3 763 (madmen not present) and 4 594.

36 For a modern analysis, R Dresser 'Missing Persons: Legal Perceptions of Incompetent Patients' (1994) 46 *Rutgers Law Review* 609.

South Africa, where a person is an absentee he or she is treated as alive but requiring of special treatment. The policy of the law in both jurisdictions is threefold: first, to protect the absentee's property against removal by third parties and to manage his or her affairs because of the absentee's seeming inability, for whatever reason, to do this himself or herself;[37] secondly, in the words of a judge from another mixed legal system, to preclude the distribution of the absentee's property 'in the hope, and expectation that he may again return';[38] and thirdly, albeit entitling the absentee to enhanced protection, the absence of that person does not augment his or her rights as regards others.[39]

One may distil from this threefold policy that, for an absentee, the law in both Scotland and South Africa generally is designed to operate in a conservative and not a distributive role.[40] Consequently, the context is generally inimical to the application of the laws of succession which, albeit such an application would have the side-effect of protecting against the unmanaged depredations of the world at large,[41] would effect a compulsory distribution of that person's net estate to a limited group of third parties – the beneficiaries. Although an absentee may still be required to pay his or her existing debts, the beneficiaries cannot force a distribution of the estate. It has been observed in the United States of America:[42]

'A person ought not lightly to be deprived of his property, and the policies of certainty involved in real property law counsel extreme caution before distributing the property of a person who may return to assert a claim to it.'

The policy identified in this quotation merits application also to moveable and incorporeal estate and can readily be applied in jurisdictions beyond

---

[37] C Demolombe *Traité de l'absence* 4e (Auguste Durand/ Hachette et Co 1870) 2–3, § 1. See also the similar view of Islamic law, *The Hedaya* (Charles Hamilton and Standish Groove Grady translation) (Premier Book House Lahore 1963) vol 2, book 13, 213–15.

[38] Supreme Court of Louisiana in *Sassman v Aime* 9 Mart (o s) 257 (La 1821) at 263–4 per Porter J.

[39] D 50.17.26. (Paul).

[40] A factor *loco absentis* was held entitled to oppose a petition of service on the ground that his principal might still be alive: *John Thomson v Dr William Sommerville* (1818) 6 Pat App 393 with prior proceedings reported at 19 May 1815 18 FC 362 case no 84. On the analogous phase in France, Demolombe *Traité de l'absence*, note 37 supra, 45 § 34 wrote: 'Il ne s'agit pas de changer, d'innover, d'améliorer même, mais de conserver seulement et d'attendre'. 'It is not a matter of changing, of innovating, or even of improving, but solely of conserving and of waiting.'

[41] This protective role of the law of succession was recognised at an early stage by the sixteenth-century English writer Swinburne who wrote that the proving of the will of an absent man and the appointment of an executor is better than 'to suffer the goods to perish, or to be subject to be purloyned by men and means unknown': H Swinburne *A Treatise of Testaments and Last Wills* 4e (George Sawbridge 1677) Part 6 S 13, 360.

[42] R B Dworkin 'Death in Context' (1972–1973) 48 *Ind L J* 623 at 634.

North America, such as South Africa and Scotland. For example, in a nineteenth-century Scottish case it was judicially observed:[43]

> 'I cannot conceive that because a man has been absent from the country for a long time, any body not having a right to his estate may nevertheless carry it off, either by being served,[44] although not the true heir, or by a false claim of debt or in some other way. There must be some remedy in such a case.'

It may be that this policy of conservation is not absolute and is subject to an exception. If this were to be the case, the exception would merit investigation as it would tend to deprive of property someone who is not deemed or presumed to be dead. Before we can examine any such exception, the implementation of the general policy must be established.

5.9 THE IMPLEMENTATION OF THE PROTECTION OF ABSENTEES

Many jurisdictions from diverse legal traditions have special provisions to protect the estates of absentees from depredation by third parties.[45] Scotland and South Africa have no specialist comprehensive code of law to deal with this situation[46] but that does not mean they do not deal with the situation in some way.

In Scotland and South Africa a certain degree of personal foresight, self-help and responsibility is encouraged. A person who anticipates he or she may be absent for some time may, in advance, set up arrangements (such as agency,[47] transfer of property to a third party,[48] or creation of subsidiary real rights in favour of third parties[49]) to deal with property. As these arrangements arise from the free will of the property owner, by definition, none of them involves any deprivation of property. However, that is also their drawback in that some of the devices, such as agency or mandate, depend for their continued efficacy on the sustained will of the absent party, and if

---

[43] *Kennedy v Maclean* (1851) 13D 705 at 710 per Lord Mackenzie.

[44] At the date of the case 'service' or being 'served' as heir was the means of having title made up as heir under the laws of heritable succession.

[45] E.g. Saskatchewan: Absentee Act R S S 1978 c A-3; *Re Kindrachuk* 2000 SKQB 325; Ontario: Absentees Act R S O 1990, c A-3; *Kamboj v Kamboj* 2007 CanLII 14932. For France see Civil Code, arts 112–32; Planiol with Ripert *Treatise on the Civil Law* note 20 supra, 368–81 §§ 611–36.

[46] Such a 'Missing Persons Code' was contemplated and rejected as a 'complex body of new law to deal with a relatively unusual state of affairs' by Scottish Law Commission *Report on Presumption of Death* (Scot Law Com No 34 1974) 14 para 36.

[47] E.g. *Phaup v Phaup* (1831) 9S 584; *Steel Ptr* (1874) 11 SLR 160. In *Ex parte Kuhr* 1940 CPD 227 the wife had a power of attorney limited to the use of her husband's bank account only.

[48] *Lawder v Goodwife of Whitekirk* (1637) Mor 1692 and Mor 3593 (assignation with backbond to count and pay to the cedent upon reappearance).

[49] *Blackwood v Cunnochie's Creditors* (1686) Mor 3596.

there is doubt about the absentee's continuance in life, the continued validity of the legal arrangement also comes into doubt. In other cases, a degree of care to deal with the special facts of absence may be taken by third parties. For example, a testamentary provision for an absentee may be made for him or her specially referring to and providing for the fact of his or her absence, as is illustrated by a provision in a trust for a person who had been absent for many years to be paid (and perhaps also to vest) only if that person reappeared.[50]

Following common Civilian roots,[51] in the case of a Scottish or South African absentee who has not made voluntary advance provision, there may be a limited role for a *negotiorum gestor*.[52] Such a person acts 'necessarily and profitably for the good of the absent',[53] or, as the Scottish institutional writer Bankton quaintly put it, a person who acts 'in the management of the affairs of an absent friend'.[54] In other cases, where an absent person is merely uncontactable but not suspected to be missing without hope of return, various interim measures may be taken to protect his or her entitlement and interests. For example, in the context of dividing up an estate, where a person who is temporarily absent is one of the beneficiaries, that absent person may have his interests sufficiently protected by the executor retaining sufficient to pay any sum due to the absent party.[55] Again, in such a case there is no deprivation of the absentee's property.

5.10 CURATOR BONIS AND FACTOR LOCO ABSENTIS

The remedies noticed in the immediately foregoing paragraphs are extrajudicial and do not involve any involvement of the state. By contrast, where there is the possibility of long-term absence with no clear evidence of a likelihood of return, the main remedy in South Africa is to apply to court to seek the appointment of a *curator bonis*[56] as regards the absentee's estate. The Scottish equivalent is virtually identical albeit the office-holder in question is known as a factor *loco absentis*.

Although cases of this nature do occur, the published reports in both jurisdictions on this matter are relatively rare and the judgments usually

---

[50] E.g. *Alexander Cuthbert and another (Special Case)* 1894 1 SLT 598.
[51] See D 3.5.10 (Ulpian) and 22 (Gaius).
[52] See the South African cases *Ex parte Pearlman* 1957 (4) SA 666 (N); *Ex parte Hattersley* 1904 TH 258; *Abroms v Minister of Railways & Harbours* 1917 WLD 51; *Ex parte Lennon Ltd* 1929 WLD 195 and the observations in the Scottish case *Agnes Martin or Grozier and others v George Downie* (1871) 9M 826; 8 SLR 563; 43 Sc Jur 456.
[53] Stair *Institutions* 1.8.3; Erskine *Institute* 3.3.52.
[54] Bankton *Institute* 1.4.25 (reprinted Stair Society vol 43 1993, 98).
[55] See, e.g. *Robert Couper and others, Petitioners* (1863) 35 Sc Jur 193.
[56] *Ex parte Thomson and Others* 1919 CPD 277; *In re Widdicombe* 1929 NPD 311; *Ex parte Shulman* 1955 (1) SA 514 (W); *Ex parte Pearlman* 1957 (4) SA (N).

brief. One suspects that, in many cases, no one bothers to seek the appointment of such an office-holder to the estate of the absentee, perhaps because the value of the estate is slight or because the estate fortuitously is already being conserved by other means.[57] Perhaps also (and this is no more than speculation), the interested parties act in a selfish manner in that they wish to avoid additional expense when they intend in due course to have the absentee presumed or declared dead as a missing person and to have the estate distributed to themselves. However, in both jurisdictions, the case reports demonstrate this appointment of a factor or curator to be an effective remedy: the application to court may be presented very quickly and the appointment by the court made as a matter of urgency. The recent South African cases illustrate a period of as little as two weeks after a disappearance until the granting of the application.[58] Where commercial interests are involved, speed is often of the essence if the value of the absentee's estate is to be preserved. This is illustrated in recent South African reports where, in one case, the petition emphasised the need to preserve the assets and goodwill of various businesses,[59] and in another, the absentee was involved in a number of ongoing contracts.[60] In Scotland the potential speed of the procedure is similar and though not illustrated as dramatically in the reported case law, there can be little doubt that the courts could respond just as quickly should the need arise. In the light of this, there can be little in the way of basis for a claim that the absentee or interested parties are deprived of an effective remedy for the difficult situation facing them.

Just as the role of curator or factor cannot subordinate the interests of the absentee, so an application to have appointed either a *curator bonis* or factor *loco absentis* cannot be used to frustrate the legitimate application of the law of succession and to stall or block the legitimate inheritance of beneficiaries. The application for the appointment of a *curator bonis* or a factor *loco absentis* is incompetent as regards a person who is already known to be dead or who is already presumed dead at common law in South Africa or Scotland[61] or declared dead in terms of the Presumption of Death (Scotland) Act 1977.[62]

The curatory or factory does not last forever: it is not a meal ticket for

---

57 This might be the case where the person was already *incapax* and benefiting from supervision such as, in Scotland, by means of intervention orders and guardianship under Adults with Incapacity (Scotland) Act 2000 ss 53 and 64.

58 *Viz* the period of two weeks between appointment of the *curator* and the date the person was last seen, in *Ex parte Sehlabaka* [2009] JLO 24112 (FB), and three weeks after he was last seen in *Ex parte Shulman* 1955 (1) SA 514 (W) and *Ex parte Pearlman* 1957 (4) SA (N).

59 *Ex parte Shulman* 1955 (1) SA 514 (W).

60 *Ex parte Sehlabaka* [2009] JLO 24112 (FB).

61 *Wardrop v Wardrop* (1846) 18 Sc Jur 540; *Chambers v Chambers or Carruthers* (1849) 21 Sc Jur 538. Cf the narrative in *John Dickson's Trs, Petitioners* 1894 2 SLT 61 where the person had been on a ship that disappeared.

62 *The Laws of Scotland: Stair Memorial Encyclopaedia* vol 24 (Butterworths 1989) para 272.

the factor or *curator*. The role of the *curator bonis* or the factor *loco absentis* will endure only until sufficient time elapses and evidence comes to light to enable a person to be declared or presumed dead[63] or until he or she has been found alive and, probably in such a case, is capable of looking after his or her affairs. Upon declaration or presumption of death, the curatory or factory, as the case may be, will terminate.[64] The curatory or factory probably needs a formal recall if the absent party is found alive. In all of this it becomes clear that it is the interests of the absentee that come first. This is confirmed in one South African case[65] where the Court conferred on the *curator bonis* powers the exercise of which had the potential to bring the curatory to an early conclusion – the powers included the right to make a payment to a detective agency to trace the absentee or to find out if he was dead.

5.11 FLEXIBILITY AND ACTIVE NATURE

The *curator bonis* and factor *loco absentis*[66] are both subject to a general duty of conservation. However, they do not impose a dead hand and the estate of the absentee is not frozen. This lessens the possibility that the proceedings may be challenged as an expropriation or deprivation of the absentee's property.[67] Albeit the proceedings are generally conservatory, they do not remove the absentee's estate entirely from commerce. Debts of the absent party may continue to be paid and existing obligations implemented. Thus the proceedings tend to safeguard the interests of third parties, including dependent family members, who depend upon the continued life and participation in commerce of the absentee.

More unusual matters can also be attended to either by seeking special powers in advance at the time the appointment is made or approaching the Court at some time thereafter when the need for powers becomes obvious.

---

[63] See N M L Walker *Judicial Factors* (W Green 1975) 28–29; *Stair Memorial Encyclopaedia* vol 24, note 62 supra, para 272. E.g. the appointment of an absentee who later was found to be murdered in *Garvie's Trs v Still* 1972 SLT 29; appointment proceedings: *Petition for Appointment of a factor loco absentis on the estate of Maxwell Robert Garvie* 1970 National Archives CS258/1970/3734. See also cases involving the common law presumption of death: *Reid v Brown* (1834) 12S 278; *Kennedy v Maclean* (1851) 13D 705; *Chambers v Carruthers* (1849) 11D 1359: factor not appointed; *Barstow v Cook* (1862) 24D 790; (1862) 34 Sc Jur 399; (1874) 11 SLR 363.

[64] See the Scottish cases *Milne v Wills* (1868) 5 SLR 189; (1868) 40 Sc Jur 221: caution required; *Barstow v Cook* (1874) 11 SLR 363; *Tait's Factor v Meikle* (1890) 17R 1182. Cf *Reid v Brown* (1834) 12S 278.

[65] *Ex parte Pearlman* 1957 (4) SA 666 (N).

[66] *Stair Memorial Encyclopaedia* vol 24, note 62 supra, para 272.

[67] Cf the remarks on the effect of the Insolvency Act 24 of 1936 and the interaction with s 28(3) of the 1993 Constitution in *Harkenson v Lane NO and Others* 1997 (11) BCLR 1489 (CC); 1998 (1) SA 3000 (CC) at paras 35–7 per Goldstone J and the criticism in A J van der Walt *Constitutional Property Clauses* (Kluwer 1999) 336–340.

This may be illustrated in both Scotland and South Africa. For example, where it is appropriate to retain the value of the estate, a Scottish factor *loco absentis* may seek authority to sell specific items of property.[68] This could prove suitable, for example, where the estate includes business premises that would deteriorate if retained.[69] Furthermore, where a factor *loco absentis* is appointed, this gives a focus for the absentee being sued by third parties. In Scotland, the absentee, by means of the factor *loco absentis* may be called as a defender in appropriate proceedings such as an action of division and sale initiated by other co-proprietors[70] and where the absentee was under an existing obligation to grant title to a third party.[71] The position of a *curator bonis* in South Africa presents almost a mirror image. Special powers may be obtained at the time of the appointment to deal with the particular circumstances then presenting.[72] In one case[73] an order of the Court at the time of appointment empowered the *curator* to make regular payment of sums for the maintenance of his family. In another,[74] the order of the Court, reflecting the rather more complex commercial interests of the absentee, was more wide-ranging and provided that the factor had power (a) to take care of, control and administer all the property and business interests of the absentee; (b) to pay all debts and expenditure incurred for the maintenance of the property and the family of the absentee and the preservation of his business interests; and (c) to reinvest all sums not immediately required for any of the foregoing. In its judgment it is possible for the court specifically to mention the entitlement of the *curator* to seek further powers as and when required[75] but such a right would exist whether referred to or not at the time of appointment.

5.12 ABSENTEE'S DEALINGS AND ACQUISITION OF RIGHTS

The generally applicable policy of conservation of the absentee's estate does not automatically require that the absent party be deprived of the right

---

[68] There are numerous examples to be found in Scottish National Archives, e.g. *James S A Jeffray factor loco absentis on estate of Thomas C Moan: Authority to Sell* 1983 National Archives CS46/1983/837; *David C Coull (Factor Loco Absentis) to Inger M Powell: Authority to Sell* 1979 National Archives CS46/1979/94.

[69] E.g. the sale of public house: *Interim decree granting authority to Colin Campbell Penney (factor loco absentis to Matthew Alexander Watson) to sell (Welltrees Bar, Maybole Ayrshire)* November 1939 National Archives CS46/1939/11/16.

[70] *Macfarlane v Greig* (1895) 22R 405; *sub nom Stewart v Macfarlane* 1895 2 SLT 516; *McLean v City of Glasgow District Council* 1987 SLT (Lands Tr) 2 at 4.

[71] Eg *Lunan v Macdonald* 1927 SLT 661; 1927 SN 148.

[72] Albeit no detail of what the powers were is given, the case report indicates certain specified powers were granted by the Court in *Ex parte Shulman* 1955 (1) SA 514 (W).

[73] *Ex parte Pearlman* 1957 (4) SA 666 (N).

[74] *Ex parte Sehlabaka* [2009] JLO 24112 (FB).

[75] E.g *Ex parte Pearlman* 1957 (4) SA 666 (N).

to deal with his or her own estate even if the absentee is doing so wholly unknown to the factor *loco absentis* or *curator bonis*. By virtue of absence alone, it appears that an absentee is not disabled by the law of South Africa or by Scots law from dealing with property, far less from acquiring property or rights. As early as the mid-seventeenth century counsel in one Scottish case successfully argued that it was 'ordinar to give Seasines to . . . absents out of the Countrey'[76] meaning that it was quite lawful for such parties to acquire land in Scotland by the then applicable procedures. This remains the position of Scots law and Scotland, and it would appear that even if an officer of court is appointed to administer the affairs of an absentee for the benefit of the absentee, that absentee may acquire heritable and moveable property by means of both *inter vivos* or *mortis causa* conveyances. So too may the absentee benefit from a promise.[77]

This general position applies also in the context of the laws of succession. By virtue of absence the absentee is not rendered unworthy as regards receiving a bequest, legacy, provision on intestacy or forced provision (known in Scotland as 'legal rights') as regards the estate of another party. This is implicit in the Scottish authority indicating that a factor *loco absentis* may be appointed to protect the interests of such a beneficiary[78] which recognises that the rights continue to vest in the absentee. It is also the subject of express provision in other legal systems.[79] This is also the law of South Africa.[80] That said, for at least a temporary period there may be a reluctance on the part of executors and trustees acting on the estate of a third party to distribute estate merely on the basis that an absentee is presumed to be alive. The Scottish courts have upheld not only the right but also the duty of trustees and executors to delay distribution in such a case.[81]

Where a lawful condition is attached to a bequest requiring it to be claimed or accepted within a short period of time, absence has the potential to disable an absent beneficiary from compliance with the timescale envisaged if no *curator bonis* or factor *loco absentis* has been appointed and no one else can act. There is a similar phenomenon where statutory discretionary

[76] *The Lady Carnagy v The Lord Cranburn* 30 January 1663, Stair *The Decisions of the Lords of Council and Session, in the Most Important Cases Debate before Them* (1683) vol 1, 166 at 167.
[77] Stair *Institutions* 1.10.4.
[78] See Stair *Institutions* 4.50.28(4); *Carmichael Petitioner* (1700) Mor 7454 (absent party known to be a ship's surgeon in the Indies); *Gilchrist Petitioner* (1752) Mor 4070 (absent party not known to be alive or dead, abroad and last heard of in service of the South Sea Company at La Vera Cruz); *James Paton Petitioner* (1785) M 4071; *Kennedy v McLean* (1851) 13D 705; *Barstow v Cook* (1862) 24D 790; (1862) 34 Sc Jur 399; *Sutherland, Petr* 1898 6 SLT 257.
[79] E.g. Québec: Civil Code art 617 and France: Civil Code art 725 as added by Law of 28 December 1977.
[80] *Ex parte Volckers* 1911 CPD 101; *Ex parte Davids* 1948 (1) SA 1018 (W).
[81] *Stewart's Trs v Stewart* (1875) 2R 488: absence for ten years, absentee would have been 46 if alive.

schemes require timeous application for provision to the applicant out of the estate of a deceased,[82] or where there requires to be made within a set timetable an election between entitlements[83] or an application for relief from forfeiture.[84] It might appear that in none of these cases is there a deprivation of property on the part of the absentee. In accordance with the Civilian principles, no one can lose what he does not have[85] – *non potest videri desisse habere, qui numquam habuit* – and in all of these cases the absentee has not complied with a precondition of a potential entitlement. However, the word 'possessions' used in article 1 of the First Protocol of the ECHR denotes an autonomous concept not limited by traditional classifications. On that basis it has been held in an English case[86] that a party disqualified by a statutory time limit to seek relief from forfeiture of a right in an inheritance could be regarded as being deprived of a possession. The potential application of such reasoning to absentees remains unexplored. It cannot be certain that Scots law would be persuaded by this reasoning[87] and there is no similar decision in South African law.

5.13 CONSERVATION VERSUS DISTRIBUTION

Eventually there comes a time when conservation of an absentee's estate is no longer appropriate. Other policies take on greater importance: first, the desirability of protecting the rights of third parties against the absentee, especially where these rights would depend upon the death of the absentee; and second, the need to avoid the economic drawback of removing assets from beneficial use for a considerable period of time. At this stage one must consider distribution of the estate of the absentee.

Albeit the importance of their application may be more widely recognised today, these policies are far from novel.[88] Over a century ago the concern at the heart of these policies was judicially identified in a Scottish context in a comment on the statutory replacement of what had become to be regarded as the unsatisfactory common law relating to declaration of death of a missing person. To this effect Lord President Inglis observed:[89]

---

[82] Family Law (Scotland) Act 2006, s 29(6).
[83] Succession (Scotland) Act 1964, ss 8(1) and 8(3) provisos.
[84] Forfeiture Act 1982.
[85] D 50.17.208 (Paulus).
[86] *Land v Land* [2007] 1 WLR 1009; [2006] EWHC 2997 per HHJ Alastair Norris QC.
[87] 'Article 1 of the First Protocol protects existing rights (and certain legitimate expectations): it does not guarantee a right to acquire what one does not already have': *Di Ciacca v The Scottish Ministers* 2003 SLT 1031 at 1046 para 53 per Lord Reed.
[88] See Demolombe *Traité de l'absence*, note 37 supra, 2 and 3, § 1.
[89] *Williamson v Williamson* (1886) 14R 226 at 228. See also the remark that the common law of disappearance 'effectively quarantined the person's property for a generation'. D R Macdonald, *Succession* 3e (W Green 2001) 2 para 1.05.

'the expediency of the statute[90] has been very generally recognised, for the old law often kept property in neutral custody for so long a time as to deprive a generation from taking any benefit from a succession which had really opened up to them.'

Only a few years previously the same concern was raised by the French writer Demolombe writing in relation to an absent person and his estate. After identifying the private interests involved he recognised:[91]

'l'intérêt général de la société, qui exige que les biens ne restent pas trop longtemps abandonnés, sans représentant et sans maître, dans une sorte de stagnation; et que le cours normal et régulier de leur transmission ne soit pas indéfinement interrompu, et, si je puis dire ainsi, barré part cet obstacle.'

'the general interest of society which may require that property does not remain abandoned without some one representing it, and without an owner in a sort of stagnation. This interest may also require that the normal and regular course of the transmission of property is not indefinitely interrupted and, if I might so put it, barred by this obstacle.'

5.14 CAUTION AND PRAGMATISM

Such comments may initially give rise to the impression that a legal system must now move to alter the status of absentees and to presume them to be dead or deem them dead so that they might be deprived of their property and to enable it to be distributed according to the law of succession. Arguably the conferring of the status of *civiliter mortuus* is a precondition for the distribution of those persons' estates. That may be logical but that is not how Scots or South African law operates.

Even whilst the absentee is presumed to be alive, both Scots law and the law of South Africa, in certain circumstances, may enable the property of the absentee to be distributed in emulation of the pattern dictated by the applicable law of succession. Considered by some commentators as a pragmatic approach,[92] this is truly a very radical but long-established possibility. It was known to our common inheritance of Roman Dutch law.[93] Even today, a virtually identical cross-jurisdictional approach is to be observed in South African and Scottish cases. These cases confirm that the property of an absentee may be transferred to those parties who would be entitled as beneficiaries under the applicable law of succession if the absentee were

---

[90] Presumption of Life Limitation (Scotland) Act 1881 now repealed.

[91] Demolombe *Traité de l'absence*, note 37 supra, 2 and 3 § 1.

[92] Anonymous 'Presumption of Life at Common Law and Its Statutory Limitations' (1888) 4 *Scot Law Review* 169 at 173.

[93] Voet *Pandects* 10.2.18 translated by Percival Gane *The Selective Voet* vol 2, 641. See the more restrictive view in Huber's *Jurisprudence of My Time* translated by Percival Gane (Butterworths 1939) vol 1, 566–7, ch 34, 3.

actually dead provided there are a considerable period of absence and some evidence of death, albeit insufficient to overcome the common law presumption of life. This is a somewhat vague test. It appears to be little more than a balancing of various factors but the case reports do not make clear when the tipping point is reached to justify distribution.

In these astonishing cases the Scottish courts have given authority to uplift and distribute the funds, on condition that the parties receiving the money took out insurance to deal with the contingency of repayment of such sums upon the reappearance of the missing person.[94] The insurance may be regarded as a fund of potential compensation to the absentee. This approach bears some functional resemblance to what are known in Common Law jurisdictions as 'Benjamin' orders.[95] As there is no clear guidance in the Scottish decisions as to the appropriate level of insurance or caution that is to be taken out, it may well be that the courts would find some guidance in the English authorities,[96] although an enthusiast for mixed legal systems would suggest South African law provides an equally good if not better exemplar for Scots law. However, one might presume that appropriate insurance cover should deal with the cost of restoring a similar item to that distributed, duly index-linked to deal with inflation or, if the thing distributed comprises money, the value of that money with interest thereon at an appropriate rate.

It must be emphasised that this is not an application of the laws of succession. Succession opens only on death or civil death. However, the approach noticed here is an emulation of the laws of succession. This emulation of the laws of succession clearly provides the possibility of an accelerated inheritance albeit the transfer effecting that is strictly speaking an *inter vivos* transfer and not a *mortis causa* transfer. The most striking illustration of how the Scottish common law approach might serve to speed up distribution of an estate is seen in one case in which the court permitted distribution upon the finding of caution, only to be informed that the party to receive the sums could not afford to provide caution. The estate could not then be distributed. Only after a further wait of nine years did the court permit distribution of the sums without caution, on the basis that the inference of death was then strong enough to overcome the common law presumption of

---

[94] Eg *Ruthven v Cleik (or Clerk)* (1628) Mor 482, 8048 and 11629; *James and Mary Renny v R Crosbie* (1822) 2S 53; *Campbell v Lamont* (1824) 3S 145; *Fettes (Ritchie's Trs) v Dr Gordon* (1825) 4S 149 (NE 150); *Hislop or Gordon Ptrs* (1830) 8S 919; *Garland v Stewart* (1841) 4D 1; *Chambers v Chambers or Carruthers* (1849) 21 Sc Jur 538.

[95] The name is taken from *Re Benjamin: Neville v Benjamin* [1902] 1 Ch 723. See Scottish Law Commission *Discussion Paper on Trustees and Trust Administration* (Scot Law Com DP 126, 2004) para 73.

[96] Viz English discussion in *Evans v Westcombe* [1999] 2 All ER 777 (ChD); P H Kenny 'A Lost Beneficiary Returns' 1999 *Conv & Prop L* 375–6.

life.[97] The beneficiaries were then entitled to succeed by virtue of the law of succession.

So too in some South African cases the *curator bonis* has been authorised to sell the absentee's property and to distribute the proceeds to the family.[98] The pattern of distribution is the one dictated by the law of succession (whether testate or intestate)[99] which would be applied if the absentee were dead. The heirs are usually required by the Court to provide sufficient security to the Master of the High Court for the return of the benefits so received, or the value thereof, should the absentee reappear. This is known as a *cautio de restituendo*.[100] Where the estate to be distributed is of a very small amount in comparison with the costs of providing such security the Court may forego the provision of the security.[101] In appropriate cases the Court may restrict the duration of the security.[102]

5.15 COMMENTS ON THE GRANTING OF THE POWER OF DISTRIBUTION

In none of the reported cases, either in Scotland or South Africa, has the power to distribute the absentee's estate been conferred immediately upon the appointment of a factor *loco absentis* or a *curator bonis* at the time of his initial appointment. Instead, in those cases the power appears to have been conferred on the curator or factor only after he or she has been in office for some considerable time. The key issue, however, is not the existing length of the curatory or factory but the length of the absence. In all the reported cases the power to distribute has been conferred only after the absentee has been absent for a significant period. The power of distribution, when granted, emulates the distribution that would be effected by the law of succession and, where the absentee has left a will, one would presume the Court would seek to style the distribution in accordance with the testate scheme of settlement (as limited, of course, by any restraints on testamentary freedom). Because of this a court is not likely to order distribution if it is likely that the property will have to be handed back by the recipients. Consequently

---

[97] *Campbell v Campbell's Trs* (1834) 12S 382.
[98] E.g. *Dempsters & Van Ryneveld v SA Mutual Life Assurance Society* (1908) 25 SC 162; 18 CTR 127; *Ex parte Volckers* 1911 CPD 101 (sister 31 years absent) referring to *In re Kannemeyer* (1899) 16 SC 407; 9 CTR 440 (man 24 years absent); *Ex parte Hepinstall* 1923 OPD 134 (husband 15 years absent); *Ex parte Estate Russell* 1926 WLD Vol. 2, 118 (34 years absence); *Ex parte Davids* 1948 (1) SA 1018 (W) (9 years absence until death of father from whom absent could inherit, followed by a further 24 years absence). The practice is discussed in *Ex parte Verster* 1956 (1) SA 409 (C) at 411 per de Villiers J P. Cf *In re Labistour* 1908 NLR 227 (death presumed after seven months).
[99] Eg *Ex parte Volckers* 1911 CPD 101.
[100] R A Jordaan and C J Davel *Law of Persons* 4e (Juta 2005) para 7.4.1.4.
[101] *Ex parte Pieters* 1993 (3) SA 379 (D).
[102] *Ex parte Davids* 1948 (1) SA 1018 (W).

a court in Scotland and South Africa is unlikely to give special powers to the *curator bonis* or factor *loco absentis* to distribute all of the property in situations where the absentee is known to be alive, or suspected to be alive but merely difficult to contact.

Albeit this ability to appoint factors *loco absentis* and grant them special powers is in no way abrogated by the Presumption of Death (Scotland) Act 1977, the enactment of that legislation may lead the Scottish courts to be slightly more reluctant to confer a power on a factor *loco absentis* to emulate the distribution that would occur upon death. One suspects that in many of the common law cases in which a distributory power was granted to factors *loco absentis*, the absentee could now be declared dead in terms of the 1977 Act. This may be attractive to a court in that the estate of a missing person who is declared dead in terms of the 1977 Act may be distributed subject to all the statutory protections.[103]

However, situations remain in which the ability of a Scottish factor *loco absentis* to distribute the estate of an absentee may be suitable. For example, where a husband has been absent for some time, his wife may not wish to have him declared dead because she does not wish technically to become a widow. At the same time, however, she may need the benefit of a complete or substantial distribution of the absent husband's estate and not a series of smaller payments 'on the drip' out of the estate. The obtaining of distributory powers by a factor *loco absentis* may assist in achieving this end without having her absent husband declared dead. That said, modern commercial and financial practice has moved on since the date of decision of many of the Scottish cases. Indeed, it would be fair to say that this practice has developed largely in ignorance of the little-known power of distribution potentially available to factors *loco absentis*. Many modern insurance providers will probably insist upon a declaration of death leading to the issuance of a death certificate before paying out on policies of life assurance. Indeed the contracts themselves may be worded in such a way. In these cases the wife may obtain a declaration of death at common law, calling the particular insurance company as a defender because such a decree is not good against the world and does not automatically terminate a marriage. To put the matter another way, Scots law has the flexibility, if such is desired, to regard an absentee as having passed on to being 'missing' and therefore dead for some purposes whilst retaining him or her in life for others.

---

[103] See, e.g., the case of *Inger Powell*, note 68 supra, in which the absentee, having had a factor *loco absentis* appointed on her disappearance eight years previously, was declared dead in terms of the 1977 Act (Court of Session: Lord Wylie): *The Glasgow Herald*, 27 September 1985, 5. See National Archives of Scotland, reference *Inger Powell: Petition for Factor Loco Absentis* CS258/1986/P754. The author thanks Dr D C Coull for this information.

5.16 HUMAN RIGHTS AND CONSTITUTIONAL ASPECTS

There has been no case reported in which the South African or Scottish courts have considered the human rights or constitutional aspects of their domestic regimes for the conservation of the estates of absentees and the distribution of their property in exceptional situations. Some guidance, however, may be sought from cases in which the American Supreme Court has addressed the constitutionality of legal regimes to deal with the property of missing persons.[104] The objections centred on jurisdiction and the protection against deprivation of property without due process in terms of the Fourteenth Amendment to the US Constitution.[105] From these decisions one may deduce that the following essential requirements must be met before one may regard as constitutional a statute permitting a declaration of death and permitting the distribution or the estate of the party declared dead. First, the court must have jurisdiction over the property of the individual. Secondly, notice to the missing party must be attempted. Thirdly, the lapse of time before the declaration of death can be obtained must be reasonable. Due process would be lacking in the case of 'an arbitrary and unreasonable presumption of death resulting from absence for a brief period'.[106] Fourthly, there must be some safeguards for the missing person should he or she return.

5.17 DUE PROCESS SATISFIED

Given the generally conservative nature of the proceedings, a petition for the appointment of a *curator bonis*[107] or a factor *loco absentis*[108] may be presented by someone who has at heart the interests of the absentee. Conversely, in Scotland, a suitable respondent (the person against whom the action is notionally raised) is a person who asserts the absentee is dead and his estate should be distributed according to the law of succession.[109] There may be the potential for a conflict of interest in such proceedings. For example, in one South African case[110] the applicant for a *curator bonis* was the next of kin and

---

[104] *Scott v McNeal* 154 US 34 14 S Ct 1108 US (1894); *Cunnius v Reading School District*, 198 US 458, 25 S Ct 721 US (1905).

[105] See, e.g., J L Carriere 'The Rights of the Living Dead: Absent Persons in the Civil Law' (1989–1990) 50 *La L Rev* 901 at 910–14.

[106] *Cunnius v Reading School District*, 198 US 458, 25 S Ct. 721 US (1905) respectively at 459, 476–7, 722 and 727.

[107] *Ex parte Volckers* 1911 CPD 101 (the absentee's sister); *Ex parte Shulman* 1955 (1) SA 514 (W) (the absentee's brother); In *Ex parte Pearlman* 1957 (4) SA 666 (N) (the absentee's father-in-law).

[108] NML Walker *Judicial Factors* (W Green 1975) 29.

[109] E.g. *White v Stevenson* (1829) 7S 555.

[110] *Ex parte Shulman* 1955 (1) SA 514 (W).

brother-in-law of the absentee. In another the applicant was the wife of the absentee and she was also appointed *curator bonis*.[111] This may be regarded by some as almost inevitable in matters involving family affairs but due process would be better served by having an independent party appointed as *curator bonis* or factor *loco absentis* as the case may be, with perhaps only small-value estates being subject to the applicant seeking self-appointment. That said, considerable comfort may be taken from the fact that appointment as factor *loco absentis* or *curator bonis* is not made on demand but only on cause shown.

The benefit of such an appointment is that, it provides an independent focus for management: the estate of the absentee is not provisionally distributed to a multiplicity of persons. The protection of the absentee's interest is enhanced in that, in Scotland, caution – a guarantee of good performance – for the factor's intromissions may be required. This is also the position in South Africa as regards the *curator bonis*.[112] Furthermore, in South Africa the *curator bonis* may be placed under the supervision of the Master,[113] whilst the Scottish equivalent is to place the factor *loco absentis* under a duty to report to the Accountant of Court. As regards the property placed in the trust of the *curator bonis* or factor *loco absentis*, these officials are therefore constituted, functionally if not formally, as types of what has become known in modern trust law as 'protectors' of the interests of the various potential beneficiaries including the absentee.

5.18 CONCLUSION

The subjection of an absent person's estate to administration by a *curator bonis* is a deprivation in terms of the South African Constitution, article 25. However, even where this involves a court granting a power to distribute the estate in emulation of the laws of succession, which are then exercised, it is not an 'arbitrary deprivation' of property in terms of article 25(1). This is because each case is considered judicially on its merits. The exercise of the Court's powers to appoint and empower a *curator bonis* may be considered a legal practice of general application and no one class of person is picked out for adverse discrimination. Compensation for the deprivation is not immediate but is potential and contingent in the form of the *cautio de restituendo*.

Likewise, in terms of article 1 of the First Protocol to the ECHR the appointment of a factor *loco absentis* to a Scottish absentee and the exercise by that factor of judicially-conferred powers to transfer the property of the

---

[111] E.g. *Ex parte Kuhr* 1940 CPD 227. See also *Hoffmeester* (1900) 17 SC 539; *Re Nicolson* 1908 TS 870; *Ex parte Halbert* 1912 OPD 134.

[112] E.g. *Ex parte Kuhr* 1940 CPD 227; *Ex parte Sehlabaka* [2009] JLO 24112 (FB).

[113] E.g. *Ex parte Kuhr* 1940 CPD 227; *Ex parte Sehlabaka* [2009] JLO 24112 (FB).

absentee in emulation of the laws of succession is a form of deprivation of the absentee's possessions. However, this deprivation is in the 'public' and 'general' interest and the central judicial role in the proceedings ensures that such a deprivation is subject to conditions provided for by law. Again, compensation of an adequate amount in a contingent form is available.

Chapter 6

The Right to Personal Security

*Anton Fagan**

6.1 INTRODUCTION

Both Scots and South African private law have a body of rules giving effect
to the right to personal security. The two bodies of rules are similar in
content, but they differ as regards their reach. The Scottish rules apply to
all bodily injuries, regardless of the manner or context wherein they have
arisen. The South African rules, by contrast, do not apply to bodily injuries
arising from motor vehicle accidents or in the workplace. To these two types
of bodily injuries, South African law applies a different collection of rules, a
collection of rules which is of a public law rather than private law nature and
which has no counterpart in Scots law.

This raises several questions of relevance to the overall theme of this
book. Is it necessary, in order for the law adequately to give effect to the right
to personal security, that – like Scots law – it offer a private law response to
all bodily injuries, no matter how or where they occur? Or is it sufficient
that – like South African law – it offer a mixed response, applying private law
rules to some kinds of bodily injuries and public law rules to others? Might
it even be sufficient, in order for the law adequately to give effect to the right
to personal security, that – unlike either Scots or South African law – it offer
an exclusively public law response to bodily injury?

The answers to these questions are not obvious. It is unlikely that
there is only one body of rules that will adequately give effect to a right
as abstract and fundamental as the right to personal security. At the same
time, it is certain to be the case that a body of rules will adequately give
effect to the right to personal security only if it possesses certain general
features. This raises a further question. Is there any general feature which
a body of rules must possess if it is adequately to give effect to the right
to personal security and which is possessed only by private law rules and
not by public law ones? The most plausible candidate for such a general
feature is the achievement of corrective justice. That is, it may be that a
body of rules cannot adequately give effect to the right to personal security

* I would like to thank my colleague Helen Scott for her helpful response to an earlier draft of
this chapter.

unless it achieves corrective justice in respect of bodily injuries. And it may be that a body of rules cannot achieve corrective justice in respect of bodily injuries unless it consists of private law rules rather than public law ones.

If so, it will be necessary, in order for the law adequately to give effect to the right to personal security, that it offer a private law response to all bodily injuries. A mixed response, applying private law rules to some kinds of bodily injuries, but public law rules to others, will not do. Nor will an exclusively public law response. To put it another way, if it is so that the right to personal security requires for its proper implementation rules achieving corrective justice in respect of all bodily injuries and that corrective justice in respect of bodily injuries can be achieved only by rules of private law and not by rules of public law, then the Scottish approach to bodily injuries is to be preferred to the South African one.

The second part of this chapter does two things. It describes the essentially identical private law rules giving effect to the right to personal security in Scots and South African law, and it explains the difference in their reach or scope of application. The third section raises the possibility that this difference – that is, the difference in the reach of the private law rules giving effect to the right to personal security – is a difference that matters, because it may mean that Scots law better or more fully implements the right to personal security than does South African law. The fourth section explores this possibility in greater detail. Drawing on recent scholarship on corrective justice and its relationship to the law of delict, it tries to show that it may well be the case: (a) that the law cannot adequately give effect to the right to personal security unless it achieves corrective justice in respect of bodily injuries; (b) that the law cannot achieve corrective justice in respect of bodily injuries unless it is prepared to characterise all bodily injuries, regardless of where and how they occurred, as delicts; and therefore (c) that the law better gives effect to the right to personal security if it offers a comprehensive private law response to bodily injuries, as does Scots law, than if it adopts a mixed private law/public law response along the lines of South African law.

6.2 THE PRIVATE LAW RULES AND THEIR REACH

There is much common ground between the rules of Scots and South African private law giving effect to the right to personal security. The extent of the convergence is shown by the fact that the following five rules are firmly established in both legal systems:

(1) A person who assaults another (that is, who intentionally and without justification applies force to another or threatens to do so) commits a wrong which grounds an obligation on the wrongdoer to compensate the

victim for the affront as well as for consequential financial loss and pain and distress.[1]

(2) A person who negligently injures another (that is, who injures another by careless conduct in breach of a duty of care) commits a wrong which grounds an obligation on the wrongdoer to compensate the victim for consequential financial loss and pain and distress.[2]

(3) A person who assaults or negligently injures another commits a wrong which grounds an obligation on the wrongdoer to compensate some third parties suffering nervous shock as a result.[3]

(4) A person who intentionally applies force to another may be justified in doing so (and thus not commit an assault) if the person to whom the force was applied consented to it or if the person applying the force was acting in self-defence or defence of another.[4]

(5) A person who injures another by a careless omission only exceptionally does so in breach of a duty of care (and thus only exceptionally is negligent).[5]

However, though these five rules exist in both Scots and South African law, they do not play the same role in each. The difference in role relates to two common kinds of bodily injury. One is bodily injury arising from the driving or use of a motor vehicle. The other is bodily injury arising out of and in the course of a person's employment.

In Scotland bodily injuries arising from the driving of motor vehicles as well as bodily injuries arising in the course of a person's employment

---

[1] On this rule in Scots law, see D M Walker *The Law of Delict in Scotland* 2e (W Green 1981) 488–9; J Thomson *Delictual Liability* 4e (Tottel 2009) 11–16; E Reid *Personality, Confidentiality and Privacy in Scots Law* (W Green 2010) paras 2.01–2.08 ; J Blackie 'Unity in Diversity: The History of Personality Rights in Scots Law' in N R Whitty and R Zimmermann (eds) *Rights of Personality in Scots Law* (Dundee University Press 2009) 31 at 104–10. On this rule in South African law, see R G McKerron *The Law of Delict* 7e (Juta 1971) 153; J Neethling and J M Potgieter *Law of Delict* 6e (LexisNexis 2010) 325–6.

[2] On this rule in Scots law, see Walker *Delict*, supra note 1, at 503–631; Thomson *Delictual Liability*, supra note 1, at 61–72; H L MacQueen and W D H Sellar 'Negligence' in K Reid and R Zimmermann (eds) *A History of Private Law in Scotland* vol II *Obligations* (Oxford University Press 2000) 517 at 536–42. On this rule in South African law, see McKerron *Delict*, supra note 1, at 25–39, 154.

[3] On this rule in Scots law, see Scottish Law Commission *Report on Damages for Psychiatric Injury* (Scot Law Com No 196, 2004) paras. 2.1–2.25; Thomson *Delictual Liability*, supra note 1, at 75–83. On this rule in South African law, see McKerron *Delict*, supra note 1, at 154–7; Neethling and Potgieter *Delict*, supra note 1, at 285–90.

[4] On this rule in Scots law, see Walker *Delict*, supra note 1, at 496–8; Thomson *Delictual Liability*, supra note 1, at 15–16. On this rule in South African law, see McKerron *Delict*, supra note 1, at 153; Neethling and Potgieter *Delict*, supra note 1, at 326.

[5] On this rule in Scots law, see Thomson *Delictual Liability*, supra note 1, at 73–5. On this rule in South African law, see McKerron *Delict*, supra note 1, at 14–25; Neethling and Potgieter *Delict*, supra note 1, at 57–76.

are subject to all five of the rules above. That is, in Scotland a driver who assaults or negligently injures another commits a wrong which grounds an obligation to compensate the injured person and to compensate some who suffer nervous shock as a result. The same is true of an employer who assaults or negligently injures his employee in the course of the latter's employment. Admittedly, Scots law has an additional rule requiring that no one drive a motor vehicle unless he is insured against the obligation to compensate others for bodily injuries arising from his doing so.[6] Scots law also has an additional rule requiring that employers insure against the obligation to compensate their employees for bodily injuries arising in their course of employment.[7] And it has an additional rule requiring that the state compensate employees at least in part for such injuries.[8] However, these additional rules do not displace or render superfluous any of the five rules above.

In South Africa, by contrast, neither rule (1) nor rule (2) above applies to bodily injuries arising from the driving of motor vehicles. For South African law adds to rules (1)–(5) two further rules:

(6) A driver who assaults or negligently injures another does not commit a wrong which grounds an obligation on the wrongdoer to compensate the victim.[9]
(7) Where a driver has assaulted or negligently injured another, the South African Road Accident Fund is under an obligation to compensate the victim for consequential financial loss (though not necessarily in full) and pain and suffering (provided the injury is a serious one).[10]

Both of these additional rules are likely to be modified in the not too distant future. Rule (6) will probably be changed so as to exempt a driver who assaults or negligently injures another not only from the obligation to compensate the victim, but also from the obligation to compensate any third party suffering nervous shock as a result.[11] Rule (7) will probably be altered in order to make the Fund's obligation to compensate a person injured as a result of the driving of a motor vehicle unconditional upon the driver's having acted intentionally and without justification, or having

---

[6] Road Traffic Act 1988, s 143.
[7] Employers' Liability (Compulsory Insurance) Act 1969, s 1.
[8] Social Security Contributions and Benefits Act 1992, s 94.
[9] Road Accident Fund Act 56 of 1996, s 21.
[10] Ibid s 17. For a summary of the key provisions of the Road Accident Fund Act, see *Law Society of South Africa and Others v Minister of Transport and Another* 2011 (1) SA 400 (CC) at paras 22–8.
[11] Department of Transport *Draft Policy Paper: Restructuring of the Road Accident Fund on a No-Fault Basis and as Compulsory Social Insurance in Relation to the Comprehensive Social Security System* Government Gazette 32940 of 12 February 2010 para 6.6.

acted carelessly in breach of a duty of care.[12] The effect of these modifications will be that, in the case of bodily injuries arising from the driving of motor vehicles, not only rules (1) and (2) but also rules (3), (4) and (5) will be inapplicable.

The situation is more or less the same in respect of bodily injuries arising in the course of a person's employment. According to South African law, neither rule (1), nor rule (2), nor rule (3) applies where an employee has been assaulted or negligently injured in the course of his employment by his employer (or by certain of his fellow employees).[13] In other words, according to South African law, an employer who assaults or negligently injures an employee in the course of the latter's employment does not commit a wrong that grounds an obligation on the employer to compensate the employee. Nor does the employer commit a wrong grounding an obligation to compensate some who suffer nervous shock as a result. Instead, the injured employee (but not a third party suffering nervous shock as result of such injury) has a right to obtain compensation from the so-called Compensation Fund (but only for consequential financial loss, and only in part).[14] The Compensation Fund's obligation to compensate an injured employee is not conditional upon the employer's having acted intentionally and without justification, or having acted carelessly in breach of a duty of care.[15] Nonetheless, rules (4) and (5) still have some application. For the compensation which the Fund is obliged to pay to an injured employee may be increased (to an amount which is equitable but not in excess of the employee's financial loss) when the injury was due to the employer's having acted intentionally and without justification, or carelessly in breach of a duty of care.[16]

The differences between the Scottish and South African responses to bodily injuries arising from the use of motor vehicles and in the course of employment are significant for three reasons. First, they mean that in Scotland a driver who assaults or negligently injures another and an employer who assaults or negligently injures an employee commit delicts. In South Africa, by contrast, they do not. Why? Because in both Scots and South African law a delict is not merely a wrong. It is a wrong that grounds an obligation on the wrongdoer to compensate the victim. It is precisely because a delict is constituted, in part, by the wrongdoer's obligation to compensate the victim, that the law of delict falls within the law of obligations.[17]

---

[12]　Ibid para 6.1.
[13]　Compensation for Occupational Injuries and Diseases Act 130 of 1993, s 35.
[14]　Ibid ss 15 and 22.
[15]　Ibid s 22.
[16]　Ibid s 56. For a summary of the key provisions of the Compensation for Occupational Injuries and Diseases Act 130 of 1993, see *Jooste v Score Supermarket Trading (Pty) Ltd (Minister of Labour Intervening)* 1999 (2) SA 1 (CC) at 11A-F.
[17]　See R Zimmermann *The Law of Obligations* (Juta 1990) 1–33; D Visser and N Whitty 'The

It is also this fact which distinguishes delicts from crimes.[18] Evidence that this is how a delict is understood by both Scots and South African law is provided by the following quotes. The first is from David Walker, writing on Scots law. The second is from F P van den Heever, writing on South African law.

> 'The fundamental concept of the modern Scottish law of delict is breach of legal duty causing unjustifiable harm. Principles and rules of statute and common law impose on every individual a large number of duties of varying standards, owed to all persons who are within the area of risk of harm if the duty is not observed, to refrain from causing, intentionally or unintentionally, by act or omission, various kinds of harm to anyone within the area of risk and thereby infringing their legally protected interests. If a duty is broken . . . the law automatically imposes a bond of obligation joining them, conferring on the wronged person a claim to reparation and imposing on the wrongdoer a duty to make reparation for the loss caused.'[19]

> 'It is sufficient for our purposes to describe a delict as an unlawful infringement of another's rights in respect of which the law allows the injured person at his own discretion to invoke the assistance of the Courts and in private proceedings to claim satisfaction from the wrong-doer.'[20]

It follows that to hold, as Scots law does, that a driver or employer who assaults or negligently injures another commits a wrong which grounds an obligation to compensate the victim is to hold, by definition, that the driver or employer commits a delict. Conversely: to hold, as South African law does, that such a driver or employer does not commit a wrong grounding an obligation to compensate the injured party is to hold, again by definition, that he does not commit a delict.

The differences between the Scottish and South African treatment of bodily injuries arising from the driving of motor vehicles and in the course of employment are important, secondly, because they mean that whereas Scots law provides a private law response to drivers and employers who assault or negligently injure others, South African law provides a public law one. Rules (1)–(5) above are part of the common law of Scotland and of South Africa. The additional rules which South African law brings to bear on assault and negligent injuring by drivers and employers, in order to shift the obligation to compensate from the drivers and employers to the Road Accident and Compensation Funds, were created by statute. However, this is not the basis

---

Structure of the Law of Delict in Historical Perspective' in Reid and Zimmermann *History*, supra note 2, 422 at 439–40; Neethling and Potgieter *Delict*, supra note 1, at 3.

[18] See F P van den Heever *Aquilian Damages in South African Law* vol I (Juta 1944) 1–2; McKerron *Delict*, supra note 1, at 1.

[19] Walker *Delict*, supra note 1, at 31. See also Thomson *Delictual Liability*, supra note 1, at 1.

[20] Van den Heever *Aquilian Damages*, supra note 18, at 3. See also McKerron *Delict*, supra note 1, at 5; G Wille *Principles of South African Law* (Juta 1937) 357.

for the assertion that while Scots law provides a private law response, South African law provides a public law one. Nor could it be. A rule cannot be characterised as private or public by reference to its source: a private law rule can be created by statute; a public law rule can be part of the common law. What is more, the additional rules which Scots law applies in order to ensure that drivers and employers are insured against the obligation to compensate those whom they assault or negligently injure, and to require the state to compensate injured employees, are also statutory. Instead, the basis for the assertion that the Scottish legal system provides a private law response, the South African legal system a public law one, is the different obligations imposed by the rules of each, and the different grounds for those obligations.

Consider first bodily injuries arising from the driving of motor vehicles. Both in Scotland and South Africa, the fact that a driver has assaulted or negligently injured another gives rise to an obligation to compensate the injured party. In Scotland that obligation rests on a private party, namely the driver. And the ground or justification for the obligation is a private wrong, namely the wrong which the driver committed against the injured party by breaching his duty not to injure him. In South Africa, by contrast, the obligation to compensate rests on the state, operating through the agency of the Road Accident Fund. And the justification for that obligation is not that the driver has wronged the injured party. It is not that the driver has breached a duty which he owed to the injured party (or infringed a right which the injured party had against him). Instead, the justification is that the imposition of this obligation is a means of giving effect to a duty resting upon the state, namely the duty to provide all its citizens with access to healthcare and social security.[21] True, it is at present a necessary condition, for the Fund's obligation to compensate to arise, that the driver committed a wrong against the injured party. But the reason for this condition is not that the Fund's obligation to compensate would be unjustified in the absence of such wrongdoing. It is only to ensure the short-term financial viability of the Fund.[22] Precisely for that reason, wrongdoing on the part of a driver will probably not remain a necessary condition for the Fund's obligation to compensate an injured party to arise.

A similar distinction applies in respect of bodily injuries arising in the course of employment. South African law responds to the fact that an employer has assaulted or negligently injured an employee by imposing an obligation to compensate, not on the employer, but on the state (working through the Compensation Fund). Moreover, the ground for this obligation on the state is not that the employer, by assaulting or negligently injuring the employee, committed a wrong against him. For it is not a necessary

---

[21] See *Law Society of South Africa and Others v Minister of Transport and Another*, supra note 10 at paras 44, 46, 52 and 54.

[22] Ibid paras 46 and 51.

condition, in order for the state's obligation to arise, that the employer actually did assault or negligently injure the employee – it is enough that the injury occurred in the course of the employee's employment. Presumably the ground for this obligation is, again, that it is a means of giving effect to the state's duty to provide everyone with access to healthcare and social security.[23] Scots law, by contrast, deals with the fact that an employer has assaulted or negligently injured an employee by imposing an obligation to compensate the employee on the employer – that is, on a private party. Admittedly, Scots law in addition requires the state to pay certain benefits to the injured employee.[24] However, this in no way detracts from or diminishes the employer's obligation to compensate his employee. For the state can recover the benefits it has paid to the employee from the employer, who in turn can deduct them from the compensation it has to pay to the employee.[25]

The differences between the Scottish and South African responses to bodily injuries arising from the driving of motor vehicles and in the course of employment matter, in the third place, because they mean that Scotland and South Africa diverge in their legal treatment of a substantial fraction of the bodily injuries occurring in each. In Scotland the overwhelming majority of bodily injuries are of these two kinds: that is, they are bodily injuries arising from the driving of motor vehicles or in the course of employment. This is to be inferred from the following extract, taken from the seventh edition of Patrick Atiyah's *Accidents, Compensation and the Law*, and dealing with the United Kingdom in general:

> 'According to CRU [the Compensation Recovery Unit] figures, more than half (by number) of all tort compensation payments are made in road accident cases, more than a quarter in cases of work-related injury and illness, around 12% in cases involving accidents in public places and on privately owned land ('public liability' cases), and less than 2% in other types of case, including medical negligence and product liability. There is no reason to think that these proportions of the various types of successful tort claims do not roughly reflect the proportions of the various types of tort claims, both successful and unsuccessful.'[26]

In South Africa, bodily injuries arising from the driving of motor vehicles or in the course of employment constitute a smaller share of the total, somewhere between a third and a half. The reason for this is a considerably higher incidence of interpersonal violence.[27] However, the incidence of bodily inju-

---

[23] See Department of Transport *Draft Policy Paper: Restructuring of the Road Accident Fund on a No-Fault Basis and as Compulsory Social Insurance in Relation to the Comprehensive Social Security System*, supra note 11 at para 4.4.

[24] Social Security Contributions and Benefits Act 1992, s 94.

[25] Social Security (Recovery of Benefits) Act 1997.

[26] P Cane *Atiyah's Accidents, Compensation and the Law* 7e (Cambridge University Press 2006) 205.

[27] See, e.g., R G Matzopoulos, M R Prinsloo, J L Bopape, A Butchart, M M Peden and C J

ries arising from the driving of motor vehicles or in the course of employment remains high. According to South Africa's Road Traffic Management Corporation, approximately 220,000 people are injured every year in traffic accidents in South Africa. Of these, around 61,000 sustain serious injuries. A further 15,000 people are killed as a result of motor vehicle collisions.[28] To put this in relative terms, according to the World Health Organisation, South Africa in 2002 ranked 33rd out of a 192 countries in the world in respect of its death rate from road accidents: 30 deaths per 100,000 compared to a world average of nineteen.[29]

In concrete terms, this means the following. If Scotland were to abandon its approach to bodily injuries arising from the driving of motor vehicles and in the course of employment in favour of the South African one, around 80 per cent of the bodily injuries currently categorised as delicts, and hence regulated by private law, in Scotland would cease to be such. Conversely, if South Africa were to adopt the approach of Scots law, the number of bodily injuries classed as delicts, and thus handled as matters of private rather than public law, would increase by as much as 100 per cent.

6.3 DEDUCTION OR *DETERMINATIO*?

The previous part of this chapter explained that, while the Scottish and South African private law rules regulating bodily injury converge to a high degree, the Scottish and South African legal systems in fact diverge greatly in their responses to bodily injury. They diverge because Scots law applies the rules of private law, particularly the law of delict, to all bodily injuries. South African law, by contrast, does not. Unlike Scots law, South African law does not regard assaults and negligent injuries committed by drivers and employers as delicts. It does not, therefore, deal with them by application of its private law. Instead, it offers a public law response to such injuries. Does this have any implications for the overall theme of this book? More specifically, does the convergence in the rules of Scots and South African private law regulating bodily injury mean anything for our understanding of the right to personal security? Conversely, does our understanding of the right to personal security have any bearing on the divergence between the two legal systems' responses to bodily injury?

It is by no means self-evident that any of these questions has a positive answer. The reason is explained by John Finnis, Professor of Law and Legal

---

Lombard 'Estimating the South African Trauma Caseload as a Basis for Injury Surveillance', available at *http://www.sahealthinfo.org/violence/injurypreventionarticle.pdf*.

[28] See Department of Transport *Draft Policy Paper: Restructuring of the Road Accident Fund on a No-Fault Basis and as Compulsory Social Insurance in Relation to the Comprehensive Social Security System*, supra note 11 at para 3.1.

[29] Ibid.

Philosophy at Oxford University and the foremost contemporary exponent of natural law theory. Drawing on the work of Thomas Aquinas, Finnis distinguishes two relationships that may hold between a right and a rule (or set of rules) of positive law that is derived from it. One is deduction. This is where moral reasoning from the right (which may, and is likely to, involve further moral premises) uniquely justifies the rule.[30] The other is *determinatio*, which Finnis translates as 'implementation', 'specification' or 'concretisation'. This is where moral reasoning from the right justifies the rule of positive law, but not uniquely. It also justifies one or more other rules which the law-maker was free to adopt instead. In this case the rule of positive law represents a choice which could, with no less justification, have been made otherwise.[31] Finnis elucidates the latter relationship, that of *determinatio* or concretisation, with a non-legal example. An architect instructed to design and build a house will have to give shape to the general idea of a house by deciding on this or that size of door and window, this or that pitch of roof, this or that configuration of rooms and passages, and so on. These specifications, says Finnis, 'are certainly derived from and shaped by the general idea but . . . could have been more or less different in many (even in every!) particular dimension and aspect, and . . . therefore require of the [architect] a multitude of choices. The [design of the house] is controlled but not fully determined by the basic idea (say, the client's order) . . .'.[32]

Another example elucidating the notion of *determinatio* is provided by Joseph Raz, formerly Professor of the Philosophy of Law at the University of Oxford and the most influential legal positivist since H L A Hart. Raz asks us to assume that the theory of democracy yields only a general principle, for example:

> 'a democratic government is one where there are formal legal mechanisms making the content of policies and the identity of those in charge of implementing them sensitive to the wishes of the governed, in a way that as far as possible does not give any individual greater political power than that enjoyed by any other.'[33]

It follows, says Raz, 'that there can be in principle many morally legitimate

---

[30] J Finnis *Natural Law and Natural Rights* (Clarendon Press 1980) 281; J Finnis 'The Truth in Legal Positivism' in R P George (ed) *The Autonomy of Law: Essays on Legal Positivism* (Clarendon Press 1996) 195 at 197, 201, 202; J Finnis 'Natural Law Theories' in *The Stanford Encyclopedia of Philosophy* 5 February 2007, available at *http://plato.stanford.edu/entries/natural-law-theories*.

[31] Finnis *Natural Law and Natural Rights*, supra note 30, at 284; Finnis 'The Truth in Legal Positivism', supra note 30 at 197–203; Finnis 'Natural Law Theories', supra note 30, at 4, 9–10.

[32] Finnis *Natural Law and Natural Rights*, supra note 30, at 284; Finnis 'The Truth in Legal Positivism', supra note 30, at 202.

[33] J Raz 'On the Authority and Interpretation of Constitutions: Some Preliminaries' in his *Between Authority and Interpretation* (Oxford University Press 2009) 323 at 347.

ways of organizing democratic governments: federal republics and unitary constitutional monarchies, single-member constituencies, and proportional representation systems, parliamentary government and elected presidential systems, and so on'.[34] According to Raz, '[a]ll these radically different systems would be adequate democratic systems of government'.[35] To use Finnis's terminology, though all these different systems can be derived from the general principle, none can be derived from it by deduction, since none is uniquely justified by it. Instead, each can be derived from the general principle only as a *determinatio* or concretisation, that is, by an exercise of choice, on the part of a particular country, from among a number of equally justified alternatives.

Finnis's distinction between deduction and *determinatio* should raise some doubt as to whether the described similarities and dissimilarities in the way that Scots and South African law deal with bodily injury have any implications for the general theme of this book. Why? Because it is possible that the five rules stated at the beginning of section 6.2 – that is, the rules governing bodily injuries both in Scots and in South African private law – are derived from the right to personal security, not by deduction, but rather by *determinatio*. In other words, it may be that, while the right to personal security justifies the five rules in question, it does not justify them uniquely. Perhaps it also justifies the alternative rules which South African law applies to assault and negligent injuring by drivers and employers. To put this another way, it may be that, while the right to personal security justifies a private law response to bodily injuries which classifies all assaults and negligent injuries as delicts, it equally justifies a public law response which does not so classify any of them, or a mixed response which classifies some assaults and negligent injuries as delicts but not others.

If so, the described convergence in the Scots and South African private law regulating bodily injury is unlikely to provide much insight into the nature of the right to personal security. For the convergence then is less likely to reflect any essential features of the right, than to reflect contingent facts in the history of Scots and South African law. An obvious contingent fact is that both Scots and South African law are mixtures of Roman and English law.[36] Conversely, the right to personal security is unlikely to shed much light upon the described divergence between Scots and South African law. In particular, the right is not going to provide a ground for critique. It will not give the private law chauvinist, trying to construct an argument against the mixed private law/public law response of South African law, his first premise. But neither will it do that for the public law chauvinist, endeav-

---

[34] Ibid.

[35] Ibid.

[36] On the mixed nature of Scots and South African private law, see R Zimmermann '"Double Cross": Comparing Scots and South African Law' in R Zimmermann, D Visser and K Reid (eds) *Mixed Legal Systems in Comparative Perspective* (Oxford University Press 2004) 1.

ouring to put together a case against the comprehensive private law response of Scots law.

The idea that the rules of Scots and South African private law dealing with bodily injury are derived from the right to personal security, not by way of deduction, but rather by way of *determinatio*, is not altogether implausible. For there are many rules of Scots and South African law which indisputably are derived in exactly this manner. An obvious example is the Scots and South African rule of the road requiring everyone to drive on the left.[37] The rule is derived from, among other rights, the right to personal security. But it is derived from the right as a *determinatio* thereof rather than a deduction therefrom. Anyone doubting this should take his right-hand-drive car for a spin down a French country lane or along the German Autobahn.

Moreover, there is reason to believe that the South African Constitutional Court sees the relationship between the right to personal security and the rules of Scots and South African private law dealing with bodily injuries more or less in this way. In *Law Society of South Africa and others v Minister of Transport and another*, the Court was required to decide whether s 21 of the Road Accident Fund Act was unconstitutional.[38] Section 21 is headed 'Abolition of certain common law claims' and holds, among other things, that '[n]o claim for compensation in respect of loss or damage resulting from bodily injury to or the death of any person caused by or arising from the driving of a motor vehicle shall lie – (a) against the owner or driver of a motor vehicle'.[39] It is s 21, in other words, which declassifies assaults and negligent injuring by drivers as delicts – thus removing these injuries from the ambit of private law. According to the applicants, the section was unconstitutional because it unjustifiably limited the right to security of the person conferred by s 12(1) of the South African Constitution.[40] The Court disagreed. Its argument went as follows:

(1) The right to personal security in s 12(1) imposes on the state a duty 'to afford an appropriate remedy to victims of motor vehicle accidents who suffer bodily injury as a result of someone else's negligence'.[41]
(2) It is sufficient, for the state to discharge this duty, that it provide every person who suffers bodily injury as a result of someone else's negligence with 'a private law delictual remedy'.[42]
(3) However, it is not necessary: as the Court put it, 'the state's constitu-

---

[37] See Finnis *Natural Law and Natural Rights*, supra note 30, at 285.
[38] *Law Society of South Africa and Others v Minister of Transport and Another*, supra note 10.
[39] Road Accident Fund Act, supra note 9.
[40] The Constitution of the Republic of South Africa, Act 108 of 1996. The applicants also had other grounds for challenging the section's constitutionality, but those are irrelevant to this paper.
[41] At paras 57, 60 and 63.
[42] At para 74.

tional duty to protect and enforce the right to security of the person need not always include a civil claim for damages in delict or indeed any private law remedy'.[43]

(4) For it is also sufficient, for the state to discharge this duty, that it 'ameliorate the plight of victims rendered vulnerable by motor accidents' by providing them with a right to be compensated – albeit not in full – by a public fund.[44]

(5) Since the state was in fact providing the victims of motor vehicle accidents with a right to compensation against a public fund, the abolition of the 'private law delictual remedy' by s 21 of the Act did not, therefore, unjustifiably limit the right to security of the person in s 12(1) of the Constitution.[45]

The Court did not use Finnis's terminology in order to make this argument. But it could have. It could have expressed its reasoning by saying that the 'private law delictual remedy' was not a deduction from the right to personal security, but rather just one of two (or more) possible *determinationes* of that right, another being the public law compensatory remedy created by the Road Accident Fund Act. And it could have gone on to say that, this being so, the right to personal security could not possibly constitute a reason to prefer one of the remedies over the other, and that the legislature was therefore free to choose between them on the basis of policy considerations extraneous to the right to personal security, without having its choice second-guessed by the Court.

Those with an iconoclastic bent are bound to find some satisfaction in the idea that the right to personal security does not necessitate a private law response to bodily injuries – a response which treats all assaults and negligent injuries as delicts, that is, as wrongs grounding an obligation on the wrongdoers to compensate the victims. The idea may also please those who regard private law in general as a regrettable anachronism, a relic from a more individualistic and less caring past. However, notwithstanding its possible appeal and its apparent endorsement by the South African Constitutional Court, the idea may yet be mistaken. The remainder of this chapter explores that possibility. That is, it investigates whether the right to personal security may not, after all, require a private law response to bodily injury and whether, therefore, the right may not in this respect be better served by Scots law than it is by South African law. Central to that investigation will be the following two propositions:

(1) It is a necessary condition, for a legal system adequately to give effect to

---

[43] At para 79.
[44] At paras 66 and 79.
[45] At para 80.

the right to personal security, that it achieve corrective justice in respect of assault and negligent injuring.

(2) It is a necessary condition, for a legal system to achieve corrective justice in respect of assault and negligent injuring, that it characterise them as delicts.

If these two propositions are true, it necessarily follows that – contrary to the apparent supposition of the South African Constitutional Court – the right to personal security does require a private law response to bodily injury. And it necessarily follows that, in this respect, Scots law better or more fully gives effect to the right to personal security than does South African law.

In passing, and lest an enquiry into the truth of these two propositions seem esoteric, it may be noted that a failure to prove their truth has implications that reach beyond the right to personal security. The right to personal security is one of the most important rights we have, certainly more so than the rights to property, reputation and privacy. If the first proposition were false, if a legal system did not have to achieve corrective justice in respect of the right to personal security, why then would it have to achieve it in respect of the right to property, or the right to reputation, or the right to privacy? Why then could a legal system not also declassify deliberate and negligent property damage as a delict, and instead just require all property owners to insure themselves against it? Why then could a legal system not declassify deliberate defamation as a delict, and instead create a 'media tribunal' with the power to order retractions and impose fines? And what about so-called pure economic loss? If a legal system were not required to achieve corrective justice in respect of negligently-caused bodily injury, it could not possibly be required to achieve it in respect of negligently-caused pure economic loss. But if that were so, how would we account for the fact that most legal systems are increasingly willing to regard the negligent causing of pure economic loss as a delict?

6.4 CORRECTIVE JUSTICE

The key concept in the two propositions above is corrective justice. It is the key concept because whether the two propositions are true depends on how corrective justice is understood.

The truth of the second proposition – that is, the proposition that a legal system cannot achieve corrective justice in respect of assault and negligent injuring unless it characterises them as delicts – depends mainly on the *nature* of corrective justice. It depends, in other words, on the answers to questions like the following: what is corrective justice? What does it require of us? What conditions have to be met before we can say that it has been done? Over the past few decades, much has been written about the nature of corrective justice, particularly by Jules Coleman, Professor of Jurisprudence and Philosophy at Yale University, and Ernest Weinrib, Professor in the Faculty of Law at the University of Toronto.[46] For a number of years, Coleman advocated an account of the nature of corrective justice – he called it the 'annulment thesis' – which was fundamentally at odds with Weinrib's. However, in the early 1990s, Coleman abandoned the annulment thesis in favour of a new account, which he calls the 'mixed conception'. Coleman's new account is considerably closer to Weinrib's, so much so that it is possible to speak, as Weinrib has, of an 'emerging consensus' on corrective justice (or at least, on its nature). As is explained below, the 'emerging consensus' entails an unambiguous affirmation of the second of our propositions. It clearly entails that, in order for a legal system to achieve corrective justice in respect of assault and negligent injuring, it must characterise them as delicts.

What about the first proposition – that is, the proposition that a legal system must achieve corrective justice in respect of assault and negligent injuring if it is adequately to give effect to the right to personal security? The truth of this proposition depends less on the nature of corrective justice than on its *justification*. It depends, in other words, on the answers to questions of the following kind: what (if anything) is corrective justice for? What (if anything) is its point or value? Why (if at all) are we required to achieve it? Until very recently, these questions – questions about the justification of corrective justice – had not been satisfactorily answered by anyone, including Coleman and Weinrib. However, John Gardner, Ronald Dworkin's successor as Professor of Jurisprudence at Oxford University, has recently published an article which goes a long way towards remedying that.[47] As will be explained presently, Gardner's explanation of corrective justice's point or value does not quite vindicate the first proposition. But it may provide the foundation for such vindication.

All contemporary explanations of corrective justice's nature build upon, and in a sense interpret, Aristotle's original explanation thereof. So it is useful to start there. Essential to Aristotle's explanation is the contrast between corrective and distributive justice. Aristotle expressed the contrast in mathematical terms. Here is how Gardner summarises it:

'Norms of distributive justice are to be understood on the 'geometric' model of

---

[46] J L Coleman 'Corrective Justice and Wrongful Gain' in his *Markets, Morals and the Law* (Oxford University Press 1988) 184, 'Tort Law and the Demands of Corrective Justice' (1992) 67 *Indiana Law Journal* 349, *Risks and Wrongs* (Oxford University Press 1992), 'The Practice of Corrective Justice' in D G Owen (ed) *The Philosophical Foundations of Tort Law* (Clarendon Press 1995) 53; E J Weinrib *The Idea of Private Law* (Harvard University Press 1995), 'Correlativity, Personality, and the Emerging Consensus on Corrective Justice' (2001) 2 *Theoretical Inquiries in Law* 107.

[47] J Gardner 'What is Tort Law For? Part 1. The Place of Corrective Justice' (2011) 30 *Law and Philosophy* 1.

division. There are several potential holders of certain goods or ills and the question is how to divide the goods or ills up among them. Norms of corrective justice, on the other hand, are to be understood on the 'arithmetic' model of addition and subtraction. Only two potential holders are in play at a time. One of them has gained certain goods or ills from, or lost certain goods or ills to, the other. The question is whether and how the transaction is to be reversed, undone, counteracted. Should we add what has been subtracted, subtract what has been added, or leave things as they are?'[48]

According to Coleman's first conception of corrective justice, that is his annulment thesis, corrective justice is achieved in respect of a wrongful loss (or gain) in so far as the loss is eliminated or rectified.[49] But, stated the thesis, to the achievement of corrective justice in respect of a wrongful loss the 'mode of rectification' – that is, the manner in which the loss is eliminated or rectified – is irrelevant.[50] It does not matter, in other words, whether the loss is rectified by the wrongdoer or by some other person or means. That being so, it is not necessary, in order for a legal system to achieve corrective justice in respect of wrongful losses, that it place wrongdoers under an obligation to compensate their victims.[51] An accident compensation scheme such as the New Zealand no-fault plan, which eliminates wrongful losses by placing the obligation to compensate on the state, could thus serve corrective justice just as well.[52]

That Coleman's annulment thesis entails the falsity of the second proposition – the proposition that a legal system cannot achieve corrective justice in respect of assault and negligent injuring unless it characterises them as delicts – is self-evident. However, Coleman has since repudiated his annulment thesis – though not in its entirety. Coleman's second conception of corrective justice, his so-called mixed conception, retains the idea that corrective justice in respect of a wrongful loss requires the elimination or rectification of the loss.[53] But it drops the idea that corrective justice is indifferent as to the mode of rectification. According to the mixed conception, it is essential, in order for corrective justice to be done in respect of a wrongful

---

[48] Gardner 'What is Tort Law For?', supra note 47, at 9. For other summaries of Aristotle's account, see Weinrib *The Idea of Private Law*, supra note 46, at 61–3; J Gordley 'Tort Law in the Aristotelian Tradition' in Owen *Philosophical Foundations*, supra note 46, 131 at 132; Finnis *Natural Law and Natural Rights*, supra note 30, at 178.

[49] Coleman 'Corrective Justice and Wrongful Gain', supra note 46, at 185, *Risks and Wrongs*, supra note 46, at 306, 314 and 365.

[50] Coleman 'Corrective Justice and Wrongful Gain', supra note 46, at 187–8, *Risks and Wrongs*, supra note 46, at 306, 309, 314 and 365.

[51] Coleman 'Corrective Justice and Wrongful Gain', supra note 46, at 197, *Risks and Wrongs*, supra note 46, at 309 and 314.

[52] Coleman *Risks and Wrongs*, supra note 46, at 493.

[53] Coleman *Risks and Wrongs*, supra note 46, at 324–6, 'The Practice of Corrective Justice', supra note 46, at 66.

loss, that the loss be eliminated *by the wrongdoer*. It is therefore also essential, in order for a legal system to achieve corrective justice in respect of wrongful losses, that it place *the wrongdoers* under an obligation to compensate the victims.[54] Here is how Coleman puts it:

> 'In the mixed view, individuals incur a duty to repair the wrongful losses for which they are responsible. The victim who has suffered a wrongful loss owing to another's agency has a right to recover and the individual whose agency is responsible for the loss has a duty to make the loss good. Doing corrective justice means imposing the victim's loss on the person who is responsible for it.'[55]

Coleman's mixed conception of corrective justice, unlike his annulment thesis, does not render the second of our two propositions false. In fact, it does quite the opposite. If the mixed conception is sound, it is a necessary condition, for a legal system to achieve corrective justice in respect of assault and negligent injuring, that it impose on the wrongdoer an obligation to compensate the victim. As was explained in section 6.2, to do that is just to characterise assault and negligent injuring as delicts.

In so far as Coleman's mixed conception accepts that corrective justice in respect of wrongful losses requires that the wrongdoers be held to a duty to compensate the victims (who in turn have a corresponding right to be compensated by the wrongdoers), it is in line with most other contemporary explanations of corrective justice.[56] Of course, agreement on the fact that corrective justice requires holding wrongdoers to an obligation to compensate their victims – and thus, by implication, requires assaults and negligent injuring to be characterised as delicts – does not entail its truth. That notwithstanding, this chapter will not investigate the nature of corrective justice, and its implications for the second of our two propositions, any further. Instead, the chapter will now move on to the enquiry into the justification of corrective justice and the bearing of that justification on the first of the two propositions. This enquiry will proceed on the assumption that the emerging consensus as to the nature of corrective justice has it right. In other words, it will be asking about the point or value of corrective justice and whether the right to personal security demands it, assuming that corrective

---

[54] Coleman *Risks and Wrongs*, supra note 46, at 366.

[55] Ibid; see also at 311–28.

[56] See, for example, Weinrib *The Idea of Private Law*, supra note 46, at 63–6, 135–6, 'Correlativity, Personality, and the Emerging Consensus on Corrective Justice', supra note 46, at 116; Gordley 'Tort Law in the Aristotelian Tradition', supra note 48, at 139; R W Wright 'Right, Justice, and Tort Law' in Owen *Philosophical Foundations*, supra note 46, 159 at 167, 176–80; A Brudner *The Unity of the Common Law: Studies in Hegelian Jurisprudence* (University of California Press 1995) 198; S R Perry 'Tort Law' in D Patterson (ed) *A Companion to Philosophy of Law and Legal Theory* (Blackwell 1996) 57 at 72–3; T Honoré 'The Morality of Tort Law: Questions and Answers' in his *Responsibility and Fault* (Hart 1999) 67 at 74–5; L Kaplow and S Shavell *Fairness versus Welfare* (Harvard University Press 2002) 41; A Beever 'Corrective Justice and Personal Responsibility in Tort Law' (2008) 28 *Oxford J of Legal Studies* 475 at 476–9.

justice does – as is now generally agreed – require that wrongdoers be obliged to compensate their victims and, consequently, that assaults and negligent injury be branded as delicts.

As was mentioned earlier, to date the most successful attempt to explain why and how much corrective justice matters is that of John Gardner. Gardner calls his explanation the 'continuity thesis' (for reasons that will become apparent in a moment). However, in developing his explanation, Gardner relies on several ideas that were first articulated and defended by Joseph Raz.[57] Gardner's contribution is in bringing those ideas directly to bear on the particular problem of corrective justice's justification. It may therefore be best to speak of the 'Raz-Gardner explanation' of the point or value of corrective justice. The main elements of that explanation are as follows:

(1) A loss is wrongful if it is in breach of a duty (or infringes a right).
(2) Not only are duties (and rights) reasons, but they are justified by reasons.[58]
(3) It is in the nature of reasons that, if one has a reason to do X (because, for example, one has promised to do X, or because of another's interest in one's doing X) and one cannot do X, then one's reason to do X is also a reason to do the next-best-thing to doing X. As Raz puts it:

> 'Practical reasons generally admit the possibility of partial compliance. If I owe you £100, giving you £30 is paying part of my debt. I do not need a special reason to pay the £30. The reason to pay the £100 is also a reason to pay the £30 . . . Agents who are responsible for failure to do what they had reason to do should, when possible, do the next best thing, in order to come as close as possible to doing what they had to do. So, if I should have cleaned your car yesterday and did not I should clean it today. The original reason is the reason for partial or second best compliance; no new reason is required.'[59]

> 'If I have reason to give you $10 and I can only give you $8, then that same reason is a reason to give you the $8.'[60]

(4) Where another's interest is a reason for one to refrain from doing X, and one does X, the next-best-thing may be and often is to compensate the person. As Raz, again, explains:

> '[I]n some cases compensation to others for harm inflicted or for rights vio-

---

[57] J Raz 'Numbers, With and Without Contractualism' (2003) 16 *Ratio* 346, 'Personal Practical Conflicts' in P Baumann and M Betzler (eds) *Practical Conflicts: New Philosophical Essays* (Cambridge University Press 2004) 172, 'Responsibility and the Negligence Standard' (2010) 30 *Oxford J of Legal Studies* 1, 'On Respect, Authority, and Neutrality: A Response' (2010) 120 *Ethics* 279.

[58] Gardner 'What is Tort Law For?, supra note 47, at 32–3.

[59] Raz 'Responsibility and the Negligence Standard' supra note 57, at 9–10.

[60] Raz 'Personal Practical Conflicts', supra note 57, at 190.

lated is . . . a natural extension of the reason to take the second best course
of action, having failed fully to conform to reason. So if I have reason not to
damage your property, and I do damage your fence, I have reason to compensate you, that is, to mitigate the consequences of failure, and this reason is the
very same reason I had initially (the reason not to trespass or not to disturb
your peace).'[61]

(5) It follows that, where a person wrongfully occasions a loss to another
by breaching a duty to refrain from doing X, the reasons for the duty to
refrain from doing X (the primary duty) may be and often are reasons for
a duty to compensate the victim (the secondary duty). In Raz's words,
once more:

'The duty to compensate is part of the 'logic' of practical reasons generally: if
you fail to completely or perfectly comply with reasons which apply to you
(be they duties or otherwise), you should do the next best thing to come as
close to complete compliance as possible. Compensation is one way of doing
so.'[62]

'[T]he derivative duty to compensate is the duty not to harm transformed by
failure to comply into a duty to do the next best thing (restore the victims to
where they should have been, or as close as possible).'[63]

(6) Corrective justice is thus not an independent moral principle, requiring
its own justification: the (secondary) duty to compensate for a wrongful
loss has the same justification as the (primary) duty, breach whereof constitutes the wrong. Gardner this time:

'How does [the foregoing] help us to solve the problem of reparation for
wrongs? How does it help to make a case for moral norms of corrective
justice? Like this. The normal reason why one has an obligation to pay for the
losses that one wrongfully occasioned . . . is that this constitutes the best still-
available conformity with, or satisfaction of, the reasons why one had that
obligation. Or to put it more tersely, the reasons why one must pay for the
losses that one occasions are the very same reasons why one must not occasion those losses in the first place, when it is true that one must not occasion
them. One's reparative act is in at least partial conformity with the original
reasons, and if one was bound to conform to the original reason then *ceteris
paribus* one is now bound, in turn, to engage in the reparative act.'[64]

The Raz-Gardner explanation goes some distance towards vindicating the

[61] Raz 'Personal Practical Conflicts', supra note 57, at 191.
[62] Raz 'On Respect, Authority, and Neutrality: A Response', supra note 57, at 296.
[63] Raz 'Responsibility and the Negligence Standard', supra note 57, at 10.
[64] Gardner 'What is Tort Law For?', supra note 47, at 33–4. See also Raz 'Personal Practical
Conflicts', supra note 57, at 191.

first proposition. It shows that, to the extent that a legal system serves corrective justice in respect of assault and negligent injuring, it succeeds in giving effect to the right to personal security. It succeeds in giving effect to the right because it achieves second-best conformity with the right (or the reasons for it) when there has not been perfect compliance with it. However, to show this is not yet to establish the truth of the first proposition. According to the first proposition, to recall, the achievement of corrective justice in respect of assault and negligent injuring is a necessary condition for a legal system adequately to give effect to the right to personal security. In other words, the first proposition supposes that nothing else − no response other than one achieving corrective justice − will do. But perhaps that is not so. Perhaps achieving corrective justice in respect of assault and negligent injuring is just one of several ways to give effect to the right to personal security. More to the point, perhaps the compensation schemes adopted by South African law in respect of motor vehicle accidents and workplace injuries, though they do not achieve corrective justice, nonetheless do succeed in giving effect to the right to personal security.

This, as was explained in the previous section, seems to be the view of the South African Constitutional Court. It also is a view that probably would be supported by Jules Coleman, even now that he has traded in his annulment thesis for his mixed conception. According to Coleman, '[t]he state has the moral authority, but not the moral duty, to implement corrective justice'.[65] Why? Because a state could adopt an accident compensation scheme like the New Zealand no-fault plan. And if it did so, claims Coleman, the need for corrective justice would fall away. In respect of the injuries for which the scheme paid out compensation, there would simply be no corrective justice to be done. Coleman's explanation for this is not that, if such a scheme were adopted, those who wrongfully injured others would still have an obligation to compensate them, but this obligation would be discharged on their behalf by the scheme. It is rather that, in the event of such a scheme being adopted, no obligation on the part of the wrongdoers to compensate their victims would arise at all. As Coleman puts it: 'If there is a comprehensive plan put into effect for dealing with [wrongful] losses by imposing them on everyone . . . then corrective justice itself imposes no duties within that community'.[66]

Let us assume for the moment that Coleman is correct. It would then follow that the first proposition would be false. Contrary to what is stated by the proposition, it would not be a necessary condition, for a legal system adequately to give effect to the right to personal security, that it achieve corrective justice in respect of assault and negligent injuring. Would it also follow that there would be nothing to choose between the Scottish and South

---

[65] Coleman *Risks and Wrongs*, supra note 46, at 367.
[66] Coleman *Risks and Wrongs*, supra note 46, at 403–4. See also at 493–4, and see Coleman 'The Practice of Corrective Justice', supra note 46, at 71.

African responses to bodily injury? Would it follow that the right to personal security would be adequately served not only by the Scottish private law approach to motor vehicle accidents and workplace injuries, but also by the South African public law one? Not quite. As Coleman concedes, even in terms of his analysis, an accident compensation scheme of the New Zealand type would eliminate the need for corrective justice only if certain further conditions were satisfied. The important one, for present purposes, is that 'the victims must be fully compensated under the alternative plan, or they must be as fully compensated under the alternative as they would be under a scheme that implements corrective justice'.[67] This condition clearly is not satisfied by the two South African compensation schemes, as both place caps on the compensation to be paid out by the relevant fund. For example, in November last year, when the South African Constitutional Court delivered its judgment in the *Law Society of South Africa* case, the amount which the Road Accident Fund was obliged to pay out for loss of earnings fell 'to be calculated, irrespective of earnings, on the basis of a maximum annual income . . . set at R182 047 per year.'[68]

However, it is doubtful that Coleman is correct.[69] To see his error, imagine that a community has a tax-funded scheme which, in respect of negligent injury, compensates victims for their financial loss (that is, medical expenses and loss of earnings) and does so in full. According to Coleman, persons who negligently injured others in such a community would have no duty, in corrective justice, to compensate their victims for any financial loss which they may suffer as a result. That surely is true. But why? The reason, it may be thought, is that in this situation the connection which Raz and Gardner identify, between the primary obligation to refrain from carelessly injuring and the secondary obligation to compensate when one has so injured, is severed. To put it in Gardner's terminology, the reason (it may be thought) is that the 'continuity' between the primary and secondary obligation has been interrupted. The financial interest which persons have in not being injured still serves as a reason for the primary duty to refrain from carelessly injuring others. But, because of the scheme's intervention, it no longer constitutes a reason for holding those who breach this duty to a secondary duty to compensate the victims for their financial loss, as a way of doing the next-best-thing.

But this explanation is mistaken. How great a financial interest a person

---

[67] Coleman *Risks and Wrongs*, supra note 46, at 493.

[68] *Law Society of South Africa and others v Minister of Transport and another*, supra note 10, at para 27.

[69] Coleman's claim – that the existence of an accident compensation scheme of the New Zealand type has the result that wrongful injury ceases to give rise to any duty, in corrective justice, on the part of the wrongdoer to compensate his victim – is explicitly rejected by Wright 'Right, Justice, and Tort Law', supra note 56, at 178–9. It is implicitly rejected by Brudner *The Unity of the Common Law*, supra note 56, at 204–10.

has in not being injured is a contingent matter. It depends on whether he is a concert pianist or a bank clerk, plays professional football or works in a call centre, and so on. Less obviously perhaps, it is also a contingent matter whether a person has any financial interest at all in not being injured, or in not being injured in a particular manner. For example, a person would have no financial interest in not being carelessly injured if his wealthy and kindly aunt had undertaken to compensate him in full for any loss he might suffer in the event of his being so injured. Nor – and for present purposes this is the point that matters – would a person have such an interest if he lived in a community like our imagined one, a community which has a tax-funded scheme which fully compensates carelessly-injured persons for their medical expenses and lost earnings. A person living in such a community would have no financial interest in not being carelessly injured because, as a result of the scheme's pay-outs, he would not suffer any financial loss as a consequence of such injury. This is why the explanation in the previous paragraph is wrong. The explanation assumes that persons in our imagined community retain a financial interest in not being carelessly injured. It then claims that this interest continues to be a reason for the primary duty to refrain from carelessly injuring others, but ceases to be a reason for holding careless injurers to the secondary duty to compensate their victims. However, as shown, persons living in such a community in fact have no financial interest in not being carelessly injured. Since they do not have this interest, it can no more serve as a reason for the primary duty not to injure carelessly than it could serve as a reason for the secondary duty to compensate in the event that one does so injure. In fact, it is precisely because this interest has fallen out of the rationale for the primary duty that it also falls out of the justification of the secondary one.

None of this yet amounts to a refutation of Coleman's claim that, where a community adopts an accident compensation scheme like the New Zealand one, the need for corrective justice falls away (provided the scheme compensates in full). On the contrary, it may seem that the preceding two paragraphs only serve to render Coleman's claim more plausible. For, so it may seem, they explain just how the adoption of such a scheme would make corrective justice unnecessary: not by eliminating the rationale for the secondary obligation to compensate while leaving standing the rationale for the primary obligation not to injure, but rather by simultaneously eliminating the rationale for both. However, things are not as they may seem, for the reasons given below.

First, the duty not to injure (or, to put it more or less the other way around, the right to personal security) is justified by interests other than merely financial ones. Were that not so, a community's adoption of the kind of scheme under discussion would automatically relieve persons in the community from the duty not to injure others (or not to injure them deliberately or carelessly). Even in a community without such a scheme, a person would be able to relieve himself of the duty not to injure others by undertaking, in advance, to compensate those he injures for their medical expenses and loss of earnings. Clearly, neither of these is the case. The duty not to injure survives the removal of persons' financial interest in not being injured – and it does so because it is justified by other interests too. Chief among them is the interest in one's autonomy. In relation to one's body, this means the interest in having control or governance over one's own body rather than having it controlled by, or subjected to the will of, another. Arguably, the autonomy interest that people have in their bodies plays a bigger part in the justification of the duty not to injure than does their financial interest.[70] But that is not an argument that has to be made here. For present purposes, it is enough that the autonomy interest be accepted as one of the interests justifying the duty not to injure.

Secondly, though (as explained) the existence of a tax-funded compensation scheme could eliminate people's financial interest in not being carelessly injured, it could not, in a similar manner, eliminate their autonomy interest therein. That is, even if a community had a scheme which paid out carelessly-injured persons both for their medical expenses and loss of earnings, and for their loss of autonomy, persons in that community would retain an autonomy interest in not being carelessly injured. This is shown by the following analogy. A, an illegal organ-trader, is about to harvest a kidney from B against B's wishes. In response to B's protestations, A undertakes, sincerely, to compensate B in full for his consequential medical expenses and loss of earnings. In that case, A's forcible removal of B's kidney will not cause B any financial loss. But it will still cause B to suffer a loss of autonomy. For, to be autonomous in respect of his body, B must have the choice whether to keep his kidney or to have his kidney removed subject to compensation for his medical expenses and loss of earnings. By forcibly removing B's kidney, A would have denied B this choice.

However, what if A were to undertake, sincerely, to compensate B not only for his medical expenses and loss of earnings, but also for depriving B of this choice, that is, the choice whether to retain his kidney or have it removed subject to compensation for his medical expenses and loss of earnings? It may seem that, in that case, A's forcible removal of B's kidney would not, after all, cause B to suffer a loss of autonomy. But that is not so. To be autonomous in respect of his body, B must also have the *further* choice whether to keep his kidney or to have his kidney removed subject to compensation both for his medical expenses and loss of earnings *and* for his loss of the choice whether to retain his kidney or to have his kidney removed

---

[70] See, for example, S R Perry 'On the Relationship Between Corrective and Distributive Justice' in J Horder (ed) *Oxford Essays in Jurisprudence 4th Series* (Oxford University Press 2000) 237 at 256: 'The main reason that personal injury constitutes harm is that it interferes with personal autonomy'.

subject to compensation for his medical expenses and loss of earnings. And, by forcibly removing B's kidney, A would have deprived B of this *further* choice.

Would it help if A were to undertake (again sincerely) to compensate B also for the loss of this *further* choice? In other words, would a loss of autonomy on B's part be avoided if A were to undertake to compensate B for all three of the following:

(1) his medical expenses and loss of earnings,
(2) his loss of the choice whether to retain his kidney or to have his kidney removed subject to compensation for (1), and
(3) his loss of the *further* choice whether to retain his kidney or to have his kidney removed subject to compensation for (1) and (2)?

No, it would not – for a reason that by now should be obvious. B will only be autonomous in respect of his body if he also has the *further further* choice whether to keep his kidney or to have his kidney removed subject to compensation for (1), (2) *and* (3). And, of course, the regress continues indefinitely.

Thirdly, it follows that, if the existence of a tax-funded compensation scheme could bring it about that those who carelessly injure others no longer are under a secondary duty, in corrective justice, to compensate them for their lost autonomy, it would have to be by virtue of a different explanation than the one previously provided in respect of financial loss. Essential to that explanation were the following two claims. One: because of the scheme's existence, people cease to have a financial interest in not being carelessly injured. Two: because people do not have this interest, it cannot be a reason for the primary duty not to injure carelessly. In respect of the autonomy interest that people have in their bodies, quite the opposite holds. As has just been shown, whatever scheme is adopted, people will continue to have an autonomy interest in not being carelessly injured. Moreover, this autonomy interest will continue to constitute a reason for the primary duty not to injure carelessly. This means that what is required in respect of the autonomy inter-est that people have in their bodies is precisely the kind of explanation that was dismissed in the respect of their financial interest. That is, what needs to be explained is how the existence of a compensation scheme could bring it about that, even though people retain an autonomy interest in not being injured and this autonomy interest continues to justify a primary duty not to injure, it ceases to justify a secondary duty, on those who breach the primary duty, to compensate their victims for their lost autonomy – as a way of doing the next-best-thing. To put it another way, it needs to be explained why the existence of the scheme severs the connection or interrupts the continuity – described by Raz and Gardner – between primary and secondary duties.

Finally, there are grounds for doubting whether such an explanation is possible. A full discussion of these grounds will have to await another occasion. Here, very briefly, they are.[71] First, the autonomy interest that people have in their bodies is in part a relational or inter-personal one. In other words, it is not merely an interest in having self-governance over one's own body – it also is an interest in not having one's body subject to control by others. It is an interest in others' not using one's body for their purposes, or treating one's body as a means to their ends. It is precisely because our autonomy interest in our bodies has this relational aspect that many of us respond with resignation to injuries brought about by natural causes, but with outrage to similar injuries deliberately or carelessly brought about by other persons. Secondly, it follows that the loss of autonomy which a person suffers when he is deliberately or carelessly injured by another is in turn a relational harm (at least in part). That is, it is a harm the suffering whereof by the victim cannot be separated from the doing whereof by the deliberate or careless injurer. In this regard, the harm that one does by denying a person his autonomy over his body is similar to the harm one does when one insults another by spitting in his face or hurling racist abuse at him. Thirdly, relational harms – by their very nature – can only be undone by action on the part of the harm-doers. That is why the harm done to my wife when a colleague calls her an 'insufferable white madam' is not undone when I, to console her, bring home an exquisite bunch of flowers – even if her pleasure at receiving the flowers is greater than her upset.

6.5 CONCLUSION

The central question in this chapter can be put several ways. Does the right to personal security require a delictual, and thus private law, response to bodily injury regardless of how and where it occurs? Does Scots law better give effect to the right to personal security than does South African law? Did the South African Constitutional Court get it wrong in the *Law Society* case? The chapter cannot claim to have provided a conclusive yes-answer to this question. But it has, hopefully, laid the foundation for one. It also, I hope, has shown that those who answer the question in the negative will have to pay closer attention to the nature and justification of corrective justice, and to the non-financial interests justifying the right to personal security, than they may hitherto have done.

To conclude, this chapter will briefly touch on a matter which it has not so far discussed, the omission whereof may appear surprising, namely the different legal status of the right to personal security in South African and

---

[71] These grounds reflect ideas to be found in Weinrib *The Idea of Private Law*, supra note 46, 'Correlativity, Personality, and the Emerging Consensus on Corrective Justice', supra note 46; Gordley 'Tort Law in the Aristotelian Tradition', supra note 48; Wright 'Right, Justice, and Tort Law', supra note 56; and Brudner *The Unity of the Common Law*, supra note 56.

Scots law. In South African law, the right appears in a Bill of Rights which not only requires that all the rights therein have so-called 'vertical' and 'indirect horizontal' application, but also allows for the possibility that any one of the rights therein has 'direct horizontal' application.[72] In Scots law, by contrast, the right was incorporated by the Human Rights Act – but as a right which has no direct horizontal application and which, if it has any indirect horizontal application, has it in much weaker a form than in South African law.[73] Given this difference, one might have expected that the right to personal security would have had greater horizontal impact in South Africa than in Scotland. Yet quite the opposite appears to be the case.

Ask yourself this: how exactly does a legal system give the right to personal security horizontal effect? It does not do so in so far as it criminally prohibits certain kinds of bodily injuring. Nor does it do so by setting up tax-funded compensation schemes for those who suffer certain kinds of bodily injury. To do these things is – clearly and uncontroversially – to give the right vertical effect. So how, to repeat the question, does a legal system give the right to personal security horizontal effect? There is only one possible answer: it does so by treating certain kinds of injuring as wrongs justifying the imposition on the wrongdoers of an obligation to compensate their victims. Or, to put it another way, it does so by treating certain kinds of injuring as delicts: as private wrongs justifying a private law response.

This has two interesting and unexpected implications. First, it means that the South African Constitutional Court, in its *Law Society* judgment, effectively (and perhaps unwittingly) 'de-horizontalised' the constitutional right to personal security. For it held (in effect) that, though the right could be horizontally applied (by means of a 'private law delictual remedy'), it did not have to be – a vertical application of the right (by means of the criminal law and a statutory compensation scheme) sufficed. Secondly, it means that, notwithstanding the fact that the South African Bill of Rights places greater emphasis on the horizontal application of rights than does Scotland's Human Rights Act, Scots law in fact gives greater horizontal effect to the right to personal security than does South African law.

---

[72] The right is recognised by s 12 of the Constitution of the Republic of South Africa, Act 108 of 1996. Vertical application is required by s 8(1); indirect horizontal application is required by s 39(2); and direct horizontal application is (conditionally) required by ss 8(2) and 8(3).

[73] See N R Whitty and R Zimmermann 'Rights of Personality in Scots Law: Issues and Options' in Whitty and Zimmermann *Rights of Personality*, supra note 1, at 8–9.

Chapter 7

Privacy

F D J Brand

7.1 INTRODUCTION

The two human rights instruments involved are the European Convention on the Protection of Human Rights (1953) in Scotland and the Bill of Rights in chapter 2 of the Constitution[1] in South Africa. With regard to the protection of privacy the provisions of the two instruments are broadly similar. Yet, the impact of these provisions had been more predictable in South Africa than in Scotland, because South African common law already protected privacy as a separate right before the advent of the Constitution, while in Scots law the protection of privacy was unclear. In the post-constitutional dispensation, the effect of these provisions has also been more prominent and noticeable in South Africa than in Scotland, because the courts of the former have been directly confronted with the constitutional protection of privacy and other personality rights, while this has not yet happened in Scotland. This makes it easier to compare the position in Scotland with what has happened in South Africa, rather than the other way round.

7.2 SOUTH AFRICAN LAW

In the same way as article 8 of the European Convention on Human Rights does, s 14 of the South African Constitution protects privacy as a separate right – that is, in addition to the protection of other personality rights.[2] Section 14 provides:

'Everyone has the right to privacy, which includes the right not to have –
(a) their person or home searched;
(b) their property searched;
(c) their possessions seized; or
(d) the privacy of their communications infringed.'

---

[1] The Constitution of the Republic of South Africa, 1996.
[2] Rather surprisingly, the more 'popular' right to one's reputation, which lies at the heart of defamation actions, enjoys no such separate protection. Thus, reputation has been held to be included, for constitutional purposes, under 'dignity' in s 10. See, e.g., *Holomisa v Argus Newspapers Ltd* 1996 (2) SA 588 (W) at 606E-F.

The first three subsections obviously seek to protect an individual from wrongful searches and seizures. Even section 14(d), which approaches a broader protection of privacy, only extends to private communications. Yet the open-ended introduction to the section has been understood as a constitutional reinforcement to our common law protection of privacy.[3] There is no doubt that section 14 has horizontal application. This measure of certainty derives from section 8 of the Constitution. According to section 8(1), the Bill of Rights applies 'to all law and binds the legislature, the executive, the judiciary and all organs of state'.[4] Moreover, s 8(2) provides that the Bill of Rights binds 'a natural or a juristic person if, and to the extent that, it is applicable, taking into account the nature of the right and the nature of any duty imposed by the right'. Rather self-evidently, the nature of the right to privacy renders it eminently suitable for application in horizontal relationships.[5]

In terms of s 8(3) courts are required to apply and, if necessary, develop the common law to the extent that legislation does not give effect to a constitutionally protected right. Accordingly, the courts are enjoined to determine first whether a common law rule gives effect to the constitutional right. If there is such a rule, that rule regulates the relationship between private persons, and, subject to the constitutionality of that rule, the Constitution's reach into the exercise of private power is through the common law.[6] If the common law does not give effect to the right, the court must develop a common law rule to do so. This means that the Constitution again only reaches into the exercise of private powers through the medium of a common law rule. In developing the common law to give effect to the right, the court may limit a constitutional right, provided the limitation accords with s 36(1).[7] Equally important in the context of private law is the

---

[3]   See, e.g., *NM v Smith (Freedom of Expression Institute as amicus curiae)* 2007 (5) SA 250 (CC) at paras 27 and 126; J Burchell *Personality Rights and Freedom of Expression – The Modern Actio Injuriarum* (Juta 1998) 372; J Neethling, J M Potgieter and P J Visser *Neethling's Law of Personality* 2e (Butterworths 2005) 220.

[4]   Section 7(1) of the Interim Constitution, Act 200 of 1993, did not include the judiciary as one of the arms of government bound by the Bill of Rights. This was understood by the Constitutional Court in *Du Plessis v De Klerk* 1996 (3) SA 850 (CC) at paras 45–7 as an indication against horizontality. So, in s 8(1) of the 1996 Constitution, the judiciary was included to put beyond doubt the intention that the Bill of Rights has horizontal application.

[5]   On the other hand, the nature of the rights contained in s 35 in respect of arrested, detained and accused persons, for example, are clearly not enforceable against private individuals. H Cheadle, D Davis and N Hayson *South African Constitutional Law: The Bill of Rights* 2e (Butterworths 2005) ch 3 at 18.

[6]   See, e.g., *Fose v Minister of Safety and Security* 1997 (3) SA 786 (CC) at paras 16–19; *NM v Smith*, supra note 3, at paras 27–8.

[7]   Section 36(1) of the Constitution provides:

   '36. Limitation of rights. – (1) The rights in the Bill of Rights may be limited only in terms of law of general application to the extent that the limitation is reasonable and justifiable

injunction to the courts in s 39(2)[8] 'to interpret legislation and to develop the common law so as to promote the spirit, purport and objects of the Bill of Rights'. This means that, even in the absence of any direct reliance on a constitutional right that binds private persons, any future development and application of the common law must give effect to the underlying values of the Bill of Rights.

With regard to s 14 of the Constitution, the majority of the Constitutional Court held in *NM v Smith*[9] that the right to privacy relied upon by the claimants in that case was sufficiently protected by the common law as it stands and that it was therefore not necessary to consider whether any development was required. According to the minority judgments in *Smith*, only slight modifications to the common law were[10] or might be[11] necessary. Despite that, the Supreme Court of Appeal more recently held that the proper protection of personality rights enshrined by the Constitution requires an amendment to the principles of our common law.[12] But, speaking generally, experience has shown, with regard to claims for patrimonial loss under the *lex Aquilia* – which, by their nature come up more frequently for consideration by the courts – that the values of the Constitution do not often require development of the principles of common law and that the values of the Constitution have a more direct impact on the application of common law principles than on the principles themselves.[13] This tends to support the notion that the South African common law is inherently just and fair.

As in the case of the United Kingdom, South African common law is largely uncodified. Like Scots law, but unlike English law, South Africa has a law of delict rather than specific torts. However, a distinction is made in principle between conduct that causes patrimonial loss (*damnum iniuria*

---

in an open and democratic society based on human dignity, equality and freedom, taking into account all relevant factors, including –

    (a) the nature of the right;
    (b) the importance of the purpose of the limitation;
    (c) the nature and extent of the limitation;
    (d) the relation between the limitation and its purpose; and
    (e) less restrictive means to achieve the purpose.'

[8] Section 39(2) of the Constitution provides: '(2) When interpreting any legislation, and when developing the common law or customary law, every court, tribunal or forum must promote the spirit, purport and objects of the Bill of Rights'.

[9] Note 3 supra, at para 57.

[10] Per Langa CJ at paras 94–5.

[11] Per O'Regan J at paras 174–7.

[12] *Le Roux v Dey* 2010 (4) SA 210 (SCA). See however, the judgment by the Constitutional Court in *Le Roux v Dey* [2011] ZACC 4 at para 137, now reported as *Le Roux v Dey (Freedom of Expression Institute and Restorative Justice Centre as* Amici Curiae) 2011 (3) SA 274 (CC).

[13] E.g. *Minister of Safety and Security v Van Duivenboden* 2002 (6) SA 431 (SCA) paras 17 and 19; *Minister of Safety and Security v Carmichele* 2004 (3) SA 305 (SCA).

datum) and that which causes injury to personality (*iniuria*).[14] The action for compensation for patrimonial loss has its origin in the *lex Aquilia*, a Roman plebiscite of about 286 BC.[15] Protection for personality rights on the other hand derives from the *actio iniuriarum* which dates back even further to the Twelve Tables of about 450 BC.[16] Following upon the threefold distinction derived from Voet,[17] personality rights protected within the framework of the *actio iniuriarum* are categorised in South African law under the headings of *corpus*, *fama* and *dignitas*, that is, bodily integrity, dignity and reputation.[18] According to this classification, infringement of bodily integrity includes assault and wrongful deprivation of liberty. *Iniuria* affecting dignity would comprise insult and infringement of privacy while reputation is protected by the law of defamation. But, of course, these interests often overlap. Thus, although assault is an infringement of bodily integrity, it will often infringe the dignity of the victim as well, whereas impairment of one's reputation will usually also constitute an affront to one's dignity. This, however, does not mean that the same conduct will attract liability under the headings of both *dignitas* and *fama* since that would amount to a splitting of actions.[19]

In the pre-constitutional era, South African law for many years protected what later became recognised as manifestations of the right to privacy, both with reference to public disclosure of private facts as well as intrusions into the private sphere.[20] Examples of recognition of intrusions included entry into a private residence; listening to private telephone conversations ('bugging');[21] the reading of private documents[22] or private correspondence;[23] the looking through the complainant's window;[24] unauthorised medical

---

[14] See, e.g., J Neethling and J M Potgieter *Law of Delict* 6e (LexisNexis Butterworths 2010) 5; J Burchell *Principles of Delict* (Juta 1993) 11–12.

[15] *Guardian National Insurance Co Ltd v Van Gool NO* 1992 (4) SA 61 (A) at 63–4.

[16] M De Villiers *The Roman and Roman-Dutch Law of Injuries* (Juta 1899) 1; R Zimmermann *The Law of Obligations* (Juta 1990) 1050 et seq; Neethling, Potgieter and Visser *Law of Personality*, note 3 supra, at 39 et seq; H Walter *Actio Iniuriarum: Der Schutz der Persönlichkeit im südafrikanischen Privatrecht* (Duncker & Humblot 1996) 42.

[17] *Commentarius ad Pandectas* 47.10.1. The triad is taken from Ulpian D. 47, 10, 1, 2 – see Zimmermann, note 16 supra, at 1064 and 1083.

[18] See, e.g., *R v Umfaan* 1908 TS 62 at 66, *Universiteit van Pretoria v Tommie Meyer Films (Edms) Bpk* 1977 (4) SA 376 (T) at 384A-B.

[19] See *Le Roux v Dey*, note 12 supra, (SCA) at paras 20–5; (Constitutional Court) at paras 140–3.

[20] See *Bernstein v Bester and Others NNO* 1996 (2) SA 751 (CC) at para 69; *Financial Mail (Pty) Ltd v Sage Holdings Ltd* 1993 (2) SA 451 (A) at 462; D McQuoid-Mason 'Invasion of Privacy: Common Law v Constitutional Delict – Does it Make a Difference?' 2000 *Acta Juridica* 227 at 229–31.

[21] *Financial Mail (Pty) Ltd v Sage Holdings Ltd* 1993 (2) SA 451 (A); *S v A* 1971 (2) SA 293 (T) at 298.

[22] *Reid-Daly v Hickman* 1981 (2) SA 315 (ZA) at 323.

[23] *S v Hammer* 1994 (2) SACR 496 (C) at 498.

[24] *S v I* 1976 (1) SA 781 (RA) at 783F-H.

examinations[25] and the taking of unauthorised blood tests.[26] Publication of private facts included disclosure of private information obtained by illegal telephone tapping;[27] publishing a story about an intimate relationship between the claimant and a famous rugby player;[28] publishing photographs of persons implicated in a crime;[29] a doctor informing colleagues on an informal occasion that the claimant suffered from AIDS;[30] and the unauthorised use of photographs.[31]

Initially the courts did not regard privacy as a separate right but as included in the concept of dignity to which they gave a wide meaning.[32] Primarily through the influence of academic writers[33] the courts came to realise, however, that privacy is a separate identifiable right. Accordingly it was held that although there is nothing insulting about suffering from a terminal disease, the disclosure of that fact can constitute an invasion of the sufferer's right to privacy.[34] On the same basis it was held that although a corporate body 'has no feelings to outrage or offend' and that it can therefore suffer no impairment of its dignity (in the narrow sense) it indeed has a right of privacy to protect. In consequence, the defendant in *Financial Mail (Pty) Ltd v Sage Holdings (Pty) Ltd*[35] was interdicted from publishing information pertaining to the business operations of the claimant-corporation which was held to be private. Following this line of reasoning, privacy of corporations has also been recognised as a value protected by s 14 read with s 8(4) of the Constitution.[36] It cannot be said that the protection of privacy is as fully developed in South African law as the protection of other rights

---

[25] *Goldberg v Union and South West Africa Insurance Co Ltd* 1980 (1) SA 160 (E) at 164.

[26] *M v R* 1989 (1) SA 416 (O) at 426–7; *C v Minister of Correctional Services* 1996 (4) SA 292 (T) at 300.

[27] *Financial Mail (Pty) Ltd v Sage Holdings Ltd*, note 21 supra, at 463.

[28] *National Media Ltd v Jooste* 1996 (3) SA 262 (A).

[29] *La Grange v Schoeman* 1980 (1) SA 885 (E).

[30] *Jansen van Vuuren and Another NNO v Kruger* 1993 (4) SA 842 (A).

[31] *Mhlongo v Bailey* 1958 (1) SA 370 (W); *O'Keeffe v Argus Printing and Publishing Co Ltd* 1954 (3) SA 244 (C); *Kidson v SA Associated Newspapers Ltd* 1957 (3) SA 461 (W).

[32] See, e.g., *O'Keeffe* at 247; *S v A*, note 21 supra, at 297G-H.

[33] See, e.g., the reference, with approval, to W A Joubert *Grondslae van die Persoonlikheidsreg* (Balkema 1953) at 130–6 in *Jansen van Vuuren v Kruger*, note 30 supra, at 849E-F, and the reference, again with approval, to J Neethling, J M Potgieter and P J Visser *Deliktereg* 2e (Butterworths 1992) at 325 in *Financial Mail (Pty) Ltd v Sage Holdings Ltd*, note 21 supra, at 462B-E.

[34] See, e.g., *Jansen van Vuuren v Kruger*, note 30 supra; *NM v Smith*, note 3 supra.

[35] Note 21 supra, at 462A-B. See also, e.g., *Janit v Motor Industry Fund Administrators (Pty) Ltd* 1995 (4) SA 293 (A).

[36] *Investigation Directorate: Serious Economic Offences v Hyundai Motor Distributors (Pty) Ltd: In re Hyundai Motor Distributors (Pty) Ltd v Smit NO* 2001 (1) SA 545 (CC) at para 18. Section 8(4) of the Constitution provides: '(4) A juristic person is entitled to the rights in the Bill of Rights to the extent required by the nature of the rights and the nature of that juristic person'.

of personality, such as dignity or reputation. In the course of developing the protection of privacy the courts have therefore often referred to more developed remedies deriving from the *actio iniuriarum*, particularly the action for defamation.[37] Following the lead of the defamation action, three requirements are traditionally formulated for liability under the *actio iniuriarum*,[38] namely (a) an infringement of a personality right; (b) wrongfulness and (c) *animus iniuriandi* or intent. Once the plaintiff establishes the infringement of a personality right, both wrongfulness and intent are presumed.[39] A defendant seeking to avoid liability must then raise a defence which rebuts either wrongfulness or intent. Until recently there was doubt as to the nature of the onus of rebuttal: whether it merely constitutes a duty to adduce evidence or a full onus.[40] That debate has now been settled in favour of a full onus: it must be discharged on a balance of probability.[41]

With regard to the infringement of the right to privacy it appears from the reported cases that the existence of the right often comes across as self-evident: the right to the seclusion of one's private home; the right to keep one's correspondence private; the right to keep one's state of health confidential, and so on. But I do not believe it can be said that South African law has yet succeeded in developing a definitive test for determining the exact nature and scope of the right to privacy. In *NM v Smith*[42] it was held that 'the nature and scope of the right [to privacy] envisage[s] a concept of the right to be left alone'. And that '[p]rivacy encompasses the right of a person to live his or her life as he or she pleases'. These definitions have, however, been criticised as too wide.[43] I tend to agree with this criticism. As was pointed out in *National Media Ltd v Jooste*,[44] an individual's right to privacy cannot be determined solely by that individual's wishes or will. The disclosure of numerous public scandals would be prevented if those involved could simply claim manifestly public information to be private, because they consider it to be so.

The test for privacy therefore requires at least an element of objectivity. On the other hand this does not mean that the will of the individual becomes irrelevant. As *National Media Ltd v Jooste*[45] further explained, though the

[37] See, e.g., *Jansen van Vuuren v Kruger*, note 30 supra; *NM v Smith*, note 3 supra.

[38] See, e.g., *R v Umfaan*, note 18 supra, at 66; *Suid-Afrikaanse Uitsaaikorporasie v O'Malley* 1977 (3) SA 394 (A) at 402 (hereafter '*SAUK v O'Malley*'); *Minister of Justice v Hofmeyr* 1993 (3) SA 131 (A) at 154; *NM v Smith*, note 3 supra, at para 55.

[39] See, e.g., *SAUK v O'Malley* at 402, *NM v Smith*, note 3 supra, at para 152–3; *National Media Ltd v Bogoshi* 1998 (4) SA 1196 (SCA) at 1201.

[40] See, e.g., *Borgin v De Villiers* 1980 (3) SA 556 (A) at 571.

[41] *Mohamed v Jassiem* 1996 (1) SA 673 (A) at 709H-I; *Hardaker v Phillips* 2005 (4) SA 515 (SCA) at para 14.

[42] Note 3 supra, at para 32–3.

[43] See, e.g., J Neethling 'The Right to Privacy, HIV/AIDS and Media Defendants' (2008) 125 *SALJ* 36 at 38–9.

[44] Note 28 supra, at 271.

[45] Note 28 supra, at 271D.

boundary of the right to privacy remains an objective question 'the general sense of justice does not require the protection of a fact that the interested party has no wish to keep private'. In this light it is likely that the courts will eventually formulate a test analogous to the one adopted for dignity (in the narrow sense) in *Delange v Costa*[46] namely, (a) the individual concerned must have a subjective expectation of privacy and (b) that expectation must be objectively reasonable.[47] As to when an expectation of privacy will be regarded as reasonable, some guidance can be attained from the notion expressed by Ackermann J in *Bernstein v Bester*[48] that the right to privacy lies on a *continuum*, where a high level of protection can be expected to the individual's intimate personal sphere. The more the individual inter-relates with the world, however, the more the right to privacy becomes attenuated.[49]

As to the requirement of *animus iniuriandi*, it has become well established in South African law that this requirement does not refer to malice, spite or ill-will; that it simply means the subjective intent to injure; and that it includes both *dolus directus* and *dolus eventualis*.[50] With regard to the action of defamation, the requirement of *animus iniuriandi* has changed over time. Under the influence of English law South African courts initially refused to accept that an action for defamation can be deflected on the grounds of absence of subjective intent to defame.[51] However, during the 1960s, the attitude of the courts began to change. It all started with a judgment of De Villiers AJ in *Maisels v Van Naeren*.[52] Eventually any remaining doubt about the issue was eliminated when the Appellate Division confirmed that *animus iniuriandi* was an essential element of defamation.[53]

Moreover, in accordance with the courts' understanding of the requirement of *animus iniuriandi*, it includes knowledge of wrongfulness. So-called 'colourless intent' does not suffice.[54] If the defendant therefore mistakenly believed that the occasion of publication was privileged where it was not, the defence of lack of *animus iniuriandi* would succeed, as it did in *Maisels*. This gave rise to problems with the media who could get away with publication of the most blatant and damaging untruths, as long as they thought that these statements were true. And it matters not how careless these mistakes turned

---

[46]　1989 (2) SA 857 (A) at 862. See also *Le Roux v Dey* – (Constitutional Court) note 12 supra, at paras 147–9; 178 et seq. Neethling, Potgieter and Visser *Law of Personality*, note 3 supra, at 221; McQuoid-Mason, note 20 supra, at 232.

[47]　As I see it, this corresponds with the test laid down by the House of Lords in *Campbell v MGN Ltd* [2004] 2 AC 457 (HL) at paras 21, 94–6, 134–7 as a yardstick for what constitutes private or confidential information.

[48]　Note 20 supra, at para 77.

[49]　See also *Hyundai*, note 36 supra, at para 15.

[50]　See, e.g., *SAUK v O'Malley*, note 38 supra, at 402G-H.

[51]　See, e.g., *Jooste v Claassens* 1916 TPD 723 at 732; *Mankowitz v Geyser* 1928 OPD 138 at 139.

[52]　1960 (4) SA 836 (C).

[53]　*SAUK v O'Malley*, note 38 supra, at 402.

[54]　See, e.g., *SAUK v O'Malley*, note 38 supra, at 403C-D.

out to be. In the result, the courts went to the other extreme with regard to the media by imposing strict or no-fault liability on them.[55] This resulted in a material constraint on the freedom of the press, as was vividly illustrated by the facts of *Neethling v Du Preez*.[56]

Following the advent of the Constitution, the South African courts were confronted with the constitutionality of the media's position. The conclusion arrived at by the Supreme Court of Appeal in *National Media Ltd v Bogoshi*[57] was that the imposition of strict liability on the media was indeed unduly restrictive of the constitutionally enshrined right to freedom of the press. At the same time, Hefer JA, writing for the court, accepted that there are compelling reasons why the media should be treated differently from ordinary members of the public and that media defendants can therefore only escape liability if the publication was reasonable.[58]

What should immediately be pointed out is that in making the defence of reasonable publication available to the press in *Bogoshi*, the court's focus was not so much on the element of fault. Its real focus was on the element of wrongfulness, to which I shall presently return. Primarily, reasonable publication was therefore introduced as a ground for justification, that is, as a defence excluding wrongfulness and not as a defence excluding fault.[59] Nonetheless, it also touched on the element of fault. As Hefer JA himself pointed out,[60] if the media could rely on absence of *animus iniuriandi* as a defence excluding fault, it would make a nonsense of the requirement under the rubric of wrongfulness that the mistake must be reasonable. From the perspective of the fault element, negligence can therefore be accepted as the criterium for media liability.[61] In *Khumalo v Holomisa*[62] the Constitutional Court held the common law of defamation, as far as liability of the media is concerned, to be in accordance with the Constitution. As formulated in *Bogoshi*, so the Constitutional Court held, the common law of defamation struck the right balance between freedom of expression of the media – protected by s 16 of the Constitution – and the right to reputation – protected by s 10. But the court expressly held that, were the Supreme Court

---

[55] *SAUK v O'Malley*, note 38 supra, at 404G-405B; *Pakendorf v De Flamingh* 1982 (3) SA 146 (A) at 156.

[56] *Neethling v Du Preez; Neethling v The Weekly Mail* 1994 (1) SA 708 (A).

[57] 1998 (4) SA 1196 (SCA).

[58] At 1214E-I.

[59] See, e.g., *Bogoshi*, note 57 supra, at 1212F-G.

[60] At 1214C-E.

[61] See, e.g., *Marais v Groenewald* 2001 (1) SA 634 (T) at 646A-B; *Mthembi-Mahanyele v Mail & Guardian Ltd* 2004 (6) SA 329 (SCA) at paras 44–6. See also J Burchell 'The Legal Protection of Privacy in South African Law: A Transplantable Hybrid' (2009) 13(1) *Electronic Journal of Comparative Law* 10, available at *http://www.ejcl.org/131/art131-2.pdf*. Cf J R Midgley 'Media Liability for Defamation' (1999) 116 *SALJ* 211 at 214–15; A Fagan 'Rethinking Wrongfulness in the Law of Delict' (2005) 122 *SALJ* 90 at 101–6.

[62] 2002 (5) SA 401 (CC).

of Appeal not to have created the defence of reasonable publication, the common law would not have made the constitutional grade.

Subsequently, it was held in *NM v Smith*[63] that the constitutional right to privacy is sufficiently protected by the common law as amended in *Bogoshi*. The cause of action relied upon by the plaintiffs in *Smith* was that their HIV-positive status had been published by the defendants without consent. The defence raised was lack of knowledge of wrongfulness. The first and third defendants – the author and publisher of the publication – were classified as 'media defendants' while the second defendant was regarded as 'an ordinary defendant'.[64] At the trial all three defendants conceded that as a fact, plaintiffs did not consent to publication.[65] The defence raised was that they were under the bona fide impression, albeit mistakenly so, that they were justified by consent and therefore had no knowledge of wrongfulness. The majority held that all three defendants were aware that the plaintiffs had not consented, or at least had reconciled themselves with the possibility that the plaintiffs had not consented, which constituted *animus iniuriandi* in the form of *dolus eventualis*.[66] Langa CJ disagreed that *dolus* had been established but found the defendants negligent in their failure to verify the consent. He therefore held the two media defendants liable but absolved the second defendant.[67] O'Regan J, on the other hand, found that the defendants were not negligent in their belief that the plaintiff had consented to the publication.[68]

However, since the decision in *Smith* the Supreme Court of Appeal's views about the requirement of knowledge of wrongfulness as part of *animus iniuriandi* have undergone a dramatic change in *Le Roux v Dey*.[69] Dey was the vice-principal of a well-known secondary school in Pretoria. The three defendants were learners at the school. They found a picture on the Internet of two naked, gay bodybuilders in a compromising position. They then manipulated the picture by posting the photograph of Dey on the face of the one bodybuilder and the face of the principal of the school on the other. Thereafter they distributed the manipulated picture at the school. One of the defences raised was lack of *animus iniuriandi* in that the defendants did not realise the wrongfulness of their conduct.[70] Harms DP went into the history as to how knowledge of wrongfulness came to be regarded as an element of *animus iniuriandi* in South African law. The conclusion he arrived at was that

---

[63] *NM v Smith*, note 3 supra. See Madala J (para 57); Langa CJ (para 94); O'Regan J (paras 170–82) Sachs J (para 203).

[64] Langa CJ (paras 98 and 99); O'Regan J (para 182).

[65] See para 123.

[66] At para 64.

[67] At paras 98 et seq.

[68] At paras 183–9.

[69] Note 12 supra.

[70] At para 26. See however, *Le Roux v Dey*, Constitutional Court, note 12 supra, at para 137.

so-called 'coloured intent' was never required in Roman-Dutch law and that it had been introduced by the continental Pandectists during the nineteenth century.[71] That development, he decided, was unfortunate. And, so he held, since it is not too late to turn back the clock, knowledge of wrongfulness should no longer be recognised as an element of *animus iniuriandi* in the South African law of delict.[72] Apart from the historical consideration, Harms DP also advanced another reason for getting rid of the concept of coloured intent, which is of perhaps even greater importance in the present context, when he said:[73]

> 'It appears to me to be incongruous that a defendant who, for example, cannot establish truth and public benefit to justify defamation, can nevertheless escape liability by relying on a belief in either the truth or public benefit. Not only that, the approach also inhibits the development of this part of the law under the Constitution.'

After *Le Roux animus iniuriandi* therefore requires no more than the intention to infringe a personal right. But that does not mean, so Harms DP explained in *Le Roux*, that mistaken belief of justification becomes irrelevant. Mistake, he said, might in appropriate circumstances justify an infringement of personal rights if it was reasonably made. With that comment, as I understand it, he did two things. First, he extended the defence of reasonable publication, which *Bogoshi* made available to the media only, to non-media defendants as well. Secondly, he essentially shifted the role of (reasonably) mistaken justification from the category of fault to that of wrongfulness.[74]

The correctness of the decision in *Le Roux* on this aspect was expressly left open by the Constitutional Court in its judgment reported under the same name.[75] As far as protection of privacy is concerned, it appears to be at odds with the approach in *Smith*. But at the moment the Supreme Court of Appeal judgment in *Le Roux* represents South African law. It undoubtedly brings a substantial change, not only with regard to defamation, but also with reference to all personality rights, including privacy. While up to now the focus has often been on the element of fault, it will now shift to wrongfulness. It is true that outside the ambit of knowledge of wrongfulness a distinction will still be drawn between the media, on the one hand, and non-media defendants on the other. For non-media defendants *dolus* will still be the requirement. For the media *culpa* will suffice. But, in practice, cases

---

[71] At para 29. J R Midgley and J C van der Walt 'Delict' in W Joubert (ed) *The Law of South Africa* 2e (LexisNexis Butterworths 2003) vol 8 (1) para 105 note 3.

[72] At para 39.

[73] At para 37. See also van Dijkhorst R in *Marais v Groenewald*, supra note 61, at 646.

[74] This shift had been predicted five years earlier by Anton Fagan in 'Rethinking Wrongfulness in the Law of Delict' (2005) 122 *SALJ* 90 at 117 et seq.

[75] *Le Roux v Dey (Freedom of Expression Institute and Restorative Justice Centre as Amici Curiae)* 2011 (3) SA 274 (CC).

where the defence of mistake will succeed, outside the field of knowledge of wrongfulness, will in my view be rare. The defence of mistake will probably still succeed in circumstances illustrated by *Hulton & Co v Jones*[76] where the defendants had published defamatory statements of a person named Artemus Jones, who they believed to be a fictitious character, but was held to refer to the plaintiff, a real person who happened to have the same name. Or where the defendant inadvertently walked into a private room or overheard a confidential conversation. Or where a letter containing private information had been delivered to the wrong address.[77] But it is the rarity of these examples, I believe, that illustrates the point.

This brings me to the element of wrongfulness, sometimes also referred to as unlawfulness, though the former appears to be the more common and juristically preferable term.[78] What is meant by wrongfulness in the present context is that the infringement of privacy is actionable. And according to established South African dogma, wrongfulness is a matter for judicial determination, involving criteria of public and legal policy consistent with constitutional norms.[79] This is therefore primarily the level for balancing the rival constitutional norms of freedom of the media, on the one hand, and the right to privacy, on the other. In defamation actions the defendant usually seeks to rebut the element of wrongfulness by relying on one or other of the well-established defences which either own their origin or bear the influence of English law, referred to as grounds of justification. These typically include privileged occasion (absolute or qualified) and fair comment.[80] But these well-established defences do not constitute a *numerus clausus*. In the final analysis the question whether conduct is adjudged wrongful or not usually depends on a balancing of conflicting rights. Nonetheless, as Scott JA said in *Hardaker v Phillips*,[81] the well-established grounds of justification remain both useful and convenient and in addition, have the advantage of affording litigants a degree of certainty.

In view of the correspondence perceived in South African law between defamation and the protection of privacy, it is not surprising that the well-established defences in the law of defamation have found their way into actions aimed at the protection of privacy. Thus, for example, in *Jansen van Vuuren v Kruger*[82] the defendant relied on qualified privilege. Another

---

[76]   *E Hulton & Co v Jones* 1910 AC 20.

[77]   *Tothill v Foster* 1925 TPD 857.

[78]   See, e.g., *Delange v Costa*, supra note 46, at 861C-D.

[79]   See, e.g., *Bogoshi*, note 57 supra, at 1204D-E; *Trustees, Two Oceans Aquarium Trust v Kantey & Templer (Pty) Ltd* 2006 (3) SA 138 (SCA) at paras 10–12.

[80]   See, e.g., H Scott 'Liability for the Mass Publication of Private Information in South African Law: *NM v Smith (Freedom of Expression Institute as Amicus Curiae)*' (2007) 18 *Stellenbosch LR* 387 at 392.

[81]   Note 41 supra, at para 15.

[82]   Note 30 supra, at 851.

defence originating from the law of defamation that has been raised in the sphere of privacy is that of truth and public benefit.[83] Of relevance with regard to this defence, however, is the fact that unlike in the English[84] and Scots[85] law of defamation, truth in itself is not a defence in South African law. In order to succeed, the defendant must also show that the publication of the (true) defamatory allegation was for the public benefit.[86] In cases aimed at the protection of privacy, the information disclosed is mostly true. In consequence the defence in this sphere mostly turns on the element of public interest.

In *Bogoshi*[87] the Supreme Court of Appeal created a new ground of justification for the media in defamation actions that came to be known as the defence of reasonable or justifiable publication.[88] This defence has since been extended by *Le Roux*[89] in two ways: first, to non-media defendants, and, secondly, to all forms of *iniuria*, including breach of privacy. Even if it should therefore be found that the publication of private information was untrue or not in the public benefit, the alternative defence of reasonable publication may be available. But the most significant ground of justification in the context of privacy will probably remain consent to publication. When this defence is raised, the issues often turn on the ambit of the consent – whether it had (expressly or impliedly) been given only for a particular purpose or only on certain terms and, if so, whether the limits thus established had been exceeded by the defendant.[90]

Since the action for invasion of privacy derives from the *actio iniuriarum*, the plaintiff has a claim for general damages. Because these damages are intended as a *solatium* and not as compensation for actual loss, proof of actual damages is not required. There is no formula for the determination of general damages. It flows from the infinite number of varying factors that may come into play.[91] As to a claim for special damages, the Supreme Court

---

[83] See, e.g., *Financial Mail (Pty) Ltd v Sage Holdings Ltd*, note 21 supra.

[84] See, e.g., *Reynolds v Times Newspapers Ltd* [2001] 2 AC 127 (HL) at 192.

[85] See, e.g., K McK Norrie *Defamation and Related Actions in Scots Law* (Butterworths 1995) 125–7; N R Whitty 'Overview of Rights of Personality' in N R Whitty and R Zimmermann (eds) *Rights of Personality in Scots Law: A Comparative Perspective* (Dundee University Press 2009) 147 at 180–1. Some Scottish writers have argued, however, for the survival of a form of verbal injury in which *veritas convicii* is not a defence. For a (rather sceptical) overview see, e.g., E C Reid *Personality, Confidentiality and Privacy in Scots Law* (W Green 2010) paras 8.01–8.15.

[86] See, e.g., *Independent Newspapers Holdings Ltd v Suliman* [2004] 3 All SA 137 (SCA); *Financial Mail (Pty) Ltd v Sage Holdings Ltd*, note 21 supra, at 463B-464G; *South African Associated Newspapers Ltd v Yutar* 1969 (2) SA 442 (A).

[87] *National Media Ltd v Bogoshi* 1998 (4) SA 1196 (SCA).

[88] See, e.g., Lewis JA in *Mthembi-Mahanyele v Mail & Guardian Ltd*, note 61 supra, at para 44.

[89] *Le Roux v Dey* 2010 (4) SA 210 (SCA).

[90] See, e.g., *O'Keeffe*, note 31 supra; *National Media Ltd v Jooste*, note 28 supra.

[91] See, e.g., *Jansen van Vuuren v Kruger*, note 31 supra, at 857J-858A.

of Appeal recently held with regard to defamation that the *actio iniuriarum* and its derivative actions, are not available for the recovery of actual loss which must be claimed under the *actio legis Aquiliae*.[92]

7.3 SCOTLAND AND ENGLAND

In common with the rest of the United Kingdom, Scotland does not have its own statement of fundamental human rights. Although the United Kingdom was a signatory to the European Convention for the Protection of Human Rights and Fundamental Freedoms (1953) there is no obvious connection between the Convention and the delict or torts of contracting states. In fact, prior to 1998 the approach of both academic lawyers and the courts in the United Kingdom was that the Convention only protected the individual against the acts of public authorities and therefore had little, if any, effect on the development of the law of tort or delict in cases between private citizens.[93] What lent impetus to the consideration of human rights in the development of private law was the passage of the Human Rights Act and the Scotland Act, both in 1998. These two statutes had been described by Lord Mance in *Somerville v The Scottish Ministers*[94] as 'essential elements of the architecture of the modern United Kingdom'.

The Convention values that are of relevance for present purposes are to be found in articles 8 and 10. The debate whether the Human Rights Act 1998 caused the provisions of the Convention to have a so-called direct or indirect horizontal effect[95] between citizens or whether that was in any event the position before that Act came into operation,[96] is of no particular concern to us. This is so because the courts in the United Kingdom, including the House of Lords, have consistently held that the values enshrined by articles 8 and 10 of the Convention are as much applicable between individuals as they are in disputes between individuals and public authorities.[97] In consequence, the courts have accepted that they are bound by article 8

---

[92]　*Media 24 Ltd v SA Taxi Securitisation (Pty) Ltd (Avusa Media Ltd and Others as* Amici Curiae) 2011 (5) SA 329 (SCA).

[93]　See H L MacQueen 'Delict, Contract, and the Bill of Rights: A Perspective from the United Kingdom' (2004) 121 *SALJ* 359; Buxton LJ in *Wainwright v Home Office* [2002] QB 1334 (CA) at para 62; Lord Hoffman in *Wainwright v Home Office* [2004] 2 AC 406 at paras 14 and 51.

[94]　[2007] UKHL 44; 2008 SC (HL) 45 at para 169.

[95]　See, e.g., S D Pattinson and D Beyleveld 'Horizontal Applicability and Horizontal Effect'(2002) 118 *Law Quarterly Review* 623; H MacQueen and D Brodie 'Private Rights, Private Law, and the Private Domain' in A Boyle, C Himsworth, H MacQueen and A Loux (eds) *Human Rights and Scots Law* (Hart 2002) 141 at 153–4; MacQueen, note 93 supra, at 366.

[96]　See, e.g., *von Hannover v Germany* (2004) 40 EHRR 1 at para 57; Resolution 1165 (1998) of the Parliamentary Assembly of the Council of Europe on the right to privacy, at para 12; *Douglas v Hello! Ltd (No 3)* [2006] QB 125 at para 47.

[97]　See, e.g., *Campbell v MGN Ltd*, note 47 supra, per Lord Nicholls (at paras 17 and 18); per Lord Hoffman (at para 50); per Lord Hope (at para 86).

(read with article 10) of the Convention to give effect to the protection of privacy.

So far the Scottish courts have not been directly confronted by the impact of article 8 on the common law. In England, on the other hand, that challenge had been presented to the Court of Appeal in the case of *Douglas v Hello! Ltd*[98] soon after the Human Rights Act came into operation on 2 October 2000. The difficulties encountered by English lawyers are well illustrated in that case. Mr Douglas and Ms Zeta-Jones, both famous film stars, were married in New York. They sold the exclusive rights to publish photographs of their wedding to the publishers of a celebrity magazine, *OK!*. But their wedding reception was infiltrated by a paparazzo who surreptitiously took photographs of the couple. He then sold the exclusive right to publish the unauthorised photographs in England to the publisher of another celebrity magazine, *Hello!*. When this was discovered by the famous couple and *OK!*, they sought and obtained an interlocutory injunction against *Hello!* restraining publication.

Hello! appealed the injunction in the Court of Appeal. In response the two film stars relied on an infringement of their right to privacy. Their difficulty was, however, that the Court of Appeal had decided in rather uncompromising terms in *Kaye v Robertson*[99] that 'in English law there is no right to privacy, and accordingly there is no right of action for breach of a person's privacy'. Though this difficulty would appear to be insurmountable, all three members of the Court of Appeal found a potential remedy for the famous couple in the equitable doctrine of breach of confidence.[100] As Brooke LJ went on to explain,[101] breach of confidence is not a tort. It had been developed by the Court of Chancery, in the exercise of its equitable jurisdiction, to restrain freedom of speech in circumstances in which it would be unconscionable to publish confidential material. The notion underlying the doctrine was therefore that once information had been obtained in confidence, the recipient's conscience was bound by that confidence not to publish the information to others.[102] Originating from this underlying notion, application of the doctrine traditionally required some relationship of confidence between the confider and the confidant.[103]

However, as the members of the court pointed out, there had been a movement away from requiring a pre-existing confidential relationship in breach of confidence actions, even before the advent of the Human Rights

[98] [2001] QB 967 (CA).
[99] [1991] FSR 62 (CA), per Glidewell LJ at 66.
[100] See Brooke LJ (at para 96); Sedley LJ (at para 126) and Keene LJ (at para 166).
[101] At para 65.
[102] See, e.g., *Stephens v Avery* [1988] Ch 449 at 456; *Attorney-General v Observer Ltd* [1998] 2 WLR 805 (CA) at 904.
[103] See, e.g., Megarry J in *Coco v A N Clark (Engineers) Ltd* [1968] FSR 415 at 419; *Campbell v MGN Ltd*, note 47 supra, at para 44.

Act.[104] What the Act has done, they said, was to lend impetus to the movement in order to give effect to the protection of privacy in article 8 of the
Convention.[105] As a result of these developments, Sedley LJ concluded,
'[W]e have reached a point at which it can be said with confidence that the
law recognises and will appropriately protect a right of personal privacy',[106]
and that, 'The law no longer needs to construct an artificial relationship
of confidentiality between intruder and victim: it can recognise privacy
itself as a legal principle drawn from the fundamental value of personal
autonomy'.[107]

These statements by Sedley LJ were relied upon by the claimants in
Wainwright v Home Office[108] in support of their contention that English law
had reached the stage of development where invasion of privacy has become
recognised as a separate tort. The complaint in *Wainwright* had nothing to
do with the publication of confidential information. The invasion of privacy
relied upon by Mrs Wainwright and her handicapped son was that, on occasion of their visit to a family member in prison, they had been strip-searched
by prison officials, contrary to prison rules and in a humiliating fashion.
Unsurprisingly in the circumstances the claimants did not seek to rely on the
action for breach of confidence, but on invasion of privacy as an independent tort. For the existence of such a tort in English law they sought to find
support in the statements of Sedley LJ in *Douglas*. But in *Wainwright*, the
Court of Appeal would have none of this. Buxton LJ firmly denied the existence of the independent tort contended for, essentially for three reasons.[109]
First, the recognition of such a tort is precluded by the earlier authority
of *Kaye v Robertson*.[110] Secondly, the creation of such a new tort would fall
outside the ambit of the courts' authority and should thus be reserved for
the legislature. Thirdly, considerations of policy did not, in his view, favour
the creation of a new tort protecting privacy in general. What Buxton LJ
found of particular concern from a policy perspective related, so it seems,
mainly to issues of conceptualisation and limitation.[111]

Broadly speaking, the House of Lords agreed with Buxton LJ.[112] Writing
for the House, Lord Hoffman likewise concluded that English law recognises
no general cause of action for invasion of privacy.[113] As to the statements by

---

[104] See, e.g., *Attorney-General v Observer Ltd* [1990] 1 AC 109 at 281.
[105] See, e.g., Sedley LJ (at paras 118 and 125) and Keene LJ (at paras 165–7).
[106] At para 110.
[107] At para 126.
[108] [2002] QB 1334 (CA) at 1340C-D and para 96.
[109] [2002] QB 1334 (CA) paras 97–111.
[110] [1991] FSR 62 (CA).
[111] See paras 108–12. See also, e.g., Jonathan Lewis 'Privacy: A Missed Opportunity' (2005) 13
       Tort Law Review 166 at176.
[112] See *Wainwright v Home Office* [2004] 2 AC 406 (HL).
[113] At para 23.

Sedley LJ in *Douglas*, relied upon by the claimants for their contention to the contrary, Lord Hoffman said the following:[114]

'I read these remarks as suggesting that, in relation to the publication of personal information obtained by intrusion, the common law breach of confidence has reached the point at which a confidential relationship has become unnecessary. As the underlying value protected is privacy, the action might as well be renamed invasion of privacy. . . . I do not understand Sedley LJ to have been advocating the creation of a high-level principle of invasion of privacy. His observations are in my opinion no more (although certainly no less) than a plea for the extension and possibly renaming of the old action for breach of confidence. As Buxton LJ pointed out in this case in the Court of Appeal,[115] . . . such an extension would go further than any English court has yet gone and would be contrary to some cases (such as *Kaye v Robertson* . . .)[116] in which it positively declined to do so. The question must wait for another day. But Sedley LJ's dictum does not support a principle of privacy so abstract as to include the circumstances of the present case.'

In consequence of the unequivocal denial in *Wainwright* of an independent tort protecting the right to privacy in general, a bright line has evolved in English law between the unauthorised publication of private information, on the one hand, and invasion by means of what can be described as intrusions into private life, on the other. On the latter category *Wainwright* had closed the door. An interesting feature of *Wainwright*, however, is that the Scots case of *Henderson v Chief Constable, Fife Police*[117] was cited to the court but not followed. In addition, it appears that *Henderson* in turn relied upon an English case, *Lindley v Rutter*,[118] which arose from an inappropriate strip-search. Again this case was cited but not followed in *Wainwright*. Why *Henderson* and *Lindley* did not even merit a mention in the *Wainwright* speeches is not clear. What they do indicate, however, is that the position in Scots and English law was not as clearly defined as *Wainwright* might suggest. Subsequently, the European Court of Human Rights decided in *Wainwright v The United Kingdom*[119] that English law, as construed by the House of Lords in that case, constituted a breach of article 8 of the Convention.

In *Watkins v Secretary of State for the Home Department*[120] prison officials deliberately broke the prison rules by reading correspondence addressed to Mr Watkins by his solicitor. Though his conduct plainly constituted an invasion of privacy, the matter was not decided on that basis. What the House of Lords essentially held was that in English law the tort of misfeasance in

---

[114] At paras 29–30.
[115] [2002] QB 1334 (CA) at paras 96–9 (note added).
[116] Note 99 supra (note added).
[117] *Henderson v Chief Constable, Fife Police* 1988 SLT 361 (OH).
[118] *Lindley v Rutter* [1981] 1 QB 128.
[119] (2007) 44 EHRR 40.
[120] [2006] 2 AC 395 (HL).

public office was not actionable without proof of special damages and that, accordingly, in the absence of any special damages caused to Mr Watkins by the actions of the prison officers, his claim for damages could not succeed. In the course of his concurring speech, Lord Hope pertinently digressed to point out that the position in Scotland has long been settled to be the same.

In rather stark contrast with their approach to intrusions, English courts have shown a notable willingness to develop and extend the breach of confidence action in order to afford protection against the invasion of informational privacy. According to Lord Woolf CJ,[121] the courts were able to achieve this result by absorbing the rights which article 8 and 10 protect into the long-established action for breach of confidence. This thesis was endorsed and enhanced by the House of Lords in *Campbell v MGN Ltd*.[122] Ms Naomi Campbell was an internationally acclaimed fashion model who, while courting publicity, volunteered information to the media that she did not take drugs. MGN then published an article in its newspaper, *The Mirror*, which disclosed that Ms Campbell was in fact a drug addict and that she had attended meetings of Narcotics Anonymous. Details were given as to the frequency of these meetings and the article was illustrated by photographs of her on the doorstep of the building where such a meeting had just taken place. The photographs were taken covertly by a freelance photographer employed by MGN for this purpose. Ms Campbell claimed damages for breach of confidence. MGN's defence was that it was entitled, in the public interest, to publish the information in order to correct the claimant's misleading public statements.

Ms Campbell was successful in the court of first instance, but the Court of Appeal found for MGN. On a further appeal, the House of Lords reverted to the former decision by a majority of three to two. As it turned out, the difference of view in the House about the outcome proved to be of little consequence with regard to the general principles of law involved. While confirming that English law did not recognise an 'overarching, all-embracing cause of action for "invasion of privacy"',[123] there was consensus that, in order to protect informational privacy, the action for breach of confidence had been extended so that '[t]he essence of the tort is better encapsulated now as misuse of private information'.[124] 'The result of these developments' so it was said,[125]

> 'has been a shift in the centre of gravity of the action for breach of confidence when it is used as a remedy for the unjustified publication of personal information. . . .

---

[121] In *A v B Plc* [2003] QB 195 (CA) at para 4.
[122] [2004] 2 AC 457 (HL).
[123] Per Lord Nicholls (at para 11). See also Lord Hoffman (at para 43); Baroness Hale (at para 133).
[124] Per Lord Nicholls (at para 14).
[125] By Lord Hoffman (at para 51).

[T]he new approach takes a different view of the underlying value which the law protects. Instead of the cause of action being based upon the duty of good faith . . . it focuses upon the protection of human autonomy and dignity . . .'

Though it was held to be unnecessary for the purposes of *Campbell* to predict the prospective consequences of these new developments,[126] the House of Lords did in fact lay down some general principles for future guidance. So, for example, it accepted as the yardstick for what constitutes 'private information' the 'objective reasonable expectation test'. Accordingly it comprises of information in respect of which the person in question had a reasonable expectation that it would not be published.[127] Consideration was also given to the balancing exercise that the court is enjoined to perform when the article 8 right to privacy comes into conflict with the right to freedom of expression, guaranteed by article 10 of the Convention. In this regard the House of Lords confirmed what had previously been declared by the Council of Europe in its Resolution 1165 (1998), para 11, namely that neither of these two fundamental rights takes preference over the other. With regard to these two rights, it was further pointed out that both are qualified and restricted by articles 8(2) and 10(2) respectively, inter alia, with reference to what is acceptable in an open and democratic society, in order to protect the rights and interests of others.[128] Broadly stated, the conclusion arrived at seems to have been that an invasion of privacy, once established, can only be justified by reliance on the right to freedom of expression if publicity of the private information can be said to have been in the public interest.[129]

About one month after the decision in *Campbell* the European Court of Human Rights handed down its signpost judgment on the right of privacy in *von Hannover v Germany*.[130] The applicant in *von Hannover* was Princess Caroline, the eldest daughter of Prince Rainier III of Monaco. Over a period of many years she had brought proceedings in German courts against newspapers which published private information about her and her family without her consent. In this case three series of photographs were in issue. These photographs were taken not just of Princess Caroline herself but also of her children and in a variety of different locations. The German Federal Court held that publication of photographs taken in a secluded place in a restaurant was in breach of her right to privacy. The Federal Constitutional Court took the matter slightly further but refused her relief in respect of

---

[126] Per Lord Hoffman (at para 52–3).

[127] See, e.g., Lord Nicholls (at para 21); Lord Hope (at paras 94–6); Baroness Hale (at para 134–7).

[128] See, e.g., Lord Nicholls (at paras 19–20); Lord Hoffman (at paras 55–56); Lord Hope (at paras 85–6, 105–7 and 113–8); Baroness Hale (at paras 137–140).

[129] Lord Hoffman (at para 56); Lord Hope (at paras 107 and 117–18).

[130] (2005) 40 EHRR 1.

photographs consisting mostly of her skiing, shopping, riding and cycling in public places.

On a further appeal the European Court of Human Rights in Strasbourg pointed out that the applicant did not complain against any action by the German government, but against the lack of state protection of her private life.[131] With reference to this complaint the Court eventually agreed with the applicant that she had been afforded insufficient protection of her private life by German law and that there had thus been a breach of article 8 of the Convention by the German government.[132] In arriving at this conclusion the court did not agree with the principle of German law that figures of contemporary society generally deserve lesser protection of their private lives than others. Though the applicant was a member of the ruling family of Monaco, so the court held, she did not exercise any official functions.[133] In consequence the public right in some circumstances to be informed of the private lives of public figures, particularly politicians, did not find application in her case.[134]

The relevance of *von Hannover* for English law flows directly from s 2(1) of the Human Rights Act 1998 which requires the courts of the United Kingdom, when determining a question arising in connection with a convention right 'to take into account' any decision of the European Court of Human Rights. What this means is that though not bound by it, English courts should follow Strasbourg jurisprudence 'no more, but certainly no less'.[135] And the position in Scotland will clearly be the same. Following on *Campbell* and *von Hannover*, protection of privacy in the sphere of information had been successfully sought in the English courts with increasing regularity, particularly by celebrities and public figures. When the *Douglas v Hello! Ltd* saga therefore returned to the Court of Appeal,[136] the court appears to have had little difficulty in upholding the award of damages for breach of informational privacy in favour of the two film stars.

Further implementation of these principles appears from the cases that followed. One such case was *Murray v Express Newspapers Plc*.[137] The claimant in *Murray* was the infant son of Mrs Joanne Murray, better known as J K Rowling, the author of the Harry Potter series of books. The claim arose from a picture covertly taken by a photographer using a long-range lens of the claimant being pushed in a buggy by his parents in a public street

---

[131] At para 56.

[132] At paras 78–80.

[133] At para 62.

[134] At paras 64–5.

[135] *R (on the application of Ullah) v Special Adjudicator* [2004] 2 AC 323 (HL) at 350.

[136] In *Douglas v Hello! Ltd (No 3)* [2006] QB 125 (CA). The further appeal to the House of Lords did not concern the claim by the two film stars but that by the publishers. See *OBG Ltd v Allan !* [2008] 1 AC 1 (HL).

[137] [2007] EWHC 1908 (Ch) reversed *Murray v Express Newspapers Plc* [2008] EMLR 12.

in Edinburgh. Though the picture had already been published once, the claimant sought an injunction against its further publication. In the court of first instance it was held that, in applying the reasonable expectation of privacy test in these circumstances, regard should be had to the reasonable expectation of the parents rather than that of the infant claimant.[138] On the application of the test in this way, the court of first instance concluded that a reasonable expectation of privacy had not been established in respect of a routine activity when conducted in a public place.[139] This decision was however overturned by the Court of Appeal because, so it was held:[140]

> 'We do not share the predisposition identified by the [court a quo] that routine acts such as a visit to a shop or a ride on a bus should not attract any reasonable expectation of privacy. All depends upon the circumstances. The position of an adult may be very different from that of a child.'

As pointed out by Hector L MacQueen,[141] the decision of the Court of Appeal appears to extend *Campbell* and move in the direction of *von Hannover* so far as photography in public places is concerned. However, the real significance of *Murray*, as I see it, is its recognition that those who are not in themselves famous but merely related to a celebrity retain a legitimate expectation of privacy, in particular during childhood.[142]

7.4 SCOTLAND

Though *Murray* had its origin in the streets of Edinburgh, proceedings were, of course, launched south of the border. So, in Scotland the crucial question remains: how will the Scottish courts respond when they are directly confronted with the impact of article 8 on the common law? Elspeth Reid predicts[143] that, with regard to liability for the infringement of informational privacy, it is doubtful that Scottish defenders will escape liability in circumstances where their English counterparts would not. On the face of it, the difficulty with this prediction is that in English law the action for breach of confidence did not derive from common law but from equity, which does not fit easily within the framework of Scots law. That much was pointed out by Lord Coulsfield in a case which preceded the Human Rights Act in 1998,

---

[138] Para 66.

[139] Ibid.

[140] *Murray v Express Newspapers Plc* [2008] (CA), note 137 supra, at para 56.

[141] H L MacQueen 'A Hitchhiker's Guide to Personality Rights in Scots Law, Mainly with Regard to Privacy' in Whitty and Zimmermann, note 85 supra, 549 at 558.

[142] *Murray v Express Newspapers Plc* [2008] (CA), note 137 supra, at paras 56–7.

[143] E Reid 'Protection of Personality Rights in the Modern Scots Law of Delict' in Whitty and Zimmermann, note 85 supra, 247 at 303; E C Reid *Personality, Confidentiality and Privacy*, note 85 above, at para 14.55.

ie *Lord Advocate v Scotsman Publications Ltd.*[144] On appeal to the Inner House this doctrinal difficulty was, however, brushed aside by Lord Ross with the comment that '[t]he courts in Scotland administered an equitable as well as a common law jurisdiction'.[145] This view was endorsed in the House of Lords by the Scottish lawyer Lord Keith when he said: 'While the juridical basis may differ to some extent in the two jurisdictions, the substance of the law in both of them is the same'.[146]

What is more, the prediction that, as far as confidential information is concerned, the Scottish courts are likely to draw on recent English precedent appears to be supported by the approach of the Outer House in *X v British Broadcasting Corporation.*[147] While making a documentary about the work of the Glasgow Sheriff Court, an agent of the BBC photographed Ms X both in and outside the Court, in situations of humiliation and embarrassment to her. Though she gave her prior consent for the pictures to be published, she sought an interim interdict preventing such publication, essentially on the basis that the consent was invalid and had in any event been exceeded by the BBC's agent. In support of her case, Ms X relied on article 8 of the Convention to which the BBC predictably responded with a reliance on article 10. In performing the balancing act between the interests protected by these two sections, Temporary Judge Thompson made liberal use of English law as formulated, for example, in *Campbell.*[148] Eventually he did not decide the merits but granted the interim interdict on the basis that Ms X had real prospects of success and that the balance of convenience was in her favour. Of real interest for present purposes, however, is the instinctive approach by both counsel and the court to automatically revert to the principles of English law.

Nonetheless, it appears to me that, particularly in the light of the decisions in the Strasbourg court in *Peck v United Kingdom*[149] and *Wainwright v United Kingdom,*[150] the Scottish courts will have no option but to extend the protection of privacy beyond the confines of confidential information. Quite recently, various suggestions have been made by the contributors in *Rights of Personality in Scots Law: A Comparative Perspective*[151] and by Elspeth Christie Reid in *Personality, Confidentiality and Privacy in Scots Law*[152] as to how the Scottish courts can best achieve this goal. I will not presume to improve on their suggestions. For present purposes the enquiry is in my view much more

---

[144] 1989 SC (HL) 122 at 134.
[145] At 141–2.
[146] At 164.
[147] 2005 SCLR 740 (OH).
[148] *Campbell v MGN Ltd* [2004] 2 AC 457 (HL).
[149] (2003) 36 EHRR 41.
[150] (2007) 44 EHRR 40.
[151] Whitty and Zimmermann, note 85 supra, at 14–19; E Reid at 303 et seq; H L McQueen at 563–5 and 587–8.
[152] Note 85 supra, at ch 17.

focused. It is this: can the South African law of privacy be of any assistance to the Scottish courts? I believe the answer is: 'Yes, it can'. But that answer, of course, requires some motivation. The tempting argument is that South African law of privacy can provide inspiration to Scots law because they share the same ancestry of the *actio iniuriarum*. Though the common ancestry is of course a weighty consideration, I think the argument loses much of its force through the developments in the modern South African action for protection of personality rights, which renders it quite different from the remedy provided for in the Twelve Tables. As I see it, the common ancestry argument in itself therefore does not render South African law any more worthy of consideration than, say, German law which also has its roots in the *actio iniuriarum*[153] and could very well have more to offer both by way of research and practical examples.[154]

But I believe there are more compelling arguments why South African law deserves special consideration by Scottish lawyers. Perhaps most important in the present context is the fact that the two systems are guided by similarly formulated human rights instruments. Unlike most other documents of this kind, but in common with the Convention, the South African Constitution has a specific protection of the right to privacy which the courts in both systems are enjoined to implement through the development of the common law.[155] Moreover, in authorising limitations to this right, article 8(2) of the Convention refers to the criterion of what 'is necessary in a democratic society', which, broadly stated, is also the criterion of the limitation clause, namely s 36(1), in the South African Constitution. Ultimately sections 14 and 16 of the South African Constitution, in the same way as articles 8 and 10 of the Convention, require a balancing act between the right to privacy and the right to freedom of expression, where the one enjoys no preference over the other.

In the context of article 8 of the Convention, Elspeth Reid regards the *animus iniuriandi* element of the *actio iniuriarum* as one of the major difficulties in reverting to this Roman instrument as a model for the development of modern Scots law.[156] As I see it, her argument is indeed supported by the changes in South African law pertaining to both defamation and protection of privacy in order to reflect the values of the Constitution. But the point is that those changes have now been effected and that consequently the

---

[153] See, e.g., R Zimmermann, *The Law of Obligations* (Juta 1990) 1090–4.

[154] See, e.g., B S Markesinis and H Unberath *The German Law of Torts: A Comparative Treatise* 4e (Hart 2002) 74–8 and 412 et seq; A Teichmann in O Jauernig *Kommentar zum Bürgerliches Gesetzbuch* 13e (C H Beck 2009) § 823 Rn 65–88; D Looschelders *Schultrecht: Besonderer Teil* 4e (Vahlen 2010) Rn124 et seq (also with reference to Swiss and Austrian law in Rn 1237).

[155] See ss 8(3) and 39(2) of the South African Constitution and s 6 of the United Kingdom's Human Rights Act 1998.

[156] *Protection of Personality Rights*, note 143 supra, 305; *Personality, Confidentiality and Privacy*, note 85 supra, at paras 17.13 and 17.14.

South African common law actions for defamation and for the protection of privacy, based on the *actio iniuriarum*, have now passed the constitutional audit.

What is more, these changes in South African law, read with the recent changes in English law, have brought the two systems closer in many areas, including in those areas where reconciliation previously appeared to be improbable. So, for example, the South African courts have stepped down from insisting that infringement of personality rights is an intentional wrong. In most respects negligence will now suffice. That brought South African law close to the 'reasonable publication' defence in *Reynolds*.[157] English courts, on the other hand, have come to acknowledge and apply the public interest defence in confidential information cases,[158] an exercise which had been performed by South African courts in defamation cases for many years.

A well-known phenomenon in South Africa, which I have not encountered in either Scots or English law, is the transposition of the principles of law of defamation onto the law of privacy.[159] Perhaps that is something Scottish lawyers may consider. If so, they will find South African law even more familiar, since many grounds of justification in defamation actions, such as privilege (qualified or absolute), fair comment, and so on[160] have their origin in English law.

But perhaps the most significant correlation between Scotland and South Africa lies in our shared tradition of *stare decisis* and its concomitant of judge-made law. Inherent in the system appears to be a resistance to change. As Sir Stephen Sedley once said,[161] the motto of an English judge is that one should never do anything for the first time. South African judges are guided by the same light.[162] The reasons for this are explained with admirable eloquence and clarity by Lord Simon in *Miliangos v George Frank (Textiles) Ltd* when he said:[163]

---

[157] *Reynolds v Times Newspapers Ltd* [2001] 2 AC 127 (HL).

[158] See, e.g., *Campbell v MGN Ltd* [2004] 2 AC 457 (HL).

[159] Though there is a tendency in English cases to use the same terminology, for example in assessing public interest for the purposes of determining whether publication of false information was reasonable or whether disclosure of private information was justified. See, e.g., *Jameel v Wallstreet Journal Europe Sprl* [2007] 1 AC 359 (HL) on defamation, Baroness Hale says (at para 147) that there is no public interest in 'vapid tittle-tattle about the activities of footballers' wives'. This very phrase is cited in *McKennitt v Ash* [2008] QB 73 (CA) at para 66.

[160] For these defences in Scots law of defamation, see, e.g., K Norrie *Defamation and Related Actions in Scots Law* (Butterworths 1995).

[161] S Sedley 'Sex, Libels and Video-Surveillance' (The Blackstone Lecture, Pembroke College, Oxford, 13 May 2006) available at *http://www.judiciary.gov.uk/media/speeches/2006/speech-sedley-lj-13052006*.

[162] See, e.g., M M Corbett 'Aspects of the Role of Policy in the Evolution of our Common Law' (1987) 104 *SALJ* 52 at 56.

[163] [1976] AC 443 (HL) at 481.

'[T]he training and qualification of a judge is to elucidate the problem immediately before him, so that its features stand out in stereoscopic clarity. But the beam of light which so illuminates the immediate scene seems to throw surrounding areas into greater obscurity: the whole landscape is distorted to the view. A penumbra can be apprehended, but not much beyond; so that when the searchlight shifts a quite unexpected scene may be disclosed.'

Maybe this fear of the unknown and of unintended consequences on the part of Scottish courts may be quelled by having regard to a kindred legal system in South Africa where a general law of privacy had been acknowledged and applied for some time. Some of the policy difficulties that persuaded Buxton LJ[164] to resist the extension of privacy protection may be found to have been resolved in South African law. Or, to mirror the words of Lord Simon, in having regard to South African law it may appear that the searchlight had already been shifted, so as to change the penumbra to greater clarity.

---

[164] In *Wainwright v Home Office* (CA), note 93 supra, at paras 108–12.

Chapter 8

Defamation and Freedom of Expression

*Jonathan Burchell**

8.1 INTRODUCTION

Earlier research on the Scots and South African law of defamation traced the origins of both systems of law, identifying common Roman threads and focusing on points of convergence and areas of divergence in later development.[1] This chapter will focus less on origins and elements of liability for defamation in each of these two mixed jurisdictions and more on the impact of human rights norms on specific areas of the law of defamation, the future direction of defamation law in both jurisdictions and its potential role in regulating cyberspace communication.

8.2 COMMON GROUND

It appears that *facets* of defamation law, under pressure to find a more viable balance between protection of reputation and freedom of expression, are in the process of being moulded by judges in the United Kingdom and Commonwealth jurisdictions into broadly compatible principles. The courts in Australia and New Zealand opted for a reasonableness test[2] for

---

* I am indebted to Elspeth Reid of the Faculty of Law, University of Edinburgh for her detailed and insightful comments on the draft of this chapter and for drawing my attention to some important authorities, both ancient and modern.

1 J Burchell 'The Protection of Personality Rights' in R Zimmermann and D Visser (eds) *Southern Cross – Civil Law and Common Law in South Africa* (Juta 1996) 639; J Blackie 'Defamation' in K Reid and R Zimmermann (eds) *A History of Private Law in Scotland* vol 2 (Oxford University Press 2000) 633; and J Burchell and K McK Norrie 'Impairment of Reputation, Dignity and Privacy' in R Zimmermann, D Visser and K Reid (eds) *Mixed Legal Systems in Comparative Perspective: Property and Obligations in Scotland and South Africa* (Oxford University Press 2004) 545.

2 *Lange v Australian Broadcasting Corporation* (1997) 189 CLR 520; *Lange v Atkinson* [1998] 3 NZLR 424. The Privy Council, [2000] 1 NZLR 257, in an appeal in the latter case handed down a decision on the same day as the House of Lords (with the same judges) decided the English case of *Reynolds v Times Newspapers Ltd* [2001] 2 AC 127, and remitted *Lange* back to the New Zealand Court of Appeal to reconsider their decision in the light of *Reynolds*. The Court of Appeal did so and confirmed their earlier decision: [2000] 3 NZLR 385.

'political discussion'. In the United Kingdom, broadening the scope of the defence of privileged occasion in *Reynolds v Times Newspapers*[3] provided the catalyst which has led, as Lord Hoffmann said in *Jameel v Wall Street Journal Europe Sprl*,[4] to more of a 'public interest'[5] than an expanded privileged occasion defence. In South Africa the Supreme Court of Appeal in *National Media Ltd v Bogoshi*[6] affirmed a 'reasonable publication' defence for the media.[7] In Canada the Supreme Court confirmed a new defence of 'responsible communication on matters of public interest' in defamation.[8] While there may be differences in emphasis between the approaches in these various Commonwealth jurisdictions,[9] the general tenor of the developments in defamation law is broadly similar: twentieth-century rules of defamation, in providing strict protection of individual reputation, have not provided adequate protection for freedom of expression. A supple, objectively-assessed criterion of 'reasonableness' holds the key to correcting the balance in favour of free expression.[10] The 'reasonable publication' or 'responsible journalism' formulation not only sets the bounds of fair journalism, but also accommodates an emphasis on a right of reply which can further the debate. Most importantly, the 'reasonable publication' or 'responsible journalism' defences can apply even in jurisdictions that opt for strict (in the sense of no-intention) liability for defamation (as they are defences excluding the unlawfulness or unreasonableness of the conduct) and they are also defences that are compatible with negligence-based liability.

In the process of giving substance to this new defence of reasonable

---

[3] Supra note 2. It seems that the 'Reynolds defence' will apply in Scots law: E Reid *Personality, Confidentiality and Privacy in Scots Law* (W Green 2010) at para 11.29, who cites *Adams v Guardian Newspapers* 2003 SC 425 per Lord Reed at para 52.

[4] [2007] 1 AC 359 at para 46.

[5] At para 46. See also the recommended new statutory defence of 'publication on matters of public interest' in the Draft Defamation Bill, infra note 53. The establishing of a public interest defence could well have the effect of providing the catalyst for the recognition of a right to privacy in the United Kingdom: see J Burchell 'The Legal Protection of Privacy in South African Law: A Transplantable Hybrid' (2009) 13(1) *Electronic Journal of Comparative Law* (available at *http://www.ejcl.org/131/art131–2.pdf*).

[6] 1998 (4) SA 1196 (SCA).

[7] In rejecting media strict liability (under *Pakendorf v De Flamingh* 1982 (3) SA 146 (A)), the Supreme Court of Appeal in *Bogoshi* appeared to opt for negligence-based liability for the media. The debate that has arisen on the scope of the *Bogoshi* judgment, in particular whether *both* a defence of 'reasonable publication' *and* absence of negligence were created by the judgment, will be canvassed infra at section 8.8.

[8] *Grant v Torstar Corp* 2009 SCC 61.

[9] For instance, the difference between an extended defence of privileged occasion and a defence of 'reasonable publication'.

[10] The *New York Times Co v Sullivan* 376 US 254 (1964) approach, based on the distinction between public officials and ordinary citizens and notoriously slippery concepts of 'malice' and 'recklessness' is rightly rejected.

publication/responsible journalism favouring free speech, which exists in addition to the standard defences of truth (in South Africa, public benefit is also required), fair comment and privileged occasion, it is encouraging to see that a common jurisprudence on the boundaries of the 'new' defence[11] is being facilitated by mutual citation of case authority in the various jurisdictions.

It is inevitable that courts in the jurisdictions that accept a defence of 'reasonable publication' or 'responsible communication on matters of public interest' will regard this defence as applicable not just to print, television and radio media, but also to the broader electronic media. In fact, Lord Hoffmann in *Jameel*[12] regarded the new defence as 'available to anyone who publishes material of public interest *in any medium*' (emphasis supplied) and the English case of *Flood v Times Newspapers*,[13] in principle,[14] extended the *Reynolds* defence to a website publication. The Canadian Supreme Court judgment in *Grant* affirms that the 'responsible communication on matters of public interest' defence would apply to 'new disseminators of news and information'[15] and it is likely that the same scope would be given to the *Bogoshi* 'reasonable publication' defence in South Africa.[16]

This shift in emphasis towards freedom of expression is of considerable significance in those civil and common law jurisdictions that have started with the protection of reputation (and, in South Africa, protection of dignity[17] and privacy,[18] as well) and then proceeded to examine the limits that free speech places on this right to an unimpaired reputation. The South African and Canadian Constitutions focus on *balancing* rights. Article 10 of the European Convention on Human Rights starts with freedom of expression and then defines the legitimate *limits* on (or *exceptions* to) this significant right, including the countervailing right to protection of

---

[11] For instance, the South African Supreme Court in *Bogoshi*, supra note 6, relies heavily on *Reynolds* in the Court of Appeal and *Lange*, supra note 2, and the Supreme Court of Canada in *Grant*, supra note 8, cites the English and Commonwealth precedent.

[12] Supra note 4, at para 54.

[13] *Flood v Times Newspapers Ltd* [2012] UKSC 11, [2012] 2 AC 273.

[14] Although the defence might fail where the web archive version had not been updated on clarification of the facts.

[15] Supra note 8, at para 96.

[16] An advantage of the South African terminology of 'reasonable publication' is that it does not, explicitly or implicitly, link the defence solely to the publication of 'journalists'. Many of the new-age publishers (such as bloggers) who need to be regulated by the defence will neither fit into the mould of journalists nor necessarily adhere to journalistic practices and ethics.

[17] See J Burchell 'Personality Rights in South Africa: Re-affirming Dignity' in N R Whitty and R Zimmermann (eds) *Rights of Personality in Scots Law: A Comparative Perspective* (Dundee University Press 2009) 349.

[18] See Burchell, supra note 5.

reputation.[19] Despite differing starting points, it seems that common ground is, nevertheless, ultimately being found.

Freedom of expression under article 10 has been extended to cover commercial speech, artistic expression and even includes the expression of information or ideas that 'offend, shock or disturb'.[20] However, the European Court and European Commission's emphasis on 'public interest' and/or 'public debate' and freedom of political debate,[21] as well as reliance on a type of 'reasonable publication' defence, based on journalistic responsibilities,[22] is fostering further commonality between Convention and Anglo-Commonwealth jurisprudence.[23]

However, despite growing common ground within Anglo-Commonwealth jurisprudence, especially in the development of a defence that underscores freedom of expression and which has some resonance in European precedent, there are considerable differences in the approach of various jurisdictions to achieving a workable balance between protection of reputation and freedom of expression. A viable balance between protection of these two valued interests (reputation and free speech) can be found not just in the scope of the new defence to an action for defamation, but also in the rules relating to title to sue; publication; defamatory matter; defences other than the 'new' defence of 'reasonable publication'; onus of proof; fault and remedies. Furthermore, freedom of communication in cyberspace has placed additional pressures to revisit the balance between protection of reputation and free speech.

A major debate is raging on whether the common law is flexible enough to accommodate new forms of communication or publication via cyberspace.[24]

---

[19] Because the starting point of the European Convention is freedom of expression, it is not surprising that the United Nations Committee on Human Rights will not stop 'short of the wholesale Americanization of defamation law': 93rd session, Geneva, July 30, 2008 (CCPR/C/GBR/CO/6 available at *http://www.unhcr.org/refworld/category,COI,HRC,,GBR,48 a9411a2,0.html*) cited in P Milmo and W V H Rogers (eds) *Gatley on Libel and Slander* 11e (Sweet & Maxwell 2008) at v.

[20] *Surek v Turkey (No 1)* (1999) ECHR 51 at paras 58 and 62.

[21] *Lingens v Austria* (1986) 8 EHRR 407; *Barthold v Germany* (1985) 7 EHRR 383.

[22] *Lindon v France* (2007) ECHR 836, which involved the alleged defamation of a politician in a novel. At para 67 the majority of the court emphasised that journalists must act in 'good faith and on an accurate factual basis and provide "reliable and precise" information in accordance with the ethics of journalism. . . . [F]reedom of expression carries with it "duties and responsibilities", which also apply to the media even with respect to matters of public concern'. Three judges, dissenting in *Lindon*, emphasised the role of artistic creation and the robustness of debate regarding politics. See also *McVicar v UK* (2002) 35 EHRR 22 at para 72.

[23] As *Gatley*, supra note 19, states, referring to the concurring opinion of Judge Loucaides in *Lindon v France* [2007] ECHR 836: '[T]here are some signs at Strasbourg of the recognition of the dangers of over-protection of freedom of expression at the expense of reputation'.

[24] See especially the judgment of Gaudron J in *Dow Jones & Company Inc v Gutnick* (2002) 210 CLR 575 at paras 111–38 setting out the reasons for and against new rules for Internet defa-

The position adopted in this chapter is that, by and large, the common law is sufficiently supple in the United Kingdom and South Africa to be able to regulate the legal consequences of new ways of communicating, although this premise does not rule out ad hoc, special legislation, for instance, to resolve, say, the debate (discussed below) on the desirability of 'single' or 'multiple' publication rules.

8.3 TERMINOLOGY

A few cautionary words on terminology are needed before comparing aspects of the law of defamation in the United Kingdom under the influence of the European Convention and, in South Africa, under the impact of the 1996 Constitution.

'Reputation' is sometimes contrasted with 'dignity'. The essence of 'reputation' is what other people think of you, the estimation they have of you. 'Dignity' is often equated with *self*-esteem. In South Africa, particularly under the influence of a Constitution that protects 'dignity' but does not, *eo nomine*, protect 'reputation', the protection of reputation has been included under an overarching concept of dignity. Modern Scots law recognises defamation as a single action protecting both reputation and dignity. Similarly, South African law has affirmed that injury to reputation and dignity may overlap and that a court can award compensation for both injuries in one action.[25] The term 'defamation' is used in this chapter as an omnibus term, including both 'libel' and 'slander'.

'Freedom of expression' is a term that is often used without any elaboration. Various premises for free expression have been offered: it helps in attaining the truth; political speech is an integral part of the democratic process; and, more recently, freedom of expression is a facet of individual autonomy.[26] Defining freedom of expression in only one of these ways will inevitably be too restrictive. For instance, the objective of attaining 'truth' does not accommodate the vital expression of 'opinion' or acknowledge that, in special circumstances, the public interest may even grant immunity to untrue statements.[27] Even giving 'political' speech its broadest meaning cannot adequately cover expression in the field of creative works and many forms of Internet communication.

---

mation. See also *H v W* 2013 (2) SA 530 (GSJ) where a South African high court applied the law of defamation and interdicts to a posting on Facebook.

[25] *Le Roux v Dey* 2010 (4) SA 210 (SCA) (hereafter '*Le Roux v Dey* – (SCA)') at para 23 where Harms DP said 'any defamation is in the first instance an affront to a person's dignity which is aggravated by publication'.

[26] See generally J Burchell 'What are the Traditional Justifications for Freedom of Expression?' in *Personality Rights and Freedom of Expression – The Modern* Actio Injuriarum (Juta 1998) 1.

[27] *Grant*, supra note 8, at para 55; *Bogoshi*, supra note 6, at paras 23 and 28.

As was said in *Grant*:[28]

'Of the three rationales for the constitutional protection of free expression, only the third, self-fulfilment, is of dubious relevance to defamatory communications on matters of public interest. This is because the plaintiff's interest in reputation may be just as worthy of protection as the defendant's interest in self-realization through unfettered expression. . . . *Charter* principles do not provide a licence to damage another person's reputation simply to fulfil one's atavistic desire to express oneself.'

Notwithstanding this reservation, it is best to give freedom of expression its broadest foundation, drawing on any one or more of these bases, where appropriate.

8.4 TITLE TO SUE

At the outset, South African and English courts deprive certain entities of title to sue for defamation. Government (or the State, as such) cannot sue for defamation for obvious reasons of freedom of speech.[29] This rule covers both central and local government.[30]

The law in South Africa and United Kingdom has, however, accorded title to sue for defamation to a trading corporation without the need to establish special damage, provided the offending statement was *calculated* to cause financial prejudice (*Dhlomo*)[31] or had a 'tendency to damage it in the way of its business' (*Jameel*).[32] In South Africa, the same protection is accorded a non-trading corporation.[33]

Controversially, South African courts have also permitted individual

[28] Supra note 8, at para 51.

[29] *Die Spoorbond v South African Railways* 1946 AD 999; *Derbyshire County Council v Sunday Times* [1993] AC 534;. K McK Norrie *Defamation and Related Actions in Scots Law* (Butterworths 1995) argues at 69 that 'it is likely that Scots law today will take its rule from the English House of Lords' (in *Derbyshire CC*).

[30] *Derbyshire CC*, supra note 29. Cf *R Rajagopal v State of Tamil Nadu* [1994] 6 SCC 632 (Supreme Court of India).

[31] *Dhlomo NO v Natal Newspapers (Pty) Ltd* 1989 (1) SA 945 (A). Traditionally, Scots law only provides a remedy for defamation of a corporation where actual *patrimonial loss* is sustained: Norrie, supra note 29, at 66 but Elspeth Reid has drawn my attention to the parallel approach in Europe (*Niemietz v Germany* (1993) 16 EHRR 97) which is echoed in the Scottish case of *Response Handling Ltd v BBC* 2008 SLT 51 that, on the authority of the article 1 of the ECHR, extends a company's right to privacy of possessions to the confidentiality of its working practices.

[32] Per Lord Bingham in the House of Lords in *Jameel*, supra note 4, at para 17.

[33] *Dhlomo*, supra note 31, at 954D. The Constitutional Court in *Investigating Directorate: Serious Economic Offences v Hyundai Motor Distributors; In Re Hyundai Motors Distributors (Pty) Ltd v Smit NO* 2001 (1) SA 545 (CC) also held that a right to privacy was applicable to juristic person's, although because a juristic person had no human dignity as such, this privacy would not be as 'intense' as that of human beings (at paras 17–18).

politicians and political parties the right to sue for defamation.[34] Allowing
political parties (although, of course, not the ruling party or parties *qua*
government) title to sue for defamation might surprise Anglo-American
lawyers, who would regard this approach as a highly questionable intrusion on freedom of expression, especially in the form of political debate.
The South African Appellate Division, in reaching the conclusion that
even a political party should not *at the outset* be deprived of title to sue for
defamation in the *IFP* case, did set certain limits: the political party could
only sue for defamatory statements *calculated* to cause them *pecuniary loss*;
an appropriate balance between freedom of expression and reputation
would still have to be struck on the facts of the case; and 'new situations' in
which it might be considered lawful to publish defamatory material could
be recognised. In other words, further elements of liability for defamation
(including the defences to these elements) serve to limit the protection of
a political party's reputation. However, in a democratic society there are
many legitimate avenues for political debate and, arguably, a court of law
is not the appropriate forum for the airing of battles between political
parties.

In keeping with this inclusive approach to title to sue, the South African
courts did not preclude judges from suing for defamation[35] in regard to criticism of their judgments or official conduct and have even accorded corporations title to sue for invasion of privacy.[36]

The South African Constitution extends the protection of the Bill of
Rights to juristic persons to the extent that the right in question is applicable
to the juristic person and 'taking into account the nature of the right and
of any duty imposed by the right'.[37] None of the judgments extending title
to sue to various juristic and, in the case of judges and politicians, natural
persons has yet been challenged in terms of the Constitutional protection of
free expression. However, each of these judgments recognises, and indeed
encourages, a specific balancing of freedom of expression against protection
of reputation (or other personality right) in an individual case.

It would seem that there is a vast difference in approach between, on the
one hand, depriving certain artificial or human persons, at the outset, of the
opportunity of invoking the law of defamation to protect their reputations
and, on the other hand, extending title to sue for defamation to all, except
the State or Government. But it all depends on the ultimate balance between
protection of reputation and free speech that is struck during the trial. The

---

[34] On political parties see *Argus Printing and Publishing Co Ltd v Inkatha Freedom Party* 1992 (3)
    SA 579 (A) and, on politicians see *Mangope v Asmal* 1997 (4) SA 277 (T).
[35] *Argus Printing and Publishing Co Ltd v Esselen's Estate* 1994 (2) SA 1 (A).
[36] *Financial Mail (Pty) Ltd v Sage Holdings Ltd* 1993 (2) SA 451 (A) and *Janit v Motor Industry
    Fund Administrators (Pty) Ltd* 1995 (4) SA 293 (A).
[37] Section 8(2).

concept of 'reasonable publication' and the balance between these competing rights of reputation and free speech that is struck within each element of liability (and its corresponding defences) will hold the key to whether there is any difference in practice between these two outwardly contrasting approaches.

8.5 PUBLICATION

In English and South African law publication (or the communication) of defamatory matter to *a third person* is crucial to defamation.[38] Merely communicating the imputation to the *injured person alone* might constitute an impairment of that person's dignity,[39] but does not amount to defamation unless the alleged defamatory matter is communicated to at least one other person. In essence, reputation is the estimation that *right-thinking persons* have of you. Most systems of law include within the concept of publication the *understanding* or *comprehension* of the defamatory content of the publication by the receiver.[40]

However, under Scots law damages for affront or insult *to the pursuer alone* is sufficient for defamation,[41] although, if there is publication to a third party, damages for economic loss can be recovered.[42] There is some dispute as to precisely when these two facets of a defamation claim were consolidated into one action: T B Smith maintains that this occurred when the jurisdictions of the commissary and the civil courts (where reparation in the form of damages could be sought) were merged with the establishment of the Jury Court; John Blackie maintains that some 50 years before the establishment of the Jury Court, the Court of Session was, in fact, 'dealing with both aspects of defamation in a single claim'.[43] Norrie, who favours the view of Blackie, has cautioned that although the two types of action may be claimed in a single action, there is still a need to separate the two types of action conceptually: only non-patrimonial loss (that is, *solatium*) can be claimed if the harmful words are not published, but are communicated to the pursuer alone; and only if the pursuer is an artificial person (such as a company) can patrimonial loss be claimed.[44]

---

[38] *Gatley*, supra note 19, at para 6.1; J M Burchell *The Law of Defamation in South Africa* (Juta 1985) 67; *Gutnick*, supra note 24, at para 25.

[39] See Burchell, supra note 17.

[40] See Burchell, supra note 17, 68–9; *Gutnick*, supra note 24, at paras 108 and 124.

[41] *Thomson v Kindell* (1910) 2 SLT 442. Perhaps the confusion of 'insult' and 'defamation' in this century-old decision is ready for reconsideration?

[42] Norrie, supra note 29, at 28–9; Reid, supra note 3, at para 10.35.

[43] K McK Norrie 'The Scots Law of Defamation: Is there a Need for Reform?' in Whitty and Zimmerman, supra note 17, 436 (citing T B Smith *A Short Commentary on the Law of Scotland* (W Green 1962) at 724–30 and Blackie, supra note 1, at 678–9).

[44] Norrie, supra note 43.

8.5.1 Single or multiple publication rule?

The rule that each publication (or communication) gives rise to a separate cause of action is part of the common law of England,[45] Australia,[46] Canada[47] and South Africa.[48] In contrast, both the common law and statutes[49] in various states in the United States adopt a single publication rule and this single publication rule applies to the Internet.

> 'In other words, it is the prevailing American doctrine that the publication of a book, periodical, or newspaper containing defamatory matter gives rise to but one cause of action for libel, which accrues at the time of the original publication, and that the statute of limitations runs from that date. It is no longer the law that every sale or delivery of a copy of the publication creates a new cause of action.'[50]

In 1975 the Faulks Committee *Report on Defamation*[51] recommended that a claim for defamation based on a single publication should constitute a single cause of action giving rise to only one award of damages. In 1979 the Commonwealth Law Reform Commission recommended that the plaintiff should be limited to a 'single action in respect of a multiple publication but only to the extent disclosed in the action'.[52] The debate on whether a 'multiple' or 'single' publication rule should apply has been exacerbated by electronic publications, especially via the Internet. Procedural and choice of law concerns about sales of multiple copies of books or newspapers giving rise to multiple claims for defamation are magnified considerably by the opportunities afforded to individuals and companies by electronic publishing, especially via the Internet. Does every Internet hit give rise to a separate cause of action?

It seems that the current 'multiple publication' rule which applies in the United Kingdom and South Africa (under which each publication of defamatory material can form the basis of a new defamation claim and which, in the context of electronic publication, would mean that a fresh action arises every

---

[45]   The origin of the rule is found in *Duke of Brunswick v Harmer* (1849) 14 QB 185, recently affirmed in *Loutchansky v Times Newspapers Ltd (Nos. 2–5)* [2002] 1 All ER 652 at paras 57, 60 and 62.

[46]   *Gutnick*, supra note 24, at para 197.

[47]   *Carter v BC Federation of Foster Parents Association* 2005 BCCA 398 at para 18.

[48]   Burchell, supra note 38, at 81.

[49]   In *Gutnick*, supra note 24, at para 29 it was estimated that 27 states of the United States, including California, Illinois, New York, Pennsylvania and Texas have by legislation or judicial decision adopted a single publication rule.

[50]   District Judge Holtzoff in *Ogden v Association of the United States Army* (1959) 177 F. Supp 498 at 502.

[51]   See *Report of the Committee on Defamation* (1975) Cmnd 5909, chaired by Faulks LJ, at paras 25 and 189–92.

[52]   The Law Reform Commission, Report no. 11 *Unfair Publication: Defamation and Privacy* (1979) at paras 109–15.

time someone accesses a website or archive) is in need of modification in order to contend with the electronic era. The Defamation Bill recently introduced in the Westminster Parliament, to take effect in England and Wales, recommends a single publication rule.[53]

Place of publication traditionally determines the forum and the choice of law applicable to the claim. Traditionally the defamation was located at the place where the damage to reputation occurred. Does this mean that in an electronic age the place of the defamation is where defamatory material is uploaded onto the Internet or where the material is downloaded on to a computer? If the first-mentioned situation prevails and the material is uploaded in the United States, then the free-speech-oriented rules of that jurisdiction apply to the defamation suit. If the last-mentioned situation applies, then the plaintiff has greater choice regarding jurisdiction and applicable legal rules.[54]

8.5.2 Publication in cyberspace

A person who creates a website and posts material on this website has clearly 'published' the material. However, is the Internet service provider which provides the services that are used to disseminate this material also liable for publication? In *Godfrey v Demon Internet Limited*[55] it was held that an Internet service provider is a 'publisher' of material it 'hosts' whether it had knowledge or not that the material was defamatory. However, where knowledge of the defamatory content was lacking, then s 1(1) of the United Kingdom Defamation Act of 1996 could come into play and provide a defence for the defendant who can show

'(a) that he was not the author, editor or publisher of the statement complained of,
(b) that he took reasonable care in relation to its publication, and
(c) that he did not know, and had no reason to believe, that what he did caused or contributed to the publication of a defamatory statement.'

Similarly, a European Community Directive, which has been transposed into English law by the Electronic Commerce (EC Directive) Regulations

---

[53] At clause 8. For full text see *http://www.services.parliament.uk/bills/2012-13/defamation.html*.

[54] The High Court of Australia in *Gutnick*, supra note 24, declined the invitation to reject the existing 'multiple publication' rule of the common law. At para 44 Gleeson CJ, McHugh, Gummow and Hayne JJ emphasised that ordinarily 'defamation is to be located at the place where the damage to reputation occurs' and damage will occur in the context of Internet communications where the person 'downloads the material'. Gaudron J, concurring, added that where a natural person was 'ordinarily resident' (para 153) and where the material is accessed was the usual indicator of the appropriate choice of law for defamation (paras 134 and 151). The Australian High Court held that the defamation law of Victoria (Australia) applied to the claim.

[55] [2001] QB 201.

2002,[56] provides exemption from liability where the internet service provision is

> 'limited to the technical process of operating and giving access to a communication network over which information made available by third parties is transmitted or temporarily stored, for the sole purpose of making the transmission more efficient; this activity is of a mere technical, automatic and passive nature, which implies that the [Internet service provider] has neither knowledge of nor control over the information which is transmitted or stored.'

Gatley points out that these Regulations do not repeal s 1 of the Defamation Act and that the two potential defences created do not necessarily cover identical ground.[57] An obvious difference in the scope of the two defences would lie in the Act's emphasis on the taking of 'reasonable care' and the Regulations' emphasis on the lack of knowledge of or control over content. A potential 'Catch 22' embedded in the Act's import is that, in order to rely on the defence in s 1(1), a web publisher has to show that it took reasonable care in regard to a publication. If reasonable care involves 'prior review', 'prior review' may be indistinguishable from exercising the editorial function which will mean the eventual loss of the defence under s 1(1)(*a*).

It would seem that the Regulations provide the best line of defence for Internet service providers,[58] although an offer of amends under ss 2–4 of the Defamation Act 1996[59] or, possibly, a defence of innocent dissemination under the common law might be available.

8.6 DEFAMATORY MATTER

There is consensus on the appropriate test for determining defamatory matter in the United Kingdom and South Africa. Lord Atkins' classic formulation in *Sim v Stretch*[60] of the test for determining defamatory matter (that is, '[W]ould the words tend to lower the plaintiff in the estimation of

---

[56] At Recital 42 of the Directive, which came into force on August 21, 2002: See *Gatley*, supra note 19, para 6.28.

[57] *Gatley on Libel and Slander*, supra note 19. The authors also observe that the two provisions do not abolish the common law defence for distributors, but they add in parenthesis 'if that still exits'. M Collins *The Law of Defamation and the Internet* 3e (Oxford University Press 2010) at para 17.53 points out that the common law defence of innocent dissemination 'is yet to be the subject of extensive consideration in an Internet context'. Collins observes that the common law defence was 'assumed to have been abrogated by the defence in section 1 of the Defamation Act 1996 (UK)' in *Godfrey v Demon Internet Limited* [2001] 1 QB 201. However, he also observes that it was 'held to have survived, but said not to be relevantly different from the section 1 defence, at least on the facts in [the] case' in *Metropolitan International Schools Ltd v Designtechnica Corp* [2009] EMLR 27.

[58] Collins, supra note 57, at paras 18.10–18.11.

[59] Collins, supra note 57.

[60] [1936] 2 All ER 1237 at 1240.

right-thinking members of society generally?') is acknowledged as expressing the test of defamatory content in both Scotland[61] and South Africa.[62] It is also acknowledged in Scotland that this criterion takes into account the 'class of persons to which the individual belongs',[63] and in South Africa that the estimation in which the plaintiff is held by the community to which he belongs (provided this section of the community constitutes a 'substantial and respectable segment' of society) can be factored into the enquiry into the estimation of 'right-thinking persons generally'. In South Africa the right-thinking person's estimation of the plaintiff must reflect the values and attitudes embodied in the Constitution[64] and the same conclusion would be valid for the influence of the European Convention on Human Rights on the views and attitudes of the right-thinking person in the United Kingdom.[65]

8.7 FALSITY

In the United Kingdom 'falsity' is an element of the action for libel and slander. Although, strictly speaking, the claimant bears the burden of proving the falsity of a defamatory statement, he or she is assisted by a rebuttable presumption of falsity after the defamatory content of the words has been established.[66] The effect of this presumption is to cast an onus onto the defendant to show truth (*veritas*, in Scots law).[67]

In the South African law of defamation, falsity is not an element of the delict of defamation. The plaintiff does not bear any burden of proving the falsity of a defamatory statement, rather the burden lies squarely on the defendant who publishes the statement to prove its truthfulness and also that the disclosure of this truth is for the public benefit. Although this might seem to place an undue fetter on freedom of expression, the South African Constitutional court in *Khumalo v Holomisa*[68] confirmed that, in the light of the development of the *Bogoshi*[69] defence of 'reasonable publication' open

---

[61] *Steele v Scottish Daily Record and Sunday Mail* 1970 SLT 53; *Thomson v News Group Newspapers* OH, Lord Kirkwood, 6 March 1992, unreported, 1992 GWD 14–825 (on which, see Norrie, supra note 29, 9 n 8); *Quilty v Windsor* 1999 SLT 346; *McCann v Scottish Media Newspapers Ltd* 2000 SLT 256; *Adams v Guardian Newspapers Ltd* 2003 SC 425; *Robertson v Newsquest (Sunday Herald) Ltd* 2006 SCLR 792 and *Curran v Scottish Daily Record and Sunday Mail Ltd* 2010 SLT 377.

[62] See *Mohamed v Jassiem* 1996 (1) SA 673 (A) at 708–9 and the other authorities cited there.

[63] Lord McLaren in *Macfarlane v Black & Co* (1887) 14 R 870 at 872–3.

[64] See Goldstein J in *Sokhulu v New Africa Publications Ltd* 2001 (4) SA 1357 (W) at para 7 (a defamation case) and, in general, *Carmichele v Minister of Safety and Security (Centre for Applied Legal Studies Intervening)* 2001 (4) SA 938 (CC).

[65] See Burchell and Norrie, supra note 1, at 553.

[66] *Gatley*, supra note 19, para 11.3.

[67] 'Veritas' or truth' is a defence in Scots law as well, at least by 1830: Norrie, supra note 29, at 126.

[68] 2002 (5) SA 401 (CC).

[69] Supra note 6, and see above section 8.2.

to the media, this rule relating to the proof of truthfulness is compatible with the constitutional demands of free speech.[70]

Allocation of onus (especially of proving falsity or truthfulness) provides a powerful tool for extending or restricting freedom of expression. There is no doubt that requiring the plaintiff in a defamation action to prove falsity on a balance of probabilities would further the freedom of the defendant's expression. That is why the burden of proving falsity rests on the public figure plaintiff in the United States.[71] In the jurisprudence of the European Court, a burden of proving the truthfulness of factual allegations on a balance of probabilities constitutes a justified restriction on freedom of expression under article 10 of the Convention (freedom of expression).[72]

The only qualification that the South African jurisprudence would add regarding onus is that in the case of an individual defendant who raises the defence of absence of intention, only an evidential burden (as opposed to a burden of proof on a balance of probabilities) rests on such a defendant in a defamation claim to support his defence,[73] and this is for reasons of freedom of expression.

8.8 FAULT

Perhaps the most vivid contrast between the Common and the Civil Law tradition in the context of the protection of personality rights is found in the English penchant for strict (no-fault) liability, alleviated somewhat by legislative regulation of innocent defamation which is combined with an offer to make amends[74] and the Roman predilection for fault (*animus iniuriandi*) liability. Actually, the conflict is between the English *irrebuttable* presumption of intention (except in the context of malice which defeats a defence of qualified privileged occasion) and a general *rebuttable* presumption of intention, or *animus iniuriandi* – as it was called in Roman law. Requiring the plaintiff to prove intention[75] or allowing the defendant to escape liability

---

[70] At para 39.

[71] The United States Congress recently enacted a statute, the Speech Act 2010, preventing United States courts from enforcing foreign judgments that would violate First Amendment free speech rights.

[72] *McVicar v UK* (2002) 35 EHRR 22 at para 87.

[73] Rumpff CJ in *Suid-Afrikaanse Uitsaaikorporasie v O'Malley* 1977 (3) SA 394 (A) at 403B-C (hereafter '*SAUK v O'Malley*').

[74] Section 4 of the United Kingdom Defamation Act of 1952, which was seldom invoked, and has been replaced with ss 2–4 of the Defamation Act 1996, discussed briefly infra at section 8.10.1.

[75] This is the position in the United States where public officials are required to prove 'malice' or 'reckless disregard' as to whether the imputation was true or false. Apart from the enormous difficulty in drawing a distinction between ordinary citizens and public figures or matters of private and public concern, the meaning of 'malice' and 'recklessness' is notoriously slippery: see Burchell, supra note 26, at 311–14.

for defamation on the grounds of absence of intention would undoubtedly encourage freedom of expression.

Early Scots law revealed its civilian roots by requiring proof of intention but, as John Blackie has observed, eventually 'slipped into strict liability'.[76] In fact, it is argued that there is evidence in pre-*Hulton v Jones*[77] Scottish cases to support the view that the strict liability approach to defamation was of older lineage in Scotland than in England.[78] Ultimately, this emphasis on strict liability for defamation was extended to defamation cases involving economic loss as well.[79]

Norrie has suggested that the Scottish law of defamation should return to its historical distinction between the two claims – a distinction historically drawn in Scotland.[80] Claims for affront/insult based on *animus* and claims for patrimonial loss based on negligence should, according to Norrie, be kept separate. This recommendation would free Scottish courts to find greater synergy with the South African law on *solatium* for insults. However, modern South African law does not draw rigid distinctions between the type of damages claimed. As Brand J has correctly stated for the majority of the Constitutional Court in *Le Roux v Dey*: 'According to established principle, an award of damages for defamation should compensate the plaintiff for both wounded feelings and loss of reputation.'[81]

The South African Supreme Court of Appeal has recently scrutinised the meaning of *animus iniuriandi* and elaborated on its definition. According to Harms DP in *Le Roux v Dey*,[82] *animus iniuriandi* in Roman law meant simply intention to injure[83] and continental Pandectists of the nineteenth century added a further element to intention to injure, namely consciousness of the wrongfulness of the act (or coloured intent).[84] Harms DP dismissed the Pandectist view in these words:

'In spite of my high regard for them [the Pandectists] it has to be conceded that by systematising the Roman-law concepts they did not necessarily state the

---

[76] See Blackie, supra note 1, 662 who submits that the development of newspapers in the eighteenth century moved the law from *animus* to strict liability. Norrie, supra note 43, at 441 suggests that the 'patrimonial' or 'loss of trade' nature of the claim in many early cases might have impelled the move to strict liability as well as the fact that corporate newspaper defendants were involved.

[77] [1910] AC 20.

[78] Norrie, supra note 43, at 440.

[79] Ibid 441.

[80] See supra section 8.5.

[81] *Le Roux v Dey (Freedom of Expression Institute and Restorative Justice Centre as* Amici Curiae) 2011 (3) SA 274 (CC) at para 151.

[82] *Le Roux v Dey –* (SCA), supra note 25.

[83] *Le Roux v Dey –* (SCA), supra note 25, at para 28.

[84] Ibid para 29. J R Midgley and J C van der Walt 'Delict' in W Joubert (ed) *The Law of South Africa* 2e (LexisNexis Butterworths 2003–4) vol 8(1) para 105 n 3.

Roman-Dutch law. This means that an adherence to the roots of our law does not necessarily require an adoption of Pandectist theories.'[85]

While, in criminal law, knowledge of unlawfulness was authoritatively regarded as a part of intention in 1977 in *S v De Blom*,[86] the presence of 'coloured' intent in the law of delict was more debatable. The then Chief Justice of South Africa, Frans Rumpff, who delivered the unanimous judgment of the Appellate Division in *De Blom*, in the very same year also pronounced in *SAUK v O'Malley*[87] (a defamation case) that knowledge of unlawfulness was part of *animus iniuriandi* in the context of defamation by an individual, as opposed to the media.[88]

Notwithstanding that in *National Media Ltd v Bogoshi*[89] Hefer JA had concluded that '[f]inally, in *O'Malley* this Court . . . expressly accepted the principle that consciousness of the wrongfulness of the publication is required', Harms DP (who, incidentally, was also part of the unanimous judgment in *Bogoshi*) held in 2010 in *Le Roux v Dey*[90] that this statement of Rumpff CJ in *O'Malley* was obiter[91] and should not be followed. Whether the statement by Rumpff CJ in *O'Malley* requiring knowledge of unlawfulness was, in fact, obiter will be debated later.[92] However, despite regarding as 'commendable' the judgment of De Villiers AJ in 1960 in *Maisel v Van Naeren*[93] (holding that knowledge of unlawfulness *was* a part of *animus iniuriandi*) Harms DP in *Le Roux v Dey* asserted:

'It appears to me to be incongruous that a defendant who, for example, cannot establish truth and public benefit to justify defamation, can nevertheless escape liability by relying on a belief in either the truth or public benefit. Not only that,

---

[85] At para 29.

[86] 1977 (3) SA 513 (A).

[87] Supra note 73, at 403C-D.

[88] The Chief Justice also stated that strict (no-fault) liability for defamation by the media should apply (at 404–5). This statement was clearly obiter as it was unnecessary for the court to change the law in this way, especially as it concluded that *animus iniuriandi* had been established on the facts anyway. It was this obiter statement pertaining to strict liability for the media that was followed by Rumpff CJ himself in *Pakendorf v De Flamingh* 1982 (3) SA 146 (A) only to be overruled in *National Media Ltd v Bogoshi* 1998 (4) SA 1196 (SCA). Perhaps it is time now (with the prevalence of electronic forms of mass publication, open even to individuals) and a resurgence of interest in personality rights for the law to move in the direction of a *culpa* or negligence-based liability for infringements of personality. See discussion infra in this section.

[89] Supra note 6, at para 11.

[90] Supra note 82.

[91] If the statement of Rumpff CJ in *O'Malley* regarding consciousness of unlawfulness as a requirement of *animus iniuriandi* was obiter and so was the statement of the then Chief Justice regarding strict liability of the media, it would seem that *O'Malley*, despite being a unanimous judgment, would be one of those perplexing judgments that lacks any *ratio* on the law.

[92] See discussion infra in this section.

[93] 1960 (4) SA 836 (C).

the approach also inhibits the development of this part of the law under the Constitution.'[94]

After evaluating the authority, both judicial and academic, on *animus iniuriandi* Harms DP concluded:

> 'The effect of this is that mistake or bona fides might in appropriate circumstances justify a defamatory statement (ie, if it were reasonable to have been made) and that it is accordingly not necessary to require coloured intent. I therefore conclude, especially in view of precedent and the constitutional emphasis on the protection of personality rights, that the *animus iniuriandi* requirement generally does not require consciousness of wrongfulness . . .'[95]

Le Roux v Dey proceeded to the Constitutional Court for adjudication, where the majority of the justices upheld the decision of the Supreme Court of Appeal that the publication was defamatory, although the quantum of damages was reduced.[96] Brand J, delivering judgment for the majority of the Constitutional Court, did not find it necessary to consider whether knowledge of unlawfulness should be part of the *animus iniuriandi* inquiry, except to conclude that the fact that the defendants foresaw the possibility of the *general* wrongfulness of their conduct (on an analogy with the concept of *dolus eventualis*/foresight of possibility in criminal law) was sufficient for liability.[97] So, Harms DP's consideration of the 'knowledge of unlawfulness' issue in the Supreme Court of Appeal still prevails. If the Supreme Court of Appeal's conclusion on this matter means that an individual (that is, non-media) defendant in a defamation case can only escape liability on the grounds of a mistake regarding the existence of a defence excluding unlawfulness (or ground of justification) where the mistake is *reasonable*,[98] but can escape liability by, for instance leading evidence of a *bona fide* (although not necessarily, reasonable) mistaken identity, accidental publication or ignorance of the meaning of the words, then this conclusion can be endorsed.[99]

---

[94] *Le Roux v Dey* – (SCA), supra note 25, at para 37.
[95] At para 39.
[96] *Le Roux v Dey* – (CC), supra note 81.
[97] At para 137.
[98] See the words in parenthesis in the quotation above.
[99] In 1985, in Burchell *Defamation in South Africa*, supra note 38, at 174, this author wrote:

> '[I]t is submitted that an individual defendant's bona fide (genuine) and essential mistake of fact or law relating to the publication of defamatory matter referring to the plaintiff can, and should, serve to rebut the inference of *animus injuriandi*. A bona fide (genuine) and essential mistake of fact or law regarding the existence of a ground of justification (defence excluding unlawfulness) should not alone be sufficient to rebut the inference of *animus injuriandi* – it should have to be reasonable as well.'

However, on a strict interpretation of the 1977 judgment of Rumpff CJ in the Appellate Division in *O'Malley*, a distinction between a mistake or ignorance relating to an element of defamation and a mistake or ignorance relating to the purported existence of a ground of

However, it is the process of reasoning by which Harms DP in *Le Roux v Dey* reached his conclusion that may be open to criticism. First, it is difficult to see the statement regarding the requirement of knowledge of unlawfulness in O'*Malley* as obiter since that court *decided* the matter on the grounds that the presumption of *animus iniuriandi* had not been rebutted.[100] Furthermore, the Supreme Court of Appeal in *Dey* concluded that, by depriving a defendant of a defence of *bona fide* mistake or ignorance regarding truth or public benefit, it would not be inhibiting 'development of this part of the law under the Constitution'. Surely, limiting the scope of a defence of mistaken belief in truth or public benefit would result in curtailing free expression – a constitutionally-protected right. If Harms DP wanted to justify the conclusion he reached, he should have specifically overruled O'*Malley* on knowledge of unlawfulness which would have raised freedom of expression implications.

In fact, it might have been unnecessary for Harms DP to have engaged in the re-definition of *animus iniuriandi*, since he was concerned that a *cellphone* had been used to publish the alleged defamatory material. The established *Bogoshi* rule applicable to mass publication via the *media* could thus have been invoked to resolve the matter, making *Le Roux v Dey* the first South African decision on cyberpublication.[101] Not only did Harms DP in *Le Roux v Dey* not invoke *Bogoshi*, he actually suggested that 'the discussion of negligence in *Bogoshi* might have complicated matters unnecessarily' and that it 'might be opportune to revisit with the wisdom of hindsight the judgment in *Bogoshi*'[102] on this point. Although Harms DP acknowledged the 'reasonable publication' defence for the media in *Bogoshi*, what the Deputy President of the Supreme Court of Appeal would seem to dispute is *Bogoshi's* creation of a further defence of absence of negligence. Harms DP states: 'Once it is found that the publication was unreasonable the next question should simply be whether it was published with the *intent* to injure'[103] (emphasis supplied).

Commentators who dispute that *Bogoshi* introduced both a 'reasonable publication' defence *and* a negligence fault criterion[104] do not, however, place sufficient emphasis on the following conclusions in the judgment in *Bogoshi* (with which Harms JA, as he then was, concurred):

justification was not drawn. Rumpff CJ would seem to have given free rein to *every* genuine lack of knowledge of unlawfulness.

[100] Even if the defendant had adduced no evidence of absence of *animus iniuriandi*, either in the form of intention to injure the plaintiff's reputation or knowledge of unlawfulness, it would still have been necessary for the court to set out the contents of the legal parameters on which the defendant would have been required to adduce evidence.

[101] See further on defamation in cyberspace, supra section 8.5.2.

[102] Supra note 25, at para 38.

[103] Ibid.

[104] J R Midgley 'Media Liability for Defamation' (1999) 116 *SALJ* 211 at 214–15 and A Fagan 'Rethinking Wrongfulness in the Law of Delict' (2005) 122 *SALJ* 90 at 101–6.

(1) Hefer JA in *Bogoshi* specifically overrules the strict liability basis for defamation by the media in *Pakendorf v De Flamingh*[105] and such overruling would be unnecessary simply in order to create a 'new' defence of 'reasonable publication' because of the already recognised principle that the list of defences excluding unlawfulness is not closed and that defences excluding unlawfulness would be available even if strict (no-fault) liability applied; and

(2) After establishing the defence of 'reasonable publication' as a defence excluding unlawfulness, Hefer JA in *Bogoshi* explicitly reverts to the 'question of fault'.[106] He then reviews the various fault options to strict liability (both intention and negligence) and concludes that the approach in other countries (that 'the media are liable unless they were not negligent') places an 'entirely reasonable' burden on the media.[107] Hefer JA also specifically emphasises that 'absence of *animus injuriandi* can plainly not be available to the [media] defendant' (that is, a genuine lack of knowledge of unlawfulness cannot alone be a defence for the media; the ignorance or mistake must be *reasonable* as well in order to excuse).[108] The judge of appeal acknowledges that counsel for the defendants rightly accepted that there were

> 'compelling reasons for holding that the media should not be treated on the same footing as ordinary members of the public by permitting them to rely on the absence of *animus injuriandi*, and that it would be appropriate to hold media defendants liable unless they were not negligent in the circumstances of the case.'[109]

Any previous reference to 'ignorance and mistake at the level of lawfulness'[110] is surely meant to refer not to the *unlawfulness* enquiry itself but rather to *fault in regard to unlawfulness* – that is, to ignorance or mistake relating to unlawfulness (or, as it is more commonly described, lack of knowledge of unlawfulness) which, in the case of negligence, would have to be reasonable in order to excuse. If ignorance or mistake must be *reasonable* in order to excuse, then the fault element required for the media cannot be subjectively-assessed intention (as it is in the case of an individual defendant), it must be objectively-assessed negligence. Reference to the word 'legality' in Hefer JA's statement that negligence 'may well be determinative of the legality of the publication'[111] is surely no more than an allusion to 'legal liability' in a broad, non-technical sense?

---

[105] 1982 (3) SA 146 (A).
[106] At para 33.
[107] At para 36.
[108] At para 35.
[109] Ibid.
[110] Ibid.
[111] Ibid.

This approach is endorsed in *Mthembi-Mahanyele v Mail & Guardian Ltd and Another*.[112] However, in this judgment Lewis JA unfortunately merged the fault and unlawfulness enquiries,[113] and this part of Lewis JA's judgment is the portion that Harms DP quotes with approval in *Le Roux v Dey*. In *Khumalo v Holomisa*[114] the Constitutional Court confirmed the constitutionality of the *Bogoshi* principles in regard to the 'new' defence of 'reasonable publication'. Although O'Regan J made no detailed comment about a negligence fault criterion, she did say: 'Hefer JA [in *Bogoshi*] therefore concluded that media defendants could not escape liability merely by establishing an absence of knowledge of unlawfulness. They would in addition have to establish that they were not negligent'.[115]

It is clear that *Bogoshi* established two defences for the media: (1) reasonable publication; *and* (2) absence of negligence (or reasonable belief). Admittedly factors of 'reasonableness' are often common to both defences. For instance, in the context of setting, say, standards of reasonable Internet publication, the steps taken to verify information would feature in both enquiries. But, the focus of the 'reasonable publication' enquiry would be on what steps were objectively-speaking available to the publisher, while the focus of the negligence enquiry would be on what the publisher *reasonably believed*. In the second enquiry, for instance, if the Internet publisher claimed that he or she believed that there were no restraints on publication in cyberspace, the court would have to determine whether it was reasonable to hold this belief in order to decide whether, in the circumstances, the publisher had been negligent in publishing the information. Similarly in the English case of *Flood*[116] the claimant had not merely been cleared of corruption charges, but he had notified *The Times* of this fact. Arguably, it was not just irresponsible but also negligent journalism to fail to update its web archive. The enquiry into negligence would focus on fault and not just whether the publication was reasonable in itself. Furthermore, there is some precedent in South Africa that, although the publisher would have to prove 'reasonable publication' as a ground of justification, he or she might only have to *adduce evidence* of absence of fault (including perhaps reasonable mistake) in order to escape liability for defamation.[117]

It is submitted that a viable balance between freedom of expression and

---

[112] 2004 (6) SA 329 (SCA) at para 46.

[113] At para 47.

[114] 2002 (5) SA 401 (CC).

[115] At para 20.

[116] See notes 13 and 14 supra. The issue of whether the website publication had ceased to be privileged was accordingly adjourned so that it could be further addressed.

[117] See the conclusion reached by Rumpff CJ in *O'Malley*, supra note 73, on the evidential burden regarding the rebuttable of the presumption of *animus*. Compare the conclusion of Hefer JA in *Bogoshi*, supra note 6, regarding the full burden of proof on a balance of probabilities resting on the media defendant to prove lack of negligence.

protection of reputation should not be based on fine distinctions between various types of harm suffered in a defamation claim (as suggested by Norrie)[118] or invoking mercurial concepts like 'malice' or 'recklessness' (as the American courts do). A distinction between the liability of the *media* for defamation (based *inter alia* on a 'reasonable publication'/'responsible journalism' defence combined with a negligence fault criterion) and liability of an *individual* for defamation (based *inter alia* on intention in regard to the elements of defamation and an objective evaluation of absence of fault regarding the existence of a recognised defence) without drawing any fine distinctions between wounded feelings (*solatium*) and patrimonial loss or 'malice' and 'recklessness' would be more defensible.[119]

8.9 FAIR (HONEST) COMMENT

The South African law of defamation borrowed the defence of fair comment from English law.[120] In English law 'malice' in the context of fair comment does not mean spite or ill-will or improper motive (as in the context of the forfeiture of the privileged occasion), but rather lack of belief in the opinion expressed – that is, the defendant was not expressing a genuinely-held opinion.[121]

Although the South African Appellate Division in *Marais v Richard*[122] in the 1980s briefly flirted with a concept of 'fairness' of the comment being equivalent to the 'reasonableness' of the comment, it is now clear that the 'reasonableness' of the comment is not the decisive criterion of 'fairness', but rather whether the comment or opinion was one that an honest person could hold (not necessarily an objectively reasonable opinion).[123] This approach which is more in keeping with original English law (and, most importantly, freedom of expression) has been affirmed by Innes CJ in *Crawford v Albu*,[124] the various judgments in *Johnson v Beckett*[125] and by Cameron J in the Constitutional Court in *The Citizen v McBride*[126] who said:

'Protected comment need thus not be 'fair or just at all' in any sense in which these terms are commonly understood. Criticism is protected even if extreme, unjust,

---

[118] Supra note 43.
[119] Greater freedom of expression for the *individual* would seem to be needed.
[120] *Marais v Richard en 'n Ander* 1981 (1) SA 1157 (A) at 1166E-F and 1167C-E
[121] *Gatley*, supra note 19, at paras 12.25 and 12.1–12.2.
[122] Supra note 120.
[123] The question of malice, which in English defamation law is said to rebut fair comment then becomes simply an inquiry into whether the belief was honestly held.
[124] 1917 AD 102 at 114.
[125] 1992 (1) SA 762 (A) at 775C-E (per van den Heever JA); at 780J-781B (per Harms AJA; and at 783B (per Corbett CJ (Hefer JA and Kriegler AJA concurring).
[126] *The Citizen 1978 (Pty) Ltd and Others v McBride (Johnstone and Others*, Amici Curiae) 2011 (4) SA 191 (CC).

unbalanced, exaggerated and prejudiced, so long as it expresses an honestly-held opinion, without malice, on a matter of public interest on facts that are true . . . Perhaps it would be clearer, and helpful in the understanding of the law, if the defence were known rather as 'protected comment' . . . [which term] may illuminate the constitutional source and extent of the protection.'[127]

Search for an appropriate label for the defence of 'fair' comment also impelled British courts to talk of 'honest comment'[128] and, more recently, 'honest opinion'.[129] Lord Phillips in *Joseph v Spiller* acknowledged that comment did not have to identify the factual matters on which it was based with sufficient particularity to enable the reader 'to judge for himself whether it was well founded'.[130] It was enough if the comment indicated, explicitly or implicitly, 'at least in general terms what it is that has led the commentator to make the comment'.[131] Lord Phillips even went as far as to suggest that the 'public interest' requirement for the defence and that the role of juries in defamation cases might be re-visited.[132] Not only did Lord Phillips and Cameron J define 'fairness' in a similar way, they also took an expansive view of the factual foundation for the comment, concluding that the facts on which the comment is made do not have to be specifically identified in the offending publication. It is sufficient if they are revealed explicitly or implicitly in general terms (Lord Phillips) or derived from previous articles in the newspaper or from the common knowledge of its readers (Cameron J).[133] There was some support (reflected in *Crawford*)[134] for a higher standard of comment requiring that the comment constitute a reasonable inference from the facts where 'wicked or dishonourable motives' were imputed. The current attitude in the United Kingdom is that this 'special rule has disappeared from the law', for obvious reasons of freedom of expression and difficulty of definition,[135] and the same should be the case for South Africa.

---

[127] At paras 83 and 84 (Brand AJ, Froneman J, Nkabinde J and Yacoob J concurring) (footnotes omitted).

[128] *British Chiropractic Assoc v Singh* [2010] EWCA Civ 350; [2011] 1 WLR 133.

[129] *Joseph v Spiller* [2010] UKSC 53; [2011] 1 AC 852. See also the statutory defence of 'honest opinion' recommended by the Draft Defamation Bill, supra note 53.

[130] At para 104.

[131] Ibid.

[132] At paras 113 and 116 respectively.

[133] *The Citizen v McBride*, supra note 126, at paras 89–95. Cf *Bladet Tromsø & Stensaas v Norway* (2000) 29 EHRR 125 at para 62: reporting 'should not be considered solely by reference to the disputed articles . . . but in the wider context of the newspaper's coverage' of the issue. See also *Bergens Tidende v Norway* (2000) 31 EHRR 16 at para 51 and *Tønsbergs Blad as and Haukom v Norway* (2008) 46 EHRR 40 at para 94.

[134] Supra note 124.

[135] See *Gately*, supra note 19, at para 12.24.

8.10 RETRACTION, APOLOGY AND REPLY

8.10.1 *Retraction and apology*

The Roman-Dutch law provided two actions: *amende profitable* and *amende honorable*. *Amende profitable* bore a distinct resemblance to the Roman law action for the recovery of pecuniary damages. *Amende honorable* took two forms: (i) a declaration by the wrongdoer retracting his words and acknowledging that they were false (*palinodia, retractio* or *recantio*); and (ii) an apology or acknowledgement of guilt and prayer for forgiveness (*deprecatio*).[136] Although there was some dispute on this matter amongst the authorities, it seems that the correct view was that the *amende honorable* was a remedy *additional*, rather than *alternative*, to damages.[137] The recantation applied to oral and written words and, if the defendant refused to make honourable amends, he could render himself liable to fine or imprisonment.[138] Leaving aside the fact that at times humiliating forms of apologies were sought, the retraction and apology did not always reach the desired audience and it was enforced by threat of punishment, the concept of retracting the offensive words and apologising for their use has some attraction from the perspective of legal and practical resolution of disputes.

There appears to be resurgence of *judicial* interest in South Africa (prompted to some extent by indigenous emphasis on restorative justice and *ubuntu*) in the *amende honourable*,[139] which was thought to have been abrogated by disuse.[140]

In *Le Roux v Dey*[141] the Constitutional Court ordered an unconditional apology, in addition to the payment of damages, for the injury caused by a defamatory picture. Cameron and Froneman JJ, regarding the wrong as an impairment of dignity rather than reputation, considered it time the South African law recognise the value of restorative justice implicit in an apology

---

[136] See Burchell, supra note 38, at 11–12.

[137] See the authorities cited in Burchell, supra note 38, at 12.

[138] Burchell, supra note 38.

[139] In *Mineworkers Investment Co (Pty) Ltd v Modimane* 2002 (6) SA 512 (W) at para 24, Willis J described the *amende honorable* as a forgotten 'little treasure lost in a nook of our legal attic'. The majority of the Constitutional Court in *Dikoko v Mokhatla* 2006 (6) SA 235 (CC) did not make a finding on the relevance of the *amende honorable* in current law, but Mokgoro J dissenting took the view that whether or not the *amende honorable* did still form part of our law, it was important that once an apology was forthcoming it be 'sincere and adequate' (at para 67). Le Grange J in *Manuel v Crawford-Browne* 2008 (3) All SA 468 (C) held that the apology would, on the facts, not be 'sincere and adequate' and that freedom of expression did not cover 'the right to falsely attack the integrity of a fellow citizen for selfish reasons or for reasons which have nothing to do with public benefit' (at para 28).

[140] On the history of *amende honorable* in the South African law and the reasons for its falling into desuetude, see Burchell, supra note 38, at 315.

[141] Supra note 81.

and retraction. The justices urged that the law should be developed in this direction.[142] On the facts of *Le Roux v Dey* a genuine apology by the schoolchildren might have been the most effective (and educationally desirable) resolution of the dispute between them and their teachers.

The issue of apology also arose in *McBride's* case but Cameron J (for the majority of the Constitutional Court) distinguished *Dey*, especially because no personal relationship needed restoring in *McBride*,[143] the media defendant in *McBride* displayed 'no remorse', and the plaintiff asserted that an apology was 'inappropriate'. According to Cameron J, the 'question of an apology where a media defendant has defamed another must await another day'.[144]

One of the potential practical difficulties in the use of retraction and apology as a defence or a remedy is that the retraction and apology might not reach the readers or hearers of the original defamatory statement. The Internet, with its immediacy and its ability to reach an audience as wide as, if not wider than, that which read (or saw) the original defamatory publication may encourage rethinking of the merits of retraction and apology in South Africa.

In older Scottish practice, *palinode* (or public retraction with acceptance that the words were untrue) could be a remedy for insult before the commissary courts where *solatium* was sought.[145] Borthwick[146] points out that although the *actio ad palinodiam* was unknown to Roman law it was derived from Roman and Greek practice, and commissary court records indicate that this practice was adopted in Scotland. Palinode was in addition to a fine and damages but was awarded with caution.[147] Borthwick points to the value of palinode in 'reconciling animosities' and 'shortening law-suits'.[148]

The United Kingdom opted for a *statutory* form of amends in sections 2–4 of the Defamation Act 1996[149] providing for an innocent[150] publisher

---

[142] At para 197 (rather than re-instating the old *amende honorable*: para 199).

[143] Supra note 126, at para 133.

[144] At para 134.

[145] Norrie, supra note 29, at 2, 125 and 164.

[146] J Borthwick *A Treatise on the Law of Libel and Slander* (W & C Tait and J & WT Clarke 1826) at 180–1. See also *Deanes v Bothwell* (1669) Mor 7577 (where having alleged that a procurator was a 'false knave', the wrongdoer was required to stand at the church door of Glencourse, acknowledge his fault and pay money to the poor and the party) and *Symmond v Williamson* (1752) Mor 3435. I am indebted to Elspeth Reid for drawing my attention to these Scottish authorities.

[147] Supra note 146, at 181–2.

[148] Supra note 146, at 183.

[149] These provisions came into operation in England and Wales on 28 February 2000 and in Scotland on 31 March 2001: Collins, supra note 57, at para 18.01.

[150] Someone who did not know and had no reason to believe (it is presumed that the offeror did not know or had no reason to believe) that the statement was likely to be understood as referring to the aggrieved party, or that the statement was both false and defamatory of that person. Eady J in *Milne v Express Newspapers* [2003] 1 WLR 927 at para 41 has interpreted the words 'no reason to believe' to mean proof of 'bad faith' or 'reckless disregard of the truth' is required (proof of negligence is not sufficient).

to rely on an exclusive defence that an offer of amends has been made. It is submitted that it is too restrictive of free speech (and, in the case of a media defendant, a possible inhibition on editorial discretion) to link the defence of lack of fault only to an offer of amends. Similarly, it may unduly restrict the pertinence of retraction and apology, in an appropriate case, to link the relevance of retraction and apology to cases where intention (or recklessness) on the part of the defendant is lacking or even to confine retraction and apology to cases of defamation, as opposed to other *iniuriae*.[151]

South African law allows greater *common law* scope for innocent defamation by a non-media defendant and, in terms of *Bogoshi*, the media are accorded, in addition to the defence of 'reasonable publication' and the standard grounds of justification that apply to everyone, a defence of absence of fault in the form of *negligence* (that is, a defence of *reasonable* ignorance of, or mistake in relation to, any of the basic elements of defamation or the existence of any justificatory defences).[152] These defences of absence of intention or negligence exist, in terms of South African law, irrespective of an offer of amends having been made.

An obvious and ideal way of giving weight to the making of amends (in the form of retraction and apology) in the context of media publication lies within the *common law* concept of 'reasonable publication' and 'responsible communication on matters of public interest' that has emerged in jurisdictions within the Commonwealth of Nations.[153] Failure to pursue, or even offer, the route of amends may, in certain circumstances, be a factor (although not necessarily decisive on its own) pointing towards unreasonable or irresponsible publication. Where an individual, rather than a media defendant, is involved and the publication takes place in some electronic form, then it may also be adjudged 'unreasonable' conduct to fail to make amends for inaccuracies, misrepresentations or even opinions.

8.10.2 Reply

A reply is perhaps the most effective way of continuing the debate and furthering freedom of expression but, like retraction and apology, there are potential problems of inhibiting editorial discretion and in determining means of enforcing a 'right of reply'.[154] It is preferable to use the term

---

[151] As noted in this section supra, retraction and apology may be particularly pertinent in cases of insult or impairment of dignity.

[152] See section 8.8 supra.

[153] See section 8.2 supra.

[154] For instance, the *droit de réponse* in France requires a newspaper that refers to a person, even in a non-defamatory way, on pain of a fine, to allow that person a right or reply. The interference with editorial discretion impelled the United States Supreme Court to hold that a right of reply infringed the First Amendment: *Rosenbloom v Metromedia Inc* 403 US 29 (1971) and *Miami Herald Publishing Co v Tornillo* 418 US 241 (1974).

'opportunity to reply' rather than 'right of reply' in order to avoid the issue of enforcing the 'duty'.

In the non-exhaustive list of factors relevant to determining whether a publication is 'reasonable', 'responsible' or 'in the public interest', the judgments in Australia,[155] South Africa,[156] Canada[157] and England[158] consider a major factor to be whether an opportunity to rebut allegations was provided. The Canadian[159] and English precedent[160] specifically includes Internet publishing. One of the features of Internet communication is that an almost immediate reply, which can reach a similar (or perhaps wider) audience, could be forthcoming. Moreover, growing opportunities are being given to ordinary persons, who do not form part of the organised media, to become 'self-publishers' of their own views by utilising modern forms of electronic social networking and blogs. While opportunities for impairing the reputations and dignities of others are compounded by electronic communication, so are the opportunities to redress the wrong. The concept of 'reasonable/ responsible' publication found in contemporary Commonwealth jurisprudence illuminates the path.

---

[155] *Lange*, supra note 2, at 574.
[156] *Bogoshi*, supra note 6, at paras 31–2G.
[157] *Grant*, supra note 8, at paras 110–19.
[158] *Reynolds*, supra note 2, at 205A-C (per Lord Nicholls of Birkenhead).
[159] Supra note 47.
[160] Supra note 55.

Chapter 9

Strict Liability

Max Loubser

9.1 INTRODUCTION

9.1.1 *The area in focus*

The concept of 'strict liability' is not exact: the level of fault required for delictual liability varies and the group of rules that are commonly regarded as applying to 'strict liability' can be plotted not at an exact point, but at a cluster of locations on a continuum between absolute and fault-based liability.[1] There are differences between the two jurisdictions regarding the strictness of liability in certain areas, for example in respect of damage-causing involving land and buildings. The focus for considering the impact of human rights on strict liability is on three prominent areas common to both jurisdictions: (1) liability for animals (statute-based in Scotland and common law-based in South Africa); (2) product liability (statute-based in both jurisdictions); and (3) vicarious liability (common law-based in both jurisdictions).

The potential impact of human rights on strict liability rules of law is in principle the same in Scotland and South Africa, despite differences in detail between the applicable human rights instruments (the Human Rights Act in Scotland and the South African Constitution). First, rules can be tested for compatibility with the applicable human rights instrument. Second, rules must be interpreted in accordance with the applicable human rights instrument. Third, when applying rules of common law in disputes between private individuals (or a private individual and the state) courts must test the rules for compatibility with the human rights instrument and consider their development to that end. Rules are particularly susceptible to such development if they involve 'open-ended norms . . . through which human rights may be filtered in legal development': it is a 'question of finding the open-ended private law norms through which the human rights can be filtered in

---

[1] E Reid and M Loubser 'Strict Liability' in R Zimmermann, D Visser and Kenneth Reid (eds) *Mixed Legal Systems in Comparative Perspective: Property and Obligations in Scotland and South Africa* (Oxford University Press 2004) 606.

the development of the law'.[2] However, there is a major imbalance between the two jurisdictions regarding the material available on human rights and strict liability – there is almost no Scottish material.

9.1.2 Fault and human rights generally

Generally the courts decline to implement major reforms such as the introduction or abolition of strict liability by a decision in a particular case, opting to leave such reform to the legislature. Attempts have been made to persuade South African courts on constitutional grounds to expand strict liability, in cases involving liability of manufacturers for defective products[3] and liability of the state for dishonest conduct of its employees,[4] but these attempts have been unsuccessful. However, there are some examples in both South African and Scots law where constitutional/human rights values have had an impact on the fault requirement in delict.

In pre-Constitution South African cases involving wrongful deprivation of liberty (mostly by arrest) and wrongful attachment of property, where common law liability is based on a form of intent, the courts have held that policy considerations concerning the protection of physical integrity and property favour a watering-down of the intent requirement. Liability still requires proof of intention, but this is an attenuated form of intention, which relates only to achieving a particular result, and not to consciousness of unlawfulness.[5] The policy underlying this approach is that more comprehensive protection should be afforded against serious encroachments upon the freedom of the individual.[6] This approach is underscored by the constitutional protection of the right to freedom and security of the person.[7] The plaintiff must prove the fact of imprisonment or arrest and that it was

---

2 H L MacQueen 'Human Rights and Private Law in Scotland: A Response to President Barak' (2003) 78 *Tulane Law Review* 363 at 377.

3 *Wagener v Pharmacare Ltd; Cuttings v Pharmacare Ltd* 2003 7 BCLR 710 (SCA); 2003 2 All SA 167 (SCA); 2003 (4) SA 285 (SCA).

4 *Phoebus Apollo Aviation CC v Minister of Safety & Security* 2003 1 BCLR 14 (CC); 2003 2 SA 34 (CC) at para 6: 'It was also contended in argument that the respondent should be held liable for the wrongful acts of the policemen whether they were acting in the course of their employment or not. No convincing argument was, however, advanced to sustain this submission, or to show why the common law should be developed so as to impose an absolute liability on the State for the conduct of its employees committed dishonestly and in pursuit of their own selfish interest'.

5 *Minister of Justice v Hofmeyr* 1993 (3) SA 131 (A) 154; *Tödt v Ipser* 1993 (3) SA 577 (A) at 588; *Minister of Finance v EBN Trading (Pty) Ltd* 1998 (2) SA 319 (N) at 328–9; *Sheriff, Pretoria East v Meevis* 2001 (3) SA 454 (SCA) para 14.

6 DJ McQuoid Mason 'Vicarious and Strict Liability' in W Joubert (ed) *The Law of South Africa* 2e (LexisNexis Butterworths 2003–) vol 30 para 71; *Shoba v Minister van Justisie* 1982 (2) SA 554 (C) 559B-D.

7 S 12 of the Constitution of the Republic of South Africa Act 108 of 1996.

unlawful and it is then for the defendant to show that the imprisonment or arrest was justified.[8] Consciousness of the unlawfulness of the arrest is not a requirement for liability. This approach is also followed in respect of detention or imprisonment, where the manner of detention may constitute an infringement of basic rights to bodily integrity and to mental and intellectual wellbeing.[9]

In effect the same phenomenon can be observed in Scots law, even prior to the introduction of the Human Rights Act. This appears from the analysis by Sheriff Principal Cox in *McKinney v Chief Constable Strathclyde Police:*[10]

> 'In my opinion the decided cases can be divided between those in which the pursuer avers that he or she has been deprived of liberty unlawfully – in which case averments of malice are unnecessary – and those in which the pursuer concedes that the constable had the power to arrest or detain but that the exercise of that power on the particular occasion was unwarranted – in which case malice must be averred and proved.'[11]

The post-Human Rights Act analysis appears to follow the same lines.[12]

For some sixteen years in the late twentieth century the South African courts accepted a regime of strict liability for defamation by the media. In 1998, in *National Media Ltd v Bogoshi,*[13] the Supreme Court of Appeal changed course and moved away from strict liability. The court based its decision on policy considerations (freedom of expression and the importance of the media in a democratic society) and also indicated that the development is compatible with constitutional/human rights values.[14] The nature of the current fault requirement is somewhat contentious, but essentially a media defendant is saddled with an onus of proof and can avoid liability for defamation by proving that it was not negligent in the circumstances of the case. Absence of knowledge of unlawfulness is a defence, but only if the media defendant can show that such lack of knowledge was reasonable, and not due to any negligent act or omission on its part.[15]

---

[8] McQuoid Mason 'Vicarious and Strict Liability', note 6 supra, at para 71; *Whittaker v Roos and Bateman; Morant v Roos and Bateman* 1912 AD 92 122–3; *Groenewald v Minister van Justisie* 1972 (3) SA 596 (O) 599; *Donono v Minister of Prisons* 1973 (4) SA 259 (C) 262; *Minister of Justice v Hofmeyr* 1993 (3) SA 131 (A).

[9] *Whittaker v Roos and Bateman; Morant v Roos and Bateman* 1912 AD 92 122–3; *Minister of Justice v Hofmeyr* 1993 (3) SA 131 (A).

[10] 1998 SLT (Sh Ct) 80 at 82.

[11] See also the recent English case of *R (on the application of Sessay) v South London and Maudsley NHS Foundation Trust* [2011] EWHC 2617 (QB).

[12] See *Beck v Chief Constable Strathclyde Police* 2005 1 SC 149.

[13] 1998 (4) SA 1196 (SCA).

[14] Ibid at 1216–1219.

[15] Ibid at 1214; 1214–1215 (SA); *Mthembi-Mahanyele v Mail & Guardian* 2004 3 All SA 511 (SCA); 2004 11 BCLR 1182 (SCA); 2004 (6) SA 329 (SCA); See also *Khumalo v Holomisa* 2002 8 BCLR 771 (CC) para 20; 2002 (5) SA 401 (CC).

In Scots law defamation remains a delict of strict liability at a formal level (the South African *Bogoshi* case was noted but not followed by Lord Nicholls in *Reynolds v Times Newspapers*).[16] However, given that most cases do involve the media, the availability of the *Reynolds* qualified privilege means that in functional terms the real focus has become whether the journalism was responsible – in other words it is a fault-based enquiry. *Reynolds* is accepted in Scots law.[17]

Against this background of a rather limited impact of constitutional/human rights values on the fault requirement in delict generally, the impact or potential impact on strict liability is examined below.

9.2 STRICT LIABILITY AND THE RIGHT TO EQUALITY

Is there a constitutional/human rights basis for the courts to decide that either strict liability or the existence of a fault requirement is inconsistent with constitutional/human rights values? The right to equality in terms of section 9 of the South African Constitution holds out such a possibility. Section 9(1) provides for a general right to equality whereas the provisions of section 9(3) and (4) prohibit a specific form of unequal treatment, namely unfair discrimination. Section 9(1) covers all forms of differentiating treatment that do not amount to unfair discrimination. This distinction is not made in article 14 of the European Convention, which provides that the enjoyment of the rights and freedoms set forth in the Convention 'shall be secured without discrimination on any ground . . .' and does not refer to a substantive right to equality. Section 9 thus raises several key questions which will be explored in the sections to follow: (1) Does the right to equality rights apply to natural and juristic persons in delict? (2) How is the right to equality relevant to strict liability in delict? (3) Can the existence or absence of strict liability in a particular case violate the right to equality? (4) Does the law that provides for strict liability meet the requirement of a rational connection to a legitimate government purpose? and (5) Could equality or discrimination arguments be raised in respect of strict liability in delict in Scotland?

9.2.1 Does the right to equality apply to natural and juristic persons in delict?

In terms of section 8(2) the Bill of Rights binds natural and juristic persons if and to the extent applicable, depending on the nature of the right and the nature of any correlative duty. The equality rights enshrined in section 9 of the Constitution apply to all law and bind all state organs. It is accepted in case law that the right to equality and most of the duties imposed by it are of

---

[16] [2001] 2 AC 127, and see discussion at sections 8.2 and 8.8 supra.
[17] See *Adams v Guardian Newspapers* 2003 SC 425.

such a nature that the right is capable of being applied to private natural and juristic persons in terms of section 8(2).[18]

9.2.2 How is the right to equality relevant to strict liability in delict?

It is arguable that the requirement to prove fault in certain cases but not in others violates the right to equality before the law and to equal protection and benefit of the law under section 9(1) of the Constitution. An argument along these lines was made to attack the validity of a shorter-than-normal (one-year) limitation period contained in section 113(1) of the Defence Act 44 of 1957 (since repealed) in actions against the state for delicts committed by members of the Defence Force, in *Mohlomi v Minister of Defence*:[19]

> 'The inequality lay, so it was said, in the discrimination between the general run of plaintiffs and those whose cases the subsection affected, to their disadvantage, and furthermore between the State when sued and in suing.'

In the *Mohlomi* case the Constitutional Court held the limitation period to be invalid for being inconsistent with the constitutional right to to have justiciable disputes settled by a court of law or other forum, under s 22 of the 1993 Constitution. There was no need, therefore, to decide the equality argument.

How could strict liability or the lack of it offend against the right to equality before the law and to equal protection and benefit of the law? From the point of view of the defendant the argument could be that the general run of defendants in delict can rely on absence of fault; and the imposition of strict liability in certain cases (harm done by an animal or by a defective product) therefore violates the right to equality before the law and to equal protection and benefit of the law under section 9(1) of the Constitution. From the point of view of the plaintiff in a case of firearm abuse, for example, the argument could be that the law recognises strict liability in cases of harm done by an animal or by a defective product; similar policy considerations apply in the case of harm done by the use of a firearm; therefore maintenance of the fault requirement in the firearm case violates the right to equality before the law and to equal protection and benefit of the law under section 9(1) of the Constitution.

9.2.3 Can the existence or absence of strict liability in a particular case violate the right to equality?

Section 9(1) guarantees a general right to equality whereas section 9(3) and (4) prohibit a specific form of unequal treatment, namely unfair discrimination.

---

[18] *Bill of Rights Compendium* (LexisNexis 1996–) para 1A57.2.
[19] 1997 (1) SA 124 (CC) para 21.

Section 9 can be said to identify three ways in which a law might differentiate between people or categories of people.[20] First, there is 'mere differentiation', which, while it does treat some people differently to others, does not amount to discrimination. Secondly, there is differentiation which amounts to unfair discrimination. Discrimination, unlike 'mere differentiation', involves differentiation on illegitimate grounds.[21] These grounds can be 'listed grounds', such as race, gender, sex, ethnic origin, or an 'analogous ground', which is one based on attributes or characteristics that have the potential to impair human dignity.[22] The third category of differentiation, implied by the second, is fair discrimination, involving law that discriminates but does not do so unfairly, taking into account the impact of the discrimination on the complainant and others in his or her situation.

Section 9(1) implies a minimum rationality requirement. The Constitutional Court has largely used section 9(1) as a basic rationality threshold for compliance with the equality right. Mere differentiation will violate section 9(1) unless it has a rational connection to a legitimate government purpose. 'Mere differentiation' in legislation and administration is common practice in any modern state that seeks to govern effectively and regulate the needs and interests of its citizens. Examples of such differentiation range from income classification for the purposes of taxation or social welfare grants to the distinctions made in regulations for the distribution of various types of drugs. The majority of these distinctions do not contravene the equality right. However, differentiation in this context will not always be constitutional. In particular, it will fall foul of the Constitution when it is arbitrary or irrational.

The application of the rationality standard is illustrated by a number of cases. In *Prinsloo v Van der Linde and Another*,[23] a case dealing with the negligence requirement in delict, the Constitutional Court considered section 84 of the Forest Act 122 of 1984, which created a presumption of negligence by landowners in respect of fires occurring in 'non-controlled areas'. The Act provided for fire control areas where compulsory fire control measures were put in place. Outside these areas landowners were not obliged to institute fire control measures but were encouraged to do so, inter alia by the section 84 presumption which operated only against landowners in 'non-controlled areas' where no control measures were put in place. In this manner the Act differentiated between landowners in 'non-controlled areas' and landowners in 'controlled areas'. This was not a differentiation on any of the 'listed grounds' or 'analogous grounds' under section 9(3) and therefore did not amount to unfair discrimination, but was the imposition of a presumption

---

[20] I Currie and J De Waal *The Bill of Rights Handbook* 5e (Juta 2005) 237.
[21] Ibid 243.
[22] Ibid 243–4.
[23] 1997 (3) SA 1012 (CC); 1997 (6) BCLR 759 (CC).

of fault a violation of the right to equality before the law or the right to equal protection and benefit of the law? A rationality standard applies, as explained by Ackerman J, as follows:[24]

'[T]he constitutional state is expected to act in a rational manner. It should not regulate in an arbitrary manner or manifest naked preferences that serve no legitimate governmental purpose, for that would be inconsistent with the rule of law and the fundamental premises of the constitutional state. The purpose of this aspect of equality is, therefore, to ensure that the state is bound to function in a rational manner. This has been said to promote the need for governmental action to relate to a defensible vision of the public good, as well as to enhance the coherence and integrity of legislation.'

In *Harksen v Lane NO and Others*[25] the Constitutional Court distilled the standard set by section 9(1) into a simple test: does the provision differentiate between people or categories of people? If so, does the differentiation bear a rational connection to a legitimate government purpose? If it does not, then there is a violation of section 9(1). Even if it does bear a rational connection, it might nevertheless amount to discrimination if it amounts to differentiation on any of the 'listed grounds' or 'analogous grounds' under section 9(3). In the *Harksen* case Goldstone J held that the stages of enquiry were the following:

'(a) Does the provision differentiate between people or categories of people? If so, does the differentiation bear a rational connection to a legitimate government purpose? If it does not then there is a violation of s 8(1). Even if it does bear a rational connection, it might nevertheless amount to discrimination.

(b) Does the differentiation amount to unfair discrimination? This requires a two-stage analysis:

(i) Firstly, does the differentiation amount to 'discrimination'? If it is on a specified ground, then discrimination will have been established. If it is not on a specified ground, then whether or not there is discrimination will depend upon whether, objectively, the ground is based on attributes and characteristics which have the potential to impair the fundamental human dignity of persons as human beings or to affect them adversely in a comparably serious manner.

(ii) If the differentiation amounts to 'discrimination', does it amount to 'unfair discrimination'? If it has been found to have been on a specified ground, then unfairness will be presumed. If on an unspecified ground, unfairness will have to be established by the complainant. The test of unfairness focuses primarily on the impact of the discrimination on the complainant and others in his or her situation.

If, at the end of this stage of the enquiry, the differentiation is found not to be unfair, then there will be no violation of s 8(2).

---

[24] At para 25.
[25] 1998 (1) SA 300 (CC) para 53.

(c) If the discrimination is found to be unfair, then a determination will have to be made as to whether the provision can be justified under the limitations clause (s 33 of the interim Constitution).'

The rationality test set out by Goldstone J in *Harksen* as the first line of enquiry involves two questions:

(a) First, has there been a differentiation between individuals or groups? The establishment of a differentiation between individuals or groups is the first step of the section 9(1) enquiry. If there is no differentiation, there can be no violation of section 9(1).
(b) Second, does the differentiation bear a rational connection to a legitimate government purpose? This entails two steps:
  (i) First, to identify a legitimate purpose. The court will evaluate the reasons given by the government to determine whether there is such a legitimate purpose. To meet the criterion of legitimacy under section 9(1), it seems that the government merely has to show that its purpose is neither arbitrary nor irrational. Legitimacy is, thus, equated with rationality. The government does not have to justify its purpose against substantive constitutional values or any conception of 'the general good' as it might under the justification enquiry contemplated in section 36 of the Constitution.
  (ii) The next step considers whether the scheme or measures chosen by Parliament or the government are rationally connected to this purpose. The question is not whether the government may have achieved its purposes more effectively in a different manner, or whether its regulation or conduct could have been more closely connected to its purpose. The test is simply whether there is a reason for the differentiation that is rationally connected to a legitimate government purpose.[26]

It appears that as the law stands, the only purpose of the rationality review is an enquiry into whether the differentiation is arbitrary or irrational, or manifests naked preference. It is irrelevant to this enquiry whether the scheme chosen by the legislature could be improved in one respect or another. This series of questions, therefore, constitutes section 9(1) as a minimum rationality threshold to the equality right. It does not entail an analysis of the impact of the impugned action or of the policy choices made. As such it has been said to be 'extremely deferential to the legislature and most laws will pass constitutional muster under this provision'.[27]

---

[26] See also *Law Society of South Africa and others v Minister for Transport and others* [2010] ZACC 25 paras 34–5.
[27] M H Cheadle, D M Davis and N R L Haysom *South African Constitutional Law: The Bill of Rights*, ch 4.6.1.1, page 4–16 (LexisNexis Online publication, accessed 3 October 2011).

The Constitutional Court in *Jooste v Score Supermarket Trading (Pty) Ltd (Minister of Labour intervening)*[28] adopted a test of equality that merely requires reasons for the legislature's decision to differentiate. The Court considered section 35 of the Compensation for Occupational Injuries and Diseases Act 130 of 1993, which limits employees who suffer injuries incurred in the course of their employment to compensation under that Act, preventing such employees from making claims against their employer under the common law. The Court found the differentiation in respect of this group to be rationally connected to the legitimate government purpose of providing compensation for disability caused by injuries sustained during the course of employment. In doing so, the Court said:[29]

> 'It is clear that the only purpose of rationality review is an inquiry into whether the differentiation is arbitrary or irrational, or manifests naked preference and it is irrelevant to this inquiry whether the scheme chosen by the legislature could be improved in one respect or another. Whether an employee ought to have retained a common law right to claim damages, either over and above or as an alternative to the advantages conferred by the Compensation Act, represents a highly debatable, controversial and complex matter of policy. It involves a policy choice which the legislature and not a court must make.'

The case of *Pretoria City Council v Walker*[30] provides an example of a failure to meet the rationality standard under section 9(1), although it was not decided as such. One of the issues facing the Court in this case was the constitutional validity of the council's selective enforcement of the debts of defaulting residents. The Court found that this practice was not based on a 'rational and coherent' policy, but was adopted and implemented in a secretive and misleading manner by council officials, on a racial basis, apparently without council authority and in conflict with a council resolution. Although the Court found this to be unfair racial discrimination, the facts clearly also support a claim that the differential treatment was irrational and arbitrary.

In *Mvumvu and others v Minister of Transport and another*[31] the Western Cape High Court considered the capping of passenger claims under the Road Accident Fund Act 56 of 1996 and held that the Act distinguishes between two broad categories of people and treats them differently: on the one hand, pedestrians and the occupiers (including passengers) of an 'innocent' vehicle who have unlimited claims for compensation and, on the other hand, passengers in an 'offending' vehicle, whose claims are capped by section 18.

Does this differentiation bear a rational connection to a legitimate government purpose? Two explanations were offered on behalf of the minister

---

[28] 1999 (2) SA 1 (CC).
[29] Para 17.
[30] 1998 (2) SA 363 (CC).
[31] [2011] 1 All SA 90 (WCC).

for the differentiation between the two classes. First, it was stated that the funding of the Road Acident Fund is not designed to compensate all victims for all losses they might suffer as a result of motor vehicle accidents. Were it otherwise, the fund would long since have been bankrupt. Capping was therefore a cost-saving measure. However, this does not constitute an explanation for differentiating between classes of innocent road accident victims, nor for explaining why the claims of some victims are singled out for very limited compensation whilst others receive full compensation. Second, the minister's representative stated that the decision as to what limitations ought to apply was a complex policy choice, resolved along the following lines: a pedestrian, or occupant of another vehicle, has no choice in choosing the driver or owner of the offending vehicle, whereas the same is not necessarily true in respect of a passenger in an offending vehicle. However, what was put up as the apparent justification for the unequal treatment appears to be unsupported by fact or logic. In the first place, it is artificial to suggest that a person in a taxi queue 'chooses' the driver of the taxi which he/she will board. The passenger seldom has knowledge of the competence of the driver or the roadworthiness of the vehicle. Similarly, employees have little or no say regarding the identity or competence of the drivers of employers' vehicles. In any event, even if one does attribute such a 'choice' to a passenger, this still provides no explanation of what rational government purpose is served by treating such a passenger differently from other people who are also innocent victims of road accidents.

The Court in *Mvumvu* held that the differentiation created by the impugned capping provision fell at the first hurdle stipulated in *Harksen* (supra) in that it bears no rational connection to a legitimate government purpose, and it is, therefore, in violation of section 9(1) of the Constitution.

9.3 RATIONALITY OF STRICT LIABILITY

Differentiating between plaintiffs in delict who need to prove some form of fault and those who do not, in cases of strict liability, does not involve discrimination on a listed or analogous ground. The test in terms of section 9(1) is therefore whether the law that provides for strict liability meets the requirement of a rational connection to a legitimate government purpose. This question will be considered below in respect of strict liability for harm done by animals, harm done by a defective products and vicarious liability.

9.3.1 *Animals*

In respect of harm done by animals the imposition of strict liability was challenged before the Supreme Court of Appeal in *Loriza Brahman v Dippenaar*.[32]

---

[32] 2002 (2) SA 477 (SCA).

In this case a company that owned a cattle stud farm, trading under the name 'Loriza Brahman', was sued for harm caused by one of their stud animals named 'Alicia' when it ran into Dippenaar and injured him while he was inspecting cattle in an enclosure prior to a cattle auction. Dippenaar instituted an *actio de pauperie* against Loriza, alleging strict liability for harm suffered and succeeding in the court *a quo*. In defence and on appeal Loriza attacked the set of rules underlying the *actio de pauperie*, arguing for this form of strict liability to be abolished. The grounds for attacking the rationality of the rules of pauperian liability emerging from this case, and from other cases and legal writing on the subject, and from the right to equal treatment under section 9(1) of the Constitution, are explained below.

9.3.1.1 Types of animal
Strict liability for harm done by animals is irrationally restricted to domestic or domesticated animals. The Animals (Scotland) Act 1987 is more rational; it creates liability for harm done by an animal of 'a species whose members generally are by virtue of their physical attributes or habits likely (unless controlled or restrained) to injure severely or kill persons or animals, or damage property to a material extent'.[33] The term 'species' includes a form or variety or subspecies of the species, identifiable by age, sex or such other criteria as are relevant to the behaviour of the animals, and a kind which is the product of hybridisation.[34] Dogs and dangerous wild animals[35] are deemed to be likely (unless controlled or restrained) to injure or kill 'by biting or otherwise savaging, attacking or harrying'[36] even if the animal has never shown any vicious tendencies in the past.

9.3.1.2 The contra naturam sui generis rule
This rule lacks a rational basis, because it is unclear what it means. It is inconsistently applied, and it creates uncertainty: is the test objective or is it subjectively based on 'fault' of the particular animal? Does *genus* refer to domestic animals generally or the particular species? Or is the standard entirely arbitrary, depending on the view of the court on the reasonableness of imposing liability? In so far as it refers to a standard related to a species such as dogs or horses, it is irrational to treat all kinds of dogs or horses according to the same standard; and it is in any event irrational to attempt to assess in human terms either the disposition of an individual animal (that is, if it is a generally placid or unruly horse), or the disposition of the species (that is, if horses or dogs are by nature aggressive). Some cases refer to the innate wildness, viciousness or perverseness (*sponte feritate commota*) of the

---

[33] S 1(1)(b).
[34] S 1(2)(a) and (b).
[35] Within the meaning of the Dangerous Wild Animals Act 1976 s 7(4).
[36] S 1(3).

particular animal (a subjective approach) while others refer to what could be expected of a well-behaved animal of its kind (an objective or 'reasonable animal' approach).[37]

Typical of the latter approach is the much discussed and even ridiculed judgment in *Da Silva v Otto*.[38] The appellant had been walking his dog on a leash in a public road in a residential area when the respondent's dog ran out of an open side gate on the respondent's premises and attacked the dog on the leash. The appellant, who carried a whip, hit the respondent's dog which then bit him. The Court found that the respondent had not acted negligently: the dog had never before bitten a person and he had taken sufficient precautions against the possibility of the dog escaping from his premises. The Court held furthermore that the appellant had also not acted negligently: he had not 'provoked' the dog by hitting it, and he was entitled to protect his dog against an attack. Nestadt J (with O'Donovan AJ) held that in such circumstances, where the injured person had acted lawfully and reasonably, the dog was presumed to have acted *contra naturam sui generis*: an objective test of the reasonable dog applies and it was expected of the dog to distinguish between a lawful attack and an unlawful attack on itself.

The Animals (Scotland) Act 1987 is more rational: the keeper of an animal is strictly liable if the injury or damage complained of is directly referable to the physical attributes or habits that make the particular species of animal likely (unless controlled or restrained) to injure or kill persons or animals, or to damage property to a material extent.[39] Thus injury as a result of being bitten by a dog is directly referable to the dog's attribute or habit to bite, but injury as a result of falling over the dog is not.[40] The case of *Fairlie v Carruthers*[41] (a dog playfully ran up to, knocked over, and injured a 66–year-old woman and liability was not imposed) indicates that the Animals (Scotland) Act 1987 is restricted to behaviour that would be described in human terms as aggressive or vicious, excluding liability for behaviour that would be described in human terms as over-friendly. There is also no strict liability for injury or damage caused by the mere fact that the animal was present on a road or in any other place,[42] or where the injury consists of 'disease transmitted by means which are unlikely to cause severe injury other than disease'.[43] Thus if an escaped animal bites a passer-by, the keeper is strictly liable to the victim, but if it runs into the road and causes a car accident, the keeper will only be liable if negligence can be proved.

---

[37] C G van der Merwe and M A Rabie 'Animals' in W Joubert (ed) *The Law of South Africa* 2e (LexisNexis Butterworths 2003) vol 1 para 334.

[38] 1986 (3) SA 538 (T).

[39] S 1(1)(b) and (c).

[40] J Thomson *Delictual Liability* 4e (Tottel 2009) para 9.3.

[41] 1996 SLT (Sh Ct) 56.

[42] S 1(5).

[43] S 1(4).

9.3.1.3 Fairness

Pauperian liability leads to unfair results, in that liability can be imposed on the owner of an animal in circumstances where the owner was in no position to contain the risks presented by keeping the animal, for example in the case of a bank financing the purchase of a stud animal and thus obtaining ownership, or an owner leasing the animal for stud services. The owner of an animal is liable even if he was not in possession of the animal at the time when it caused harm, but the owner can rely on the negligence of the keeper of the animal at the time as a defence.[44] The special risk of animals in a human environment is their instinctive, unpredictable behaviour and mobility. The keeper of an animal is a party to creating or maintaining this risk and is in a position to contain the risk by controlling or restraining the animal; and may benefit from keeping the animal. Therefore the policy considerations underlying the recognition of strict liability for harm done by animals indicate that liability should include keepers and not be restricted to owners. There is an important difference between South African and Scots law in this regard.

The Animals (Scotland) Act 1987 provides that a person is a keeper of an animal if he owns the animal or has possession of it; or has actual care and control of a child under the age of sixteen who owns the animal or has possession of it; or was the owner or possessor at the time when the animal was abandoned or escaped. A person temporarily detaining an animal to protect it or to protect another person or animal or to restore it to its owner as soon as reasonably practicable shall not be regarded as having possession of it. The effect of these provisions is that, in so far as more than one person qualifes as keeper, liability will be joint and several.

The Apportionment of Damages Act 34 of 1956 does not apply to pauperian claims. Instead an all-or-nothing rule applies[45] which leads to unfair results. The Animals (Scotland) Act 1987 is more rational: contributory negligence may result in the apportionment of damages.[46]

9.3.1.4 Animals: conclusion

In the *Loriza Brahman* case the Court (per Olivier JA) held[47] that the requirements for the *actio de pauperie* have been controversial but this form of strict liability has existed for about 2,500 years and remains part of South African law. Strict liability based on creation of risk is on the increase in modern legal systems and performs a useful function. As long as this form of liability is not unconstitutional or *contra bonos mores* or has not fallen into disuse,

---

[44] *Lever v Purdy* 1993 (3) SA 17 (A).
[45] *South African Railways and Harbours v Edwards* 1930 AD 3 op 10; and also *Svamvur v Portwood* 1970 (1) SA 144 (R) 145; *Swart v Honeyborne* 1981 (1) SA 974 (C) 976B.
[46] s 2(1)(a).
[47] Para 15.

it will not be abolished by the court. The task of the court is rather, where necessary, to adapt, extend or limit it.

The courts will not undertake abolition of an established form of strict liability lightly. Should there be some irrationality and inconsistencies, as appear in the rules relating to strict liability for harm done by animals, the court will endeavour to rationalise the rules, by adapting, extending or limiting them, rather than abolishing strict liability outright, as appears from the *Loriza Brahman* case. For abolition additional constitutional/human rights reasons will be required, as appears from the *Bogoshi* case, where the value of freedom of speech played a decisive role.

9.3.2 Product liability

9.3.2.1 The Wagener case

In South Africa the statutory introduction of strict product liability was foreshadowed by the case of *Wagener and Cuttings v Pharmacare Ltd*,[48] in which the South African Supreme Court of Appeal declined to introduce strict product liability judicially. *Wagener* involved a defective batch of a local anaesthetic named 'Regibloc' which, when administered, caused the plaintiffs to suffer necrosis and paralysis. The plaintiffs referred to strict product liability regimes in Europe and the US and argued that the law in South Africa had reached the stage where such liability should be imposed; and that there was a constitutional imperative to develop the common law in this regard, to give proper effect to the constitutional right to bodily integrity. However, the Court confirmed the common law requirement of negligence in the manufacture, sale or distribution of the product and refused to recognise liability where the manufacturer's fault had not been proved. The Court acknowledged its role in developing the common law, but concluded that 'if strict liability is to be imposed it is the legislature that must do it'.[49]

The Court in *Wagener* confirmed that the constitutional protection of the right to bodily integrity enjoins the court to consider developing the law in accordance with the Constitution's spirit, purport and objects. On the difficulty of proof under the Aquilian action, which could operate unduly harshly in the case of defective manufacture of a medical product, the court said that, even if strict liability applied, a plaintiff would still have to prove not only that the product was defective when used but defective when it left the manufacturer's control. In the case of a medical product, for example, that burden would in any event probably require expert evidence involving, no doubt, some complexities of scientific analysis.[50]

To illustrate the dilemma involved in trying to 'legislate' judicially in

---

[48] 2003 7 BCLR 710 (SCA); 2003 2 All SA 167 (SCA); 2003 (4) SA 285 (SCA).
[49] Para 38.
[50] Para 19.

this complex field the court referred to several questions that could arise.[51] Single instances of litigation cannot possibly provide the opportunity for the breadth and depth of investigation, analysis and determination that is necessary to produce, for use across the manufacturing industry, a cohesive and effective structure by which to impose strict liability. The court therefore confirmed that the only available remedy was the Aquilian action, which adequately protected the right to bodily integrity and which allowed the opportunity for incremental development of the approach to *res ipsa loquitur* and to the incidence of the onus. If strict liability was to be imposed, it was the legislature that had to do it.[52]

9.3.2.2 The Consumer Protection Act 68 of 2008

This has Act in section 61 introduced strict product liability, with effect from 1 April 2011. The standards for imposing strict liability, based on the concepts 'defect', 'unsafe', 'hazard' and 'failure' as defined in section 53, are to some extent irrational. To determine whether particular goods are 'unsafe', for example, could involve a bewildering array of alternative and overlapping standards. It could also involve standards bordering on the absurd. If the question is whether goods are 'unsafe' on account of a 'hazard', the court will have to determine whether the particular goods present an 'extreme risk' of personal injury or property damage, owing to a characteristic that presents a 'significant risk' of personal injury to any person, or damage to property. This does not make good sense. Even if it did make sense to link 'extreme risk' and 'significant risk' in this convoluted way, it is difficult to see why a claimant would rely on an 'extreme risk' situation (involving the definition of 'unsafe') if it is also possible to rely on a 'significant risk' situation (involving the definition of 'hazard'). A claimant would simply rely on what in the circumstances appears to be the lowest of the various vague and general standards contained in the definitions of 'defect', 'failure' or 'hazard'. Nevertheless, the courts are likely to find a core of rationality in the various standards, probably built on the characteristic of being unreasonably dangerous.

9.3.2.3 Policy considerations

Is there any moral, economic, or social reason why the victims of defective products in South Africa should be accorded any more special treatment than, for instance, the victims of road accidents, medical misadventures or environmental pollution? The differentiation created by the legislature for defective products will pass constitutional muster provided it has some rational basis. The rational basis must be sought in the policy considerations underlying strict product liability.

[51] Para 35.
[52] Para 38.

(a) Although the Court in *Wagener* ruled that there was no basis in existing case law for a finding of strict liability, it nevertheless remarked of
the arguments in favour of strict liability 'that virtually without exception they would hold good were imposition to be by the legislature'.[53]
Numerous arguments based on considerations of fairness, equity and
economic efficiency support the view that manufacturers or suppliers
should be liable on a no-fault basis for harm resulting from defectively
manufactured products.

(b) The ultimate consumer is normally unable to analyse or scrutinise
products for safety, and implicitly takes it on trust that a product will
not endanger life, health or property. The European Product Liability
Directive 85/374/EEC states in this regard that 'liability without fault
on the part of the producer is the sole means of adequately solving the
problem, peculiar to our age of increasing technicality, of a fair apportionment of the risks inherent in modern technological production . . .'.

(c) According to the US *Restatement Third, Torts: Products Liability* the
argument for strict liability for manufacturing defects rests on several
important fairness concerns.[54] In many cases manufacturing defects are
in fact caused by the manufacturer's negligence, but plaintiffs have difficulty proving it. Strict liability therefore comes to the aid of consumers
harmed by defective products where proof of negligence would be difficult or impossible.

(d) The basic utilitarian or efficiency-based argument for strict liability is
that 'the burden of losses consequent upon use of defective articles is
borne by those who are in a position to either control the danger or
make an equitable distribution of the losses when they do occur . . .'.[55]
Manufacturers invest in quality control at consciously chosen levels and
often know that a predictable number of flawed products will enter the
marketplace, with predictable potential harm to consumers. The manufacturer is the 'least cost avoider' – the party who can most effectively
take steps to avoid the risk of damage or to minimise its effects. The
manufacturer and other businesses forming part of the product supply
chain can spread the costs of improved quality and safety control, either
through insurance or through increased prices: 'The cost of an injury
and the loss of time or health may be an overwhelming misfortune to the
person injured, and a needless one, for the risk of injury can be insured
by the manufacturer and distributed among the public as a cost of doing
business'.[56]

(e) It should be conceded that strict liability might not always achieve

---

[53] Per Howie P at para 29.
[54] Para 2 comment (a).
[55] *Henningsen v Bloomfield Motors Inc* 161 A 2d 69 (1960) 81.
[56] Per Traynor J in *Escola v Coca-Cola Bottling Co of Fresno* 150 P 2d 436 (1944) 440.

optimal economic efficiency. Some risks are unavoidable, particularly those arising from hidden design defects. A strict liability regime
that holds the manufacturer automatically liable for harm resulting
from defects might lead to manufacturers taking excessive precautions,
pushing prices up beyond the level which reflects the potential costs to
society of product defects, or driving producers out of the market. Also,
product innovation may be inhibited by the threat of high damages
awards based on strict liability.[57] However, empirical evidence of such
inefficiencies is hard to come by and such potential drawbacks are probably unavoidable, representing the trade-off for allocating the risk of a
potentially overwhelming individual misfortune to the manufacturer or
supplier.

(f)   It must also be recognised from an insurance point of view that manu-
      facturers are not always best placed to assess particular risks and to take
      out appropriate insurance.[58] As far as physical damage to property is
      concerned, the consumer, who has more information about the value of
      the property and the uses to which it is put, is in a better position to take
      out insurance covering the potential loss. Household property is often
      covered by first-party or loss insurance, and strict liability that imposes
      upon the manufacturer what is in essence a requirement to take out
      third-party or liability insurance may create the potential for a wasteful
      double insurance of the loss in question.[59] However, this kind of inef-
      ficiency is to an extent unavoidable and is mostly limited to property
      insurance.

(g)   Apart from the 'down-stream', corrective or compensatory function
      of strict liability for defective products there is also an 'up-stream',
      preventative or deterrence function. In the USA in particular product
      liability litigation is seen as a powerful means to induce product safety,
      whereas in many other jurisdictions product safety is regarded as belong-
      ing primarily in the domain of public regulation.[60] The comment on the
      US *Restatement Third, Torts: Products Liability* refers in this regard to the
      premise that tort law serves the instrumental function of creating safety
      incentives. Imposing strict liability on manufacturers for harm caused by
      manufacturing defects encourages greater investment in product safety
      than does a regime of fault-based liability under which sellers may escape
      their appropriate share of responsibility.

(h)   Not only manufacturer behaviour but also consumer behaviour should

---

[57]   S Deakin et al *Markesinis and Deakin's Tort* Law 5e (Oxford University Press 2003), 620;
       C Hodges 'Development Risks: Unanswered Questions' (1998) 61 *MLR* 560.
[58]   See generally J Stapleton *Product Liability* (Butterworths 1994) ch 5.
[59]   Deakin et al, note 57 supra, at 620–1.
[60]   M Reimann 'Product Liability in a Global Context: The Hollow Victory of the European
       Model' 2003(2) *European Review of Private Law* 128 at 152–3.

be tested according to a standard of reasonableness. It is fair to require that individual consumers bear reasonable responsibility for proper use of products. This prevents careless consumers from being subsidised by more careful ones, when the former are paid damages out of funds to which the latter are forced to contribute through higher prices. Therefore, the introduction of strict liability should not exclude reliance on contributory negligence on the part of the consumer.

The policy considerations referred to above indicate that there is economic and moral justification for imposing a form of strict liability for defective products, to ease the shifting of loss from an individual consumer, for whom the concentration of the loss can prove catastrophic, to the 'deep-pocket' manufacturer, for whom the loss would be far less disruptive.[61] A strict form of product liability is conducive to a fair apportionment of the risks inherent in the mass production of goods in the modern economy. Gerhard Wagner has summed it up as follows:[62]

> 'As things stand today, economic analysis is the only discipline that can offer a comprehensive and consistent explanation for strict liability. According to economic wisdom, strict liability achieves the same level of deterrence with regard to precautions, but goes further than that because it also affects the activity levels chosen by potential tortfeasors. Because, under strict liability, the tortfeasor must compensate even those losses that are impossible to avoid at a reasonable cost he has an incentive to balance gains derived from the particular activity against its total cost. From there it follows easily that strict liability is the appropriate regime where the activity in question causes a substantial risk of harm even if all reasonable measures of safety have been observed.'

This constitutes a sufficiently rational basis for the liability differentiation in respect of defective products.

9.3.3 Vicarious liability

The same general set of rules on vicarious liability is applied in Scotland and South Africa, namely that an employer is vicariously liable for the delicts of his employee committed in the course and scope of his employment.[63] Both the set of rules constituting this form of liability and the justification for strict liability must have a rational basis.

Arguably there are some irrational aspects to the rules governing vicari-

---

[61] Stapleton, note 58 supra, at 93–4.

[62] G Wagner 'Comparative Tort Law' in M Reimann and R Zimmermann (eds) *The Oxford Handbook of Comparative Law* (Oxford University Press 2006) 1034.

[63] See Thomson, note 40 supra, at paras 12.5 ff; D H Sheldon 'Obligations Arising from a Wrongful Act' in *The Laws of Scotland, Stair Memorial Encyclopaedia* vol 15 (Butterworths 1996) para 243; McQuoid Mason 'Vicarious and Strict Liability', note 6 supra, at para 255.

ous liability, notably in the formulation of the so-called 'standard test' or traditional criterion for determining whether a delict was committed in the course and scope of the wrongdoer's employment.[64] However, there is a certain rational core to these rules, around which a large body of case law has developed, establishing reasonably clear guidelines.

Is there any moral, economic, or social reason why strict liability should be imposed on persons or entities engaging employees for the purposes of their enterprise, but not on persons or entities engaging independent contractors? The differentiation created by the rules on vicarious liability will pass constitutional muster provided it has a rational basis. The rational basis must be sought in the policy considerations underlying vicarious liability.

(a) In 1874 De Villiers CJ described the rule in respect of the vicarious liability of a principal for his agent as being 'founded upon public policy and convenience; for in no other way could there be any safety to third persons in their dealings either directly or indirectly with him through the instrumentality of agents'.[65]

(b) Emphasis has been placed on the actual or potential control exercised or exercisable by an employer over an employee in many cases on vicarious liability, both as a factor indicating the existence of the employment relationship and indirectly as a justification for the existence of strict liability.

(c) It has been accepted by the courts that the employer through the employment relationship creates a risk for its own ends[66] and that the employer's liability is therefore 'co-extensive and identical in every respect with the liability of the servant';[67] or that the employer is considered to be the actor himself where he acts through an employee – *qui facit per alium facit per se*.[68] Consequently, an employer who is liable as a result of a delict committed by an employee is bound *in solidum* with the employee to compensate the person who suffers damage as a result of the employee's delict.[69]

(d) Other policy considerations underlying the doctrine of vicarious liability are the following:[70] the employer can account for the risk in the

---

[64] See S Wagener 'An Assessment of the Normative Bases for the Doctrine of Vicarious Liability in South African Law, and the Implications for its Application' unpublished D Phil thesis University of Cape Town (2011) 87–96.

[65] *Gifford v Table Bay Dock and Breakwater Management Commission* (1874) 4 Buch 96 114.

[66] McQuoid Mason 'Vicarious and Strict Liability', note 6 supra, at para 257.

[67] *Botes v Van Deventer* 1966 (3) SA 182 (A) 205.

[68] Sheldon 'Obligations arising from a wrongful act', note 63 supra, at para 243 n 2.

[69] Sheldon 'Obligations arising from a wrongful act', note 63 supra, at para 243; McQuoid Mason 'Vicarious and Strict Liability', note 6 supra, at para 257.

[70] See K Zweigert and H Kötz *Introduction to Comparative Law* 3e (tr T Weir Clarendon Press 1998) 643–5.

structuring of the employee's compensation package; and employers
are the best 'risk-absorbers' because they can cost-effectively distribute
the risk of accidents by insurance and take precautionary measures
by resource allocation or incentive devices tailored to their type of
enterprise.

(e) In *K v Minister of Safety and Security*[71] the rationale for vicarious liability
was said to rest on a range of underlying principles. An important one
is the desirability of affording claimants efficacious remedies for harm
suffered. Another is the need to use legal remedies to incite employers to
take active steps to prevent their employees from harming members of
the broader community. There is a countervailing principle too, which is
that damages should not be borne by employers in all circumstances, but
only in those circumstances in which it is fair to require them to do so.[72]

The policy considerations referred to above indicate that there is some
economic and moral justification for imposing a form of strict liability on
employers for delicts committed by employees within the scope of their
employment. These considerations will probably continue to be regarded
as a sufficiently rational basis for the liability differentiation in respect of
employers, for delicts committed by employees. Should there be some
irrationality and inconsistency, the courts will endeavour to rationalise the
rules, by adapting, extending or limiting them, rather than abolishing vicarious liability outright.

9.3.4 *Could equality and rationality arguments be raised in Scotland?*

Article 14 of the European Convention provides that the enjoyment of the
rights and freedoms set forth in the Convention 'shall be secured without
discrimination on any ground such as sex, race, colour, language, religion,
political or other opinion, national or social origin, association with a
national minority, property, birth or other status'. Article 14 thus guarantees that everyone shall enjoy the Convention rights, without discrimination. However, article 14 is not a general 'equal treatment' guarantee. The
Convention contains no generally applicable free-standing prohibition on
discrimination. It requires only that the enjoyment of other Convention
rights be secured without discrimination: in effect it is a guarantee of equality
before the law of the Convention. This means that it can operate only within
the ambit of other Convention rights.[73]

---

[71] 2005 (6) SA 419 (CC).
[72] Para 21.
[73] R Reed and J Murdoch *Human Rights Law in Scotland* 3e (Bloomsbury Professional 2011)
para 3. 90.

9.4 CONSTITUTIONAL/HUMAN RIGHTS ARGUMENTS RELATING SPECIFICALLY TO VICARIOUS LIABILITY

Does vicarious liability raise constitutional/human rights issues other than equality and rationality? This question has arisen in recent South African cases before the Constitutional Court, involving criminal conduct by the police. The jurisdiction of the Constitutional Court in these cases depended on a finding that vicarious liability raises constitutional issues.

In *Phoebus Apollo Aviation CC v Minister of Safety and Security*[74] the plaintiff sought to hold the Minister of Safety and Security liable in delict for damages arising from the theft by certain policemen of property of the appellant. It was common cause that the appellant was robbed of a large sum of money by an armed gang. The investigating officer traced the proceeds of the robbery but when he arrived he discovered that the money had already been taken by three dishonest policemen. It was not clear where these three policemen had come by the information concerning the location of the stolen money, but it was clear that they had not been responsible for the investigation of the robbery, nor had they been on duty when they went to recover it, nor had they been in uniform although they had induced the man guarding the money to hand it over because they were policemen. The plaintiff did not argue either that the rules of vicarious liability were in conflict with the Constitution or that they failed to give effect to the spirit, purport and objects of the Bill of Rights. The Court concluded that the matter did not raise a constitutional issue and dismissed the appeal. In doing so, Kriegler J on behalf of a unanimous Court explained:[75]

> 'It is not suggested that in determining the question of vicarious liability the SCA applied any principle which is inconsistent with the Constitution. Nor is there any suggestion that any such principle needs to be adapted or evolved to bring it into harmony with the spirit, purport or objects of the Bill of Rights. On the contrary, counsel for the appellant expressly conceded that the common-law test for vicarious liability, as it stands, is consistent with the Constitution. It has long been accepted that the application of this test to the facts of a particular case is not a question of law but one of fact, pure and simple. The thrust of the argument presented on behalf of the appellant was essentially that though the SCA has set the correct test, it had applied that test incorrectly – which is of course not ordinarily a constitutional issue. This Court's jurisdiction is confined to constitutional matters and issues connected with decisions on constitutional matters. It is not for it to agree or disagree with the manner in which the SCA applied a constitutionally acceptable common-law test to the facts of the present case. (Footnotes omitted.)'

[74] 2003 (2) CC 34 (CC).
[75] At para 9.

In *K v Minister of Safety and Security*[76] Ms K, who was raped by three uniformed policemen who had given her a lift, applied for leave to appeal against a judgment of the Supreme Court of Appeal that held that the state was not vicariously liable for policemen's conduct. The applicant's appeal was based on the arguments that first, if, on a proper application of the ordinary common law rule of vicarious liability, the state is not liable for the applicant's damages, that rule should be developed to render it consistent with the spirit, purport and objects of the Bill of Rights; and, secondly, in developing the rule, the Court should consider the applicant's constitutional right to freedom and security of the person, and in particular, the right to be free from all forms of violence from either public or private sources as well as her right to dignity, right to privacy and right to substantive equality.

In her judgment O'Regan J said that the influence of the fundamental constitutional values on the common law is mandated by s 39(2) of the Constitution. It is within the matrix of this objective normative value system that the common law must be developed. The Court then considered the question what constitutes 'development' of the common law for the purposes of s 39(2). The Court accepted that the issue of wrongfulness in delict was not at issue in this case as it was in *Carmichele*, but the obligations imposed upon courts by sections 8(1) and 39(2) of the Constitution are also applicable when considering the common law principles of vicarious liability, and the question of whether that law needs to be developed in that area.[77] The common law develops incrementally through the rules of precedent. From time to time a common law rule is changed altogether, or a new rule is introduced, and this clearly constitutes the development of the common law. More commonly, however, courts decide cases within the framework of an existing rule. In this regard the Court said the following:[78]

> 'There are at least two possibilities in such cases: firstly, a court may merely have to apply the rule to a set of facts which it is clear fall within the terms of the rule or existing authority. The rule is then not developed but merely applied to facts bound by the rule. Secondly, however, a court may have to determine whether a new set of facts falls within or beyond the scope of an existing rule. The precise ambit of each rule is therefore clarified in relation to each new set of facts. A court faced with a new set of facts, not on all fours with any set of facts previously adjudicated, must decide whether a common-law rule applies to this new factual situation or not. If it holds that the new set of facts falls within the rule, the ambit of the rule is extended. If it holds that it does not, the ambit of the rule is restricted, not extended.'

---

[76] 2005 (6) SA 419 (CC).
[77] Para 19.
[78] Para 16.

Did the Court interpret the general effect of s 39(2) correctly? In his article 'The Confusions of K',[79] Anton Fagan lists the errors of the Constitutional Court, indicating how the Court misread, misunderstood and misapplied s 39(2) of the Constitution in this case: the values referred to in the section are not the values of the Constitution as a whole, but of the Bill of Rights – one of the fourteen chapters of the Constitution; the obligation imposed by s 39(2) is not an obligation to develop the common law whenever that would promote the values of the Bill of Rights, but rather an obligation to promote the values of the Bill of Rights whenever it becomes necessary in terms of s 8(3) to develop the common law.

Furthermore, is it correct to say that the common law rules of vicarious liability develop incrementally when applied to a new set of facts? The Court maintained:

> 'The question is whether one characterises such cases as development of the common law for the purposes of s 39(2). The overall purpose of s 39(2) is to ensure that our common law is infused with the values of the Constitution. It is not only in cases where existing rules are clearly inconsistent with the Constitution that such an infusion is required. The normative influence of the Constitution must be felt throughout the common law. Courts making decisions which involve the incremental development of the rules of the common law in cases where the values of the Constitution are relevant are therefore also bound by the terms of s 39(2). The obligation imposed upon courts by s 39(2) of the Constitution is thus extensive, requiring courts to be alert to the normative framework of the Constitution not only when some startling new development of the common law is in issue, but in all cases where the incremental development of the rule is in issue.'[80]

The notion that law is made when the courts apply an existing common law rule or set of rules to a new set of facts is questionable, as indicated by numerous judicial statements on the non-law-making and precedent-setting effect of applying the rules of negligence, legal causation and wrongfulness to new sets of facts.[81] At most, in the words of Boberg, 'the regular recurrence of typical factual patterns yields a jurisprudence of rulings which, though not strictly binding, enjoys equivalent respect'.[82] O'Regan J's explanation of 'incremental development' is not clear:[83]

> 'The precise ambit of each rule is therefore clarified in relation to each new set of facts. A court faced with a new set of facts, not on all fours with any set of facts previously adjudicated, must decide whether a common-law rule applies to this new factual situation or not. If it holds that the new set of facts falls within the

---

[79] A Fagan "The Confusions of *K*" (2009) 126 *SALJ* 156 at 195–196.
[80] At para 17.
[81] Fagan, note 79 supra, at 184–92.
[82] P Q R Boberg *The Law of Delict* (Juta 1984) 367.
[83] At para 16.

rule, the ambit of the rule is extended. If it holds that it does not, the ambit of the rule is restricted, not extended.'

The correctness of this passage is questionable, but even if an argument can be made that 'incremental development' of the rules on vicarious liability is a matter of both fact and law and subject to constitutional scrutiny, what are the relevant constitutional rights and duties and values of the Bill of Rights shaping such development?

On the relevant constitutional rights and duties the Court said that the question of the protection of *K*'s rights to security of the person, dignity, privacy and substantive equality are of profound constitutional importance. In addition, it was part of the three policemen's work to ensure the safety and security of all South Africans and to prevent crime. Referring to the Constitutional Court's judgment in *Carmichele*, the Court affirmed that few things can be more important to women than freedom from the threat of sexual violence and that the police is one of the primary agencies of the state responsible for the protection of the public in general and women and children in particular against the invasion of their fundamental rights by perpetrators of violent crime. All the specific rights referred to in these passages underscore the wrongdoing by the policemen, the invasion of *K*'s rights, the policemen's duties towards *K* and the horrific nature of the crime, but none of this was in dispute. The Court specifically accepted that the issue of wrongfulness in delict was not at issue in this case. The rights and duties referred to are: the security of the person; dignity; privacy; substantive equality; women's right to be free from the threat of sexual violence; the duty of the police to ensure the safety and security of all South Africans and to prevent crime; and the role of the police as one of the primary state agencies responsible for the protection of the public in general and women and children in particular against the invasion of their fundamental rights by perpetrators of violent crime.

It is abundantly clear that the policemen by their abhorrent wrongdoing violated *K*'s constitutional rights. None of this was ever in dispute. The question was why the violation of constitutional rights should result in vicarious liability of the state. The nature of the rights violated cannot render wrongdoing closer to or further away from the wrongdoer's employment, and neither can the degree of the violation.[84] On the effect of breach of duty, more is said below.

On relevant values of the Constitution (the correct reference should have been to values of the Bill of Rights) the Court said that as a matter of law and social regulation, the principles of vicarious liability are imbued with social policy and normative content.[85] The principles of vicarious liability and their

---

[84] Wagener, note 64 supra, at 118.
[85] Para 22.

application must be developed to accord more fully with the spirit, purport and objects of the Constitution. The Court thus professed to apply and adhere to 'the spirit, purport and objects of the Bill of Rights', 'the normative framework of our Constitution', 'the objective normative value system', and 'the values the Constitution seeks to promote',[86] but the judgment lacks specific reasoning on precisely how this value-awareness forges a connection between the policemen's conduct and their employment.

In its final conclusions on application of the common law principles of vicarious liability the Court accepted the 'standard' test set out in *Minister of Police v Rabie*,[87] involving two questions. The first is whether the wrongful acts were done solely for the purposes of the employee. This question requires a subjective consideration of the employee's state of mind and is a purely factual question. Even if it is answered in the affirmative, however, the employer may nevertheless be liable vicariously if the second question, an objective one, is answered affirmatively. That question is whether, even though the acts have been done solely for the purpose of the employee, there is nevertheless a sufficiently close link between the employee's acts for his own interests and the purposes and the business of the employer. This question does not raise purely factual questions, but mixed questions of fact and law. The questions of law it raises relate to what is 'sufficiently close' to give rise to vicarious liability. It is in answering this question that a court should consider the need to give effect to the spirit, purport and objects of the Bill of Rights.[88]

After undertaking a comparative review the Court concluded that the test set in *Rabie*, with its focus both on the subjective state of mind of the employee and the objective question whether the deviant conduct is nevertheless sufficiently connected to the employer's enterprise, is a test very similar to that employed in other jurisdictions. The objective element of the test which relates to the connection between the deviant conduct and the employment, approached with the spirit, purport and objects of the Constitution in mind, is sufficiently flexible to incorporate not only constitutional norms, but other norms as well. It requires a court when applying it to articulate its reasoning for its conclusions as to whether there is a sufficient connection between the wrongful conduct and the employment or not. 'Thus developed, by the explicit recognition of the normative content of the objective stage of the test, its application should not offend the Bill of Rights or be at odds with our constitutional order'.[89]

The application of the test set in *Rabie* finally proceeded as follows. The three policemen did not further the state's purposes or obligations by the

[86] Para 22–23.
[87] 1986 (1) SA 117 (A).
[88] Para 32.
[89] Para 44.

rape. They were, subjectively viewed, acting in pursuit entirely of their own objectives and not those of their employer. However, their conduct was found sufficiently close to their employer's business to render the state vicariously liable for the following considerations. First, the policemen all bore a statutory and constitutional duty to prevent crime and protect the members of the public. That duty is a duty which also rests on their employer and they were employed by their employer to perform that obligation.[90] Second, in addition to the general duty to protect the public, the police here had offered to assist the applicant and she had accepted their offer. In so doing, she placed her trust in the policemen although she did not know them personally. One of the purposes of wearing uniforms is to make police officers more identifiable to members of the public who find themselves in need of assistance. The Constitution mandates members of the police to protect members of the community and to prevent crime. It is an important mandate which should quite legitimately and reasonably result in the trust of the police by members of the community. Where such trust is established, the achievement of the tasks of the police will be facilitated. In determining whether the minister is liable in these circumstances, courts must take account of the importance of the constitutional role entrusted to the police and the importance of nurturing the confidence and trust of the community in the police in order to ensure that their role is successfully performed. In this case, and viewed objectively, it was reasonable for the applicant to place her trust in the policemen who were in uniform and offered to assist her.[91] Third, the conduct of the policemen which caused harm constituted a simultaneous commission and omission. The Court referred to the example given by Watermeyer CJ in *Feldman v Mall* of a railway gate keeper who, on a hot day, deserts his post to get refreshment, and while he is away an accident occurs, in which case the 'servant's indulgence in a frolic may in itself constitute a neglect to perform his master's work properly, and may be the cause of the damage'. In such circumstances, Watermeyer CJ implied the employer would be vicariously liable. The Court held that there can be no doubt that this reasoning is correct. An employee can at the same time be committing a delict for his or her own purposes, and neglecting to perform his or her duties as an employee. In this case it is clear that the rape was a deviation from the policemen's duties and, when committing the rape, the policemen were simultaneously omitting to perform their duties as policemen. The question of the simultaneous omission and commission is relevant to answering the second question set in *Rabie*: was there a sufficiently close connection between that delict and the purposes and business of the employer?[92] In this case the commission lay in their brutal rape of the applicant. Their

[90] Para 51.
[91] Paras 48–9.
[92] Paras 51–2.

simultaneous omission lay in their failing while on duty to protect her from harm, something which they bore a general duty to do, and a special duty on the facts of this case.[93] After concluding that the state was vicariously liable for the conduct of the policemen, the Court found it unnecessary to consider the argument that the state was directly liable in delict to the applicant.[94]

On breach of duty by the policemen the Court's reasoning was essentially that the policemen failed in their constitutional duty to protect K from harm and that this was the link between their wrongdoing and their employment. The idea that a breach of a duty imposed by an employer upon its employee can forge a connection between wrongdoing by the employee (in breach of that duty) and his employment is questionable. It seems to follow from this argument that the greater the breach by the employee the closer would be the connection between the wrongdoing and the employment.[95]

Furthermore, what was the nature of their breach of duty? The policemen did not fail to protect the victim from external danger – they failed to protect her from themselves. Breach of duty in this case is simply another way of describing their positive wrongdoing. It does not establish a link between their wrongdoing and their employment, let alone a link based on constitutional values. It was the rape itself, which is also of course at the same time a failure to desist from rape, that constituted the wrongdoing, and the wrongdoing was not in dispute. Describing the rape as a failure of duty does not establish a link between the wrongdoing and their employment; and to advance this simultaneous-commission-and-omission argument for meeting the 'close connection' test was rightly described by Lord Millett in *Lister v Hesley Hall Limited*[96] as 'indulging in sophistry'.

This simultaneous-commission-and-omission argument for meeting the 'close connection' test arose again in the recent case of *The Minister of Safety*

---

[93] Para 53.

[94] Para 58.

[95] Fagan, note 79 supra, at 195–6.

[96] [2002] 1 AC 215 at para 84: 'I would hold the school vicariously liable for the warden's intentional assaults, not (as was suggested in argument) for his failure to perform his duty to take care of the boys. That is an artificial approach based on a misreading of *Morris v Martin*. The cleaners were vicariously liable for their employee's conversion of the fur, not for his negligence in failing to look after it. Similarly in *Photo Production v Securicor Transport Ltd* the security firm was vicariously liable for the patrolman's arson, not for his negligence. The law is mature enough to hold an employer vicariously liable for deliberate, criminal wrongdoing on the part of an employee without indulging in sophistry of this kind. I would also not base liability on the warden's failure to report his own wrongdoing to his employer, an approach which I regard as both artificial and unrealistic. Even if such a duty did exist, on which I prefer to express no opinion, I am inclined to think that it would be a duty owed exclusively to the employer and not a duty for breach of which the employer could be vicariously liable. The same reasoning would not, of course, necessarily apply to the duty to report the wrong-doing of fellow employees, but it is not necessary to decide this'.

and Security v F,[97] which also concerned rape by a policeman, who, while off-duty but on 'standby', offered a lift to a stranded young girl. Mogoeng J, who wrote the majority judgment, found that there was a sufficiently close link between the policeman's employment and the wrongdoing. Use of a police vehicle facilitated its commission, F placed her trust in the defendant because he was a police official, and the state has a constitutional obligation to protect the public against crime. Froneman J in a separate concurring judgment agreed with the outcome, but found that the Minister's liability was direct, rather than vicarious, because the actions of state officials are in effect the state's own actions and the normative considerations for determining liability may be appropriately assessed as part of the wrongfulness enquiry.[98] In a minority judgment Yacoob and Jafta JJ applied the same test as the majority but concluded there was an insufficient link between the delict and the policeman's employment, since it was too far removed in space and time.

My conclusion is that the constitutional arguments advanced by the court in *K*, such as they are, add nothing meaningful to the principles of vicarious liability. The references to constitutional rights, duties and values are vague and general and appear to be a constitutional garnish added to conclusions reached on other grounds.

Are the outcomes in *K* and *F* justifiable if shorn of constitutional/human rights arguments? The 'close connection' test requires a value judgment on the degree of closeness, but this judgment must be capable of analysis and verifiable – the court is not absolved from the need for an open and structured process of reasoning, with reference to specific factors and policy considerations taken into account. It is not a test that can be based solely on economic analysis, enterprise liability or statistical risk theory.[99] In my view there is a sufficiently close connection between the rape and the policemen's employment in *K*, because they were on duty, in uniform and using a police vehicle. In these circumstances Ms K placed her trust in them to take her home safely and therefore a connection exists between their employment as policemen at that time and the rape. The facts relevant to application of the 'close connection' test were different in *F*, because the policeman was off duty, not in uniform and the car was not marked as a police car; and therefore the result in that case also seems to me to be justified. However, in neither case is the value judgment in terms of the 'close connection' test in my view meaningfully informed by constitutional values or human rights arguments.

Human rights arguments have not featured at all in Scottish or English cases on vicarious liability and, for the reasons advanced above, such arguments are unlikely to succeed.

---

[97] 2012 (1) SA 536 (CC).
[98] Para 39.
[99] *Contra* Fagan, note 79 supra, at 199–204.

9.5 CONCLUSIONS

The impact of human rights on strict liability is examined mainly with reference to three instances of strict liability common to both jurisdictions: (1) liability for animals (statute-based in Scotland and common law-based in South Africa); (2) product liability (statute-based in both jurisdictions); and (3) vicarious liability (common law-based in both jurisdictions).

The potential impact of human rights on strict liability rules of law are in principle the same in Scotland and South Africa, despite differences in detail between the respectively applicable human rights instruments (the Human Rights Act in Scotland and the South African Constitution). There is a major imbalance between the two jurisdictions regarding the material available on human rights and strict liability – there is almost no Scottish material. Generally the courts have declined to implement major reforms such as the introduction or abolition of strict liability by a decision in a particular case, opting to leave such reform to the legislature.

The right to equality under section 9 of the South African Constitution provides a constitutional/human rights basis for the courts to decide that either strict liability or the existence of a fault requirement is inconsistent with constitutional/human rights values. It is arguable that the requirement to prove fault in certain cases but not in others violates the right to equality before the law and to equal protection and benefit of the law under section 9(1) of the Constitution unless such differentiation has a rational connection to a legitimate government purpose. The imposition of strict liability in certain cases but not in others will fall foul of the Constitution if such differentiation is arbitrary or irrational. To meet the criterion of legitimacy under section 9(1), the government merely has to show that its purpose is neither arbitrary nor irrational. Legitimacy is thus equated with rationality. It is irrelevant to this enquiry whether the legislation or rule of law could be improved in one respect or another. The minimum rationality threshold under section 9(1) does not entail an analysis of the impact of the impugned rule or of the policy choices made. As such it has been said to be 'extremely deferential to the legislature and most laws will pass constitutional muster under this provision'.

If the minimum rationality test is applied to the underlying policy considerations and main rules of the three prominent instances of strict liability in South African law, it appears that there are irrational aspects to the rules, but on the whole these instances of strict liability are likely to pass constitutional muster.

The constitutional arguments advanced by the South African Constitutional court in *K v Minister of Safety and Security*[100] add nothing meaningful to the principles of vicarious liability. The references to consti-

---

[100] 2005 (6) SA 419 (CC).

tutional rights, duties and values are vague and appear to be a constitutional gloss added to conclusions reached on other grounds.

Article 14 of the European Convention guarantees that everyone shall enjoy the Convention rights without discrimination. However, article 14 is not a general 'equal treatment' guarantee or generally applicable free-standing prohibition on discrimination. It requires only that the enjoyment of other Convention rights be secured without discrimination and does not provide a minimum rationality test as section 9 of the South African Constitution does. Under Scots law the underlying policy considerations and main rules of forms of strict liability cannot therefore similarly be tested for rationality.

Chapter 10

Liability of Public Authorities and Public Officials

John Blackie

10.1 INTRODUCTION

Actions for damages against public authorities or public officials are not a new phenomenon. There is an extensive body of authority in Scotland on the liability of roads authorities dating from the end of the eighteenth century. A significant body of case law in South Africa also goes back some way in time, though not as far as in Scotland. Here and there isolated cases of liability in other contexts involving public bodies or officials can be found in both jurisdictions before the twentieth century. However, until the second half of the twentieth century the literature concerning actions of damages against public authorities or public officials was not prominent in considerations of the taxonomy of delict in either jurisdiction. Its development, and the search for legal principle to rationalise the cases coming through the courts, was thus a relatively recent concern when human rights regimes came to impact directly upon the domestic law of both jurisdictions.

The way in which human rights law affects the law of delict in relation to the liability of public authorities and their officials is inevitably different from its impact on the law of delict in the context of liability of private individuals and entities: with public bodies and officials the relationship is between the state and citizens. This raises fundamental questions about the relation of public law to private law, and, through vertical applicability of human rights regimes to state obligations, the relation between specific human rights enforceable against the state on the one hand, and the private law of delict as a way of enforcing rights on the other.

There are utterly different ways in which a legal system might decide to deal with these large questions. It could see actions against the state or its officials as coming solely within public law. Then the rules and remedies of delict in this context would reflect the legal policies of administrative and constitutional law. Neither Scotland nor South Africa has taken this approach, though a modified version of it was recommended by the Law Commission for England and Wales,[1] which, following adverse commen-

---

[1] Law Commission *Administrative Redress: Public Bodies and the Citizen* (Law Com Con Paper No 187, 2008).

tary, was later abandoned.[2] A second model could be that where a human right of a citizen is infringed by the state or a public official, the relevant law is constitutional law as incorporating the protection of human rights. A third model would be to consider the area not to be regulated by public law at all, but by the private law of delict, with human rights law playing the role that it has assumed in various area of delict, such as defamation and the protection of dignitary interests. In that model the human rights dimension has moulded the development of delictual rules and principles. A fourth model would be to treat it as falling at one and the same time under both the law of delict and administrative and constitutional law including human rights law. Neither Scotland nor South Africa has adopted the first possibility of treating the whole question as one of administrative law, nor the third possibility of treating it as solely within private law. Accordingly what has emerged is a relatively complex picture.

10.2 GOVERNMENTAL LIABILITY AND THE CONCEPT OF 'PUBLIC' IN DELICT

A contextual area within tort law of 'governmental [or government] liability' was identified in English writing in the middle of the twentieth century,[3] and it is fair to say that this reflected at least a reformist agenda.[4] In Scotland, following that lead, this development came a bit later.[5] In both these jurisdictions this occurred well before there was any need to think of human rights law. In South Africa such terms have come to be used more recently and the impact of human rights law, and in some respects the wider Constitution beyond the Bill of Rights, can be seen as having promoted its recognition.[6] However, even without that, it is almost certain that South African writers would have followed the lead of the literature in other English-speaking jurisdictions in examining the public dimension in the law of delict. The context is relevant in private law to determining both whether there can be a case at all, i.e. in Scotland the duty of care in negligence question and what for the sake of simplicity one may call the 'other delicts' question, and in South Africa, following the dominant opinion, the wrongfulness question. It is pertinent, too, to the nature of the conduct question. It may also be

---

[2] Law Commission *Administrative Redress: Public Bodies and the Citizen* (Law Com Report No 322, 2010).

[3] In particular through C Harlow *Compensation and Government Torts* (Sweet and Maxwell 1982).

[4] F du Bois 'State Liability in South Africa A Constitutional Remix' (2010) 25 *Tulane European and Civil Law Forum* 139 at 148.

[5] See J Blackie 'Scots Law: General Principles or Diverse Rules?' in J Bell and A Bradley (eds) *Governmental Liability: A Comparative Study* (UKNCCL 1991) 45.

[6] C Okpaluba and P Chukwunweike Osode *Government Liability: South Africa and the Commonwealth* (Juta 2010) appears to be the first book with this title.

relevant to some other issues in the law of delict, as with vicarious liability in South Africa.[7]

To give more precision to this contextual area, and to determine what effect as a context it has on the rules and principles of the law of delict and their application, it is necessary to have some concept of what gives a dispute a 'public' element. The approach here has, however, been influenced in both jurisdictions by the different reasons why courts have considered the question. In South Africa the principal reason has been the recent one of the need for the Constitutional Court to address the question of its jurisdiction. In a negligence case it is the wrongfulness issue that triggers the Constitutional Court's jurisdiction where there is a 'public' dimension.[8] But other dimensions of the question of what is public have been held to be reasons for the Court having jurisdiction, namely, that the defendant's acts were in the exercise of a power derived from the Constitution, and from 'legislation in pursuit of constitutional goals'. So it held that it had jurisdiction in a negligence claim by a disappointed tenderer for a contract with a public body, which the Supreme Court of Appeal had dismissed on the ground of no wrongfulness.[9] As considered further below, the South African consideration of the liability of public officials for infringements of personality rights, in particular of the rights to bodily integrity and physical liberty, has been to analyse the law with little or no reference to the fact that there is a 'public' element. In Scotland, on the other hand, much of the earlier consideration of the liability of public bodies and public officials was indeed in such contexts, as well as in others where the alleged wrongful conduct complained of was not negligence.

The history of what gives a delictual case a public element in Scotland has never produced a coherent body of doctrine. Moreover, it has generally had no impact today, though the requirements of the delicts of wrongous imprisonment and wrongous arrest can be connected loosely with one of the approaches expressed for other contexts. This approach was that a person or body was public if the body or person's function was to act in the public interest. This was extended during the nineteenth century from its original application to those involved in the administration of justice,[10] first to categorise members giving information to these authorities as acting for 'public' benefit,[11] then later to medical practitioners giving their opinion in criminal cases where the proof of the crime depended on evidence of the physical condition of the victim.[12] Acting in the public interest was the concept used also

---

[7] *K v Minister of Safety and Security* 2005 (6) SA 419 (CC).
[8] *Steenkamp NO v The Provincial Tender Board for the Eastern Cape* 2006 (3) SA 151 (SCA) per Mosenke DCJ at para 19; per Lange CJ and Regan J (not dissenting on this point) at para 56.
[9] *Steenkamp NO v Provincial Tender Board, Eastern Cape* 2006 (3) SA 151 (SCA).
[10] Erskine, *Institute* 4.4.31.
[11] *Beaton v Ivory* (1887) 14 R 1057 per Lord President Inglis at 1062.
[12] *Urquhart v Grigor* (1864) 3M 283.

to characterise cases involving the bodies of governance of the established (Presbyterian) Church of Scotland as 'public'.[13] This may have been because they were (and are) technically 'courts' of the church. But in any event such cases were looked on as raising constitutional issues.[14]

A second, quite different, approach, which first appears in the late nineteenth century (in roads cases), was to categorise a person or body as public where there was a statutory background to his, her or its existence or role. The recognition of its potential significance followed the creation of a comprehensive statutory code of legislation for roads authorities, and contemporaneously in other areas of local authority activity the statutory creation of completely new bodies with powers and duties, notably in the state school education system. There was then an obvious tension between seeing 'public' dimension as fundamentally arising from having a statutory background, and from 'acting in the public interest'. The attempted resolution was unsatisfactory. It led to a crude doctrine that, generally speaking, the body was liable if it failed to follow the legislative provisions in question, but a 'minor' failure did not give rise to liability. The rationale was stated in an education case drawing on the concept of the public interest: 'a public body like this school board' acts 'not in the least in their [sic] own interests, but entirely in the interest of the public'.[15]

10.3 PUBLIC BODIES AND THEIR OFFICIALS – GROUNDS OF LIABILITY IN DELICT OTHER THAN NEGLIGENCE

The law regulating the liability of public bodies and their officials where the conduct element is not negligence has always incorporated rules that in a more or less appropriate way are about a balance between the citizen and the exercise of state power. Much of what public bodies and their officials do is to regulate the conduct of individuals or activities. In carrying out those functions they have to act to the detriment of individual people and private entities. In Scotland in the earlier nineteenth century, reflecting much earlier ideas, there was a concept of 'illegality and oppression' that may have been capable of applying whenever the type of interest capable of protection by the law of delict was invaded by a public official.[16] However, that did not survive. As in South Africa, the general principles of the law of delict are therefore applied to this public context. The interaction of human rights law and private law is, however, distinct between the two

---

[13] In particular in *Ferguson v Kinnoull* (1843) 1 Bell 662.
[14] Lord Rodger of Earlsferry *The Courts, the Church and the Constitution: Aspects of the Disruption of 1843* (EUP 2008).
[15] *Macaulay v North Uist School Board* (1887) 15 R 99.
[16] J Blackie 'Scots Law: General Principles or Diverse Rules?' in J Bell and A Bradley (eds) *Governmental Liability: A Comparative Study* (UKNCCL 1991) 45 at 57.

jurisdictions for two reasons above all. The *actio iniuriarum* (together with aquilian liability for patrimonial loss) in South Africa in contexts involving public bodies or officials had already largely achieved the goals of the Bill of Rights and there are no free-standing additional or collateral human rights claims. In Scotland the common law of delict has long been underdeveloped in this area. On one view it needs development inspired by human rights law.

10.3.1 Protection of property and economic rights

Delictual liability in respect of invasions of property and economic rights by public officials has been given less attention than liability in respect of invasion of personality rights. A number of the Scottish cases discussed above in connection with considering what gives a case a 'public' element, on issues such as the denial of a liquor licence or the demolition of a building, were of this sort. However, today the facts of the latter seem inconceivable and situations such as that in the former would not be dealt with under the law of delict, but within a process of judicial review. It is, however, convenient to consider invasions of these rights before invasions of personality rights because the English tort of misfeasance in a public official has been borrowed particularly for this context. The absence of this element of English tort law from South African law is taken to show that South Africa has a generalised law of delict[17] and does not incorporate 'nominate wrongs'. The Scots law of delict is certainly not nominate-wrong-proof, however. To assert that Scots law has borrowed this tort is to follow a first-instance decision from the 1980s.[18] There is no further case law since then. In that case the owner of a ship refused entry by the harbourmaster to the large public harbour at Sullom Voe in Shetland sought to recover damages for the consequent economic loss through the ship accordingly been delayed. Absent any Scottish case law on intentional wrongful acts being put to the court,[19] a passage in Walker on *Delict*,[20] which adopted the English tort, was applied. There was an attempt by counsel to link this somehow to the concept of *culpa*. But in truth it is a transplant. The law as formulated in this case was:

> 'deliberate misuse of statutory powers by a public body would be actionable under the law of Scotland at the instance of a third party (*sic*) who has suffered loss and damage in consequence of the misuse of statutory powers, provided that there was proof of malice or proof that the action had been taken by the public

[17] Du Bois 'State Liability', supra note 4 at 165.
[18] *Micosta SA v Shetlands Island Council* 1986 SLT 193.
[19] The very old cases on 'oppression' could have been cited but they would not have been readily discovered by counsel.
[20] D M Walker *The Law of Delict in Scotland* 2e (W Green 1981) 9 and 878.

authority in the full knowledge that it did not possess the power which it pur-ported to exercise'.[21]

The meaning of 'malice' is not explored, but it can be assumed that it has the meaning in the English tort, namely 'targeted malice . . . conduct specifically intended to injure. . . [involving] bad faith in the sense of the exercise of public power for an improper or ulterior motive'.[22] Scots law has not bor-rowed one aspect of this tort, namely the right where the loss is patrimonial[23] to be awarded exemplary damages. The reason is simply that its adoption would be inconsistent with the general approach to damages in delict, which is to conceive of them as solely compensatory.

10.3.2 Protection of the right to bodily integrity

Police officers routinely invade individuals' bodily integrity. Other public officials, for instance prison staff, do this too, at least on occasion.[24] The South African Bill of Rights expressly extends to the 'right to bodily and psy-chological integrity'[25] and with that 'the right to . . . security of the person', which includes the right 'to be free from all forms of violence . . . from public . . . sources'.[26] There is no exact equivalent in the European Convention on Human Rights (ECHR). But it is accepted that the Convention right not to be subject to 'inhuman and degrading treatment'[27] is engaged when there is an assault by police.[28] However, it is in Scotland rather than South Africa where the impact of human rights law is potentially significant. In South Africa the Bill of Rights has not been influential in developing the common law of assault. This appears to be because it is unnecessary. The common law achieves the necessary level of protection. The 'wrongfulness' requirement is met by 'factual infringement of the physical-mental body'.[29] The extension of the integrity of *corpus* to mental integrity is well established, and not con-fined to protection against developing mental illness. The *animus iniuriandi* requirement in at least one type of case involving *iniuria* through invasion bodily and psychological integrity does not need to be shown, namely where prison officers hold a prisoner in conditions which affected his or her bodily

[21] Per Lord Ross at 198.
[22] *Three Rivers District Council v Bank of England (No 3)* [2003] 2 AC 1 per Lord Steyn at 191.
[23] *Kuddus v Chief Constable of Leicestershire Constabulary* [2002] 2 AC 122.
[24] *Minister of Justice v Hofmeyr* 1999 (3) SA 131 (AD).
[25] S12(2).
[26] S12(1)(c).
[27] Article 2 ECHR. The South African Bill of Rights, s 12(1) lists this as one of the rights that the wider right of 'freedom and security of the person' includes.
[28] *Ruddy v Chief Constable of Strathclyde* [2012] UKSC 57. Also accepted in England: *ZH v Commissioner of Police for the Metropolis* [2012] EWHC 604 (QB).
[29] J Neethling, J M Potgieter and P J Visser *The Law of Delict* 5 e (LexisNexis 2006) 302.

integrity.[30] In cases of police assaults it is not likely to be difficult to show this anyhow. In Scotland there is no concept equivalent to the South African concept of wrongfulness other than in negligence law (where much of its work is done by 'duty of care'). The law on intention is doubtful, lacking rigorous analysis, and in the case of invasions by public officials, confused. Human rights law has a potential effect on all these issues in Scotland where the delict is committed by a public official. First, it can provide additional support for the view that in civil assault at least where committed by a public official[31] there is automatic liability, with the onus of proof shifting to the defender to establish a defence that what was done was lawful, or otherwise justified. It can, if support is needed, make clear that those authorities[32] that say it is necessary to prove 'malice and want of probable cause' in cases against the police are incorrect.[33] There is a free-standing[34] human rights claim which now routinely included in cases of police assault, as it is in England for 'just satisfaction'. However, it is never likely to result in a separate award, as the delictual damages will themselves be sufficient to satisfy that.[35] Treating human rights claims as distinct from delict claims nonetheless has a real functional impact here. It can operate as a form of substitute for not extending the range of personality rights protected, even though the approach to damages may give less than if the right were protected by the common law of delict. Thus, though the Scottish common law conception of physical integrity does not extend to the 'mental body' (other than where mental illness is caused) a free-standing human rights claim can functionally extend the protection of the law, even though it is highly unlikely that the concept of physical integrity could be extended in the common law of delict under the influence of human rights.[36] Article 3 ECHR may be breached without physical harm or mental illness being caused,[37] as has been

---

[30] *Minister of Justice v Hofmeyr* 1999 (3) SA 131 (AD).

[31] In England it has been argued that this is or should be the case without making that distinction on the basis of the nature of the defendant: D Priel 'A Public Role of the Intentional Torts' (2011) 22 KLJ 183. The principal case prompting the author's consideration was *Ashley v Chief Constable of Sussex Police* [2008] 1 AC 962 – a police assault case.

[32] *Ward v Chief Constable of Strathclyde* 1991 SLT 292; *Mckie v Orr* 2002 Rep L R 137 aff'd 2003 SC 317.

[33] See E Reid *Personality, Confidentiality and Privacy in Scots Law* (W Green 2010) paras 2.35–2.36 for their being anyhow incorrect.

[34] See in particular *Docherty v Scottish Ministers* 2012 SC 150. The human rights claim is not covered by the same rules of prescription as a delict claim.

[35] *Ruddy v Chief Constable of Strathclyde* [2012] UKSC 57; also accepted in England: *ZH v Commissioner of Police for the Metropolis* [2012] EWHC 604 (QB).

[36] That is a logically possible effect of a human rights regime on a law of delict (see A Price 'The Influence of Human Rights on Private Common Law' 2011 SALJ 330 at 353) but the example of the development of confidentiality to include privacy involves extending an interest rather than recognising a completely new one.

[37] *Greens Petitioner* 2012 SLT 549 per Lady Dorrian at para 257 summarising the case law of the ECtHR.

recognised by several cases where claims have been successful in respect of the lack of full toilet facilities in Scottish jails.[38]

10.3.3 *Protection of the right to physical liberty*

The contrasting ways in which the two jurisdictions deal with infringement of physical liberty by public officials reflect that the concept of wrongfulness in South Africa has application to the whole of delict, while in Scotland there is no equivalent other than in negligence. In both jurisdictions invasions of the right to physical liberty by public officials are analysed distinctly from invasions of that right by other people. In South African law there is a delict of malicious deprivation of liberty but it is only relevant where 'the actual deprivation of liberty is . . . carried out . . . by the machinery of the state through a valid judicial process';[39] and where the action is directed at a private party who set that in train it is necessary to show that the defendant acted with malice (meaning *animo iniuriandi*) and without probable cause. However, general wrongful deprivation of liberty by a public official is based upon an application of the general common law of deprivation of liberty. This has led to a dispute in the literature at to whether liability entails proof of intention, which would normally be required for an *actio iniuriarum*, or whether liability is strict with the *onus* then being on the defendant to prove a lawful justification for the act. Given that instances of legally contested deprivation of liberty are nowadays usually by a public official, such as by a police officer or by prison staff,[40] the latter view has been convincingly argued to be supported by the Bill of Rights, as the relationship between the parties 'is one of complete inequality' – an inequality that arises from there being on the one side 'the almost defenceless individual' and on the other 'the powerful, faceless state with its overpowering compulsive measures and virtually unlimited financial resources.'[41] What counts as a legal justification for deprivation of liberty will normally be that the public official had a power *qua* public official. In South Africa in this field, accordingly, the only situation where the person who is deprived of liberty has to prove something more in a case directly against a public official or body is where a valid power was validly exercised. The extra element required is suggested as being proof of 'an improper motive', such as where a police officer acting validly under a power to arrest did so with a purpose other than bringing the arrested person properly to trial.[42] Here it needs to be emphasised that rather

---

[38] *Napier v Scottish Ministers* 2005 1 SC 307; *Docherty v Scottish Ministers* 2012 SC 150.

[39] Neethling, Potgieter, and Visser, supra note 29 at 306.

[40] As in *Minister of Correctional Services v Tobani* 2003 (5) SA 126 (E).

[41] J Neethling 'Constitutional Compatibility of the Common Law of Wrongful and Malicious Deprivation of Liberty as Injuriae' (2004) 121 SALJ 711 at 715.

[42] Neethling, Potgieter and Visser, supra note 29, 305, citing *Duncan v Minister of Law and Order* 1986 (2) SA 805 (A) 820.

than acting as a restriction on the rights of a person to sue for wrongful deprivation of liberty where there is no lawful justification for it, the right is extended, though that extension is limited in a particular way. In Scotland it may be that the impact of article 5 of the ECHR (right to liberty and security) means that the law is correctly stated as it is in South Africa in cases where deprivation of liberty is by a public official. Thus arrest without a warrant or without any other justification is actionable in Scottish common law.[43] There is no requirement in South African law to show 'malice and want of probable cause'. However, in Scotland the matter is not so simple, as these requirements were forcibly transplanted into the Scots law of deprivation of 'wrongous imprisonment', which meant deprivation of liberty by a public official, but could also extend to a private party who had instigated this,[44] even though their origins (and in South Africa their sole role) are in the (English) law of malicious prosecution. The questions now are: when, if ever, is it necessary to establish both of these requirements against a public official for a case in respect of deprivation of liberty? When, if ever, is it necessary to establish lack of probable cause but not malice? And when, if ever, is it necessary to establish malice that is unrelated to lack of probable cause?

The answers to these questions also involve defining what is meant by malice. A series of cases starting in the late nineteenth century suggest that both requirements must always be satisfied in a case against a public official, and that malice is some subjective state, though this has varied from 'spite' or 'improper motive' to 'malevolence or ill-will'. However, the position in the modern law has been argued convincingly to be that where the public official has acted 'without legal authority' then 'malice' is just 'inferred from the wrongful act', and the requirement to prove some form of subjective malice is only where there was a 'legal authority'. If there is any doubt that this analysis is not where the confused case law had got to, the impact of article 5 of the ECHR must be to confirm that it is correct.[45] This would leave 'malice' as the label of the subjective requirement in the latter situation. The South African position that recognises the possibility of liability in this situation based on proof of 'an improper motive' has the added virtue that it separates the law regarding the liability of public officials from that of private individuals who trigger the acts of public officials. This is an area where more generally the law should distinguish between public officials and private individuals. It is the existence of legal powers of deprivation that is a fundamental reason for treating the law as distinct from

---

[43] See in particular *Pringle v Bremner and Stirling* (1867) 5 M (HL) 55 and Reid *Personality*, supra note 33 at para 5.20.

[44] By reference to an early nineteenth-century House of Lords case, *Arbuckle v Taylor* (1815) 3 Dow 160.

[45] Reid *Personality*, supra note 33, para 5.12.

that applicable to invasions of liberty by private parties. The same is true where there is a statutory code that regulates the powers of parties who, though not public officials, act under that code. This applies, for example, to mental health professionals, who are liable if they act without a power given by legislation, even where a private individual would be permitted to detain a person honestly believing it was appropriate for that person's protection.[46]

10.3.4 Protection of intangible personality rights – dignity – privacy etc

In both Scotland and South Africa public bodies and officials were liable for invasions of privacy under the law of delict before the impact of human rights law. Such cases before the Bill of Rights in South Africa, and the incorporation of the ECHR in Scottish domestic law generally did not particularly focus on the fact that the defender was not a private party.[47] There is an important Scottish case which is an exception to this,[48] where it was held that the police might potentially be liable for carrying out surveillance with a view to collecting evidence relevant to a disciplinary procedure against a police officer, and where the court considered the extent of police powers, including the statutory background, which was necessary in considering the (successful) defence proposition that actual malice had to be shown. However, today the public element seems more naturally focused through recognising that a human right is infringed.[49] In Scotland, where analysis of the law of personality rights protection in the law of delict has generally been rather thin in the case law, it should have the further effect of securing the recognition of the right as protected by the law. There may, however, be some free-standing role for human rights law supporting a distinct human rights claim. This has been indicated as a possibility in English cases where it has been alleged that police passed on incorrect information with regard to a person's criminal record.[50]

---

[46] See the Scottish case *Black v Forsey* 1988 SC (HL) 28 imposing liability where a patient was detained after the then short-term period for compulsory detention in a mental hospital had expired, when he was becoming ill again, and it was too late to instigate before the end of that period the court process which was necessary for longer-term compulsory detention for treatment.

[47] *Minister of Police v Mbilini* 1983 (3) SA 705 (A): insulting words; *Dalgliesh v Lothian and Border Police* 1992 SLT 721: public authority revealing employee's address to a taxation authority; *Henderson v Chief Constable Fife Police* 1981 SLT 361: requiring removal of underwear when in police custody.

[48] *Robertson v Keith* 1936 SC 29.

[49] *McKie v Chief Constable of Strathclyde* 2002 Rep L Rep 137 (aff'd 2003 SC 317).

[50] Cases pled on the basis that there was duty of care in negligence law have failed: *Desmond v Chief Constable of Nottinghamshire Police* [2011] EWCA Civ 3 per Sir Anthony May P at para 51.

10.4 VICARIOUS LIABILITY

Both Scotland and South Africa impose vicarious liability upon employers for delicts committed by employees within the scope of their employment. The two concepts open to judicial development are thus, what counts as a relationship of employer and employee and what is covered by the scope of employment. The traditional model of negligence liability for public authorities has incorporated vicarious liability and the public dimension of the context has not impacted on the understanding of vicarious liability. However, it is not in vicarious liability for negligence that the law has been dynamic but in vicarious liability for delicts other than negligence. The United Kingdom is currently particularly focused not only upon case law but upon the wider culture on historic child abuse. In South African case law a central concern is rape. That the employment background is public in nature logically could be relevant to the issues of employment and scope in the law of delict. Many public employments provide opportunities for public officials to commit wrongdoing, for instance workers in care homes for children, support workers more generally and the police. In these contexts there is an obvious contrast between the official's function to protect and the conduct being the opposite of that. The impact of the public dimension on the development and application of the legal rules, as well as the impact of human rights law, has been radical in South Africa.[51] In Scotland, following the rest of the United Kingdom, not only has there been no human rights law impact, there has been no overt consideration of the context having a public dimension.

In South Africa the leading new cases involve police. They have, therefore, indisputably a public context. They involve rapes by officials on duty,[52] and off duty, though using with permission a police vehicle.[53] The rules laid down in these cases have been directly inspired by a particular view of the role of the South African Bill of Rights as enjoining the courts actively to develop the law.[54] Anton Fagan[55] has put forward the view that this was both unnecessary and underpinned by an unjustified reading of the role the court is required by the Bill of Rights to adopt in developing the common law. However, it is clear from the second of these cases that the approach will not change; the majority makes no mention of the literature. Another judgment that supports the outcome of the majority on a different ground, extending the concept of direct as opposed to vicarious liability of the state to cover this type of situation simply notes that there is literature 'both critical and

---

[51] On this see also discussion in preceding chapter at section 9.4.
[52] *K v Minister of Safety and Security* 2005 (6) SA 419 (CC).
[53] *F v Minister of Safety and Security* 2012 (1) SA 536 (CC).
[54] *K v Minister of Safety and Security* 2005 (6) SA 419 (CC).
[55] A Fagan 'The Confusions of K' (2009) 126 SALJ 156.

favourable'.[56] In the South African approach the constitutional obligations of the state to prevent crime and to protect members of the public, as well as the constitutional rights to freedom and security of the person and to dignity, are treated as the 'prism' through which the question of state vicarious liability 'should be conducted'.[57]

That even the possible significance of the wrongdoer being a public official has not been discussed in the United Kingdom may be an accident of the fact that the leading new cases have not concerned acts by people who, like the police, are public employees. One Privy Council appeal from Jamaica[58] applied the general law in finding vicarious liability for an off-duty official who demanded the use of a public telephone for his own purposes, shouting 'police', and shot the plaintiff when he did not give way. In that case, however, it is striking that relevance was attached to the police body having created a context of risk. The analysis of the South African Court of Appeal in *Minister of Police v Rabie*[59] was followed,[60] i.e. an authority that has been built upon further in the new post-Bill of Rights South African cases.

In the child abuse cases, which have in the last decade driven the development of vicarious liability in the United Kingdom, there has been in one sense a public dimension to the context. The children would not have been in the particular institutional environment but for the fact that private bodies employing the abuser provided facilities that were used by the state in discharging its statutory obligations to children,[61] or in fulfilling its obligations to provide institutions for children sentenced by criminal courts.[62] The recent cases have not been about the scope of employment question but about which body or bodies would count as employer.[63] The 'public' dimension may not change the nature of the relationship between the body in question and the person who committed the delict, though in one English

---

56   F, note 53 supra, Froneman J at para 89 note 54, listing in addition to Fagan's work, 'Neethling and Potgieter 'Middellike Aanspreeklikheid van die Staat vir Vekragting deur Polisiebeamptes' (2005) TSAR 595; T J Scott 'K v Minister of Safety and Security' (2006) *De Iure* 471; S Wagener 'K v Minister of Safety and Security and the Increasingly Blurred Line Between Personal and Vicarious Liability' (2008) 125 (4) SALJ 673; and du Bois 'State Liability', supra note 4.

57   F, note 53 supra, per Mogoeng J at para 54.

58   *Bernard v Attorney General of Jamaica* [2005] IRLR 398.

59   1986 (1) SA 117.

60   Though expressly aware that the reasoning of Jansen JA had been criticised in subsequent case *Minister of Law and Order v Ngobo* 1992 (4) SA 822; *Ess Kay Electronics v FNB* 2001 (1) SA 1214 (SCA); and *Bezuidenhout NO v Eskom* 2003 (3) SA 83.

61   In the leading case on scope of employment in this context *Lister v Hesley Hall Ltd* [2002]1 AC 215 the children were '[i]n the main children with emotional and behavioural difficulties were sent to the school by local authorities' (per Lord Steyn at para 2).

62   In M *v Hendron sub nom McE v De La Salle Brothers* 2007 SC 566 there was consideration of a distinct case of liability for negligence by the Scottish Government as responsible for schools (which was unsuccessful).

63   *Various Claimants v Institute of the Brothers of the Christian Schools* [2012] UKSC 56.

first-instance case[64] on the point there was a passing reference to *Minister of Police v Rabie* (without further noting the more recent developments in South Africa). But it would be capable of being relevant to the scope of employment question. However, children in other institutional or other structured environments where they interact with adults in charge are in the same situation of potential vulnerability. To refer to the public dimension may therefore give with one hand a benefit to one group of vulnerable people, and run the risk of being seen as implying that this different group should not have that assistance. The emphasis in the leading South African cases on the public background may, indeed, give rise to unwanted problems when such backgrounds give rise to the same forms of abuse.

10.5 NEGLIGENCE – PUBLIC AUTHORITIES AND THEIR OFFICIALS

The area of activity in which liability of public bodies and their officials first clearly developed in both South Africa and Scotland is liability for the state of public roads. This apparently routine area of negligence liability provides the backdrop, in differing ways in both jurisdictions, to the modern development of public authority negligence law. In South Africa roads authorities cases are analogised to private occupiers' duties. In Scotland they once were,[65] but have not been for some time. But in Scotland the consequences from that analogy for legal doctrine were different. A statutory regime for roads authorities was first developed in the late nineteenth century, and consolidated around a century later.[66] However, its relevance to negligence claims against roads authorities was just that statutory powers enabled the authority to do certain things to fulfil its common law duty.[67] The placing of certain specific duties in the statutory regime, such as to 'take such steps as they consider reasonable to prevent snow and ice endangering the safe passage of pedestrians and vehicles over public roads' have been held not to create a duty beyond that of common law negligence.[68]

The shift from what was basically occupiers' liability did not come about because of some shift from a wider acceptance of liability for omissions. It is true that the distinction between misfeasance and nonfeasance that historically limited English roads authorities' liability in negligence to the former was never part of Scots law. But the very absence of consideration by Scots courts played no part either in expanding or restricting the liability of roads

---

[64] *E v English Province of Our Lady of Charity* [2012] 2 WLR 709 per MacDuff J at para 24.
[65] Already by the end of the eighteenth century: *Innes v Magistrates of Edinburgh* (1798) Mor 13189 and 13967.
[66] Roads (Scotland) Act 1984.
[67] *Fraser v Glasgow Corporation* 1972 SLT 177.
[68] *Grant v Lothian Regional Council* 1988 SLT 553.

authorities in the course of time. English authority was simply not referred to. As considered further below, Scotland unlike South Africa was never particularly open to developing liability for omissions. Scots law subtly moved from what was essentially occupiers' liability to a distinct type of road authority liability, which would not in its nature provide a basis for developing a general doctrine of liability of public authorities for omissions. In private occupiers' liability the focus was solely on the particular hazard. In road authority cases it came to be on the system of roads as a whole. The hazard had to be seen in the light of the inevitability that there would be some hazards in the system. The practice of other local authorities in their prioritisation within the whole system was accepted as relevant.[69] That led to a subtle shift in the general test for negligence in this area, to being not whether the authority acted reasonably but whether it 'was reasonable and practicable' for the authority to have done what the pursuer averred it should have done to eliminate the particular hazard.[70] With this it has come to be overtly recognised that authority resources are finite and so have to prioritise in their activities to deal with hazards that are caused by the elements.[71] There has now been a further shift to seeking to distinguish between policy and operational decisions in roads cases. It has been stated at first instance that:[72]

> 'the allocation of finite resources among competing demands is entrusted to the discretion of the roads authority and the reasonableness of the policy decisions made by the authority is not subject to review by the Court in an action for damages unless the decision is so unreasonable as to fall outwith the ambit of discretion and relates to operational matters.'

In this form the law represents a particular application of modern doctrine developed principally through English case law to determine whether a duty of care of a particular scope exists on the part of a public authority for the activity in question.

There are various factors that played a part in Scottish roads authority liability law developing into an area with its own particular rules that are not a source for building a wide doctrine of liability for omissions, but not all of these would on their own have brought this about. In South Africa, too, it has long been recognised that the authorities are limited and relevant.[73] However, the impact of that obvious factual truism was different. Its sig-

---

[69]   *Gibson v Strathclyde Regional Council* 1993 SLT 1243 per LJC Ross at 1246 and Lord Weir at 1247.

[70]   Ibid; *Nugent v Glasgow City Council* [2009] CSOH 88 per Lord Brodie at para 23.

[71]   See *Grant v Lothian Regional Council* 1988 SLT 533 per Lord Prosser at 534, cited in *Syme v Scottish Borders Council* 2003 SLT 601 per Lord Clarke at para 21.

[72]   *Hutchison v North Lanarkshire Council* 7 February 2007 unreported per Lord Brodie, repeated in *Nugent v Glasgow City Council* [2009] CSOH 88 per Lord Brodie at para 23.

[73]   *Moulang v Port Elizabeth Municipality* 1958 (2) SA 518(A) 522.

nificance was reinterpreted in South Africa. In contrast to Scotland roads authority cases had originally reflected the historic English roads authority doctrine distinguishing between misfeasance and nonfeasance. But South African lawyers later 'came to see municipalities' immunity from liability for nonfeasance as a *failure* to treat them on all fours with private persons, justified, if at all, by municipalities' need to use their scarce resources in the broader public interest'.[74] Whether this makes any difference to the outcome of cases averring hazards in the physical state of the roads is doubt-ful. Local authorities in Scotland do sometimes, for example, compensate cyclists who are injured through hitting[75] or avoiding potholes, as they do in South Africa.[76] However, the rhetoric in the South African authority points to the possibility of a broader acceptance that a wider range of protective duties could give rise to a claim, and specifically there is liability for negli-gently failing to warn by 'appropriate signs or other means'.[77]

A great deal of what public authorities and their officials do is to support and protect members of the public. As a Scottish commentator pointed out five years ago, logically the distinction between commission and omission is 'much less relevant in the context of public authorities since those bodies are established by the legislature to fulfil prescribed aims'.[78] South Africa has been open to this view. Scotland has not been. It is not only that the significance of the distinction between omission and commission is today in Scotland certainly the same as in England. It is that there is no historical mate-rial to support a difference in the past, except the fact that it was not referred to in Scottish roads authority cases. François du Bois has shown that for South Africa its civilian heritage has led to fundamental divergence between it and English law, so that 'behind the façade' of 'conceptual similarity' there is recognition in South Africa of preventive duties and a more open accept-ance of liability for omissions.[79] There is no Scottish heritage of this sort. A distinguished first-instance judge five years ago,[80] in not following an English decision[81] and in holding that there could be a duty of care on a fire authority that had failed to check properly that it had completely extinguished a fire, did express the view that the distinction between commission and omission

---

[74] Du Bois, 'State Liability', supra note 4 at 161.

[75] The author successfully assisted one of his Delict students in the 1980s to obtain a payment from the local authority for this.

[76] *McIntosh v Premier of the Province of KwaZulu-Natal* 2008 (6) SA 1 (SCA) highlighted in du Bois, 'State Liability', supra note 4 at 164 as showing a different approach to English law.

[77] *Cape Municipality v Bakkerud* 1997 (4) SA 356 (C), cited in du Bois, 'State Liability', supra note 4 at 163.

[78] D Brodie 'Public Authority Liability: The Scottish Approach' (2007) EdinLR 254 at 255.

[79] Du Bois 'State Liability', supra note 4 at 162–3.

[80] *Burnett v Grampian Fire and Rescue Service* 2007 SLT 61 per Lord Macphail at para 34.

[81] Distinguishing *Capital and Counties plc v Hampshire County Council* [1997] QB 1004 (CA).

was not followed in the same way in Scotland as in England.[82] But at best that can only be supported by a negative – the absence in older Scottish writing and case law of any reference to it. It is really impossible to say what view was taken on this question before the late twentieth century. A passage in Stair,[83] never referred to in case law or delict texts, perhaps because it is not located within his treatment of delict, actually states that there is no legal obligation to assist those 'in hazard'. What part of the civilian tradition that derives from waits to be researched. Perhaps it represents a different civilian tradition, an earlier version of the limited view found in Voet that 'liability should only be imposed for an omission connected with a prior positive act, or where there had been an express assumption of a duty',[84] which is no longer followed in South Africa. Neither Scottish case law nor legal writing addressed these questions. In any event, if they had, it has long been clear that English and Scots law is the same in the area of negligence.

There are within the wider absence of a Scottish heritage four specific reasons why there is this divergence between Scotland and South Africa. First is the impact of a recent leading Scottish case[85] decided by the House of Lords. In this it was held that a local authority as landlords of a tenant who murdered a neighbouring tenant of the same authority had no duty of care in respect of having failed to take preventive measures to avoid this. In that case, it is true, the House of Lords did not place particular emphasis on the fact that the defender was a local authority.[86] But that just serves to under-line a general lack of openness to recognising protective duties. Secondly, the duty of care concept is seen as common to Scots law and English law. Thirdly, and consequentially, English House of Lords decisions holding there is no duty on a roads authority with regard to the design of a road junction,[87] or to keep visible painted warning lines which it had put at a road junction[88] are taken as authoritative in Scotland. The latter is paralleled by an earlier Scottish first-instance decision,[89] and has now been followed in another similar Scottish case.[90] The former has been distinguished at first instance, but on grounds that do not entail a greater openness to liability for omissions.[91] Some cases that perhaps could have been argued as reflecting a

---

[82] Cf du Bois 'State Liability', supra note 4 at 165 note 130.
[83] *Institutions* 1.30.40.
[84] Du Bois 'State Liability', supra note 4, at 162.
[85] *Mitchell v Glasgow City Council* 2009 SC (HL) 21.
[86] See especially per Lord Hope of Craighead.
[87] *Stovin v Wise* [1996] AC 923.
[88] *Gorringe v Calderdale Metropolitan Borough Council* [2004] 1 WLR 1057.
[89] *Murray v Nicholls* 1983 SLT 194 not cited by counsel but followed in *Gorringe* per Lord Rodger of Earlsferry at para 83.
[90] *MacDonald v Aberdeenshire Council* 2012 SLT 863.
[91] *Bennett v J Lamont & Sons* 2000 SLT 17 (Temporary Judge TG Coutts QC) – no foreseeability on part of local authority that farmers in the Highlands would not take appropriate steps to keep cows of the road, and not fair, just and reasonable to require the provision of miles of

certain level of openness to recognise liability for omissions could anyway have been reasoned in the same way in England, for example, a Scottish[92] appellate decision[93] holding the police had a duty of care once they had taken control of a road in the context of a flood. An English judgment holding that an ambulance authority has a duty of care once it has received an emergency call[94] had been followed in Scotland. If a fire authority case were to be considered at an appellate level in Scotland or in England, the process of reasoning, whatever the outcome,[95] would be the same.

The openness of the South African common law of delict to liability for omissions has been shown to have facilitated its development of the law of delict in the area of the protective duties imposed on public authorities.[96] There are many decisions that would not have resulted in liability in Scotland, strikingly for example, *Local Transitional Council of Delmas v Boschoff*[97] holding a local authority liable for failure to protect a community from harm done by those living in an 'informal township' next door. This type of attitude to liability for omissions has made the law receptive to direct development in this area by reference to the Bill of Rights. The current position in South Africa is premised upon the idea that 'it is usually the very business of a public authority or functionary to serve the interests of others, and its duty to do so will differentiate it from others who similarly fail to act to avert harm'.[98] As in the law of delict more generally the controlling concept of wrongfulness has to reflect in its application the legal convictions of the community,[99] particularly in relation to liability for a negligent omission. That has to be 'informed and guided by the norms and values which have been enshrined in the Bill of Rights, because norms or values which are inconsistent with the Constitution, have no validity'.[100] This is reinforced by the specific provision in the Constitution[101] that provides '[w]hen interpreting any legislation, and when developing the common law . . . courts . . . must promote the spirit, purport and objects of the Bill of Rights'. In applying these principles in a recent case a prison authority was held liable for

---

fences; *McKnight v Clydeside Buses Ltd* 1998 (OH) (Lady Cosgrove) – double decker bus on road under bridge hitting the bridge, negligence in the course of erection of warning signs.

[92] But approved in England (*Van Colle v Chief Constable of Hertfordshire Police* [2009] 1 AC 225 per Lord Bingham of Cornhill at para 53).

[93] *Gibson v Orr* 1999 SC 420.

[94] *Kent v Griffiths* [2001] QB 36 (CA).

[95] The English case was doubted in *Van Colle* per Lord Bingham at para 55.

[96] Du Bois 'State Liability', supra note 4.

[97] [2005] 4 All SA 175 (SCA) referred to in du Bois, 'State Liability', 165 note 128

[98] *Minister of Safety and Security v Van Duivenboden* 2002 (6) SA 431 (SCA) per Nugent JA at para 19.

[99] *Minister of Polisie v Ewels* 1975 (3) SA 590 (A) at 597A-B.

[100] *Minister of Safety and Security v Van Duivenboden* 2002 (6) SA 431 (SCA) per Nugent JA at para 17; *Carmichele v Minister of Safety and Security* 2001 (4) SA 938 (CC) at 961.

[101] S 39.

negligently failing to take reasonable steps to protect the plaintiff from being exposed to TB, and so becoming infected.[102]

The Scottish position is that the rules of the law of negligence are not influenced by the fact that a human right is affected. If it is, a separate body of rules additionally or alternatively provides a distinct basis of liability. Consequently, in any question of public authority liability where there is, for example, an impact on the party's right to life, as in the case of the local authority landlord, discussed above, or on private and family life, it is necessary to consider separately when a common law negligence claim fails, or if it was not pleaded at all, whether there is liability on this separate ground. There is, however, little point in basing a claim on this ground where the common law case is one of negligence, since the test that has been developed for the human rights claim is that it is necessary to show that there was a 'real and immediate risk' of the right being impacted on. It seems that in cases where a negligence claim has failed or would have failed if separately pled, not on the ground of a lack of duty of care, but on the ground that that duty of care was not breached, it would be unlikely that this different basis of liability could be established on the facts. For instance, where a family member sought to make an English health authority liable after a patient compulsorily detained in a mental hospital got out and committed suicide,[103] it was accepted there was a duty of care in negligence, but in the circumstances it was not breached. It was held there were obligations with respect to article 2 ECHR (right to life) to have a proper system for supervising patients,[104] and a 'further "operational" obligation where there is a "real and immediate" risk of suicide' to do all that can reasonably be expected to prevent the patient from committing suicide.[105] But as that is more difficult to prove than that there was negligence, there seems no point from the litigant's standpoint of knowing this. Where a negligence claim fails because there is no duty of care, or is not pled in anticipation of that, the human rights ground of liability is the only possible one. As the human rights obligation will not generally apply in such a situation, it would be necessary to proceed on the 'operational' obligation where there is 'real and immediate risk'. However, such claims are likely to fail on the facts even in cases against the police for the consequences of failure to take protective steps when a person has reported threats against himself or herself, and where there is some scepticism about the public policy grounds which exclude a common law duty of care on the part of the police.[106] Further, almost all negligence claims for personal injury or death that would succeed will be settled. As the human rights claim will

---

[102] *Lee v Minister of Correctional Services* [2011] ZAWCHC 12.
[103] *Savage v South Essex Partnership NHS Foundation Trust* [2009] 1 AC 681.
[104] Per Lord Rodger of Earlsferry at para 69.
[105] Per Lord Rodger of Earlsferry at para 72.
[106] *Van Colle v Chief Constable of Hertfordshire Police* [2009] 1 AC 225.

add nothing to what is obtained in the settlement, it will therefore play no practical role in the vast majority of these cases.

The idea of a vindicatory claim is unreal in this context. There are other much more meaningful ways in which defenders as part of a settlement will satisfy the pursuer's desire for vindication, in particular by providing a full explanation, accepting formally that what occurred should not have occurred, and making an apology. However, if those are part of the settlement, it will then have the effect of making any free-standing human rights claim worth nothing. Both the adequacy of any monetary settlements and whether there was an apology are factors to be taken into account in determining whether there was effective redress given for any human rights claims, or as alternatively put, whether the pursuer is any longer a 'victim' of the breach.[107]

Generally academic comment on United Kingdom on the separation of human rights liability from the law of negligence has been unfavourable.[108] There has been no distinctively Scottish commentary on the question. That unfavourable comment has not been related to the practical unimportance of the free-standing human rights claim. It springs, rather, from the background of some dissatisfaction with the law of negligence as it has been applied to public authorities. With the exception of a very small number of cases, the effect of applying the general tests of whether there is or is not proximity, and considering whether it is 'fair just and reasonable' for a duty of care to be recognised, has been severely to restrict claims on the ground of negligence against public authorities. As already considered, an important factor is that there has been the general hostility to recognise protective duties except in very limited circumstances. Those that have been recognised all have in common that the public authority in question had entered into a direct relationship with the party, notably in one case where the claimant had been in local authority care throughout his childhood and adolescence, and claimed that the delivery of that care had materially contributed to his on-going state of mental ill-health in adult life.[109] In another (based on vicarious liability for the breach of duty of the public official)[110] the pursuer was a school child with dyslexia who later sued in respect of the failure of an educational psychologist properly to recognise that condition. The cases of failures in the provision of an ambulance or in firefighting are borderline because of the difficulty of determining exactly when a relationship has been entered into with the member of the public.

However, there are also cases where a relationship had been entered into

---

[107] *Rabone v Pennine Care NHS Trust* [2010] EWCA Civ 698 per Jackson LJ at 105.

[108] In particular J Steele 'Damages in tort and under the Human Rights Act: Remedial or Functional Separation?' (2008) 67 *Cambridge Law Journal* 606.

[109] *Barrett v Enfield LBC* [2001] 2 AC 550.

[110] *Phelps Hillingdon LBC* [2001] 2 AC 619.

and where, nonetheless, there is no duty of care, notably the cases involv-ing social workers, and those police cases of the type where members of the public have reported threats made against them. In the social worker cases the decisions, which can be justified as a matter of legal policy, now stand essentially on the open-ended criterion of whether it is 'fair just and reasonable'.[111] The police cases are still affected by the line of authority going back to the first modern case,[112] which adopted what at least in some respects has been criticised as an over-simplistic weighing[113] of the disadvan-tages to the police service if claims were to be more generally recognised. It has also been suggested that the separation of human rights claims from the law of negligence was based on a rather crude distinction between the fun-damentally vindicatory function of the former, and that of the latter being compensatory.

Recently, however, François du Bois has argued forcibly that the generally unfavourable academic comment in the United Kingdom is unjustified.[114] Instead separation of delict and human rights in this area is appropriate, essentially because delict is generally concerned with corrective justice, and human rights law with distributive justice. It is accepted that at least in the consideration of whether a duty of care exists in negligence law issues of dis-tributive justice are appropriately considered, and indeed this has often been done in decisions on this topic in the United Kingdom. 'But it is one thing to treat distributive justice as a constraining value, sometimes inhibiting the pursuit of corrective justice . . . and quite another to promote it to the status of the basic criterion for determining liability'.[115] This is convincing analysis. However, there is a practical problem here. The United Kingdom experi-ence, as we have seen earlier in this section, shows that free-standing human rights claims add nothing of practical use to a litigant to whom there is no duty of care in delict, or where there is, but there is no breach of that duty.

10.6 CONCLUSION

South African law has seen an extensive development of liability directly and overtly responding to the Bill of Rights on the ground of an alleged negligent failure by a public authority or its officials to protect. It has also seen a development of the law of vicarious liability of public officials, again directly and overtly responding to the Bill of Rights. Scotland, along with the rest of the United Kingdom, has not experienced this. In the rest of the Scots

---

[111] Starting with X *v Bedfordshire County Council* [1995] 2 AC 633.
[112] *Hill v Chief Constable of West Yorkshire* [1989] AC 53.
[113] Recognised to an extent judicially *Van Colle* per Lord Hope and per Lord Bingham dissenting.
[114] F du Bois 'Human Rights and the Tort Liability of Public Authorities' (2011) LQR 589.
[115] At 598.

law of delict as it affects public bodies, notably the protection of personality rights from infringements by public officials, however, the position is the opposite. South African law has here not drawn significantly on the Bill of Rights. The reason is that it has not had to. The equivalent area of the Scots law of delict is underdeveloped, and in some respects, unless developed in certain ways, would result in a common law claim being denied while the free-standing human rights claim would succeed. The impact of human rights law, therefore, in the field of the liability of public bodies is influenced by the expansiveness or otherwise of the common law of delict, as has been shown to be the case with recognising protective duties in South Africa against a background of an openness to liability for negligent omissions as already established in its common law.

It is possible for legal systems reasonably to differ on the level of protection for which public authorities should be responsible, and on the role of delictual damages actions in promoting such protective duties. Whether in this context a human rights claim is treated as separate from (as in Scotland and the United Kingdom more generally) or intertwined with a common law claim (as in South Africa) is less important than the attitude the legal system takes to such claims anyway. However, it is a central issue where a legal system such as Scotland's has lacked a structured development in the common law, with regard, for example, to the protection of the citizen against invasions of bodily integrity or physical liberty by public officials. Human rights law may remain separate from delict but its background effect is to prevent the common law from persisting with doctrines, such as the requirement to show 'malice' and 'lack of probable cause', which can anyhow be shown to be historically unjustifiable. An appeal to human rights has simply a stronger impact than an appeal to pre-nineteenth-century Scottish doctrinal legal history.

Chapter 11

Nuisance

*Hanri Mostert**

11.1 INTRODUCTION

In law, 'nuisance' refers to conduct causing actual or potential damage, discomfort or injury to neighbours.[1] The rules governing an allegation of nuisance respond to the duty to refrain from using one's property in a way that causes unreasonable prejudice to a neighbour or the community.[2] Offending conduct may include emissions (such as smoke, dust, smells and noise) emanating from the neighbouring property, or disturbances caused by the neighbours. The offended neighbour may apply for abatement of the conduct. Where the public at large, or a particular part of it, is affected, a public authority may move to suppress the offending conduct or disturbance.[3] Jurisdictions that have legal rules to deal with nuisance correspond on these points even though the models of nuisance law may differ.

In some jurisdictions the law of nuisance is seen to stem from a specific delict or tort.[4] In others it is developed from a rule of property law, derived from the maxim *sic utere tuo ut alienum non laedas*.[5] Sometimes it is regarded as a legal doctrine covering a generic concept.[6] In some jurisdictions, the

* I am greatly indebted to Meyer van den Berg, Janine Howard and Cheri-Leigh Young for research assistance, made possible by the National Research Foundation, and to Anne Pope, Elspeth Reid, Niall Whitty, Andrew Steven, Robin Evans-Jones, Leon Verstappen, Michael Milo, Alison Dundes Renteln and Albert Verheij for their advice, comments and criticisms. I take responsibility for the views expressed here and the errors that remain.

1 D van der Merwe 'Neighbour Law' in R Zimmermann and D Visser (eds) *Southern Cross – Civil Law and Common Law in South Africa* (Juta 1996) 759.
2 D M Sanchez Galera and J Zehetner 'Action Against Emissions: Fundamental Rights and the Extension of the Right to Sue in Private Nuisance to Non-owners' in G Brüggemeier, A Colombi Ciacchi and G Comandé (eds) *Fundamental Rights and Private Law in the European Union* (Cambridge University Press 2010) 304, 306–7.
3 J Church and J Church 'Nuisance' in W Joubert (ed) *The Law of South Africa* 2e (LexisNexis Butterworths 2003) vol 19(1), para 211; A J van der Walt *The Law of Neighbours* (Juta 2010) 302.
4 J R L Milton 'The Law of Neighbours in South Africa' 1969 *Acta Juridica* 123 at 143.
5 Van der Walt, note 3 supra, 237.
6 E.g. in Milton, note 4 supra, at 142.

concept extends to interference with the free flow of water or the surface and lateral support of the neighbouring land.[7] In other jurisdictions, these are treated under specific rules of neighbour law.[8] Some jurisdictions distinguish between public nuisance and private nuisance,[9] whereas others make no such distinction.[10]

The frequency of nuisance-type disturbances is high, judging by the number of matters litigated in any given jurisdiction,[11] and so one expects nuisance law to be well developed. Even so, nuisance law knows several areas of contention. In the United States, the doctrine of nuisance is described as 'muddled and confusing.'[12] Scots commentators refer to the 'inherent ambiguity' of the term nuisance, the loose legal usage thereof,[13] the fact that

---

[7]   E.g. English law, see *Leakey and Others v National Trust for Place of Historic Interest or Natural Beauty* [1980] 1 All ER 17; *Home Brewery plc v William Davis & Co (Loughborough) Ltd* [1987] 1 All ER 637.

[8]   E.g. South Africa, see van der Walt, note 3 supra, 204 ff; C G van der Merwe 'Things' in W Joubert (ed) *The Law of South Africa* 2e (LexisNexis Butterworths 2003) vol 27(1), para 315; C G van der Merwe and A Pope 'Property' in F du Bois (ed) *Wille's Principles of South African Law* 9e (Juta 2007) 476; P Badenhorst, J M Pienaar and H Mostert *Silberberg and Schoeman's The Law of Property* 5e (Butterworths, LexisNexis 2006) 122; H Mostert and A Pope (eds) *The Principles of the Law of Property in South Africa* (Oxford University Press 2010) 139. For Scots law see N R Whitty 'Nuisance' in *The Laws of Scotland: Stair Memorial Encyclopaedia*, Reissue (2001) para 91.

[9]   E.g. South Africa, England. In South Africa, the public nuisance mechanism is regarded as underdeveloped, and unnecessary. In England, public nuisance is an important mechanism to curb conduct with property that may be harmful to the community. Whitty, note 8 supra, para 20.

[10]   E.g. Scotland. See Bell *Principles* §§ 973–8; Whitty, note 8 supra, paras 159,165–6.

[11]   South African courts have over the past fifteen years heard nuisance-related arguments in e.g. *Wingaardt and Others v Grobler and Another* 2010 (6) SA 148 (ECG); *Botha v Andrade and Others* 2009 (1) 259 (SCA); *Van Rensburg and Another NNO v Nelson Mandela Metropolitan Municipality and Others* 2008 (2) SA 8 (SE); *Allaclass Investments (Pty) Ltd and Another v Milnerton Golf Club Estate (Stelzner and Others intervening)* 2007 (2) SA 40 (C); *Laskey and Another v Showzone CC and Others* 2007 (2) SA 48 (C); *Nelson Mandela Metropolitan Municipality and Others v Greyvenouw CC* 2004 (2) SA 81 (SE); *Hichange Investments (Pty) Ltd v Cape Produce Company (Pty) Ltd t/a Pelts Products and Others* [2004] JOL 12538 (E); *Wright and Another v Cockin and Others* 2004 (4) SA 207 (E); *Clark v Faraday and Another* 2004 (4) SA 564 (C); *Mkangeli and Others v Joubert and Others* 2002 (4) SA 36 (SCA); *Dorland and Another v Smits* 2002 5 SA 374 (C); *Three Rivers Ratepayer's Association and Others v Northern Metropolitan* 2000 (4) SA 377 (W); *Garden Cities Incorporated Association Not For Gain v Northpine Islamic Society* 1999 (2) SA 268 (C); *Body Corporate of the Laguna Ridge Scheme No 152/1987 v Dorse* 1999 (2) SA 512 (D); *Rademeyer and Others v Western Districts Council and Others* 1998 3 SA 1011 (SE). Recent judgments in Scots law include: *King v The Advocate General for Scotland* [2009] CSOH 169; *Morris Amusements Ltd v Glasgow City Council & ORS* 2009 SLT 697; *Viewpoint Housing Association Ltd v Edinburgh Council* [2007] CSOH 114, 2007 SLT 772; *Canmore Housing Association Ltd v Bairnsfather (t/a B R Autos)* 2004 SLT 673.

[12]   Halper 'Untangling the Nuisance Knot' 1998 *Boston College Environmental Affairs Law Review* 89ff.

[13]   Whitty, note 8 supra, para 1.

it 'defies exact definition',[14] and the 'bewildering diversity of views'[15] about when an owner's use and enjoyment of property would be appropriate. South African scholars are only now, after more than four decades, coming to terms with the realisation that the search for a 'unifying normative frame-work'[16] in neighbour law is futile, because social dynamics would render the framework 'elusive at best'.[17]

In many ways, uneasiness in private law circles concerning the messiness, ambiguities and lack of exactness in the taxonomy of nuisance law resonates on a much broader scale where courts are constitutionally mandated (and obliged) to develop common law to bring it in line with constitutional goals. Societies are becoming more diverse and yet people must live more closely together. Disputes between neighbours often have their cause in incompatible personality traits or temperaments. Wealth, envy and boredom may fuel grievances. Where there are such deeper underlying causes, it is unlikely that the process of law will be able to address the root of the problem.[18]

Yet, in a constitutional framework that supports human rights the demand may be for the development of a society based on 'good neigh-bourliness and shared concern'[19] to promote fundamental values such as dignity, equality and freedom in an open democracy. The discerning feature of nuisance law – its support of flexibility in resolving disputes and solving problems – is one that fits well into a constitutional paradigm, especially one supporting human rights. The commitment to reasonableness in the balancing of competing interests is, after all, as prevalent in human rights law as it is in nuisance law. What complicates an analysis of such issues, however, is that nuisance law, as human rights law, is closely tied to life itself, which at the best of times can be messy and inexact. This is bound to influence the applicable laws, especially where flexibility is essential for reaching fair outcomes.

Under investigation in this essay are the laws of Scotland and South Africa, where nuisance law has developed in very similar ways, over a long period, being influenced by both Civil Law and Common Law. In both jurisdictions introduction of justiciable human rights affects the general understanding of legal rules and principles; yet the law of nuisance in both these jurisdictions

---

[14] Ibid, relying on *Central Motors (St Andrews) Ltd v St Andrews Magistrates* 1961 SLT 290 at 295;

[15] D Johnston 'Owners and Neighbours: From Rome to Scotland' in R Evans-Jones (ed) *The Civil Law Tradition in Scotland* (The Stair Society 1995) 176.

[16] Van der Walt, note 3 supra, 385.

[17] Ibid.

[18] L Verstappen *Heerenheibel in de Heerlijkheid Beek – Rondom de Berg en Dalse Watertorenarresten* (Stichting tot Behoud van Monumenten en Landschap in de Gemeente Ubbergen 2004) 13; and see the author's particularly telling account (16ff) of the neighbourhood dispute in *HR 13 maart 1936* 1936 NJ 415 and *HR 2 april 1937* 1937 NJ 639 .

[19] *Port Elizabeth Municipality v Various Occupiers* 2004 (12) BCLR 1268 (CC) at para 37.

apparently remains largely unaffected by human rights considerations. One may want to ascribe this lack of alignment to the 'chalk and cheese' quality of an attempt to equate the rules of nuisance law with the values espoused by human rights. Where such exercises had already been undertaken, it has been labelled 'privatist' and risky,[20] especially where private law principles have been compromised politically. The South African case is a good example, given that human rights law is expected to rectify the inequities of apartheid, rather than entrench or protect the interests that were furthered by the old political regime. In the face of these pressures, it is understandable that for some even an attempt at balancing conflicting private rights would be suspect.[21]

Whether balancing different interests is a matter of private law or human rights, is not the point of interest in this chapter. It is accepted that the common law functions within a particular constitutional context where it can be influenced by constitutional values. This chapter concerns itself with what the spheres of human rights and nuisance law have to offer to achieve a better understanding of the balancing exercise that occurs in both contexts. It focuses on only one question, namely whether the common law reasonableness or tolerability standard which determines the acceptability of particular conduct is to be understood differently because of the influence of human rights rules.[22] Other issues, such as whether development or reform of the notion of public nuisance is necessary,[23] and whether it is necessary to develop a statutory mechanism to deal with the intersection of nuisance and human rights,[24] are dealt with only in passing.

The laws of Scotland and South Africa have peculiarly similar legal roots. They are mixed jurisdictions. Their laws on nuisance were shaped by Roman law principles and influenced to varying extents by the notion of equity which featured in English law at the time of reception.[25] In both jurisdictions, the principles of both property law and delict (or tort) law determine the standard of liability and the relief available in nuisance cases.[26] Here the

---

[20] See the comments of van der Walt, note 3 supra, 314–16 to F du Bois and E Reid 'Nuisance' in R Zimmermann D Visser and K Reid (eds) *Mixed Legal Systems in Comparative Perspective: Property and Obligations in Scotland and South Africa* (Oxford University Press 2004) 596ff, qualified by his commendations of their conclusions.

[21] Van der Walt, note 3 supra, 315.

[22] Du Bois and Reid, note 20 supra, 598–9.

[23] Van der Walt, note 3 supra, at 318 argues that public nuisance should not be used to object to the establishment of new neighbourhoods or housing developments, as this mechanism was developed and used for different purposes and it allows too much for under-regulated interference with the exercise of legitimate government functions, sanctioned and required by the Constitution.

[24] Ibid.

[25] For Scotland, see, e.g., du Bois and Reid, note 20 supra, 98–121; Johnston, note 15 supra, 176–97.

[26] For South Africa, see, e.g., Milton, note 4 supra, 131–2; van der Merwe, note 8 supra, paras

similarities end. The laws of Scotland and South Africa operate in very different social contexts. The South African human rights experience is informed
quite significantly by fairly recent political history, which is hallmarked by
discrimination, inequality and violations of human dignity.[27] Scotland has
not had a similar experience. It is bound to its own context, within Europe,
where the move towards closer political and economic cooperation between
and cohesion of European states had an influence on law-making.[28]

The very different social contexts of South Africa and Scotland constitute one factor that may complicate the analysis.[29] Another is that very
few sources exist in either South Africa or Scotland that deal directly with
the interchange between nuisance law and human rights. Whilst a small
number of scholarly works raise the issue, the examples from case law are
few and far between. In other European jurisdictions, such as England and
the Netherlands, and more so in the overarching European law sphere, the
intersection of nuisance issues with human rights has at least been considered judicially. Regard is thus had to a broader source base, as the literature
on fundamental rights and private law in the European Union more broadly
may be instructive. There, it is accepted that a broad range of constitutionally protected rights and interests (such as the rights to life, health, privacy,
enjoyment of property, personal development, and exercise of a profession)
ought to be considered in private nuisance claims.[30]

The chapter refers briefly to these experiences, well aware that taking
a cue from other contexts may be problematic.[31] It is obvious that
constitutionally-entrenched rights and interests of different parties may
clash, but how these rights are described constitutionally may differ from one
context to another, and whether they are indeed entrenched on a constitutional level would also depend on the specific context. The level of protection
also differs from one right to another.[32] What is acceptable in one jurisdic-

302 and 314; Mostert and Pope, note 8 supra, 134; Badenhorst, Pienaar and Mostert, note 8
supra, 114–16. For Scotland, see, e.g., Whitty, note 8 supra, paras 97, 104; see also paras 17,
87–8.

[27] See, e.g., *S v Makwanyane* 1995 (3) SA 391 (CC) at para 7 and see R Davenport and C
Saunders *South Africa: A Modern History* 5e (Antony Rowe 2000) 570, and more generally H
Giliomee and B Mbenga *New History of South Africa* (NB Publishers Tafelberg 2007) 396–411.

[28] Writing from the English perspective, P Sparkes *European Land Law* (Hart 2007) at xi comments that 'Brussels has constructed a law capable of flooding into all the nooks and crannies
of [the English] domestic property system'.

[29] Du Bois and Reid, note 20 supra, at 594 have already observed that contextual difference will
affect the implementation of the shared underlying principle of nuisance law.

[30] Sanchez Galera and Zehetner, note 2 supra, 308.

[31] See, e.g., G D L Cameron 'Scots and English Nuisance . . . Much the Same Thing?' (2005)
9 *EdinLR* 98 at115ff on the inadequacy of the perception that the Scots and English laws of
nuisance are congruent.

[32] L S Underkuffler 'When should Rights "Trump"? An Examination of Speech and Property'
(2000) 52 *Maine Law Review* 311 at 322 argues persuasively, for instance, that the constitu-

tion may not be so in another, because of different social contexts, different concerns and different lifestyles. Before these issues are considered, however, it is necessary to understand the standard by which nuisance is determined, as well as the human rights contexts in the two jurisdictions being compared.

11.2 THE NUISANCE TEST AND CONSEQUENCES

The origins of nuisance[33] and the way in which it was received into Scots[34] and South African[35] law have been the subject of several scholarly analyses, and hence need not be discussed at length here. As a point of departure, it is accepted that in both South Africa and Scotland a mechanism, referred to as nuisance under the influence of English law,[36] exists to deal with invasion of interests in land,[37] resulting from the use of neighbouring property. It addresses the occurrence of actual or potential damage, discomfort or injury[38] by offering solutions ranging from the (prohibitory or mandatory) interdict,[39] to the declaratory order[40] and even court-ordered damages in lieu of an interdict.[41]

11.2.1 Locus standi: *Owners and land users*

In both Scotland and South Africa nuisance law assumes that at least two properties are involved. These may be land in private hands,[42] or public spaces.[43] The owner or user of the land (such as tenant in occupation or lessees)[44] may bring a claim in nuisance. Where a non-owner suffers from the nuisance, it is typically expected that a valid entitlement or authorisation to be present on, occupy, use or enjoy the land should exist.[45]

---

tional right to property is not as 'invariably powerful' as is presumed, because of its distributive features and its interconnectedness with the particular political system in which it functions.

[33] See van der Merwe, note 1 supra, 759.

[34] Whitty, 'Nuisance' note 8 supra, paras 1, 7–16; N R Whitty 'The Source of the Plus Quam Tolerabile Concept in Nuisance' (2003) 7 *EdinLR* 218.

[35] Van der Merwe, note 1 supra, 759.

[36] Ibid 760.

[37] Whitty, note 8 supra, para 5. Milton, note 4 supra, 137; van der Walt, note 3 supra, 237.

[38] Van der Merwe, note 1 supra, 759.

[39] Whitty, note 8 supra, paras 144–7.

[40] Ibid para 149.

[41] Ibid paras 150–6.

[42] For SA law: van der Walt, note 3 supra, 240; For Scots law: Whitty, note 8 supra, para 2.

[43] For SA law: van der Walt, note 3 supra, 240; *Malherbe v Ceres Municipality* 1951 (4) SA 510 (A). For Scots law: Whitty, note 8 supra, para 2.

[44] For SA law: C G van der Merwe and M J De Waal *The Law of Things and Servitudes* (Butterworths 1993) para 314; For Scots law: Whitty, note 8 supra, para 133.

[45] For SA law: van der Walt, note 3 supra, 241; For Scots law: Whitty, note 8 supra, paras 133, 134.

Nuisance can be caused by the owner or occupier of the land, or even occasional visitors to the premises.[46] It would usually be the owner or entitled occupier who would be liable.[47]

11.2.2 Standard: Reasonableness/Tolerability

The test to assess whether specific conduct amounts to nuisance is one that balances the interests of neighbours. This is determined, in South Africa, by an 'objective criterion of reasonableness'[48] determining whether conduct under the given circumstances was 'proper, becoming and socially adequate'[49] as against the 'prevailing views of the community'.[50] In Scots law, the similar test is phrased as one of tolerability:[51] the invasion of interests must be 'so unreasonable that the complainer should not be required to tolerate it'.[52] From an analysis of the Scottish cases on this topic,[53] the tenets of the test may be deduced as follows: reasonableness/tolerability is judged according to the usages of the particular society,[54] and assessed against all the 'surrounding circumstances of the offensive conduct and its effects'.[55] Determining liability in nuisance cases is therefore a 'weighing process' in which the 'leading principle is one of reasonable compromise between neighbours'.[56] This corresponds largely with the sentiment in South African case law where it is said that the idea of mutuality,[57] summarised by the phrase 'give and take, live and let live',[58] is at the core of the law.[59]

---

[46] Van der Walt, note 3 supra, at 241.

[47] Ibid.

[48] Van der Merwe and De Waal, note 44 supra, paras 111–13; updated in van der Merwe, note 8 supra, para 304; van der Merwe and Pope, note 8 supra, 478.

[49] Van der Merwe and De Waal, note 44 supra, para 112; updated in van der Merwe, note 8 supra, para 304.

[50] Ibid.

[51] W M Gordon *Scottish Land Law* 2e (W Green 1999) para 26–21. Whitty, note 34 supra, demonstrates that the bases for this reasonableness standard (being, in South Africa and elsewhere, the maxim *sic utere tuo ut alienum non laedas*, and in Scotland the *plus quam tolerabile* concept) derive from different principles.

[52] Whitty, 'Nuisance' note 8 supra, para 39.

[53] Ibid.

[54] *Sedleigh-Denfield v O'Callaghan* [1940] 3 All ER 349 at 364.

[55] *Watt v Jamieson* 1958 SC 56 at 58.

[56] Whitty, note 8 supra, para 40.

[57] I.e. 'mutual and reciprocal neighbourly tolerance and forbearance': A J van der Walt 'The Give-and-Take Spirit of Neighbour Law' in H Mostert and M De Waal (eds) *Essays in Honour of CG van der Merwe* (Butterworths, Lexis Nexis 2011) 68.

[58] See, e.g., *Allaclass Investments (Pty) Ltd and Another v Milnerton Golf Club Estate (Stelzner and Others intervening)* 2007 (2) SA 40 (C) at para 21; van der Merwe, note 8 supra, para 189, Mostert and Pope, note 8 supra, 137.

[59] The same appears in case law relied upon in Scotland. E.g. in *Bamford v Turnley* 1862 3 B & S 62 at 80; *Cavey v Ledbitter* 1863 13 CB(NS) 470 at 476 per Erle CJ; *Wilson v Gibb* 1902 10 SLT 293 at 293–4, per Lord Stormonth Darling.

In both Scots and South African law the determination of reasonableness is objective and relies on a number of relevant considerations.[60] This means that the offending conduct must be regarded as unacceptable by ordinary, rather than overly-sensitive, persons under the same circumstances, when viewing it objectively and impartially.[61] The objective criteria considered by courts in Scotland and South Africa include factors that evaluate both the conduct of the defendant/defender and the gravity of the harm suffered.[62] On the one hand, the reasonableness of the conduct may be assessed by considering, among others,[63] the milieu (locality or neighbourhood) in which the conduct occurs;[64] the sensitivity of the persons or property affected;[65] the type, extent and gravity of the harm or potential harm to the neighbour;[66]

---

[60] For SA law: van der Merwe and De Waal, note 44 supra, para 112, updated in van der Merwe, note 8 supra, para 304. For Scots law: Whitty, note 8 supra, para 41.

[61] For SA law: van der Merwe and De Waal, note 44 supra, para 112; van der Merwe, note 8 supra, para 304; For Scots law: Whitty, note 8 supra, para 41.

[62] Du Bois and Reid, note 20 supra, 583–5.

[63] The list is taken from van der Merwe and De Waal, note 44 supra, para 113. See updated discussion in van der Merwe, note 8 supra, para 305.

[64] For SA law: van der Merwe and De Waal, note 44 supra, para 115; van der Merwe, note 8 supra, para 306; *Gien v Gien* 1979 (2) SA 1113 (T); *Du Toit v De Bot; Du Toit v Zuidmeer* 1883–1884 2 SC 213; *Liss Shoe Co (Pty) Ltd v Moffet Building & Contracting (Pty) Ltd* 1952 2 All SA 425 (O); *Die Vereniging van Advokate (TPA) v Moskeeplein (Edms) Bpk* 1982 (3) SA 159 (T); *Vogel v Crewe and Another* 2003 (4) SA 509 (T). For Scots law: Whitty, note 8 supra, paras 56–9; and see, e.g., *Maguire v Charles M'Neil Ltd* 1922 SC 174 at 188, 192 per Lord Mackenzie; *Lochrane v Allan* 1895 11 Sh Ct Rep 89; *Bosworth-Smith v Gwynnes Ltd* 1919 89 LJ Ch 368; *Hislop v Fleming* (1882) 10 R 462, per Lord Justice-Clerk Moncreiff; *Allen v Gulf Oil Refining Ltd* [1981] AC 1001; *Gillingham Borough Council v Medway (Chatham) Dock Co Ltd* [1993] QB 343; *Wheeler v J J Saunders Ltd* [1995] 3 WLR 466; *Hunter v Canary Wharf Ltd* [1997] 2 All ER 426.

[65] For SA law: van der Merwe and De Waal, note 44 supra, para 116; van der Merwe, note 8 supra, para 308; *Prinsloo v Shaw* 1938 AD 570; *Leith v Port Elizabeth Museum Trustees* 1934 EDL 211; *Van den Berg v OVS Landbou Ingenieurs (Edms) Bpk* 1956 (4) SA 391 (O); *Die Vereniging van Advokate (TPA) v Moskeeplein (Edms) Bpk* 1982 (3) SA 159 (T); *De Charmoy v Day Star Hatchery (Pty) Ltd* 1967 4 SA 188 (D). For Scots law: Whitty, note 8 supra, paras 60–6; and see, e.g., *Heath v Brighton Corpn* 1908 98 LT 718; *Gaunt v Fynney* 1872 8 Ch App 8; *Simpson v Millar* 1923 39 Sh Ct Rep 182; *Armistead v Bowernab* (1888) 15 R 814; *Robinson v Kilert* 1889 41 CH D 88 (CA); *Mackinnon Industries Ltd v Walker* 1951 3 DLR 577 (PC).

[66] For SA law: van der Merwe and De Waal, note 44 supra, para 114, updated in van der Merwe, note 8 supra, para 307; Church and Church, note 3 supra, paras 174–80; see also, e.g., *Holland v Scott* 1882 2 EDC 307 at 313 318 330 332; *Blacker v Carter* 1905 19 EDC 223 at 230; *Whittaker v Hime* 1912 NPD 72 at 76; *Graham v Dittman & Son* 1917 TPD 288 at 290; *Leith v Port Elizabeth Museum Trustees* 1934 EDL 211 at 213; *R v Bilse* 1953 (2) SA 770 (O) at 779; *South African Motor Racing Co Ltd v Peri-Urban Areas Health Board* 1955 (1) SA 334 (T) at 339G; *Van den Berg v OVS Landbou Ingenieurs (Edms) Bpk* 1956 (4) SA 391 (O) at 400; *De Charmoy v Day Star Hatchery (Pty) Ltd* 1967 (4) SA 188 (D) at 192; *Die Vereniging van Advokate (TPA) v Moskeeplein (Edms) Bpk* 1982 (3) SA 159 (T) at 163. For Scots law: Whitty, note 8 supra, paras 44–54; and see, e.g., *Fleming v Gemmil* 1908 SC 340; *Ralston v Pettigrew* (1768) Mor 12808; *Gaunt v Fynney* 1872 8 Ch App 8; *Hole v Barlow* 1858 4 CB(NS) 334; *Duke of Buccleuch v Alexander Cowan & Sons* (1886) 6 M 214; *Webster v Lord Advocate* 1984 SLT 13.

whether other, less invasive activities could have achieved the landowner's purpose;[67] whether it was practicable to abate or prevent the nuisance, or to take protective or remedial measures.[68] On the other hand, factors relating to the defendant/defender include the motive behind a particular activity;[69] the benefit entailed for the landowner by the activity;[70] the social utility of the conduct (that is, whether it serves some public purpose);[71] whether the conduct was sanctioned statutorily.[72] Aesthetic considerations[73] and the remote possibility of danger[74] are generally not considered.

Du Bois and Reid conclude, on comparing the reasonableness or tolerability standards in South African and Scots law, that the test is utterly flexible, 'alive in its implementation to the concrete circumstances in which the specific parties found themselves'.[75] Their comparison[76] of nuanced

---

[67] For SA law: van der Merwe and De Waal, note 44 supra, para 120; updated in van der Merwe, note 8 supra, para 311. Further C G van der Merwe and M Blumberg 'For Whom the Bell Tolls' (1998) 3 *Stell LR* 351 at 355–356. And see, e.g., *Starfield & Starfield v Randles Bros & Hudson* 1911 WLD 175 at 180; *Die Vereniging van Advokate (TPA) v Moskeeplein (Edms) Bpk* 1982 (3) SA 159 (T) at 164. For Scots law: Whitty, note 8 supra, para 132.

[68] For SA law: van der Merwe and De Waal, note 44 supra, para 121; updated in van der Merwe, note 8 supra, para 312. See further van der Merwe and Blumberg, note 67 supra, 356. And see, e.g., *Bloemfontein Town Council v Richter* 1938 AD 195; *Regal v African Superslate (Pty) Ltd* 1963 (1) SA 102 (A) at 111–12 116–18. For Scots law: Whitty, note 8 supra, paras 64–6, 74, 76 and see, e.g., *Wilson v Gibb* 1902 10 SLT 293; *Collins v Hamilton* (1837) 15 S 895; *Ralston v Pettigrew* (1768) Mor 12808; *Overseas Tankship (UK) Ltd v Miller Steamship Co Pty (The Wagon Mound (No 2))* [1967] AC 617.

[69] For SA law: Milton, note 4 supra, 162–5; van der Merwe and De Waal, note 44 supra, para 117; updated in van der Merwe, note 8 supra, para 309. See, e.g., *Blacker v Carter* 1905 19 EDC 223 at 234–5; *Ingelthorpe v Sackville-West* 1908 EDC 159 at 161; *Kirsch v Pincus* 1927 TPD 199; *Regal v African Superslate (Pty) Ltd* 1963 (1) SA 102 (A) at 107–8; *Gien v Gien* 1979 2 SA 1113 (T) at 1121. For Scots law: Whitty, note 8 supra, paras 68–73; and e.g. *Armistead v Bowernab* (1888) 15 R 814; *Ralston v Pettigrew* (1768) Mor 12808.

[70] For SA law: van der Merwe and De Waal, note 44 supra, para 118; updated in van der Merwe, note 8 supra, para 307. See further van der Merwe and Blumberg, note 67 supra, 353–4. For Scots law: Whitty, note 8 supra, para 132.

[71] For SA law: van der Merwe and De Waal, note 44 supra, para 119; updated in van der Merwe, note 8 supra, para 310; van der Merwe and Blumberg, note 67 supra, 355. For Scots law: Whitty, note 8 supra, paras 55, 72–3; *Swinton v Pedi* (1837) 15 S 775; *Ralston v Pettigrew* (1768) Mor 12808.

[72] For Scots law: Whitty, note 8 supra, para 75 and see, e.g., *Hasley v Esso Petroleum Co Ltd* [1961] 2 All ER 145; *Farley v G Adam of Hillington* 1977 SLT (Sh Ct) 81.

[73] For SA law: *Dorland and Another v Smits* 2002 (5) SA 374 (C) 383G-I; Mostert and Pope, note 8 supra, 139–40. For Scots law: Whitty, note 8 supra, para 84; and see, e.g., *Paterson v Beatie* (1845) 7 D 561; *Bland v Mosely* (1587) cited in *Aldred's Case* (1610) 9 Co Rep 57b at 58a.

[74] *Dorland and Another v Smits* 2002 (5) SA 374 (C).

[75] Du Bois and Reid, note 20 supra, 585. They explain: 'A and B may complain of the same interference, but if there are differences in the conduct or circumstances of C and D, their respective neighbours, or in respect of the locations where the collisions of interest took place, then only one of them may be held to have suffered a nuisance. Likewise, identical conduct by C and D will not result in both of them being held to have committed a nuisance

variations in interpretation of the individual factors in South African and Scots law renders further elaboration here superfluous. Their close scrutiny of the reasonableness or tolerability tests in South Africa and Scotland and the implications thereof for specific matters such as whether and/or when liability for payment of damages results[77] need simply be noted here.

11.2.3 Liability

South African law accepts liability in neighbour law even in the absence of negligence.[78] As *Regal v African Superslate* suggests, negligence is not even an element of the enquiry.[79] Whether such liability is suitable to the purposes of nuisance law has been a source of scholarly disagreement for quite some time in South African law.[80] More recent analyses[81] explain by distinguishing between the consequences of a finding of nuisance in the narrow sense of annoyance and nuisance in the wide sense of abuse of rights respectively.[82]

There are two main types of consequence: narrowly, nuisance relates to a neighbour's infringement with another neighbour's entitlement to use and enjoy her property, usually affecting wealth, comfort and convenience.[83] In a wider sense, nuisance also refers to abnormal or unusual use of land

---

if the circumstances of A and B are different. Not even identical outcomes produced by identical conduct will necessarily be treated the same'. (Footnotes omitted.)

[76] Ibid 582–6.

[77] For more detail, see ibid 582–92; van der Walt, note 3 supra, 291–6.

[78] Ibid 32–4, 256–7.

[79] Ibid 256–9.

[80] Ibid 257. See especially *Regal v African Superslate (Pty) Ltd* 1963 (1) SA 102 (A) at 109 and 112.

[81] Mostert and Pope, note 8 supra, 134–9; van der Walt, note 3 supra, 292.

[82] Van der Walt, note 3 supra, 292–3. E Reid 'The Doctrine of Abuse of Rights: Perspective from a Mixed Jurisdiction' (2004) 8.3 *Electronic Journal of Comparative Law* at 5; E Reid 'Abuse of Rights in Scots Law' (1998) 2 *EdinLR* 129 at 155. In SA law, further distinction is made between instances of nuisance as described above, and other transgressions catered for in neighbour law, such as encroachment (trespass). In SA, encroachment is an area governed by special remedies due to its historical background. Strictly speaking, encroachment does not form part of the scope of the analysis. However, there has been more academic activity on the matter of encroachment under the Constitution than in any other aspect of neighbour law, nuisance included. The reason for this is the decision in *Trustees of the Brian Lackey Trust v Annandale* 2003 (4) SA 528 (C) a case involving a massive (80 per cent) encroachment of a new luxury home onto the neighbouring property. The outcome was a decision ordering the neighbour to accept compensation for the encroachment and surrendering the ownership of the land to the encroaching builder. Though the remedy available for encroachment differs significantly from the remedy for nuisance, scholars commenting on the unfortunate outcome of the *Lackey Trust* case do take into account the reasonableness standard underlying neighbour law. In this sense it is necessary to distinguish the two areas and the respective remedies.

[83] For SA law: Milton, note 4 supra, 149–50; See also Mostert and Pope, note 8 supra, 134; Badenhorst, Pienaar and Mostert, note 8 supra, 111; and see *Vogel v Crewe and Another* 2003 (4) SA 509 (T) at 511H–512A. For Scots law: Whitty, note 8 supra, para 3

that results in actual damage to the neighbour.[84] Comparison of the narrow and wide senses of nuisance in recent literature and cases demonstrates that annoyance/disturbance is generally addressed by reliance on an interdict,[85] while loss and *culpa* would found a claim based in Aquilian liability.[86] Some commentators add that an interdict may also be employed in the latter context to prevent a continuation of the offensive conduct.[87]

This tendency, apparent in recent case law, has spurred van der Walt[88] to comment that the notion of 'give and take' is limited to 'annoyance-type nuisance . . ., which does not amount to or cause actual physical harm or personal injury for neighbours.' He explains[89] that determining reasonableness in this context helps to 'indicate when otherwise lawful use of one's property becomes unlawful and actionable.' This is to be contrasted with nuisance in the wide sense, where the action itself is unlawful to begin with, because it is 'contrary to other norms of social acceptability':[90] it may be 'inherently unnatural and unlawful' conduct, or it may cause (the threat of) 'actual and significant physical damage or loss or personal injury'.[91] Van der Walt points out that in respect of the latter type of conduct, it is inappropriate to expect an owner to tolerate the conduct by invoking a reasonableness standard.

In Scots law,[92] as du Bois and Reid[93] demonstrate, a comparable approach is followed: a test seeking to establish negligence only would relate to negligent nuisance, whereas a test seeking to establish both wrongfulness and blameworthiness of the conduct (that is, malicious; or deliberate in the knowledge that the conduct would cause harm; or reckless)[94] would relate to intentional nuisance. Tolerability would be the standard only in cases of intentional nuisance.[95]

A tight, categorical distinction between those cases that attract damages and those that do not does not resolve difficulties in establishing the basis of liability. Du Bois and Reid[96] indicate that the approaches in South African

---

[84] *Regal v African Superslate (Pty) Ltd* 1963 (1) SA 102 (A) at 120G; *East London Western Districts Farmers Association v Minister of Education and Development Aid* 1989 (2) SA 63 (A) at 67H–J; Milton, note 4 supra, 150ff.
[85] Mostert and Pope, note 8 supra, 136; van der Walt, note 3 supra, 292.
[86] Van der Merwe and Pope, note 8 supra, 481; Mostert and Pope, note 8 supra, 137; van der Walt, note 3 supra, 292; and see *Dorland and Another v Smits* 2002 (5) SA 374 (C).
[87] *Rademeyer and Others v Western Districts Council and Others* 1998 (3) SA 1011 (SE) at 1017; and see Mostert and Pope, note 3 supra, 137.
[88] Van der Walt, note 57 supra, 68.
[89] Ibid.
[90] Ibid.
[91] Ibid.
[92] See especially Whitty, note 8 supra, paras 89 and 104–6.
[93] Du Bois and Reid, note 20 supra, 587.
[94] *Kennedy v Glenbelle* 1996 SC 95 at 100–1.
[95] Whitty, note 8 supra, para 89; *Kennedy v Glenbelle* 1996 SC 95 at 100–1.
[96] Du Bois and Reid, note 20 supra, 587–92.

and Scots law diverge formally, although the results are substantially similar, if not identical: the restrictive definition of nuisance in South Africa removes the likelihood of 'once-off disturbances' most likely to be negligent outside its scope.[97] Scots law may have a more encompassing definition of nuisance, 'which includes non-recurrent and non-continuous harm', but there are subtle variations in the application of the principles.[98] This demonstrates, they argue, that the reasonableness standard in the case of nuisance and the reasonableness standard in the case of negligence practically are 'mutually exclusive alternatives', which operate in different contexts.[99] So although the underlying justification for liability in both the 'once-off disturbance' and 'harm' contexts may be the same, different applications are justified because of the different contexts. The range of interests that can potentially be affected in the neighbour context is much narrower than in the general delictual context:[100] nuisance law deals with 'fixed, certain and enduring relationships' that require physical proximity and always involve use and enjoyment of land.[101]

The distinction hence is between those actions by a person in exercising property rights that *affect the use and enjoyment* of the neighbour's land, and those actions that *cause actual harm*. In the former case, where use of one's property affects the use of another's, the range of interests affected are much narrower than in the latter case, where use of property can cause harm more broadly. It is against this backdrop that one must assess the impact of human rights principles on the rules of nuisance.

11.3 THE HUMAN RIGHTS ANGLE

To understand the human rights imperatives of South African and Scots law, a brief reference to the paradigm in which human rights mechanisms operate in each jurisdiction is necessary. Thereafter, the effect of human rights on nuisance disputes may be explored.

11.3.1 *Paradigm*

Though the introduction of human rights in South Africa and Scotland occurred in very different ways and for different reasons, the human rights paradigms created thereby for property law are comparable. In their constitutional frameworks, constitutionally entrenched human rights enjoy

---

[97] Ibid.

[98] Ibid.

[99] Ibid 592–3.

[100] Ibid 592–5.

[101] See also Sanchez Galera and Zehetner, note 2 supra, 307; U Mattei *Basic Principles of Property Law: A Comparative Legal and Economic Introduction* (Greenwood Press 2000) 148.

a particular standing. These rights bind the state but may also be invoked, albeit in different ways, by parties in private disputes.

11.3.1.1 Constitutional framework

The South African Constitution of 1996 is the supreme law of the country,[102] introduced, amongst other reasons,[103] in order to 'heal the divisions of the past and establish a society based on democratic values, social justice and fundamental human rights'.[104] Its chapter 2, the 'Bill of Rights', applies to all law and binds the legislature, executive, judiciary and all organs of state.[105] It also binds natural or juristic persons where applicable, and with due regard to the right which may be at stake and duties imposed by it. The judiciary is given the task to apply or develop the common law (for which it is given inherent power)[106] where legislation does not give effect to the rights in chapter 2, or where rights need to be limited in terms of the general limitations clause of section 36(1).

In *Port Elizabeth Municipality v Various Occupiers*[107] the South African Constitutional Court stated that 'the Constitution imposes new obligations on the courts concerning rights relating to property not previously recognised by the common law'. This judgment goes on to demonstrate that the property regime has changed to embody goals of social justice[108] embodied in the Constitution.[109] Issues of property law must be decided keeping in mind the recognition of socio-economic fundamental (human) rights and of the state's obligation progressively to realise these.[110]

As discussed in the Introduction to this volume, human rights became a feature of Scots law through the Scotland Act 1998 and the Human Rights Act of 1998 ('the HRA') which incorporated most of the ECHR into UK law.[111] UK courts must consider the decisions of the European Court of Human Rights (ECtHR) when deciding issues relating to the Convention

---

[102] Constitution s 2.

[103] Such as 'lay the foundations for a democratic and open society in which government is based on the will of the people and every citizen is equally protected by law'; 'improve the quality of life of all citizens and the free the potential of each person'; and 'build a united and democratic South Africa able to take its rightful place as a sovereign state in the family of nations'.

[104] Preamble to the Constitution.

[105] Constitution s 8(1).

[106] Constitution s 173.

[107] *Port Elizabeth Municipality v Various Occupiers* 2004 (12) BCLR 1268 (CC) at para 16.

[108] *Port Elizabeth Municipality v Various Occupiers* 2004 (12) BCLR 1268 (CC) at para 16.

[109] A J van der Walt *Property in the Margins* (Hart 2009) 212.

[110] Badenhorst, Pienaar and Mostert, note 8 supra, 93–4.

[111] See section 1.3 supra; also A J M Steven 'Property Law and Human Rights' 2005 *Juridical Review* 293.

rights.[112] The ECHR has direct effect against the state or any part of it.[113] An action based on breach of Convention rights by a public authority may be brought by anyone who suffered as a result.[114] If a breach is found, the court may order relief or a remedy considered just and appropriate,[115] including damages in specific circumstances.[116] As far as possible, legislation must be interpreted to comply with the ECHR.[117] Where a compliant interpretation is impossible, the consequences for laws emanating from Westminster and from the Scottish Parliament differ. In England a higher court may declare the legislation incompatible with the ECHR, which means that remedial law-making becomes necessary.[118] In a Scots court, a law which is found to contravene the ECHR will be found to be unenforceable (void).[119] This particular point has relevance for the question of whether human rights are horizontally applicable.

11.3.1.2 Horizontality
In the South African context the majority of authors accept that the Bill of Rights has direct horizontal applicability.[120] For Scotland the situation at this point is less clear-cut: Gretton[121] postulates that although the ECtHR does not accord horizontal applicability to the Convention,[122] the requirement in section 6 of the HRA that public authorities must act in conformity with the ECHR, results in horizontality. Steven agrees,[123] pointing out that a broad interpretation of this section 'would mean that one private individual could raise a successful action against another individual for breach

---

[112] HRA s 2.

[113] HRA s 6. Steven, note 111 supra, 295.

[114] HRA s 7. Steven, note 111 supra, 295.

[115] Damages may be awarded to afford 'just satisfaction' for the applicant, by courts with the power to award damages or order payment of compensation in civil proceedings. HRA s 8(1).

[116] HRA ss 8(2), 8(3).

[117] HRA s 3.

[118] HRA s 4(6). Steven, note 111 supra, 294.

[119] Scotland Act 1998 s 29(1)(d) (hereafter 'Scotland Act'). Steven, note 111 supra, 294–5.

[120] See, e.g., S Woolman 'Application' in S Woolman and M Chaskalson *Constitutional Law of South Africa* 2e (Juta 2004) ch 31; I Currie and J De Waal *The Bill of Rights Handbook* (Juta 2005) 34. It has been illustrated convincingly by A J van der Walt 'Transformative Constitutionalism and the Development of South African Property Law (part 1)' 2005 *Tydskrif vir die Suid-Afrikaanse Reg* 655–89 and A J van der Walt 'Transformative Consitutionalism and the Development of South African Property Law (part 2)' 2006 *Tydskrif vir die Suid-Afrikaanse Reg* 1–31, for instance, that the 'doctrine' of state duty has overridden the debate about horizontal applicability of fundamental rights.

[121] G L Gretton 'The Protection of Property Rights' in A Boyle, C Himsworth, A Loux and H MacQueen (eds) *Human Rights and Scots Law* (Hart 2002) 285.

[122] See also T Raphael 'The Problem of Horizontal Effect' (2000) 5 *European Human Rights Law Review* 493.

[123] Steven, note 111 supra, 296.

of a Convention right, because . . . if the court did not uphold the claim, it would be acting in a manner incompatible with a Convention right'. He adds that, although the broad approach has been favoured in some English judgments,[124] this view of section 6 is not shared by the majority of Scots scholars, who prefer to think of Convention rights as new grounds of defence in actions under general law.[125] For Steven[126] other considerations that point to some measure of horizontality are the requirement for ECHR-compliant interpretations of legislation, even where no public body is party to a particular dispute,[127] and the provision in the Scotland Act[128] that ECHR-incompatible legislation is void, regardless of whether the dispute about the law is between a public body and an individual, or between two individuals *inter se*.

If a nuisance enquiry were to be based on article 8 of the ECHR (the right to respect for family life), for instance, it would relate to how the law may foster the development of a protective environment in which individuals may choose to live in a particular way without external interference. Article 8 does not guarantee the right to a clean and peaceful environment, but if a person is directly and significantly affected by noise or other emissions, this can point to a transgression of the right to respect for family life.[129] Here the question arises how the human rights mechanism applies: if it applies only vertically, to protect citizens from government, and the infringement does not result from state action, unconstitutionality is not an issue. Yet the state has the positive duty to protect the rights of individuals under article 8 of the ECHR.[130] For this reason, it may be argued, it does not really matter whether the infringement is direct or indirect (that is, a breach of the duty to protect). The applicable principles are similar: the state is compelled to restrict the infringement as far as possible, to seek alternatives that impose less serious infringements, and to act as mediator.[131]

11.3.1.3 Development of common law
It would be a mistake to assume that constitutional transformation has little to offer the development of neighbour relationships, on the basis that private owners and land users can negotiate these relationships themselves

---

[124] *Campbell v MGN Newspapers* [2004] 2 AC 457 at 494, per Lady Hale; and see H L MacQueen 'Protecting Privacy' (2004) 8 *EdinLR* 420 at 422.

[125] See, e.g., R Clayton and H Tomlinson *The Law of Human Rights* 2e (Oxford University Press 2009) 232–238.

[126] Steven, note 111 supra, 296.

[127] HRA s 3(1). Steven, note 111 supra, 296.

[128] Scotland Act s 29(1)(d).

[129] See, e.g., *López Ostra v Spain* (1995) 20 EHRR 277; *Mileva and Others v Bulgaria*, App No 43449/02, 25 November 2010.

[130] Ibid.

[131] *Hatton and Others v The United Kingdom* (2002) 34 EHRR 1.

and that the state should adopt a 'hands-off' approach.[132] Similarly, it would be wrong to equate the balancing of interests that is a frequent feature of human rights adjudication with the standard of reasonableness/tolerability in a nuisance dispute,[133] simply because it, too, requires flexibility in the weighing of various interests at stake.[134]

The law of nuisance could certainly be influenced by human rights mechanisms, even if there are currently few (if any) cases that deal directly with the issue in either Scotland or South Africa. Van der Walt argues, for the South African context, that the state must allow the courts, legislature and administrative organs to transform neighbour law more broadly by ensuring that it 'embodies and represents an element of good neighbourliness, of citizenship, of community, that reflects the transformative intentions of the Constitution'.[135] For van der Walt, neighbour law is about more than the purely private or economic relationships, the localised community relationships and the mutual understanding of reciprocal respect for neighbours' rights.[136] The idea of neighbourliness in the broader metaphorical sense already resonates in the 'give and take, live and let live' spirit endorsed by the South African courts in the nuisance context. But van der Walt writes for a broader context – one that sees 'living together as new neighbours'[137] as an element of the transforming South African society – in which 'good neighbourliness' is a metaphor for the kind of citizenship envisaged by the Constitutional Court.[138] This suggests that 'give and take, live and let live' is an outlook not limited to the narrow area of nuisance.

To understand how a constitutional, human rights paradigm may intersect with nuisance law, one has to come to terms with constitutional expectations as to how people are to live together as neighbours in the broader, general sense of the word. This raises expectations around the 'lifestyles' endorsed in a human rights context. Property rights and interests of different parties generally may be difficult to reconcile. Moreover, other constitutionally-entrenched rights may conflict with property rights in given situations. These may include the rights to life, health, privacy, and personal security and development, and also the right to exercise a profession.[139]

---

[132] Van der Walt, note 3 supra, 5.

[133] See du Bois and Reid, note 20 supra, 598ff; van der Walt, note 3 supra, 314v

[134] Du Bois and Reid, note 20 supra, 597; Van der Walt, note 3 supra, 313.

[135] Van der Walt, note 3 supra, 5–6.

[136] Ibid, relying on G S Alexander and E M Peñalver 'Properties of Community' (2009) 10 *Theoretical Inquiries in Law* 127–80.

[137] Van der Walt, note 3 supra, 51.

[138] H Mostert 'Engaged Citizenship and the Enabling State as Factors Determining the Interference Parameter of Property: A Comparison of German and South African Law' (2010) 127 *South African Law Journal* 238 at 243.

[139] Sanchez Galera and Zehetner, note 2 supra, 308.

Du Bois and Reid's[140] identification of the limitations of the reasonableness test for nuisance renders it necessary to seek out the most likely agents for constitutional development of nuisance law. In the South African context it is the rights to equality (section 9), environment (section 24), property (section 25), housing (section 26) and cultural/religious freedom (section 31) that could influence the understanding of the reasonableness standard in nuisance law. The provisions of the ECHR most likely to influence Scots property law are those that:[141] protect property rights (article 1 of the First Protocol); provide procedural guarantees in the determination of rights (article 6); and protect family life and the home (article 8). The guarantee against discrimination in the enjoyment of Convention rights and freedoms (article 14) is also cited as a possible agent for development of Scottish property law.[142]

The 'lifestyle issues' at stake in South Africa and Scotland may be very different. This may have an influence on how 'good neighbourliness' is understood. In South Africa, one major constitutional concern is the elimination of discrimination and the establishment of a just and equitable society based on human dignity, equality and freedom. One concern in the broader European context is embodied by the expectation that personal freedom includes the obligation to protect and enhance the freedom of others. In matters relating to property, this is referred to as the 'social obligation' of property.[143] How the social obligation of property translates into country-specific rules, is a question that complicates the analysis.

The real challenge for present purposes, however, is how to deal with the lack of relevant case law in this analysis. As for South African law, there are certain constraints in transposing into nuisance law conclusions from related contexts that deal with 'neighbourliness' more broadly, such as eviction and impoundment. As concerns the dearth of Scots cases – especially as regards the interaction between public interest considerations espoused by common law, and the proportionality consideration envisaged by article 8 – one may look to English case law for guidance, though some points of tension remain. These are explored further below.

11.3.2 *Effect of the human rights paradigm on nuisance disputes*

When viewed from the human rights perspective, the challenge for the development of neighbour law is that it 'has to support and embody a notion of neighbourliness that extends beyond the sum total of the individual interests of each neighbour or the localised interests of small, neighbourhood

---

[140] Du Bois and Reid, note 20 supra, 595.
[141] Steven, note 111 supra, 293; Gretton, note 122 supra, 275.
[142] Steven, note 111 supra, 293.
[143] Sanchez Galera and Zehetner, note 2 supra, 301.

communities'.[144] The strength is that neighbour law, especially nuisance law, already accepts that landownership is inherently subject to limitations, which eliminates the need to 'indulge in constitutional justification analysis'[145] time and again.

The context of the neighbourhood puts a particular spin on enquiries into the liability for use of one's property in a way harmful to others.[146] Neighbours' interests may vary significantly,[147] but even so, the range of interests – all of which are aligned with land use and enjoyment – is comparatively much narrower and the liability for abuse much more stringent when compared against other interests.[148] Underkuffler explains[149] that property rights are often allocative: they demand intervention based on policy choices, as to who may have, use and enjoy, and who may not. Redistributive schemes (such as taxation or welfare programmes) are justified on the basis of the allocative nature of property rights. Certain underlying values determine the policy choices made in allocating property rights, and in redistributing schemes. If the value underlying a particular redistributive intervention is the same value that upholds the property right in the first place, the property right loses any potentially presumptive power it may have had.[150] The value underlying nuisance disputes, she indicates, is in the idea that one person's use and enjoyment of land cannot impair the use and enjoyment of another.[151] In such cases, the values that the relevant rights involve are aligned with the public interest, and so there is no basis for concluding that one right is normatively superior to the other.[152] This is different, Underkuffler claims, to situations where, for instance, the right to free speech conflicts with a government's need to stop the publication of information in the interests of national security, where the underlying values supporting free speech and national security are not the same.[153] This analysis assists in determining why human rights have thus far had such an apparently negligible influence on the development of nuisance law. The following sections explore this idea further.

---

[144] Van der Walt, note 3 supra, 6.

[145] Ibid 47.

[146] Mattei, note 101 supra, 148.

[147] Du Bois and Reid, note 20 supra, 595.

[148] Ibid; Mattei, note 101 supra, 148.

[149] Underkuffler, note 37 supra, 321.

[150] Ibid 320 uses the example of a property claim which conflicts with redistributive activity of the state (e.g. by creating a welfare programme), explaining that the value underlying the property claim here – the need for security of wealth – is the same as the one addressed by the redistributive intervention – the creation of similar security for the less affluent.

[151] Ibid 318.

[152] Ibid 316.

[153] Ibid 316.

11.3.2.1 South Africa: defeating exclusion and discrimination

Some South African lifestyle issues[154] have a bearing on implementation of an open and democratic society based on human dignity, freedom and equality.[155] For example, the phenomenon of 'gated' communities (such as security villages) reflects a major concern in South African daily life, namely how to secure the home and neighbourhood against violent crime. The dilemma, as van der Walt points out, is that enclosure or privatisation of neighbourhoods entrenches exclusivity, compromises openness, diversity and community,[156] and sacrifices public property, citizenship and political space when it encourages 'cocooning'.[157] The point is that constitutionally-inspired development of neighbour law should not reinforce separation and exclusion, but should rather strive to reach the constitutional ideal of an open democracy founded on human dignity, equality and freedom.[158]

Van der Walt reinforces his argument by referring to a number of cases: in *V&A Waterfront v Police Commissioner, Western Cape*[159] the court opted for an order prohibiting offensive conduct, rather than one removing the offending persons permanently from an area which practically amounts to a public space.[160] Arguing that exclusionary practices relating to purely private land should similarly be rejected, or at least be considered to be rejected, he discusses a series of attempts by predominantly white landowners and land users to prevent the establishment of new, predominantly black residential areas close to their established neighbourhoods,[161] by engaging in eviction proceedings. Though the decisions focused on eviction issues, the nature of the cases induced rhetoric[162] that for van der Walt demonstrates 'the danger that neigh-

---

[154] Van der Walt, note 3 supra, 49–61.

[155] See, e.g., *Minister of Public Works v Kyalami Ridge* 2001 (3) SA 1151 (CC) which highlights issues about the responsibility of the landowner towards neighbours and the community at large. Cases such as these demonstrate that abating nuisance is no longer a wholly private matter, to be governed solely by private law.

[156] Van der Walt, note 3 supra, 50.

[157] Ibid 50–1.

[158] Ibid 50.

[159] *V&A Waterfront v Police Commissioner, Western Cape* 2004 (1) All SA 579 (C) did not deal with a claim based on nuisance, but rather the owners' right to exclude certain individuals from the area, the clashing interests embodied by the right to property and the right to movement were considered.

[160] Discussions in van der Walt, note 3 supra, 52; Badenhorst, Pienaar and Mostert, note 8 supra, 524 n 21.

[161] *East London Western Districts Farmers Association v Minister of Education and Development Aid* 1989 (2) SA 63 (A); *Diepsloot Residents' and Landowners' Association v Administrator Transvaal* 1993 (1) SA 577 (T); *Diepsloot Residents' and Landowners' Association v Administrator, Transvaal* 1993 (3) SA 49 (T); *Diepsloot Residents' and Landowners' Association v Adminsitrator Transvaal* 1994 (3) SA 336 (A); *Minister of Public Works and Others v Kyalami Ridge Environmental Association and Others* 2001 (7) BCLR 652 (CC).

[162] The settlements were mostly of the 'informal' kind, and the conduct complained of included emissions of noise and dust, pollution and potential increase in crime in the surrounding

bour law could be used to entrench the kind of sameness and homogeneity in which an economic and exclusive version of the reasonableness principle can flourish'.[163] He illustrates further by referring to the impoundment of stray cattle[164] in the rural context. A constitutionality issue arises, it is argued, where impoundment of stray cattle – a crucial mechanism to deal with neighbourly conflicts – is abused, allowing exclusion and marginalisation of black farmers to be perpetuated.[165] In these contexts, van der Walt's analysis demonstrates, ownership is protected but not allowed to 'trump the nonexistent or weak interests of beggars, labourers or homeless people'.[166]

None of the case examples van der Walt uses as a basis for his argument is a nuisance case. They all deal more broadly with owners' rights to exclude 'weak, non-owners' (that is, vagrants, farm labourers, homeless persons) from gaining access or entry to land themselves or through their cattle. In this sense the enquiry in these cases is rather different from that undertaken in nuisance disputes, which is not about access or entry but rather about mutual limitation of rights and interests in (use and enjoyment of) property. What is present in nuisance cases, much more so than in eviction or impoundment cases, is greater parity between the parties to the dispute.

The pitfalls of using access/entry cases to develop nuisance law according to human rights standards do not prevent van der Walt from exploring the importance of the rhetoric of the access/entry cases for the broader neighbour law context.[167] He argues for a more 'distributive approach'[168] even if the core of neighbour law is not altered by the constitutional paradigm. His argument is one against exclusion on the basis of difference.[169] To this effect, it targets the manner in which the reasonableness criterion in nuisance relies on the views of a particularly localised community. Van der Walt indicates that this constitutional principle would essentially still amount to the imperative entailed in the maxim *sic utere tuo ut alienum non laedas*, but that it would be decidedly 'non-racial, anti-discrimination and transformation-oriented'.[170]

Van der Walt is correct in stating that existing rules are lacking where they

neighbourhoods. This induced the inhabitants of the settled (white) neighbourhoods to argue that establishing the informal settlements would create a public nuisance. See, e.g., decision of the court *a quo* in *Joubert v Van Rensburg* 2001 (1) SA 753 (W) in which the decision turned upon whether or not a community of informal settlers could be evicted from private land held in trust for them.

[163] Van der Walt, note 3 supra, 54–5.
[164] Relying on *Zondi v Member of the Executive Council for Traditional and Local Government Affairs and Others* 2005 (3) SA 589 (CC).
[165] Van der Walt, note 3 supra, 57.
[166] Ibid.
[167] Ibid 58.
[168] Ibid 58; Alexander and Peñalver, note 137 supra, 146.
[169] Van der Walt, note 3 supra, 58.
[170] Ibid 61.

are expected to guide decisions that involve exclusion and discriminatory behaviour and activities.[171] For the broader neighbour law context about which van der Walt writes, the *status quo* of the past twenty years has been problematic. In the narrower nuisance context, however, the problem is a different one. The difficulty with making nuisance law specifically conform to a revisionist approach is that exclusion and discrimination do not feature in the same way in disputes about acceptable use and enjoyment of land by neighbours, as they do in eviction or even impoundment cases. Nuisance disputes typically involve conflicting and offending uses of different pieces of land by their respective owners or users, rather than attempts by an owner to exclude others from use of or access to her land.

Further, the objective reasonableness standard at the heart of the nuisance enquiry already has the in-built feature of balancing competing interests, which is what a constitutional analysis would seek to achieve. Despite the high frequency of litigation on nuisance matters over the past fifteen years or so,[172] South African courts have had very little opportunity to test the current meaning of nuisance against constitutional standards, or to implement the idea of a non-racial, non-discriminatory, transformation-based nuisance law. The dearth of jurisprudence on this matter is a positive reflection on how interest-balancing is undertaken by the courts when considering nuisance allegations.

It does not mean, however, that opportunities cannot or will not arise. Du Bois and Reid[173] as well as van der Walt[174] discuss the possibility that the (effects of the) use of property on neighbours may be found to be unreasonable because of an exclusionary or discriminatory social context:[175] their example is developed from the facts of *Worcester Muslim Jamaa v Valley*,[176] in which disruption of the religious practices of one group by another group on the same property lead to a dispute. The hypothetical question developed is whether a muezzin's amplified call to prayer could be found unreasonable in a neighbourhood where the practices of Christianity would be more widespread than those of other religions and the chiming church bells would hence be regarded as reasonable.[177] The concern is that the noise created by an amplified prayer call may be regarded as unacceptable by those in the neighbourhood, objectively and impartially considered. Given that spatial separation of race and culture was a feature of the discriminatory, pre-constitutional regime in South Africa, and that communities are still to a very large extent

---

[171] Ibid 58.
[172] A superficial survey revealed at least eighteen reported cases in which nuisance issues were raised since 1996. See among others the cases listed in note 11 supra.
[173] Du Bois and Reid, note 20 supra, 599.
[174] Van der Walt, note 3 supra, 316.
[175] Du Bois and Reid, note 20 supra, 598–9.
[176] *Worcester Muslim Jamaa v Valley* 2002 (6) BCLR 591 (C).
[177] Van der Walt, note 3 supra, 316.

geographically separated along racial and cultural lines, the concern is understandable. Considerations of the inherent cultural and racial attributes of locality are to be taken into account in determining reasonableness in a nuisance dispute, as should the effects of the noise, the prevailing views of the community, and the constitutional goals of creating a non-discriminatory society supporting human dignity, equality and freedom. This does not mean, however, that the amplified call to prayer would pass the reasonableness test.

In *Garden Cities Incorporated v Northpine Islamic Society*[178] considering the validity of a contractual clause excluding use of amplified sound for the call to prayer, the Cape High Court rejected the argument that the clause, concluded in the pre-constitutional era, was contrary to the defendant's constitutionally protected religious freedom. The decisive consideration was that the contract did not exclude the particular religious activity altogether. The clause sought to limit noise in the interests of the community by restricting calls to prayer to the unassisted human voice. Unable to affirm that electronic amplification of the call to prayer had become 'a precept of the Islamic religion', the court upheld the clause. Although, given the context of the case, the court was not expected to weigh the constitutionally protected interests of one segment of the society against another, its reasoning highlights that even conduct forming part of an activity protected by the religious freedom clause of the Constitution may be unreasonable.

The inference that could be drawn from the example above is that where an activity (such as religious activity) is entrenched by one of the rights or freedoms under the Constitution, this fact must form part of the enquiry as to the reasonableness of the conduct. The human rights consideration cannot, however, trump other relevant considerations.

Growthpoint Properties Ltd v SACCAWU,[179] though not decided on the common law principles of nuisance, affirms this inference. The owner of a shopping mall sought an interdict against striking workers, whose picketing created noise in the form of shouting, singing, chanting, ululating, blowing whistles and horns and banging various instruments and objects. Amplified by the covered parking garage where the strikers had gathered, the noise reportedly disturbed and intimidated members of the public and disrupted normal business operations.[180] The stance of the trade union representing the striking workers was that the conduct formed part of their constitutionally protected right to take industrial action. The dispute hence turned upon a weighing-up of the constitutional property rights of owners and occupiers, and their rights to the environment and to trade, which conflicted with the

---

[178] *Garden Cities Incorporated Association Not For Gain v Northpine Islamic Society* 1999 (2) SA 268 (C).

[179] *Growthpoint Properties Limited v SA Commercial Catering & Allied Workers Union & Others* [2010] 31 JOL 26099 (KZD).

[180] Ibid para 5.

right of strikers to freedom of expression, to bargain collectively, and to picket, protest and demonstrate peacefully.[181]

The Kwa-Zulu Natal High Court carefully analysed the range of constitutional rights available to strikers, focusing specifically on the right to freedom of expression and the right to demonstrate, bargain collectively, strike and picket. It concluded that protests and demonstrations are 'part of the fabric of everyday life' and some tolerance is expected of parties outside the action, but that even such expected tolerance has its limits. Accepting that picketing, which is statutorily permitted, is normally a noisy affair, and acknowledging that the common law of nuisance which regulates the conduct of neighbours does not apply to picketers, the court indicated that the outcome of the decision turned on the question whether the conduct was too noisy.[182] Intolerable noise levels can be objectively determined.[183] The legal limit set by the regulation governing noise-induced hearing loss is 85 decibels.[184] The court found that in the particular case, the noise constituted a nuisance, because it was beyond what tolerance could be expected.[185] The order was for the picketing strikers to lower their noise level; they could continue 'demonstrating, picketing, carrying placards, singing and chanting softly'.[186]

Following on from these examples, one may ask whether South African courts would be inclined to view a nuisance dispute differently if the dispute had a racial flavour. This is a particularly sensitive issue in South African society, because of the disparity historically drawn between people from different racial groups. In a society where redress and the rectifying of past wrongs have been translated into various policies to ensure black economic empowerment and to achieve parity between individuals regardless of personal attributes, it may be expected that eradication of racial discrimination is paramount. Because apartheid was so much reliant on the geographical

---

[181] Ibid para 1.

[182] Ibid paras 10–11.

[183] See, e.g., the consideration of the registered occupational hygienist's report of the noise levels in the shopping mall: ibid para 6.

[184] Reg 3, Noise-induced Hearing Loss Regulations in terms of the Occupational Health and Safety Act 85 of 1993, Government Notice R307 in Government Gazette 24967 of 2003.03.07. Referred to in *Growthpoint Properties Limited v SA Commercial Catering & Allied Workers Union & Others* [2010] 31 JOL 26099 (KZD) at para 6.

[185] Ibid para 59 summarises the reasoning as follows: 'Tolerance levels are exceeded when Growthpoint and its tenants cannot conduct their business. The noise emanating from the picketers was unacceptably high; it disturbed tenants and the public. The evidence of the expert and tenants of Growthpoint shows that a persistent, loud noise was intolerable. Growthpoint, its tenants and customers were inconvenienced and prejudiced. Businesses not party to the labour dispute suffered a loss of revenue as the public took its custom elsewhere. The noise of the picketers also created an unhealthy environment and impeded Growthpoint and its tenants from using their properties.'

[186] Ibid para 61.

separation of different race groups, there are still many neighbourhoods in which the lack of diversity reminds us of the divisions of former times. In other neighbourhoods life has moved on, and has brought with it the kind of diversity that is envisaged and fostered by the Constitution.

In both such 'old' and 'new' neighbourhoods activities may be perceived by some to be disruptive simply because they are different from those familiar and tolerated in a particular area. The range of possible examples here is vast and if the inference drawn from the abovementioned examples is correct, what human rights considerations may be relevant would form part of the palette of factors to be taken into account to determine reasonableness from case to case. The scope here does not permit an exhaustive consideration of the possibilities; one example must suffice.

Where the noise from a Camps Bay nightclub was tolerated in the past but (after a change in the nightclub's management) has escalated to the point of being persistently unbearable to the clients of the neighbouring hotel,[187] constitutional considerations of non-racialism, anti-discrimination and transformation may not add any value. This would not be the first incident of its kind, and the private law rules of nuisance are flexible enough to allow the courts to find an equitable solution[188] where the parties are unable to resolve the situation without recourse to litigation. But if the on-going dispute between the hotel management and the nightclub had a racial character,[189] would this invoke constitutional intervention? Should it matter that the nightclub owner is the first (or only) black business owner in the particular area, and that he believes he is being targeted as a result?[190] The nuisance – again noise, where tolerability levels are objectively measurable – does not seem to stem from the racial attributes of either of the parties: the area in which the dispute is located is known for its trendy nightlife which attracts a diverse range of visitors, and a certain level of noise in this regard is to be expected. It seems difficult to justify that the noise levels should soar above

---

[187] Example taken from reports about a similar incident in Camps Bay, an area regarded as an affluent suburb of Cape Town, attracting many tourists both foreign and local, for beach holidays. It has a trendy nightlife. (On the High Court's roll the case is recorded as *Village and Life Limited v Ste Yves Beach Club CC* (11948/11) 2011 unreported (C).) The matter was eventually thrown out for being brought prematurely, because both the hotel and nightclub were already busy implementing noise-reduction measures. Hence the court did not have the opportunity to test the meaning or implement the idea of a non-discriminatory, transformation-based neighbour law.

[188] In the earlier decision of *Laskey and Another v Showzone CC and Others* 2007 (2) SA 48 (C), for instance, the court afforded a nightclub a reasonable time to implement noise-reducing measures to respect the interests of the particular area's residents, whilst being realistic about what city-centre residents could reasonably expect by way of noise reduction.

[189] The nightclub owner also claimed in his court papers that one of the hotel managers had told him he should 'move to Gugulethu'. See the report of L Samodien 'Camps Bay Spat over "Rowdy Music" Gets Louder' *The Cape Times* 8 August 2011.

[190] Ibid.

the expected tolerability threshold in the area, simply on the basis of the race of one of the parties.

In this context it is again useful to refer to Underkuffler's analysis.[191] She reminds us that the value behind nuisance disputes lies in the idea that one person's use of land cannot impair the use of another.[192] Even where constitutional considerations become part of the reasonableness enquiry in nuisance cases, the underlying value remains the positioning of one's use against that of another. The public interest ultimately is in ensuring that both parties get to exercise their rights in an acceptable way. This explains why considerations such as religious freedom or the creation of a non-racial society may be relevant circumstances, objectively to be considered when establishing the reasonableness of particular conduct, but may not amount to superior considerations with presumptive power. It also explains why allegations of racial discrimination by themselves may not be sufficient to change what would otherwise be regarded as reasonable or unreasonable under specific conditions.

The lifestyle issues at the heart of some nuisance disputes may resonate well with issues promoted by the Constitution. They draw attention to the 'give-and-take' nature of solutions, either judicially crafted or amicably achieved. In *Nowers NO v Burmeister*[193] the soured relations between neighbours led to litigation involving, among others, a makeshift structure, erected on a common boundary, to block off the view of the security surveillance cameras on the Nowers' property, which allegedly looked into the backyard and entertainment area of the Burmeisters' property. A tension here is the extent to which a neighbour's privacy may be compromised by the need for securing a safe living environment at home. Both privacy and personal security are considerations for which it is easy to find constitutional support. But as with the previous example, the rules of nuisance could resolve the issue with reference to several of the factors determining reasonableness: even if the structure was ugly, aesthetics would be too subjective a consideration upon which to base a finding of unreasonableness.[194] Less invasive means[195] could have been devised to protect the claimant's need for security at home.[196] What is more, use of property with an intention to harm the neighbour would disallow conduct.[197] This particular considera-

---

[191] Underkuffler, note 37 supra, 321.
[192] Underkuffler, note 37 supra, 318.
[193] *Nowers NO v Burmeister* (EL 1038/08) 2 August 2011 unreported (ECD).
[194] *Dorland and Another v Smits* 2002 (5) SA 374 (C).
[195] *Gien v Gien* 1979 (2) SA 1113 (T).
[196] Surprisingly, though evidence was led that the cameras were not looking into the Burmeisters' property, the court nevertheless found that it was not sufficient. The court required an affidavit from the company that installed the cameras. This stance is questionable, given that the evidence was led under oath.
[197] *Kirsch v Pincus* 1927 TPD 199.

tion must have been prevalent in this particular case, given the historical rift between the parties.

As was demonstrated above, here too the underlying value consideration for protecting property rights on either side of the fence is use and enjoyment of the property. This means that both privacy and security become considerations to be taken into account in determining the reasonableness of the conduct complained of, but that neither would have presumptive power in the absence of other supporting considerations already prevalent in the inherently flexible test to determine reasonableness.

Issues such as these demonstrate that nuisance law, even if it is messy and lacks exactness, strives to find just and equitable solutions for conflicts arising in the neighbourhood. Constitutional considerations may become part of the process to determine the reasonableness of one's use and enjoyment against that of another, but as yet there is no indication that such considerations are likely to trump other relevant factors in the attempt to determine reasonableness of conduct in a given scenario. Where there is a greater likelihood of constitutional development of the reasonableness test, as the comparative analysis below suggests, is where a court needs to determine the content of the public interest served by upholding or rejecting particular conduct in the nuisance context; or the extent of state involvement in nuisance disputes.

11.3.2.2 Europe: social obligation and public interest

Undertaking a 'comparative mapping' of the interaction between nuisance rules and fundamental rights in Europe, Sanchez Galera and Zehetner[198] focus on the remedies available and on the *locus standi* issue, pointing out that requiring the person bringing an action in nuisance to own land may leave non-owners who have comparable interests without recourse. They illustrate how this inequity has been remedied by recourse to ordinary law in many European jurisdictions, and by recourse to fundamental rights in others. Their analysis does not cover, however, a consideration of the substantive requirements for nuisance and how this may be influenced by fundamental rights. They and other scholars of property law in Europe note, nevertheless, a shift away from a primarily individualistic conception of property.[199]

The shift requires that more reliance is placed on the 'collective dimension' of property.[200] It is manifested, for instance, in the rules that place a person, with his particular interests, within a neighbourhood where such interests must bow to measures protecting the neighbourhood against

---

[198] Sanchez Galera and Zehetner, note 2 supra, 306–19.
[199] Mattei, note 101 supra, 58–60; Sanchez Galera and Zehetner, note 2 supra, 301.
[200] Sanchez Galera and Zehetner, note 2 supra, 301.

emissions or other harmful conduct.[201] In the twentieth century, this shift away from an individualistic conception of property occurred alongside two other trends: the first was that an increased reliance was placed upon social guarantees, with the rise of the social state;[202] the second was the broad move to include the right to property in constitutional texts, which served to 'constitutionalise' property across the private and public law contexts.[203] Accordingly, in many of the jurisdictions across Europe, the 'social function' of property – that is, the principle that 'property obligates'[204] – is seen as an element of the constitutionally entrenched right to property. This entails the responsibility not to abuse the right of ownership[205] (and, one could add, any interest worthy of protection under constitutional property law).[206]

The social function of property 'modifies the entire content of the right to property to make it compatible with so-called "general interest"'.[207] In this regard, it may have an impact on how the reasonableness standard in nuisance law is to be understood, as the general public ('collective') interest may be considered more pointedly, especially where such collective interests are represented by other constitutionally-entrenched rights essential to fulfilment of state duties (such as rights to health, clean environment, equality). This is in line with the general trend in civil-law jurisdictions, where nuisance is mostly regarded as an aspect of property law, which must 'demarcate' rights to allow each to develop to its fullest potential, despite possible conflict with other 'equally valid' rights.[208]

Where nuisance intersects with human rights considerations, such demarcation frequently involves defining and circumscribing the ambits of both individual and public interest. In this regard Dutch law provides some examples of actions which have been found to constitute nuisance, but which had to be tolerated nevertheless because of the way in which the public interest is understood. A claim for compensation would lie, however, particularly since it has become settled for nuisance disputes to be treated under tort law rather than property law.[209] One such example could be found in the *Voorste Stroom* case,[210] where a municipality was permitted to continue draining sewerage into a river, thus perpetuating pollution thereof, contrary to

---

[201] Ibid 302.

[202] Mattei, note 101 supra, 20, 33.

[203] Sanchez Galera and Zehetner, note 2 supra, 301–2.

[204] Wording of art 14 II, Grundgesetz für die Bundesrepublik Deutschland (Basic Law) of 1949. Similar notion entailed in art 42, Italian Constitution of 1947.

[205] Sanchez Galera and Zehetner, note 2 supra, 301.

[206] France, Spain and Sweden here are the exceptions. Ibid 310–11.

[207] Ibid 301.

[208] Ibid 306–7.

[209] See the exposition in A Verheij 'Fault Liability between Neighbours in the Netherlands 1850–2000' in J Gordley (ed) *Comparative Studies in the Development of the Law of Torts in Europe*, vol 2: *The Development of Liability between Neighbours* (2010) 110–15.

[210] HR 19 december 1952 (*Voorste Stroom*) 19 December 1952, 1953 NJ 642.

the interests of the neighbouring owners. As abatement was found not to be appropriate under the circumstances, a damages award was made. It was found that the relevant municipality was obliged by the public interest to find cost-effective means of disposing of sewerage, even if this would amount to nuisance for individual owners. Dutch tort law has since been developed to provide for this kind of scenario. Art. 6: 168 lid 1 BW now provides that where an injunction is sought to prohibit specific tortious conduct, the court may reject the action where the conduct 'must be tolerated for compelling reasons of public interest'. A claim for compensation lies.

A range of other, more recent cases define activities that should be tolerated because they are in the public interest: the development of a nature reserve;[211] normal commercial activities;[212] activities preventing the outbreak of cattle disease;[213] and the establishment of a centre for the care and treatment of drug addicts.[214] Most recently the development of social housing was found to be an important public interest, to the extent that considerations for the wellbeing and health of neighbours were not sufficient to substantiate a prohibition of the development on the basis of nuisance.[215] It has been pointed out that Dutch law does not readily accept the idea of nuisance as an invasion of privacy invoking damages.[216]

In this sense the jurisprudence emanating from the constitutional paradigm of the broader European sphere challenges certain established views prevalent in the laws of the United Kingdom. Already more than half a century ago, the English judiciary was criticised[217] for endorsing a 'spirit of unrestricted egoism' and being 'too much inspired by the nineteenth-century liberalistic economic outlook'[218] when, in the nineteenth-century case of *Mayor of Bradford v Pickles*,[219] adjudicating the propriety of an owner's (apparently wilful)[220] pollution of his fellow townsfolk's water supply, it indicated that although the conduct may be morally and philosophically deplorable, the law did not prohibit him from being 'churlish, selfish and grasping'.[221]

In view of the jurisprudence from the broader constitutional context of Europe, it is surprising that *Bradford v Pickles* – displaying as it does the

---

[211] *HR 15 februari 1991* 15 February 1991, 1992 NJ 639.

[212] *HR 3 april 1987* 3 April 1987 NJ 703.

[213] *HR 18 januari 1991* 18 January 1991 NJ 638.

[214] *Rb. Arnhem 18 januari 1996* 18 January 1996, 1997 NJ 142.

[215] *Rb 's-Hertogenbosch (vzr)* (LJN BH7428) 26 March 2009.

[216] Verheij, 'Fault Liability between Neighbours' note 209 supra, 121.

[217] H C Gutteridge 'Abuse of Rights' (1933) 5 *Cambridge Law Journal* 22.

[218] J E Scholtens 'Abuse of Rights' (1958) 75 *South African Law Journal* 39 at 49.

[219] *Mayor of Bradford v Pickles* [1895] AC 587 .

[220] See the discussion in Reid 'Abuse of Rights in Scots Law', note 82 supra, 143ff.

[221] *Mayor of Bradford v Pickles* [1895] AC 587 at 600; and see also *Allen v Flood* [1898] AC 1 at 46, which endorsed a similar position in respect of contract law. Reid, 'The Doctrine of Abuse of Rights', note 82 supra, 4.

'political and economic philosophy of late Victorian England'[222] – still is authoritative in English law in respect of depriving neighbours of amenities or prospects.[223] Its position in respect of the offending owner's motives and intentions was reconfirmed by *Stephens v Anglian Water Authority.*[224] Antisocial developments, Reid points out,[225] are nowadays curbed mostly by public law controls[226] which limit the frequency of complaints such as the one in *Bradford v Pickles*.

In Scots law the actions of a proprietor in depriving a neighbour of an amenity such as water may be addressed under the doctrine of *aemulatio vicini*.[227] Moreover, it has been indicated that a court in any civilian jurisdiction would, on the basis of the *Pickles* facts, have found a clear and actionable case of abuse of rights.[228] Demonstrating how *aemulatio vicini* amounts to a restricted[229] form of abuse of rights, Reid[230] argues that in disputes over land use, where its modern application lies,[231] this doctrine sets Scots law apart from English law. It targets, however, malicious conduct[232] and hence deals with what may be seen to be extreme cases in the nuisance context.[233] The cases that do not involve an element of malice seem to reinforce the individual freedom of an owner to use land, and they do so from the viewpoint of the defender, rather than from that of the pursuer.[234] This is illustrated below by a discussion of some of the English cases that were decided under the Human Rights Act 1998, and a comparison of the principles endorsed therein with existing precedent in the Scots law on nuisance.

The predominant example in sources considering the intersection of nuisance and human rights in the European context, like the sources on the Human Rights Act 1998, is that of environmental regulation,[235] especially with regard to the right to private and family life.[236] Although it has been

---

[222] Reid, 'Abuse of Rights in Scots Law', note 82 supra, 144.

[223] Ibid; Reid, 'The Doctrine of Abuse of Rights', note 82 supra, 9.

[224] *Stephens v Anglian Water Authority* [1987] 3 All ER 379.

[225] Reid, 'The Doctrine of Abuse of Rights', note 82 supra, 3.

[226] See further also T Allen *Property and the Human Rights Act 1998* (Hart 2005) 215–18.

[227] Reid, 'The Doctrine of Abuse of Rights', note 82 supra, 5; Reid, 'Abuse of Rights in Scots Law', note 82 supra, 129–57.

[228] Reid, 'Abuse of Rights in Scots Law', note 82 supra, 144.

[229] Ibid 155.

[230] Ibid 151–7.

[231] Johnston, note 15 supra, 188.

[232] Ibid 194.

[233] Reid, 'Abuse of Rights in Scots Law', note 82 supra, commenting on Johnston, note 15 supra, at 194, points out that the doctrine will be available also where reasonable conduct (i.e. which is not *plus quam tolerabile*) is nevertheless malicious.

[234] Reid, 'The Doctrine of Abuse of Rights, note 82 supra, 6.

[235] R G Lee 'Resources, Rights, and Environmental Regulation' (2005) 32 *Journal of Law and Society* 110; Sanchez Galera and Zehetner, note 2 supra, 298.

[236] M Poustie 'Environment' in *The Laws of Scotland: Stair Memorial Encyclopaedia* Reissue (2001) para 55.

remarked that the impact of international law may not have much direct impact on the internal law of Scotland, it is recognised that problems such as pollution require international measures.[237] In a few instances the Human Rights Act 1998 has been invoked in the context of nuisance in the English courts: for instance, with regard to a complaint about regular overflowing of a garden with foul water from overloaded sewers owned by the statutory water authority, it was held in *Marcic v Thames Water Utilities Ltd*[238] that no claim lay in private nuisance. The House of Lords also overturned the Court of Appeal's finding in this matter that the public authority acted in a way which was irreconcilable with the complainant's right to respect for his private and family life and his entitlement to enjoy his possessions peacefully,[239] arguing that the interests of the individual and the community at large were to be balanced primarily by Parliament, not the judiciary.[240] A relevant consideration that arises from the judicial treatment of *Marcic* seems to be the experience of the single (or group of) afflicted landowner(s) measured against the greater purpose of a particular activity, especially in achieving justice.[241] A further factor is that the event inevitably resulted from the exercise of a statutory power, or the fulfilment of a statutory duty.[242] In *Marcic* a distinction was drawn between the duties of public bodies operating under statutory powers on the one hand, and the duties of private landowners on the other.[243] The judgment went in favour of Thames Water on the basis of its performance of statutory powers and duties, even though the company was privatised. The statutory scheme in terms of which it operated was also set on ensuring appropriate allocation of the resources available to improve the sewer systems.[244] The company had, by the time the matter had reached the House of Lords, invested considerable funds in establishing a programme that would deal with the overflow problem, and that affected the area in which Marcic's property was situated.

The Scots decision in *RHM Bakeries (Scotland) Ltd v Strathclyde Regional Council*[245] demonstrates that sewage overflow could in principle constitute a nuisance. It also shows, however, the difficulties of establishing liability for this sort of utility. The tension between the English position as represented by *Marcic* and the Scots position as represented by *RHM* may be attributable

---

[237] Gordon, note 51 supra, para 26–38.

[238] *Marcic v Thames Water Utilities Ltd* [2003] UKHL 66; J O'Sullivan 'Nuisance, Human Rights and Sewage – Closing the Floodgates' (2004) 63 *Cambridge Law Journal* 552.

[239] Ibid.

[240] O'Sullivan, note 238 supra, 553.

[241] Allen, note 226 supra, 157.

[242] Ibid 215.

[243] O'Sullivan, note 238 supra, 554.

[244] Allen, note 226 supra, 213–16.

[245] See *RHM Bakeries v Strathclyde Regional Council* 1985 SLT 3 where the difficulties of establishing common law liability against such utility providers are highlighted.

to the distinction between English and Scots law on nuisance, where the latter does not differentiate between public and private nuisance in the manner the former does.[246] In England public nuisance is a criminal offence, whereas this is not the case in Scotland.[247] This has an impact on who may sue, and for what.[248] Moreover, the reasonableness test inherent in a typical nuisance dispute is stretched to its limit in cases demanding the judiciary to make a call on the propriety of capital expenditure involving public utilities. In such cases the outcome would affect not only the complaining party, but everyone receiving the service. The question of reasonableness for the individual then becomes one about what is in the public interest.[249] In this regard, the private law approach seems to dominate: Allen comments on the striking resemblance between the analysis of the nuisance claim in private law and the human rights analysis in *Marcic*, pointing out that although public interest 'may enter into the private law balance', the repercussions of a particular finding for the broader consumer base and for shareholders involved remain a marginal consideration.[250]

On the European level, an intervention with an individual's right must be quite severe to found a violation of the right to respect for the home, private and family life. In *López Ostra v Spain*,[251] referring to the 'fair balance . . . to be struck between the competing interests of the individual and of the community as a whole', the Court considered that the nuisance created in this particular case (a waste-treatment plant located close to the applicant's home)[252] was caused by activities responding to a larger pollution problem in the relevant area. Because of the severity of the harm suffered in relation to the municipality's remedial attempts, a violation of the right to respect for the home, private and family life was nevertheless found to exist. The nature of the ECtHR's jurisdiction allows for a different slant on the issue of

---

[246] Ibid, with reference to *Fleming v Hislop* (1886) 13 R 43 (HL) at 48.

[247] Bell *Prin* § 974; Whitty, note 8 supra, para 159; but see Cameron, note 31 supra, 98–9.

[248] See further Whitty, note 8 supra, paras 160–7 and esp para 166.

[249] *Marcic v Thames Water Utilities Ltd* [2003] UKHL 66 at para 63.

[250] Allen, note 226 supra, 215.

[251] In *López Ostra v Spain* (1995) 20 EHRR 277 at para 57 the ECtHR specifically considered the role of the local authority in ensuring that the fundamental rights of the applicant were protected, noting that the measures that were put in place (partial closing of the waste plant and eventual assistance in temporary relocation of the applicant) were not sufficient as 'complete redress' for the nuisance and inconveniences caused. This line of reasoning (para 57) was extended subsequently, with the state's involvement coming to be regarded as more than simply the duty to refrain from interfering, but rather to take positive steps to protect the fundamental rights of the individual. See, e.g., *Öneryildiz v Turkey* (2005) 41 EHRR 20 at para 134. The case involved a landslide caused by a methane explosion, in which lives were lost and property destroyed. The authorities' failure to reduce a reported risk was at the core of the case.

[252] It was found that the relevant municipal authority's inertia to address the nuisance violated the right to respect for her home, private and family life (article 8(1) and (3) ECHR).

private interest as opposed to public interest. The Court sees its task in this regard as determining whether domestic law had been applied appropriately to the matter,[253] and so is careful to pronounce on the substantive issues of nuisance law itself. In a couple of decisions concerning the extension of nuclear power plant licences in Switzerland, the Court paid attention not to engage with the question whether the power plants constituted a nuisance, indicating that this is a matter to be determined on the domestic law level.[254] Other cases before the ECtHR that involved nuisance considerations placed in question state interventions with individuals' rights on the basis of article 6(1) of the ECHR (the right to be heard) and article 13 of the ECHR (the right to an effective remedy), and demonstrate how important the link is between the substantive rights, such as those entrenched by article 8, and other rights upholding the structural aspect of human rights in Europe, such as articles 6 and 13. In particular, article 6(1) states the principles of reasonableness, fairness and impartiality in the determining of (among others) a person's civil rights and obligations. *Mileva v Bulgaria*[255] is a good example of the significance of the link between the substantive rights and the rights determining the structure of ECHR protection in individual cases.[256] There, damages was awarded for the state's failure to determine the impact of authorising the running of a business inside an apartment building causing nuisance to the residents, and for its failure to take effective steps to contain the nuisance.

Hatton v The United Kingdom[257] demonstrates, however, that the ECtHR's consideration is not limited to structural issues only. The complaint involved the rise in night noise levels due to increased air traffic around Heathrow airport, which caused sleep deprivation and thus, it was argued, violated the article 8 rights under the ECHR. In this matter there was no element of

---

[253] *Mileva and Others v Bulgaria*, App No 43449/02, 25 November 2010.

[254] In *Balmer-Schafroth and Others v Switzerland* (1998) 25 EHRR 598 para 40, the Court found that the applicants could not show the continued operation of the power plant would expose them to an imminent, serious and specific danger. In *Athanassoglou and Others v Switzerland* (2001) 31 EHRR 13 para 42, the Court followed up, indicating that the ECHR's article 6 – the right to be heard – does not found a right to contest the use of nuclear energy *per se*; and the state law against nuisance and *de facto* expropriation should sufficiently govern the issue.

[255] The ECtHR here found (para 108) that the relevant authorities did not discharge their obligation to take steps to abate nuisance created by an (at first illegally) operating computer club in an apartment building, for suspending the enforcement of an administrative decision taken in this regard. The police and municipal authorities also failed to take effective steps to determine how the club's round-the-clock operations affected neighbours. The club, created for gaming and Internet surfing, was reportedly frequented by teenagers and young adults, who displayed noisy and unruly behaviour, including drug and alcohol abuse, in and around the building. It operated without a permit at first, and the permit that was eventually granted was contested for imposing impossible conditions around access. The applicants were awarded non-pecuniary damages.

[256] See also *Benthem v The Netherlands* (1986) 8 EHRR 1; *Balmer-Schafroth and Others v Switzerland* (1998) 25 EHRR 598.

[257] *Hatton and Others v The United Kingdom* (2002) 34 EHRR 1.

domestic irregularity involved: it was not denied that the United Kingdom's policy on night flights (which had already been challenged and subsequently amended on the domestic level) was compatible with domestic law. In considering how a fair balance is to be struck between competing individual and communal interests, the ECtHR acknowledges that a whole range of material considerations is relevant. These included actions already taken to mitigate nuisance and whether the activity complained of (increased night flights) was demonstrably beneficial to the economy. In holding that the right to respect for the home, private and family life had been violated, the Court awarded non-pecuniary damages and compensation. A similar outcome was reached in *Dennis v Ministry of Defence*[258] where the noise created by jet fighters on a military pilot training base was found to be a private nuisance as well as a violation of the right to respect for private and family life and the right to enjoy possessions peacefully. Owing to the public interest in allowing the activity (training of fighter pilots) to be continued, however, damages were ordered in lieu of abatement.[259] The Court added that the claim under the Human Rights Act would be relevant if the finding of nuisance was prevented by the public interest.

The solution achieved in *Dennis* may not be possible in other jurisdictions, however. The award in *Dennis* of damages in lieu of injunction would probably not be competent in the Scots courts, which do not have power to award prospective damages in lieu of an interdict.[260] Following the example of the ECtHR, this is a possible area for development of Scots law.

Though public interest considerations may affect the outcome of decisions in a constitutional order, the treatment of public interest considerations themselves may vary significantly between different jurisdictions in Europe. This is demonstrated well by the tension inherent in using the English examples to project judgments in neighbouring Scotland.[261] The stance of the Scots courts hitherto is that in the law of nuisance, 'public interest cannot overrule law.'[262] This contrasts starkly with the approach to uphold public interest considerations under the proportionality test for the purposes of article 8. Cases such as *Marcic* and *Hatton* demonstrate that the public interest may override specific rights, but neither of these examples involved such severe consequences as to cause the property to lose its entire economic value and/or use.[263] The more severe infringe-

---

[258] *Dennis v Ministry of Defence* [2003] EWHC 793, per Buckley J.

[259] J Elvin 'The Law of Nuisance and the Human Rights Act' (2003) 62 *Cambridge Law Journal* 546.

[260] See Whitty, note 8 supra, para 150.

[261] See, e.g., *Webster v Lord Advocate* 1984 SLT 13, in which an interdict was suspended for a period to allow the defenders to reduce their noise levels.

[262] *Webster v Lord Advocate* 1984 SLT 13 per Lord Stott at 15; and see also *Ben Nevis Distillery v North British Aluminium* 1948 SC 592.

[263] Allen, note 226 supra, 216.

ment in *López Ostra*[264] resulted in a decision in favour of the individual interest.

In Scots law the treatment of reasonableness generally still favours the individual interest and plays down the public interest factors: Whitty's analysis[265] of a range of Scots cases indicates that even the necessary social utility of potentially annoying establishments[266] on which the 'prosperity or health of the nation depend' may be diminished if they are inappropriately situated. *Ben Nevis Distillery (Fort William) Ltd v North British Aluminium Co Ltd*[267] is the example *par excellence*. There, an interdict was granted to an owner of property injured by fumes from a nearby aluminium factory, despite the harsh consequences that this would have had on the industry in terms of unemployment and loss of profit. In a judgment which unequivocally placed the individual's interests first, the Court remarked that, in its opinion, the expectation that improvements to manufacturers' property may not injure their neighbours does not result in 'undue or injurious restriction upon the adventure or the invention or the enterprise of the commercial public' even from a public and social vantage point.[268] More recent judgments still rely on this stance.

This suggests that Scots common law provides better protection for the individual, because of how it plays down public interest factors in favour of individual liberty. If this is so, the possible future implementation of article 8 ECHR jurisprudence in Scotland will have far-reaching consequences for the development of Scots law on nuisance. That said, the importance of the public interest consideration should not be overemphasised. Although the ECHR and Dutch jurisprudence suggest that public interest may be informed by the manner in which human rights are endorsed in a particular context, the public interest consideration does not categorically override individual concerns. The sentiments expressed by the ECtHR reflect, instead, the sustained approach of a carefully weighed consideration of relevant factors, taking into account individual interests, the public interest and also the duty upon the state to respect human rights.

11.4 STATE DUTY AND CITIZENSHIP IN THE NUISANCE CONTEXT

Despite the distinctly different concerns that are raised in the South African and European contexts, including England and Scotland, a theme that emerges in all contexts is the relation between citizenship and the

---

[264] *López Ostra v Spain* (1995) 20 EHRR 277 discussed supra note 251.
[265] Whitty, note 8 supra, para 74.
[266] Such as factories, slaughterhouses, sewage treatment works and hospitals for infectious diseases.
[267] *Ben Nevis Distillery v North British Aluminium* 1948 SC 592.
[268] *Fraser's Trustees v Cran* (1879) 6 R 451 at 453.

'give-and-take' nature of the law pertaining to nuisance. Elsewhere[269] analysis of a range of South African Constitutional Court decisions demonstrated the expectation for owners to be 'engaged' citizens: to be not only tolerant of inroads upon their rights, for the sake of the broader public good, but also to be both *proactive* and *resourceful* in finding solutions to property problems with significant socio-political dimensions. However, the state remains both responsible for and instrumental in creating a society based on constitutional values. Most of all, it is expected to enable engaged citizenship by being involved, facilitative and mediating in resolving the tensions between the public interest and private rights.[270]

Often, however, as the ECHR jurisprudence specifically demonstrates, state involvement may complicate rather than simplify a dispute. Other possible examples are where extraction of minerals, occurring in terms of an exercise of a state-granted mining right, impairs the neighbouring land's stability or the viability of activities such as dairy farming,[271] or where it does not sustain valuable natural resources such as the water table.[272] This latter example arises from the cases with facts such as *Bradford v Pickles*, mentioned above,[273] because it involves a state authority. Another similar example may be where a licence to conduct a business is granted on ecologically sensitive land, and where the actual business activities impair the biodiversity on the neighbouring owners' land.[274] In these contexts conduct which may be patently unreasonable in terms of nuisance law is sanctioned by state involvement, in the granting of mining rights or trading licences, usually after consideration of the impact that the granting of such rights would have on the surroundings.

The pertinent question here is whether the introduction of a public authority into the relationship between neighbours affects the manner in

---

[269] Mostert, note 139 supra, 271–3.

[270] Ibid.

[271] Developed from the facts of *Swartland Municipality v Louw NO & Others* 2010 JOL 26136 (WC) which was not decided on the issue of nuisance.

[272] E.g. South African Press Association 'No Confusion on Karoo Fracking' *Times Live* 26 April 2011; J Stephen 'Fracking: Vat Jou Goed en Pak, Vrak' *The Media Online* 5 May 2011; M Gosling 'Kramer Takes Stand against Fracking' *Independent On Line* 12 May 2011; S Blaine 'Shell Fracking Application in Karoo "Illegal"' *Business Day* 25 March 2011; L Steyn 'Fracking Opens Deep Divisions' *Mail & Guardian* 27 May 2011; D Alfreds D 'Earthlife Africa Slams Karoo Fracking' *News24* 30 May 2011. On Shell's Environmental Management Plan see F Bekker *Review of the Draft EMP in Support of an Application for Gas Exploration in the Western Karoo (Central Precinct) by Shell Exploration Company* (Clean Stream Environmental Services 2011); L Havemann, J Glazewski and S Brownlie *A Critical Review of the Application for Karoo Gas Exploration Right by Shell Exploration Company BV* (Havemann Inc 2011).

[273] Section 11.3.2.2 supra.

[274] *Fuel Retailers Association of South Africa (Pty) Ltd v Director-General Environmental Management Mpumalanga and Others* 2007 (2) SA 163 (SCA).

which reasonableness and liability should be determined and assessed. Two principles identified by Alexander and Peñalver provide a basis on which to determine the extent of state intervention here.[275] On the one hand, private or local solutions should be favoured where possible: the state should not assume functions for itself that can be performed equally well on an inter-personal, or more intimate community level. On the other hand, individual dignity must be safeguarded by prohibiting arbitrary state action.

11.5 CONCLUDING OBSERVATIONS

Scholars who have commented on the effect of a human rights paradigm on nuisance law agree that there is bound to be an effect.[276] The range of interests weighed and balanced may be expanded to include interests sanctioned in a human rights context.[277] The human rights context may also redefine the relationship between public and private interest in this area of the law.[278] This chapter does not contest these conclusions. Instead, it accepts that the prin-ciples of nuisance and the values of human rights may intersect: (a) where the conflict arises between private parties, because they both attempt to exercise their human rights through the use of their properties; or (b) where the conflict arises because the exercise of a state-granted right over property infringes on the human rights of a neighbour. This paper is more concerned with what the spheres of human rights and nuisance law have to offer to achieve a better understanding of the balancing exercise that occurs in both contexts.

One observation, gained from the preceding analysis, is the extent to which the state is drawn into disputes that would in the past have had a purely private law character. The constitutional, human rights documents that formed part of this analysis displayed the general tendency of obliging the state to protect individual relations with property and to protect the privacy of individuals. It also has a duty not to interfere with the rights thus created unduly. This raises a third dimension of liability, beyond the private law relief of abatement and/or damages, in the context of nuisance. This

[275] Alexander and Peñalver, note 137 supra, 148–9.
[276] Du Bois and Reid, note 20 supra, at 598 indicated that 'gaps between common law nui-sance principles and human rights principles may lead to the adaptation of nuisance'. Van der Walt, note 3 supra, at 315 opts for a seemingly less 'privatist' approach, and indicates that 'to assume identity or similarity between [nuisance principles and human rights] . . . is fraught with deep political, moral and justice problems'. He agrees (at 318), neverthe-less, with the conclusion of du Bois and Reid that the reasonableness standard is likely to be influenced by human rights values where it could possibly entrench 'constitutionally suspect patterns of exclusion and discrimination', and that it is in the field of public nui-sance where strong constitutional development may be expected.
[277] Du Bois and Reid, note 20 supra, 598–9.
[278] Van der Walt, note 3 supra, 381–5.

third dimension, state liability based on the constitutional provisions, is well illustrated in cases such as *Mileva*, *Hatton* and *López Ostra*.

In view of the analysis above, another observation is that nuisance law applies to a limited category of disputes, mostly those which involve use and enjoyment of one person's land in a way that offends or harms another. Although the rhetoric of neighbourliness is prevalent in disputes involving access to or eviction from land, the standards developed there are not easily transposed to the narrower context of nuisance. The main hurdle is that the underlying values to be protected are different for the two categories of dispute. With regard to the transformative rhetoric of good neighbourliness prevalent in the South African access and eviction cases, the conflicting values are use or ownership versus access. In the narrower nuisance context, where similar rhetoric is absent for want of consideration of the human rights matrix as such, the underlying value to be protected amounts to use on either side of the dispute.

This does not mean that the neighbourliness rhetoric has nothing to offer by way of contributing to the development of nuisance law. Especially in the manner in which the notion is explored in the South African Constitutional Court jurisprudence, it signifies broader acceptance of the idea that property law needs to be conceptualised around the responsibilities that property entails, and not only in view of the rights entrenched by it. Nuisance law, in which the mutuality of rights and duties in respect of one's property has been paramount all along, can demonstrate the 'give-and-take' spirit of this conception of property law excellently. At the same time, nuisance law itself can be enhanced by a constitutional endorsement of such a more relativist conception of property law.

Another way of dealing with the increased influence of constitutional or human rights considerations on this aspect of property law is to develop statutory mechanisms to address claims about the inviolability of the individual property rights as against the broader public. As some European scholars have demonstrated,[279] the *Bradford v Pickles* dilemma is thus avoided by legislating on areas of broader social concern, in which nuisance and human rights are likely to intersect. To some extent this is already the case where environmental protection measures are built into, for instance, South African mineral law. Van der Walt[280] argues that a broader statutory mechanism would render it easier to make a decision based on reasonableness of the conduct. I submit that the existing common law mechanism for nuisance is sufficient on a general level, and that it is unnecessary to replace the existing, standard reasonableness test through statutory intervention. Where more specific – and/or stricter – regulatory intervention is necessary (such

---

[279] Reid, 'The Doctrine of Abuse of Rights', note 82 supra; Allen, note 226 supra (see discussion supra).
[280] Van der Walt, note 3 supra, 318.

as in the mineral law or environmental law contexts), statutory regulation could play a more significant role but a shift in how the rules of nuisance are utilised may occur. At the very least, the human rights paradigm will force a consideration of the fact that the standard of reasonableness or tolerability is not merely there to measure and reconcile opposing individual rights. Instead, it reminds us of the social and legal norms by which rights to own and use land are inherently and contextually restricted.[281] The human rights context reminds us of the social and democratic responsibilities inherent in owning and using land, and reinforces and enhances the reciprocal nature or mutuality of owners' ability to use and enjoy land as expressed in the phrase 'give and take, live and let live'.

---

[281] J Singer 'How Property Norms Construct the Externalities of Ownership' in G Alexander and E M Peñalver (eds) *Property and Community* (Oxford University Press 2010) 59–60; van der Walt, note 3 supra, 48; Alexander and Peñalver, note 137 supra, 143.

Chapter 12

Contract Law and Human Rights

Peter Webster

12.1 INTRODUCTION

This chapter seeks to consider the impact of human rights upon contract law. A Scots lawyer might be forgiven for asking 'what influence?' There are no Scottish cases of which I am aware in which the interplay between these two areas of law has been considered in detail. In the various books published around the time that the Scotland Act 1998 and the Human Rights Act 1998 came into effect, contract law does not feature heavily, if at all.[1] It is easy to see why. As Professor MacQueen has remarked:

> 'The law [i.e. contract law] is founded on ideas of transactional equality, private autonomy, and voluntary inter-action, in which, within very broad limits, individuals strike their own balance of interests, rather than have it set for them by external, social or public standards.'[2]

Freedom of contract is seen as the dominant principle.[3] That has various aspects. As a general proposition, parties are free to decide not to contract with each other for whatever reason; if they do contract, the law will enforce whatever terms they agree.[4] Of course, neither of those propositions is absolute, but nevertheless the idea of fundamental rights which parties must respect sits ill with the general principle. Further, human rights are seen as primarily controlling state action and not that of individuals. The merest of glances at South African law, or at other European legal systems which have

---

[1] A Boyle, C Himsworth, A Loux and H MacQueen (eds) *Human Rights and Scots Law* (Hart 2002); R Reed and J Murdoch *A Practical Guide to Human Rights Law in Scotland* (W Green 2001) (now in its third edition of 2011).

[2] H L MacQueen 'Delict, Contract, and the Bill of Rights: A Perspective from the United Kingdom' 2004 SALJ 359 at 376.

[3] For judicial recognition in Scottish cases, see, e.g., *EFT Commercial Ltd v Security Change Ltd* 1992 SC 414 at 422 (OH – Lord Coulsfield) and 428 (IH – Lord President Hope). In South Africa, see, e.g., *Sasfin (Pty) Ltd v Beukes* 1989 (1) SA 1 (AD) 9E.

[4] These two different aspects to freedom of contract are distinguished in German law as *Abschlussfreiheit* and *Inhaltsfreiheit*: D Coester-Waltjen 'Discrimination in Private Law' in K S Ziegler (ed) *Human Rights and Private Law* (Hart 2007) 117 at 124; P Schlechtriem & M Schmidt-Kessel *Schuldrecht: Allgemeiner Teil* 6e (Mohr Siebeck 2005) 34–48.

had domestically-enforceable constitutional rights for longer than the UK,[5] suggests that any view that contract law will not be affected by human rights jurisprudence is misplaced. The question is what effect that is to be.

There is already a rich seam of South African case law and academic literature in this field. There is far less Scottish material, although there is now some English case law and there are also relevant decisions of the European Court of Human Rights (ECtHR). In light of the different stages of development of each legal system, this chapter analyses each separately. It first summarises the developments in South African law, with a view to identifying the key issues that have arisen in the debate there about the constitutionalisation of contract law. It then turns to Scots law, considering first how what might be called 'human rights issues' in a broad sense are addressed by well-established rules (such as those against discrimination and unfair terms), and then how human rights points in the narrower, more technical sense can be expected to be dealt with now that rights recognised by the European Convention on Human Rights (ECHR) are enforceable domestically.

12.2 SOUTH AFRICA

12.2.1 Introduction

Various cases have considered the impact of the Constitution upon contract law and this has been the subject of vigorous academic debate.[6] Three cases, in particular, have been the focus of attention, for they established

---

[5] Four English texts in respect of other European legal systems are T Barkhuysen and S Lindenbergh (eds) *Constitutionalisation of Private Law* (Martinus Nijhoff 2006); O O Cherednychenko *Fundamental Rights, Contract Law and the Protection of the Weaker Party* (Sellier 2007); S Grundmann (ed) *Constitutional Values and European Contract Law* (Wolters Kluwer 2008); and C Mak *Fundamental Rights in European Contract Law: A Comparison of the Impact of Fundamental Rights on Contract Law in Germany, the Netherlands, Italy and England* (Wolters Kluwer 2008).

[6] Notable contributions are: G Lubbe 'Taking Fundamental Rights Seriously: The Bill of Rights and its Implications for the Development of Contract Law' (2004) 121 SALJ 395; D Bhana and M Pieterse 'Towards a Reconciliation of Contract Law and Constitutional Values: *Brisley* and *Afrox* Revisited' (2005) 122 SALJ 865; D Bhana 'The Law of Contract and the Constitution: *Napier v Barkhuizen* (SCA)' (2007) 124 SALJ 269; S Woolman 'The Amazing, Vanishing Bill of Rights' (2007) 124 SALJ 762; P J Sutherland 'Ensuring Contractual Fairness in Consumer Contracts After *Barkhuizen v Napier* 2007 5 SA 323 (CC)' Part 1 (2008) 19 Stell LR 390 and Part 2 (2009) 20 Stell LR 50; D Moseneke 'Transformative Constitutionalism: Its Implication for the Law of Contract' (2009) 20 Stell LR 3; I M Rautenbach 'Constitution and Contract – Exploring "the Possibility that Certain Rights may Apply Directly to Contractual Terms or the Common Law that Underlies Them"' 2009 TSAR 613; F J D Brand 'The Role of Good Faith, Equity and Fairness in the South African Law of Contract: The Influence of the Common Law and the Constitution' (2009) 126 SALJ 71.

the current position: *Brisley v Drotsky*,[7] *Afrox Healthcare Bpk v Styrdom*[8] and *Napier v Barkhuizen*.[9] A variety of arguments have been advanced. The initial tendency was to submit that the Constitution required particular rules of contract law, or even the approach of contract law generally, to be changed, for example by affording the doctrine of good faith a broader role. These broader arguments have not succeeded: courts have been keen to maintain contract law as a regime of legal certainty, to the dismay of some commentators who perceive this as affording too much weight to laissez-faire liberalism and perpetuating the inequality which they perceive the Constitution as being designed to address.[10] Significantly, however, the courts have accepted that the common law of contract is subject to the Constitution and that constitutional values inform the doctrine of public policy. Oddly (at least to this outsider), arguments that reaching a particular result in a particular case would infringe a particular constitutional right have been less common.

12.2.2 Exposition

12.2.2.1 Constitutional framework

There are two ways in which the Constitution can be of relevance in disputes between private parties.[11] The first is by direct application, provided for by section 8(2). Section 8 provides:

> '(1) The Bill of Rights applies to all law, and binds the legislature, the executive, the judiciary and all organs of state.
>
> (2) A provision of the Bill of Rights binds a natural or a juristic person if, and to the extent that, it is applicable, taking into account the nature of the right and the nature of any duty imposed by the right.
>
> (3) When applying a provision of the Bill of Rights to a natural or juristic person in terms of subsection (2), a court
>
> a. in order to give effect to a right in the Bill, must apply, or if necessary, develop, the common law to the extent that legislation does not give effect to that right; and
>
> b. may develop rules of the common law to limit the right, provided that the limitation is in accordance with section 36(1).'

Section 8(2) has been described as a 'rather awkward provision'.[12] It does not make clear which provisions of the Bill of Rights are, and which are not, capable of direct application. The Constitution also makes provision for it

---

[7] 2002 (4) SA 1 (SCA).
[8] 2002 (6) SA 21 (SCA).
[9] 2006 (4) SA 1 (SCA), 2007 (5) SA 323 (CC).
[10] See, e.g., Bhana and Pieterse, note 6 supra.
[11] See, in general, I Currie and J De Waal *The Bill of Rights Handbook* 5e (Juta 2005) 50–5, 67–72.
[12] M du Plessis and J Ford 'Developing the Common Law Progressively – Horizontality, the Human Rights Act and the South African Experience' 2004 *European Human Rights Law Review* 286 at 291.

to have what has been described as a 'radiating influence'[13] upon the legal system generally. More prosaically, this is described as indirect application or sometimes as indirect normative effect.[14] Section 39(2) provides: 'When interpreting any legislation, and when developing the common law or customary law, every court, tribunal or forum must promote the spirit, purport and objects of the Bill of Rights'. It has been held that this applies in two circumstances: first, when a common law rule is actually inconsistent with a constitutional provision; secondly, where, although not actually inconsistent with a constitutional provision, a common law rule falls short of its spirit, purport and objects. In those circumstances, the law must be adapted so that it grows in harmony with the 'objective value system' of the Constitution.[15]

In judgments in the contractual arena to date, the second type of argument has been more prominent than the first, reflecting a broader trend in cases between private parties in which the Bill of Rights is invoked.[16]

12.2.2.2 Good faith and reasonableness
One of the first arguments to be advanced about the impact of the Constitution upon contract law was that it required a greater role to be afforded to abstract notions of good faith and reasonableness, so that courts should refuse to give effect to contractual terms viewed as imperilling those values. There was already some support in the case law for an active doctrine of good faith, founding mostly upon the minority opinion of Oliver JA in *Eerste Nasionale Bank van Suidelike Afrika Bpk v Saayman*.[17] That had been interpreted in various decisions of the Cape High Court[18] as permitting courts not to apply a particular rule of contract law if the result was unfair.[19] In *Mort NO V Henry Shields-Chiat*[20] Davis J argued that the constitutional obligation to develop the common law in accordance with the principles of

---

[13] Du Plessis and Ford, note 12 supra, 292. The term stems from the famous German *Lüth* case, in which the German Constitutional Court held that the Basic Law establishes an 'objective order of values' affecting all areas of law, via an '*Ausstrahlungswirkung*': (1958) 7 BVerfGE 198, 207.

[14] K O'Regan 'The Best of Both Worlds? Some Reflections on the Interaction between the Common Law and the Bill of Rights in our New Constitution' (available from *http://www. ajol.info/index.php/pelj/article/viewFile/43507/27042*) 9.

[15] *Carmichele v Minister of Safety and Security* 2001 (4) SA 938 (CC); *S v Thebus* 2003 (6) SA 505 (CC) para 28.

[16] Currie and De Waal, note 11 supra, 61. They suggest, however, that *Khumalo v Holomisa* 2002 (5) SA 401 (CC) marks a change in approach: there article 16 of the Bill of Rights was applied directly between private parties in a defamation dispute.

[17] 1997 (4) SA 302 (SCA).

[18] *Mort NO v Henry Shields-Chiat* 2001 (1) SA 464 (C) 474J – 475I; *Miller & another NNO v Dannecker* 2001 (1) SA 928 (C) at para 19.

[19] See Brand, note 6 supra, 78–80 and F Brand and D Brodie 'Good Faith in Contract Law' in R Zimmermann, D Visser & K Reid (eds) *Mixed Legal Systems in Comparative Perspective* (Oxford University Press 2004) 94 at 98–106.

[20] 2001 (1) SA 464 (C) 474-5

equality and dignity required the courts to establish an active doctrine of good faith. This argument was considered, and rejected, by the Supreme Court of Appeal in *Brisley v Drotsky*.[21] South African law had decided in the 1960s, after some debate, that a 'non-variation' or 'entrenchment' clause (which provides, for example, that any variations to a contract are valid only if recorded in writing) is enforceable: *SA Sentrale Ko-Op Graanmaatskappy Bpk v Shifren*.[22] In *Brisley*, a tenant sought to resist eviction for non-payment of rent on the basis that the landlord had orally agreed to the rent being paid late. The landlord relied upon an 'entrenchment clause'. The tenant argued that to apply the *Shifren* principle would yield unfair results, and be contrary to *bona fides* and Constitutional values.[23] The court unanimously found for the landlord, but was not unanimous as to the role which good faith should play in contract law. The majority held that good faith and reasonableness do not provide a free-standing basis for refusing to give effect to a contract and that *Shifren* remains good law. In a joint judgment, Harms, Streicher and Brand JJA accepted that the 1996 Constitution required the development of common law principles in order to reflect the spirit, purpose and objects of the Constitution but that this did not require development of the concept of good faith. Allowing judges to refuse to apply contractual provisions when unfair or unreasonable would unacceptably subjectivise decision-making and render contract law insufficiently certain. Cameron JA agreed. Significantly, as we shall see,[24] he drew support for this approach from the Constitution itself, arguing that constitutional notions of equality, dignity and freedom favour a restrained approach to striking down contractual provisions. Olivier JA concurred in the result, but would have accorded good faith, modelled upon constitutional values, a broader role, in line with his earlier judgment in *Saayman*.

---

[21] 2002 (4) SA 1 (SCA). The majority's and Oliver JA's opinions are in Afrikaans. I rely upon the headnote and the analysis in Lubbe, note 6 supra, and Bhana and Pieterse, note 6 supra, in this portrayal.

[22] 1964 (4) SA 760 (A).

[23] The tenant also advanced arguments more particularly focused upon section 26(3) of the Constitution, which provides that no one may be evicted from their home without an order of court made after considering all the relevant circumstances. These were also unsuccessful. The court accepted that section 26(3) applies horizontally but held that the personal circumstances of the lessee and the availability of alternative accommodation are not 'relevant circumstances' for its purposes. Private law controlled whether an ejectment order would be granted. It remains to be seen what the approach of courts in the UK and Europe will be to this issue. In leases from a public authority landlord, the Strasbourg court has held that there must be an assessment of 'proportionality' of the eviction before a court order can be granted removing a tenant. This involves more than an assessment of whether the private law right to occupy the property has been validly terminated. It is not yet clear whether the same is required in private sector tenancies, but there are some signs that the Strasbourg court will hold that it is. See, generally, *Pinnock v Manchester City Council* [2011] 2 AC 104, in particular para 50.

[24] Discussed in more detail in section 12.2.2.3.1 infra.

The Supreme Court of Appeal has therefore adopted a position where, as explained by Lubbe, good faith does not operate on the black-letter or doctrinal level as an open norm:[25]

> '[t]he ethical principle of good faith does not directly intervene in contract law, but is realized through the instrumentality of the technical, black-letter rules and institutions of contract doctrine, in which it is discounted and balanced against other principles and policy concerns relevant to the overall aims of contract law.'

In *Napier v Barkhuizen* the Constitutional Court reserved its opinion as to whether the role which the Supreme Court has been willing to afford good faith is compatible with the Constitution.[26] The majority suggested that there was a 'compelling argument' that the enforcement of time limitation clauses should be subject to a requirement of good faith.[27] It has been argued in various cases that the Constitutional Court's decision in *Barkhuizen* does permit a broad-ranging enquiry into the 'fairness' or 'reasonableness' of any contract term. Although it certainly contains some broad passages,[28] it is thought that, properly interpreted, *Barkhuizen* is not authority for such a proposition.[29] Certainly, the Supreme Court of Appeal has since reiterated its stance, stating that unless and until the Constitutional Court holds otherwise, fairness, reasonableness or good faith are not free-standing grounds for refusing to give effect to the provisions of a contract.[30] Just how the Constitutional Court will decide this issue when it does require to be addressed remains to be seen. Contract lawyers typically trumpet the virtue

---

[25] Lubbe, note 6 supra, 398. D Hutchison 'Non-variation Clauses in Contract: Any Escape from the *Shifren* Straightjacket' (2001) 118 SALJ 721 at 746, referred to with approval by the SCA in *Brisley* at para 26, expresses a similar view.

[26] 2007 (5) SA 323 (CC) para 82 (Ncgobo J, with whom Madala J, Mkabinde J, Skweyiya J, van der Westhuizen J and Yacoob J concurred); para 120 (O'Regan J, who concurred with the outcome, but expressly reserved her opinion on this point). Moseneke DCJ (with whom Mokgoro J concurred) and Sachs J did not address this point. In *The Crown Restaurant CC v Gold Reef City Theme Park (Pty) Ltd*, an applicant sought leave to appeal to the Constitutional Court, arguing that the Constitution required the reintroduction of the *exceptio doli generalis* (a now-abolished defence against the 'unfair' enforcement of a contract), but leave to appeal was refused as the point had not been raised in the courts below: judgment 6 March 2007.

[27] Ibid para 83.

[28] Such as paras 48 and 73 ('public policy would preclude the enforcement of a contractual term if its enforcement would be unjust or unfair').

[29] Whether the clause was unfair or unjust was only relevant as part of the court's assessment of whether the clause was compatible with the particular constitutional values in question and not as part of a general enquiry into whether the clause could be enforced. It might be said, however, that the values of one of the sections of the Constitution will frequently be in play: if that permits an assessment of the 'fairness' and 'reasonableness' of a contractual provision, the SCA's concern to maintain certainty may easily be undone.

[30] *Bredenkamp v Standard Bank of SA Ltd* [2010] ZASCA 75 para 50; *Maphango (Mgidlana) and others v Aengus Lifestyle Properties (Pty) Ltd* [2011] ZASCA 191 para 25; *Potgieter v Potgieter* [2011] ZASCA 181 para 32.

of certainty because it facilitates commercial transactions. In *Bredenkamp v Standard Bank of SA Ltd*, Harms DP reminded us that an even more fundamental principle is at stake:[31] '[a] constitutional principle that tends to be overlooked when generalized resort to constitutional values is made is the principle of legality. Making rules of law discretionary or subject to value judgments may be destructive of the rule of law'.

12.2.2.3 Public policy and constitutional values: objectionable contractual terms

12.2.2.3.1 Public policy as a doctrinal gateway: two arguments
In the same decisions in which the Supreme Court of Appeal denied that the Constitution requires good faith or reasonableness to be given a broader role in contract law, it accepted that the Constitution informs the doctrine of public policy.[32] The Constitutional Court approved this approach in *Barkhuizen*. As it has been put by Brand JA, writing extra-judicially, 'the concept of public policy forms the doctrinal gateway for the importation of constitutional values into the law of contract'.[33] There remain uncertainties, however, about the exact manner in which the Constitution informs public policy and the weight to be given to freedom of contract in the analysis. There are two types of argument. In early cases they were not always kept distinct.[34] The first relies upon the general values expounded by section 1 of the Constitution as those upon which the Republic of South Africa is founded. They include (a) human dignity, the achievement of equality and the advancement of human rights and freedoms and (b) non-racialism and non-sexism.[35] The second approach is to rely upon the values of particular substantive provisions, such as the right to healthcare (section 27) or to housing (section 26) or of access to courts (section 34), as giving content to public policy.

The foundation for each argument is Cameron JA's judgment in *Brisley*, where he stated, that public policy is 'rooted in our constitution and the fundamental values it enshrines'[36] and that contracts which offend against

---

[31] Ibid para 39.
[32] *Brisley*, note 7 supra, para 92, *Afrox*, note 8 supra, *Barkhuizen* (SCA), note 9 supra, para 7, *Bredenkamp*, note 30 supra, para 39, *Maphango*, note 30 supra, paras 26–8, *African Dawn Properties Finance 2 (Pty) Ltd v Dreams Travel and Tours CC* [2011] ZASCA 45 para 22. In *Bredenkamp* it was said that this is now 'trite' (at para 39).
[33] Brand, note 6 supra, 84.
[34] They are distinguished most clearly in the SCA judgment in *Barkhuizen*, note 9 supra.
[35] These feature again as substantive provisions of the Bill of Rights: section 9 is the right to equality (which will be breached by sexist or racist conduct) and section 10 the right to have one's dignity respected. It is therefore not entirely clear what treating section 1 as the basis for a separate type of argument adds.
[36] *Brisley*, note 7 supra, para 91.

these fundamentals will be struck down. He explained, however, that the values of dignity, equality and freedom required the courts to approach their task of striking down contracts or declining to enforce them with 'perceptive restraint'.[37] In *Brisley* the focus of the argument was upon more general constitutional values (and not so much, as one might have expected, on the values which section 34 – the right to housing – aims to promote). The more general argument failed. Cameron JA concluded that:

> '[t]he Constitution requires that its values be employed to achieve a careful balance between the unacceptable excesses of contractual "freedom", and securing a framework within which the ability to contract enhances rather than diminishes our self-respect and dignity. The issues in the present appeal do not imperil that balance.'

In fact, it was noted that the institution of contract actually promotes constitutional values: '[s]horn of its obscene excesses, contractual autonomy informs also the constitutional value of dignity'.[38] In *Afrox* the weight to be given to contractual autonomy was strengthened further.[39] Brand JA held that contractual freedom was itself a Constitutional value, which encompassed the doctrine of *pacta sunt servanda*.[40] It was in the public interest that contracts concluded freely and with serious intent be enforced. The constitutional challenge failed in that case, in large part because there was no evidence of an inequality of bargaining power between the parties.

Both types of values argument were run at different stages of *Barkhuizen v Napier*,[41] the most significant case in this field. Given the significance of the case, its facts should be outlined. It concerned the enforceability of a time limitation clause in an insurance contract. Barkhuizen insured his car with a syndicate of Lloyds, represented in South Africa by Napier. Clause 5.2.5 of their contract provided that if the insurer rejected liability for any claim under the policy, it would be released from liability unless a court summons was served on it within 90 days of the repudiation. Napier repudiated a claim made by Barkhuizen. Two years later Barkuizen initiated proceedings against Napier. When Napier sought to rely upon clause 5.2.5, Barkuizen responded that it was contrary to public policy as it infringed his right of access to

---

[37] Ibid para 94.

[38] Ibid. In the later case of *Maphango*, note 30 supra, contractual autonomy was described as 'a real and meaningful incident of freedom' (at para 28).

[39] In *Afrox*, note 8 supra, the plaintiff sought damages for alleged negligent treatment by the defendant private hospital. The defendant relied upon an exemption clause in the contract which the plaintiff had signed prior to admission. The plaintiff argued, inter alia, that the clause conflicted with the spirit, purpose and object of section 27(1)(a), the right to healthcare.

[40] *Afrox*, note 8 supra, para 23. (I rely upon the translation given by Lubbe, note 6 supra, n 147).

[41] Indeed, it was also argued that to give effect to the provision would actually contravene the Constitution, on which see part 12.2.2.4 infra.

court. Specifically, he argued that the clause was contrary to section 34 of the Constitution, which guarantees that right. The case was heard by both the Supreme Court of Appeal and by the Constitutional Court, both of which found for Napier.

12.2.2.3.2 Inconsistency with the Constitutional values of dignity and equality
The Supreme Court of Appeal treated there as being two grounds of constitutional challenge in *Barkhuizen*. The first was the broader one: that the terms of the contract, and the bargaining positions of the parties, were such that to enforce the contract would infringe the insured's constitutional rights to dignity and equality. Cameron JA gave the judgment of the court. It accepted that 'the Constitution requires us to employ its values to achieve a balance that strikes down the unacceptable accesses of "freedom of contract", while seeking to permit individuals the dignity and autonomy of regulating their own lives'.[42] Cameron JA acknowledged that although it was 'relatively easy' to see how the foundational values of non-sexism and non-racialism could lead to invalidation of a contractual term, it was less immediately obvious how the values of human dignity, the achievement of equality and the advancement of human rights and freedoms would do so. However, the court held that this was what *Brisley* and *Afrox* had accepted the Constitution required. Inequality of bargaining power was an important factor in this analysis and Barkhuizen had failed to establish that he and the insurer were not of equal bargaining power. There had been no evidence about, for example, the nature of the market in short-term insurance products, whether most insurers impose a time bar, and, if so, whether all do so on the same terms, and whether the car was an optional convenience or an essential attribute of life. These all bore on the question 'whether the plaintiff was in effect forced to contract with the insurer on terms that infringed his constitutional rights to dignity and equality in a way that requires this Court to develop the common law of contract so as to invalidate the term'.[43] The Supreme Court therefore rejected this element of the argument. It seems that the court wishes to preserve the possibility of refusing to enforce a contract on the ground that it would be contrary to one of the parties' dignity, but that it will require exceptional circumstances, and detailed evidence, to support such a claim. This broad equality/dignity argument was not pursued in Barkhuizen's application to the Constitutional Court.

The Supreme Court's acceptance that this argument can be made is, in itself, noteworthy. It is an attempt to keep open the possibility of a constitutional argument similar to that which succeeded in the famous German *Bürgschaft* case,[44] in which the German Federal Constitutional Court held

---

[42] 2006 (4) SA 1 (SCA) para 13.
[43] Ibid para 16.
[44] BVerfG 19 October 1993 89 BVerfGE 214.

that to enforce a guarantee given by a daughter of her father's (by then, substantial) business debts would be inconsistent with the protection of her private autonomy guaranteed by article 2 of the *Grundgesetz* (Basic Law).[45]

12.2.2.3.3 *Inconsistency with the values of section 34: the proper basis for applying the Constitution in contractual cases*

The second ground of challenge, as perceived by the Supreme Court of Appeal, focused upon section 34 of the Constitution, which guarantees a right of access to courts. Barkhuizen maintained that to enforce the clause and hold that his action had been raised too late would be inconsistent with his constitutional right of access to court. The Supreme Court of Appeal sought to apply existing Constitutional Court jurisprudence regarding limitation periods[46] to the time limitation provision in the contract. It concluded that, because a contractual limitation period means that the right to insurance had been limited from its inception, it need not be treated in the same way as a statutory limitation period imposed upon a pre-existing claim. Section 34 did not prohibit clause 5.2.5. For the purposes of this chapter, the court's analysis of the constitutional right is of less interest than the basis on which it applied the Constitution to a contractual term. The Supreme Court of Appeal did not consider this in much detail, but it appears that the values of section 34 were used to give content to the contractual doctrine of public policy. The High Court had addressed this point in detail, as did the Constitutional Court upon Barkhuizen's subsequent application. Indeed, the Constitutional Court identified the proper approach to constitutional challenges to contractual terms as a 'threshold issue' in the case. Barkhuizen had argued, successfully before the High Court, that it was possible to apply section 34 directly to the terms of contracts via section 8. The Constitutional Court rejected that argument, for reasons explored in more detail below.[47] Instead, the majority of that court held that:[48]

'the proper approach to the constitutional challenges to contractual terms is to determine whether the term challenged is contrary to public policy as evidenced by the constitutional values, in particular, those found in the Bill of Rights. This approach leaves space for the doctrine of *pacta sunt servanda* to operate, but at the same time allows courts to decline to enforce contractual terms that are in conflict

45 There is a discussion (in English) in C Mak, note 5 supra, 75–82. South Africa has already had a case of its own along these lines: *Sasfin (Pty) Ltd v Beukes* 1989 (1) SA 1 (A), where a deed of cession, which effectively gave control of all Dr Beukes' professional earnings to a creditor, was declared contrary to public policy.
46 Primarily *Mohlomi v Minister of Defence* 1991 (1) SA 124 (CC) and *Moise v Greater Germiston Transitional Local Council* 2001 (4) SA 491 (CC).
47 Part 12.2.2.4.
48 2007 (5) SA 323 (CC) para 30.

with the constitutional values even though the parties may have consented to them.'

12.2.2.3.4 *Constitutional scrutiny of the content of a contractual term*

On the Constitutional Court's approach, it was not simply a case of applying the test established in the jurisprudence regarding section 34 to the term of the contract. Instead, the test set down in cases concerning section 34 was paraphrased. It was said that 'broadly speaking' the test is whether a provision 'affords a claimant an adequate and fair opportunity to seek judicial redress'.[49] That was used to give content to the contractual doctrine of public policy. The court disapproved of the Supreme Court's 'narrow and formalistic' reasoning that, because the limitation on the right of access to court was inherent in Barkhuizen's contractual right, it was unobjectionable. The general standard which the court applied to assessing the clause was one of fairness, which it divided into two further questions. First, was the clause itself unreasonable?[50] Secondly, if the clause was reasonable, should it be enforced in light of the circumstances which prevented compliance with the time limitation clause?[51] Inequality of bargaining power was a relevant consideration in respect of both issues.[52] The court broke down the first question into two further stages. The first was directed to the objective terms of the contract: were they themselves incompatible with public policy?[53] The second asked whether the terms were contrary to public policy in light of the relative situation of the parties. The Constitutional Court approved the Supreme Court of Appeal's approach of taking *pacta sunt servanda* into account as part of the public policy analysis (although noticeably it did not elevate freedom of contract to the status of a constitutional value as Brand JA had done in *Afrox*).[54] The extent to which the contract was freely and voluntarily concluded was said to be vital to determining the weight to be afforded

---

[49] *Barkhuizen* (CC), note 9 supra, para 51, drawing on *Mohlomi v Minister of Defence* 1991 (1) SA 124 (CC), one of the leading cases on section 34 and limitation periods.

[50] Considered at *Barkhuizen*, note 9 supra, paras 62–7.

[51] Considered at ibid paras 68–86.

[52] Cf ibid paras 58–9, which might be taken to suggest that inequality of bargaining power is relevant only to the second question. Paras 65 and 66, however, refer to inequality of bargaining power in the context of answering the first question.

[53] In *The Johannesburg Country Club v Stott* 2004 (5) SA 511 (SCA) para 12, it was suggested that a term excluding liability for damages for negligently caused death would per se be contrary to public policy. That argument was not advanced in *Afrox*, note 8 supra, where enforcement of an exclusion clause in a contract for treatment at a private hospital was held not to breach the Constitution. Brand JA has suggested, extra-judicially, that had it been, the result in *Afrox* might have been different: Brand, note 6 supra, 89.

[54] The weight which should be afforded to the notion of contractual autonomy has remained controversial. See, e.g., *Advtech Resourcing (Pty) Ltd t/a Communicate Personnel Group v Kuhn* 2008 (2) SA 375 (C) para 30 where it is described as 'a heavily value laden concept employed in an individualistic, autonomous fashion'.

to the values of freedom and dignity when considering whether a term was enforceable.[55] It would, therefore, be possible to dislodge the weight which *pacta sunt servanda* presumptively bore by establishing that the contract was not freely concluded. To do so would, however, require evidence and, like the Supreme Court of Appeal, the Constitutional Court concluded that no evidence of an inequality of bargaining power had been presented in this case.[56] In light of that, the majority concluded that the time limitation clause was not itself contrary to public policy.[57]

12.2.2.3.5 *Constitutional scrutiny of the enforcement of a contractual term*

The final stage of analysis in *Barkhuizen* was to consider whether, even if the term was reasonable in itself, its application to the facts was not.[58] The majority[59] accepted that, in principle, there could be a constitutional challenge to the operation of a term which, in the abstract, is unobjectionable.[60] They give the example of an insured who had lapsed into a coma shortly after the repudiation and had been prevented from raising a claim in time.[61] Again, however, this type of argument would require to be supported by evidence of the term's operation in practice and no evidence had been provided of why Barkhuizen had failed to comply with the clause's requirements.

In this context (that is, a challenge to the constitutionality of how a term operated in practice) the court considered the common law doctrines of impossibility[62] and good faith. Napier argued that these two doctrines were sufficient to ensure that an objectively reasonable clause would not be applied so as to produce unreasonable results and so there was no need for further development of the law to provide a constitutionally-based public policy challenge to the enforcement of a clause which – in the abstract – was reasonable.[63] The majority held that, given the lack of evidence on this point, these issues did not require to be addressed.[64] It is not clear (to this writer, at least) how those doctrines, if they were to be developed, would interact

---

[55] Ibid 57.

[56] Ibid 66.

[57] Ibid 67.

[58] This was considered under the heading 'Inflexibility' at *Barkhuizen*, note 9 supra, paras 68–86. It is different from concluding that the term is objectively unreasonable because it provides for no flexibility in its operation (ibid at para 69).

[59] O'Regan J, who concurred with the rest of Ngcobo J's judgment, viewed it as unnecessary to decide this point (ibid at para 120).

[60] See, in particular para 72, where the Constitutional Court contrasts its approach with that of the Supreme Court of Appeal which, on one interpretation, was unconcerned with the results which a reasonable clause produced.

[61] Ibid para 69.

[62] I.e. that the law will not compel a person to do what is impossible

[63] Here, therefore, there is the oddity that it was the party defending the constitutional challenge who was arguing for a more active role for good faith.

[64] *Barkhuizen*, note 9 supra, para 83.

with the rule of public policy which the majority did accept, namely that a term will not be enforced if it would be contrary to public policy to do so.[65]

In various cases since *Barkhuizen*, the Supreme Court of Appeal has accepted that there can be a constitutionally-inspired public policy challenge to the enforcement of a *prima facie* reasonable contractual term. In *Bredenkamp v Standard Bank of South Africa*,[66] for example, the challenge was to a bank's exercise of a contractual power to close accounts.[67] It failed, because the aggrieved customer had not invoked a particular provision of the Constitution which, it was said, the closure of his accounts contravened, and there was no general obligation to exercise a contractual power fairly. But the court accepted the principle, as it did in *Maphango (Mgidlana) v Aengus Lifestyle Properties (Pty) Ltd*.[68]

12.2.2.3.6 *Barkhuizen: dissentient voices*
The approach of the majority in *Barkhuizen* requires courts to take into account the individual circumstances of the parties as part of the public policy analysis. Moseneke DCJ dissented, opining that ordinarily the determination of a question of public policy should not depend upon such factors. Instead, the question should have been whether the provision itself unreasonably or unjustifiably limited the right to seek judicial redress.[69] That was the traditional approach of the public policy doctrine, which looked to the *tendency* of a clause to have a particular effect. On the majority's approach, identical stipulations in different contracts could be good or bad depending upon the relative situations of the parties to contracts, which rendered whimsical the reasonableness standard of public policy.[70] Moseneke DCJ would have held that clause 5.2.5 was unconstitutional: the period allowed for raising a claim was too short,[71] there was no legitimate purpose for the limitation,[72] and it was insufficiently flexible, as it required strict compliance with the time limits whatever the circumstances.[73] It is suggested below that there is some weight to these criticisms.

---

[65] Ibid para 120.

[66] [2010] ZASCA 75.

[67] The customers concerned were international commodities traders whose accounts were closed after they were listed as 'Specially Designated Nationals' by the United States Department of Treasury's Office of Foreign Asset Control, which administers economic and trade sanctions. They were alleged to have provided financial and logistical support to Mugabe's regime in Zimbabwe.

[68] [2011] ZASCA 191: an unsuccessful challenge to the constitutionality of a landlord's exercise of a power to terminate a lease.

[69] *Barkhuizen*, note 9 supra, para 96.

[70] Ibid para 98.

[71] Ibid para 112.

[72] Ibid para 113.

[73] Ibid para 118.

Sachs J also dissented and would have decided the case on the basis of an objective analysis, as opposed to a consideration of the parties' particular positions. Although section 34 of the Constitution provided the backdrop to his analysis, there was little discussion of the content of that right. Instead, his focus was upon the law's treatment of standard form contracts. A question posed at the outset set the tone for the judgment:[74]

> 'Should considerations of public policy in our present constitutional era compel courts to refuse to give legal effect to an imposed, onerous and one-sided ancillary term buried in a standard form contract that unilaterally and without corresponding advantage, limits the enjoyment of an important constitutionally protected right, namely, that of access to court?'

Sachs J reviewed much of the international debate concerning such contracts, in order to demonstrate that there need be no genuine consensus between the parties to them on all of their terms. He noted that many jurisdictions do not hold all provisions of standard form contracts to be binding[75] and that there had been proposals for statutory reform in South Africa.[76] Far from promoting autonomy, standard form contracts were said to induce automatism.[77] This was all relied upon as giving content to public policy. Sachs J listed a variety of objective factors which established that this clause was contrary to public policy, which included that it was in a standard form document; that it was not one of the actual terms on which reliance was placed when the agreement had been reached; that the time limit was for a period of less than 10 per cent of the statutory limitation period for a contractual claim; and that it significantly limited the right to have a dispute settled by a court, which was a constitutionally guaranteed right.[78] The court did not require further evidence to be able to conclude that enforcing the clause would be contrary to public policy. He rejected the Supreme Court of Appeal's analysis that this was a freely made bargain which contained, at its heart, a limitation of the insured's rights. There is much in the analysis with which one would agree. Indeed, it would be hard not to, given that it has formed the basis for legislative intervention in this field in so many jurisdictions. One wonders, however, whether judicial intervention can provide as effective (or as legitimate) a control for the problem posed by standard form contracts as well-drafted legislation can.

---

[74] Ibid para 123.
[75] He referred to the UK's Unfair Contract Terms Act 1977 and the Council Directive 93/13/EEC on Unfair Terms in Consumer Contracts OJ 1993 L95/29 (ibid at para 164).
[76] Ibid paras 169–74. There has now been legislation in the field: the Consumer Protection Act 2008.
[77] Ibid para 155.
[78] The full list of twelve points is at para 183.

12.2.2.4 Direct application of the Constitution to contractual terms?

We have seen that the predominant approach is to apply the Constitution indirectly, via section 39, and to view constitutional values as giving content to the common law doctrine of public policy. *Barkhuizen* also considered whether the Constitution could be applied directly to contractual terms. The majority of the Constitutional Court, reversing on this point the High Court, held that it could not be. Before the High Court the insured had argued successfully that the time limitation clause could be tested directly against the Constitution. One difficulty which the court had to overcome to reach this result concerned how section 36, which deals with whether the limitation of a constitutional right is justified, could be applied.[79] One of the requirements for a limitation to be permissible is that it must be 'in terms of law of general application'. A contractual term itself could not be tested against section 36, for it is not a law of general application. Instead, the High Court identified the law of general application that was being challenged as the common law rule that contracts are binding and will be enforced. In substance, however, the High Court was testing the content of the limitation clause itself against sections 34 and 36 of the Constitution. Having found that the term in question limited the insured's right under section 34, and that this was not justified, the High Court concluded that the clause (and not the common law principle) fell foul of section 34. Section 172 of the Constitution requires a court to declare 'any law or conduct which is inconsistent with the Constitution' to be invalid. The clause was not 'conduct' and so the High Court held that it was law, and declared that it was inconsistent with the Constitution.

The majority of the Constitutional Court held that this reasoning was flawed. It viewed the dispute as being about whether the clause itself (and not a broader rule of contract law) was inconsistent with section 34. This was what the High Court ultimately found. However, it did so only by holding the clause itself to be 'law' for the purposes of granting a remedy under section 172(1)(a), which was the very thing which earlier in the analysis it had refused to do for the purposes of section 36. The majority of the Constitutional Court viewed these difficulties as indicating that directly testing contractual provisions against provisions of the Bill of Rights was inappropriate.[80] The Chief Justice, however, although concurring in the majority's opinion, reserved his opinion on this point.

---

[79] Section 36(1) provides '[t]he rights in the Bill of Rights may be limited only in terms of law of general application to the extent that the limitation is reasonable and justifiable in an open and democratic society based on human dignity, equality and freedom, taking into account all relevant factors, including: a) the nature of the right; b) the importance of the purpose of the limitation; c) the nature and extent of the limitation; d) the relation between the limitation and its purpose; and e) less restrictive means to achieve the purpose'.

[80] A view followed, and shared, by Wallis AJ in *Den Braven SA (Pty) Limited v Pillay and another* 2008 (6) SA 229 (D) para 30.

12.2.2.5 Beyond public policy

The impact of the Constitution upon the doctrine of public policy has been the focus of commentary, and, indeed, the case law, but it does not exhaust the ways in which the Constitution may affect contract law.[81] Compliance with the Constitution may require more than refusing to give effect to contractual terms (which is what an application of public policy achieves). Various cases bear this out. Constitutional issues can arise in respect of interpretation (for example: does 'family' in a contract include long-term homosexual partners?)[82] Or they may concern particular rules of contract law. In some areas, within the confines of public policy, the law has crystallised into particular rules and these have been subject to constitutional challenge. *African Dawn Properties Finance 2 (Pty) Ltd v Dreams Travel and Tours CC*,[83] for example, considered whether the common law definition of 'usury'[84] required to be revisited in light of the Constitution. Reversing the High Court, the Supreme Court of Appeal concluded that it did not.[85] It has been suggested that the traditional doctrines of duress and undue influence may require to be amended so as properly to give effect to constitutional notions of equality and dignity.[86] Given the wide interpretation of the equality clause of the Constitution (which does not proceed, as does UK discrimination law, by reference to certain protected characteristics), if a party can identify an area where the common law treats him differently from someone in an analogous position, the possibility of a constitutional argument presents itself. In *Janse van Rensburg v Grieve Trust CC*[87] the right to equality in section 9 was relied upon by the Cape Provincial Division in a contract case that is, one might think, as far as it is possible to be from a 'constitutional' case. It concerned the availability of the *actio quanti minoris* to the seller in respect of defects in a trade-in item. It may also be that the constitutional impropriety lies in the parties *not* having contracted, as in *Hoffmann v South*

---

[81] Lubbe, note 6 supra, 404–7. See too the chapter by Laing and Visser in this volume at section 13.3.

[82] *Farr v Mutual & Federal Insurance Co Ltd* 2000 (3) SA 684: a motor insurance policy excluded liability for bodily injuries caused to a member of the policy-holder's family normally resident with him. Applying normal principles of interpretation, this was held to cover a long-term homosexual partner of the policy-holder. Louw J suggested that such an interpretation would also have followed from applying the values of the Bill of Rights. Excluding homosexual partners from the definition of family would not have been in keeping with Constitutional values.

[83] [2011] ZASCA 45.

[84] As requiring either extortion or oppression or something akin to fraud.

[85] Another example are rules concerning the enforceability of covenants in restraint of trade, which have also been the subject of constitutional argument: e.g. *Advtech Resourcing (Pty) Ltd t/a/ Communicate Personnel Group v Kuhn* 2008 (2) SA 375; *Den Braven S.A. (Pty) Limited v Pillay* 2008 (6) SA 229 (D); *Mozart Ice Cream Classic Franchises (Pty) Ltd v Davidoff* 2009 (3) SA 78 (C).

[86] R H Christie *The Law of Contract in South Africa* 5e (LexisNexis 2006) 18–19.

[87] 2000 (1) SA 315.

African Airways,[88] where an applicant for the position of cabin attendant was rejected because he had HIV, which the Constitutional Court held to be unjustified discrimination. There are, therefore, many ways – beyond a challenge to the substance of a contractual term – in which the Constitution can be relevant to contract law.

12.2.3 Observations

Before turning to Scots law, it is useful to highlight some areas of the South African approach which have proven to be particularly controversial. One is the reluctance to apply the Constitution directly in contract cases and a preference instead for using a 'values' analysis to develop the common law. This has been strongly criticised.[89] The process of indirect application envisaged by section 39(2), Woolman argues, was intended as a supplement to and not a substitute for direct application. It was to enable courts to go further than what was required to ensure compliance with constitutional rights, which was the task of section 8. Direct application would entail a black-letter constitutional analysis which asks whether a particular outcome would interfere with the content of a particular constitutional right and whether that interference was justified in terms of the limitation provision of section 36. This would give content to the substantive provisions of the Constitution.[90] Of course, if a court which engages in section 39(2) 'indirect application' asks whether the right is engaged and whether any infringement is justified in terms of section 36, then there is little difference between the two approaches.[91] But it seems more likely that a 'values' analysis will be less rigorous, allowing the exact content of constitutional rights to go unnoticed or more easily to be compromised in favour of other factors which are not recognised by section 36 as grounds for justifying interference with a constitutional right. It permits an interpretative strategy which 'floats so free of the text that it makes any analysis of the specific substantive rights in ss 9–35 superfluous'.[92] Woolman goes as far as to suggest that the current 'values'

---

[88] 2001 (1) SA 1. There the respondent was an emanation of the state, but it is thought that the same approach would have been taken had it been a private employer.

[89] In particular by Woolman, note 6 supra, 762–3, 769, 772–81; Sutherland, note 6 supra, 391–406; Rautenbach, note 6 supra. Other commentators, however, express a preference for the methodology of indirect application: e.g. Bhana and Pieterse, note 6 supra, 870.

[90] Which, one might add, is particularly important in the early years of a constitutional document.

[91] There is some evidence of the courts doing this: *Maphango*, note 30 supra, para 26. If, however, that is the full extent of the court's s 39(2) analysis, it would, presumably, mean that that section is being denied its full effect. It is commonly said that direct and indirect application will not frequently produce different results: Langa CJ in *Barkhuizen* (CC), note 9 supra, para 186; Bhana and Pieterse, note 6 supra, 870.

[92] Woolman, note 6 supra, 771. See, too, Sutherland, note 6 supra, 40, who suggests that it results in the 'dilution' of constitutional rights.

approach is not conducive to the rule of law, because it is insufficiently certain.[93]

It is not immediately clear (to this writer, at least) what is wrong with the High Court's approach in *Barkhuizen* that, when the enforceability of a contractual term is challenged as being incompatible with the Constitution, what is being challenged is the rule of contract law which permits the term to be enforced (or, put another way, the absence of a rule of contract law which provides that the particular term is unenforceable in the circumstances). The difficulties posed by section 172 (and its requirement to declare 'law or conduct' incompatible with the Constitution) can be avoided by the court developing contract law so as to prevent the Constitution from being infringed. If the court declares the term to be unenforceable as a matter of contract law, there is no constitutional incompatibility which need be declared under section 172. The difficulties perceived by the Constitutional Court in identifying the 'law' which is to be declared unconstitutional do not arise. If the court develops the common law of contract to render the contract unenforceable, it prevents there from being any infringement of the Constitution. Furthermore, the term is declared unenforceable because of a rule of contract law, not because of the Constitution. It also seems possible to give the principle *pacta sunt servanda* sufficient weight as part of the section 36 limitation analysis. Analysing the matter through the prism of section 36 would force the courts to engage more with the question of the extent to which the contract in question resulted from an exercise of free will and whether the doctrine of *pacta sunt servanda* justified an interference with the Constitutional right in question.

A second group of observations relates to the focus upon public policy as the means used to ensure that contract law complies with the Constitution. Of course, courts only decide the cases which are litigated and most, so far, have been cases that lend themselves to a public policy analysis. As noted above, however, there is an acceptance that the Constitution can be relevant in other types of case. One wonders whether the same approach of abjuring direct application will be taken in a case where the challenge is to some other rule of contract law. There the Constitutional Court's objection in *Barkhuizen* to direct application (namely, that it was a contractual term and not a rule of contract law which was being tested against the Constitution) would not arise. It might also be suggested that in some types of case public policy is being relied upon where another doctrine of contract law might more suitably provide the private law response to constitutional concerns. Short of the case in which the terms of a contract are so extreme that to enforce it would be an affront to the constitutionally protected right to dignity, one wonders whether giving effect to the constitutional demands of dignity might be better done by means

---

[93] Ibid 763.

of developing the law about defects of consent, duties of information and the like than by relying on the relatively undeveloped tool of public policy.[94]

Even where public policy is the best private law 'tool', it is important to note that, in its constitutional guise, it operates differently from how it does in traditional common law cases.[95] *Barkhuizen* requires a court to consider the parties' bargaining position to assess whether the contract resulted from an exercise of genuine freedom of contract (in which case it will be more difficult to hold a term to be contrary to public policy) or it did not (in which case it will be struck down more easily). This is a more complex analysis than public policy has traditionally required and, although it has logical appeal, one wonders how practical it is. It also means that decisions are more difficult to use as precedents. Further, when public policy is extended to allow challenges to the enforceability of a *prima facie* unobjectionable term because of the circumstances in which it is being enforced, public policy has little in common with 'traditional' public policy doctrine. In fact, it has more in common with the *exceptio doli generalis*, abolished in *Bank of Lisbon and South Africa Ltd*,[96] which had provided a defence to the unfair enforcement of a contract.[97] Presumably courts are reluctant to recreate a free-standing private law concept of 'unconstitutional enforcement' for fear that it would lead to arguments by analogy that the *exceptio doli* should be reintroduced.

A final point to note, indeed the most significant from a comparative perspective, is the emphasis that has been placed upon freedom of contract in the constitutional analysis. Of course, that principle has always been qualified in various respects based either upon the contract's content[98] or the circumstances in which it was concluded.[99] But it is the founding principle of contract law. As well as giving effect to the moral principle that people should keep their promises, the doctrine enhances autonomy and provides the backbone of commerce. It was thought that some way must be found of affording freedom of contract constitutional status itself (either as a value in its own right or as implicit in other recognised rights), for otherwise, in competition with any constitutional right, the balance would always come down in favour of the constitutional right. Courts have striven to find some way to recognise its importance in any constitutional arguments about contract law. Both the Supreme Court of Appeal and the Constitutional Court linked freedom of contract to the constitutional values of freedom and

---

[94] As, indeed, Christie has argued: Christie *The Law of Contract*, note 86 supra, 18–19.
[95] As Moseneke DCJ remarked in *Barkhuizen*, note 9 supra, paras 98 and 104.
[96] 1988 (3) SA 580 (A).
[97] See G Glover 'Lazarus in the Constitutional Court: An Exhumation of the *Exceptio Doli Generalis?*' (2007) 124 SALJ 449.
[98] Via the public policy doctrine.
[99] Via rules regarding duress, misrepresentation, undue influence and the like.

dignity. And both courts, it appears, consider a contract to be an exercise of genuine freedom of contract (and therefore worthy of protection) unless it is demonstrated otherwise by evidence. They differ, however, in the exact weight that they would afford to the concept. The Supreme Court appeared to have viewed a genuine exercise of freedom of contract as trumping any other constitutional rights.[100] Applied literally, this would mean that parties could contract out of *any* constitutional right. The Constitutional Court's approach was different. It recognised that freedom of contract informs the constitutional values of freedom and dignity and that the extent to which the contract was freely and voluntarily concluded is a vital factor that will determine the weight that should be afforded to those values.[101] There was, however, no suggestion, that in order for a constitutional argument to succeed, it must be shown that the contract was not freely concluded. Instead it was said that inequality of bargaining power would *often be* a relevant consideration in the public policy analysis.[102] That is the preferable approach. What is striking, however, about both courts is their apparent willingness to presume that (in the absence of evidence to the contrary) a standard form contract was as much a genuine exercise of freedom of contract as an individually negotiated one.[103] With respect, that appears unrealistic. It may also make litigation prohibitively expensive: it would require evidence to be led, often on very complex issues such as the state of the market and whether a contract on different terms could have been obtained from any other business in the market. Although it is useful that the courts have made clear the types of issue on which they would wish to hear evidence, their breadth is such that such arguments will be difficult and very costly to advance. For many, this approach symbolises the courts' failure to act sufficiently radically in using the Constitution to transform contract law. One does not need to subscribe to that view to be of the opinion that a court which gives 'freedom of contract' the same weight whether the case involves a standard form contract or an individually negotiated contract is not engaging as rigorously as it might do with the balancing exercise inherent in considering whether an interference with a constitutional right is justified.

---

[100] *Barkhuizen* (SCA), note 9 supra, para 27, where it was said that the constitutional challenge would not succeed unless it was shown that the contract had been concluded other than freely.

[101] *Barkhuizen v Napier* (CC), note 9 supra, para 57.

[102] Ibid para 65.

[103] So in *Afrox*, note 8 supra, and *Barkhuizen* the constitutional arguments failed because of a lack of evidence about the respective bargaining power of the parties. Bhana and Pieterse have criticised the assumption of formal equality of bargaining power as in fact entrenching inequality (note 6 supra at 887).

12.3 SCOTLAND

12.3.1 Introduction

The 'constitutionalisation' of contract law has not been nearly as prominent an issue in Scots law as it has been in South African. However, despite the lack of a developed literature, there remains a fair amount to report from Scotland. First, many of the issues which are now being addressed in South Africa as constitutional issues have been addressed in Scotland (as in other parts of the UK) by legislation since the 1960s. Secondly, although there are few Scottish cases in which human rights issues have been addressed in a contractual context, there are now some decisions of English courts grappling with the issues. The framework of human rights protection and these cases form the second aspect of this part of the chapter. Thirdly, questions of the application of the European Convention on Human Rights in a contractual context are beginning to be addressed by the Strasbourg court.[104]

12.3.2 Existing legislation

12.3.2.1 Unfair contractual terms

To a certain extent, constitutional arguments in South Africa have been used to attempt to redress the imbalance of bargaining power which often exists in modern contracts, especially standard forms. As Sachs J illustrated in his dissent in *Barkhuizen*, this issue has been addressed in many countries by legislation. There are two planks to that which apply in Scotland. First on the scene was the Unfair Contract Terms Act 1977 which, despite its name, does not confer a general power on courts to deal with unfair or oppressive terms. Its focus is mostly on terms which seek to 'exclude or restrict' liabil-

---

[104] Another area which might increasingly be relied upon to give effect to human rights principles is EU law. Following the Court of Justice's judgments in Case C-144/04 *Mangold v Helm* [2005] E.C.R. I-9981 and Case C-555/07 *Kücükdeveci v Swedex GmbH & Co KG* [2011] 2 CMLR 27 there has been considerable debate about the extent to which the principle of equality (recognised as a fundamental principle of EU law) has horizontal effect (so as to enable one individual to rely upon it against another in a dispute which comes within the scope of EU law). With the coming into effect of the Charter of Fundamental Rights of the European Union, the influence of EU law appears set to increase. Recently the Grand Chamber of the CJEU held that insurers may not take into account the sex of an insured when calculating risk (Case C-236/09 *Association belge des Consommateurs Test-Achats ASBL and others v Conseil des ministres* [2011] 2 CMLR 38). For reasons of space, issues of EU law are not considered here. For discussion, see T Papadopoulos 'Criticising the Horizontal Direct Effect of the EU General Principle of Equality' [2011] European Human Rights Law Review 437, and O Cherednychenko 'EU Fundamental Rights, EC Fundamental Freedoms and Private Law' [2006] European Review of Private Law 23. For an overview of the provisions of the EU Charter, including a useful comparison with the provisions of the European Convention on Human Rights, see K Beal & T Hickman '*Beano* No More: the EU Charter of Rights After Lisbon' [2011] Judicial Review 113.

ity. It only applies to particular types of contract (most significantly, those to provide services).[105] A term which purports to exclude or restrict liability for breach of duty is void where the exclusion or restriction is in respect of death or personal injury and, in any other case, has no effect if either it was not fair and reasonable to incorporate the term in the contract or if it is not fair and reasonable to allow reliance on the provision.[106] Further protection is provided in respect of consumer or standard form contracts. If it was not fair and reasonable to incorporate a term into such a contract, it cannot have particular effects, such as excluding or restricting liability for breach or allowing a party to render performance substantially different from what the other party reasonably expected from the contract.[107] There are various other provisions, which are not detailed here.

The second plank of the legislation has a broader reach. The Unfair Terms in Consumer Contracts Regulations 1999, passed to implement in the UK an EU Directive on the topic,[108] applies to terms in contracts concluded between a seller or a supplier and a consumer.[109] Unfair terms are not binding upon a consumer.[110] A term is regarded as unfair if, contrary to the requirement of good faith, it causes significant imbalance in the parties' rights and obligations arising under the contract, to the detriment of the consumer. The Regulations provide an indicative list of terms that may be regarded as unfair.[111] This obviously provides a significant control over the content of consumer contracts. An important limitation, however, is that in so far as a term is expressed in plain intelligible language the assessment of fairness shall not relate to certain 'core' areas, namely (a) the definition of the main subject matter of the contract or (b) the adequacy of the price or remuneration, as against the goods or services supplied in exchange.[112]

12.3.2.2 Prohibition upon discrimination

There are also broad statutory prohibitions upon discrimination. Their history began in the 1960s. An increasingly diverse spread of legislation was recently consolidated by the Equality Act 2010.[113] The area of law is too broad to explore in depth here. In overview, the structure of the Act

---

[105] The full list is in s 15(2).

[106] S 16.

[107] S 17.

[108] Council Directive 93/13/EEC on Unfair Terms in Consumer Contracts OJ 1993 L95/29.

[109] Reg 4(1).

[110] Reg 8(1).

[111] Sch 2. Interestingly, in light of *Barkhuizen*, note 9 supra, it includes at (q) 'excluding or hindering the consumer's right to take legal action'. The various examples which it provides do not, however, include subjecting any legal action to short time limits.

[112] Reg 6. Controversially, it was held in *Office of Fair Trading v Abbey National* [2010] 1 AC 696 that bank overdraft charges fell within this exception, as they were part of the overall consideration given by customers for the operation of their accounts.

[113] For analysis and history see B Hepple *Equality: The New Legal Framework* (Hart 2011).

is to stipulate certain 'protected characteristics' (on the grounds of which discrimination is unlawful), to prohibit certain types of conduct in respect of those protected characteristics (direct discrimination, indirect discrimination, harassment and victimisation) and to identify certain circumstances in which the prohibition applies. There is, however, no general prohibition of discrimination. The protected characteristics are: age; disability; gender reassignment; marriage and civil partnership; pregnancy and maternity; race; religion or belief; sex; and sexual orientation.[114] The prohibitions apply, amongst other things, to the provision of services to the public,[115] to the disposal and management of property,[116] and to work (which includes employment and some categories of self-employment).[117] So, for example, a landlord could not refuse to lease premises to a person because he or she was black,[118] or exercise a power under an existing lease for that reason.[119]

12.3.3 The UK framework for applying human rights

Against that backdrop, we turn to consider how arguments relying on the European Convention on Human Rights could be advanced in a contractual context. How can it be said that the Convention, which provides individuals with rights against states, is relevant to contractual disputes between private parties at all? Although the Convention is targeted at states, as its article 1 makes clear, it has been interpreted not only as creating negative obligations on states to refrain from interfering with individuals' rights, but also, in some circumstances, as imposing positive obligations on states to protect Convention rights, including against interference by other private parties. This may require a state to make a particular legal remedy available in a particular situation.

A similar question may be asked of the Human Rights Act 1998, which provides a mechanism for enforcing Convention rights domestically. It, too, is focused upon public bodies: section 6 makes it unlawful for a public authority to act in a way that is incompatible with a Convention right. As Chapter 1 has discussed,[120] there has been a considerable debate about whether the Act can have horizontal effect and, if so, the exact way in which it does so. No doubt this debate is not yet complete, but some points are now clear. First, the obligation imposed by section 3 of the Human Rights Act to interpret legislation compatibly with Convention rights, so far as possible,

---

[114] Equality Act 2010 s 4.
[115] Part 3.
[116] Part 4.
[117] Part 5.
[118] Ss 33(1) and 38.
[119] S 35.
[120] See section 1.3 supra.

applies in cases between private individuals.[121] Secondly, the same is true of the limit on the legislative competence of the Scottish Parliament, which prevents it from legislating incompatibly with Convention rights: that applies even to legislation affecting the relationship between private parties.[122] Thirdly, because courts are themselves public authorities for the purposes of section 6, if the Convention requires a particular outcome, courts are bound not to act incompatibly with that in determining common law claims.[123] This may require the law to be developed (although there may be limits, inherent in the common law method, to how far that development can be made by judges as opposed to by Parliament). Fourthly, when assessing how UK courts are likely to react to arguments based upon the Convention, it is important to bear in mind what has become known as the '*Ullah* principle' or the 'mirror principle'.[124] In *R (on the application of Ullah) v Special Adjudicator*[125] Lord Bingham famously said that '[t]he duty of national courts is to keep pace with Strasbourg jurisprudence as it evolves over time: no more, but certainly no less'. When giving content to the 'Convention rights' which the Human Rights Act rendered enforceable in the UK, British courts will not, as a rule, go further than the Strasbourg jurisprudence has gone.[126] That has obvious consequences for a field such as contract law, where there is, as yet, little Strasbourg jurisprudence.

---

[121] See, e.g., *Ghaidan v Godin Mendoza* [2004] UKHL 30, [2004] 2 AC 557, which concerned the compatibility of provisions of the Rent Act 1977 regarding succession to a tenancy, and *Wilson v First County Trust Ltd (No 2)* [2003] UKHL 40, [2004] 1 AC 816, which concerned the compatibility of provisions of the Consumer Credit Act 1974 (discussed in more detail at note 130 infra.) In *Ghaidan*, Keene LJ addressed the relevance of the fact that the dispute was between private parties in the Court of Appeal: [2003] Ch 380 paras 37–8.

[122] *Salvesen v Riddel* [2012] CSIH 26 is an illustration of this obvious point. Provisions of the Agricultural Holdings (Scotland) Act 2003 relating to the security of tenure of agricultural tenants were held to be incompatible with article 1 of the First Protocol of the European Convention (which protects property). The case involved two private parties. The outcome of an appeal to the Supreme Court is awaited

[123] *McKennitt v Ash* [2006] EWCA Civ 1714, [2008] QB 73 paras 9–10, citing, in particular, *Campbell v MGN Ltd* [2004] UKHL 22, [2004] 2 AC 457 para 132. Cf the more restrictive approach adopted in *Karl Construction Karl Construction Ltd v Palisade Properties Plc* 2002 SC 270 paras 75–6.

[124] Because it means that 'Convention rights' in the Human Rights Act exactly mirror those which the Strasbourg court recognises.

[125] [2004] UKHL 26; [2004] 2 AC 323 para 20. For a recent application in a Scottish case, see *Ambrose v Harris* [2011] UKSC 43, 2011 SLT 1005, in particular paras 17–20.

[126] The principle is controversial and has been the subject of much recent discussion. See, e.g., J Lewis 'The European Ceiling on Human Rights' [2007] *Public Law* 720; Lord Irvine 'A British Interpretation of Convention Rights' [2012] *Public Law* 237; P Sales 'Strasbourg Jurisprudence and the Human Rights Act: A Response to Lord Irvine' 2012 *Public Law* 253. Given the comments in *Sugar v BBC* [2012] UKSC 4, [2012] 1 WLR 439 at para 59 and *Rabone v Pennine Care NHS Trust* [2012] UKSC 2, [2012] 2 WLR 381, paras 111–14, it may not be long until the point is considered in some detail by the Supreme Court.

12.3.4 Domestic case law

As far as I am aware, human rights points have been raised in only two Scottish contract cases, and in neither were they decisive so they were not explored in any detail. In *Robertson v Anderson*[127] Lord Reed raised the possibility that article 6 (which guarantees a right of access to court for the determination of civil rights and obligations) would have needed to be addressed had the court held that a contract to share the winnings of a bingo game was unenforceable.[128] In *X v BBC*[129] interim interdict proceedings were raised to prevent the BBC from broadcasting TV footage of the pursuer. One aspect of the argument was that the contract by which she had consented to the footage being used should be reduced because she had lacked capacity to contract. There were also arguments about whether the broadcast would have interfered with the pursuer's article 8 rights. As these were interim interdict proceedings, the points of law were not definitively resolved. The argument could have been advanced that to enforce the contract and broadcast the material would have infringed the pursuer's article 8 rights (to respect for private and family life) and so should not have been enforced.

12.3.4.1 Compatibility of rule of contract law which renders contract unenforceable

The interplay between human rights and contract law has been addressed slightly more frequently in England, in decisions that would almost certainly be followed in Scotland (even although they are not technically binding). Contract law has many rules that render agreements unenforceable or void in certain circumstances. The House of Lords' decision in *Wilson v First Country Trust Ltd (No 2)*[130] provides some guidance as to whether such rules engage Convention rights. It considered whether provisions of the Consumer Credit Act 1974, which rendered a credit agreement unenforceable if it did not comply with certain formalities,[131] were compatible with article 6 (the right to a fair trial), and article 1 of the First Protocol (the protection of property). The discussion was *obiter*, as the contract had been entered into and litigation in respect of it commenced before the Human Rights Act came into effect.[132] The lender argued that section 127(3) infringed article 6 as it denied recourse to court to determine whether the loan agreement should be enforced. The court expressed the unanimous view that article 6 was not engaged: it was a procedural guarantee and did not guarantee the substantive

---

[127] 2003 SLT 235 (IH).
[128] As the court held that the contract was enforceable, the point did not require to be addressed.
[129] 2005 SLT 796 (OH).
[130] [2003] UKHL 40, [2004] 1 AC 816.
[131] S 127(3), combined with s 65. S 127(3) was repealed by the Consumer Credit Act 2006.
[132] Ibid paras 20, 102, 219–20.

content of rights.[133] The court was also unanimous that there had been no breach of article 1 of the First Protocol in this case, but its reasoning was diverse. Lords Nicholls reasoned that article 1 was engaged[134] – because there was an interference with possessions – but that the interference was justified as it served, and was proportionate to, legitimate policy aims. However, Lords Hope, Hobhouse and Scott[135] would have accepted the argument that article 1 was not engaged by a rule which renders contractual rights unenforceable in particular circumstances, as the rights had been limited by law from their inception. As it was put by Lord Scott, '[n]o authority has been cited ... for the proposition that a statutory provision which prevents a transaction from having the quality of legal enforceability can be regarded as an interference for article 1 purposes with the possessions of the party who would have benefited if the transaction had had that quality'.[136] This is an argument that remains to be determined in a future contractual case. A leading English contract textbook favours Lord Nicholls' approach.[137] Certainly, if one considers the example of a rule of unenforceability which operated in a discriminatory way (perhaps by only rendering agreements made by those of a particular religion or sex unenforceable),[138] this points strongly to article 1 being engaged.

12.3.4.2 Testing the substance of contractual terms against the Convention

English courts have also considered whether a contract should receive effect where the substance of its terms is said to be incompatible with a Convention right. Were such a challenge to succeed, it seems that it would be recognised as giving rise to a new category of contractual illegality.[139] *Stretford v*

---

[133] Ibid paras 32–7, 104–5, 132, 165–6 and 215. Cf *Entico Corp Ltd v UNESCO* [2008] EWHC 531 (Comm) where it was argued that the immunity afforded by UK law to UNESCO which prevented it (in this case) from being sued for breach of contract was in breach of article 6. The English High Court expressed no concluded view on whether article 6 was engaged by such an immunity and held that, even if it was, the infringement pursued the legitimate aim of implementing international obligations in domestic law.

[134] Ibid paras 39–44.

[135] Ibid paras 107, 137 and 168 respectively.

[136] Ibid para 168.

[137] H Beale (ed) *Chitty on Contracts* 30e (Sweet and Maxwell 2008) at para 1–046.

[138] Of which there were certainly examples in Scots law in the past, e.g. the restricted contractual capacity of women and the restrictions imposed on the legal capacity of Catholics. The former rules regarding the capacity of married women are detailed in John L Wark 'Husband and Wife' in Viscount Dunedin (ed) *Encyclopaedia of the Laws of Scotland* vol VII (W Green 1929) paras 1704–1718. For details of the statutory prohibitions upon Catholics holding leases, not abolished until 1829, see J Rankine *A Treatise on the Law of Leases in Scotland* 3e (W Green 1916) 20.

[139] *Chitty on Contracts*, note 137 supra, para 1–056.

Football Association Ltd[140] and *Sumukan Ltd v Commonwealth Secretariat*[141] both considered whether to enforce an agreement to arbitrate would be incompatible with a party's rights under article 6 of the ECHR. Stretford was a football agent. In order to be allowed to negotiate with football players and clubs, he was required to obtain a licence from the (English) Football Association (FA). The licence required him to observe the rules of the FA. It was accepted that this licence amounted to a contract between Stretford and the FA. Rule K contained an agreement to arbitration (which provided that neither party could appeal).[142] Later, the FA instituted disciplinary proceedings against Stretford, who contended that the proceedings did not comply with article 6. He sought a declaration to that effect from the English High Court. The matter fell within the scope of the arbitration clause and the FA sought to have the court proceedings stayed (sisted) in favour of arbitration.[143] *Sumukan* was a commercial contract dispute. Sumukan's predecessor in title had contracted to provide the Commonwealth Secretariat with IT services. The contract provided for the settlement of disputes by arbitration in accordance with the Commonwealth Secretariat Arbitral Tribunal's statute, which contained a clause providing that the judgment of the Tribunal would be final and not subject to appeal. Sumukan sought to appeal the arbitral decision on a point of law to the High Court. The Secretariat argued that it was not entitled to do so.[144] Sumukan argued that the exclusion of a right of appeal would infringe its rights under article 6.

Stretford and *Sumukan* each therefore raise similar issues: first, whether the agreement to arbitrate had been incorporated into the parties' contracts; secondly, if it had been, whether to enforce that agreement would infringe article 6, or, put another way, whether the agreement to arbitrate amounted to a valid waiver of article 6 rights of access to court. In each case the court held that, applying well-established law on the incorporation of terms by reference, the arbitration clauses had been incorporated into the contracts. Although some clauses are so unusual or onerous that they require to be specifically drawn to the attention of the other party in order to be incorporated by reference,[145] these arbitration clauses were not of that type.[146] Further, the

---

[140] [2007] EWCA Civ 238, [2007] Bus LR 1052. The High Court decision (upheld on appeal) is [2007] EWHC 479 (Ch).

[141] [2007] EWCA Civ 243, [2007] Bus LR 1075.

[142] *Stretford* (High Court), note 140 supra, para 20.

[143] Under s 9 Arbitration Act 1996. S 10 Arbitration (Scotland) Act 2010 is the equivalent Scottish provision.

[144] S 69 Arbitration Act 1996 provides for an appeal on a point of law *unless otherwise agreed* by the parties. Rule 69 of the Scottish Arbitration Rules (Sch 1 to Arbitration (Scotland) Act 2010) is the equivalent Scottish provision.

[145] A principle seen most clearly in *Interfoto Picture Library Ltd v Stiletto Visual Programmes Ltd* [1989] QB 433 (CA) 438 and 445.

[146] *Stretford* (High Court), note 140 supra, paras 12–27 (the point was not pursued on appeal); *Sumukan*, note 141 supra, paras 35–52.

Court of Appeal held that to enforce them would not breach article 6. Three points may be observed. First, the Court of Appeal accepted that the Human Rights Act is relevant to a contractual dispute on the basis the court was a public body and is bound to give effect to Convention rights, even in a dispute between private parties. Indeed, the point was not even disputed.[147] Secondly, the court was willing to consider whether common law principles required to be re-interpreted in order to comply with the Convention. In *Sukuman*, for example, it asked whether article 6 considerations would alter the conclusion that the clause was not 'onerous' or 'unusual' when determining whether it had been incorporated by reference into the contract.[148] Thirdly, in both cases the court found the agreement to arbitrate to be a valid waiver of the right to a judicial determination in face of arguments that consent to the contract containing the arbitration clause was not voluntary. On the Court of Appeal's analysis, the Strasbourg case law establishes that certain (but possibly not all) of the component rights in article 6 may be waived. In order for a waiver to be valid, it must have been voluntary and not compulsory and (which was viewed as amounting to the same thing) it must have been given without constraint.[149] In each case, the claimant argued that these requirements had not been met, relying upon the imbalance of power between the contracting parties. This was particularly clear in *Stretford*. Mr Stretford had no option but to accept the term if he wished to continue his business as a players' agent.[150] The Court of Appeal's approach was that, although the Strasbourg jurisprudence does not explain precisely what is meant by constraint, if the agreement to arbitrate was an enforceable contract as a matter of domestic law, that would meet the Convention's requirements. The court noted the existence of principles of duress, undue influence and mistake and also the rules about when terms can be taken to be incorporated into contracts.[151] There was no appetite for an argument that a contractual waiver was not one which was 'freely' agreed for the purposes of the Convention.[152]

---

[147] The point is expressly addressed in *Stretford* (High Court), note 140 supra, para 41. It was a matter of agreement between counsel that, notwithstanding that the FA was not a public body, the article 6 point was relevant.

[148] *Sumukan*, note 141 supra, para 60.

[149] *Stretford*, note 140 supra, paras 45–53; *Sumukan*, note 141 supra, para 57. See S Woolman 'Category Mistakes and the Waiver of Constitutional Rights: A Response to Deeksha Bhana on *Barkhuizen*' (2008) 125 SALJ 10 for an argument that it makes no sense to speak of the 'waiver' of constitutional rights.

[150] *Stretford* (High Court), note 140 supra, para 42.

[151] Ibid para 53.

[152] See, too, Lord Hoffmann's brief treatment of an article 6 argument in *Fiona Trust and Holding Corpn v Privalov* [2007] UKHL 40, [2007] Bus LR 1719 at para 20: 'The European Convention was not intended to destroy arbitration. Arbitration is based upon agreement and the parties can by agreement waive the right to a court. If it appears upon a fair construction of the charter that they have agreed to the arbitration of a particular dispute, there is no infringement of their Convention right.'

One wonders what Sachs J would have made of this aspect of the decision, or what Strasbourg would. It seems unlikely that it can hold true as an absolute proposition that consent to waive a Convention right will be accepted as genuine because it is contained in an enforceable contract. However, the reluctance to probe the genuineness of consent is mitigated by the fact that the nature of consent to the waiver is only one factor in assessing whether it is valid: the arbitral regime for which the contract provided was also relevant. In England (as in Scotland), the law contains various protections against defects in the arbitration procedure that the court took into account in concluding that the parties' agreement to use arbitration instead of court proceedings did not result in a breach of article 6.[153]

English courts have therefore accepted that the Convention can be relevant even in a contractual dispute between private parties: rules of contract law must be Convention-compliant, and the terms of contracts themselves can be challenged if to enforce the contract would infringe the Convention. It is thought that Scottish courts would reach the same conclusion.

12.3.5 Convention case law

Courts in the UK are bound to 'take into account' decisions of the European Court of Human Rights when determining human rights points.[154] Although there are few decisions which consider how the Convention applies to contract law, there are two relatively recent, and significant, decisions which establish that the rules of private law relevant to contract law (such as interpretation) are subject to the Convention and that to enforce the term of a contract can be contrary to the Convention.[155]

12.3.5.1 Interpretation of a private law act contrary to the Convention

Pla & Puncernau v Andorra[156] is a controversial decision which, if interpreted widely, would have profound consequences for freedom of contract. It concerned the interpretation of a will, executed in 1939, by which a testatrix left her estate to her son as tenant in life. The will required him in turn to leave the estate to 'a son or grandson of a lawful and canonical marriage', failing which the children and grandchildren of the remaindermen under the

---

[153] In England an arbitral award may be challenged on the grounds that the arbitrators exceeded their jurisdiction (s 67 Arbitration Act 1996) or that there was a serious irregularity (s 68). In Scotland, the equivalent provisions are rule 67 (jurisdiction) and rule 68 (serious irregularity) Scottish Arbitration Rules (Sch 1 to Arbitration (Scotland) Act 2010).

[154] S 2 Human Rights Act 1998.

[155] See, in addition, the admissibility decision in *X v The Netherlands*, App No 9322/81, 3 May 1983 in which the Commission stated that it was arguable that a state had a duty to ensure that rules adopted by a private association (in that case, the Dutch football association) do not run contrary to the provision of the Convention.

[156] (2006) 42 EHRR 25.

testatrix's settlement were to inherit the estate. The son had no biological children but had adopted and he left the assets that he had inherited from his mother to his adopted son, Antoni. There ensued litigation in Andorra about whether an adopted child qualified as a 'son or grandson of a lawful and canonical marriage'. The first-instance court (the *Tribunal des Batlles*) held that Antoni did fall within that clause but this was reversed on appeal to the High Court. Both courts agreed that the task was to ascertain the testatrix's intention but reached different conclusions as to what that was. The High Court noted that adoption was practically unheard of in Andorra and so concluded that the testatrix was unlikely to have intended to include adopted children within the clause. It also said (and this may have been the fatal line when the matter was considered by the Strasbourg Court) that 'the purpose of a family settlement *si sine liberis decesserit* under Catalan law is to keep the family estate in the legitimate or married family and Catalan legal tradition has always favoured the exclusion of adopted children from such family settlements'.[157] The Fourth Section of the Strasbourg Court held (by majority) that there had been a breach of article 14 in conjunction with article 8.[158]

The case is controversial, for it appears to go further than previous decisions in respect of discrimination against adopted children in the field of succession. The argument was not that Andorra's succession law generally discriminated against adopted children.[159] Rather, the breach lay in the High Court having given effect to this particular will in the way that it did. The concern has been voiced that this decision might open the door to greater intrusion into parties' individual freedom of testation (and, by analogy, of contract).[160] It is tolerably clear, however, that the majority did not hold that the article 14 prohibition upon discrimination applied horizontally, so that there would be an infringement if a testator (or a party to a contract) included a discriminatory term in a will or contract and that was then enforced by a court. The court emphasised that 'no question relating to the testatrix's free will is in issue in the present case'.[161] In a powerful dissent, Sir Nicolas Bratza makes the same point, although he does say that in exceptional cases the Convention may intervene if the term that is sought to be enforced is 'repugnant to the fundamental ideals of the

---

[157] Ibid para 18.

[158] Article 14 prohibits discrimination in the enjoyment of the rights conferred by the Convention. There need be no breach of the 'primary' right before there can be discrimination in respect of it: it suffices that the matters fall within the scope of the primary right.

[159] The type of situation considered in *Marckx v Belgium* (1979) 2 EHRR 330.

[160] R S Kay 'The European Convention on Human Rights and the Control of Private Law' [2005] EHRLR 466.

[161] *Pla and Puncernau*, note 156 supra, para 57. For criticism of the Common Law's approach to discriminatory settlements, see M Harding 'Some Arguments against Discriminatory Gifts and Trusts' (2011) 31 OJLS 303.

Convention' or aims at the 'destruction of the rights and freedoms set forth therein'.[162]

Instead, the basis for the majority's decision was that the Andorran's High Court's interpretation of the will was incorrect: 'son' did not, as it had held, mean only 'biological son'.[163] This meant that its interpretation did not pursue a legitimate aim and had no objective and reasonable justification, both of which are prerequisites to justification under article 14. The majority's readiness to reach this conclusion sits ill with the orthodox assertion that domestic courts are best placed to construe and apply domestic law[164] and that Strasbourg's role is not to provide a further appeal against the determination of domestic law by national courts. It justified its intervention in reliance upon the following passage, which one suspects will become one of those repeated in Strasbourg cases:[165]

> 'Admittedly, the Court is not in theory required to settle disputes of a purely private nature. That being said, in exercising the European supervision incumbent on it, it cannot remain passive where a national court's interpretation of a legal act, be it a testamentary disposition, a private contract, a public document, a statutory provision or an administrative practice appears unreasonable, arbitrary or, as in the present case, blatantly inconsistent with the prohibition of discrimination established by article 14 and more broadly with the principles underlying the Convention.'

The focus by Strasbourg on the national court's *interpretation* of the legal act and its compatibility with the Convention, as opposed to the legal act itself, is welcome. It makes clear that the court was not asserting that article 14 affected the parties' freedom of contract. Much of the criticism of the majority's decision fails to draw this distinction. It proceeds on the basis that interpretation is concerned only with ascertaining intention and that this is simply a question of fact: having ascertained parties' intentions, courts give effect to them. Would that it were that simple. Interpretation, at least in Scotland (and England too), is a question of fact and law.[166] There are rules of law that guide the interpretative process: what Lord Hoffmann referred to as the 'intellectual baggage of "legal" interpretation'.[167] Many of these rules have been discarded in recent years but some remain. There is a difference between a testatrix providing that only a biological child may inherit and a court enforcing that will, and a testatrix providing that any child of the marriage may inherit and the court interpreting that will as meaning that only a biological child may inherit (especially if it does so in reliance upon

---

[162] Ibid para 4 of Sir Nicolas Bratza's dissent.

[163] Ibid para 58.

[164] Ibid para 46.

[165] Ibid 59. See, too, the similar passage at para 46.

[166] *Chitty on Contracts*, note 137 supra, para 12–046; W W McBryde *The Law of Contract in Scotland* 3e (W Green 2007) para 8–11.

[167] *Investors Compensation Scheme v West Bromwich Building Society* [1998] 1 WLR 896 at 912.

statements such as that 'the Catalan legal tradition has always favoured the exclusion of adopted children from such family settlements'). Viewed in that light, as a decision preventing courts from exercising their legal powers of interpretation in a discriminatory manner, the principle of the decision becomes (it seems to me) unobjectionable, Sir Nicolas Bratza's powerful dissent notwithstanding.

12.3.5.2 Contractual terms inconsistent with a substantive provision of the Convention

The Strasbourg court has also held that it can be incompatible with the Convention for the terms of a contract between private parties to be judicially enforced. In *Khurshid Mustafa and Tarzibachi v Sweden*[168] it held that article 10 of the ECHR had been infringed when the private tenants of a private landlord were evicted for breach of a term of their lease which prohibited the erection of outdoor antennae without the landlord's permission. The case is of clear significance for the domestic contract laws of the contracting states. There are, however, real concerns with its approach.

The applicants were of Iraqi origin. As tenants, they used a dish mounted on the outside of their flat to receive TV programmes in Arabic and Farsi. In 2003 a new landlord demanded that they remove the dish. When the tenants refused to do so, the landlord terminated the tenancy and raised proceedings to enforce the termination notice. When the domestic tribunals considered whether to enforce the termination notice which the landlord had served, they engaged in a balancing exercise of the landlord's and tenants' respective interests. The first-instance Rent Review Board found for the tenants, but this was overturned on appeal and the tenants applied to the European Court of Human Rights, alleging infringement of their right to respect for the home under article 8 and their freedom to receive information under article 10.

The first significant aspect of the case is that the court rejected the argument that the complaint was inadmissible because this was simply a contractual dispute. The Swedish Government submitted that the Convention did not apply as all that the Swedish courts had done was interpret and apply the provisions of a contract.[169] The court held both complaints admissible (although it only determined the article 10 complaint).[170] Article 10 can impose a positive obligation on the state to protect the right against interference by private persons.[171] It relied upon the passage quoted above from *Pla & Puncernau v Andorra*[172] and noted that the national court had applied

---

[168] (2011) 52 EHRR 24.

[169] Ibid para 26.

[170] Ibid paras 35, 53.

[171] See, e.g., *Appleby v UK*, App No 44306/98, 6 May 2003 paras 39, 40.

[172] *Mustafa*, note 168 supra, para 33. The wording had changed slightly to become: 'unreasonable, arbitrary, discriminatory or, more broadly, inconsistent with the principles underlying the Convention'. The original quotation is at note 165 supra.

a provision of domestic legislation relating to land and that 'in effect, the applicants' eviction was the result of the court's ruling.' This was sufficient for the Convention to be engaged.

When assessing the merits of the case, the court applied its usual approach to determining an article 10 complaint. It asked first whether there had been an interference with the applicants' article 10 rights. Here, there had been: the applicants' tenancy had been terminated as a result of their having exer-cised their freedom to receive information. Secondly, it asked whether that interference had been 'prescribed by law' and concluded that it had been: by domestic land law and the tenancy agreement. It then moved to the core of the infringement analysis, to ask whether the interference pursued a legitimate aim and whether it was 'necessary in a democratic society', namely whether it was in response to a pressing social need and was proportionate to the legitimate aim. The legitimate aim identified was the landlord's interest in upholding order and good custom.[173] The Strasbourg court, however, held that the interference with the applicants' right was not justified as a response to that aim and that the state had exceeded its margin of appreciation in ordering the tenants' eviction. The court conducted a detailed analysis of the tenants' interest in being able to use the dish,[174] and the impact on them of their eviction, and weighed these against the interests of the landlord which it was said that the prohibition sought to protect.[175] It concluded that none of the interests which the landlord advanced was substantiated and that the interference with the tenants' rights was therefore not justified. This is a very detailed proportionality analysis, weighing one individual's interests directly against another's. However, it appears that the crucial defect with the Swedish Court of Appeal's analysis was that it had held that the appli-cant's right to freedom of information was of no real importance in the case. This allowed the Strasbourg court to conclude that the national court had failed to engage in the requisite balancing exercise. It therefore proceeded to strike the balance for itself, without affording the national court the margin of appreciation that it usually would.[176]

12.3.5.3 Conclusions regarding Strasbourg case law

Mustafa is a Third Section decision and appears to be the first case in which the Strasbourg court has considered whether a state's role enforcing a con-

---

[173] This was viewed as being aimed at the 'protection of the . . . rights of others', within article 10(2).

[174] It emphasised the importance to the applicants of being able to use the dish to maintain contact with the culture and language of their country of origin, especially given they had children.

[175] Protecting against physical and aesthetic damage to the property; protecting the landlord against the risk of being held liable for injuries to others; and preserving emergency access to the flat.

[176] *Mustafa*, note 168 supra, para 48.

tract between private parties can be incompatible with the Convention. As more cases arise, one can expect the arguments to be refined and for there to be continued challenges by states to the applicability of the Convention to purely contractual disputes. This is such a significant issue that some states may push for it to be addressed by a Grand Chamber. However, those states whose laws already recognise that constitutional rights influence contract law are likely to be less concerned by Strasbourg's intervention.[177] The Strasbourg court had not yet clearly articulated the basis on which the Convention applies to contractual cases. The passage from *Pla and Puncernau*, currently used as a justification for the application of the Convention to matters of private law, is vague. Is any 'unreasonable' or 'arbitrary' decision of a national court sufficient? One suspects not. What do those standards require? It is not clear what, if anything, the difference is between something being 'inconsistent with the principles underlying the Convention' and being in breach of the terms of one of the articles of the Convention. Nor is it clear what the passage from *Pla and Puncernau* adds to the more traditional assertion that, in some circumstances, articles of the Convention impose positive duties on states to protect Convention rights even against action by private parties. From *Mustafa* it seems likely that Strasbourg will hold that the Convention is applicable whenever the enforcement of a contract would result in an interference with a Convention right which the State had a positive duty to protect.

A Scottish contract lawyer might be tempted to say that that, leaving aside the possibility of challenging the enforceability of the contract or some of its terms at common law or via unfair contract terms legislation, the parties' contract is determinative of how they have struck the balance between their competing interests. *Mustafa* demonstrates that where there is a Convention right in play, that is not sufficient. However, the court's approach may be criticised because, although the fact that the case involved a contract featured prominently in the court's consideration of the admissibility of the complaint, it was given no weight at all in the court's analysis of whether the interference with the right was justified. The court applied a 'legitimate aim'/'justification' test designed for application to state action directly to the parties' individual interests.[178] It asked whether the landlord had a legitimate aim in including a particular term and weighed that against the impact on the tenant of enforcing the term. In so doing, the court did exactly what it was at pains to emphasise in *Pla and Puncernau* that it would not do: interfere

---

[177] The decision in Mustafa is, for example, strikingly similar to that in a German decision: *Parabolantennae* 2006 *Neue Juristen Wochenschrift* 1062. One doubts, therefore, that German lawyers would find the idea of the Convention being relevant to this type of dispute as odd as lawyers from the UK do.

[178] One wonders why it was not argued that the landlord's article 1 of the First Protocol rights should have been considered as part of the balance.

with the parties' free will. No weight was afforded to the *public* interest in enforcing contracts and in maintaining the freedom of contract (emphasised so clearly in the South African cases).[179] Of course, once one does recognise the value of freedom of contract, the difficulty arises of determining how much weight should be afforded to it, in particular in cases where it is thought that the contract was not freely concluded because it is a contract of adhesion. It must, however, receive *some* weight and, in *Mustafa*, it did not.[180]

12.4 CONCLUSION

What lessons, if any, may Scotland and South Africa learn from each other? When it comes to the substance of rights, directly controlling the outcome of a contractual dispute, the scope for mutual learning appears limited. The South African Constitution and the European Convention on Human Rights are very different instruments, the former by far the broader of the two, in particular in its recognition of various social and economic rights. Further, the South African Constitution recognises a right to dignity and a free-standing right to equality, both of which feature heavily in the jurisprudence concerning contracts. The European Convention recognises neither. The fact that in a South African case, say, a particular argument was advanced based on the right to healthcare is interesting, no doubt, for a Scots contract lawyer, but not particularly relevant to a case on which he or she is advising given the absence of a similar right in the European Convention. And from the South African perspective, the fact that any argument that the European Convention requires states to recognise a general duty of good faith between contracting parties would certainly fail before Strasbourg is of no real relevance to a South African lawyer seeking to argue that the South African Constitution requires such a rule to be adopted in South Africa. These structural differences mean that it is not just a question of time before Scotland, and Europe, 'catches up' with South Africa in this field. Although the UK Human Rights Act is fairly recent, the European Convention itself is a well-established instrument. Of course, Strasbourg jurisprudence is constantly evolving, but experience over the period in which the Convention has been in force bears out that its relevance for contract cases is inherently more limited than that of the South African Constitution. For various reasons, not least the different socio-political backdrop which meant that there was a real impetus to argue for reform, it is

---

[179] See text to notes 36–40, 48, 54–6, 98–103 supra.
[180] Even had it done so, the result in *Mustafa* may not have been different since the largest problem with the Swedish Court of Appeal's decision was that it had failed to accept that the applicant's freedom to receive information was a real consideration at all: (note 168 supra, at 48).

genuinely possible to talk in South Africa of a 'constitutionalisation' of contract law (that is, a process by which the rules of contract law are reformed so that they are compatible with the values and rules of the Constitution). In this writer's view, at least, use of such a term would be unjustified in Scotland.[181]

All that having been said, Scots courts will almost certainly have to deal with a contract case which raises human rights elements, just as the Strasbourg and English courts have done.[182] There will be an influence upon contract law, but it will be on a far smaller scale than in South Africa. Scots (like other European) lawyers can learn a lot from considering *how* South African courts are approaching issues of human rights that arise in a contractual context – the structure of their analysis – even if the substantive arguments about the contents of rights are of less relevance. The position reached in South Africa, of recognising that constitutional rights can be relevant both for challenging a rule of contract law and in order to challenge a term of a contract, via a flexible concept of illegality or public policy, is useful. It would almost certainly be followed in Scotland. It is thought, however, that Scots law would, and should, abjure the 'values-based' analysis which has been taken in South African cases in favour of a more rigorous analysis of whether one of the Convention rights is engaged and, if so, whether the interference with it is justified. South African courts, too, might wish to give thought to that approach. By far the most important issue which the South African courts have grappled with when establishing the framework for analysing human rights issues in contractual disputes is the question of how much weight should be afforded to the value of freedom of contract in a human rights balancing exercise. The South African jurisprudence serves as a clear reminder of the importance of this concept, even if the exact weight that it should bear in the constitutional balancing exercise is yet to be worked out. The Strasbourg court has yet seriously to engage with this issue, and so have the courts in Scotland and elsewhere in the UK. This may be one point on which, when the next chapter such as this comes to be written, there will be enough material from Scotland, England and the Strasbourg court to allow the comparative exercise to be more balanced.

---

[181] Although there has been more general discussion of the 'constitutionalisation' of private law: Lord Reed 'The Constitutionalisation of Private Law: Scotland' (2001) 5 EJCL (available at *http://www.ejcl.org/52/art52–4.html*).

[182] One issue which seems almost guaranteed to arise – albeit that it would probably be viewed more as an issue of property than contract law – is whether the (supposedly, but self-evidently not, purely procedural) requirement imposed by article 8 that a tenant be able to challenge the proportionality of his or her eviction will apply to eviction by private landlords. When that point is considered by Strasbourg, there will be an opportunity for further insight into how that court views the Convention as applying to purely private law disputes between private parties.

Chapter 13

Principles, Policy and Practice: Human Rights and the Law of Contract

Sheldon Laing and Daniel Visser

13.1 THE PRESSURE OF THE PUBLIC ON THE PRIVATE

The experience of the post-Second-World-War period in countries that have adopted human-rights instruments has been a pervasive pressure (either at the time of drafting or at some time after promulgation) to extend, in one form or another, the rights in such instruments to the dealings between private individuals and/or corporations. South Africa was no exception. Because this country came to democratic constitution-making only at the end of the twentieth century, it had the benefit of much comparative learning and decided to include in its post-apartheid Constitution a Bill of Rights which expressly brought the constitutional values into the private sphere. On the one hand, the advantage of being able to learn from the experience of others allowed South Africa to nail down some issues more quickly than many countries that had to struggle with the same questions without comparative guidance. On the other hand, the suddenness of the constitutionalisation of private law in South Africa also means that the legal system as a whole has not fully come to terms with the process of bringing constitutional values into the dealings between individuals. Thus we still have some learning to do – and a central part of this learning, we believe, is to think harder about, first, *what we really seek to achieve* when we apply a human rights instrument to the relationship between parties where one is not the state, and, secondly, *how we should apply* that instrument in different conditions.

The purpose of this chapter is to address these two issues, but before doing so, it is important to note that our chapter is one of two dealing with the law of contract in this book. Peter Webster has made a comprehensive and elegant analysis of both Scots and South African law in Chapter 12 of this volume, and that affords us the opportunity to devote this chapter to a second interpretation of the state of the application of human rights to the law of contract in South Africa. Webster (quite correctly) states that, because of the differences between the relevant human-rights instruments applicable in South Africa and Scotland – respectively, the South African Constitution and the European Convention on Human Rights (ECHR) – it is unlikely that there will be direct influence of the one on the other in a conventional, substantive sense. Rather, he says, 'Scots (like other European) lawyers can learn a lot from considering *how* South African courts are approaching issues of human rights which arise in a contractual context – the structure of their analysis – even if the substantive arguments about the contents of rights are of less relevance.'[1] The central aim of this chapter ties into this objective, because its purpose is exactly to look more closely at the importance of *how* to do the job of bringing human rights into the law of contract – and therefore we think it will be of relevance to both Scots and South African lawyers. (At the same time, the fact that Scotland is able to maintain an efficient system of contract with very little emphasis on human-rights instruments is in itself an object lesson for South Africa, in that it demonstrates that, even though the influence of the Constitution in the contract arena has been less than in, say, delict or property, it has nevertheless been appreciable when compared to other countries.)

Let us now turn to the two issues that form the burden of this contribution.

13.2 WHAT WE SEEK TO ACHIEVE WHEN APPLYING A HUMAN RIGHTS INSTRUMENT TO PRIVATE LAW: THE RELEVANCE OF THEORY

Bringing human rights into private law, we believe, is intimately linked to the theoretical underpinnings of the law. To this end, we consider, first, the importance of certainty and coherence in the law of contract and, secondly, what kind of justice it is that the law is seeking to promote – since finding the right balance between certainty (which is vital to the success of the law of contract in any economy) and justice (which is the primary aim of the constitution) lies at the heart of an appropriate contract regime in the constitutional era.

13.2.1 Certainty and coherence

It is useful to outline the context in which the courts may develop the common law so as to lay bare the limitations they face. In a system of precedent such as our own, consistency is highly valued, but so too is development to adapt to the changing needs of society. Joseph Raz sets up a structural tension between the values of legal certainty and coherence on the one hand, and those of equity and legal development on the other. The insistence on upholding the values of certainty and coherence – that is to say, the insistence on consistency – is not merely the defensive rumblings of conservative, formalist judges: these values can also be seen to be located in the Constitution, as Harms DP notes in *Bredenkamp v Standard Bank of South Africa Ltd*:

---

[1] See section 12.4 infra.

'A constitutional principle that tends to be overlooked when generalised resort to constitutional values is made is the principle of legality. Making rules of law discretionary or subject to value judgments may be destructive of the rule of law.'[2]

On the other hand, a powerful argument can also be made in favour of a lesser role for constraints on the exercise of the courts' power. In an influential article, Lubbe notes that

'the perception that the elasticity and flexibility of decision-making based on open norms should be restricted in order to protect legal doctrine is . . . misconceived. Denying flexible instruments a role in the regulation of contractual conduct would . . . stand in the way of treating unlike cases differently, and so heighten the risk of injustice in particular cases.'[3]

However, the adjudication of private-law disputes in a constitutional setting need not amount to a choice between legal certainty and flexibility: after all, the requirement of certainty has a bearing on *which* flexible instruments will be used and *how* they will be employed – for example, the value of certainty has clearly played a role in the rejection of good faith in favour of public policy as the open-norm of choice in South Africa.

The insistence on certainty and coherence is, furthermore, a rejection of the notion of parallel streams of law. We adopt as our starting point the statement of Justice O'Regan in *Khumalo v Holomisa*,[4] namely *that there is one law in South Africa* – not a Constitution and, separate from it, private law. This sentiment contains the clue to incorporating human rights into a legal system in a way that will preserve the essential requirements of consistency and coherence – without which there is little point in having a legal system. The advantage of law as we know it is that it is predictable. If it did not have that quality, we might as well just choose wise men to rule on our disputes according to their own lights. That we have this facility of a predictable set of rules to govern our disputes is Rome's gift to us; if instead we had inherited the approach of ancient Greece – which was far less clear about the dividing line between law and morality – we would not have had quite the same sharp tool that has served the world so well. And predictability means that precedent, in one form or another, is necessary to ensure that the system as a whole remains integrated and coherent. The principle of one law also means that where legislation gives effect to a right, it is not necessary to develop the common law. We will return to this point below when considering how legislation has altered the future landscape of common-law development.

---

[2] 2010 (4) SA 468 (SCA) para 39.
[3] G Lubbe 'Taking Fundamental Rights Seriously: The Bill of Rights and its Implications for the Development of Contract Law' (2004) 121 SALJ 395 at 417.
[4] 2002 (5) SA 401 (CC).

13.2.2 *Corrective justice versus distributive justice*

It is often said that private law is based on notions of corrective justice, in terms of which the courts restore a pre-existing balance between two parties, one or both of which have had their rights disturbed in some way. Corrective justice assumes that a state of equality or balance pre-existed the disturbance, be it a delict, a breach of contract or something of a similar nature, and seeks to restore the parties to the positions they were in before the disturbance occurred. The animating principle of correlativity requires restoring the wrongful or unjust gain from the person who benefits from a wrong to the person who has suffered a loss. Corrective justice, then, is about restoring a pre-existing and value-neutral balance and is contrasted with distributive justice, in terms of which external criteria of merit or need determine how rights and duties are to be apportioned. Corrective justice provides an attractive account of some aspects of private law,[5] such as unjustified enrichment, but it is by no means a complete one. A wholesale commitment to a corrective-justice explanation of private law takes for granted the primacy of the pre-existing balance or existence of rights, thereby ignoring the courts' distributive and inescapably political role in recognising new rights and duties. Left unchallenged, an over-reliance on this understanding of private law, and contract in particular, can have a stifling effect on legal development. To quote our former Chief Justice: 'There is no longer place for assertions that the law can be kept isolated from politics. While they are not the same, they are inherently and necessarily linked.'[6]

We take this to mean that the courts in some instances, namely those that involve recognising new legal rights and duties, are not merely neutral arbiters restoring balance, but are engaged in 'political' decisions about how to apportion rights and duties in accordance with the demands of the Constitution. While the reluctance to engage in more extensive development may also be explicable in terms of a legal culture which underemphasises the political or distributive role played by the courts, such an explanation is best used sparingly. In this regard, accusations that notions of formalism and conservatism are behind those instances where there is a lack of development in our law are disingenuous, since they overlook constraints such as the rule of law and separation of powers, which rightfully restrict more activist interventions. The question, then, is how are judges to engage appropriately with the political or distributive aspects of the law?

To begin, the courts must become acutely aware of those aspects of the law that have come to embody particular values or political stances. As Lubbe notes:

---

[5] In particular the procedural/transactional aspects of delict and breach of contract.
[6] P Langa 'Transformative Constitutionalism' (2006) 17 Stellenbosch LR 351 at 353.

'Above all, there is a need to understand the ethical principles and social policies underlying even the most technical rules and concepts of the common law. This should enable better evaluation of the adequacy of traditional doctrine against the constitutional value-system that now provides the direction in which solutions are to be found.'[7]

The degree to which the constitutional value system provides judges with clear directions varies. In some cases the facts are such, and the rights in question are clearly sufficiently articulated, that the Constitution does in fact provide direction to the courts; but in others the open-ended nature of the applicable rights does not provide indisputable direction to the courts and they are required to make political, or if you prefer, policy, decisions – even if they would sometimes prefer not to do so. The then Deputy President of the Supreme Court of Appeal, Mr Justice Louis Harms, in a 2007 speech entitled 'Judging under a Bill of Rights', took aim at the legislature for forcing the courts to make the difficult political decisions it does not want to make: 'Politicians who are unwilling to make difficult or unpopular decisions that are able to hide behind a bill of rights, not only when drafting it but also thereafter'.[8] What is clear, however, is that the courts are, on a regular basis, faced with the challenge of having to align private law to the values of the Constitution, and they have made considerable strides in doing so. The remainder of this contribution is devoted to how the courts have thus far – and should in future – manage this alignment.

13.3 HOW TO INSERT HUMAN RIGHTS INTO THE LAW OF CONTRACT

13.3.1 *The role of 'fairness', 'good faith', 'equity' and 'public policy'*

13.3.1.1 The historical development and the emergence of public policy as the preferred device

The rise in South African law of public policy as the primary device to alleviate contractual excess (and the concomitant restriction of fairness, good faith and equity as 'free-floating' principles) must be our starting point when considering the practical means by which human rights are inserted into the body of private law. The rejection by the Appellate Division – as it then was – of the general equitable defence, the *exceptio doli generalis*, available in Roman law and for some time under South African law, is the beginning of this story. In *Bank of Lisbon v De Ornelas*[9] the majority of the court, per Joubert JA, after careful examination, concluded that this rule was never

---

[7] Lubbe, note 3 supra, at 423.
[8] L Harms 'Judging under a Bill of Rights' (2009) 12 *Potchefstroom Electronic LJ* 16.
[9] 1988 (3) SA 580 (A).

received into our law and consequently barred its future application. The decision sparked much debate. Some viewed the demise of the *exceptio* as a loss of judicial discretion to temper the strict application of *pacta servanda sunt*.[10] The concern over the majority judgment in *Bank of Lisbon* is understandable: Zimmermann points out that the *exceptio* was variously used to 'legitimize the introduction'[11] of the doctrine of estoppel, to make 'the equitable remedy [of rectification] palatable to South African lawyers',[12] and to 'provide a convenient screen behind which an entirely new doctrine [of innocent misrepresentation] could be introduced'[13] into South African law. Since the *exceptio* has, over time, come to be equated with the various equitable doctrines it helped to infuse into the South African common law, there was of course a danger that the revocation of this 'passport'[14] (the *exceptio*) could endanger the legal citizenship of the aforementioned doctrines which had since become naturalised in South African Law. Indeed, Jansen JA's dissenting judgment in *Bank of Lisbon* supports Zimmermann's characterisation of the *exceptio* as a temporary guide on the road to a more equitable law of contract, but he felt that it was too soon to do away with it altogether:

> 'In our law the requisite of good faith has not as yet absorbed the principles of the *exceptio doli* nor has the concept of *contra bonos mores* as yet been specifically applied in this field. To deny the *exceptio* right of place would leave a vacuum.'[15]

Jansen JA identifies the elements of *contra bonos mores* or public policy[16] and good faith as two avenues for development which may, given more time, more naturally have replaced the *exceptio*. The courts were quick to develop further[17] the avenue of public policy, beginning with *Sasfin v Beukes*,[18] which, according to Christie, 'may be taken as the starting point of the modern law of illegality or unenforceability of contracts by common law'.[19] More

---

[10] A J Kerr has repeatedly called for its reintroduction and suggested that the courts have gone so far as to resurrect the *exceptio*, if under different names: see 1991 (108) *SALJ* 583 on *Van der Merwe v Meade* , Kerr 2008 (125) *SALJ* 241 on *Barkhuizen v Napier* 2007 (5) SA 323 (CC).

[11] R Zimmermann 'Good Faith and Equity' in R Zimmermann and D Visser (eds) *Southern Cross: Civil Law and Common Law in South Africa* (Oxford University Press 1996) 223.

[12] Ibid 228.

[13] Ibid 230.

[14] Trollip JA at note 45 in *Connock's Motors v Sentraal Westelike Ko-operatiewe Maatskappy Bpk* 1964 (2) SA 47 (T); see also Zimmermann, note 11 supra, at 223.

[15] Jansen JA in *Bank of Lisbon*, note 9 supra, at 616 C-D.

[16] Smalberger JA in *Sasfin (Pty) Ltd v Beukes* 1989 (1) SA 1 (A) recognised that the terms *contra bonos mores* and public policy were interchangeable in the context of contracts that are illegal or unenforceable at common law. See also S W J van der Merwe, L F van Huyssteen, M F B Reynecke and G F Lubbe *Contract: General Principles* 4e (2012) 166–8 and the case cited therein.

[17] Develop further because our courts have long held that contracts which are contrary to public policy or the *boni mores* are illegal or unenforceable.

[18] 1989 (1) SA 1 (A).

[19] R H Christie *The Law of Contract in South Africa* 5e (Butterworths 2006) 343. Jansen JA

recently the court has reiterated[20] that the element of good faith will have no direct role in filling Jansen JA's perceived vacuum: in *Brisley v Drotsky*[21] (later confirmed in *Afrox Healthcare Bpk v Strydom)*[22] the Supreme Court of Appeal stressed that even under the Constitution, principles of good faith, justice and reasonableness could not operate on their own to override the sanctity of contract, but must instead inform existing rules on contract law.[23] Parties could not seek to escape liability on the grounds that to impose liability is not fair, for these values and principles do not operate in isolation and must instead be 'discounted and balanced against other principles and policy concerns relevant to the overall aims of contract law'.[24] Crucially, the device of public policy was identified as an avenue through which constitutional values may be given effect.[25] Of further significance in *Brisley* and *Afrox* is the location of the principle of *pacta sunt servanda*, long a core requirement of public policy, in the web of constitutional values. In *Brisley v Drotsky* Cameron JA in the Supreme Court of Appeal stated that 'the Constitution's values of dignity and equality and freedom require that the courts approach their task of striking down contracts or declining to enforce them with perceptive restraint', and added that

> 'one of the reasons, as Davis J has pointed out, is that contractual autonomy is part of freedom. Shorn of its obscene excesses, contractual autonomy informs also the constitutional value of dignity.'[26]

This theme was taken up by the SCA in *Afrox Healthcare Bpk v Strydom*,[27] a case about an exemption clause exonerating a hospital from liability for negligence, where Brand JA confirmed the elevation of contractual freedom (and within it the principle of *pacta sunt servanda*) to a constitutional principle.

Cameron JA in *Napier v Barkhuizen* (SCA decision) reiterated that the law of contract was subject to the Constitution, that constitutional values had to be taken into account when developing the law, and that public policy – rooted in the Constitution – allowed the courts to strike down contractual

---

opined in *Bank of Lisbon* at 617 F-H that the *exceptio* is closely related to the defences based on public policy (interest) or *boni mores* and that [c]onceivably they may overlap: to enforce a grossly unreasonable contract may in appropriate circumstances be considered as against public policy or *boni mores*.

20 Although there is much recent case law on this point, fairness as a general ground to resist the enforcement of contracts was rejected over a century ago in *Burger v Central South African Railways* 1903 TS 571 LA.

21 2002 (4) SA 1 (SCA).

22 2002 (6) SA 21 (SCA).

23 Lubbe, note 3 supra, at 397–8.

24 Ibid at 398.

25 Cameron JA commenting on *Brisley* in *Napier v Barkhuizen* 2006 (4) SA 1 (SCA) para 6.

26 *Brisley v Drotsky*, supra note 22, at para 94.

27 2002 (6) SA 21 (SCA).

terms thought to violate constitutional rights.[28] The Constitutional Court[29] affirmed, per Ngcobo J,[30] that the public policy approach to challenging allegedly unconstitutional contractual terms was correct.[31] One argument advanced in support of this affirmation was that such an 'approach would allow proper space for balancing the principle of freedom of contract against the values enshrined in the Constitution'.[32] On the facts, the majority held that a time-bar clause in a contract of insurance was not *per se* against public policy, nor would it be against public policy to enforce it in the particular circumstances. The decision to enforce the term was reached on account of a lack of evidence to illustrate that it would be against public policy to enforce it in the circumstances – and the court expressly mentioned the lack of evidence relating to the relative bargaining power of each party.[33] This leaves open the possibility that there may be instances in which the courts would decline to enforce such a term in the future. Ngcobo J refers to the hypothetical situation in which the insured was unable to act within the time limitation due to being in a coma,[34] although Harms DP rightly points out in *Bredenkamp v Standard Bank of South Africa Ltd*[35] that 'application of the *lex non cogit ad impossibilia* rule could conceivably solve the problem'[36] of that example. He suggests as a better hypothetical example a situation in which there was lack of compliance because the defendant, or the plaintiff as the case may be, was unable to afford a lawyer.[37]

In *Barkhuizen* a majority in the Constitutional Court set out a test and then applied that test to make its finding on the facts. This constitutes the highest precedent in South African law on the general principles of validity and enforceability of terms alleged to be contrary to public policy, and more specifically on time-bar clauses. *Barkhuizen*'s two-stage test brought together (a) the long-standing principle that contractual terms which are contrary to public policy are invalid and (b) the courts' power to decline to enforce an otherwise valid term where to do so would be against public policy.[38]

---

[28] P J Sutherland 'Ensuring Contractual Fairness in Consumer Contracts after *Barkhuizen v Napier*' 2007 (5) SA 323 (CC)' – Part 1 (2008) 19 Stellenbosch LR 390 at 393.

[29] In *Barkhuizen v Napier* 2007 (5) SA 323 (CC).

[30] The dissenting judgments of Sachs J and Mosoneke J (concurred in by Mokgoro J) also treat the public policy approach as the correct one. Only Langa CJ's separate concurring judgment raised the possibility that contractual provisions could be tested directly against the Constitution in some instances: see Sutherland, supra note 28, at 395.

[31] *Barkhuizen v Napier*, supra note 29, at para 30.

[32] Sutherland, supra note 28, at 394–5.

[33] *Barkhuizen*, supra note 29, at para 66.

[34] Ibid at para 69.

[35] 2010 (4) SA 468 (SCA).

[36] Ibid at para 46.

[37] Ibid.

[38] In *Brisley v Drotsky* the majority recognised and adopted the approach to public policy in *Magna Alloys* and seemed to be prepared to accept that the *Sasfin* principle applied not

Bredenkamp is also important for Harms DP's reiteration that fairness cannot be relied upon directly as a general principle in the law of contract[39] and that considerations of fairness, where relevant, must find expression through the public policy approach.[40]

Finding clauses to be unenforceable 'in light of the circumstances' encompasses subjective factors pertaining to the particular circumstances of the parties at the time that enforcement is sought and has led some to suggest that it is, in substance, much the same as the *exceptio doli generalis*.[41] Others have suggested that the effect of *Barkhuizen* was to revive the *exceptio*. This contention was strongly rejected in *Bredenkamp* by Harms DP. In doing so, and seeking to explain the references to the *exceptio* in a series of cases, the learned judge notes that '[a]s in German law . . . [it] was simply a convenient label for a number of rules but it had no specific content'[42]

(It is worth interpolating at this stage the caveat that, while our focus here is specifically on the role of constitutional principles in determining public policy, this focus should not create the impression that the Constitution is the sole source of public policy. While public policy is now firmly rooted in the Constitution, it is not the only source of the content of public policy, with considerations of social and economic expediency remaining very relevant. Indeed, it must constantly be kept in mind that public policy is a very wide and all-encompassing term, which gives tremendous flexibility to judges.)

13.3.1.2 Why public policy rather than good faith?

It is now clear that there is no *numerus clausus* of types of contracts or contractual terms the validity, and more importantly the enforceability, of which a court will enquire into when a public policy consideration can be identified. Considering the wide variety of criteria that have been identified as relevant to a consideration of what public policy requires,[43] it is fair to say that in almost every conceivable case a party could challenge, if not the validity, then the enforcement of a term. What then of legal certainty? The rejection of the *exceptio doli*, and more importantly of good faith and fairness as free-floating values, owes much to the court's insistence on legal certainty and the dangers of allowing judges to impart their individual sense of fairness to contractual disputes. But if the enforcement of almost every contractual

---

merely to cases where the provision was in itself illegal (op sigself . . . ongeldig), but that it could be extended to prevent the enforcement of a provision that was not in itself contrary to public policy (Lubbe, supra note 3, at 413).

[39] *Bredenkamp*, supra note 35, at paras 27–30.

[40] Ibid at para 51.

[41] See G Glover 'Lazarus in the Constitutional Court: An Exhumation of the *exceptio doli generalis*?' (2007) 124 SALJ 449.

[42] *Bredenkamp*, supra note 35, at para 34.

[43] Sutherland, supra note 28, at 407.

term is open to challenge, how can the courts honestly insist that certainty is not compromised? Furthermore, what is there to recommend the public policy approach over the avenues that the courts have rejected? [44] As Davis J notes:

'[T]he courts have never offered a plausible justification as to why good faith should be regarded as so imprecise and vague a notion that it cannot be employed as compared, for example, to public policy which is rooted in human dignity, the achievement of equality and the advancement of human rights and freedoms, non-racialism and non-sexism. To be sure, the concept of dignity has hardly been immune from such critique, but that has not proved an obstacle to its employment.'[45]

However, insisting on an approach based on public policy has some benefits, at least one of which is that it accords with the notion of retaining an economy of concepts in the common law. But having fewer doctrinal labels is of little use when this comes at the expense of clarity and certainty. A better argument in support of the present line of development is that public policy, although an open-ended norm, is one that has received greater attention from our courts than the competing alternatives. While there is no comprehensive delineation of what constitutes illegality,[46] there is an established body of case law in a variety of factual settings which may serve to guide the courts. Admittedly there is less certainty at present regarding the likely enforcement of time-bar clauses than there is in other areas of contract law such as restraints of trade or contracts that undermine marriage, but this is a function of the relative novelty of challenges to such clauses – and common-law development is of course always gradual.

13.3.1.3 The future: challenges to the development of public policy as a device

First, in developing public policy in the future, it will be important to keep the following extra-curial observation by Mr Justice Brand in mind:

'Further development and fine tuning of public policy as an instrument in the present context, will also require greater awareness and imagination on the part of practitioners. Take *Afrox* as an example. If it had been pleaded and argued that any contractual exemption from liability for death and/or personal injury is per se contrary to public policy, the result may very well have been different. It may also have made a difference – both in *Afrox* and in *Barkhuizen* – if the response had been pertinently raised and then supported by the evidence, that the indemnity clauses were unnecessary and/or unduly oppressive, and/or that the bargaining

---

[44] Sutherland, ibid at 403, regards the justifications offered in support of the public-policy approach as unconvincing.

[45] *Mort NO v Henry Shields-Chiat* 2001 (1) SA 464 (C) 475B-F.

[46] See generally van der Merwe et al, supra note 16, at 165ff.

position of parties was so unequal that the plaintiff in reality had no say at all. And maybe the fine tuning of "public policy" may also require greater activism and ingenuity on the part of the judiciary than they have hitherto displayed.'[47]

Secondly, there is a need to concretise public policy in as many instances as possible – the move from the general to the specific and thus to build incrementally the profile of public policy in each of the typical contractual contexts in which it might play a role. In this context of incremental change, Lubbe points to the successes of the German *Fallgruppen* approach to developing the law and calls for its application in the South African context:

> 'Here [i.e. in Germany] the experience has been that open norms such as that embodied in § 242 BGB often yield large numbers of decided cases. In order to reduce the resulting complexity, these decisions are initially loosely classified into sub-groups on the basis of perceived factual commonalities. Further analysis of such provisional classificatory schemes often brings to light deeper fact patterns and variable features that are normatively significant. These refined distinctions in turn yield legal principles underlying the cases, which then form the bases for the development of new juridical categories and detailed technical rules.'[48]

The device of public policy will continue to be used to craft adequate responses to individual cases, and over time patterns will emerge based on factual similarities which can then be further deduced into black-letter law or clear rules. We know of no bar to a *Fallgruppen*-type approach and it seems that our courts and academic writers engage in a similar approach, as is evident from the multitude of decisions regarding the enforceability of contracts in restraint of trade and the categories, rules and tests that have emerged therefrom. It is not unusual to find references to restraint-of-trade cases in discussions about developing other areas of the law of contract (both in judgments and scholarly publications). This is presumably because the case law on enforcing restraint of trade is an excellent example of how the device of public policy may be used to develop relatively coherent and certain legal principles which ordinary citizens can use to guide their conduct, while at the same time alleviating the inequitable excesses that a stringent emphasis on the sanctity of contract might produce.

Thirdly, for the sake of certainty, our courts need to be ready to engage in the public-policy enquiry rather than avoid it through 'convenient findings of fact'. Take for example the following dictum of Harms DP in *Bredenkamp*:

> 'I would be surprised if the judgment of Ngcobo J holds that an agreement to pay a loan on demand or on a given agreed day requires for enforcement an inquiry into

---

[47] F D J Brand, 'The Role of Good Faith, Equity and Fairness in the South African Law of Contract: The Influence of the Common Law and the Constitution' (2009) 126 SALJ 71 at 89 (footnotes omitted).

[48] Lubbe, supra note 2, at 404–5 (footnotes omitted).

the reasonableness of the creditor's decision to rely on the contractual right. It would mean that the debtor could argue that he needs time to pay; that the creditor does not require the money on the given day; and that enforcement could lead to the debtor's sequestration – all very unfair.'[49]

Of course the judge is correct in saying that these clauses normally require nothing more to be enforceable – but if a relevant public policy criterion can be identified as being implicated 'in light of the circumstances',[50] and we have already pointed out the wide variety of factors which may be relevant to such an enquiry – then the court must make a finding of what public policy requires in the circumstances. Of course the reasonableness enquiry would have to be conducted through the public-policy approach and reasonableness or fairness could not be relied upon directly, or as the sole criterion in the public-policy enquiry. But it would remain open to a debtor, on our reading of *Barkhuizen*, to challenge the enforcement of the loan agreement. Such a challenge would of course involve other policy considerations, one of which would be considerations of social and economic expediency, which would most likely work against the debtor.[51] Challenges such as the hypothetical examples given by Harms DP will probably quickly result in the realisation that in loan agreements, public policy will mostly require enforcing the contract. If, however, there are circumstances in which the enquiry yields a different outcome, these will, over time, crystallise into clear guidelines for debtors and creditors, the practitioners who represent them and the courts asked to decide disputes.

Fourthly, it is important to guard against an overreliance on the principle of *pacta sunt servanda*. That they have done precisely this is perhaps the most important criticism of the approach of the courts thus far. This heavy reliance was made possible by its constitutionalisation and privileged status as a consideration of public policy. The courts have taken *pacta sunt servanda*, nowhere expressly mentioned in the Constitution, and elevated it to the status of a constitutional value, locating its roots in the rights to freedom, dignity and equality. They then used this constitutionalised value, already described as 'the one thing that public policy requires above all else', as a counterweight to those policy factors that favour declining to enforce the term. To the value of *pacta sunt servanda* is added 'requirements of social and economic expediency' to balance out the factors further in favour of escaping the contractual obligation.

The problem with this structuring of the balancing process is twofold.

---

[49] *Bredenkamp v Standard Bank of South Africa Ltd*, supra note 35, at para 28.

[50] Ibid at para 50: 'With all due respect, I do not believe that the judgment held or purported to hold that the enforcement of a valid contractual term must be fair and reasonable even if no public policy consideration found in the Constitution or elsewhere is implicated'.

[51] Because to decline to enforce the term would lead to uncertainty in loan agreements affecting the availability of credit to consumers.

First, the better formulation of the principle of *pacta sunt servanda* is that agreements *freely entered into* should be honoured. Thus it is inappropriate for the courts to rely on the principle when the agreement was not freely entered into in the first place. The fact is that there is no such thing as abso-lute or unrestricted freedom of will and that in all contracts the 'freedom' of one or both of the parties is constrained to some degree.[52] The challenge for the law of contract is to find acceptable limits to the constraints on that freedom.[53]

The second problem is related and goes to the constitutional rights and values identified in the process: while dignity and freedom can be said to underlie the value of *pacta sunt servanda*, that is not their only role. The point is expressed well by Mr Justice Brand (who penned the judgment in *Afrox*) in a recent article when he notes that

> 'although I concurred with Cameron JA in *Brisley* and *Afrox*, I now, upon consid-eration, tend to agree with Professor Gerhard Lubbe that the values of "dignity" and "freedom" display a perplexing capacity to pull in several directions at the same time and may accordingly fulfil very different roles. By their very nature these values are simply too vague to provide a decisive answer in deciding cases. Fortunately, I do not believe that we need to find a specific constitutional value, expressly referred to in the Constitution, to underpin every rule of contract law. In the present context, the inquiry works the other way around, namely: is there anything in the approach formulated by the Supreme Court of Appeal with regard to the role of good faith, reasonableness and fairness in our contract law which is in conflict with the constitutional value system? The short answer, I believe, is that there is none.'[54]

We agree with Brand that it is not necessary to constitutionalise *pacta sunt servanda* or other principles of contract law, as the public-policy enquiry makes it possible to take account of both constitutional rights and values and other relevant considerations. And yet, while it may not be *necessary*, a further interrogation of the values underlying a principle such as *pacta sunt servanda* may help to give better effect to it by ensuring it is only relied upon where appropriate.[55] That is to say, where the dignity or freedom of a party

---

[52] See Nugent JAs passing remark to this effect in paragraph 18 of *Medscheme Holdings v Bhamjee* 2005 (5) SA 339 (SCA) at para 18.

[53] S N Thal 'The Inequality of Bargaining Power Doctrine: The Problem of Defining Contractual Unfairness' (1988) 8 *Oxford Journal of Legal Studies* 17 at 22. See further *African Dawn Property Finance 2 (Pty) Ltd v Dreams Travel and Tours CC* 2011(3) SA 511 (SCA), where the SCA held that a loan was not usurious and that the transaction in question passed con-stitutional muster, amongst other things because the borrower was relatively pecunious and there had been no inducement to take the loan. On other words, the borrower's will had not been constrained.

[54] Brand, supra note 47, at 86.

[55] Sutherland, supra note 28, expresses concern that it allows for the watering-down of consti-

to a contract was impaired in the process of attaining consensus, the courts would be wrong to place strong reliance on the principle of *pacta sunt servanda*. The judgment of Ngcobo J in *Barkhuizen* exemplifies the value of such an approach:

> 'Self-autonomy, or the ability to regulate one's own affairs, even to one's own detriment, is the very essence of freedom and a vital part of dignity. The extent to which the contract was freely and voluntarily concluded is clearly a vital factor as it will determine the weight that should be afforded to the values of freedom and dignity.'[56]

While it is true that the law of contract sometimes relies on the fiction of consensus, this dictum illustrates that our courts are moving away from a crude, formalistic approach and refusing to recognise a contractual setting in inappropriate instances. In the context of administrative law, Cameron JA in *Logbro Properties CC v Bedderson NO* refused to recognise the acceptance by a company of tender conditions as constituting a contract in circumstances where the agreement precluded the application of administrative-justice duties on the part of the provincial government.[57] We may take as a further example the *obiter* remarks of Harms JA (as he then was) on the breach of promise action raised in *Van Jaarsveld v Bridges*:

> 'I do not accept the proposition that parties, when promising to marry each other, contemplate that a breach of their engagement would have financial consequences as if they had in fact married. They assume that their marital regime will be determined by their wedding. An engagement is, in my view, more of an unenforceable *pactum de contrahendo* providing a *spatium deliberandi* – a time to get to know each other better and to decide whether or not to marry finally.'[58]

tutional rights to the level of ordinary rights and values. Put differently the argument seems to proceed: but for the constitutionalisation of *pacta sunt servanda*, rights in the Bill of Rights would trump freedom of contract in all (or at least most) public policy enquiries. This is not the case as the balancing process is not a simple binary and includes a multitude of factors, one of which is considerations of social and economic expediency. Thus even if we accord more weight to a particular right than we do to a non-constitutional public policy factor (as we should do), it is far from settled that that right will always win so to speak. In any event this is an unproductive line of argument to engage in, as there is no exact law and economics calculus that can be applied to the public policy enquiry to yield the correct outcome. It is a political enquiry that proceeds on a case by case basis, and the best the courts can do is to identify the various factors they will consider and stress how important they are in the scheme of the enquiry. Clearly *pacta sunt servanda* is a very important consideration, whether it is expressly underpinned by constitutional rights and values or not.

[56] *Barkhuizen v Napier*, supra note 29, at para 57, quoted with approval by Harms J in para 50 of *Bredenkamp*, supra note 35. See also *African Dawn Property Finance 2 (Pty) Ltd v Dreams Travel and Tours CC*, supra note 53, at para 15.

[57] 2003 (2) SA 460 (SCA) paras 9–14.

[58] 2010 (4) SA 558 (SCA) para 8.

We suggest then that use of a constitutionally-located principle of *pacta sunt servanda* in public policy considerations has resulted in, and will continue to result in, greater scrutiny of the true degree of consensus underlying the alleged agreements.

13.3.1.4 Conclusion

The public policy approach after *Barkhuizen* is an appropriate and sufficient vehicle to give effect to constitutional rights. The considerations that go into deciding what public policy requires provide sufficient flexibility to the courts to address any constitutional right relied upon. It is important also to keep in mind that giving effect to constitutional rights may involve more than deciding which terms will be upheld and which will not. There may conceivably be instances in which the relief sought will not be possible without reading a term into a contract,[59] giving a particular interpretation to an existing term, or applying the rules on reasonable reliance, duress and undue influence.

13.3.2 Implied terms

Implied terms, or *ex lege*[60] terms, are those that are automatically imported into contracts and are distinguishable from tacit terms.[61] Implied terms are ultimately based on policy considerations.[62] As such it is easy to see how implied terms are a possible doctrinal device for the constitutional development of the law of contract. But as a general device to import constitutional values into the law of contract, implied terms lack the flexibility of a public-policy-based approach to enforceability.[63] This is because implied terms have to be capable of being formulated in words and, once found to exist, will by default apply to all further contracts. A degree of flexibility is introduced by confining the implied terms to contracts of a particular type, such as contracts of sale, employment and lease, and by employing the principle that parties are usually free to contract out of these terms expressly or even tacitly. Yet the potential range of application of implied terms remains considerable: the courts will, through recognising an implied term, establish a default legal rule that apportions rights and duties between the parties apart

---

[59] For example in *Murray v Minister of Defence* 2009(3) SA 130 (SCA).

[60] See van der Merwe et al, supra note 16, at 241.

[61] Tacit terms are those where the parties did not expressly agree on/discuss but which both would regard as part of their agreement. There is still a consensual basis for finding that such a term operates, whereas implied terms are applicable even where neither party considered or desired the term to form part of the agreement. Caveat: you can expressly exclude certain implied terms.

[62] Christie, supra note 19, at 160, quoting de Villiers J in the 2006 decision of *Anglo Operations Ltd v Sandhurst Estates (Pty) Ltd* 2006 (1) SA 350 (T) 374.

[63] As noted by R H Christie *Bill of Rights Compendium* (Butterworths 1996) at 3H-23.

from those expressly or even tacitly considered by them. Implied terms may prove particularly useful for importing statutory protections into the common law, but not where this would amount to the creation of parallel streams of law – that is, where the right in question is already given effect to by legislation.

However, the use of implied terms has its limitations in the context. The case of *South African Forestry Co Ltd v York Timbers*[64] (*Safcol*), although not expressly concerned with constitutional influence, illustrates these limitations (and like *Brisley*, *Afrox* and *Bredenkamp*) stresses that good faith, reasonableness and fairness are informing and underlying values rather than rules of contract law.[65] In *Safcol* the court declined to recognise an implied term formulated as requiring that the parties to the contract exercise their rights and fulfil their duties in accordance with the dictates of reasonableness, fairness and good faith.[66] In doing so Brand JA expressly mentions that such an implied term would have to be read into all future contracts:

> '[A] term cannot be implied merely because it is reasonable or to promote fairness and justice between the parties in a particular case. It can be implied only if it is considered to be *good law in general*. The particular parties and set of facts can serve only as catalysts in the process of legal development.'[67]

Brand JA added: 'To say that terms can be implied if dictated by fairness and good faith does not mean that these abstract values themselves will be imposed as terms of the contract'. Ultimately the court decided the case by interpreting the ambiguous terms of the contract 'on the basis that they negotiated with one another in good faith'.[68] They achieved the same result that would have been achieved had the implied term been recognised, but did so without laying down a generally binding future rule. This is in accordance with the courts' development of the public-policy-based power to decline to enforce a contract in the specific circumstances of the case – both retain flexibility and allow the court to avoid laying down generally applicable rules in future cases, which in effect would amount to judicial legislation.

Against the background of these general limitations, we can explore some cases in which an argument was made for the recognition of an implied term in order to give effect to constitutional rights or values.

In *Harper v Morgan Guarantee Trust Co of New York, Johannesburg* Harper argued for the development of the law to recognise an implied term of good faith, either generally governing the exercise of contractual powers in contracts of employment, or more specifically limiting the employer's power,

---

[64] 2005 (3) SA 323 (SCA).
[65] Ibid at paras 28–30.
[66] Ibid at para 26.
[67] Ibid at para 28.
[68] Ibid at para 32.

in terms of the contract, to terminate on notice.[69] This case illustrates why, in some circumstances, a public-policy approach to deny enforceability may not be able to provide appropriate relief: Harper claimed damages for breach of contract (in the form of a repudiation which she elected to accept and sue upon). The presence of a term requiring good-faith exercise of the right to terminate, or a more general requirement that the powers be exercised in good faith, would have been necessary for there to have been a breach in the given circumstances. The court was unwilling to recognise that an implied term of good faith governed the conduct of the parties to the contract, as outlined in *Safcol*. Flemming DJP in rejecting the argument for recognition of either of the implied terms held:

'One observes that in all the discussions of good faith as an element of contract, the concept remains without defined edge. While contractual terms normally have "tangible" content by way of conveying what may be done or what may not be done, the obligation to maintain good faith has no "content". It is a duty about another obligation which either creates an area where the impact of the law differs from Judge to Judge or its meaning is determined by what the specific parties regarded as not being "good faith" and so one returns to the contemplation of the parties. In such circumstances there is little to commend bending the law rather than using common equitable sense.'[70]

In a commentary on this case, Hawthorne[71] observes that the Deputy Judge President fails to distinguish between subjective and objective conceptions of good faith, relying on the problems presented by the former as a bar to applying the latter. As far as lacking a defined edge, Hawthorne points out that this is because the courts have declined to hone one. The judgment would probably have benefited from a clearer discussion of the approach to developing the common law in light of the Constitution and arguably should have made greater reference to any relevant constitutional rights and values. That having been said, it is important to note the judgment's finding that the appellant's pleadings were poorly drafted and that the relief claimed was not clearly set out, leaving the judge to frame the issue. Ultimately Flemming DJP held that the development was neither appropriate nor required by the Constitution.

In *South African Maritime Safety Authority v McKenzie*[72] the respondent on appeal (plaintiff in the *court a quo*) McKenzie sought damages for breach of contract on the basis of an express, implied or tacit term that he would not be dismissed without just cause or unfairly. Wallis AJA dealt swiftly

---

[69] 2004 (3) SA 253 (W) para 7.1.
[70] Ibid at para 9.5.
[71] L Hawthorne 'Abuse of a Right to Dismiss not Contrary to Good Faith' (2005) 17 *South African Mercantile LJ* 214–21.
[72] 2010 (3) SA 601 (SCA).

with the arguments for an express or tacit term, both of which were not present,[73] before considering whether an implied term should be recognised. In support of the implied term, reliance was placed on section 185 of the Labour Relations Act[74] (LRA), which deals with unfair dismissal, and also on section 39(2) of the Constitution, requiring the courts to promote the spirit, purport and objects of the Constitution when developing the law or interpreting legislation. The judgment dealt primarily with the argument that the LRA incorporated into all contracts of employment a right not to be unfairly dismissed. In a carefully reasoned judgment setting out when and where statutes could be said to give rise to implied terms in contracts, the court rejected the argument, noting that McKenzie sought to incorporate only the section 185 right into the contract without the statutorily provided remedies and limitations on compensation. Clearly, in this instance that would be to go against the policy considerations that animated the legislature in enacting the section and its accompanying remedies.

This case, importantly, demonstrates that where a statutory regime gives effect to a right there is no need for constitutional development of the common law:

> 'While the Constitution guarantees to everyone "the right to fair labour prac-
> tices", and also calls upon courts, when developing the common law, to promote
> the spirit, purport and objects of the Bill of Rights', it does not follow that courts
> are thereby enjoined to develop the common law contract of employment by
> simply incorporating in it the constitutional guarantee. Where the common-law,
> as supplemented by legislation, accords to employees the constitutional right
> to fair labour practices there is no constitutional imperative that calls for the
> common law to be developed. Indeed, to duplicate rights that exist by statute does
> no more than to create the 'jurisdictional quagmire . . .'[75]

In the course of his judgment Wallis AJA refers to the 2009 SCA case of *Murray v Minister of Defence*.[76] This was an appeal from a dismissal of a case in the Cape High Court, in which Murray, a military police officer with the rank of Commander, sought damages for constructive dismissal from the South African Navy. The provisions of the LRA, which would normally govern the employment relationship, were not addressed as the Act does not apply to Defence Force members. Murray instead relied directly on his section 23 right to fair labour practices, as well as his right to dignity. Cameron JA placed the reliance on these rights in the context of developing the common-law contract of employment, which 'must be held to impose on all employers a duty of fair dealing at all times with their employees – even

[73] Ibid at paras 10–12.
[74] Act 66 of 1995.
[75] *SAMSA v McKenzie*, supra note 72, at para 35.
[76] 2009 (3) SA 130 (SCA).

those the LRA does not cover'.[77] Murray was not sacked from his position and sought to rely on the notion of constructive dismissal for which the LRA provides. Cameron JA, after tracing the history of the doctrine of constructive dismissal, went on to note that 'the constitutional guarantee of fair labour practices continues to cover a non-LRA employee who resigns because of intolerable conduct by the employer, and to offer protection through the constitutionally developed common law'.[78] It is not immediately apparent from the judgment in *Murray* whether the court merely applied existing pre-LRA common law on constructive dismissal or whether the common law of employment was developed under constitutional motivation. Wallis AJA in *McKenzie* seems to take the latter view, although he expresses the opinion that such 'development' may not have been necessary.[79] This is an illustration of the importance of the courts' clearly setting out whether they are actually developing the law or whether they are merely applying existing principles.

The judgments of the SCA in *Murray* and *McKenzie*, taken together, provide important guidance as to how our courts might rely on the constitutional rights and values that underpin legislation to develop the common law of contract in general, and, through implied terms in particular,[80] to protect those litigants who, for appropriate reasons,[81] are unable to rely on that specific legislation.

13.3.3 Interpretation of contracts

The scope for judicial interpretation of contracts is curtailed by the general principle of contract law that requires the courts to give expression to the intention of the parties. Thus, in interpreting (written) contracts, our courts must seek to find the common intention of the parties as expressed by the plain meaning of the words read in conformity with the document as a whole.[82] Where the meaning of a particular term is still unclear, the parties

---

[77] Ibid at para 5.

[78] Ibid at para 9.

[79] At para 54: 'I am not sure that the common law required development in order to reach that conclusion, but that is by the by.'

[80] See *SAMSA v McKenzie*, supra note 72, at para 54 where Wallis AJA seems to be of the view that protection from unfair dismissal was incorporated by way of an implied term in *Murray v Minister of Defence*, supra note 76, notwithstanding the lack of clarity on the nature of the development in *Murray*.

[81] One caveat: to the degree that the Acts seek to protect vulnerable and disadvantaged consumers, it would hardly be appropriate for a court to rely on the remedies in the Acts to develop the common law where the Acts do not apply because the party concerned is a large, juristic person and thus presumably unaffected by the disadvantages the Acts seek to address.

[82] D Hutchison et al, *The Law of Contract in South Africa* (OUP 2010) 253–5; Christie, supra note 19, at 192.

may adduce evidence as to the background or surrounding circumstances.[83] Only where ambiguity then still remains do the other techniques of interpretation become relevant in determining the meaning.[84]

In such a case a court can construe the remaining ambiguity in a way which is consistent with constitutional values. Take, for example, the cases in which the courts have construed discretionary powers afforded to one party in the contract as being subject to the requirement that they be exercised in accordance with the judgment of a reasonable adjudicator – *arbitrium boni viri*.[85] This external, equitable, standard of conduct superimposed upon a power conferred by a contract has the potential, if elevated from the rungs of a secondary rule of interpretation, to give effect to constitutional rights. However, this will need to be done with care, because the downside is that such an elevation may 'unduly disturb the existing doctrinal machinery' unless qualified in some way.

A further technique of interpretation is to construe the provision in such a way that it will be valid and legal – *ut res magis valeat quam pereat* – and, as Maxwell suggests,[86] this should apply equally where the interpretation is one of constitutional validity or invalidity. Such an approach would be useful in a situation where the success of a litigant's claim hinges on a term (such as a claim for damages for breach) and appropriate relief cannot be achieved by way of an implied term (because of its normative consequences) or via the existing public policy approach (because this is used to invalidate terms or their enforceability, not to give an interpretation to them).

13.3.4 Legislation

The development of the common law to give effect to constitutional rights is of course a residual or backstop procedure. Section 8(3) of the Constitution clearly sees legislation as the first port of call in giving effect to rights, with common-law development arising only where the legislation is deficient in achieving that task. Thus, any analysis of the future development of the common law of contract would be incomplete without enquiring into legislation designed to give effect to constitutional rights in the contractual

---

[83] A strong *obiter* statement in KPMG *v Securefin* 2009 (4) SA 399 (SCA) has all but done away with the previous distinction between background and surrounding circumstances.
[84] Van der Merwe et al, supra note 16, at 266–8. See also generally on the interpretation of documents *Natal Joint Municipal Pension Fund v Endumeni Municipality* 2012 (4) SA 593 (SCA).
[85] *NBS Boland Bank v One Berg River Drive* 1999 (4) SA 928 (SCA); *Machanick v Simon* 1920 CPD 333.
[86] In Hutchison et al, supra note 82, at 264–5 with reference to a dictum of Marais JA in *FNB SA Ltd v Rosenblum and another* 2001 (4) SA 189 (SCA).

setting.[87] The developments that have taken place, particularly in the realm of public-policy-based enforceability and validity, have been necessary because there has not, until recently, been legislation specifically designed to control contractual excesses, particularly in respect of standard-form consumer contracts. Both the courts[88] and academic commentators have recognised the need for legislation on unfair contract terms, and the introduction of the Consumer Protection Act (CPA), brings South Africa into line with a host of other jurisdictions that have preferred legislative measures to address the problems posed by standard-form contracts. Also relevant are the LRA and the Basic Conditions of Employment Act,[89] in respect of employment agreements, as well as the Promotion of Administrative Justice Act[90] (PAJA), which regulates the exercise of executive power and applies also to powers exercised in terms of a contract.

These Acts have exerted, and will continue to exert, a strong influence on the future development of the common law. This development is likely to follow two broad avenues: first, the courts will need to interpret the legislative provisions and reconcile the common law with the acts so as to avoid the development of parallel streams of law; secondly, the courts will be faced with instances in which, for a variety of reasons, these acts do not apply and the development of the common law – to give effect to constitutional rights – will have to be considered.

As to the first avenue, while the CPA will relieve the courts of some of the burden of developing a consumerist jurisprudence, that is by no means the end of the Act's impact on the common law. Van Eeden notes that '[t]here is a symbiosis between common law and that evolving statute law'[91] and 'while private law may be an inadequate tool of consumer protection, it is still an indispensable part of the legal framework for the consumer market'.[92] The CPA will need to be reconciled with existing common-law remedies, and the effect of the Act's section 4(2)(a) 'mandate' for the courts further to develop the common law to realise consumer rights needs to be properly interrogated and understood. The statute relies on some common-law terms and devices and alters others, while certain provisions reveal a misunderstanding of the common law by the drafters. Most important, perhaps, will be how the courts come to interpret the open-ended terms 'unjust, unreasonable and unfair' in section 48 as they relate to contract terms and prices. While the section provides some guidance as to how to interpret these terms, this

---

[87] See Hutchison et al, supra note 82, at 243–4 for a list of legislation that has a bearing on contracts.

[88] See *Johannesburg City Council v Stott* 2003 (4) SA 559 (T) and *Wagener v Pharmacare* 2003 (4) SA 285 (SCA).

[89] Act 75 of 1997.

[90] Act of 2000.

[91] E van Eeden *A Guide to the Consumer Protection Act* (LexisNexis 2009) 57.

[92] Ibid.

guidance is not exhaustive and the courts will need to engage further with the concepts – perhaps by employing existing common law approaches or by referring to foreign law.

As to the second broad avenue of development: what is less immediately obvious is the effect that the consumerist legislation's focus on inequality will have on the development of private law in general and on the law of contract in particular. One possibility is that the acts may provide remedies and solutions that the courts could utilise by developing the common law of contract where the act is not applicable; that is, they may develop the common law in situations analogous to, but not covered by, the legislation. Furthermore, these acts, and the CPA in particular, may have some influence as sources of law beyond their express terms of application.[93] The persuasive power of these statutes may be particularly important where they were expressly enacted to give effect to constitutional rights or values. The case of *Murray v Minister of Defence*, discussed above, illustrates how the statutory rights afforded to one class of persons in order to give effect to a constitutional right may be taken as an example of how to develop the common law to give effect to those same rights for persons not covered by the statue in question.

The influence of statutes on common-law development may, then, proceed by a more indirect route, namely by influencing what the courts regard as the requirements of public policy, or at least by influencing the weighting accorded to the various criteria considered in the enquiry. Considerations of unequal bargaining power are already provided for in the public policy enquiry, but it has been argued that the courts have paid insufficient attention to this element and have instead over-relied on *pacta sunt servanda*. All the legislation referred to is expressly concerned with inequality of bargaining power and goes to great lengths to address it. The inequality inherent in the employment relationship and in the relationship between citizen and state (catered for in the PAJA) is self-evident.

The CPA and National Credit Act[94] (NCA) are both concerned with addressing the inequality of bargaining power that plagues standard-form contractual agreements/consumer contracts. This is explicit in the preamble to the CPA, where it is noted that 'apartheid and discriminatory laws of the past have burdened the nation with unacceptably high levels of poverty, illiteracy and other forms of social and economic inequality'.[95] Section 3, which sets out the Act's purposes, places special emphasis on reducing the

---

[93] J Beatson 'The Role of Statute in the Development of Common Law Doctrine' (2001) 117 LQR 247 at 251, cited in B Hepple *The Common Law and Statutory Rights in Rights at Work: Global, European and British Perspectives* (Sweet and Maxwell 2005) at 3 (available at *http://ucl. ac.uk/laws/hamlyn/hamlyn04_3.pdf*).

[94] Act 34 of 2005.

[95] Consumer Protection Act 62 of 2008.

.

disadvantages faced by certain vulnerable groups in consumer contracts[96] and stresses protection from conduct which is variously described as unjust, unfair, unconscionable or unreasonable.[97] Consumer protection legislation (including credit-agreements legislation) is concerned with addressing inequality of bargaining power between supplier or credit providers and consumers[98] and the NCA is no exception. In a 2005 policy document on credit industry regulation, the Department of Trade and Industry noted that

> '[t]here is a considerable imbalance of power between consumers and credit providers, consumer education levels are frequently low, consumers are poorly informed about their rights and unable to enforce such rights through either negotiation or legal action. Commission-driven agents, deceptive marketing practices and weak disclosure can easily cause consumers to enter into unaffordable credit contracts'.[99]

It is highly relevant that addressing inequality is a concern of the NCA and CPA, respectively, as both acts mandate purposive interpretation and application of the provisions by courts and tribunals as the case may be.

A potential response to a call for recognising the effect of these acts beyond their express terms, especially as indicative of the requirements of public policy, is that the legislature expressly chose to confine their application to certain classes of persons or specific transactions. Thus juristic persons with a turnover in excess of R3 million will not be protected under the CPA, nor will juristic persons engaged in 'large credit transactions'. However all franchise agreements, irrespective of the size of the franchise, are covered by the CPA. This indicates that inequality of bargaining power does not cease to operate once the weaker party meets certain numerical criteria. Rather, inequality may be inherent in the nature of the agreement and this concept is always relative to the parties to transactions. While the thresholds in the CPA may be good starting points to protect the weakest of consumers, they should not be taken as the end of the matter. In due course the courts may be confronted with cases where a party to a contract, although not meeting the CPA definition of a consumer, is nevertheless deserving of some protection against contractual exploitation.[100] Similar situations may arise in respect of transactions that are not properly called consumer transactions.

---

[96] Ibid, ss 3(1)(b)(i)-(iv), covering variously consumers who are minors, seniors, illiterate or similarly disadvantaged, low-income and those who live in remote areas.

[97] Consumer Protection Act, ss 3(1)(b) and (c).

[98] P N Stoop 'South African Consumer Credit Policy: Measures Indirectly Aimed at Preventing Consumer Over-indebtedness' (2009) 21 *South African Mercantile LJ* 365.

[99] Department of Trade and Industry South Africa *Consumer Credit Law Reform: Policy Framework for Consumer Credit* (DTI 2004) 7.

[100] See in this regard *Everfresh Market Virginia (Pty) Ltd v Shoprite Checkers (Pty) Ltd* 2010 (1) SA 256 (CC) at para 24 (Yacoob J).

13.4 APPLYING THE PRINCIPLES IN SPECIFIC SITUATIONS: CREATING THE 'FALLGRUPPEN'

We now move on to examine two examples of particular areas of application (or 'Fallgruppen') to illustrate the application of the principles discussed above. For this purpose we have chosen, first, the category of agreements known variously as *pacta de quota litis* or champertous agreements (we will use these terms interchangeably) because we believe these agreements provide solid terrain for exploring the principles raised in the preceding section, not least because they have been addressed by both South African and Scottish courts in recent times. Secondly, we will consider clauses exempting a person or entity from liability for personal injury or death and discuss briefly how the introduction of the Consumer Protection Act might influence future common law development of public policy in this sphere.

13.4.1 Pacta de quotis litis *or champertous agreements*

Under South African law agreements by one party to finance the litigation of another in exchange for a share of the proceeds have long been held to be contrary to public policy and therefore unenforceable,[101] save for certain exceptional circumstances. Those exceptional circumstances are where the potential litigant's impecuniosity operates as the only bar to the bringing of a claim and a third party agrees to provide financial assistance to that litigant in exchange for a reasonable consideration or share of the proceeds of any award or settlement.[102] In *Goodgold Jewellery (Pty) Ltd v Brevadau CC*[103] the applicant had sold jewellery on credit and then sought an order winding up the respondent close corporation. The relationship between the parties was based on an extensive written contract, in terms of which the respondent undertook debt collection on the applicant's behalf in return for a share of the recovered amounts. Significantly, the contract provided for the respondent to recover by undertaking legal action in its own name, which was made possible by way of cession of the applicant's claims against the debtors to the respondent. Stegmann J *meru motu* raised the issue of whether or not the agreement between the applicant and respondent was contrary to public policy as constituting a *pacta de quotis litis* and came to the conclusion that it was. The reasons for this finding included the speculative nature of the agreement, the potential conflict of interest that might arise when the respondent

---

[101] *Green v De Villiers, Leyds NO & Rand Exploring Syndicate* (1895) 2 OR 289 at 293–4; *Schweizers Claimholders Rights Syndicate Limited v Rand Exploring Syndicate, Limited* [1896] 3 OR 140 at 144–5; *CVJJ Platteau v Grobler* (1897) 4 OR 389 at 394–396; *Campbell v Welverdiend Diamonds, Ltd* 1930 TPD 287 at 292–4.

[102] For example *Thomas and Möller NO v Transvaal Loan, Finance and Mortgage Company* (1894) 1 OR 336 at 339–341.

[103] 1992 (4) SA 474 (W).

was undertaking legal action against the applicant's debtors, and the fact that the respondent's services were neither necessary, nor was the applicant impecunious.[104]

While in *Goodgold Jewellery* Stegmann J expressed doubt that the exception for impecunious litigants could extend to an impecunious corporation,[105] the SCA decision in *Price Waterhouse Coopers Inc v National Potato Co-operative Ltd*[106] did just that – and that presents a significant departure from the traditional approach to *pacta de quota litis*. *Price Waterhouse* illustrates the changing nature of public policy considerations as well as the influence of the Constitution and legislation in determining what is and is not contrary to public policy with respect to contractual provisions.

In the course of its judgment, the SCA, per Southwood AJA, discussed the factors underlying the traditional aversion to champertous agreements and noted that the judicial system both in England and South Africa is now sophisticated and independent enough to guard effectively against many of the evils associated with champerty.

It is plain from the judgment that the Constitution and legislation have influenced the content of what public policy requires in these types of agreements. The right of access to courts in section 34 of the Constitution is specifically relied upon,[107] as is the legislature's partial endorsement of champerty in the form of the Contingency Fees Act 1997.[108]

Of further significance is Southwood AJA's reliance on 'the constitutional value of freedom of contract'[109] which was not, as has sometimes been the case, misplaced: the facts of the case indicate a completely voluntary and negotiated agreement between the litigant and the corporation set up to finance the litigation, with members of the former sitting on the board of the latter.

Human v CMC Chemicals (EDMS) BPK[110] illustrates, however, that *Price Waterhouse Coopers* has not had the effect of making all *pacta de quota litis* enforceable. In *Human* the plaintiff was a loss assessor who had agreed to assist the defendants in assessing the extent of their losses in the course of negotiations with their insurance company which had repudiated liability under the insurance contract. In exchange for his services Mr Human was to receive 10 per cent of the award or any settlement but contracted with the defendants to limit their right to settle with the insurance company without his approval. In the event that the defendants breached the agreement he was entitled to a R300,000 penalty fee but would receive nothing if the claim

---

[104] *Goodgold Jewellery (Pty) Ltd v Brevadau CC* at 487–88.
[105] Ibid at 486A.
[106] 2004 (6) SA 66 (SCA).
[107] Ibid para 50.
[108] Ibid para 41.
[109] Ibid para 44.
[110] (9832/2007) [2011] ZAGPPHC 21.

proceeded and was unsuccessful. The court held that this clearly constituted a *pactum de quota litis*, as it was not strictly necessary in order for the defendants to proceed in their claim against their insurers (there was no evidence demonstrating their inability to finance the litigation unassisted). The court also held it to be contrary to public policy in that it precluded the litigants from otherwise reaching a settlement agreement.[111]

Pacta de quota litis will not be contrary to public policy then where their use helps to give litigants access to court when they would otherwise not be able to bring a claim (provided that the parties exercised true contractual freedom). Although the courts have used the phrase 'reasonable compensation or interest' it is not clear what the limits would be: in *Price Waterhouse* the third party corporation set up to finance the litigation would have received 45 per cent of any award or settlement in a case where the parties had alleged damages in excess of R200 million. In *Human* the interest was only 10 per cent on claims together totalling less than R6 million.

While in *Human* the financer's contractual right to block a settlement between the parties was deemed to be against public policy, a similar right[112] in *Price Waterhouse* did not appear to have the same effect. This apparent inconsistency can perhaps be reconciled when the substantial privity of interest and of identity between the litigant and the financer in *Price Waterhouse* (several members of the litigant cooperative where also directors of the company set up to finance the litigation) is borne in mind. In *Goodgold Jewellery* the cession of the claims to the debt collector, so that the latter could undertake litigation in its own name, was a factor contrary to public policy and no doubt influenced the respondent's decision in *Price Waterhouse* to reverse an earlier cession of its claim to the financer and to undertake the action in its own name.

Against this background we may briefly compare the Scottish case of *Quantum Claims Compensation Specialists Ltd v Powell*[113] which concerned an agreement between Powell, who had a claim for personal injury, and Quantum Claims Compensation Specialists, which was in the business of negotiating, settling and prosecuting claims for damages against third parties

---

[111] A significant difference between *Human v CMC Chemicals (EDMS) BPK*, supra note 110, and *Price Waterhouse Coopers*, supra note 106, was that in the former the potential litigants' relationship with Mr Human had broken down and they resisted his enforcement of the agreement, whereas in the latter case the relationship between the respondent litigants and the financers remained amicable and it was the applicants (against whom the respondents brought a large breach of contract claim) who sought to raise the existence of a champertous agreement as a defence against liability.

[112] It may be that the nature of this limitation on settlement provision is distinguishable, as in *Price Waterhouse Coopers* the court describes it as: 'the Co-operative was not permitted to accept an offer of settlement or make a counter-offer *without consulting* [the financers]' (emphasis added).

[113] 1998 SC 316.

on behalf of its clients. The court proceeds from the premise that the unenforceability of *pacta de quota litis* is a restriction of the default position of freedom of contract and thereafter seeks to 'find a basis or *ratio* for such a denial of freedom to contract, founded upon some relevant characteristic of the persons in question, or of the function or role which they are performing'. The court ultimately confines the restriction on *pacta de quota litis* to legal professionals (solicitors in particular) providing professional services to litigants.

Restrictions on *pacta de quota litis* in South Africa as exemplified in *Human* and *Goodgold Jewellery* seem to be based on similar considerations to those raised by the court in *Quantum Claims*. The restrictions would, however, appear to be wider in South Africa, extending as they do beyond legal professionals to include, for example, debt collectors or claims quantifiers assisting in and thereby exercising considerable control over the litigation. (*Price Waterhouse* concerned itself only with a company set up to provide financing to a litigating party which would not otherwise be able to have access to court. But we cannot rule out the possibility that the *Price Waterhouse* decision could be extended to a situation where a party provides services instead of, or in combination with, financial assistance, so long as such services are necessary for the claim to proceed and do not come at the expense of the litigant's control over the action.) It is important to note that the differences between the Scottish and South African approaches are not attributable to the fact that the South African courts explicitly employ human-rights reasoning in this context while the Scottish courts do not. We think that this illustrates that courts will obviously tend to – and must – use applicable human-rights instruments in their reasoning when these are available, but this does not prevent courts in systems where such instruments are not available (or are less directly implicated) to fashion appropriate policies and reach very similar results. However, the value of the presence of a human-rights instrument applicable to private law relations is obviously that it focuses the mind of the court and ensures that these issues are dealt with explicitly.

13.4.2 *Exemption and limitation clauses*

In the area of exemption clauses, the courts have relied heavily on the principle of *pacta sunt servanda*. In certain instances they have used it to uphold quite stringent and onerous provisions, and judgments in which this has happened have elicited strong criticism (as is most obvious from the decision in *Afrox Healthcare Bpk v Strydom*).[114] We do not intend to contribute further to the debate about whether the *Afrox* judgment was ultimately right or wrong. Rather, we approach the matter of exemption and limitation clauses on the

---

[114] 2002 (6) SA 21 (SCA).

basis of the considerations that should be taken into account and weighed against each other in matters involving such clauses.

It is clear that identifying a constitutional right that is infringed or limited by an exemption clause is not sufficient by itself to render that clause contrary to public policy. This is even more true when one considers that freedom of contract has itself been (even if perhaps unnecessarily, as some argue) elevated to a constitutional principle. In this stalemate of competing constitutional rights and values, other aspects of public policy, such as considerations of social and economic expediency, become highly relevant to determining outcomes.

After discussing how an *Afrox*-type exemption clause would be invalid under Scots law in terms of section 16 of the Unfair Contract Terms Act 1977, Brand and Brodie turn their attention to possible avenues of dealing with such clauses in South Africa:

> 'It was not argued on behalf of Strydom – maybe unfortunately – that an exclusion of liability for personal injuries and death is *per se* contrary to public policy. Nor was it argued that, having regard to the underlying considerations of good faith, the unlimited enforcement of a clause excluding liability for death or personal injury cannot be tolerated and should therefore be qualified or set aside. In the absence of any statutory limitation of the ambit of exemption clauses, it is not inconceivable that either of these arguments may in the future find favour with South African courts.'[115]

This serves as a point of departure for two observations. First, South Africa now has statutory limitations on the ambit of exemption clauses in the form of the CPA. While the restriction on exemption clauses has not been as extensive as under the comparable Scottish legislation, the effects may be the same when coupled with the importance of the right to life and to safety and to security of the person. Secondly, while good faith has not been directly relied upon, the argument that such clauses are contrary to public policy and thus unenforceable has been considered in a number of significant *obiter dicta*, even if the approach has not as yet been applied to hold an exemption clause unenforceable.

We proceed chronologically and begin with Harms JA's *obiter* statement in *Johannesburg Country Club v Stott*,[116] where it was suggested that it *may* be that the exclusion of liability for negligently causing the death of another, in light of the weight accorded to the right to life in the Constitution, could be against public policy.[117] The separate concurring judgment of Marais

---

[115] F Brand and D Brodie 'Good Faith in Contract Law' in R Zimmerman, D Visser and K Reid (eds) *Mixed Legal Systems in Comparative Perspective: Property and Obligations in Scots and South African Law* (OUP 2005) 94 at 115.

[116] 2004 (5) SA 511 (SCA).

[117] Ibid para 12.

JA, however, expressed reservations about reaching such a conclusion – although the judge's brief comments hint at which factors would be relevant to making such a finding: (1) the type of conduct or degree of fault from which exemption from liability is sought and (2) whether the agreement was entered into voluntarily and with knowledge of the term in question.[118]

These factors appear again in what is perhaps the most illuminating judicial treatment on the unenforceability of exemption clauses contrary to public policy, namely the *obiter* statements of Wallis J in the Durban High Court in *Swinburne v Newbee Investments (Pty) Ltd*.[119] In that case the plaintiff was a tenant who sued the landlord owner of the flat in which he lived for damages he sustained as a result of the latter's negligent failure to install a handrail adjacent to a short flight of stairs. In addition to denying negligence, the defendant raised two exemption clauses in the lease agreement excluding liability in very wide terms. Wallis J dispatched with the contractual provisions (which he found to be ambiguous) by interpreting them *contra proferentem* and limited only to property damage and therefore not extending to physical injury (in much the same way as Harms JA dealt with the exemption clause in *Johannesburg Country Club*). Wallis J then proceeded to address briefly the potential merits of a claim that such a clause, if it were to extend to limit liability for personal injury, may in the circumstances be contrary to public policy. It is worth quoting from his judgment:

'The conclusion that I have reached renders it unnecessary to enter upon this terrain or to exercise any degree of greater activism and ingenuity than has been displayed by judges in the past. I need only say that on the facts of the present case, if the exemption contained in clause 26 of the lease had applied to exclude Newbee Investments' liability for Mr Swinburne's claim, I think the argument based upon public policy would have had some force. I say this for the following reasons. First, the lease is manifestly what is commonly called a contract of adhesion in regard to the terms of which Mr Swinburne had no real bargaining power. He was presented with the lease to sign on the basis that if he wanted the flat these were the terms on which it was available to him. Second, the terms of the exclusion are buried in the fine print of the document and were not explained to him in advance of his signing the lease. He was accordingly not alerted to the need to provide his own insurance against the eventuality that occurred. Third, the exemption is contrary to the common-law right that a tenant has against the landlord that the latter take reasonable steps to ensure that the leased premises and the building

---

[118] Ibid para 15: 'Slight negligence may have no consequences in one case; in another it may have catastrophic consequences. Death is but one of them. I would need considerable persuasion before concluding that a party to a contract who wishes to protect himself or herself against the possibility that a moment's inattention may result in an enormous civil liability for damages, is to be prohibited by law from doing so despite the other party's willingness to contract on that basis.'

[119] [2010] JOL 25350 (KZD).

in which they are situated are safe for persons living in the building. Fourth, a landlord in the position of Newbee Investments is able to protect itself in two ways against this type of liability. It can take steps to ensure as best it can that the premises are safe for use by the tenants and it can, as did Newbee Investments, insure against liability occasioned by its negligence. Fifth, the constitutional right to bodily integrity ought to be given weight in the consideration of the impact of public policy on this type of clause. However, it is unnecessary for me to weigh the precise impact of these factors on the question of the enforceability of the exemption clause in the light of my finding that it does not exclude liability for Mr Swinburne's claim.'[120]

Although only *obiter*, Wallis J's approach identifies many of the policy considerations that are hinted at in earlier cases: the extent to which the provision was freely negotiated (that is the inequality of bargaining power of the parties) and the party's knowledge of the existence of the provision. Both of these considerations have a direct bearing on when it will be appropriate for a court to rely on *pacta sunt servanda* and hold a party to such an exemption clause. Considerations of 'social and economic expediency' are also raised as evidenced from questions of which party is best positioned to guard against the loss.

The nature of the contractual agreement and the degree to which the exemption clause departs from the fundamental provisions of contracts of that type are raised by Wallis J as relevant factors. (In this regard, the treatment of exemption clauses suggested by Naudé and Lubbe [121] – by comparing their scope to the *essentialia* and *naturalia* of the type of contract in which they operate – is particularly instructive.) Finally, and perhaps most importantly, Wallis J identifies constitutional rights (in this case the right to bodily integrity) as relevant, although in this case it would appear not to have been decisive.

While the arrival of the CPA with its fairly comprehensive provisions on exemption and exclusion clauses is to be welcomed, it is far from a panacea for contractual excess. Significantly, section 4(2)(a) of the Act mandates that the courts develop the common law as necessary to improve the rights of consumers generally. In this way the courts are free to rely on the Act to influence what public policy requires in areas outside the Act's strict scope of application – such as in contracts between two businesses or where a small business not protected by the Act contracts with a much larger and more powerful entity on onerous terms. It seems likely, then, that in future the dicta in *Stott* and *Swinburne*, the relevant constitutional rights, and the policy preferences expressed by the legislature in passing the CPA will combine to

---

[120] Ibid at para 37.
[121] T Naudé and G Lubbe 'Exemption Clauses – A Rethink Occasioned by *Afrox Healthcare Bpk v Strydom*' (2005) 122 SALJ 441.

further develop a jurisprudence of public-policy-based unenforceability of exemption clauses in those cases where the CPA does not apply.

Wallis J's dictum in *Swinburne* in particular and the case law on public policy enforceability in general provide a set of criteria for scrutinising such clauses, but the Act will be taken to be reflective – at least in part – of public policy and will add to the weight given to factors such as the type of risk or conduct in respect of which liability is exempted, the extent of inequality of bargaining power, and the party's knowledge and understanding of the relevant clause and its effects. For example, the Act makes it unlawful for a supplier to limit or exempt him- or herself from liability resulting from gross negligence[122] and lays down stringent requirements[123] for notifying consumers of clauses that in any way limit the liability of the supplier,[124] thereby ensuring that the consumer is aware of and understands the extent of the clause in question.

13.5 CONCLUSION

Now that the necessary and important academic debate on the direct/indirect application of the Bill of Rights to contract law has been largely settled by the trilogy of *Brisley v Drotsky*, *Afrox Healthcare Bpk v Strydom* and *Napier v Barkhuizen*,[125] it is clear that the next step in the development of the application of the Constitution to the law of contract is to build, over time, an increasingly clear profile of the courts' preferred vehicle – public policy – in as many typically occurring situations as possible. This will support the all-important value of certainty and predictability in contract as well as the courts' ability to ensure the ongoing orderly constitutionalisation of the common law of contract. As the examples that we have cited show, the courts have tools to do this – and they are already using them.

---

[122] Consumer Protection Act, s 51(c).
[123] Ibid s 49(3)-(5).
[124] Ibid s 49(1).
[125] See the literature cited by Peter Webster in Chapter 12 at note 6.

Chapter 14

Juristic Persons and Fundamental Rights

Ross Gilbert Anderson*

14.1 INTRODUCTION

Can juristic persons hold human rights? They are not human. And yet juristic persons are among the most enthusiastic pursuers of fundamental rights, in private law matters, before domestic courts.[1] The application of fundamental rights to juristic persons asks questions which go to the core of the nature of human, constitutional and fundamental rights;[2] and the relationship between these rights and private law. Questions arise on at least two levels. In the first place there are the vexed questions of the extent to which juristic persons may be the subjects or objects of fundamental rights. In the second place there is the parallel between fundamental rights and the internal regulation of juristic persons – in particular, the limited company – whether between (1) the members *inter se* or (2) the relationship between members and their government, the board. The subject is huge and the present discussion must be selective. It will be possible to make only passing mention, for example, of the various economic rights – 'fundamental' to businesses – conferred on juristic persons by, for example, the European Union (EU) or the World Trade Organization (WTO).[3]

14.2 RIGHTS: HUMAN, FUNDAMENTAL, CONSTITUTIONAL

Human rights are universal. They apply (or certainly ought to apply) to human beings irrespective of nationality, creed or colour. Unlike most

---

* I am grateful to Fritz Brand and Jonathan Burchell for various suggestions. The usual caveat applies.

1 Cf A Tomkins, 'Introduction' in T Campbell, K Ewing and A Tomkins (eds) *Sceptical Essays on Human Rights* (Oxford University Press 2001) 4.

2 W Blackstone *Commentaries on the Laws of England* vol 1 (1765) 140 referred to the 'rights, or, as they are more frequently termed, the liberties of Englishmen: liberties more generally talked of, than thoroughly understood'.

3 Fortunately more detailed discussions are available elsewhere. See, e.g., Danny Nicol, 'Business Rights as Human Rights' in T Campbell, K D Ewing and A Tomkins (eds) *The Legal Protection of Human Rights: Sceptical Essays* (Oxford University Press 2011) 229; Danny Nicol 'Europe's Lochner Moment' [2011] *Public Law* 308; Danny Nicol *The Constitutional Protection of Capitalism* (Hart Publishing 2010).

patrimonial rights, human rights are regularly expressed to be 'inalienable'. 'Constitutional rights', in contrast, at least in the UK, are more difficult: accorded by nation states, and often, perhaps normally, only to the citizens of that nation state, references to 'constitutional rights' have largely dried up since the incorporation of the European Convention on Human Rights (ECHR).[4] The South African Constitution limits 'citizenship' rights under the Constitution,[5] unsurprisingly, to citizens but fundamental rights are not so limited.[6] Although some republican scholars detest the idea of being a 'subject' of a monarchy,[7] the very word 'legal subject' indicates someone *holds* rights (*Rechtssubjekt*) rather than being an *object* (*Rechtsobjekt*) of them. It is for this reason that one of the most extreme sanctions that a state can impose on a citizen is to remove its recognition of the citizen as a citizen protected by the constitution: the citizen is declared an 'outlaw'.[8] The South African Constitution has an express prohibition on such an extreme sanction.[9]

It is now established that many of the 'fundamental freedoms' conferred by the ECHR – so-called 'human rights' – are exercisable by juristic persons. And, of course, many of the most important fundamental rights, particularly those arising as a result of supranational institutional agreements – the EU, the WTO and so on – have rather little to do with human beings at all.

14.3 HISTORY OF FUNDAMENTAL RIGHTS AND COMMERCE

In his magisterial work *Human Rights and the End of Empire* the late Brian Simpson suggested that 'human rights' was not a concept much referred to before the Second World War. There are various references to the idea of fundamental human rights – sometimes oblique, sometimes beguiling – in earlier writers, such as Germany's Samuel Pufendorf[10] and Scotland's John Millar.[11] Simpson shows that those historical examples that can be found

---

[4] *Watkins v Secretary of State for the Home Department* [2006] 2 AC 395 at para 58: 'there is, however, no magic in the term 'constitutional right'; and at para 64 *per* Lord Rodger of Earlsferry.

[5] Article 3.

[6] *Khosa v Minister of Social Development* 2004 (6) SA 505 (CC) (right to social assistance not limited to South African citizens but applied also to permanent residents).

[7] See, for example, A Tomkins *Our Republican Constitution* (Hart Publishing 2005).

[8] The term is English; the Scottish term was 'denunciation as a rebel', following a process of 'horning': Stair *Institutions* 3.3.1; G Watson (ed) *Bell's Dictionary and Digest of the Law of Scotland* 7e (Bell & Bradfute 1890) s.v. 'Denunciation'; and *Lord Advocate v Marquis of Zetland* 1920 SC (HL) 1 at 27 *per* Lord Shaw of Dunfermline.

[9] Article 20.

[10] *De iure naturae et gentium* (1672) 2.1.5 cited in U Wesel, *Geschichte des Rechts* 3e (C H Beck 2006) § 249. The best overview is in H Coing 'Der Rechtsbegriff der Menschlichen Person und die Theorien der Menschenrechte' in E Wolff (ed) *Beiträge zur Rechtsforschung* (W de Gruyte 1950) 191.

[11] See A Tomkins 'On Republican Constitutionalism in the Age of Commerce: Reflections

where the fundamental rights of minorities were to be protected almost always went hand-in-hand with the protection of private law rights:[12] the *'capitulations'* entered into between the French and the Ottomans in 1535, for instance, which allowed the rights of Christians to hold property and trade to be guaranteed; security of the person was added almost as an afterthought. Similar provisions are found in the Treaties of Nijmegen (1678), Warsaw (1773), Vienna (1814) and Paris (1858), and, before then, in European sources of the Middle Ages.[13] One of the great triumphs of humanity in the nineteenth century – the abolition of the involvement of the major powers in the slave trade – could not have occurred without the support of the commercial undertakings, many of them juristic persons.[14] Some references to the protection of property rights, in particular, can also be found in Blackstone[15] as well as in Scottish sources.[16] The earliest example of the term 'human right' I have found in the Scottish sources is in a posthumous article by a Swiss jurist in English translation which appeared in a Scottish law journal in 1888. Unsurprisingly, the right to which he was referring was the right of 'absolute dominion'.[17]

Moving into the twentieth century, it is equally difficult to find, prior to 1950, references in case law to human rights. The courts and much of the legal profession too were unenthusiastic. References, prior to 1950, to 'fundamental rights'[18] or 'human rights' in British cases are few and far between.

from the Scottish Enlightenment' in S Besson and J L Martí (eds) *Legal Republicanism: National and International Perspectives* (Oxford University Press 2009) 326.

[12] See, for all these examples, A W B Simpson *Human Rights and the End of Empire* (Oxford University Press 2001) 109–18.

[13] R von Keller *Freiheitsgarantien für Person und Eigentum im Mittelalter* (C Winter 1933). This is a work of considerable quality, despite what W Schmale, *Archaölogie der Grund- und Menschenrechte in der Frühen Neuzeit: ein deutsch-französisches Paradigma* (R Oldenbourg 1997) 67, calls the occasional 'pathetic' nod to the contemporary political *Zeitgeist*.

[14] S R Ratner 'Corporations and Human Rights: A Theory of Legal Responsibility' (2001) 111 *Yale LJ* 443 at 465.

[15] W Blackstone *Commentaries on the Laws of England* vol 1 (1765) 134–6.

[16] J Erskine *An Institute of the Laws of Scotland* [1773] 8e (1871) 2.1.2: 'persons deprived of their property ought to have a full equivalent given them for quitting it'. See too comments in *Thom v Black* (1828) 7 S 158 at 159 *per* Lord Gillies; and at 165 *per* Lord Corehouse (although both judges were dissenting).

[17] [Johann Caspar] Bluntschli 'Ownership and Property' (1888) 32 *Journal of Jurisprudence* 135 at 139. There is no indication of whether this paper is a translation and, if so, by whom and from what. For Bluntschli, see G Meyer von Knonau 'J C Bluntschli' in *Allgemeine Deutsche Biographie* vol 47 (Duncker & Humblot 1903), 29–39; M Stolleis *Juristen: ein biographisches Lexikon* (Beck 2001) 89. Bluntschli died in 1881.

[18] Three exceptional references are (1) *Keith v Lauder* (1905) 8 F 356 *per* Sheriff Substitute (Henderson Begg): 'In an industrial country like ours, "leave to toil" is one of the most fundamental rights of everyone who has to earn his living, whether with his hands or with his brains; and any interference with this right by employer, fellow-servant, or outsider, is, and ought to be, most jealously regarded by our Courts of law'. The Sheriff was reversed by the Court of Session. (2) *Lyon v Daily Telegraph Ltd* [1943] KB 746 at 753 *per* Scott LJ: 'It is

And in the first case I have traced where the ECHR was cited to the House of Lords, the instrument appeared sufficiently foreign and unfamiliar to the *Appeal Cases* reporter – a product of the upheavals of 1848 perhaps – that counsel's submission on article 6 was recorded as being to the European Convention of '1850'.[19] It was 1980 before the ECHR was first cited in the Scottish courts, but their Lordships effectively discouraged the habit.[20] By the time the First Division of the Court of Session took the opportunity to encourage a more proactive engagement with human rights law in 1997,[21] however, political developments had overtaken the courts with the Scotland Act 1998. Under the Scotland Act, the Scottish Parliament has no power to pass any legislation that is incompatible with either Convention rights or EU law.[22]

14.4 PRIVATE FUNDAMENTAL RIGHTS

Certain norms of private law have fundamental status, although often those norms are not actually written down.[23] Privity of contract is fundamental; so too is the need for publicity in order to create real rights (which, being absolute, affect one and all whether or not they were parties to the juridical act creating, varying, transferring or extinguishing a real right). Another is the principle that private persons cannot usually create a new legal person without the intervention of the state. Part of the rationale for this is creditor protection, for a fundamental principle of patrimonial law is that a creditor can look only to the assets of his debtor for satisfaction of the creditor's claim. Once juristic persons, easily formed, are admitted, the law must place some restriction on how they are formed, in order to protect creditors.[24] In

---

one of the *fundamental rights of free speech and writing* which are so dear to the British nation, and it is of vital importance to the rule of law on which we depend for our personal freedom that the courts should preserve the right of "fair comment" undiminished and unimpaired' (my emphasis). And (3) *Pollok School Company Limited v Glasgow Town Clerk* 1946 SLT 125 at 126 *per* Lord Birnam: 'In such an emergency [WWII] the *fundamental rights of life, liberty and property, which are the birthright of every citizen of this country*, had temporarily to be sacrificed or restricted in order that the nation itself might survive' (my emphasis). Lord Birnam's decision on the facts was reversed by the First Division: 1946 SC 373.

[19] *Royal Government of Greece v Governor of Brixton Prison* [1971] AC 250 at 276E-F reporting, hopefully inaccurately, the submissions of leading counsel.

[20] *Kaur v Lord Advocate* 1980 SC 319 and *Moore v Secretary of State for Scotland* 1985 SLT 38. Compare the unreported Outer House decision of Lord Morison in *Budh Singh, Petr*, 13 July 1988 discussed in J L Murdoch, 'The European Convention on Human Rights and Scots Law' [1991] *Public Law* 40.

[21] *T, Petitioner* 1997 SLT 724.

[22] Scotland Act 1998, s 29(2)(d) (as amended).

[23] V Arangio Ruiz 'La règle de droit et la loi dans l'antiquité classique' (1938) reproduced in V Arangio Ruiz *Scritti di diritto Romano* (Jovene 1977) vol 3, 197.

[24] This approach would explain why the partners of a Scottish firm, itself a juristic person, are nonetheless personally liable for its debts: Partnership Act 1890, s 4(2) and s 9.

this light it might be questioned why the law in Scotland or South Africa (or, for that matter, England) allows private parties to create trusts (which, although not benefiting from legal personality, nonetheless have many of the effects of a legal person). To this issue we shall have cause to return.

14.5 FUNDAMENTAL RIGHTS AND ECONOMIC FREEDOMS

14.5.1 The EU

A few words need to be said about the 'two legal Europes'. Over and above the ECHR is the EU. The EU, betraying its genesis as an economic union, is based on the 'four freedoms'. But these are economic freedoms: freedom of movement for persons, goods and capital; and the freedom to establish and provide services. Freedom of establishment is crucial for juristic persons: undertakings are free to choose which corporate vehicle to employ, and, once incorporated, the vehicle is free to trade anywhere in the EU.[25]

In the EU, therefore, it is economic freedoms that form the foundational core, not fundamental rights. Indeed, one of the foundational EU law cases conferring individual rights on European citizens, *van Gend en Loos*,[26] in fact involved the rights of a juristic person – a Dutch *naamloze vennootschap* – not a citizen. As Danny Nicol has observed, in cases where human rights conflict with one of the four freedoms, the ECJ tends to opt for an analysis whereby a human right needs to be justified in light of the economic freedom, rather than the economic freedom having to be justified in light of the human right.[27] The difficulty here is that, in terms of the EU settlement, economic values entrenched in EU law cannot be altered by national parliaments.[28]

The Treaty on the Functioning of the European Union imposes an obligation on the EU itself to accede to the ECHR[29] and the Court of Justice of the European Union claims a fundamental rights jurisdiction. The development can be traced through decisions of the ECJ,[30] through to the Charter of

---

25 Case C-212/97 *Centros Ltd. v Erhvervs-og Selskabsstyrelsen* [1999] ECR I-1459; Case C-208/00 *Überseering BV v Nordic Construction Baumanagement GmbH* [2002] ECR I-9919; Case C-167/01 *Kamer van Koophandel en Fabriken voor Amsterdam v Inspire Art Ltd* [2003] ECR I-10155; Case C-210/06 *Cartesio Oktato es Szolgaltato bt* [2009] Ch 354.

26 *NV Algemene Transport- en Expeditie Onderneming van Gend en Loos v Nederlandse Administratie der Belastingen* [1963] ECR 649.

27 D Nicol 'Europe's Lochner Moment' [2011] *Public Law* 308 at 321.

28 Historically, the English courts in applying constitutional principles paid less attention than they do today to Parliament: see J W Gough *Fundamental Law in English Constitutional History* (Clarendon Press 1955).

29 TEU, art 6(2).

30 Case 4/73 *Nold v Commission* [1974] ECR 491; Case 36–75 *Rutili v Minister of the Interior* [1975] ECR 1219; Case C-299/95 *Kremzow v Austria* [1997] ECR I-2629. See generally A Metzger *Extra legem, intra ius: Allgemeine Rechtsgrundsätze im europäischen Privatrecht* (Mohr Siebeck 2009) 425ff.

Fundamental Rights of the European Union. Adopted in December 2007,[31] the Charter has the same 'legal value' as the Treaties.[32] Again, however, an expanding economic core is evident: for the first time, the 'right to run a business'[33] is included in addition to the right to property (which also now explicitly includes the protection of intellectual property).[34]

14.5.2 South Africa

Matters are simpler in South Africa. The Constitution expressly provides, in a general provision, that a juristic person is entitled to the rights in the Bill of Rights.[35] With capacity, however, comes responsibility: juristic persons are also potentially objects of fundamental rights.[36] But despite the differences between the EU and South Africa, there is one area that the Scottish Parliament, the UK Parliament and the South African Parliament have in common. Each is now generally powerless to overturn by legislation a fundamental rights decision: the UK institutions for the reasons given above, the South African Parliament because it too is bound by the Constitution.[37]

14.5.3 Law, democracy, isonomy

Both the ECHR and the Constitution place considerable emphasis on democracy, without actually articulating democracy, as a political system, or the right to participate in a democracy, as a fundamental right.[38] But if this is an omission, it is perhaps a deliberate one, for fundamental rights exist to protect despised individuals or groups *against* democracy: from the mob, from the majority gone mad.[39]

There is much that could be said. Two observations suffice. The first is that the Athenian idea of democracy has all but supplanted the related, but equally important, ideal of *isonomy*: the 'equality of laws to all manner of persons'.[40] The second observation is that, whereas fundamental rights

---

[31] [2000] C364/1 (adopted 18 December 2000).

[32] TEU, art 6(1).

[33] Charter of Fundamental Rights in the European Union, art 16.

[34] Charter of Fundamental Rights in the European Union, art 17.

[35] Constitution, art 8(4).

[36] Constitution, art 8(2).

[37] Constitution, art 8(1).

[38] M Emberland *The Human Rights of Companies* (Oxford University Press 2006) 39–44.

[39] See, for example, *Chassagnou v France* (2000) 29 EHRR 615 at para 112: 'Although individual interests must on occasion be subordinated to those of a group, democracy does not simply mean that the views of a majority must always prevail: a balance must be achieved which ensures the fair and proper treatment of minorities and avoids any abuse of a dominant position'. Cf a rare law review article by F Rodell 'Judicial Activists, Judicial Self-deniers, Judicial Review and the First Amendment' (1958) 47 *Georgetown Law Journal* 483 at 486–7.

[40] See F A von Hayek *The Constitution of Liberty* (Routledge & Kegan Paul 1960) 11.2ff for

may be seen as an expression of human personality and dignity (as with the right to vote), companies and other juristic persons may express very little in the way of human personality; similarly their claims to dignity are tenuous.[41] Conversely juristic persons hold neither the right to vote nor other democratic rights. But perhaps because of, rather than in spite of, the fact that juristic persons are not subject to the certainty of mortality, they are subjected to that other certainty – taxes.[42] The brocard 'no taxation without representation' applies only to natural persons.[43] And rightly so: corporations are constituted by the people, for the people; it is not the other way around, a point worth emphasising.[44] In the EU, however, legal persons do have the right to petition the European Parliament.[45]

14.6 STANDING OF JURISTIC PERSONS

14.6.1 History

If the modern idea of human rights can be traced to the Universal Declaration of Human Rights ('Universal Declaration') in 1948, it is worth noting the persons in whose favour the Universal Declaration was drafted. The recitals refer to 'human beings'; 'all members of the human family'; the 'human person'. Considering the Universal Declaration was drafted in the aftermath of the Holocaust, with the stench of inhumanity overpowering, the Universal Declaration focused on human beings. No corporations, after all, went to the gas chambers; no companies were exterminated by death squads; no unit trusts were degraded in Gestapo interrogations. But it is perhaps only because of such express references to 'human beings' in

---

further references; and, in particular, a lucid passage from J Huizinga *Geschonden Wereld* (H D Tjeenk Willink 1945), in German translation as *Wenn die Waffen Schweigen* (Burgverlag 1945) 94–95, 'Das Wort Demokratie'. Only the German translation was available to me.

[41] See section 14.6.4 below.

[42] The English Statute of Mortemain was passed in 1279 so that feudal superiors could not be so easily deprived of the feudal privileges due to them on the death or conviction of a vassal, by land falling into the hands of corporations.

[43] The principle 'no taxation without representation' is sometimes said to derive from Magna Carta, chs 12 and 15; but the link is tenuous, there being then no modern system of taxation: W S McKechnie *Magna Carta: A Commentary on the Great Charter of King John with an Historical Introduction* 2e (B Franklin 1914, repr 1958) 239–40; J C Holt *Magna Carta* 2e (Cambridge University Press 1992).

[44] Sir Karl Popper, *The Open Society and its Enemies* 5e (Routledge & Kegan Paul 1965) vol 2, 17.V wrote that 'economic power must not be permitted to dominate political power' and that 'it rests entirely with us to see that much more stringent laws [on electioneering expenditure] are introduced'. Cf the bare majority decision of the US Supreme Court allowing US corporations to engage in electioneering: *Citizens United v Federal Election Commission* 558 US 50 (2010).

[45] Charter of Fundamental Rights of the European Union, art 44.

the text of the Universal Declaration that juristic persons are excluded. For even before the onslaught of industrial warfare, at the turn of the twentieth century the US Supreme Court, without hearing argument and without giving any reasons, accepted that corporations were protected by the terms of the US Constitution.[46]

Under the ECHR, in contrast, it was thought that the point may be open for debate. So, in _Air Canada v UK_,[47] counsel conceded in his opening statement that 'we are not human . . . the question whether we have any rights, remains for your Lordships' decision'.[48] Their Lordships have generally answered the general question in the affirmative. But there is some doubt, not just in Europe but in many other systems (South Africa is an exception), whether it was ever intended that corporations should be able to benefit from constitutional rights or other fundamental rights provisions. In 1993 the then UK Labour Party leader – the Scottish advocate John Smith – recommended the incorporation of the ECHR into domestic law, but he wanted to leave companies unprotected.[49] The fear – sometimes rational, sometimes not – is that corporate actors may abuse fundamental rights to undermine the democratic process.[50]

Suffice it to record that, since the HRA came into force in Scotland, it is mainly juristic persons that have sought to invoke their Convention rights in private law matters[51] (as well as in criminal cases)[52]. Three recent examples include: insurance companies challenging legislation deeming a certain medical condition to amount to _damnum_ for the purposes of the law

---

[46] _Santa Clara County v Southern Pacific Railroad Co_ 118 US 394 (1886) at 396 _per_ Waite CJ: 'The Court does not want to hear argument on the question [of whether a corporation is protected by the Constitution] . . . We are all of the opinion that it does'. It was with similar sleight of hand that freedom of contract was elevated to a constitutionally protected principle in the US: see _Allgeyer v Louisiana_ 165 US 578 (1897) where Peckham J, on the basis of the Fourteenth Amendment, held that the liberty extended to 'enter into all contracts which may be proper, necessary, and essential to his carrying out to a successful conclusion the purposes above mentioned'. The Fourteenth Amendment, like the Fifth, contains the so-called 'due process' clause: the Fifth Amendment is directed at the federal government; the Fourteenth at states.

[47] (1995) 20 EHRR 150.

[48] Quoted in N Bratza 'The Implications of the Human Rights Act 1998 for Commercial Practice' [2000] _EHRLR_ 1. Sir Nicholas Bratza QC, the British judge at the Strasbourg court, is presently the Court's President.

[49] Emberland, note 38 supra, 29.

[50] S Sedley 'Opinion: A Bill of Rights for Britain' [1997] _EHRLR_ 458 at 464.

[51] _Lafarge Redland Aggregates Ltd v Scottish Ministers_ 2001 SC 298; _County Properties Ltd v Scottish Ministers_ 2002 SC 79; _Karl Construction Ltd v Palisade Properties Plc_ 2002 SC 270; _Fab Tek Engineering Ltd v Carillion Construction Ltd_ 2002 SLT (Sh Ct) 113; _Strathclyde Joint Police Board v Elderslie Estates Ltd_ 2002 SLT (Lands Tr) 2; _Catscratch Ltd v Glasgow City Licensing Board (No.2)_ 2002 SLT 503; _Baden-Württembergische Bank AG, Petitioner_ [2009] CSIH 47. Other cases will be referred to below.

[52] _Transco plc (No 2) v HM Advocate_ 2005 1 JC 44.

of delict;[53] a tobacco company seeking relief against a law restricting tobacco advertising;[54] and manufacturers of alcoholic drinks invoking competition laws to challenge legislation setting minimum pricing for alcohol on public health grounds.[55]

14.6.2 *References to juristic persons*

The ECHR applies to 'everyone'. But on one view 'everyone', without more, does not include juristic persons since there are a number of provisions which make special provision for juristic persons: *expressio unis, exclusio alteris*. Article 1(1) of the First Protocol to the ECHR, protecting property rights, is expressly formulated to apply to 'every natural or legal person'. Article 10(1) ECHR indicates that 'media enterprises'[56] are protected by the right of freedom of expression. And article 34 ECHR – the victimhood provision – confers a right of private petition upon 'any person, non-governmental organisation or group of individuals'. But 'person', in this provision, *cannot* include a juristic person, because the French text refers to '*personne physique*'. So, if juristic persons, including companies, have a right of individual petition under the Convention it is because, for the purposes of article 34, they are considered, somewhat artificially, to be 'non-governmental organisations'.[57] Such an analysis – hidden from the reader of the English text – was adopted by the European Commission on Human Rights.[58] That the French text limits protection to physical or natural persons may indicate that, elsewhere in the ECHR, the protection of juristic persons was not intended; and not least because, elsewhere, particular articles expressly apply to natural and juristic persons alike: such as the right of 'association'[59] or the right to a fair hearing.[60]

---

[53] *Axa General Insurance Ltd, Petitioners* [2011] UKSC 46 reviewing the Damages (Asbestos-related Conditions) (Scotland) Act 2009. The challenge was unsuccessful.

[54] *Imperial Tobacco Ltd, Petitioner* [2012] UKSC 61, reviewing the Tobacco and Primary Medical Services (Scotland) Act 2010. The challenge was unsuccessful.

[55] The Scotch Whisky Association is presently reviewing the Alcohol (Minimum Pricing) (Scotland) Act 2012. An alcohol charity (a company limited by guarantee) has been allowed to intervene: *Scotch Whisky Association Petitioner* [2012] CSOH 156.

[56] This term has been held to include companies: *Autronic AG v Switzerland* Series A No 178 (1990) 12 EHRR 486 at para 47. The BBC invoked this right before the Court of Session in *Response Handling Ltd v BBC* 2008 SLT 51. Cf *South African Broadcasting Corporation v Avusa Ltd* 2010 (1) SA 280 (GSJ).

[57] For a summary of the *travaux preparatoires* and the evolution of the text from 'any natural or corporate person' to the present, see Emberland, note 38 supra, 35

[58] App 11921/86 *Verein, Kontakt-Information-Therapie' (KIT) and Hagen v Austria* (1988) 57 DR 81 at paras 1(4) and 2.

[59] ECHR art 11, for which, see generally Emberland, note 38 supra, 42.

[60] ECHR art 6, for which see *Her Majesty's Secretary of State for Business Enterprise and Regulatory Reform, Petitioner* 2011 SC 115.

14.6.3 South Africa

The Constitution, we have seen, has general provisions applying the Constitution to juristic persons. As a result, unless the contrary intention appears, articles that apply to everyone apply also to juristic persons. So 'freedom of movement'[61] and the right to leave the Republic, being conferred on 'everyone',[62] can, in principle, be exercised by juristic persons. Compare the important economic freedom to choose a 'trade, occupation or profession freely': this freedom derogates from the general provision in article 8(4) and is conferred only on citizens.[63] In addition, the Constitution expressly confers social and economic rights. These too are conferred on 'everyone/*Elkeen*'. So 'everyone has the right to have access to adequate housing'[64] and everyone has the right to have access to healthcare, food and water and social security.[65] The rights – perhaps with one exception[66] – are not, however, absolute.[67] If it was envisaged that only citizens may invoke these Constitutional rights, it is an intention that is not reflected in the words of the Constitution. So, since 'everyone' has 'inherent dignity', juristic persons as well as natural persons are entitled to have their dignity respected and protected.[68]

Despite the refined terms of the South African Bill of Rights, it is again striking that, as in the US and the EU, the extension of fundamental rights to juristic persons has largely occurred on the nod: the application of fundamental rights to juristic persons is asserted rather than justified.[69] Denying juristic persons the benefits of the Constitution, it has been observed, would 'lead to grave disruptions and would undermine the very fabric of our democratic state';[70] 'it would have a disastrous impact on the business world generally, on creditors of companies and, more especially, on shareholders in companies.'[71] At the same time, however, the courts have recognised that

---

[61] Constitution, art 21(1); Afrikaans: '*Elkeen*'.
[62] Constitution, art 21(2).
[63] Constitution, art 22.
[64] Constitution, art 26.
[65] Constitution, art 27.
[66] Constitution, art 27(3): 'no one may be refused emergency medical treatment'.
[67] *Minister of Health v Treatment Action Campaign (No 2)* 2002 (5) SA 721 (CC) (the right to healthcare) and *Mazibuko v City of Johannesburg* 2010 (4) SA 1 (CC) (right to water).
[68] See J H Neethling, ' 'n Vergelyking tussen die individuele en korporatiewe persoonlikheidsreg op identiteit' 2011 *TSAR* 62 at 64, notes 17 and 18, and at 73 approved in *Media 24 Ltd v SA Taxi Securitisation (Pty) Ltd* 2011 (5) SA 329 at para 43 *per* Brand JA. EU law recognises only *human* dignity as a fundamental right: Charter of Fundamental Rights, art 1.
[69] So corporations are entitled to the benefits of art 34 (due process): *Findevco (Pty) Ltd v Faceformat SA (Pty) Ltd* 2001 (1) SA 251.
[70] *Investigating Directorate: Serious Economic Offences v Hyundai Motor Distributors (Pty) Ltd* 2001 (1) SA 545 at paras 17 and 18 *per* Langa DP.
[71] *First National Bank of SA Ltd t/a Wesbank v Commissioner, South African Revenue Service* 2002 (4) SA 768 (CC) at para 45 *per* Ackermann J.

juristic persons' rights to enjoyment are 'not the same as natural persons'.[72] But this recognition repeats rather than illuminates the caveat in article 8(4) that a juristic person is entitled to the rights in the Bill of Rights only *'to the extent required by the nature of the right and the nature of the juristic person'*.[73]

14.6.4 Wider implications of recognition

Standing, in the context of juristic persons, has two additional aspects. The first is that, at common law, they are entitled to avail themselves of ordinary private law remedies: so a juristic person is even entitled to protect its reputation,[74] although the law recognises that corporations cannot claim *solatium*, only patrimonial loss.[75] But patrimonial loss may extend to the most intangible asset of all: goodwill. And corporations are no more required to prove *actual* patrimonial loss than natural persons.[76] In a memorable case note, however, the late Tony Weir questioned whether preferring the corporate image to freedom of speech was not a 'grim perversion of values.'[77]

The second issue of standing relates to a classic principle of English company law and all systems that have drawn from it. Only the company itself is the proper claimant to prosecute claims for wrongs done to the company: this is the so-called 'rule in *Foss v Harbottle*'.[78] As we will see below, both Scots and South African domestic laws have now developed sophisticated exceptions to this principle: minority protection and the derivative action (and this is one area where Scots company law is somewhat different to English law).[79] This principle of domestic law has found its way into even customary public international law,[80] as well as the European Court of Human

---

[72] *Investigating Directorate*, note 70 supra, at para 18 *per* Langa DP.

[73] Afrikaans: 'in die mate waarin die aard van die regte en die aard van daardie regspersoon dit vereis'. This caveat bears similarities to art 19(3) of the German *Grundgesetz*, and German cases and literature may be useful. For references see H Bergbach *Anteilseigentum* (Sellier 2010) 97ff.

[74] *Jameel v Wall Street Journal Europe Sprl* [2007] 1 AC 359; *Media 24 Ltd v SA Taxi Securitisation (Pty) Ltd* 2011 (5) SA 329. In *Jameel*, Lord Hope, at paras 95–6 indicated that companies should be treated no differently than natural persons, trades unions or charities. (A 'charity', however, is a status rather than a category of person.)

[75] *Rubber Improvement Ltd v Daily Telegraph Ltd* [1964] AC 234 at 262 *per* Lord Reid.

[76] *Dhlomo v Natal Newspapers (Pty) Ltd* 1989 (1) SA 945 (A) at 953D *per* Rabie AJA.

[77] J A Weir 'Local Authority v Critical Ratepayer – A Suit in Defamation' (1972) 52 *Cambridge LJ* 238 at 240 (quoted by Baroness Hale in *Jameel* at para 154). Cf the effect of the *Jameel* decision, note 74 supra: C Binham 'Business Libel Cases Treble' *Financial Times* 25 August 2011.

[78] (1843) 2 Hare 461; 67 ER 189.

[79] Companies Act 2006, ss 265 and 994; Companies Act 2008 (71 of 2008) s 165, which develops s 266 of the Companies Act 1973.

[80] *Case Concerning Barcelona Traction, Light & Power Co Ltd (Belgium v Spain) (Merits)* [1970] ICJ Rep 3.

Rights (ECtHR)[81] and South African law. Those who most usually wish to bring a claim for a breach of their fundamental rights in a corporate context – the shareholders – are, as a general rule, therefore excluded from doing so.

14.7 JURISTIC PERSONS: ONSHORE AND OFFSHORE

14.7.1 Immortal, invisible

Citizenship is a mutual relationship of right and obligation between, for the one part, citizens *inter se*, and, for the other part, citizen and state. The citizen, who abrogates his or her responsibilities to his fellow citizens, may lose some of the benefits of being a citizen. In modern law, such a citizen may lose his or her liberty and some of her constitutional rights.[82] In principle, this can happen with entities too. Terrorist 'groups', for instance, are not only deprived of basic legal rights, but are proscribed. States can petition to have companies removed from the register and liquidated. But companies give rise to special challenges in two particular aspects. In the first place, although companies can be wound up, they need not be: they may never die; they are potentially immortal.[83] Secondly, the undertaking in corporate form can be well-nigh invisible. The particular corporate form, assuming it is identifiable, is a façade; the economic interests that lie underneath are hidden from view and highly moveable: vehicles can be changed with the sleight of hand of a mask. A regulatory swipe at a corporate mask may disclose no more than a puff of smoke. A recent study – much criticised by officials in offshore jurisdictions – points to the phenomenon of 'flipping' domiciles: local laws that permit an offshore entity (normally with a trust at the top of the ladder) to change its domicile on the occurrence of a future specified event: so-called 'Castro clauses'.[84] The offshore phenomenon is eye-watering in its extent. In 2009, when US President, Barack Obama sought to garner international support for action against offshore tax havens, he highlighted a modest office in the Cayman Islands – a Crown dependency – where, he

---

[81] *Agrotexim Hellas SA v Greece* (1996) 21 EHRR 250; *Olczak v Poland*, 7 November 2002 (ECtHR, admissibility decision).

[82] E.g. *Hirst v the United Kingdom (No 2)* [2005] ECHR 681; (2006) 42 EHHR 41, concerning the incompatibility of the UK Representation of the People Act 1983, whereby criminals sentenced to periods of imprisonment lose the right to vote, was incompatible with art 3 of Protocol 1 ECHR. A South African equivalent is *Minister of Home Affairs v National Institute for Crime Prevention and the re-integration of Offenders* 2005 (3) SA 280 (CC).

[83] The Aberdeen Harbour Board is reputedly the oldest legal person in the UK, tracing its origins to 1136: J Micklethwait and A Woodridge *The Company: A Short History of a Revolutionary Idea* (Weidenfeld & Nicholson 2003) 23.

[84] N Shaxson *Treasure Islands: Tax Havens and the Men who Stole the World* (Bodley Head 2011) 119. Whether any court – even in an offshore jurisdiction – would uphold such a clause is another question. But such jurisdictions are scrupulous in upholding formal legal arrangements: the letter of the law, not its spirit, is everything.

observed, there are some 12,000 companies registered. The Chairman of the Cayman Islands Financial Services Authority retorted immediately. An office in North Orange Street, Wilmington in Delaware, he observed, must be even larger: for it is the registered office for no less than 217,000 US corporations.

The phenomenon is important. Such is the drive from major international businesses to lower their tax burden, there can be few multinational businesses whose corporate structures do not take advantage of potential immortality and, also, the invisibility offered by offshore corporate structures. The Scottish Law Commission is trying to work out how the law should respond to a Scottish general partnership – a juristic person – avoiding criminal proceedings by the simple expedient of dissolving before service of the indictment.[85] And if dealing with invisibility is difficult domestically, it is well-nigh impossible with non-transparent offshore jurisdictions spread around the globe. An international business that goes to such lengths, at considerable cost, to structure its affairs to reduce its tax bill by a few dozen million dollars is perhaps unlikely to be scrupulous in its approach to respecting fundamental rights. Less cynically but equally prosaically, even where such an undertaking is held bound to respect fundamental rights, corporate structures are often 'judgment proof'.[86]

14.7.2 Non-persons: trusts

Companies are just one type of juristic person. But there is a wider question of which entities can be fundamental rights subjects or objects. It is a fundamental principle of private law that without legal personality there can be neither active nor passive transactional capacity. A non-person, therefore, can be neither the subject nor the object of patrimonial rights: neither creditor nor debtor. Fundamental rights jurisprudence, however, takes a more flexible approach to legal personality. Companies are at least juristic persons. The existence of most juristic persons can be confirmed or denied by reference to a public register.[87] But there are other vehicles that are allowed to

---

[85] *Balmer v HM Advocate* 2008 SLT 799, which is the subject of a report by the Scottish Law Commission: *Report on the Criminal Liability of Partnerships* (SLC No 224, 2011).

[86] A classic case is *Adams v Cape Industries plc* [1990] Ch 433: a UK company, Cape, was involved in mining asbestos in South Africa. The English court held that it would not pierce the corporate veil to hold Cape liable for a judgment against an asset-poor subsidiary in respect of employee damages claims for asbestosis. But compare *Chandler v Cape plc* [2012] EWCA Civ 525 where a parent was held to owe a duty of care to its subsidiary's employees. For discussion of the regulation of multinational corporate structures, see P Sutherland 'Globalization and Corporate Law' in M Faure and A J van der Walt (eds) *Globalization and Private Law: The Way Forward* (Edward Elgar 2010) 255.

[87] Not always: the Scottish general partnership, for instance, is a juristic person, but there is no register of partnerships.

masquerade behind legal personality without being a body corporate and that are thus not always entered on any register.[88] More difficult still are the 'non-entities' which crowd commercial life. Non-entities are extremely attractive because of their invisibility. English partnerships and limited partnerships, as well as Jersey and Guernsey partnerships and limited partnerships, are good examples. But it is in trusts that we find the most extreme consequences. The Standard Oil Trust, for instance, was employed as a holding entity in order to evade the regulatory requirements of corporate law.

> '[The trust] made no agreements, signed no contracts, kept no books. It had no legal existence. It was a force as powerful as gravitation and as intangible. You could argue its existence from its effects, but you could not prove it. You could no more grasp it than you could an eel.'[89]

The anomaly whereby the 'trust' was able to evade company law is summarised thus:

> 'But consider the anomaly of the situation. Thirty-nine corporations, each of them having a legal existence, obliged by the laws of the state creating it to limit its operations to certain lines and to make certain reports, had turned over their affairs to an organisation having no legal existence, independent of all authority, able to do anything it wanted anywhere; and to this point working in absolute darkness. Under their agreement, which as unrecognized by the state, a few men had united to do things which no incorporated company could do. It was a situation as puzzling as new.'[90]

Now, the question of whether trusts – as opposed to the trustees – can hold patrimonial rights is controversial. Both Scotland and South Africa admit the trust.[91] The standard answer is: no legal personality, no transactional capacity. And without legal capacity, the trust cannot hold patrimonial rights. But, as has been seen, for fundamental rights purposes, the law takes a more flexible approach. A claim that a trust was the holder of constitutional rights in South Africa was abandoned in one case that reached the Supreme Court of Appeal.[92] But the right to associate, for instance,

---

[88] Some jurisdictions have a full suite of possibilities. So Jersey law, for instance, has three types of limited partnership alone, offering a choice between: (1) no legal personality; (2) legal personality but not a body corporate; (3) a body corporate. See, respectively, the Limited Partnerships (Jersey) Law 1994; Separate Limited Partnerships (Jersey) Law 2011; and the Incorporated Limited Partnerships (Jersey) Law 2011.

[89] I Tarbell *History of the Standard Oil Company* (McClure, Phillips & Co 1904) vol 2, 141.

[90] Ibid, vol 2, 136. The Trust Agreement of 1882 is reproduced at vol 2, 364. It is not by accident that US competition law is 'anti-trust' law.

[91] Cf B Wunsh 'Trading and Business Trusts' (1986) 103 *SALJ* 561; D Davis et al *Companies and other Business Structures in South Africa* 2e (Oxford University Press 2010) 345ff.

[92] *Bredenkamp, Breco International Ltd, Hamilton Place Trust and International Cigarette Manufacturers (Pty) Ltd* 2010 (4) SA 468.

has been accorded even to bodies that have no legal personality at all;[93] although, admittedly, there was little consideration of whether the right is conferred upon the individuals who have exercised the right to associate or on the association itself.[94] In Germany too the Constitutional court, ignoring any existential and eschatological difficulties, accepts that *Stiftungen* – funds with legal personality but no members – may even exercise the fundamental right of freedom of religion.[95]

14.8 JURISTIC PERSONS AS FUNDAMENTAL RIGHTS SUBJECTS

14.8.1 *'Juristic persons'*

In South Africa juristic persons are entitled to the rights conferred by the Bill of Rights.[96] In the UK, juristic persons have always been considered to be subjects of basic constitutional rights, such as the right to due process and a fair trial.[97] So too does the German *Grundgesetz* expressly provide that German juristic persons may hold constitutional rights.[98]

What, then, about the greatest juristic person of all: the state (the Crown)? Fundamental rights, we have seen, were originally conferred in large measure to protect persons – juristic as well as natural – *against* the state. The state can be conceptualised at different levels. Some have viewed the state as the essential institution for a legal system in the first place. Law and state, to take the views of one distinguished scholar, Paul Vinogradoff, are but different sides of the same coin.[99] But more recent scholarship has convincingly demonstrated that law has existed, does exist and may exist without the state, at least in the sense of the modern conception of state.[100] The UK lacks a

---

[93] In *Wishart Arch Defenders Loyal Orange Lodge 404 v Angus Council* 2002 SLT (Sh Ct) 43 it was assumed without argument that an unincorporated association of Orangemen could be the holder of human rights of assembly and association.

[94] Cf Lord Radcliffe, 'Law and the Democratic State' in *Not in Feather Beds* (Hamish Hamilton 1968) 45 at 58: 'It is all very well to speak of the right to free association. That is the personal side of it. But the rights of the association are equally important and equally entitled to respect'.

[95] H Bergbach, *Anteilseigentum* (Sellier 2010) 100 and cases there cited.

[96] Constitution, s 8(4): 'A juristic person is entitled to the rights in the Bill of Rights to the extent required by the nature of the rights and the nature of that juristic person'.

[97] Cf *Her Majesty's Secretary of State for Business Enterprise and Regulatory Reform, Petitioner* 2011 SC 115 (companies not allowed to appear as party litigants, represented by an officer of the company; no breach of art 6 ECHR; companies were already suitably protected).

[98] *Grundgesetz* art 19(3): 'Die Grundrechte gelten auch für inländische juristische Personen, soweit sie ihrem Wesen nach auf diese anwendbar sind.'

[99] P Vinogradoff 'The Juridical Nature of the State' (1924) 23 *Michigan Law Review* 1, reproduced in H L A Fischer (ed) *Collected Papers of Paul Vinogradoff* (Clarendon Press 1928) vol 2, 350 at 360–1.

[100] N Jansen and R Michaels 'Private Law and the State: Comparative Perceptions and

modern *Staatslehre*, primarily because of the personification of the state in the Crown. As Maitland pointed out, although the monarch is not the state, there is much statutory authority holding that the state is 'Her Majesty'.[101] The moral, however, is rather that, if we would not concede either to the Crown or to the state, as the case may be, the privilege of holding fundamental rights, still less should we accord fundamental rights to any old juristic person. We do well to remember, for instance, that in July 2011 even Uncle Sam, at one point, held less cash than Apple Inc.[102]

14.8.2 Economic rights as constitutional rights

Because corporations cannot vote, their most important constitutional rights are economic. So although 'compulsory acquisition of property is an institution common to all civilized nations',[103] laws in different places and at different times have consistently accepted the view that expropriation should have a neutral patrimonial effect: the state, assuming that it had the power to expropriate, is bound to pay for the assets expropriated.

In the UK the classic example of constitutional protection of property rights of a corporation at common law is the litigation that arose in *Burmah Oil Co (Burma Trading) Ltd v Lord Advocate*.[104] The company, incorporated in Scotland, owned a number of oil installations in Burma, then a Crown colony. With the advance of the Japanese armies in 1942, the military decision was taken that, in the event that it was not possible to defend Burma, the oil installations belonging to the company should be destroyed. The company brought an action in 1961 against the Crown arguing that, at common law, it was entitled to compensation for the destruction of its property. The crucial point was that the installations were not destroyed by enemy action but by the Crown, in prosecution of what Lord Reid described as a 'form of economic warfare',[105] in order to stop them falling into enemy hands. Lord Reid, giving the leading speech, held that, at common law, Scots law was found in the writings of Grotius[106] and Bynkershoek;[107] and

---

Historical Observations' (2007) 71 *RabelsZ* 345 at 356–357; C Donahue 'Private Law without the State and during its Formation' (2008) 56 *AJCL* 541.

[101] F W Maitland 'The Crown as a Corporation' (1901) 17 *LQR* 131, reproduced in H A L Fisher (ed) *The Collected Papers of Frederic William Maitland* (Cambridge University Press 1911) vol 3, 244 at 259.

[102] The figures were first publicised by the Canadian journalist, M Hartley, 'US Balance now less than Apple Cash' *Financial Post*, 29 July 2011, available at *http://business.financialpost. com/2011/07/28/u-s-balance-now-less-than-apple-cash/*

[103] F A Mann 'The Effect in England of the Compulsory Acquisition by a Foreign State of the Shares in a Foreign Company' (1986) 102 *LQR* 191 and (1987) 103 *LQR* 26.

[104] 1964 SC (HL) 117.

[105] 1964 SC (HL) 117 at 129.

[106] *De iure belli ac pacis* ([1625] English Carnegie edition, 1913–1925) vol 2, 807.

[107] *Quaestiones Juris Publici* ([1737] English Carnegie edition, 1930) 221–3.

had been accurately stated by the judges of the Court of Session where Lord Guthrie, for example, had formulated the general principle: 'where an individual is deprived of his property under the lawful authority of the Sovereign for the public good, the loss to the individual must be made good at the public expense'.[108]

The result, however, was unpalatable: a company would be compensated for economic losses where millions of families, which had sacrificed the lives of fathers, sons and brothers, would not be. Parliament acted: the War Damage Act 1965 was passed in haste to ensure, retrospectively, that no compensation would be payable, on the basis of the common law, in times of war.[109] The whole episode – involving retrospective legislation – is an important one in the history of human rights law in the UK: it was because of perceived claims by the company that the UK government postponed acceding to article 1 of the First Protocol to the ECHR, dealing with the protection against deprivation of possessions ('nul ne peut être privé de sa propriété')[110] and which, furthermore, is one of only two provisions to be expressly formulated to extend to 'legal persons'.

Parliament's solution to the *Burmah Oil Co* decision – legislation – under the present constitutional arrangements, however, may now be subject to review by the ECJ and domestic courts.[111]

14.9 SHOULD JURISTIC PERSONS BE SUBJECTS OF FUNDAMENTAL RIGHTS?

There is room on this question for reasonable views to differ. In the United States, for instance, it was assumed, from the late nineteenth century, that corporations were entitled to the protection of the Constitution.[112] As two Supreme Court Justices, Black and Douglas JJ, pointed out in 1949, however, 'there was no history, logic, or reason given to support that view. Nor was the result so obvious that explanation was unnecessary'.[113] But the

---

[108] 1963 SC 410 at 475 rev'd 1964 SC (HL) 117.

[109] Section 1 provided for the abolition of the ancient common law right to compensation: 'in respect of damage to, or destruction of, property caused (whether before or after the passing of this Act, within or outside the United Kingdom) by acts lawfully done by, or on the authority of, the Crown during, or in contemplation of the outbreak of, a war in which the Sovereign was, or is, engaged'.

[110] Article 1, First Protocol ECHR.

[111] Compare *Axa General Insurance Ltd v Lord Advocate* [2011] UKSC 46 (dealing with an Act of the Scottish Parliament) and *Test Claimants in the FII Group Litigation v Revenue and Customs Commissioners* [2012] UKSC 19; [2012] 2 AC 337 (dealing with compatibility of a Westminster Act with EU law). The UKSC has referred the matter to the CJEU.

[112] *Santa Clara County v Southern Pacific Railroad Co* note 46 supra.

[113] *Wheeling Steel Corporation v Glander* 337 US 563 (1949) at 577 *per* Black and Douglas JJ (dissenting); compare Jackson J's note on the point at 574–5. See too the earlier dissenting

predominant view in the US Supreme Court, at least at the time of writing, is that corporations are as much entitled to constitutional protection as anyone else. The constitution does not, for instance, allow the government to prevent corporations from electioneering. This approach, says Kennedy J, is consistent with basic democratic principles: allowing the government to place controls on particular speakers is tantamount to censoring the content of speech;[114] and 'the fact that a corporation, or any other speaker, is willing to spend money to try to persuade voters presupposes that the people have the ultimate influence over elected officials'.[115] Similarly, since much private property is held through various corporate vehicles, fundamental rights protection of private property – which has long gone hand in hand with the protection of individual liberty – would be all but impossible if corporate entities could not benefit from fundamental rights. With the exception of the *Air Canada v UK* case, there has been no serious argument before the court in Scotland (or, for that matter, anywhere else in Europe) that companies should not be entitled to benefit from fundamental rights: not least because, in Europe, freedom of establishment is one of the four freedoms; while, in South Africa, the express terms of the Constitution confer constitutional rights on juristic persons.[116] If there is room for argument in Europe, there is none in South Africa.

14.10 JURISTIC PERSONS AS FUNDAMENTAL RIGHTS OBJECTS

14.10.1 Policy

Suppose corporations can be the objects of human rights. The law must then deal with the same attribution issues that arise in the civil law under, for example, contract and delict, and in the criminal law with regard to attribution of responsibility.[117] It might be argued, however, that the most effective way of rendering corporations accountable is through private law remedies. Criminal remedies indicate the moral opprobrium of a particular state. Ultimately, however, criminal sanctions are felt to bite only if the executives of large corporations are held personally to account: that they 'get the jail'. But it might be questioned whether criminal conviction, with sentences

---

opinion of Black J in *Connecticut General Legal Insurance Co v Johnson* 303 US 77 (1938) at 85–90.

[114] *Citizens United*, note 44 supra, *per* Kennedy J at 24 (slip opinion).

[115] Ibid *per* Kennedy J at 44 (slip opinion).

[116] Constitution, art 8.

[117] For discussion of attribution of the 'directing mind' of a company to a particular officer, see: *Tesco Supermarkets Ltd v Nattrass* [1972] AC 153; *Meridian Global Funds Management Asia Ltd v Securities Commission* [1995] 2 AC 500 (PC); *Transco plc v HM Advocate* 2004 JC 29.

to modest terms of imprisonment for individual executives, is enough.[118] Corporations are commercial undertakings. The one law they understand is the bottom line. It is of interest, therefore, that the South African Truth and Reconciliation Commission, in discussing the possible reparations due by private enterprises for their conduct during apartheid, regularly referred to private law concepts: private law provided both the conceptual apparatus and the remedies to hold such corporations to account.[119]

But whereas juristic persons have been quick to prosecute claims that they hold, there is considerable equivocation about the extent to which companies, in Europe, may be the objects of fundamental rights. The author of one leading monograph, for instance, accepts that the 'the Convention exclusively concerns the bestowment of rights, not duties, on private persons'.[120] There is an immediate contrast with the South African position where the terms of the Constitution are unambiguous: article 8(2) says that a 'provision of the Bill of Rights binds a natural or juristic person taking into account the nature of the right and the nature of any duty imposed by the right'.[121]

14.10.2 South Africa

In *Rail Commuters Action Group v Transnet Ltd t/a Metrorail*[122] a number of commuters, in the course of using municipal transport, had been the victims of violent crime. They sought to establish that the entity responsible for providing the public transport services in question was under a positive obligation (whether under contract, delict or the Constitution) to protect the personal safety of rail commuters who used its stations and trains. The Constitutional Court observed that the defendants held an effective monopoly over the provision of the relevant transport services. The issue of whether the defendants were the objects of the plaintiffs' constitutional rights because they were effectively an organ of the state[123] or because all juristic persons are the objects of fundamental rights, was not focused. As

---

[118] For examples of criminal liability being imposed on corporations, see the cases prosecuted by the occupying Allied powers of German undertakings following the Second World War, the so-called Second Nurnberg trials: Ratner, note 14 supra, 477–8.

[119] *Truth and Reconciliation Commission of South Africa*, Final Report (2003) (available at *http://www.info.gov.za/otherdocs/2003/trc/*): volume 6, section 2, chapter 5, paras [24] and [60] referring respectively to liability in contract and unjustified enrichment in respect of fixing reparations to be paid by businesses complicit in apartheid policies.

[120] Emberland, note 38 supra, 74.

[121] See too the provisions of art 8(3). For an initial assessment of these provisions, see G J Pienaar 'Regspersone as staatsorgane en nie-staatsorgane ingevolge die Grondwet' (1998) 1 *Potchefstroom Electronic Law Journal* 5.

[122] 2005 (2) SA 359.

[123] Constitution, Art 8(1). For the application of the Constitution to 'staatsorgane', see Pienaar, note 120 supra.

evidence showed, it was overwhelmingly the case that it was the poorest and most vulnerable members of society who, as a result of past racist housing policies, were often housed far from the main urban centres of employment. Such commuters have no choice but to use public transport. As a result, the defendants were bound to ensure that their constitutional rights to personal safety and dignity were respected. The Court thus declared that the defendants were obliged to ensure that reasonable measures were taken to provide for the security of rail commuters using their services.

The duty imposed by the Constitution is little different from an obligation which *could* have been imposed under the law of delict, whereby a public service provider would be under a duty to take reasonable care for citizens who chose to use its service. Such a duty could also arise concurrently as an implied term of the contract of carriage. Yet, before the High Court and the SCA, the commuters had failed to demonstrate that the constitutional rights they enjoyed were either an implied term of the contract[124] or, indeed, that they were owed a concomitant duty under the law of delict, although, on the latter point, that was only because the court indicated that it would need to hear evidence before it could determine whether such a delictual duty existed.[125] The plaintiffs were essentially denied private law redress because civil procedure generally requires a plaintiff to plead and, if necessary, *prove* facts relevant to support a legal claim. Where these facts are disputed, the plaintiff will have to go to trial. The Constitution, in contrast, because it guarantees fundamental rights in the abstract, can hold that a right is engaged and then throw the onus onto the party bound by the right to demonstrate that the disputed acts or omissions comply with the Constitution.[126] It may be that private law has something to learn from this 'rights-based' approach (although experience in defamation cases suggests the procedure can also be unfair on defendants).

14.10.3 UK

Because only 'public authorities' are the objects of fundamental rights under the Human Rights Act 1998, section 6, it is generally difficult to establish that private companies are bound to respect fundamental rights. Had the facts of the *Rail Commuters* case arisen in Scotland, it may actually have been possible to do so, because it appeared that the state was the only shareholder in the defendant company. But, in the absence of that quirk, a juristic person can be bound by fundamental rights only by way of the convoluted Human

---

[124] *Transnet Ltd t/a Metrorail and Others v Rail Commuters Action Group and Others* 2003 (6) SA 349 (SCA) at para 19 *per* Howie P and Cloete JA; at para 46 *per* Streicher JA; at para 70 *per* Farlam and Navsa JJA.
[125] 2003 (6) SA 349 (SCA) paras 19 to 29; and at para 72 *per* Farlam JA and Navsa JA.
[126] *Mazibuko v City of Johannesburg* 2010 (4) SA 1 (CC) at paras 161–2 *per* O'Regan J.

Rights Act provisions: the juristic person must be a 'person certain of whose functions are functions of a public nature';[127] save that, 'in relation to a particular act, a person is not a public authority by virtue only of subsection (3)(b) if the nature of the act is private'.[128] The point assumes significance in the context of privatisation of many public services.

One example from the case law which demonstrates the point is the appropriately named *YL v Birmingham City Council and Southern Cross Healthcare Ltd*.[129] The case concerned a private residential care home for the elderly owned by a company. A public authority paid the company to look after residents whom the council had a statutory obligation to support. There was therefore a contractual relationship between the local authority and the care home company. Such residents had no contractual relations with the company in contrast to those residents who had the means to pay the fees from their own resources. The company then sought to evict one of the residents – an 84–year-old suffering from Alzheimer's disease whose fees were paid for by the council – on the basis of its standard contractual terms, which allowed it to terminate the agreement for 'good reason'. The resident's family sought to establish that the care home was carrying out a 'public function'.

The House of Lords held that the company was a commercial undertaking that happened to have residents whose fees were paid by a public authority – but the company running the care home was not itself carrying out an inherently public function.[130] As a result, the company was not bound to respect a resident's Convention rights. Apart from anything else, to hold that the company was bound to respect the Convention rights of the residents who happened to require state assistance to pay the fees, when it would not be bound to respect the Convention rights of the residents who happened to be able to pay the fees from their own means, the House held, would be an absurd result.

Parliament responded quickly by passing legislation to hold that such private care homes should be considered to be providing services of a public nature, irrespective of who happens to pay for the service.[131] So whereas Parliament cannot act to reduce the scope of Convention rights, it can act to extend the scope of Convention rights. Subsequent events have proved

---

127 HRA, s 6(3)(b).

128 HRA, s 6(5).

129 [2008] 1 AC 95.

130 E.g. [2008] 1 AC 95 at para 26 *per* Lord Scott: 'Southern Cross is a company carrying on a socially useful business for profit. It is neither a charity nor a philanthropist . . . it is operating in a commercial market with commercial competitors'.

131 Health and Social Care Act 2008, s 145. An example of a housing association – incorporated as an Industrial and Provident Society – being considered by the courts to be providing services of public nature and therefore bound to respect fundamental rights is *R (Weaver) v London and Quadrant Housing Trust* [2010] 1 WLR 363.

Parliament's action to be prescient. In 2011 the respondent corporate group, Southern Cross, which owned almost 750 care homes in the UK with tens of thousands of vulnerable residents in its care, became insolvent. The episode highlights in a very real way – old age comes to us all – how private sector corporations providing services once provided by the state should be regulated.[132] How can an insolvent corporation respect the human dignity of those in its care?

It is of interest that the South African courts have taken a similar approach, and have declined to define, for example, what amounts to 'sufficient water' for the purposes of article 27 of the Constitution, considering that this is a standard best addressed by a democratically elected executive.[133]

14.10.4 Discussion

On one view, the UK approach, turning on the public function test, can appear arbitrary. There can be little doubt that the South African Constitutional Court would have reached a different conclusion from the House of Lords in *Southern Cross*. But that is perhaps not the point. For the application of fundamental rights to private law must, to a large extent, turn on the social context in which the court is operating. There must be a considerable margin of appreciation. And the courts must be careful not to make apparently innocuous decisions of legal principle that may have sweeping consequences for an executive struggling to satisfy, from insufficient resources, a flood of legitimate claims. The move, therefore, to formulate constitutional duties in relative terms recognisable to the law of delict – duties to take *reasonable* measures, and so on – are thus to be welcomed. For where there are insufficient resources to go round, decisions have to be made about allocation that are bound to be controversial, particularly to those whose claims have not been satisfied. The courts' role is to establish whether persons have a claim. But it is better for decisions on allocation to be made an official who is politically accountable.[134]

More generally, however, Scots lawyers are likely to look to South Africa for inspiration not for establishing whether a company is exercising a 'public function', but on how the constitutional duties are actually formulated; for examples of what, in the private sphere, the Constitution actually requires.

---

[132] J Kay 'New Rules Needed to Protect the Many from the Few' *Financial Times* 12 June 2011 has suggested that: 'General insolvency rules are inadequate when a care home, or a bank, or a water supply company fails. The first priority in these cases must be the residents, depositors and customers: creditors come after. We need special regimes for such businesses . . .'.

[133] *Mazibuko v City of Johannesburg* 2010 (4) SA 1 (CC) at para 61 *per* O'Regan J.

[134] D Oliver 'Human Rights and the Private Sphere' (2008) 1 *UCL Human Rights Review* 8 at 14.

14.11 CONSTITUTIONALISM AND COMPANIES: INTERNAL GOVERNANCE

The limited company is, in many ways, the perfect microcosm to examine the constitutionalisation of private law. Company law is private law *par excellence*. A company, however, can also be seen as a mini-polity; and one where the electorate, the members, have rights to hold the management to account.[135] Indeed, such are the powers of the people – the members – to hold the board to account, it has been suggested that the 'the individual is somewhat better protected in his voluntary association with the economic mini-state of the company than in his voluntary association with the political state'.[136] Under UK company law a unanimous decision of the members can be given effect irrespective of a failure to adhere to internal company law procedures.[137]

But the analogy with political states may be over-stated. For although companies' internal workings are governed by a constitution and basic democratic principles, it is often easy to manipulate voting to achieve desired ends: this is the so-called cyclical problem. Voters may prefer A to B and B to C but, perversely, prefer C to A. As a result, everything can turn on the order in which votes are taken – something experienced chairmen know only too well.[138] And, in one particular, membership of a mini-polity is quite different from citizenship, for a member dissatisfied with the governance of the board may (at least in a publicly listed company) sell his interest in the polity and leave. In private companies, in contrast, the member is, in practical terms, denied even the right to leave since there tends to be no market in the securities of private companies.

The influx of more general principles of constitutional review of internal corporate decisions – whether of the board or of the members in general meeting – is therefore natural. There are many piecemeal provisions that seek to ensure such protection of minorities who may, in certain ituations,

---

[135] Most pragmatically by removing the director by ordinary resolution: Companies Act 2006, s 168; Companies Act 2008 (71 of 2008), s 71.

[136] J A Usher 'The Rights of Individual Shareholders in Companies' in J W Bridge et al (eds) *Fundamental Rights* (Sweet & Maxwell 1974) 254 at 274.

[137] *Re Duomatic Ltd* [1969] 2 Ch 365; for a recent application see *Schofield v Schofield* [2011] EWCA Civ 154. The rule operates on the rationale that a unanimous decision of the members, even if inconsistent with the constitution, amounts to an alteration of the articles. But under s 30 of the 2006 Act, any resolution to change the articles must be registered with the Registrar of Companies within fifteen days or the company and every officer of the company commits a criminal offence. I think there is no reason in principle why the *Duomatic* principle cannot apply under the Companies Act 71 of 2008, despite what s 15(7) says (although a similar issue arises, with respect to filing the change in the memorandum, under s 16(7), where the period is only ten days: Companies Regulations 2011, reg 15(3)).

[138] S Brittan, "Why Democracy is Overrated" (2009) (available at: <*www.samuelbrittan.co.uk/spee56_p.html*). Cf G Szpiro *Numbers Rule: The Vexing Mathematics of Democracy from Plato to the Present* (Princeton University Press 2010).

be particularly vulnerable.[139] Indeed, one of the earliest examples of a reference to 'human rights' in domestic case law, is found in a well-known company law case, still cited today:[140]

> 'At one time our progress was thought to be from status to contract, from restriction to liberty. But now status seems to be crushing out contract and liberty. And what we have to find is, according to a recent writer, a theory that will "ensure the certainty required for the economic order, and yet permit the flexibility required for the individual human life". Is the State to restrain contracts and lesson liberty to save persons from their own folly or inadequacy of outlook? The case of *Allen v Flood*[141] showed what a great difference of judicial outlook there was as to the rights of individuals, and how *human rights* were more regarded than they were a century ago. And our statutes give us many examples how status overrides contracts.'

This approach can be seen too in the South African Companies Act 71 of 2008 which proclaims as its first purpose to 'promote compliance with the Bill of Rights as provided for in the Constitution, in the application of company law'.[142]

The application of fundamental rights to companies is a large subject. I propose to focus in the remaining parts of the paper on only two issues. The first concerns identification issues: the extent to which individual shareholders (who will often be natural persons) can avail themselves of fundamental rights that are primarily held by the company. This point may seem technical but, in the event, is illuminating since it provides an example of how fundamental rights jurisprudence has accepted a basic principle of private law doctrine: separate legal personality. The second issue concerns the protection of minority shareholders.

14.11.1 *The corporate veil and fundamental rights*

The starting point is the judgment of the International Court of Justice (ICJ) in *Barcelona Traction*.[143] The Barcelona Traction, Light and Power Co

---

[139] As with class rights; schemes of arrangement; company voluntary arrangements; minority protection in the UK; and the business rescue provisions in South Africa.

[140] *Shalfoon v Cheddar Valley Co-operative Dairy Co Ltd* [1924] NZLR 561 at 563 *per* Stout CJ (emphasis added), rev'd by the NZCA on a different point, of which the judgment by Salmond J, at 574–7, contains a classic description of the statutory contract in a company's articles of association. (Salmond J gave his name to the famous *Salmond on Jurisprudence*.)

[141] [1898] AC 1.

[142] Companies Act 71 of 2008, s 7(a).

[143] *Case Concerning Barcelona Traction, Light & Power Co Ltd (Belgium v Spain) (Merits)* [1970] ICJ Rep 3. The critical commentaries on the case by H H Briggs and F A Mann are particularly interesting, since each acted as counsel in the case, to Spain and Belgium respectively: H H Briggs 'Barcelona Traction: The Jus Standi of Belgium' (1971) 65 *American Journal of International Law* 327 and F A Mann, 'The Protection of Shareholders' Interests in Light of the *Barcelona Traction* Case' (1973) 67 *American Journal of International Law* 259.

Ltd (the 'Company') was a holding company incorporated in Canada, with its head office in Toronto. The company held shares in many subsidiaries, Canadian and Spanish. The company went into insolvency proceedings in Spain, which proceedings were not recognised elsewhere. In terms of those proceedings, the whole property and assets of the company were adjudged in favour of the insolvency administrator. Many of the shareholders in the Company were Belgian nationals.[144] They complained of various wrongs under international law and, as a result, Belgium instituted proceedings against Spain, claiming, inter alia, that the Belgian shareholders were entitled to diplomatic immunity from confiscation of their assets under Spanish law. The issues raised by the case are many. I consider just two.

In the first place the ICJ set out a list of what they considered to be 'shareholder rights', as opposed to the company's rights, as including the right to any declared dividend, the right to attend and vote at meetings, and the right to the residual assets of the company on liquidation.[145] The ICJ's list 'most probably . . . articulates also those rights regarded as shareholder rights in the [ECHR]'.[146] And it is clear that shares are protected as 'possessions' under article 1 of the First Protocol to the ECHR.[147] Looking at South African law, however, it may be that the Constitutional Court has not yet had occasion to consider the *Barcelona Traction* principle, for in the *Wesbank* case, the Court explained that one of the rationales for holding that juristic persons could benefit from fundamental rights was to avoid a 'disastrous impact' on, *inter alios*, shareholders.[148] That is curious reasoning. There are three possible analyses. One is that the Constitutional Court saw shareholder protection as a rationale because of the reflective benefit that shareholders in the company would receive. Secondly, it may be that the court had corporate shareholders in mind. Thirdly, however, it is possible that not having been referred to the *Barcelona Traction* principle, the Court may have confused the distinction between the company and its shareholders. As *Barcelona Traction* shows, the whole point of allowing juristic persons to benefit from fundamental rights is, for *Foss v Harbottle* reasons, to ensure that only the company, not its shareholders, can prosecute the company's fundamental rights claims.

In addition, the ICJ in *Barcelona Traction* founded on a distinction between shareholder rights and shareholder interests 'whenever a shareholder's interests are harmed by an act done to the company, it is to the latter that he must look to institute appropriate action: for although two separate entities may have suffered from the same wrong, it is only one entity

---

[144] This is to oversimplify the matter; the shareholding structure was complex and disputed.
[145] *Barcelona Traction*, note 143 supra, at 36 (para 47).
[146] Emberland, note 38 supra, 72.
[147] *Olczak v Poland*, ECtHR, 7 November 2002 (final decision on admissibility), cited in Emberland, note 38 supra, 70–4.
[148] *First National Bank of SA Ltd, t/a Wesbank v Minister of Finance* 2002 (4) SA 768 (CC) at para 45 *per* Ackermann J.

whose rights have been infringed'.[149] One of the rationales for this principle is that the shareholders' limited interest in the company's assets is a corollary of shareholders' limited liability for the company's debts.[150] With privilege comes responsibility.

Barcelona Traction is thus a milestone in fundamental rights protection for company shareholders. The Strasbourg Court has held that it will disregard the corporate veil only in exceptional circumstances, 'in particular where it is clearly established that it is impossible for the company to apply to the Convention institutions through the organs set up under its articles of incorporation or – in the event of liquidation – through its liquidators'.[151] Importantly, this test has been applied to an application in respect of an article 6 violation (fair trial and due process) and not just to applications for deprivation of property rights *qua* shareholder. The result is that the European Court has favoured a test based on domestic legal doctrine – the corporate veil – rather than developing an autonomous concept for fundamental rights purposes.

14.11.2 *Oppression and minority protection*

The provisions in both the South African Companies Act 71 of 2008[152] and the UK Companies Act 2006[153] on minority protection are perhaps paradigm examples of provisions providing a private law remedy for the protection of what might be termed a 'private constitutional right'. The right is conferred only on shareholders of the company, as opposed to creditors, employees or other stakeholders.[154] The remedy is included without any concomitant prior norm regarding an obligation not to act in an unfairly prejudicial manner. George Gretton and Niall Whitty have suggested that such a provision is not only un-civilian, but un-juridical.[155] And there are other aspects of the remedy that perplex. The remedy was once said to be 'inalienable': it 'cannot be diminished or removed by contract or otherwise'.[156] But 'inalienable', even

---

149   *Barcelona Traction*, note 141 supra, 35 (para 44, last sentence) adopted by the Strasbourg court in *Agrotexim Hellas SA v Greece* (1996) 21 EHRR 250 at para 66.

150   Ibid 35 at para 42.

151   *Agrotexim Hellas SA v Greece* (1996) 21 EHRR 250 at para 66.

152   Companies Act 71 of 2008, s 163. The provision reflects, to some extent, the famous dicta of Lord President Cooper in *Meyer v Scottish Co-operative Wholesale Society Ltd* 1954 SC 381 at 391.

153   Companies Act 2006, s 994.

154   Similar provisions exist, for example, in s 895 CA 2006 on schemes of arrangement, where a right of review may be conferred upon a creditor or other stakeholder.

155   G L Gretton 'Reception without Integration: Floating Charges in Mixed Legal Systems' (2003) 78 *Tulane LR* 307; N Whitty 'Borrowing from English Equity and Minority Shareholders' Actions' in E Reid and D Carey Miller (eds) *A Mixed Legal System in Transition: T B Smith and Progress of Scots Law* (Edinburgh University Press 2005) 100.

156   *Exeter City Association Football Club Ltd. v. Football Conference Ltd* [2004] 1 WLR 2910 at para 23 *per* HHJ Weeks QC.

on that analysis, would apply only to any agreement between a shareholder and a company, for members of an LLP, in contrast, are accorded the privilege of waiving such a fundamental right.[157] And perhaps under this influence the English courts have now arrived at the conclusion that, if the prevailing principle is party autonomy, shareholders are able to contract out of their right to bring disputes, including those for unfair prejudice, before the courts.[158]

Which interpretation is correct? It is here that constitutional review principles are useful. They provide minimum standards where private law tends to provide certain remedies. The general principle of minority protection that can be divined from the cases is that a company, acting through its board, should act in good faith in its dealings with its shareholders.[159] There is much to be said for this principle being given statutory expression, not least because it would address the difficulties highlighted by Whitty and Gretton. But such a principle also assists in determining whether it is possible for a minority shareholder to contract out of his or her rights to bring a claim for unfair prejudice. The answer must be that, in principle, he or she can, but only where the agreement to do so was concluded in good faith. Such an approach is not far removed from the principles of constitutional review. And, in this vein, it is of interest that, in derivative action proceedings to ensure the accountability of the board to minority shareholders, the courts are careful to ensure that basic procedural safeguards – article 6, or 'due process' rights, if you will – are respected.[160]

The minority protection provisions have conferred a significant discretion on judges to develop a jurisprudence of fairness – constitutionalisation of the company – in an incremental way. The South African courts will have to do the same under the Companies Act 71 of 2008. Indeed, it is particularly striking to a Scots lawyer to see even more open-textured provisions in the Companies Act 2008. Thus: 'When determining a matter brought before it in terms of this Act, or making an order contemplated in this Act – (a) a court must develop the common law as necessary to improve the realization and enjoyment of rights established by this Act'.[161] In addition, any relevant tribunal or court 'must promote the spirit, purpose and objects' of the Act; and

'if any provision of this Act, or other document in terms of this Act, read in its context, can be reasonably construed to have more than one meaning, must prefer

---

[157] Limited Liability Partnerships (Application of Companies Act 2006) Regulations 2009 (SI 2009/1804), reg 48.

[158] *Fulham Football Club (1987) Ltd v Richards* [2011] Ch 208, not following *Exeter City* supra note 156, at para 78 *per* Vos J: 'the statutory right . . . is not an inalienable one. Members of companies and the companies themselves can agree to refer disputes that might otherwise support unfair prejudice petitions to arbitration, provided that third parties are not to be bound by the award . . .', aff'd [2011] EWCA Civ 855.

[159] *O'Neill v Phillips* [1999] 1 WLR 1092 at 1098–1099 *per* Lord Hoffmann.

[160] *Wishart v Castlecroft Securities Ltd* 2010 SC 16 at para 17 *per* Lord Reed.

[161] Companies Act 2008, s 158(a).

the meaning that best promotes the spirit and purpose of this Act, and will best improve the realisation and enjoyment of rights'.

These provisions – both on minority and protection and interpretation – are constitutional provisions, within private law, *par excellence*. The challenge for private lawyers is to engage in normal doctrinal analysis to provide a map for how these provisions should be applied.

14.12 CONCLUSIONS

The specialist human rights scholar may question, or view with reservation, a book such as this. There is a view that Roman-Dutch law is somehow irretrievably tainted with apartheid; and Scots law with anti-English, anti-Catholic prejudice.[162] A more realistic assessment is that no one legal tradition is better or more just than another.[163] For such criticisms can be made of any legal system: the English courts too have failed to control the executive in times of crisis.[164] No legal system has perfectly protected fundamental rights. In a secular world, however, fundamental rights provide a sort of moral-legal compass:

'La différence, et elle est capitale, est que la situation est inverse. C'était autrefois la morale qui était une source de droit, c'est maintenant le droit qui est la source de la morale. La moralité consistera dans le respect de l'ordre social établi par le droit ; l'immoralité se confondra avec la violation de la loi.'[165]

'Legality', in other words, '. . . has become a touchstone for legitimacy'.[166] But this observation, though perceptive, is inadequate: for compliance with

---

[162] Cf D Osler 'The Fantasy Men' (2007) 10 *Rechtsgeschichte* 169.

[163] K O'Regan 'Best of Both Worlds? Some Reflections on the Interaction between the Common Law and the Bill of Rights in our New Constitution' (1999) 1 *Potchefstroom Electronic Law Journal*.

[164] A W B Simpson *In the Highest Degree Odious: Detention without Trial in Wartime Britain* (Clarendon Press 1992); C Gearty *Can Human Rights Survive?* (Cambridge University Press 2006); D Dyzenhaus *The Constitution of Law: Legality in Time of Emergency* (Cambridge University Press 2006) 17: 'as a matter of fact the judicial record in enforcing the rule of law [in cases dealing with national security] is at worst dismal, at best ambiguous'. See too A Tomkins 'National Security and the Role of the Court' (2010) 126 *LQR* 543. In *Rossow v (Albie) Sachs* 1964 (2) SA 551 at 562–563, Oglivie Thomson JA founded on English prisons law for support of a notorious apartheid law; while in *Goldberg v Minister of Prisons* 1979 (1) SA 14 at 38ff, Corbett JA appealed to the equity of Roman-Dutch law; an opinion to which President Mandela referred on the occasion of Corbett CJ's retiral.

[165] G Ripert *Les forces créatrices du droit* (Librairie Générale de Droit et de Jurisprudence 1955) 173: 'The difference, and it is key, is that the situation is inverted. Whereas morality was once a source of law, now the law is a source of morality. Morality consists in respect for the social order established by the law; immorality has become confused with violation of the law'.

[166] M A Glendon *Rights Talk: The Impoverishment of Political Discourse* (Free Press 1991) 3.

the letter of legislation (*loi, Gesetz*) can never ensure justice.[167] The challenge for private law is how to ensure its many unwritten fundamental principles are not forgotten. For too long, perhaps, has the private law focus been on those who shout the loudest: too much development based on the rarely articulated economic theories of those who pay the fees.[168]

Fifteen years or so of interaction between fundamental rights and private law has not had particularly profound effects in either Scotland or South Africa. Even with the Constitutional Court's decision in *Barkhuizen*, the possibility of a radical revision of private law has not generally materialised. But fundamental rights ideas have forced private lawyers at least to re-examine principles that for too long had not been critically reviewed.[169]

A positive view of the horizontal application of fundamental rights is that such a review may lead to a renewed interest in basic private law doctrines. I would suggest that a positive approach is essential: private lawyers who think that fundamental rights can be excluded or ignored are guilty of wilful blindness rather than wishful thinking. Private lawyers can, and must, review private law rules and, if necessary, restate them in fundamental-rights-compliant private law terms. The tools are everywhere. Some principles, such as good faith,[170] or abuse of rights,[171] may provide particularly dynamic private law mechanisms whereby fundamental rights can be better protected. Two thousand years of hard-nosed experience of justice suggests that private law is likely to be particularly, perhaps better, suited to providing practical fundamental rights protection to citizens and legal persons alike.

One major issue is highlighted by the *Rail Commuters* decision.[172] It concerns not substantive law, but, as is so often the case in legal practice, procedure. The main reason for claimants preferring to found on fundamental rights, though a private law remedy is readily available, is procedural. In most fundamental rights cases, ordinary rules of civil procedure do not

---

[167] Arangio-Ruiz note 23 supra.

[168] Although I do not always agree with their conclusions, A Supiot makes this point well in 'Law and Labour' (2006) 36 *New Left Review* 109 at 115; and see too Paddy Ireland's perceptive essay 'History, Critical Legal Studies and the Mysterious Disappearance of Capitalism' (an extended review of R Harris, *Industrializing English Law* (Cambridge University Press 2000)) (2002) 65 *Modern LR* 120 at 130–1.

[169] Cf A Tomkins, note 11 supra.

[170] *Barkhuizen v Napier* 2007 (5) SA 323 (CC) at paras 73–83 *per* Ncobo J. A majority of the court concurred in his opinion. O'Regen J, however, expressly refused to approve of these *obiter dicta* being, as they were, unnecessary for the decision in the case. There is also an elegant and more wide-ranging dissent by Sachs J. Cf F Brand 'The Role of Good Faith, Equity and Fairness in the South African Law of Contract' (2009) 126 *SALJ* 71 and *Southern Era Resources Ltd v Frandell* 2010 (4) SA 200 (SCA).

[171] Charter of Fundamental Rights of the EU, art 54; *Bredenkamp, Breco International Ltd, Hamilton Place Trust and International Cigarette Manufacturers (Pty) Ltd* 2010 (4) SA 468 at para 24 (footnote) *per* Harms DP.

[172] Note 123 supra.

apply. Generally speaking, there is no need to prove the facts averred in a long and expensive trial which the state or corporations can spin out until the pursuers run out of patience or funds or both. The role of procedure, in my view, may be the most important aspect of discussions on the interaction between fundamental rights and private law in the future. Some Scottish legislative provisions, now Convention-compliant, show what can be done.[173]

All legal systems must address the application of fundamental rights to juristic persons. In the main, these issues have concerned legal standing, expropriation and procedural fairness. Domestic private laws have developed rules of review which are just as refined, and sometimes more so, than the dictates of fundamental rights instruments and jurisprudence. These issues are peculiar neither to Scotland nor to South Africa. They are international. International legal problems traditionally have had local solutions. But comparative law may have a useful role in assisting local lawyers to revise their domestic solutions. Company law is particularly ripe for comparative discussion because the issues and building blocks of the law are functionally similar the world over.[174] Company law, in both Scotland and South Africa, is already much constitutionalised and no worse for it. The subject thus provides a paradigm example of what can be done within the confines of private law itself.

---

[173] E.g. Debtors (Scotland) Act 1987, s 15K(10), inverting the burden of proof where a debtor applies for recall of an arrestment. The burden remains on the arrester.

[174] Cf M Delmas-Marty's stimulating *Les forces imaginantes du droit: le relatif et l'universel* (2004).

Chapter 15

Examining the Labour Law and Social Dimension of Human Rights: The UK and South Africa

David Cabrelli

15.1 INTRODUCTION

In this chapter the trajectory of development of labour law in the UK and South Africa will be traced in light of recent attempts in both jurisdictions to 'humanise' the employment sphere and enhance worker protection via the prophylactic of constitutional human rights. With the coming into force of the Human Rights Act 1998 (HRA) in the UK in the year 2000, the European Convention on Human Rights (ECHR) was incorporated into UK law. Since the ECHR consists principally of civil and political rights, and the HRA only compels public authorities to act in a way that is compatible with the ECHR rights, a number of commentators were sceptical about the likely impact of the HRA on the workplace. Indeed, there were suggestions that the traditionally individualistic, rights-based approach of the ECHR would be counter-protective and instead serve to undermine the collective bargaining power and interests of workers through trade unions.[1] The position in the UK can be contrasted sharply with South Africa, where a much bolder approach was taken around about the same time, in the sense that labour and social rights were constitutionalised in the South African Constitution (SAC). Section 23(1) of the SAC is drawn at a very general level of abstraction and directs that 'everyone has the right to fair labour practices'. Coupled with the fact that the labour rights in the SAC are entrenched and of horizontal effect, the position adopted in South Africa would appear on the face of it to offer greater scope for redress to individual workers as well as enhancing the collective interests of trade unions and other worker representative groups. However, such a rationalisation of the position is too simplistic and it is necessary to give closer attention to possible parallels in the experiences of the UK and South Africa. This assessment will be undertaken within the context of a central debate throughout the academy and beyond about the utility of harnessing human rights rhetoric in the field of labour law.

---

[1] K D Ewing 'The Human Rights Act and Labour Law' (1998) 27 *Industrial Law Journal* 275.

15.2 LABOUR RIGHTS AS HUMAN RIGHTS OR CONSTITUTIONAL RIGHTS

Before embarking on an analysis of the impact of treating labour rights as human rights in both the UK and South Africa, it is important to pause and ask what kind of positive effects human rights discourse might have for the interests of workers. There are a number of perceived advantages, but it is sufficient for these purposes to limit discussion to four of the most significant attractions.[2] First, it has been suggested that one of the appeals of drawing labour rights as human rights or constitutional rights lies in its potential to humanise the workplace. Classifying them in this way entails a retreat from the now orthodox neo-liberal view that the workplace must be subjected to the laws of the free market and globalisation,[3] and that labour laws are ill-adapted to the needs of the marketplace, economic efficiency, competitiveness and flexibility.[4] To that extent, the rhetoric that labour rights *are* human rights is an important means by which proponents of social justice seek to recalibrate the balance of power between labour and the now extremely mobile forces of capital.[5] Secondly, the language of human rights also has the added attraction of recognising the dignity, identity and autonomy of the individual employee, for example that individual's values, sense of self-worth as an individual human being and his or her identity.[6] This dignitarian and identitarian strand of human rights discourse ties in with the recent judicial acknowledgements in the UK and Canada of the social reality that a worker's employment is a significant and meaningful part of his or her life and that it confers an identity and a measure of self-

---

[2] See K D Ewing 'Laws against Strikes Revisited' in C Barnard, S Deakin and G Morris (eds) *The Future of Labour Law: Liber Amicorum Bob Hepple* QC (Hart Publishing 2004) 41 at 46–52.

[3] For an introduction to neo-liberalist thought, see R Plant *The Neo-liberal State* (Oxford University Press 2010).

[4] R Dukes 'Constitutionalising Employment Relations: Sinzheimer, Kahn-Freund and the Role of Labour Law' (2008) 35 *Journal of Law and Society* 341 at 341–342, 361–362; H Arthurs 'The Constitutionalization of Employment Relations: Multiple Models, Pernicious Problems' (2010) 19 *Social & Legal Studies* 403 at 404; R Dukes 'The Constitutional Function of Labour Law in the European Union' in N Walker, J Shaw and S Tierney (eds) *Europe's Constitutional Mosaic* (Hart Publishing 2011) 341; J Fudge 'The New Discourse of Labour Rights: From Social to Fundamental Rights' (2007) 29 *Comparative Labour Law and Policy Journal* 29 at 29–32; P Alston 'Labour Rights as Human Rights: The Not So Happy State of the Art' in P Alston (ed) *Labour Rights as Human Rights* (Oxford University Press 2005) 1 at 4–5. In the South African context, see C Fenwick, E Kalula and I Landau 'Labour Law: A Southern African perspective' in T Teklé (ed) *Labour Law and Worker Protection in Developing Countries* (Hart Publishing, 2010) 175 at 196–7.

[5] Lord Wedderburn 'Labour Law 2008: 40 Years on' (2007) 36 *Industrial Law Journal* 397 at 404. Arthurs, note 4 supra, at 405–15.

[6] S Fredman, *Discrimination Law* 2e (Oxford University Press 2011) at 19–25; B Hepple *Equality: The New Legal Framework* (Hart Publishing 2011) at 14–16; and H Collins 'Theories of Rights as Justifications' in G Davidov and B Langille (eds) *The Idea of Labour Law* (Oxford University Press 2011) 137 at 151–3.

esteem.[7] The transformative potential of classifying labour rights as constitutional human rights is also said to be grounded in its ability to entrench those rights in the sense that they are rendered inderogable, immutable and supreme. Therefore, when they clash or come into contact with the rights or freedoms of employers narrated in the written contract of employment or recognised by the common law or labour legislation, the latter will gave way to the constitutionally guaranteed labour rights. Moreover, the express disapplication or waiver of such rights in the contract of employment or some other agreement would be precluded.[8] However, by far the most powerful argument in favour of conceptualising labour rights as constitutional human rights is grounded in the legitimising function performed by the latter and is what Collins has referred to as the 'potential trumping power of [human] rights'.[9] This leitmotif is a reference to the undoubted value, weight and respect attached to a right which has achieved the 'numinous' status[10] of a human right. As Fenwick and Novitz have noted:

> 'The imperative to present [worker's] claims as human rights comes from the desire to utilise the potentially powerful legal methods of securing advantage to pursue their claims, and also from the perceived need to respond to employers' willingness to use these arguments and tools themselves.'[11]

Thus, by deploying the vocabulary of human rights, the argument is that the legitimacy of worker demands for protection will be enhanced and given greater credence in policy circles.

However, not all labour law scholars are convinced of the potential for

---

[7] *Johnson v Unisys Ltd* [2003] 1 AC 518 (HL), 539B-D and 549B-D per Lords Hoffmann and Millett and *Reference re Public Service Employee Relations Act* [1987] 1 SCR 313 at 368 (Dickson CJ), approved in *Wallace v United Grain Growers Ltd* [1997] 3 SCR 701 at 742 (Iacobucci J).

[8] However, it is not clear that this is the position in the UK in terms of the HRA and to date, the courts have had no opportunity to pronounce on the issue in the employment context, on which see the discussion in G Morris 'Fundamental Rights: Exclusion by Agreement?' (2001) 30 *Industrial Law Journal* 49 at 51–60; and M Freedland 'Privacy, Employment and the Human Rights Act 1998' in K Ziegler (ed) *Human Rights and Private Law: Privacy as Autonomy* (Hart Publishing 2007) 141 at 152–5. Nevertheless, it has been accepted in Scotland that human rights may be waived if done so in an unequivocal manner, e.g. *Clancy v Caird* 2000 SC 441 and *Robertson v Higson* 2006 SC (PC) 22 and the European Court of Human Rights has held that articles 9 and 10 of the ECHR on the freedom of religion and expression in the employment sphere may be waived, as per *Vereinigung Rechtswinkels Utrecht v Netherlands* (1986) 46 DR 200. For further details, see R Reed and J Murdoch, *A Guide to Human Rights Law in Scotland* 3e (Butterworths LexisNexis 2011) at para 7.26.

[9] Collins, note 6 supra, at 139; and C McCrudden 'Human Dignity and Judicial Interpretation of Human Rights' (2008) 19 *European Journal of International Law* 655 at 677–8.

[10] K Kolben 'Labor Rights as Human Rights' (2009) 50 *Virginia Journal of International Law* 450 at 461–2.

[11] C Fenwick and T Novitz 'Conclusion: Regulating to Protect Workers' Human Rights' in C Fenwick and T Novitz (eds) *Human Rights at Work: Perspectives on Law and Regulation* (Hart Publishing 2010) 585 at 587–8.

human rights or constitutional rights to advance the interests of labour. The most prominent scholar is Arthurs who points to the deficiencies of relying on human rights, with their traditional focus on individual, rather than collective, rights, and the inaccessibility of the rights-based, litigation-driven model.[12] In the following excerpt, Arthurs expertly captures the main counter-arguments and seeks to introduce a measure of realism into the claims that trumpet the potential of human rights discourse:

> 'Yes, it's true: workers are human; they are not commodities; they are not factors of production. People with an interest in human rights should therefore be as interested in the oppression of workers as they in the oppression of people of colour or women or disabled people. But labour rights and human rights are not easily collapsed into a single category. Labour rights have historically been framed as collective, human rights as individual; labour rights are class-based; human rights claim to be universal in their justification and application. Labour rights have generally been vindicated through economic and political action; human rights have been advanced through cultural and social change and, more recently, through litigation. Labour has tended to assert its rights at the level of the workplace and the nation state; human rights movements in recent years have tended to be trans-national. And a point of some importance: Labour rights have tended to be marginalized in the shaping of the new global economic order, while human rights have been embraced by adherents of the Washington consensus as both a precondition and consequence of global capitalism.'[13]

Arthurs advances other arguments which caution against the realignment of labour rights as human rights, namely that human rights generally operate to constrain state, rather than private, power and that the judiciary whose role it would be to police constitutional human rights infringements are not best placed to reach decisions which serve to redistribute wealth, resources and power away from economic actors towards individual employees and their collective representatives. Finally, not the least potent of the arguments is that with its emphasis on the individual, human rights discourse flies in the face of democracy, that is, it unjustifiably interferes with the democratic will of the majority which finds its expression in labour legislation promulgated by Parliament.

Many of these arguments and counter-arguments have been advanced in the abstract without consideration of the merits and demerits of the respective arguments in the context of empirical evidence. Therefore, in this chapter the focus will be on the extent to which the introduction of human rights protections in the UK and the constitutionalisation of labour rights in South Africa have advanced the cause of workers' interests. At the same

---

[12] Arthurs, note 4 supra, at 405–6.
[13] H Arthurs, 'The Constitutionalisation of Labour Rights' SSRN (available at: *http://papers. ssrn.com/sol3/papers.cfm?abstract_id=1531326*).

time, the chapter will compare the positions in the UK and South Africa within the context of the ideas rehearsed above regarding the merits and demerits of casting labour rights as human rights. To that extent, the chapter aims to make a modest contribution to the 'labour rights as human rights' debate and to test some of the issues emerging from that debate in the crucible of the UK and South African experiences.

15.3 THE UK

15.3.1 Introduction

In the UK, the common law traditionally has been perceived as the 'enemy of social justice . . . [with] deep roots'[14] and labour lawyers have tended to be suspicious of the courts, characterising their approach as hostile to the interests of workers.[15] Indeed, recent judicial dicta have recognised the fact that the common law is principally concerned with protecting the employer's private law rights from outside interference.[16] The UK Parliament has responded over the past 40 years by introducing labour legislation to bolster employment protection and has done so by 'graft[ing those] statutory protections on to the stem of the common law contract'.[17] However, not all of the statutory protections have been as radical as they might have appeared at first sight[18] and the judiciary has intervened on a number of occasions to dilute their wider social impact.[19] Therefore, one would think that the introduction of the HRA would have been welcomed by labour lawyers in the UK on the ground that it would offer an opportunity to challenge and possibly uproot some of the fundamental conceptions ingrained within the common law culture. However, not so. On one side of the debate were the commentators who argued that the individualist approach traditionally adopted in the jurisprudence of the European Court of Human Rights (ECtHR) would undermine the collective interests of labour channelled through the medium

---

[14] K D Ewing 'The Sense of Measure': Old Wine in New Bottles, or New Wine in Old Bottles, or New Wine in New Bottles?' in E Christodoulidis and R Dukes 'Dialogue and Debate: Labour, Constitution and A Sense of Measure: A Debate with Alain Supiot' (2010) 19 *Social & Legal Studies* 217–52 at 234.

[15] A Davies 'Judicial Self-restraint in Labour Law' (2009) 38 *Industrial Law Journal* 278–305 at 287; Arthurs, note 4 supra, at 405–6.

[16] *National Union of Rail, Maritime & Transport Workers v Serco, ASLEF v London & Birmingham Railway Ltd* [2011] EWCA Civ 226, [2011] IRLR 399 (CA) at 402 (Elias LJ).

[17] *Buckland v Bournemouth University Higher Education Corp* [2010] EWCA Civ 121, [2010] IRLR 445 (CA) at 447 (Sedley LJ).

[18] E.g., rather than a right to flexible working, the Employment Rights Act 1996, ss 80F-80I provides the employee with a right *to request* flexible working.

[19] This has been achieved by denying substantive rights to the worker, e.g. the emergence of the 'range of reasonable responses' test in the context of the statutory unfair dismissal regime in the Employment Rights Act 1996, Part X.

of procedural trade union rights.[20] Here, there was scepticism about the ability of the ECHR to radiate behavioural expectations about the conduct of employers given the fact that the rights contained therein were drawn at a very general level and largely made subject to qualifications. On the other hand, other commentators welcomed the coming into force of the HRA, contending that '[s]tatutory interpretation and the common law will benefit by being redrawn in categories which reflect fundamental social values'.[21] After more than ten years, it has transpired that neither of these predictions falls close to the mark. Instead, in the absence of the emergence of what Fredman and Davies have referred to as a 'human rights culture',[22] there are few signs that the ECHR has had any effect on substantive and procedural labour law in the UK. As we will see, this is despite recent step changes in the approach of the ECtHR.

15.3.2 *The scheme of the HRA*

At this juncture it is salutary to examine the basic architecture of the HRA and consider its relevance to employment relations. Section 2 of the HRA specifically directs that a court or tribunal must take into account the jurisprudence and judgments of the ECtHR so far as is possible when it is required to determine the application of the ECHR rights in a domestic dispute.[23] Section 3 provides that primary and subordinate legislation of the UK Parliament must be read and given effect to in a way which is compatible with the ECHR rights, and in terms of section 4, a court may make a declaration of incompatibility in respect of primary legislation where it is not possible to read down that legislation in accordance with the ECHR rights under section 3. However, a declaration of incompatibility does not affect the legal validity of that primary legislation – that is, it is still in full force and effect, albeit inconsistent with the ECHR. One of the key debates at the time the HRA came into force[24] was whether it had horizontal effect, since section 6 of the HRA seemed to impose a duty on public authorities only to act in accordance with the ECHR. It was questioned whether private parties would be required to act in a way that did not infringe the ECHR rights, or whether the application of ECHR rights was restricted to vertical relations between

---

[20] Ewing, note 1 supra.
[21] B Hepple 'Human Rights and Employment Law' (1998) (8) *Amicus Curiae* 19–23 .
[22] S Fredman *Human Rights Transformed* (Oxford University Press 2008); and A Davies, 'Workers' Human Rights in English Law' in C Fenwick and T Novitz (eds) *Human Rights at Work: Perspectives on Law and Regulation* (Hart Publishing 2010) 171–94 at 183–4.
[23] See *Ghaidan v Godin-Mendoza* [2004] UKHL 30, [2004] 2 AC 557 (HL).
[24] See W Wade 'Horizons of Horizontality' (2000) 116 *LQR* 217–224; R Buxton 'The Human Rights Act and Private Law' (2000) 116 *LQR* 48–65; D Pannick and A Lester 'The Impact of the Human Rights Act on Private Law: The Knight's Move' (2000) 116 *LQR* 380–5.

the state and private parties.[25] The general weight of opinion pointed to indirect horizontal effect in the case of Scots private law,[26] and in 2004 the impact of the HRA on private employers was specifically addressed by the Court of Appeal in the case of X v Y.[27] In X v Y Mummery LJ clarified that, as public authorities, courts, employment tribunals and the Employment Appeal Tribunal (EAT) have an obligation under section 3 of the HRA to interpret labour legislation in a way that is compatible with the ECHR rights and that no distinction should be drawn between public authority and private sector employers.[28] This is particularly applicable where the state has a positive duty to secure enjoyment of the relevant ECHR rights between private persons, as is the case in respect of the relevant articles of the ECHR which have had an impact on labour law in the UK, namely, articles 6 (the right to a fair trial), 8 (the right to privacy and a family life) and 11 (freedom of assembly and association).[29] As a result, it is now clear that the ECHR rights have indirect horizontal effect and apply in the context of the relationship between private employers and employees.

15.3.3 The impact of ECHR articles 6, 8, and 11 on the workplace

Another ongoing debate at the time the HRA came into force was whether the indirect horizontal effect of the ECHR rights would be 'weak' or 'strong':

> '[Weak indirect horizontal effect] involves the courts taking into account the values embodied in the [ECHR] rights in applying and developing the existing law, while [strong indirect horizontal effect] compels them to make the existing law compatible with the ECHR, the difference lying essentially in the degree to which the courts will be bound by the ECHR in handling private litigation.'[30]

Thus, the 'weak' conceptualisation would restrict an adjudicator to consideration of the ECHR as an aid to development of the law, whilst the latter approach would furnish the court with a licence to apply it in order to rupture the fabric of the law. The latter might appear to be less likely to represent the UK approach, given the command in sections 3 and 4 of the HRA to deploy the ECHR rights in order to interpret legislation or declare

---

[25] This links in with Arthurs' point above that human rights are principally designed to constrain state, rather than private, power.

[26] See R Reed and J Murdoch *A Guide to Human Rights Law in Scotland* (Butterworths LexisNexis, 2001) (now in its third edition) at 36–7; and H L MacQueen and D Brodie 'Private Rights, Private Law and the Private Domain' in A Boyle, C Himsworth, A Loux and H L MacQueen (eds) *Human Rights and Scots Law* (Hart Publishing 2002) 141–76.

[27] [2004] EWCA Civ 662, [2004] IRLR 625 (CA).

[28] Ibid at 630–632 (Mummery LJ).

[29] Ibid at 633 (Mummery LJ) and *Copsey v WWB Devon Clays Ltd* [2005] EWCA Civ 932, [2005] IRLR 811 (CA) at 815 (Mummery LJ).

[30] MacQueen and Brodie, note 26 supra, at 154.

it incompatible, rather than deprive it of legal effect. Indeed, one could claim that there was evidence of the 'weak' version in the judgments of the Court of Appeal in cases such as *Kulkarni v Milton Keynes Hospital NHS Trust*[31] and *R (on the application of G) v Governors of X School*.[32] Here, the Court of Appeal adopted a robust approach in relation to the applicability of article 6 of the ECHR (right to a fair trial) as a means of providing procedural protection to workers and their representatives which was additional to that set out in UK labour legislation. Section 10 of the Employment Relations Act 1999 (ERelA) confers a right upon an employee to be represented at a disciplinary hearing by a fellow worker or a trade union official, and the employee's companion is furnished with the right to speak at that hearing. However, crucially, that statutory provision does not permit the employee to be accompanied by a legal representative, such as a solicitor or barrister. In *Kulkarni v Milton Keynes Hospital NHS Trust* and *R (on the application of G) v Governors of X School*, notwithstanding the restricted scope of these statutory provisions, the Court of Appeal ruled that article 6 was engaged where disciplinary hearings had been scheduled to consider serious allegations of sexual assault and inappropriate conduct against a doctor and teacher respectively.[33] Since in both cases the charges were of considerable gravity and, if proven, would effectively bar the employees from practising their professions, the Court of Appeal implied a right in favour of those employees to be legally represented. In these cases, it is arguable that the Court of Appeal was essentially engaged in adopting the 'weak' approach to indirect horizontal effect, since it was making the existing law in section 10 of the ERelA compatible with the ECHR by interpolating supplementary procedural protection to workers. However, the duration of this 'weak' approach was short-lived and was cut off when the Supreme Court in *R (on the application of G) v Governors of X School*[34] (*G v X*) ruled that the teacher in issue was not entitled to legal representation since article 6 was not engaged. Therefore, the procedural safeguard which the Court of Appeal had furnished the teacher was ruled to be unavailable, since the majority[35] of the Supreme Court took the view that the employer's disciplinary proceedings would not have a substantial influence or effect on the determination by a regulator of the teacher's civil right to practise his profession in a second set of proceedings.

---

[31] [2009] EWCA Civ 789, [2009] IRLR 829 (CA). See also *R (on the application of Kirk) v Middlesborough Borough Council* [2010] EWHC 1035 (Admin), [2010] IRLR 699 (HC) and *R (on the application of Puri) v Bradford Teaching Hospitals NHS Foundation Trust* [2011] EWHC 970 (Admin), [2011] IRLR 582 (HC).

[32] [2010] EWCA Civ 1, [2010] 2 All ER 555 (CA).

[33] Where the outcome of the disciplinary proceedings was such that the employee would lose his job rather than be effectively deprived of his ability to practise his profession, it was held that article 6 was not engaged: *R (on the application of Puri)*, note 31 supra.

[34] [2011] UKSC 30, [2012] 1 AC 167.

[35] Lord Kerr delivered a dissenting opinion.

Only in cases where the disciplinary proceedings would determine, or have a substantial effect on, subsequent regulatory proceedings would Article 6 of the ECHR be applicable.

Article 6 of the ECHR can be contrasted with article 8 of the ECHR, which safeguards the employee's right to respect for his or her private and family life. The article 8 right to privacy has great potential to act as a catalyst for the evolution of the content of the law of the contract of employment, particularly in light of the pervasiveness of the Internet, digital media and social networking websites in the workplace.[36] Although the employment relationship is characterised by the subordination of the worker to the control and direction of the employer,[37] the 'wage-work' bargain[38] which is struck between the employee and management is by no means pervasive. The formation of that bargain does not necessarily mean that the employee has negotiated away all freedom to engage in any activities he or she pleases in the private sphere.[39] An individual's private life offers space, solitude and a welcome opportunity to 'retreat from the world'. For that reason, some sanctuary from the workplace should be secured and one means of safeguarding that privilege would be the development of a right of privacy under the auspices of article 8 of the ECHR.[40]

On the other hand, is it not the case that employers have a legitimate commercial interest in the private lives of their employees and that the wage-work bargain should permit them to discipline and dismiss those workers in circumstances where their private activities have a deteriorative effect on the employer's reputation?[41] There is perhaps nothing unusual in this argument, since, in the past, the courts and tribunals have demonstrated their

---

[36] For example, the Advisory, Conciliation and Arbitration Service (ACAS) in the UK has issued guidance for UK employers on the use of Internet and social networking sites in the workplace: *http://www.acas.org.uk/media/pdf/b/d/1111_Workplaces_and_Social_Networking.pdf*.

[37] One finds the classic exposition of this in P Davies and M Freedland *Kahn-Freund's Labour and the Law* 3e (Stevens & Sons 1983) at 17–18.

[38] The 'wage-work' bargain is a shorthand for the employee's contractual obligation to the employer to perform in accordance with the latter's instructions, in return for the employer's corresponding obligation to pay the employee a wage.

[39] There is an element of disjuncture between the increasing acknowledgement of the significance of family-friendly policy initiatives and the work-life balance by government through labour legislation (see, e.g., the UK Government's recent consultation paper, entitled 'Consultation on Modern Workplaces', May 2011, available at *http://c561635.r35.cf2.rackcdn.com/11–699–consultation-modern-workplaces.pdf*) on the one hand, and the expansion of the managerial prerogative into the private lives of employees, particularly in light of the reality that the fear of facing potential disciplinary action will undoubtedly constrain or curtail an employee's activities during his or her private life.

[40] W S Warren and L D Brandeis 'The Right to Privacy' (1890) 4 *Harvard Law Review* 193 at 196, and M W Finkin 'Life Away From Work' (2006) 66 *Louisiana Law Review* 945 at 952–3.

[41] For a wider discussion, see J Craig *Privacy and Employment Law* (Hart Publishing 2002) at 26–33.

willingness to uphold the managerial prerogative and hold that a dismissal was fair under section 98(4) of the ERA on the grounds that the discharged employees were having an affair[42] or had remarried[43] which was detrimental to the employer's interests. Moreover, any restrictions placed upon workers in their leisure time by the wage-work bargain are not open-ended, since they will cease to exist if and when the worker decides that the trade-off between his or her remuneration package is no longer worth bearing those constraints and he or she exercises his or her freedom to terminate the contract of employment.[44]

In practice, in the UK, the courts have generally applied article 8 in a way that serves to limit or qualify the protection available to employees. For example, in X v Y[45] it was held that article 8 was irrelevant where an employee was dismissed after having been arrested and cautioned by police for committing a sex offence in a transport café lavatory in his own private time with another man. Mummery LJ adopted a spatial or 'zonal' conceptualisation[46] of what is understood by the term 'private life':

> 'The applicant's conduct did not take place in his private life nor was it within the scope of application of the right to respect for it. It happened in a place to which the public had, and were permitted to have, access; it was a criminal offence, which is normally a matter of legitimate concern to the public; a criminal offence is not a purely private matter; and it led to a caution for the offence, which was relevant to his employment and should have been disclosed by him to his employer as a matter of legitimate concern to it. The applicant wished to keep the matter private. That does not make it part of his private life or deprive it of its public aspect.'[47]

A similar approach was taken by the EAT in *Pay v Lancashire Probation Service*[48] where the EAT held that article 8 was not invoked where an employee probation officer working with sex offenders in prisons had a proclivity for sado-masochistic activities and performances in fetish clubs

---

[42] *Spiller v FJ Wallis Ltd* [1975] IRLR 362 (IT), and see L Clarke 'Sexual Relationships and Sexual Conduct in the Workplace' (2006) 26 *Legal Studies* 347.

[43] *Jones v Lee* [1980] ICR 310 (CA).

[44] The European Court of Human Rights has adopted this approach in the past, e.g. see *Ahmad v United Kingdom* (1982) 4 EHRR 126 and *Stedman v United Kingdom* (1997) 23 EHRR CD 168.

[45] X v Y, note 27 supra.

[46] This 'zonal' approach, whereby spheres of activity are divided, appears to have been adopted in other jurisdictions, on which see the discussion in Craig *Privacy and Employment Law*, note 41 supra, at 15–19.

[47] X v Y, note 27 supra, at 631.

[48] [2004] ICR 187 (EAT). This can be contrasted with the domestic court's understanding of the scope of private life (where certain public zones of interaction were deemed to be private) in cases arising outside the context of the workplace such as *McKennitt v Ash* [2005] EWHC 3003 (QB), aff'd [2008] QB 73, per Eady J at para 50, and *Murray v Express Newspapers Plc* [2008] EWCA Civ 446, [2009] Ch 481.

and posted inappropriate images of himself in fetish and bondage gear on the Internet. The EAT ruled that those pictures were accessible in a public arena and so there was no scope for article 8 to apply to the case. However, when Pay appealed his case to the ECtHR,[49] the Court adopted a more purposive interpretation. It held that article 8 of the ECHR was engaged in such circumstances since Pay's performances had taken place in a club which was likely to be frequented only by a self-selecting group of like-minded individuals. Nevertheless, the ECtHR ruled that the employer's decision to dismiss on the facts was proportionate in terms of article 8(2) since the employer had a legitimate aim in protecting its reputation and that aim outweighed the harm to the employee.

The decisions in *X v Y*[50] and *Pay v UK*[51] have been criticised on the basis that they misunderstand the value of privacy, which should be based on protection from employer domination, so that off-duty conduct should only be invoked by the employer as grounds for dismissal where the employee's conduct would harm the legitimate interests of the employer.[52] For instance, as Justice Blackman queried in the US Supreme Court decision of *O'Connor v Ortega*, is it really the case that the deployment of a zonal analysis offers any great assistance as to what occurs in the private or public sphere?[53]

> '[T]he reality of work in modern times . . . reveals why a public employers' expectation of privacy in the workplace should be carefully safeguarded and not lightly set-aside. It is, unfortunately, all too true that the workplace has become another home for most working Americans. Many employees spend the better part of their days and much of their evenings at work . . . consequently, an employee's private life must intersect with the workplace . . . As a result, the tidy distinctions . . . between the workplace and professional affairs, on the one hand, and personal possessions and private activities, on the other, do not exist in reality.'

To date, there is nothing to suggest that the UK courts have shifted their approach to something that better reflects the issues identified in the passage above. Therefore, it can be concluded that the UK courts' treatment to date of article 8 is such that it has had little impact upon labour law.

The article 11 right to freedom of association is another area in which the ECHR might be expected to have implications for the development of UK labour law. Indeed, there is evidence that the ECtHR has in recent years been more willing to listen to, and uphold, the rights of trade unions than in the

---

[49] *Pay v UK* [2009] IRLR 139 (ECtHR).

[50] *X v Y*, note 27 supra.

[51] *Pay v UK*, note 49 supra.

[52] See H Collins 'The Protection of Civil Liberties in the Workplace' (2006) 69 *Modern Law Review* 619; V Mantouvalou 'Human Rights and Unfair Dismissal: Private Acts in Public Spaces' (2008) 71 *Modern Law Review* 912; and H Collins and V Mantouvalou 'Private Life and Dismissal: *Pay v UK*' (2009) 38 *Industrial Law Journal* 133.

[53] 480 US 709 (1987); 107 S Ct 1492 (1989).

past. In a series of recent cases[54] the ECtHR deviated from its earlier jurisprudence[55] on the means by which member states of the Council of Europe
should guarantee the article 11 right to freedom of association. The ECtHR
has ruled that trade unions have the right not to be prohibited from engaging in collective bargaining with employers and that this right also includes
a right to strike and take collective action. By holding in the case of *Demir
and Baykara v Turkey* that the right to collective bargaining was an essential
right protected by article 11, the ECtHR referred[56] to the pivotal interpretative role played by international and European labour standards, such as the
International Labour Organisation (ILO) Conventions 98 and 151, article 6
of Europe's Social Charter of 1961 (ESC) and article 28 of the EU Charter of
Fundamental Rights of 2000.[57] Moreover, in *Enerji Yapi-Yol Sen*,[58] like the
South African Constitutional Court in the case of *In Re Certification of the
Constitution of South Africa*,[59] the ECtHR recognised the close relationship
between the right to collective bargaining and the right to strike, holding that
the latter was a necessary element towards the enjoyment of the former.[60]

In light of the various cases decided by the UK courts since the ECtHR's
path-breaking decisions in *Demir and Baykara v Turkey* and *Enerji Yapi-Yol
Sen*, and the direction in section 2(1) of the Human Rights Act 1998 that a
'court or tribunal determining a question which has arisen in connection
with a Convention right must take into account any judgment, [or] decision
of the [ECtHR]', one would expect to find that this change in position at the
European level would have filtered down to the UK courts. However, that
has not happened. The judiciary in the UK, wedded to traditional common
law reasoning, have resisted the application of the ECtHR's recent jurisprudence and generally treat the common law position as the point of departure
from which any subsequent statutory intervention should be understood:[61]

> 'The common law confers no right to strike in this country. Workers who take
> strike action will usually be acting in breach of their contracts of employment . . .

---

[54] *Demir and Baykara v Turkey* (2009) 48 EHRR 54; *Enerji Yapi-Yol Sen*, App No 68959/01, 21
April 2009 (ECtHR); and *Danilenkov v Russia*, App No 67336/01, 30 July 2009 (ECtHR).
See KD Ewing and J Hendy 'The Dramatic Implications of Demir and Baykara' (2010) 39
Industrial Law Journal 1.
[55] *Swedish Engine Drivers' Union v Sweden* (1976) 1 EHRR 617; *National Union of Belgian Police
v Belgium* (1975) 1 EHRR 578.
[56] *Demir*, note 54 supra, at 781.
[57] Now replaced by article 28 of the Charter of Fundamental Rights of the European Union of
2010 (OJ C 83, 30.3.2010, 389).
[58] Note 54 supra.
[59] 1996 (4) SA 744; 1996 *ILJ* (South Africa) 821 (CC) at para 66.
[60] In the case of *Unison v UK* [2002] IRLR 497 (ECtHR), the ECtHR laid the groundwork for
its decision in *Enerji*, note 54 supra, as it recognised there the principle that the prohibition
of a strike could represent an interference with a trade union's right to protect its members,
and so amount to a restriction of its article 11 right.
[61] See Ewing and Hendy, note 54 supra, at 20 and 34.

The common law's focus on the protection of property and contractual rights is necessarily antithetical to any form of industrial action since the purpose of the action is to interfere with the employer's rights.'[62]

The absence of a right to strike in the common law was first addressed by the UK Parliament at the dawn of the twentieth century when it passed the Trade Disputes Act 1906. The relevant provisions are now found in the Trade Union and Labour Relations (Consolidation) Act 1992 ('the 1992 Act') which provide trade unions with certain statutory immunities from tortious and delictual liabilities suffered by employers and third parties as a result of collective action. However, the enjoyment of the statutory immunities is subject to conditions. The two most significant conditions are first that the collective action must be taken in 'contemplation or furtherance of a trade dispute' – that is, the dispute must be industrial rather than political[63] – and secondly, the highly technical pre-strike balloting and notice requirements imposed on trade unions, set out in sections 226 to 235A of the 1992 Act, must be complied with in advance of any industrial action. Cases concerning the trade union's right to the enjoyment of statutory immunity from liability have historically revolved around the first condition. However, in the wave of industrial action which has been ongoing in response to recent public sector cuts, the decided cases have concerned whether the trade union had observed the statutory balloting and notice requirements. Employers have sought interim injunctions and full injunctions against the trade unions in order to thwart planned industrial action on the grounds that the requirements in sections 226 and 234A of the 1992 Act[64] had been breached. In response, the trade unions contended that they had satisfied the pre-strike balloting and notice requirements, but interestingly, they also sought to harness article 11 of the ECHR in aid of their case, by arguing that the balloting provisions represented a disproportionate interference with their right to freedom of association.

This trend is particularly evident in the recent high-profile cases of *Metrobus v UNITE*,[65] *BA v UNITE*[66] and *National Union of Rail, Maritime & Transport Workers v Serco, ASLEF v London & Birmingham Railway Ltd*.[67] In *Metrobus v UNITE*[68] the Court of Appeal rejected the trade union's argument that the intricate pre-strike balloting and notice requirements represented a disproportionate interference with their article 11 right to freedom

---

[62] *National Union of Rail, Maritime & Transport*, note 16 supra, at 401–2 (Elias LJ).

[63] Trade Union and Labour Relations (Consolidation) Act 1992, ss 219(1) and 244.

[64] These statutory provisions concern the detailed rules for the holding of ballots and voting, as well as the required content of the notices of the outcome of the ballot.

[65] [2009] EWCA Civ 829, [2009] IRLR 851 (CA). See R Dukes, 'The Right to Strike under UK Law: Not Much More Than a Slogan?' (2010) 39 *Industrial Law Journal* 82.

[66] [2010] EWCA Civ 669, [2010] ICR 1316 (CA).

[67] *National Union of Rail, Maritime & Transport*, note 16 supra. See R Dukes, 'The Right to Strike under UK Law: Something More Than a Slogan?' (2011) 40 *Industrial Law Journal* 302.

[68] *Metrobus*, note 65 supra.

of association. Holding that article 11 had no application to the case, on the grounds that the legislation had been carefully adapted over the years in order to strike a balance between the interests of employers, unions and members of the public, the Court of Appeal expressed doubt whether *Enerji Yapi-Yol Sen* was good authority for the proposition that the article 11 right to freedom of association incorporated the right to strike.[69] The Court of Appeal pointed to the fact that *Enerji Yapi-Yol Sen* contained a 'less fully articulated judgment' than that of the Grand Chamber in *Demir and Baykara v Turkey*. Moreover, the Court of Appeal was dismissive of the relevance of, and the assistance to be derived from, instruments of the ILO and the ESC, and in a now famous passage in his judgment, Kay LJ expressed the view that: '[i]n this country, the right to strike has never been much more than a slogan or a legal metaphor. Such a right has not been bestowed by statute'.[70]

In the subsequent case of *BA v UNITE*,[71] recognising that he was bound by the decision of the Court of Appeal in *Metrobus v UNITE*, Justice Cox nonetheless stated that:

> '[s]ooner or later, the extent to which the current statutory regime is in compliance with [the UK's] international obligations [in ILO Convention No 87 on the Freedom of Association and Protection of the Right to Organise] and with relevant international jurisprudence will fall to be carefully reconsidered.'[72]

When *BA v UNITE*[73] was appealed to the Court of Appeal, the issue of the applicability of article 11 was bypassed, the Court of Appeal holding that the trade union had complied with the statutory procedural requirements. In *National Union of Rail, Maritime & Transport Workers v Serco, ASLEF v London & Birmingham Railway Ltd.*,[74] however, whilst holding that the question of the compatibility of the pre-strike balloting and notice requirements with article 11 of the ECHR should not be revisited as it had been settled by the Court of Appeal in *Metrobus v UNITE*, Elias LJ did recognise that the ECtHR had:

> 'in a number of cases confirmed that the right to strike is conferred as an element of the right to freedom of association conferred by article 11(1) of the European Convention on Human Rights which in turn is given effect by the Human Rights Act.'[75]

This is a particularly telling passage from Elias LJ's judgment as it represents the first time that the Court of Appeal has come close to acknowledging

---

[69] *Metrobus*, note 65 supra, at 858 (Lloyd LJ).
[70] *Metrobus*, note 65 supra, at 868 (Kay LJ).
[71] [2009] EWHC 3541 (QB), [2010] IRLR 423 (HC).
[72] Ibid at 426 (Cox J).
[73] [2010] EWCA Civ 669; [2010] ICR 1316 (CA).
[74] *National Union of Rail, Maritime & Transport*, note 16 supra.
[75] *National Union of Rail, Maritime & Transport*, note 16 supra, at 401–2.

something a little short of a revolution in the jurisprudence of the ECtHR concerning trade union rights pursuant to article 11. It may be the lynchpin upon which a subsequent decision of the Supreme Court explicitly recognising the right to strike and collective bargaining in the UK will hang. However, it may be that the trade unions will bypass the UK Supreme Court and instead seek a definitive ruling on the matter from the ECtHR. Indeed, it is understood that an application has been made by the National Union of Rail, Maritime and Transport Workers to the ECtHR, seeking a declaration that the provisions in the 1992 Act on pre-strike balloting and notice are indeed a disproportionate interference with their right to engage in collective action.[76] A judgment to that effect from the ECtHR would obviate the need to wait for any further development of the thinking of the common law courts in the UK in the direction of greater trade union rights.

If the ECtHR were to hold that UK legislation was incompatible with article 11, it would not be for the first time. For example, in the case of *ASLEF v United Kingdom*,[77] the ECtHR held that the provisions in section 174 of the 1992 Act, which prohibited trade unions from excluding or expelling their members for the reason of a member's political affiliation, were unduly restrictive. When the trade union had expelled a member for the reason that he was a member of a far-right political party, an employment tribunal had forced the trade union to re-admit him to membership, on the ground that section 174 of the 1992 Act precluded the individual's expulsion. The trade union applied to the ECtHR, who ruled that section 174 violated the article 11 right to freedom of association and to form and join a trade union.[78] The article 11 right included a right of non-association, as well as association.

The case of *Wilson v UK*[79] is another example of legislation being declared incompatible with article 11. In *Wilson* the provisions in Part III of the 1992 Act, which precluded an employer from subjecting an employee to a detriment on grounds of participation in trade union activities or from refusing to employ a person on grounds of trade union membership or lack of trade union membership, were deemed by the ECtHR to be inadequate: they failed to protect employees who had been offered financial and other inducements by their employer not to become, or to cease to be, a trade union member. As a result, the ECtHR declared that, in allowing employers to

---

[76] See Dukes, note 65 supra, at 310–11.

[77] [2007] IRLR 361 (ECtHR).

[78] For commentary on this case as it worked its way through the court system, on to the ECtHR, and the UK Parliamentary response in amending the legislation, see J Hendy QC and KD Ewing, 'Trade Unions, Human Rights and the BNP' (2005) 34 *Industrial Law Journal* 197; KD Ewing, 'The Implications of the ASLEF case' (2007) 36 *Industrial Law Journal* 425; and KD Ewing, 'Employment Act 2008: Implementing the ASLEF Decision – A Victory for the BNP?' (2009) 39 *Industrial Law Journal* 50.

[79] (2002) 35 EHRR 20.

offer such financial incentives, the UK was in breach of the right to freedom of association under article 11.[80]

15.3.4 Conclusion

The extent to which the courts in the UK have applied ECHR rights as an aid to development of the substantive law of employment has been far from progressive. If anything, there is little evidence of the courts adopting either the 'weak' or 'strong' conceptualisations of indirect horizontal effect considered above. Furthermore, there is also scant sign of the UK courts adapting the law to provide additional procedural safeguards in favour of employees in light of ECHR rights: initial movements in that direction were stymied by the decision of the Supreme Court in G v X.[81] This is in spite of reformist tendencies in the recent judgments of the ECtHR, which although radical, should not be taken for granted, since history reveals that the ECtHR has not always been so.[82] The relationship between UK labour law, with its common law and statutory sources on the one hand, and the ECHR on the other hand can perhaps be depicted as one of 'oil and water' where little crossover between the two separate streams has occurred to date. It is also noteworthy that there has been no resort in the UK case law to article 14 of the ECHR, which outlaws discrimination in respect of the enjoyment of the rights or freedoms in the ECHR. This may be attributable to the robust statutory regime which exists in the UK in respect of equality in the workplace, but can be contrasted with the position in South Africa. Overall, one can reach the conclusion that the approach of the UK courts contributes little to the debate about the merits of constitutionalising labour rights: to date, the impact of the HRA on the workplace has been marginal at best, and more time is needed before a final assessment can be made. If anything, it may be that the European Union's recent accession to the ECHR and its adoption of the Charter of Fundamental Rights of the European Union ('Charter of Fundamental Rights')[83] will provide the catalyst for the UK courts to take a more interventionist approach. For example, in the recent case of *Seda Kucukdeveci v Swedex GmbH & Co KG*,[84] the European Court of Justice referred to a particular provision of the Charter of Fundamental Rights as one of the grounds for their decision in favour of an employee. Since it is an axiomatic principle that European Union law is supreme, there is the possibility that the UK courts will have no option but to apply

---

80 The UK Government responded by introducing sections 145A-145F of the 1992 Act to prohibit employer inducements.
81 G v X, note 34 supra.
82 The case of *Wilson v UK*, note 79 supra, was the first time the Strasbourg Court upheld a claim relating to trade union rights under article 11.
83 OJ C 83, 30.3.2010, p 389.
84 [2010] 2 CMLR 874, [2010] IRLR 346 (ECJ).

the ECHR more actively in the future in order to develop domestic labour law.[85]

15.4 SOUTH AFRICA

15.4.1 Introduction

The South African labour market is undoubtedly markedly different to that pertaining in Scotland or the UK. For example, rather than being highly diversified, it is segmented, with a core of protected public and private sector workers, surrounded by a much larger informal economy with a sustained influx of formal and informal labour migrants from the rest of the African continent.[86] Moreover, most of those working in the informal economy fall outside the scope of labour protection laws.[87] There is also a significant number of marginalised unemployed. Therefore, when comparing and contrasting labour laws in South Africa and Scotland, it is important to be mindful of the wider social and economic context within which those laws are operating. The historical context is also key: it is not controversial to assert that much of the struggle against the apartheid regime was conducted by unionised workers who took industrial action against their employers in order to exercise their democratic voices of protest.[88] The prioritisation of equality and dignity in South Africa post-apartheid was an unsurprising response and can only be properly understood within the context of the pre-1990s national experience.

The 'touchstone'[89] of the new political order in South Africa is the protection of human dignity in the SAC, which is in keeping with the notion of labour rights as human rights, discussed at the beginning of this chapter.

---

[85] However, some commentators are sceptical that the EU's accession to the ECHR and its adoption of the Charter will have any lasting impact on EU law or the law of the EU member states, on which see P Syrpis 'The Treaty of Lisbon: Much Ado . . . But About What?' (2008) 37 *Industrial Law Journal* 219. Another point raised by those who doubt the scope for such impact is that the social/labour rights in the Charter of Fundamental Rights merely guarantee rights which are already conferred upon workers under EU or member state law, i.e. they do not provide additional protection, but form the bases or grounds upon which more specific and detailed member state and European legislation can be understood.

[86] See South African National Planning Commission 'Diagnostic Overview' (2011) at 12 (available at *http://www.npconline.co.za/MediaLib/Downloads/Home/Tabs/Diagnostic/Diagnostic%20 Overview.pdf*).

[87] C Fenwick, E Kalula and I Landau 'Labour Law: A Southern African perspective' in T Teklé (ed) *Labour Law and Worker Protection in Developing Countries*, note 4 supra, at 199–205.

[88] S van Eck 'Constitutionalisation of South African Labour Law' in C Fenwick and T Novitz (eds) *Human Rights at Work: Perspectives on Law and Regulation* (Hart Publishing 2010) at 260–2; P Benjamin 'Ideas of Labour Law – Views From the South' in G Davidov and B Langille *The Idea of Labour Law* (Oxford University Press 2011) at 209–11.

[89] *S v Makwanyane* 1995 (3) SA 391 (CC) at para 329 per Judge Kate O'Regan.

This is reflected in section 10 of the SAC which directs that everyone 'has inherent dignity and the right to have their dignity respected and protected'. This dignitarian foundation filters down to section 9 which promotes equality and prohibits unfair discrimination. The link between dignity, equality and non-discrimination was expressly recognised by Judge Kate O'Regan in *S v Makwanyane*,[90] and in *National Coalition for Gay and Lesbian Equality v Minister of Justice*[91] where Judge Sachs expressly refused to sever it. Section 9 provides for equal protection and affirmative action and abolishes unfair discrimination based on race, gender, sex, pregnancy, marital status, ethnic or social origin, colour, sexual orientation, age, disability, religion, conscience, belief, culture, language or birth. Great store was also placed on the role of human rights in the SAC and an appropriate ideological connection was forged between those fundamental rights and the field of labour law.[92] This nexus finds its expression in section 23(1) of the SAC, which proudly declares that '[e]veryone has the right to fair labour practices'. Section 23 then goes on to confer a suite of individual and collective labour rights in favour of workers and trade unions. For example, section 23(2)(a) sets up a right to form and join a trade union, participate in the activities and programmes of a trade union, and, most significantly of all, confers on workers a right to strike. Section 23(5) goes on to provide that trade unions, employers and employers' organisations are entitled to engage in collective bargaining. Like the position of human rights law in the UK, the SAC is indirectly applicable between private parties – that is, it is not simply vertical in orientation. Moreover, in terms of section 39(2) of the SAC, it can be harnessed as an interpretative aid in respect of legislation and can be deployed in order to develop the common law. Common law rules that are incompatible with the provisions in the SAC are superseded[93] and the social rights in the SAC adopt a hierarchical structure, forming a single body of law, with the common law subordinate to the supreme law as expressed in constitutional norms.[94]

These higher order constitutional principles filter down to the statutory level and are instantiated in the Labour Relations Act 66 of 1995 (LRA), the Basic Conditions of Employment Equity Act 75 of 1997 (BCEE) and the Employment Equity Act 55 of 1998 (EEA). As van der Westhuizen J recognised in the case of *Gcaba v Minister for Safety & Security & others*,[95] the

---

[90] Ibid.

[91] 1999 (1) SA 6 (CC) at paras 120–9.

[92] E Kalula 'Labour Market Regulation and Labour Law in Southern Africa' in C Barnard, S Deakin and G Morris (eds) *The Future of Labour Law: Liber Amicorum Bob Hepple QC* (Hart Publishing 2004) at 282.

[93] SAC, s 39(3).

[94] See SAC, ss 2 and 8(2)-(3) and *Pharmaceutical Manufacturers Association of SA: In re: ex p President of the Republic of South Africa* 2000 (2) SA 674 (CC) at para 44.

[95] 2010 (1) SA 238 (CC), (2010) 31 ILJ 296 (CC).

'LRA was promulgated . . . to provide particularity and content to section 23 [of the SAC]'.[96] The LRA recognises freedom of association and the protection of the worker's right to strike, provides a model for collective bargaining, promotes industrial democracy through the adoption of workplace forums, regulates unfair dismissals and establishes specialist labour dispute resolution courts. In particular, it also guarantees the right to 'fair labour practices'.[97] The BCEE sets out a floor of employment rights in respect of maximum hours of work and minimum annual leave provisions and adopts controls in respect of those workers not covered by collective bargaining agreements. The EEA, by contrast, builds on section 9 of the SAC to outlaw unfair discrimination and sanction affirmative action.

15.4.2 The impact of sections 23 and 9 of the SAC

In South Africa therefore, with the entrenchment and declared supremacy in the SAC of labour rights over common law or statutory rights, labour rights have been constitutionalised. There is an argument that this has been counterproductive and that the manner in which section 23 has been construed threatens to rupture the uniform fabric of labour law. This feeds into a wider debate amongst South African labour lawyers about the decompartmentalisation and fragmentation of labour law. The concern is that labour law as an autonomous body of learning is in grave danger of becoming extinct and generally subsumed by the burgeoning disciplines of public law, human rights or constitutional law.[98] The point being made here can be best articulated within the framework of a discussion which assesses the interplay between the constitutional rights in section 23 of the SAC on the one hand and the statutory rights in the LRA and common law employment rights on the other hand.

Turning first to the LRA, it is envisaged that the specialist labour courts will be the final arbiters in respect of the resolution of disputes concerning the statutory rights of employees. For instance, section 167(2) and Schedule 7, item 22(6) of the LRA provide that '[t]he Labour Appeal Court is the final court of appeal in respect of all judgments and orders made by the Labour Court in respect of the matters within its exclusive jurisdiction' and '. . . no

---

[96] Ibid at para 10.
[97] LRA, s 186(2).
[98] Van Eck, note 88 supra, at 290; P Pretorius and A Myburgh 'A Dual System of Dismissal Law: Comment on *Boxer Superstores Mthatha and another v Mbenya*' (2007) 28 *ILJ* (South Africa) 2209 and (2007) 28 *ILJ* (South Africa) 2172 at 2174 and 2176; D du Toit 'Oil on Troubled Waters? The Slippery Interface between the Contract of Employment and Statutory Labour Law' (2008) 125 *SALJ* 95 at 96–7. However, other commentators are more relaxed about this process, referring to the future relationship between the common law, labour law and public law as one of enlightened 'cross-fertilization', on which see J Grogan *Workplace Law* 9e (Juta 2007) at 14.

appeal will lie against any judgment or order given or made by the Labour Appeal Court.' The idea underpinning this approach is that a self-contained body of jurisprudence which served to interpret the statutory labour rights in the LRA would be built up incrementally by the specialist labour courts. However, in *NUMSA v Fry's Metals (Pty) Ltd*[99] the Supreme Court of Appeal (SCA) held that these provisions in the LRA had to be interpreted in accordance with the SAC and thus more or less opened the door for unsuccessful litigants to appeal the decisions of the Labour Appeal Court upwards to the Constitutional Court via the SCA. Moreover, the cases of *SA Commercial Catering & Allied Workers Union v Irvin & Johnson Ltd*[100] and *NEHAWU v University of Cape Town & others*[101] decided that since the statutory right to fair labour practices in section 186(2) of the LRA gives effect to a constitutional right, the proper interpretation of this provision may raise a constitutional issue involving the application of section 23 of the SAC. The consequence of that analysis is that, subject to the Constitutional Court's approval, it is permissible to appeal the decisions of the Labour Appeal Court to the Constitutional Court on any question arising from or connected to the Labour Appeal Court's interpretation of the section 186(2) LRA right to fair labour practices. An employee must establish that it is in the 'interests of justice' that he or she be given leave from the Constitutional Court to appeal a decision of the Labour Appeal Court.[102] However, where it is claimed that the Labour Appeal Court's interpretation of a provision of the LRA is too narrow and inconsistent with the employee's constitutional right to strike enshrined in section 23 of the SAC, something akin to a presumption applies that it is in the public interest for the Constitutional Court to grant leave.[103] The effect appears to be that in cases concerning the right to strike, the Constitutional Court will take a liberal approach in granting leave to appeal the decision of the Labour Appeal Court. The end result has been to subvert any desire to develop a uniform body of industrial jurisprudence on the scope and content of statutory employment rights in the LRA.

Moreover, fragmentation is also one of the effects of the approaches in *Boxer Superstores Mthatha v Mbenya*[104] and *Old Mutual Life Assurance Co SA Ltd v Gumbi.*[105] In these two cases the SCA recognised that the common law can be developed by analogy with the section 23 rights in the SAC. *Boxer*

---

[99] [2005] 3 All SA 318 (SCA).

[100] 2000 (3) SA 705 (CC) at para 4 (Cameron AJ).

[101] 2003 (3) SA 1 (CC), (2003) 24 *ILJ* 95 (CC).

[102] *NUMSA & others v Bader Pop (Pty) Ltd. & another* 2003 (3) SA 513 (CC), (2003) 24 ILJ 305 (CC); *Khumalo v Holomisa* 2002 (5) SA 401 (CC) at para 14; and *NUMSA v Bader Bop (Pty) Ltd.* 2003 (3) SA 513 (CC) at para 16.

[103] *South African Police Service v Police and Prisons Civil Rights Union* [2011] ZACC 21; [2011] 9 BLLR 831 (CC); 2011 (9) BCLR 992 (CC).

[104] [2007] 8 BLLR 693 (SCA).

[105] [2007] 4 All SA 866 (SCA).

Superstores and *Old Mutual* demonstrate that the constitutional right to 'fair labour practices' in section 23 affected the common law of the contract of employment to the extent that it conferred on an employee the right to a hearing prior to the employer taking any decision to dismiss him or her. This was the legal position notwithstanding the existence of the statutory regime of unfair dismissal in the LRA and despite the fact that this new common law pre-dismissal right mirrored one of the procedural guarantees conferred by the statutory regime. Likewise in the case of *Murray v MOD*[106] a military police officer who was not covered by the statutory unfair dismissal protections of the LRA was successful in persuading the SCA to develop the common law in accordance with the constitutional right in section 23 of the SAC. This enabled the employee to claim constructive dismissal along the same lines as that set out in the LRA for a breach of a common law implied term imposing a duty on employers to engage in fair dealing conduct with their employees. Some commentators went as far as to say that these decisions taken to their conclusion would lead to the emergence of a common law right not to be unfairly dismissed, that is, a contractually enforceable right.[107] However, the SCA engaged in a measure of retrenchment in the case of *South African Maritime Safety Authority v McKenzie*.[108] In *McKenzie* Wallis AJA in the SCA rejected the argument that the common law ought to evolve to provide for an implied term not to be unfairly dismissed along the same scheme as the statutory protections in the LRA. Instead, Wallis AJA could see 'no justification for mechanically duplicating statutory rights by importing them into the contract [of employment]'.[109] In the context of this discussion the sentiment of van den Westhuizen J in *Gcaba v Minister for Safety & Security & others*[110] is noteworthy, namely that fragmentation can give rise to 'parallel systems of law, duplicate jurisdiction and forum shopping'. In much the same vein, one cannot help but recall the warning of Lord Millett in *Johnson v Unisys Ltd*:[111]

> 'And, even more importantly, the coexistence of two systems, overlapping but varying in matters of detail and heard by different tribunals, would be a recipe for chaos. All coherence in our employment laws would be lost.'[112]

---

[106] [2008] 3 All SA 66 (SCA).

[107] T Cohen 'Implying Fairness into the Employment Contract' (2009) 30 *ILJ* (South Africa) 2271.

[108] 2010 (3) SA 601 (SCA), [2010] 3 All SA 1 (SCA), (2010) 31 ILJ 529 (SCA).

[109] Ibid at para 36.

[110] 2010 (1) SA 238 (CC), (2010) 31 ILJ 296 (CC) at para 69 per van den Westhuizen J.

[111] [2003] 1 AC 518 (HL).

[112] Ibid at 550D-E per Lord Millett. Lord Millett used this argument to refuse an extension of the common law of wrongful dismissal to furnish a remedy where one was already available under the statutory regime of unfair dismissal contained in the Employment Rights Act 1996, Part X.

Hence the approach of the SCA and the Constitutional Court in the cases discussed above, coupled with the fact that the civil courts have jurisdiction to hear constitutional issues in terms of section 169 of the SAC, has resulted in fragmentation between the jurisdiction of the specialist labour courts in matters governed by the LRA and the civil courts in constitutional matters.

The impact of section 23 of the SAC has not been restricted to acting as an engine for the evolution of statutory and common law labour rights. In conjunction with section 18 of the SAC which guarantees 'everyone' the right to freedom of association and the right to join a trade union, section 23 of the SAC has been deployed in order to strike down statutory provisions. For example, in the case of *SANDU v Ministry of Defence*[113] sections 18 and 23(2)(a) of the SAC were applied in order to overturn a legislative ban on soldiers joining a trade union in section 126B(1) of the Defence Act 44 of 1957. It was held that the ban was unreasonable and unjustifiable. This remarkable step can be contrasted sharply with the approach of the UK courts, where the most that can be done is to declare a UK statutory provision incompatible with the ECHR.[114] Indeed, no UK court has ever taken such a course of action in the context of labour law and it has been left to the ECtHR to do so.[115]

Section 23(5) of SAC also provides that 'every trade union, employers' organisation and employer has the right to engage in collective bargaining'. In the case of *SANDU v Ministry of Defence*[116] the Constitutional Court ruled that section 23(5) offered an employee an absolute right to collective bargaining and imposed a corresponding duty on the employer to enter into negotiations with employees or their trade unions and enter into a collective agreement. This was despite the absence of any enforceable right to collective bargaining in the LRA. The decision in *SANDU v Ministry of Defence*[117] is therefore similar to that of the ECtHR in *Demir and Baykara v Turkey*.[118] Of course, as we noted above, the corollary of the right to collective bargaining is the right to strike and in Europe, the ECtHR recognised this point in *Enerji Yapi-Yol Sen*.[119] Accordingly it is perhaps unsurprising that section 23(2)(c) of the SAC prescribes that every employee has the right to strike. The case of *ex p Chairperson of the Constitutional Assembly: In Re Certification of the Constitution of the Republic of South Africa*[120] interpreted section 23(2)(c) of the SAC as conferring that right in favour of an individual employee, but held that it does not confer a corresponding right upon an employer to exercise

---

[113] (1999) 20 *ILJ* (South Africa) 2279 (CC).
[114] By contrast any Act of the Scottish Parliament that is incompatible with Convention rights is outside of its competence and is 'not law', Scotland Act 1998, s 29(1).
[115] See, e.g., *ASLEF*, note 77 supra.
[116] 2007 (5) SA 400 (CC).
[117] Ibid.
[118] *Demir and Baykara*, note 54 supra, and see Ewing and Hendy, note 54 supra, at 2.
[119] *Enerji*, note 54 supra.
[120] (1996) 17 *ILJ* (South Africa) 821 (CC).

a lock-out.[121] Therefore, section 23(2)(c) of the SAC does not furnish a col-lective right to strike in favour of a trade union and therefore, trade unions enjoy no inderogable and entrenched collective right to strike.

The principle of equality in section 9 of the SAC which stipulates that '[e]veryone is equal before the law' has given rise to a number of develop-ments in the field of South African labour law. For example, in one of the earlier cases decided after the introduction of the SAC, section 9 of the SAC was applied by the Constitutional Court as a means of rendering an employer liable for unfair discrimination when it rejected an individual's application for a position as a flight attendant on the grounds that he was HIV-positive.[122] As we noted above, this can be contrasted with the position in the UK where article 14 of the ECHR, which outlaws discrimination in respect of the enjoyment of the rights or freedoms in the ECHR, has had little impact on the workplace. Since section 9(2) of the SAC empowers the state and private parties to promote affirmative action in order 'to protect or advance persons, or categories of persons, disadvantaged by unfair dis-crimination', it is not particularly surprising that the SAC has been con-strued as an instrument one of the aims of which is to achieve substantive, rather than formal or symmetrical, equality.[123] Substantive equality strives towards equality of outcomes for constituencies who have traditionally been systematically or institutionally under-privileged, under-represented or disadvantaged in the workplace, and it may entail an element of positive dis-crimination in their favour.[124] Thus, section 9(2) of the SAC has a redistribu-tive function and seeks to achieve distributive justice. This can be contrasted with formal/symmetrical equality – which is the general approach adopted in the UK[125] – whereby it is sufficient to ensure that a member of an under-

---

[121] However, rather bizarrely, the LRA, s 64(1) explicitly confers the right to lock-out in favour of the employer.

[122] *Hoffmann v South African Airways* 2001 (1) SA 1 (CC). See C Fenwick, E Kalula and I Landau 'Labour Law: A Southern African perspective' in T Teklé (ed), *Labour Law and Worker Protection in Developing Countries*, note 4 supra, at 191–2.

[123] *Minister of Finance v Van Heerden* 2004 (6) SA 121 (CC), 2004 25 *ILJ* (South Africa) 1593 (CC) at para 31 (Moseneke J); *National Coalition for Gay and Lesbian Equality*, note 91 supra, at para 62 (Ackermann J).

[124] Fredman, note 6 supra, at 25–33; Hepple, note 6 supra, at 19–23; S Fredman 'Reversing Discrimination' (1997) 113 *LQR* 575; C Barnard and B Hepple 'Substantive Equality' (2000) *Cambridge LJ* 562.

[125] There are some exceptions, e.g. (1) ss 20–22 of the Equality Act 2010 enjoin employers to make reasonable adjustments to the workplace and employment terms in favour of disabled employees, (2) employers must treat certain employees more favourably on account of their being pregnant or on maternity leave and (3) employers are permitted (but not required) to engage in 'positive action' in terms of ss 158–9 of the Equality Act 2010, i.e. favouring persons falling within a disadvantaged or under-represented group for the purposes of recruitment, promotion or the taking of action generally, where such recruitment, promo-tion or action would serve to overcome or minimise those disadvantages or enable or encour-age those persons in the under-represented group to participate in the activity in question.

represented or disadvantaged group in the workplace is treated consistently with members not forming part of that group.[126]

By definition, substantive equality results in members of the otherwise advantaged group being discriminated against and the Constitutional Court in South Africa has had to grapple with the difficulties engendered by that inevitability. In the case of *Minister of Finance v Van Heerden*[127] it was held that the means adopted to achieve affirmative action/substantive equality would be lawful if they carried a reasonable likelihood of meeting that end. Hence, the Constitutional Court rejected a necessity test – that is, that the means must be *necessary* to achieve the end – failing which those measures would be unlawful.[128] Furthermore, in the case of *Harmse v City of Cape Town*[129] decided by the Labour Court, it was held that the affirmative action concept not only functioned to provide the employer of institutionally under-privileged, under-represented or disadvantaged employees with a defence to any claim by a white, able-bodied, and straight male employee of unfair discrimination,[130] but that it went further and conferred individual rights to affirmative action in favour of the former constituency. This was rejected by the Labour Appeal Court in *Dudley v City of Cape Town*,[131] with Zondo JP agreeing with the prior judgment of the Labour Court that there was no constitutional or statutory right to affirmative action.[132] However, this may not be the last word on the matter, since it is likely that the Constitutional Court will be asked at some future point to form a view. In light of its past record, it is submitted that there is sufficient cause to believe that the Constitutional Court will adopt a pro-employee construction of the scope of section 9(2) of the SAC and confer individual employment rights to positive discrimination in the workplace.

15.4.3 Conclusion

To an independent observer unschooled in the vagaries of South African labour law, who is subjecting the position to close analysis, three particular

---

126 See P Westen 'The Empty Idea of Equality' (1981) 95 *Harvard Law Review* 537 at 542–8; D Schiek, L Waddington and M Bell *Cases, Materials and Text on National, Supranational and International Non-Discrimination Law* (Hart Publishing 2007) at 26–31; Hepple, note 6 supra, at 18–19.

127 2004 (6) SA 121 (CC); (2004) 25 *ILJ* (South Africa) 1593 (CC) at para 42 (Moseneke J).

128 This is the equivalent of the 'least restrictive means' test found in EU law in the cases of *Bilka-Kaufhaus v Weber von Hartz* [1986] ECR 1607 and *Enderby v Frenchay Health Authority* [1993] ECR I-5535.

129 (2003) 24 *ILJ* (South Africa) 1130 (LC) at para 46 (Waglay J).

130 This is not the position in the UK in the case of pregnant employees or employees on maternity leave, on which see *Eversheds Legal Services Ltd v De Belin* [2011] IRLR 448 (EAT).

131 [2008] ZALAC 10; [2008] 12 BLLR 1155 (LAC) at paras 51–4 (Zondo JP).

132 See discussion in O Dupper, C Garbers, AA Landman, M Christianson, AC Basson and EML Strydom *Essential Employment Discrimination Law* (Juta 2007) at 285–6.

matters stand out. First, one is struck by the fact that the approach of the South African Courts towards the relationship between the SAC on the one hand and statutory provisions and the common law on the other hand appears to be slightly inconsistent. For example, the court will intervene and use section 23 of the SAC in order to actively increase the scope of employment protection under the common law, as in *Murray v MoD*,[133] where section 23(1) of the SAC was applied to confer upon an employee a common law right of constructive dismissal along the same lines as the statutory incarnation of that concept set out in section 186(1(e) of the LRA. Moreover, in cases such as *Boxer Superstores Mthatha v Mbenya*[134] and *Old Mutual Life Assurance Co SA Ltd v Gumbi*,[135] it was held that section 23 of the SAC could be deployed to confer a common-law-based pre-dismissal hearing in favour of an employee, notwithstanding that this could serve to outflank the specifically crafted statutory unfair dismissal machinery in the LRA. At the same time, the courts engaged in an opposite movement in the case of *South African Maritime Safety Authority v McKenzie*[136] where Wallis AJA refused to allow the common law to develop an implied term which would furnish an employee with a right not to be dismissed without just cause, by analogy with the statutory right of unfair dismissal under section 185 of the LRA. A similar approach was taken in *Chirwa v Transnet Ltd & others*[137] and *Gcaba v Minister for Safety & Security & others*[138] where public sector workers were denied recourse to administrative law protections to review their dismissals in the civil courts. In *Gcaba v Minister for Safety & Security & others* the Constitutional Court ruled that the specialist labour courts tasked with resolving statutory employment disputes were the only bodies with jurisdiction to review unfair dismissals, whereas in its judgment in *NUMSA v Fry's Metals (Pty) Ltd*[139] the SCA led the way for litigants to appeal decisions of the Labour Appeal Court to the SCA and, thus, onwards to the Constitutional Court.

A second matter which the present writer has noted is the extent to which the South African courts are prepared to deploy the SAC as a means of overturning legislative provisions. The cases of *SANDU v Ministry of Defence*[140] and *SANDU v Ministry of Defence*[141] are the prime examples. Here, the Constitutional Court agreed to invalidate provisions within primary and subordinate legislation. These remarkable decisions can be contrasted with

[133] *Murray*, note 106 supra.
[134] *Boxer Superstores*, note 104 supra.
[135] *Old Mutual*, note 105 supra.
[136] *South African Maritime Safety Authority*, note 108 supra.
[137] 2008 (4) SA 367 (CC).
[138] *Gcaba*, note 95 supra, at para 69 (van den Westhuizen J).
[139] *NUMSA*, note 99 supra.
[140] *SANDU*, note 113 supra.
[141] *SANDU*, note 116 supra.

the position in the UK. In the UK the courts may not strike down statutory provisions, since section 4 of the HRA gives them the power only to declare legislation incompatible with the ECHR.[142] As we have noted, the UK courts are nonetheless reluctant to declare UK labour legislation incompatible with the ECHR. Indeed, there is scant evidence of the ECHR having had any degree of impact on UK labour law, particularly in light of the decisions of the Supreme Court and the Court of Appeal in *G v X*,[143] *X v Y*[144] and *Metrobus v UNITE*,[145] where the UK courts refused to use the ECHR to increase the scope of statutory employment rights. Instead, it has been the ECtHR which has stepped in to declare UK statutory provisions as inconsistent with ECHR rights conferring greater protection upon workers.

The third and final point which this writer would comment upon is the degree to which the concept of substantive equality has permeated the reasoning of the courts in South Africa. This differs markedly from the approach adopted by the courts in the UK where the emphasis is predominantly on the achievement of formal equality. The redistributive function associated with substantive equality in cases such as *Minister of Finance v Van Heerden*[146] serves to underscore the degree to which the South African courts have accepted that section 9 of the SAC has a transformative role to play in the workplace.

15.5 COMPARATIVE CONCLUSION

The discussion in this chapter has demonstrated that the impact of the HRA on UK labour law has been modest to negligible at best. The courts in the UK have displayed no appetite to increase the scope and content of statutory and common law employment rights by analogy with the various articles of the ECHR. This approach on the part of the UK courts has been maintained in the teeth of certain ground-breaking judgments of the ECtHR. In light of this, and somewhat paradoxically, the fear that the incorporation of the ECHR into UK law would undermine the collective interests of workers has not come to fruition. Instead, the ECtHR has shown itself willing to apply article 11 of the ECHR as a means of enhancing such interests and it has been the UK courts which have resisted various attempts to have the implications of those ECtHR decisions incorporated into UK law by the requisite means. The UK position can be compared with the interpretation of sections 9 and 23 of the SAC in South Africa, which has undoubtedly enhanced worker and trade union rights. However, at times, it would appear that these devel-

---

[142] On Scottish legislation see note 114 supra.
[143] *G v X*, note 32 supra.
[144] *X v Y*, note 27 supra.
[145] *Metrobus*, note 65 supra.
[146] *Minister of Finance v Van Heerden*, note 127 supra.

opments have been achieved at the expense of doctrinal coherence. The presence of overlapping jurisdictions for employment claims in the context of different, and sometimes nominally the same, employment rights appears to have led to some confusion and the potential for forum-shopping between the specialist labour courts and the civil courts. Indeed, some commentators have argued that this could lead to the discipline of labour law becoming eclipsed by constitutional law. However, in cases such as *Maritime Safety Authority v McKenzie*[147] the courts have shown that they are alive to the dangers of the emergence of parallel systems of law. Leaving that point to the side, however, when one examines the South African legal position in the round in light of the debate about the merits of constitutionalising labour rights, one is particularly struck by the extent to which the courts have been prepared to take decisions which redistribute resources and wealth away from employers and the state towards the workforce. This has been particularly evident in the context of the use of the principle of equality in section 9 of the SAC, where the courts have resorted to conceptions of substantive equality. To that extent, one can reach the conclusion that the South African experience furnishes some support for those who argue that casting labour rights as human rights has the potential to reclaim territory lost in recent decades to the neo-liberal imperatives of economic competitiveness, efficiency and flexibility.

---

[147] *South African Maritime Safety Authority*, note 108 supra.

Chapter 16

Rights in Security

*Andrew J M Steven**

16.1 INTRODUCTION

Superficially, rights in security appears to be a legal area located firmly in the spheres of commercial law and property law.[1] Academics and practitioners working in the area traditionally have not had human rights concerns at the forefront of their minds. Part of the reason for this is that such rights were not directly enforceable in Scotland until relatively recently when the Human Rights Act 1998 made much of the European Convention on Human Rights (ECHR) part of Scots law.[2] The requirement for legislation of the Scottish Parliament, established in 1999, to comply with the ECHR or be invalid has also had a noticeable impact.[3] In South Africa there was of course no explicit recognition of human rights until the post-apartheid constitutional settlement.[4] Another part of the reason for not immediately linking human rights to security rights is that the former on one view are a matter between the state and private individuals – in other words, they have 'vertical' application. Most security cases do not involve the state. It is accepted, however, both in Scotland and South Africa that human rights are enforceable at least to some extent in cases between private individuals – that is, they have 'horizontal' application.[5]

---

* I am very grateful to Megan Dewart and Mitzi Wiese for their assistance.

1 See A J M Steven 'Real Security Rights: Time for Cinderella to Go to the Ball?' (2011) available at *http://papers.ssrn.com/sol3/papers.cfm?abstract_id=1837533*.

2 See, e.g., R Reed and J A Murdoch, *Guide to Human Rights Law in Scotland* 3e (Bloomsbury Professional 2011) ch 1.

3 See A J M Steven 'Property Law and Human Rights' 2005 *Juridical Review* 293. See also A O'Neill 'Human Rights and People and Society' in E E Sutherland, K E Goodall, G F M Little and F P Davidson (eds) *Law Making and the Scottish Parliament: The Early Years* (Edinburgh University Press 2011) 35–57.

4 Constitution of the Republic of South Africa Act 1996. See H Mostert and A Pope (eds) *The Principles of The Law of Property in South Africa* (OUP 2010) at 15: 'The Constitution of the Republic of South Africa is now the founding and directional document for the country's legal system . . . all sources of law must be viewed in light of the Constitution'. See P J Badenhorst, J M Pienaar, and H Mostert *Silberberg and Schoeman's The Law of Property* 5e (LexisNexis Butterworths 2006) ch 21.

5 See, e.g., Reed and Murdoch *Guide to Human Rights Law*, supra note 2, para 1.76, and Badenhorst, Pienaar and Mostert *Silberberg and Schoeman's The Law of Property*, supra note 4, 525–7.

Much of rights in security law remains untouched by human rights juris-prudence. Thus the types of security which are recognised, be they express or tacit, are a matter for private law and so too is the extent to which under-lying property law principles such as accessoriness, publicity and specificity are obeyed.[6] Where, however, human rights clearly matter is in relation to the *enforcement* of securities. Security rights are often never enforced. Most people buying a house with the help of secured loan finance will manage to keep up with the repayments. The loan will eventually be repaid and the mortgage discharged. Mortgage protection insurance may provide a safety net where the debtor struggles as a result of unanticipated illness or unem-ployment. Another option may be for the debtor to 'downsize' and pay off the lender by selling the house and moving to a less expensive property. In such cases the security is not actually enforced.

Of course this is not always the position. The debtor may be so much in debt that buying another property is not feasible. The creditor may have no option but to enforce. Sadly, with the world economic downturn of recent years this has become a more likely occurrence.[7] Human rights issues are then engaged. Must a creditor always obtain a court order, to comply with the debtor's right to a fair hearing? To what extent is a debtor assisted by a property protection clause? What is the position in relation to the debtor's right to a private and family life and home under the ECHR[8] or right to housing under the South African Constitution?[9] This chapter will seek to consider these questions by critically examining the law in both Scotland and South Africa and by attempting to see if there are lessons for the respec-tive jurisdictions from each other. The first thing which strikes the author as a Scottish lawyer is that there have been several cases in South Africa specifically on constitutional rights and rights in security, but in Scotland there have almost been none.[10] This is a theme to which this chapter will return.

16.2 CREDITORS AND DEBTORS

In the same way as a superficial consideration might not see the immediate connection between rights in security and human rights, equally superficiality

---

[6] See, e.g., G L Gretton and A J M Steven *Property, Trusts and Succession* (Tottel 2009) ch 20 and Mostert and Pope (eds) *Principles of The Law of Property*, supra note 4, ch 12.

[7] See, e.g., Council of Mortgage Lenders Annual Report for 2010 (UK) at 16, available at *http:// www.cml.org.uk/cml/home*.

[8] ECHR art 6. See, e.g., Reed and Murdoch *Guide to Human Rights Law*, supra note 2, paras 6.24–6.52.

[9] Constitution of the Republic of South Africa Act 1996 s 26. See, e.g., A J van der Walt *Constitutional Property Law* 3e (Juta 2011) 142–3.

[10] But see *Wilmington Trust Co v Rolls-Royce plc* [2011] CSOH 151 where a human rights argument was unsuccessfully made in the context of lien.

would probably lead to believing that constitutional protection is something aimed only at *debtors*. This is not correct. Thus the European Court of Human Rights made it plain in the case of *Gasus Dosier und Fördertechnik GmbH v Netherlands*[11] that a security right amounted to a 'possession' within article 1 of the First Protocol to the ECHR and was thus capable of being protected by this provision.[12] Another example is the English case of *Wilson v First County Trust (No 2)*,[13] which concerned the Consumer Credit Act 1974, a piece of legislation in force in both Scotland and England. An individual had pledged her motor car to a pawnbroking company, but it had failed to use the correct documentation required by the Act. It was held by a majority in the House of Lords that the company had been deprived of its contractual rights (and thus its security) by the legislation. Since, however, moneylending transactions could give rise to significant social problems[14] and bargaining power lay with the lender, it was legitimate for Parliament to impose procedural requirements. There was no breach of the ECHR.[15]

A further point must be made. There is perhaps a tendency to view a debtor as a vulnerable private individual and a creditor as a bank or other corporate entity. But of course this is not always true. Companies often borrow money and indeed in Scotland one of the most important security rights in practice, the floating charge, is limited to corporate debtors.[16] Likewise natural persons may lend money. A parent might lend a student child capital to buy a flat. Human rights, notwithstanding the name, are not restricted to human creditors and debtors. Thus article 1 of the First Protocol protects the property rights of 'every natural or legal person'.[17] A leading example is the Scottish case of *Karl Construction Ltd v Palisade Properties plc*,[18] which involved unsecured rather than secured creditors. Both parties to the action were companies. The counterpart provision in the South African

---

11   (1995) 20 EHRR 403 at 431–2.

12   But note the mischievous argument of George Gretton in 'The Protection of Property Rights' in A Boyle, C Himsworth, A Loux and H MacQueen (eds) *Human Rights and Scots Law* (Hart 2002) 275 at 284–5.

13   [2004] 1 AC 816.

14   This rather harks back to the statement of the famous Scottish economist Adam Smith that the licensing of pawnbrokers is 'one of the greatest nuisances in the English constitution, especially in great cities'. See *Lectures on Jurisprudence* eds R L Meek, D D Raphael and P G Stein (Liberty Fund 1978) 80.

15   Strictly, this was *obiter* as the main ground of the decision was that the loan pre-dated the Human Rights Act 1998, which did not apply retrospectively.

16   See in particular the Companies Act 1985 s 462. See also the Bankruptcy and Diligence etc (Scotland) Act 2007 s 38 (not in force).

17   See, e.g., J Strachan 'The Human Rights Act 1998 and Commercial Law in the United Kingdom' in S Bottomley and D Kinley *Commercial Law and Human Rights* (Ashgate 2002) 161 at 184.

18   2002 SC 270. See A J M Steven 'The Progress of Article 1 Protocol 1 in Scotland' (2002) 6 *EdinLR* 396.

Constitution, section 25, does not specifically refer to legal persons, but the issue is covered by section 8(4) of the same legislation: 'A juristic person is entitled to the rights in the Bill of Rights to the extent required by the nature of the rights and the nature of that juristic person'. In *First National Bank of SA Ltd t/a Wesbank v Commissioner of the South African Revenue Service*; *First National Bank of SA Ltd t/a Wesbank v Minister of Finance*,[19] a case on security rights to which we will return below,[20] the Constitutional Court made it clear that section 25 does apply to juristic persons and gave the following reasons:

> '[D]enying companies entitlement to property rights would "lead to grave disruptions and would undermine the very fabric of our democratic State". It would have a disastrous impact on the business world generally, on creditors of companies and, more especially, on shareholders in companies.'[21]

Similarly, it is now uncontroversial that the right to a fair hearing under ECHR article 6[22] and the right of access to the courts under the South African Constitution section 34 apply to juristic persons.[23] On the other hand, ECHR article 8 (right to a private and family life and home) and section 26 of the Constitution (right to housing) are aimed at natural persons. These potentially assist debtors who are private individuals.

16.3 ENFORCEMENT: MUST THE COURTS BE INVOLVED?

16.3.1 *The Land Bank cases*

Much of the South African constitutional case law in relation to security rights has concerned the right of access to the courts.[24] The starting point is the decision of the Constitutional Court in *Chief Lesapo v North West Agricultural Bank*.[25] The bank is a public body which can provide farmers with loan finance. Chief Lesapo borrowed R60,000 to purchase farming implements. The loan was made under the North West Agricultural Bank Act 14 of 1981. The Chief 'pledged' two tractors, a planter, a trailer, a chisel plough and a soil master in security of the loan, but there was no delivery.[26]

---

[19] 2002 (4) SA 768 (CC).

[20] See infra, at 16.5.1.

[21] 2002 (4) SA 768 (CC) at para 45. The quote is from *Investigating Directorate: Serious Economic Offences and Others v Hyundai Motor Distributors (Pty) Ltd and Others: In re Hyundai Motor Distributors (Pty) Ltd and Others v Smit NO and Others* 2001 (1) SA 545 (CC) at para 18. See further A Kok 'Why the Finding that Juristic Persons are Entitled to the Property Rights Protected by Section 25 of the Constitution?' 2004 THRHR 683.

[22] E.g. *County Properties Ltd v The Scottish Ministers* 2002 SC 79.

[23] E.g. *Findevco (Pty) Ltd v Faceformat SA (Pty) Ltd* 2001 (1) SA 251 (E).

[24] Constitution of the Republic of South Africa Act 1996 s 34.

[25] 2000 (1) SA 409 (CC). For discussion, see M Kelly 'Constitutionality of Executions by Agricultural Banks without Debtors having Recourse to a Court' (2008) 8 Juta's Bus L 167.

[26] It was only on default that the bank attempted to seize the property.

When he fell into arrears, the bank sought to exercise its powers under section 38(2) of the Act to seize and sell the property. The provision permitted the bank to proceed 'without recourse to a court of law'. It was authorised to sell the property by public auction of which fourteen days' notice had to be given. Chief Lesapo applied to the court for an order that the provision contravened the Constitution, in particular the right of access to the courts.

The Constitutional Court unanimously granted the application, the decision being given by Mokgoro J. She set out the rationale for the right to a hearing before a court, stressing that '[t]aking the law into one's own hands is . . . inconsistent with the fundamental principles of our law'.[27] She pointed out that the normal method of enforcing a debt was by execution, which involved a court process.[28] Further, '[t]he Bank, as an organ of State, should be exemplary in its compliance with the fundamental constitutional principle that proscribes self help'.[29] Instead:

'Section 38(2) authorises the Bank, an adversary of the debtor, to decide the outcome of the dispute. The Bank thus becomes a judge in its own cause . . . The Bank itself decides whether it has an enforceable claim against the debtor; the Bank itself decides the outcome of the dispute and the subsequent relief; and the Bank itself enforces its own decision, thereby usurping the powers and functions of the courts.'[30]

The court was unwilling to accept that the need of the bank to enforce debts speedily and with low costs justified the provision under the Constitution.[31] A similar result was reached a few months later by the same court in the conjoined cases of *First National Bank of South Africa Ltd v Land and Agricultural Bank of South Africa* and *Sheard v Land and Agricultural Bank of South Africa*.[32] These concerned the power of the Land Bank to attach and sell movable and immovable property in execution extra-judicially under the Land Bank Act 13 of 1944. The offending legislation has now been repealed and replaced by the Land and Agricultural Development Bank Act 15 of 2002.[33]

The following comments may be made. First, there is no counterpart legislation in Scotland, hence the lack of a similar type of challenge. Secondly, since the Land Banks are part of the state apparatus, these are cases of 'vertical' application of constitutional rights, rather than 'horizon-

---

27 2000 (1) SA 409 (CC) at para 11.
28 Ibid at paras 13 and 19.
29 Ibid at para 17.
30 Ibid at para 20.
31 Ibid at paras 23–29.
32 2000 (3) SA 626 (CC). See also *First National Bank of South Africa v Land and Agricultural Bank* 2000 6 BCLR 586 (O).
33 See Badenhorst, Pienaar and Mostert, *Silberberg and Schoeman's The Law of Property*, supra note 4, 409–10; M Kelly 'The new Land Bank Act' (2003) 11 *Juta's Bus L* 99; and M Kelly, 'More about the new Land Bank Act' (2003) 11 *Juta's Bus L* 182.

tal' application.[34] As mentioned at the outset,[35] most cases involving rights in security do not involve the state as a party and money is normally lent by private entities. None of the Land Bank cases is strictly about security rights. Rather, they are about debt enforcement procedures, broadly equivalent to diligence in Scotland. The 'pledge' of the implements in *Chief Lesapo* was unaccompanied by delivery, so it was not a valid pledge. The power that the Land Bank was seeking to enforce was a right of seizure.

16.3.2 The parate executie *cases*

'*Parate executie*' is a term that is not familiar to the Scottish lawyer,[36] but commonly understood in South Africa. Literally it means 'immediate execution'[37] and allows the creditor to enforce a security without judicial permission. The question is whether an agreement between debtor and creditor permitting such an arrangement is compatible with the right of access to the courts. In the words of Professor Susan Scott, the case which 'let the cat loose in the pigeon cote'[38] was *Findevco (Pty) Ltd v Faceformat SA (Pty) Ltd*.[39] It concerned a general notarial bond over movable property, a type of security which is not recognised in Scotland.[40] The creditor had successfully obtained a court order authorising it to take possession of the debtor's movables in order to make its security into a real right – i.e. to 'perfect' it.[41] The bond had a clause allowing the creditor to do this. The debtor was given time to provide any reason why it should not have to pay the costs of the application and why the creditor should not be allowed to proceed to a public auction of the property as permitted by the bond. At the subsequent hearing the debtor did not appear but the judge, Froneman J, raised the issue of whether the clause enabling the creditor to send the property to auction was compatible with the right of access to the courts under section 34 of the Constitution. Under reference to the *Land Bank* cases he held that it was not:

[34] See S Scott 'Summary Execution Clauses in Pledges and Perfecting Clauses in Notarial Bonds' 2002 THRHR 656 at 659.

[35] See 16.1 supra.

[36] The author first met it when looking at South African law during his doctoral studies. See A J M Steven, *Pledge and Lien* (Edinburgh Legal Education Trust 2008) paras 8–07 and 8–12.

[37] See W G Schulze '*Parate Executie* and Public Policy' 2005 *Obiter* 710 and H Schulze 'When May Creditors Help Themselves?' (2005) 13 *Juta's Bus L* 110.

[38] Scott 'Summary Execution Clauses in Pledge and Perfecting Clauses in Notarial Bonds', supra note 34.

[39] 2001 (1) SA 251 (E).

[40] See G Pienaar and A J M Steven, 'Rights in Security' in R Zimmermann, D Visser and K Reid (eds), *Mixed Legal Systems in Comparative Perspective: Property and Obligations in Scotland and South Africa* (Oxford University Press 2004) 758 at 766–8.

[41] See J Roos 'The Perfecting of Securities Held under a General Notarial Bond' 1995 SALJ 169.

'If legislation which allows the attachment and sale of movable goods given as security without recourse to the courts is unconstitutional, even where there is no dispute about the debtor's indebtedness, why should the common law allow it? I can see no valid reason why it should.'[42]

The decision was 'trenchantly criticised'[43] by Scott.[44] She highlighted the differences between the *Land Bank* cases and this one. In particular she noted that the earlier decisions involved an organ of the state and were thus instances of vertical application of the Constitution. She emphasised the distinctions between (a) statutory provisions allowing the Land Bank to seize and sell both immovable and movable property, (b) perfection clauses (as in *Findevco*) and (c) summary execution clauses in pledge agreements (that is, *parate executie*: a contractual agreement giving pledgees a power of extra-judicial realisation). In (b) and (c) the creditor's powers have been given by agreement. In (a) the state took the powers by statute. She contested that (b) and (c) do not contravene the Constitution, commenting that requiring a court order in all cases would increase costs and adversely affect the debtor.

Scott's arguments are convincing.[45] The decision of Froneman J in *Findevco* lacks sufficient analysis of the differences between the forms of enforcement measure. The Supreme Court of Appeal was therefore correct to depart from it in *Bock v Duburoro Investments*.[46] The case involved the pledge of shares in a company to a bank. The pledge permitted the bank upon default by the debtor to sell the shares or to acquire them for a 'fair value'.[47] In his judgment Harms JA distinguished between (a) *parate executie*; (b) the contractual right of the creditor to acquire the secured asset – a *pactum commissorium*; and (c) a quasi-conditional sale allowing the creditor to acquire the secured asset at a fair price.[48] It was clearly settled that (b) is void.[49] This remedy was originally prohibited by the Emperor Constantine and the South African rule is the same as in many other

---

[42] 2001 (1) SA 251 (E) at 256.

[43] *Contract Forwarding (Pty) Ltd v Chesterfin (Pty) Ltd* 2003 (2) SA 253 (SCA) at para 12 per Harms JA.

[44] Scott 'Summary Execution Clauses in Pledge and Perfecting Clauses in Notarial Bonds', supra note 34.

[45] Although not to everyone. See S Cook and G Quixley 'Parate Executie Clauses: Is the Debate Dead?' 2004 *SALJ* 719. And see Scott's reply: 'A Private-Law Dinosaur's Evaluation of Summary Execution Clauses in Light of the Constitution' 2007 THRHR 289.

[46] 2004 (2) SA 242 (SCA). See L Steyn 'Perfection Clauses, Summary Execution (*Parate Executie*) Clauses, Forfeiture Clauses (*Pacta Commissoria*) and Conditional Sales in Pledge Agreements and Notarial Bonds – The Position Clarified' 2004 *Obiter* 443.

[47] 2004 (2) SA 242 (SCA) at para 5.

[48] 2004 (2) SA 242 (SCA) at para 6.

[49] Reference was made to the most recent case of *Graf v Buechel* 2003 (4) SA 378 (SCA). See also *Mapenduka v Ashington* 1919 AD 343.

jurisdictions.[50] On the other hand (c) is valid, at least in the context of movables.[51]

The position as regards (b) – *parate executie* – is more complicated. First of all, a distinction is made between pledges (of movables) and mortgage bonds (of immovable property). In the former the pledge agreement allowing the creditor to sell the property upon default without a court order is valid, but the debtor is entitled to go to court if the creditor acts in a way that is prejudicial to the debtor.[52] In contrast, such a clause in a mortgage bond is invalid.[53] Harms JA then states:

> 'Nevertheless, after default the mortgagor may grant the bondholder the necessary authority to realise the bonded property. It does not matter whether the goods are immovable or movable: in the latter instance, to perfect the security, the court's imprimatur is required.'[54]

The first sentence is justified by a reference to the earlier case of *Iscor Housing Utility Co v Chief Registrar of Deeds*.[55] There the court viewed an agreement to sale made only on default as not being potentially prejudicial to the debtor in the same way as a right of *parate executie* in the bond might be. In the latter, the creditor might be mistaken that the debtor was in default yet proceed to sell without notifying that party. While there is some force in this example, a better approach might be to allow earlier agreements but make it mandatory for there to be a notice of intention to sell, thus allowing the debtor an opportunity to seek injunctive relief. The author also struggles with the second sentence of Harms JA quoted above. What are 'immovable goods'? If 'the court's imprimatur is required', does that defeat the point of the debtor and creditor entering into an agreement rather than the creditor going to court? However, what is actually meant by this is that if the goods are in the debtor's possession, as will typically be the case with the notarial bond, the creditor can only remove them with the debtor's permission or by obtaining a court order.[56] The approach taken in *Bock* to *parate executie* was followed by the Supreme Court of Appeal in the subsequent case of *SA Bank of Athens Ltd v Van Zyl*.[57]

---

[50] See *Sun Life Assurance Co of Canada v Kuranda* 1924 AD 20 at 24; Steven *Pledge and Lien*, supra note 36, paras 8–14–8–17, and S Scott 'A Comparison between Belgian, Dutch and South African Law Dealing with Pledge and Execution Measures' 2010 *CILSA* 93 at 100.

[51] 2004 (2) SA 242 (SCA) at para 9. Harms JA refers again to *Graf v Buechel* 2003 (4) SA 378 (SCA). The law as to immovable property is not discussed.

[52] 2004 (2) SA 242 (SCA) at para 7 citing *Osry v Hirsch, Loubser & Co Ltd* 1922 CPD 531 at 547.

[53] 2004 (2) SA 242 (SCA) at para 7 citing *Iscor Housing Utility Co v Chief Registrar of Deeds* 1971 (1) SA 613 (T).

[54] 2004 (2) SA 242 (SCA) at para 7.

[55] 1971 (1) SA 613 (T).

[56] *Juglal NO v Shoprite Checkers t/a OK Franchise Division* 2004 (5) SA 248 (SCA) at para 25 per Heher JA.

[57] 2005 (5) SA 93 (SCA). See W G Schulze '*Parate Executie* and Public Policy. The Supreme

16.3.3 Observations

From the case law what can be concluded as to the need for court involvement in the enforcement of security rights? The obvious first point is that
there has been no equivalent debate in Scotland. To some extent this is
because the categories of security right differ. Rather than the notarial bond,
Scotland has the floating charge. Enforcement of it outside of insolvency
proceedings requires the appointment of either a receiver or an administrator and both of these individuals are subject to court supervision.[58] For
pledges of corporeal movables, licensed pawnbrokers have power to auction
without the need to go to court,[59] but they would no doubt lose their licence
if they acted in a manner unfair to debtors. For standard securities (the
equivalent of mortgages) there are detailed statutory rules on enforcement
procedures[60] and in the case of residential property, which will be discussed
further below,[61] a court order is mandatory.

Moreover, in South Africa the *Findevco* case was effectively a one-off
decision. The courts departed from it subsequently on the basis that *parate
executie* is compatible with the Constitution. The contrary arguments were
relatively weak. Were it to be otherwise, similar cases might also have arisen
in Scotland. The closest Scottish parallel in terms of actual case law is *Karl
Construction Ltd v Palisade Properties plc*,[62] where it was held that the ability of
an unsecured creditor to carry out the procedure of diligence on the dependence without any judicial involvement was contrary to article 1 of the First
Protocol to the ECHR. The procedure effectively gave the creditor power to
freeze the debtor's assets by merely raising a court action for payment.[63] The

---

Court of Appeal Provides Further Guidelines' 2005 *Obiter* 710; and Schulze, 'When May
Creditors Help Themselves?', supra note 37.

[58] The law here is complicated. In summary a receiver only has to consider the interests of the
charge holder, but an administrator must take account of those of other parties. For most
floating charges created since the Enterprise Act 2002 s 250 came into force, an administrator must be appointed. See generally I M Fletcher and R Roxburgh, *Law and Practice of
Receivership in Scotland* 3e (Tottel 2005).

[59] Consumer Credit Act 1974 ss 116(1)-(3) and 121(1); Consumer Credit (Realisation of Pawn)
Regulations 1983 SI 1983/1568.

[60] Under the Conveyancing and Feudal Reform (Scotland) Act 1970. See, e.g., D J Cusine and
R Rennie, *Standard Securities* (Butterworths 2002) ch 8. In the recent landmark case of *Royal
Bank of Scotland v Wilson* [2010] UKSC 50 the court stressed the need for debtor protection.
See, e.g., Lady Hale at para 81: 'A debtor should be given an opportunity of remedying his
default before he is dispossessed. It is not much to ask'.

[61] See section 16.4 infra.

[62] 2002 SC 270. See section 16.2 supra.

[63] In *Karl* it was held that the ECHR meant there had to be a hearing before a judge. This
requirement was diluted by the subsequent case of *Advocate General for Scotland v Taylor*
2003 SLT 1340 which ruled that it was sufficient for the matter to be considered by a judge
without an actual hearing.

law has been reformed so that the approval of a judge is required.[64] There is also an enforcement mechanism in Scotland known as 'summary diligence'. This is commonly met in commercial leases. The tenant will consent to registration of the lease for 'preservation and execution' in a register known as the Books of Council and Session. It is then possible to obtain an official copy of the lease from the register known as an 'extract'. If the tenant is in debt to the landlord, diligence can be carried out against its assets without any court order. The question may be asked whether summary diligence is compatible with article 1 of the First Protocol and article 6 of the ECHR. As far as the author is aware, no challenge has been made. The principal argument against there being a breach of Convention rights is that the tenant has voluntarily agreed to the remedy.[65] On that basis, a leading authority on human rights law in Scotland, Lord Reed, has expressed the view extra-judicially that a challenge would fail.[66] It is settled that individuals can waive at least some of their human rights, and the right to a court hearing is one of these.[67] In such circumstances, however, the waiver will probably not be valid without legal advice.[68] Therefore landlords should ensure that tenants are told to obtain independent legal advice before agreeing to such a clause. A debtor who believes that summary diligence is being used unjustly can invoke the help of the court,[69] in rather a similar way to the South African debtor who has agreed to *parate executie*. In this way the law guarantees the right of a debtor to a hearing and an important human right is respected.

Finally, there is disquiet in South Africa among some commentators on the validity of *parate executie* in pledge agreements (movable property) but not mortgage bonds (immovable property). Scott contends that this arises from the historical thinking that land is more valuable, whereas this is not always the case.[70] She suggests a distinction based on whether the creditor has control – that is, natural possession of the property – or not. Steyn argues that the law should provide more protection in the case of movables, because there are already more procedural safeguards in the case of land such as the requirement for written consent to the transfer by the owner (the debtor) under the Deed Registries Act 47 of 1937.[71] Certainly, Scott's view

---

[64] Bankruptcy and Diligence etc (Scotland) Act 2007 Pt 6.

[65] A McAllister *Scottish Law of Leases* 3e (Butterworths 2002) para 5.83.

[66] See Steven 'Property Law and Human Rights', supra note 3, at 302.

[67] *Pfeiffer and Planckl v Austria* (1992) 14 EHRR 692. In Scotland see *Clancy v Caird* 2000 SC 441 and *Robertson v Higson* 2006 SC (PC) 22.

[68] For discussion, see Reed and Murdoch, *A Guide to Human Rights Law in Scotland*, supra note 2, para 3.35.

[69] G L Gretton 'Diligence' in *The Laws of Scotland: Stair Memorial Encyclopaedia*, vol 8 (Butterworths 1992) para 122.

[70] Scott 'Summary Execution Clauses in Pledges and Perfecting Clauses in Notarial Bonds', supra note 34 at 664.

[71] Steyn 'Perfection Clauses' supra note 46 at 454.

that a court order should be required if the debtor will not surrender the property voluntarily is sound. Typically for land the creditor will not be in natural possession of the property unless the debtor defaults and hands over the keys. There is also, however, a further argument for ensuring that a court order must be obtained where the property is the debtor's residence. Here there is the matter of the right to housing. To this we now turn.

16.4 RESIDENTIAL PROPERTY

When considering the human rights of a debtor and those of a creditor who wants to enforce the mortgage held over the debtor's house, clearly a balance must be struck as between the interests of the parties. Thus in *Wood v UK*[72] the applicant invoked the property protection clause in the ECHR when she defaulted on her mortgage and her home was repossessed. The European Commission on Human Rights dismissed the case:

> 'In so far as the repossession constituted an interference with the applicant's home, the Commission finds that this was in accordance with the terms of the loan and the domestic law and was necessary for the protection of the rights and freedoms of others, namely the lender. To the extent that the applicant is deprived of her possessions by the repossession, the Commission considers that this deprivation is in the public interest, that is the public interest in ensuring payment of contractual debts, and is also in accordance with the rules provided for by law.'[73]

This does not mean, however, that the specific procedures for enforcing a security can ignore the debtor's human rights,[74] particularly where the secured property is his or her home. The South African case of *Standard Bank of South Africa Ltd v Saunderson*[75] in its application of the earlier important case of *Jaftha v Schoeman*[76] demonstrates the point. *Jaftha* concerned the legislation on levying execution and its compatibility with the right to adequate housing under section 26 of the Constitution. It was held that for execution sales of residential properties a requirement for 'judicial oversight' had to be read into the legislation, meaning that a court had to determine whether the procedure was justified in the circumstances of the case.[77] In

---

[72] (1997) 24 EHRR CD 69.

[73] (1997) 24 EHRR CD 69 at 70–1.

[74] See, e.g., the decision of the European Court of Human Rights in *Zehentner v Austria* (2011) 52 EHRR 22. See also *Kay v Lambeth LBC* [2006] 2 AC 465.

[75] 2006 (2) SA 264 (SCA). See also *Nedbank Ltd v Mortinson* 2005 (6) SA 462 (W).

[76] *Jaftha v Schoeman; Van Rooyen v Stoltz* 2005 2 SA 140 (CC). See L Steyn '"Safe as Houses"? – Balancing a Mortgagee's Security Interest with a Homeowner's Security of Tenure' (2007) 11 *Law Democracy and Citizenship* 101, and M Kelly-Louw 'The Right of Access to Adequate Housing' (2007) 15 Juta's Bus L 35.

[77] See also *Mkhise v Umvoti Municipality* 2012 (1) SA 1 (SCA).

Jaftha the creditor was unsecured and debt involved was 'trifling'.[78] The court drew a distinction with where a debtor granted a mortgage:

> 'If the judgment debtor willingly put his or her house up in some or other manner as security for the debt, a sale in execution should ordinarily be permitted where there has not been an abuse of court procedure. The need to ensure that homes may be used by people to raise capital is an important aspect of the value of a home which courts must be careful to acknowledge.'[79]

In *Saunderson* the creditor did have a mortgage bond and the question which the Supreme Court had to resolve, in what effectively was a test case, was whether there could be execution without breaching the debtor's right to adequate housing. The court followed *Jaftha* but drew factual distinctions with that earlier decision. Here the debtor had voluntarily granted the security.[80] The court stressed the value of a mortgage as 'an indispensable tool for spreading home ownership'[81] adding that 'the value of a mortgage bond as an instrument of security lies in confidence that the law will give effect to its terms'.[82] It expressed the view that it would be 'rare'[83] for the right to adequate housing to prevent the execution of a mortgage bond. The court held that the Registrar of the High Court could grant orders declaring that the properties in the current case were executable because none of the debtors had made a constitutional challenge, but it issued a practice direction requiring executing creditors in future to refer to the right to adequate housing in the summons issued to the debtor. The direction requires debtors who believe that their right is being infringed 'to place information supporting the claim before the Court'.[84]

The University of KwaZulu-Natal's Campus Law Clinic sought leave from the Constitutional Court to appeal the Supreme Court's judgment.[85] Alternatively it asked the Constitutional Court for an order stating that it was unconstitutional for the registrar to have power to grant an order declaring that execution can be carried out against immovable property. It argued that judicial oversight was required in order to protect the rights of children under section 28 of the Constitution (adequate housing being necessary for a child's best interests) and the right to human dignity under section 10 (execution could affect innocent members of the debtor's family such as

---

[78] 2005 (2) SA 140 (CC) at para 40 per Mokgoro J. There were two debtors. One had a debt of R250. The other's was R190.

[79] 2005 (2) SA 140 (CC) at para 58 per Mokgoro J. See, similarly on the value of mortgage funding, M Higgins, *The Enforcement of Heritable Securities* (W Green 2010) para 10.4.

[80] See also *Nedbank Ltd v Mortinson* 2005 (6) SA 462 (W) at para 25 per Joffe J.

[81] 2006 (2) SA 264 (SCA) at para 1 per Cameron JA and Nugent JA.

[82] 2006 (2) SA 264 (SCA) at para 3 per Cameron JA and Nugent JA.

[83] 2006 (2) SA 264 (SCA) at para 19 per Cameron JA and Nugent JA.

[84] 2006 (2) SA 264 (SCA) at para 27 per Cameron JA and Nugent JA.

[85] *Campus Law Clinic, University of KwaZulu-Natal v Standard Bank Ltd* 2006 (6) SA 103 (CC).

elderly relatives). The Constitutional Court decided that it was not in the interests of justice to grant the leave or the order sought by the Law Clinic, pointing out that a number of the issues raised had not been discussed by the Supreme Court. It stated: 'On many occasions this Court has indicated that it is undesirable to determine important constitutional questions as a Court of first and last instance'.[86] Thus, for the moment, the Supreme Court's decision stood and it was for the debtor to raise an argument that the right to adequate housing was being breached by the creditor's action.

Absa Bank Ltd v Ntsane[87] provides an example of such an argument being upheld. The principal sum of R62,043.42 was owed to the bank. The debtor had intermittently been behind on his repayments, but when the bank apparently lost its patience and commenced court action he was only in arrears to the extent of R18.46 plus interest. Giving judgment, Bertelsmann J described this amount as 'minute'.[88] Enforcement in such circumstances would conflict with section 26 of the Constitution.[89] Even were he to be wrong on this point, he stated that the bank's claim 'constitutes a *prima facie* abuse of the right to claim an outstanding amount that can be easily obtained by way of execution against movable assets'.[90]

This can be contrasted with the recent decision in *FirstRand Bank Ltd v Meyer*.[91] In that case the principal sum was R154,337.41. The married debtors had obtained a restructuring order in terms of section 87 of the National Credit Act 34 of 2005 reducing the monthly repayment from R1,722.54 per month to R1,134.10. They defaulted on the order and at the time the bank sought to enforce the arrears were R2,922.36. Thus the amount owing was considerably greater than in *Ntsane*. The debtors sought to rely on the right to adequate housing and the decision in *Jaftha*. They stated that they were both pensioners in poor health. They had occupied the house since 1983 and had nowhere else to go. The limited pension of the husband and the cost of his medical expenses meant that they could not afford alternative accommodation. The court, however, noting the reprieve that the couple already had obtained because of the restructuring order and the fact that the arrears were not 'trifling',[92] unlike in *Jaftha*, granted the order.

Then came the landmark case of *Gundwana v Steko Development CC*[93] where the applicant constitutionally challenged the power of the registrar to make an order declaring mortgaged property as specially executable. Elsie

---

[86] 2006 (6) SA 103 (CC) at para 26.
[87] 2007 (3) SA 554 (T).
[88] 2007 (3) SA 554 (T) at para 81.
[89] 2007 (3) SA 554 (T) at para 86, but compare *Nedbank Ltd v Fraser* 2011 (4) SA 363 (GSJ).
[90] 2007 (3) SA 554 (T) at para 91.
[91] [2011] ZAECPEHC 8.
[92] [2011] ZAECPEHC 8 at para 36.
[93] 2011 (3) SA 608 (CC).

Gundwana had bought a property in 1995 with the help of a R25,000 loan from Nedcor Bank, which was secured by a mortgaged bond. She fell into arrears and in 2003, following an application made by the bank, the registrar granted default judgment against her and declared the property executable for the sum outstanding. The bank did not take further action for about four years and in the meantime Ms Gundwana made occasional repayments. In 2007 the property was sold in execution to Steko Development CC which commenced eviction proceedings in 2008. An eviction order was eventually granted and unsuccessfully appealed, but Ms Gundwana then sought rescission of the 2003 default judgment. These proceedings were suspended until the determination of the case before the Constitutional Court. The court invited the Banking Association of South Africa to become a party to the case, but it declined. The National Consumer Forum and the Minister for Justice and Constitutional Development were, however, parties and the court concluded that now was the appropriate time to give judgment on the matter: 'Finality on the substantive constitutional issue will be to the benefit of all concerned'.[94] The applicant was thus given direct access to the court.

The decision of the Constitutional Court was that the registrar's power was unconstitutional. It considered two main reasons why the challenge must succeed. First, the summons checked by the registrar did not give him or her sufficient information to determine whether *Jaftha* was engaged. Moreover, the constitutional validity of the power had to be determined objectively, rather than by reference to the facts affecting a particular individual such as Ms Gundwana.[95] Thus it did not achieve anything for the bank to argue that Ms Gundwana's individual constitutional rights were not breached in the circumstances. Secondly, the court looked at the issue of the applicant having voluntarily granted the mortgage, in contrast to the facts of *Jaftha*. Froneman J, with whom the other justices unanimously concurred, considered the matter and stated:

> 'I conclude that the willingness of mortgagors to put their homes forward as security for the loans they acquire is not by itself sufficient to put those cases beyond the reach of *Jaftha*. An evaluation of the facts of each case is necessary in order to determine whether a declaration that hypothecated property constituting a person's home is specially executable, may be made. It is a kind of evaluation that must be done by a court of law, not the registrar.'[96]

Ironically, this was to return the law to its position before 1994, when a court order was required.[97] The rules of court were subsequently amended

---

[94] 2011 (3) SA 608 (CC) at para 32; see A J van der Walt and R Brits 'Judicial Oversight over the Sale in Execution of Mortgaged Property' 2012 THRHR 322.
[95] Ibid at para 43.
[96] Ibid at para 49.
[97] Ibid at para 53.

to give effect to the judgment.[98] While in principle the ruling is retrospective, previous orders by the registrar will stand unless the debtor applies for them to be set aside.[99] The court thought it unlikely that many debtors would do this as they would have to explain their reason for not doing so earlier and provide a defence to the claim against them.[100] Froneman J was moved also to say:

'It must be accepted that execution in itself is not an odious thing. It is part and parcel of normal economic life. It is only when there is disproportionality between the means used in the execution process to exact payment of the judgment debt, compared to other available means to attain the same purpose, that alarm bells should start ringing. If there are no other proportionate means to attain the same end, execution may not be avoided.'[101]

Thus it is important that there are adequate judicial resources to ensure that a creditor's right to execute can be exercised at relative speed and without high costs.

What can be concluded from these cases is that the interests of the creditor will be protected, but the right to adequate housing means that for residential mortgages the balance as between the parties is shifted in the direction of the debtor in ensuring appropriate procedures and the possibility of enforcement being stopped or delayed if the facts require this.[102]

In Scotland a rather different approach has been taken, but one which has had much the same result. The legislation for the equivalent of the mortgage bond, the standard security, dates from 1970. There was no requirement under it for a creditor to obtain a court order in order to enforce the security. Such an order was only actually required if the debtor was in residence and refused to move.[103] The position was ameliorated by the Mortgage Rights (Scotland) Act 2001 which allowed debtors to apply to the court seeking suspension of enforcement where proceedings related to their home. The judge had discretion to do so having regard to certain prescribed factors, including the debtor's ability to find alternative accommodation for him or herself and any persons living at the property, including children. This, however,

---

[98] Uniform Rules of Court rule 46(1). See *Nedbank Ltd v Fraser* 2011 (4) SA 363 (GSJ) and *Standard Bank of South Africa Ltd v Bekker* 2011 (6) SA 111 (WSC).

[99] Cf *First National Bank Ltd v Woods* 2011 (5) SA 356 (ECP). See also L Mills 'Judges, not Registrars, to Declare Homes Executable' 2011 *De Rebus* June/50.

[100] 2011 (3) SA 608 (CC) at para 59.

[101] 2011 (3) SA 608 (CC) at para 54. See also *Nedbank Ltd v Fraser* 2011 (4) SA 363 (GSJ) at para 17 per Peter AJ and *ABSA Bank Ltd v Zimele Plant Hire CC* [2013] ZAWCHC 42. Cf *Nkomo v Firstrand Bank Ltd* [2012] ZAGPPHC 108 where the property was not the debtors' primary residence.

[102] See L Fox *Conceptualising Home: Theories, Laws and Policies* (Hart 2006) 96. See also A J van der Walt 'Property, Social Justice and Citizenship: Property Law in Post-Apartheid South Africa' 2008 Stell LR 325 at 328–33.

[103] Cusine and Rennie *Standard Securities*, supra note 60, para 8.33; Higgins *The Enforcement of Heritable Securities*, supra note 79, para 4.6.

necessitated the debtor raising proceedings. As a matter of public policy, not least because of the economic downturn, this was felt to offer insufficient protection for debtors, and the Scottish Parliament recently passed the Home Owner and Debtor Protection (Scotland) Act 2010.[104] It now requires an enforcing creditor in the case of residential property to obtain a court order.[105] Moreover, that party must consider reasonable alternatives to enforcement,[106] and the court must have regard to the extent to which that obligation has been fulfilled before authorising enforcement.[107] The court must also take account of the factors that were originally in the 2001 Act. There are clear echoes here of *Jaftha*. The difference is that in the policy papers which led the way to the legislation, the notion of human rights is implicit rather than explicit.[108] There is no specific reference to article 8 of the ECHR. This is the nearest equivalent to the South African right to adequate housing, as it requires respect for the family home. Scottish legislators felt it was right to change the law as a matter of public policy and not because the ECHR required it.[109]

16.5 THIRD PARTY PROPERTY

16.5.1 *Tax cases*

The constitutional or human right to protection of property can be used as a basis for questioning the validity of security rights attaching to property which does not belong to the debtor and where the owner has not consented to the security. In relation to article 1 of the First Protocol to the ECHR the leading case is *Gasus Dosier und Fördertechnik GmbH v Netherlands*.[110] A German company sold a concrete mixer to a Dutch company. The goods

---

[104] See generally M Higgins 'An Orchestra of Instruments' 2010 *Journal of the Law Society of Scotland* Oct 22; Higgins *The Enforcement of Heritable Securities*, supra note 79, chs 5 and 6, and K G C Reid and G L Gretton *Conveyancing 2010* (Avizandum 2011) 150–4.

[105] Conveyancing and Feudal Reform (Scotland) Act 1970 ss 20(2A), 23(4) and 24 (as amended by the 2010 Act).

[106] 1970 Act s 24A and the Applications by Creditors (Pre-Action Requirements) (Scotland) Order 2010 SSI 2010/317. See *Northern Rock (Asset Management) plc v Millar* 2012 SLT (Sh Ct) 58.

[107] 1970 Act s 24(7). There is also the new possibility of approved lay representation for the debtor at the hearing. See 1970 Act s 24E and the Lay Representation in Proceedings relating to Residential Property (Scotland) Order 2010 SSI 2010/264.

[108] Scottish Government, Home Owner and Debtor Protection (Scotland) Bill Policy Memorandum (2009) available at *http://www.scottish.parliament.uk/s3/bills/32–homeOwner/ b32s3–introd-pm.pdf*; Debt Action Forum Final Report (2009) available at *http://www.aib.gov. uk/About/DAF/DebtActionForumFinalRepo*. The latter includes a Report by a Repossession Sub-Group in Annex B.

[109] It has been argued that the Scottish law here is ECHR compatible: Higgins *The Enforcement of Heritable Securities*, supra note 79, para 10.8.

[110] (1995) 20 EHRR 403. See 16.2 supra.

were delivered but they were subject to a retention of title clause until the price was paid. Without having made payment, the buyer became insolvent and the Dutch tax authorities seized the property for unpaid taxes. They were entitled to do so in respect of 'furnishings' in the company's premises, even where these did not belong to the debtor. The power of seizure was challenged in the European Court of Human Rights. The challenge was unsuccessful with six of the nine judges finding in favour of the Netherlands. The court held that the power was proportionate to the legitimate aim of recovering taxes. It placed stress on the fact that the tax authorities, unlike other creditors, were unable to take alternative forms of security in respect of debts.[111] The sellers had allowed the machinery to become part of the 'furnishings' of the premises.[112] The court opined that what the seller was truly interested in was the purchase price rather than the property itself.[113] But what coloured the court's whole judgment was the fact that the second paragraph of article 1 of the First Protocol expressly reserves the right of states 'to control the use of property in accordance with the general interest or to secure the payment of taxes or other contributions or penalties'.[114]

Strictly speaking, *Gasus* is a case on seizure rather than security rights, but it is clearly the closest comparator to the South African consolidated cases of *First National Bank of SA Ltd t/a Wesbank v Commissioner of the South African Revenue Service; First National Bank of SA Ltd t/a Wesbank v Minister of Finance.*[115] The appellant had leased two vehicles and sold a third under an instalment sale agreement to two companies. These were delivered to the purchasers. The Commissioner subsequently detained the vehicles for debts due by the companies and therefore established a lien over them under section 114 of the Customs and Excise Act 91 of 1964. The appellant contended that this amounted to an arbitrary deprivation of property in breach of section 25 of the Constitution. The Constitutional Court agreed and issued an order declaring section 114 invalid to the extent that it applied to property not owned by the debtor. While payment of a customs debt was a legitimate legislative purpose, section 114 'cast the net too wide'.[116] It allowed deprivation (a) where the property owner had no connection with the transaction which gave rise to the debt; (b) where the property had no connection to the debt; and (c) where the property owner did not give the Commissioner a misleading impression as to the ownership.

---

[111] (1995) 20 EHRR 403 at para 71.

[112] (1995) 20 EHRR 403 at para 70.

[113] (1995) 20 EHRR 403 at para 68.

[114] The court glossed over the point of whether the seizure was a 'deprivation' within the first paragraph of article 1 of the First Protocol rather than a 'control' within the second.

[115] 2002 (4) SA 768 (CC). See Mostert and Pope (eds), *Principles of The Law of Property*, supra note 4, and A J van der Walt 'Negating Grotius – The Constitutional Validity of Statutory Security Rights in Favour of the State' 2002 SAJHR 86.

[116] 2002 (4) SA 768 (CC) at para 108 per Ackermann J.

What is fascinating about the case is that the court discusses the *Gasus* decision and expressly distinguishes it. The South African court dismisses the reasoning of the Strasbourg court that the owner's right should not be protected when economically its interest is actually in the purchase price:

> 'Neither the subjective interest of the owner in the thing owned, nor the economic value of the right of ownership, having regard to the other terms of the agreement, can determine the characterisation of the right. It does not matter that the owner would rather have the purchase price than the vehicle'.[117]

The court further referred to the express mention of taxes within article 1 of the First Protocol and also the fact that the motor vehicles in the current case, unlike the concrete mixer in *Gasus*, could not be regarded as 'furnishings'.[118]

16.5.2 Landlord's hypothec

The main common law (as opposed to statutory) example of a security which is capable of attaching to third party property is the landlord's (or lessor's) hypothec. It traditionally can cover goods in leased premises which do not actually belong to the tenant.[119] The author argued in the past that this aspect of the hypothec in Scotland was contrary to article 1 of the First Protocol to the ECHR and that the *Gasus* case was of little relevance, given the express reliance on the tax exception by the Strasbourg court.[120] This was apparently accepted by the Scottish Executive. The Bankruptcy and Diligence etc (Scotland) Act 2007 ends the ability of the landlord's hypothec to attach to goods not belonging to the tenant.[121] The South African lessor's hypothec, which can extend to third party property, may also be vulnerable to a constitutional rights challenge.[122] None has been reported to date. One reason for this may be that the standard practice of owners of movables that are in the possession of lessees is to give notice to the lessor. The effect is to exempt the goods from the hypothec. Another factor is that the hypothec is excluded by statute in cases where property is encumbered by a notarial bond or is the subject of an instalment agreement (in effect acquired under hire purchase).[123]

---

[117] 2002 (4) SA 768 (CC) at para 56 per Ackermann J.

[118] 2002 (4) SA 768 (CC) at para 107 per Ackermann J.

[119] A J M Steven 'The Landlord's Hypothec in Comparative Perspective' 2008 Stell LR 278 at 286–96.

[120] See A J M Steven 'Goodbye to the Landlord's Hypothec?' 2002 SLT (News) 177. See also McAllister *Scottish Law of Leases*, supra note 65, para 5.48.

[121] Bankruptcy and Diligence etc (Scotland) Act 2007 s 208(4). See Scottish Executive, Bankruptcy and Diligence etc (Scotland) Bill Policy Memorandum (2005) para 1010. See also Gretton and Steven, *Property, Trusts and Succession*, supra note 6, para 20.65.

[122] Steven 'The Landlord's Hypothec in Comparative Perspective', supra note 119, at 295; D Smith 'The Constitutionality of the Lessor's Hypothec: Attachment of a Third Party's Goods' (2011) 27 SAJHR 308.

[123] The author is grateful to Tjakie Naudé for this suggestion.

16.6 CONCLUSION

It can be seen from the areas examined that human rights have impacted upon the area of rights in security law both in Scotland and South Africa. Seeking protection based on these rights has been considerably more noticeable in the southern hemisphere jurisdiction than its northern counterpart. This can be seen from the respective case law, or rather lack of case law, in Scotland. And yet the underlying theme of appropriately balancing the human rights of both debtors and creditors is apparent in both jurisdictions. In particular, future developments as to enforcement of mortgages over residential properties are awaited with interest as to deciding exactly where that balance should lie.

Chapter 17

Access to Credit, the Law of Suretyship and Unfair Suretyships

J T Pretorius

17.1 INTRODUCTION

Chapter 2 of the Constitution of the Republic of South Africa of 1996 is comprised of a list of human rights, referred to as the 'Bill of Rights'.[1] Section 22 of the Bill of Rights provides that '[e]very citizen has the right to choose their trade, occupation or profession freely'.[2] This 'right of occupational freedom' embraces the right to commercial activity. This is a crucial element of individual autonomy and constitutes a basis for the exercise of other rights and freedoms.[3] It has been argued that the right of occupational freedom is 'more than a right to provide materially for oneself, but is aimed at enabling individuals to live profitable, dignified and fulfilling lives'.[4] The right to provide materially for oneself would in turn imply the right to engage in economic activity to further one's livelihood. Logically speaking, to be economically active, one requires the financial or monetary

---

[1] See Chapter 1 supra.

[2] S 26(1) of the Constitution of the Republic of South Africa Act 200 of 1993 (the 'interim constitution') provided that '[e]very person shall have the right freely to engage in economic activity and pursue a livelihood anywhere in the national territory'. The proviso to this section is that measures may be taken to protect economic growth, social justice, fair labour practices, equal opportunities, and so on, provided they are justifiable in an open and democratic society based on freedom and equality. See W J Hosten, A B Edwards, F Bosman and J Church *Introduction to South African Law and Legal Theory* 2e (LexisNexis 1997) at 972ff for a discussion of the provisions of the interim constitution. Although the European Convention on Human Rights (ECHR) was incorporated into the domestic law of the United Kingdom and also in Scotland (C Ashton and V Finch *Human Rights and Scots Law* (W Green 2002) 5ff), it is interesting to note that there is no real mention in the ECHR of social or economic rights, such as the right to work or the right to be paid a fair wage. It also does not say anything about 'a right to enough food and shelter to keep body and soul together' or 'a wholesome environment' which may be regarded as a fundamental human right (N Parpworth *Constitutional and Administrative Law* 6e (Oxford University Press 2010) para 16.41 at 425).

[3] I Currie and J De Waal *The Bill of Rights Handbook* 5e (Juta 2005) 490. The authors point out that in 'one sense, all limitations on commercial freedom impact on occupational freedom in one way or another' (ibid).

[4] Ibid 491. See also I Kull 'Unfair Contracts of Suretyship – A Question about the Horizontal Effect of Fundamental Rights or about the Application of Contract Principles?' (2007) 12 *Juridica International* 36.

means to allow one meaningfully and gainfully to participate in economic activity.[5]

One can obtain money or monetary means or capital in a number of ways.[6] Selling one's labour or participating in the economy are the most common methods.[7] Borrowing money is also an option, but, in the words of Shakespeare: 'Neither a borrower nor a lender be. For a loan oft loses both itself and friend, [a]nd borrowing dulls the edge of husbandry'.[8]

17.2 CONTROL OVER THE AVAILABILITY OF CREDIT

Money lending, the availability of credit and the payment of interest on such loans have been and are the subject of various rules, regulations and legislation since time immemorial.[9] In *Desert Star Trading 145 (Pty) Ltd & another v No 11 Flamboyant Edleen CC & another*[10] the court remarked:

'Increased consumption, a desire-based need for credit, attractive borrowing options and alluring methods of repayment have all contributed to many of us not living our lives by that aphorism. Our modern consumer driven society does however come at a cost. As recently as 2005 it was reported that South Africa's consumer debt crisis was costing the country around R12 billion annually and that 40 per cent of households nationally were experiencing financial difficulty as they were unable to meet loan repayments to micro lenders and other service provid-

---

[5]　J Buchan *Frozen Desire: An Inquiry into the Meaning of Money* (Picador 1997) 5ff; J Weatherford *The History of Money* (Crown 1997) 2ff; N Ferguson *The Ascent of Money: A Financial History of the World* (Allen Lane 2008) 65ff; and G Crowther *An Outline of Money* (Nelson 1940) 13ff.

[6]　H B Falkena *Banking on Happiness* (South African Financial Sector Forum 1999) 1ff; W Bernstein *A Splendid Exchange: How Trade Shaped the World* (Atlantic 2008) 43ff; R H Frank *The Return of the Economic Naturalist: How Economics Helps Make Sense of your World* (Virgin Books 2009) 61ff. But, in the words of Bruce Springsteen: 'You're born with nothing, and better off that way. Soon as you've got something they send someone to try and take it away' (Bruce Springsteen 'Something in the Night' on *Darkness on the Edge of Town* (1978)).

[7]　J Kay *The Truth about Markets: Their Genius, Their Limits, Their Follies* (Allen Lane 2004) 55ff.

[8]　*Hamlet* (Act 1, Scene 3). In *Desert Star Trading 145 (Pty) Ltd & another v No 11 Flamboyant Edleen CC & another* 2011 (2) SA 266 (SCA) para 1 at 267G-H the court quoted the above excerpt from *Hamlet*.

[9]　D J Joubert rev J J Henning 'Loans' in W Joubert (ed) *The Law of South Africa* 2e (LexisNexis Butterworths 2003–) vol 15(2) para 304. See also G Noodt *The Three Books on Interest-Bearing Loans and Interest (Foenus et Usurae)* (Pretoria University Press 2009) by D M Kriel (translator) and D H van Zyl (editor) 26ff. At common law, unless the parties agreed otherwise, the lender became entitled to receive interest on a stipulated future date as soon as he made the funds available to the borrower (*Cactus Investments (Pty) Ltd v Commissioner for Inland Revenue* 1999 (1) SA 315 (SCA).

[10]　Note 8 supra at 267–8. Over-indebtedness is a problem that is not unique to South Africa. See L J Smith 'Scotland' in A C Ciacchi and S Weatherill *Regulating Unfair Banking Practices in Europe: The Case of Personal Suretyships* (Oxford University Press 2010) 493 who points out that '[o]ver-indebtedness, along with the recession, have given rise to new schemes to alleviate the socio-economic impact of debt enforcement in Scotland' (at 493).

ers. The protection of the consumer has become a common feature in many legal systems. Many countries have adopted consumer protection legislation to regulate credit grantor–credit consumer relationships because they can and do give rise to abuse and exploitation.'

The South African National Credit Act[11] seeks to regulate credit-grantor and consumer relationships in South Africa. The attempt to regulate the granting of credit is a worldwide phenomenon.[12] The aim of the South African Act is to provide a mechanism and structure to protect the consumer by prescribing formalities for contracts, prohibiting certain terms and regulating certain consequences of the contractual relationship between consumers and credit providers. Section 3 states that the purposes of the Act are to 'promote and advance the social and economic welfare of South Africans, promote a fair, transparent, competitive, sustainable, responsible, efficient, effective and accessible credit market and industry, and to protect consumers'. The Act introduces a whole range of measures to prevent possible overspending by consumers and also to prevent moneylenders from lending money to borrowers who cannot afford to repay either the loan amount or the interest thereon.[13]

---

[11] Act 34 of 2005. In *Nedbank Ltd & others v National Credit Regulator & another* 2011 (3) SA 581 (SCA) Malan JA pointed out that the National Credit Act is not an amendment of previous legislation dealing with consumer credit. The Act seeks to achieve much more and replaces legislation that governed consumer credit for more than a quarter of a century (para 1). (His Lordship also remarked in passing that, unfortunately, the Act 'cannot be described as the "best drafted Act of Parliament which was ever passed," nor can the draftsman be said to have been blessed with the "draftsmanship of a Chalmers". Numerous drafting errors, untidy expressions and inconsistencies make its interpretation a particularly trying exercise' (para 2). The reference to Chalmers is, of course, to Sir Mackenzie Dalzell Chalmers who was the draftsman of the British Bills of Exchange Act 1882.) Smith, note 10 supra, points out that over-indebtedness 'remains a major cause for concern within the UK. Statistics show similar patterns of debt between England and Scotland, although the levels in Scotland are slightly lower on account of the generally lower level of salary' (at 496).

[12] M Kelly-Louw, J P Nehf and Peter Rott (eds) *The Future of Consumer Credit Regulation* (Ashgate 2008) 3ff.

[13] It is not the intention of this paper to deal with the provisions of the National Credit Act in detail. See, in general, J W Scholtz in J W Scholtz, J M Otto, E van Zyl, C M van Heerden and N Campbell *Guide to the National Credit Act* (LexisNexis 2008) Service Issue 2 at 2–1; J M Otto and R L Otto *The National Credit Act Explained* 2e (LexisNexis 2010) 3ff; M Kelly-Louw 'Consumer Credit' in *The Law of South Africa*, note 9 supra, vol 5(1). The Act may in some instances provide some relief to sureties. In general and subject to certain exceptions, the Act applies to every credit agreement between parties dealing at arm's length (s 4). 'Credit agreement' is defined in s 8. It includes a 'credit facility'; or a 'credit transaction'; or a 'credit guarantee'; or any combination of the aforementioned. A 'credit guarantee' is an agreement in terms whereof 'a person undertakes or promises to satisfy upon demand any obligation of another consumer in terms of a credit facility or a credit transaction' to which the Act applies (section 8(5)). An ordinary contract of suretyship in terms of which the surety provides personal security for the debts of another person will meet the definition of a 'credit guarantee' if the principal debt is a debt that is subject to the provisions of the Act (Otto and Otto at 24ff; JW Scholtz et al para 4.1; P Stoop and M Kelly-Louw 'The National Credit Act

17.3 SECURITY FOR LOANS AND SURETYSHIP

A creditor will often not be prepared to lend money to another in the absence of some form of security that the debt will be repaid.[14] A debtor whose creditor requires security for the payment of a debt ordinarily has

regarding Suretyships and Reckless Lending' (2011) 14 *Potchefstroom Electronic LJ* 67 but cf D Mostert 'Must Suretyship Agreement Comply with the NCA?' 2009 (June) *De Rebus* 53). In *First Rand Bank Ltd v Carl Beck Estates (Pty) Ltd & another* 2009 (3) SA 384 (T) Satchwell J remarked that there is no doubt that suretyship obligations would fall under the definition of a credit guarantee as defined in the National Credit Act (para 18). Such a surety would thus be entitled to rely on the various protection mechanisms of the Act by raising, e.g., the defence that the credit guarantee itself amounted to the 'granting of reckless credit' in terms of s 80. Where the principal debt is not a 'credit agreement' so that it does not fall under the provisions of the Act, the suretyship will fall under the common law and the surety will not be entitled to raise any of the defences or provisions of the National Credit Act. Also, if the principal debtor does not qualify as a 'consumer' in terms of the National Credit Act, the surety would not be entitled to rely on the protection afforded by the Act (*First Rand Bank Ltd v Carl Beck Estates (Pty) Ltd & another*, supra para 24). See also *Standard Bank of SA Ltd v Hunkydory Investments (Pty) Ltd & another* 2010 (1) SA 627 (C) at paras 13–14; *Slip Knot Investments 777 (Pty) Ltd v Project Law Prop (Pty) Ltd & another* (case 36018/2009 dated 1 April 2011 (SGHC)) para 10. In Scotland various schemes have been introduced over the past few years allowing individual debtors to seek the advice of professional consumer debt counselling and re-organisation services (Smith, note 8 supra, at 496). The Debt Arrangement Scheme (Scotland) Regulations 2011/141 allow personal bankruptcy to be forestalled and replaced by an individual undertaking to repay debts according to an agreed schedule. The provisions of the Consumer Credit Act 1974, now amended by the Consumer Credit Act 2006, apply to credit agreements in Scotland and regulate loan agreements, including those over heritable (immovable) property. The Scots law of cautionary obligations (see below) falls within the general law of obligations, as supplemented by rules of consumer protection that may apply on an individual basis to situations where the cautioner is acting as a consumer. See also K Heine and R Janal 'Suretyships and Consumer Protection in the European Union through the Glasses of Law and Economics' in Ciacchi and Weatherill, note 10 supra, 3ff.

14　Voet *Commentarius ad Pandectas* (P Gane's translation *sub nom The Selective Voet, being the Commentary on the Pandects* (Butterworth 1955) vol 3) 20.1.25 states: 'A needy debtor, pressed by tightness of ready cash, will readily allow any hard and inhuman terms to be written down against him. He promises himself smoother times and better fortune before the day put into the commissary term, and thus hopes to avert the harshness of the agreement by payment; though such a hope, quite slippery and deceptive as it is, not seldom finds nothing at all to encourage it in the aftermath'. This passage was referred to in *Graf v Buechel* 2003 (4) SA 378 (SCA) para 12 and *Desert Star Trading 145 (Pty) Ltd & another v No 11 Flamboyant Edleen CC & another* 2011 (2) SA 266 (SCA) para 1. See also M L Vession 'The Preponderance of the Reckless Consumer – The National Credit Bill 2005' (2006) 69 *THRHR* 649 at 650ff who calls for a balancing of the interests of both credit consumers and credit grantors. Most financial institutions will insist on some form of suretyship or guarantee in the case of personal loans or the granting of overdraft facilities, *especially* when dealing with a company or a close corporation. In the commercial world business people naturally conduct business on the basis that their commercial dealings will be completed successfully. But it is usually sensible to take the view that the transaction may go wrong. Foremost is the risk that the other party to a transaction may become insolvent. Another factor is the risk that a debtor who regrets ever entering into the transaction may become reluctant to repay the debt.

two courses of action: the debtor may provide real security by setting aside a particular corporeal asset (by means of mortgage, pledge or cession) which can be sold in execution by the creditor if the debt is not paid,[15] or he may provide personal security by persuading a third person to bind himself as against the creditor to pay the debt if the debtor fails to do so.[16] The personal security may be in the form of a contract of suretyship.[17] Caney[18] defines

---

[15] This form of security is known as real security and denotes a situation in which an asset belonging to a debtor, or to someone acting on the debtor's behalf, is earmarked for the satisfaction of the creditor's claim. See G F Lubbe rev T J Scott 'Mortgage and Pledge' in *The Law of South Africa*, note 9 supra, vol 17(2) para 325 for the kinds of real security. See also S Scott 'A Step towards a more Sympathetic Credit Security Dispensation in South Africa' (2008) 71 *THRHR* 373. In Scots Law a right in security is a real right if it gives the creditor a nexus ('bond') over some property, heritable or moveable, with the result that he can resort to that property for satisfaction of the debt in so far as it has not been paid. The general principle of Scots law as to rights in security over property is that there must be some form of delivery of the property to the security holder. See D Cabrelli 'The Case against the Floating Charge in Scotland' (2004–2005) 9 *EdinLR* 407 on some of the difficulties of obtaining security over moveable property.

[16] It is possible that the personal security may be in the form of a performance bond, an indemnity, insurance or even a guarantee. See S Eden and J T Pretorius 'Suretyship and Cautionary Obligations' in R Zimmermann, D Visser and K Reid (eds) *Mixed Legal Systems in Comparative Perspective: Property and Obligations in Scotland and South Africa* (OUP 2004) 335 at 337–8 and J T Pretorius 'Suretyships and Indemnity' (2001) 13 *SA Merc LJ* 95 on the terminology in this regard.

[17] In Scots Law suretyship is known as 'caution' and the contract of suretyship is known as a 'cautionary obligation' (S M Eden and A Clark 'Cautionary Obligations and Representations to Credit' in *The Laws of Scotland: Stair Memorial Encyclopaedia* vol 3 (1990) para 801; Eden and Pretorius, note 16 supra, 337. See also A D M Forte 'Good Faith and Utmost Good Faith: Insurance and Cautionary Obligations in Scots Law' in A D M Forte (ed) *Good Faith in Contract and Property* (Hart 1999) 87 on the role that good faith plays in cautionary obligations. The contract of suretyship is one of the most ancient contracts known to western civilisation. See in this regard W D Morgan 'The History and Economics of Suretyship' (1927) 12 *Cornell Law Quarterly* 153, 487; D E Phillipson 'Development of the Roman Law of Debt Security' (1968) 20 *Stanford Law Review* 1230; R Zimmermann *The Law of Obligations* (Juta 1990) 114ff; C F Forsyth 'Suretyship' in R Zimmermann and D Visser (eds) *Southern Cross: Civil Law and Common Law in South Africa* (Oxford University Press 1996) 417ff; W H Woods 'Historical Development of Suretyship' in E G Gallagher (ed) *The Law of Suretyship* (American Bar Association 1993) at 2–1ff; T Hewitson *Suretyship, its Origin and History: An Outline* (Law Book Co of Australasia 1927).

[18] C F Forsyth and J T Pretorius *Caney's The Law of Suretyship in South Africa* 6e (Juta 2010) 28–9. This definition by *Caney* has been accepted by the Appellate Division on a number of occasions: (1) by Corbett JA (Jansen JA concurring) in *Trust Bank of Africa Ltd v Frysch* 1977 (3) SA 562 (A) at 584F; (2) by Trengove AJA (Wessels ACJ, Jansen, Muller and Joubert JJA concurring) in *Sapirstein & others v Anglo African Shipping Co (SA) Ltd* 1978 (4) SA 1 (A) at 11H; and (3) by Corbett CJ (Hefer, Nestadt, Grosskopf JJA and Nicholas AJA concurring) in *Nedbank Ltd v Van Zyl* 1990 (2) SA 469 (A) at 473I. Eden and Clark, note 17 supra, state that a 'cautionary obligation is a form of personal security for the performance of obligations under a contract. It is a collateral undertaking in the sense that there must always be an independent contract to which it relates, and is an undertaking by one person, the cautioner, that a second person known as the debtor will perform his obligations under the principal

the contract of suretyship as 'an accessory contract by which a person (the surety) undertakes to the creditor of another (the principal debtor), primarily that the principal debtor, who remains bound, will perform his obligation to the creditor and, secondarily, that if and so far as the principal debtor fails to do so, the surety will perform it or, failing that, indemnify the creditor'.

In *Jans v Nedcor Bank Ltd*[19] the court said that '[b]y its very nature a contract of suretyship is burdensome. The surety undertakes responsibility for the fulfilment of another's obligation'. The fact that one is actually willing to undertake responsibility for another's obligation does not seem 'rational' and one can only assume that the surety has his own reasons for doing so and that he is well aware of the 'risks' involved.[20] It is submitted that very few sureties would contemplate or anticipate as a *fait accompli* that they will in fact be performing the debtor's obligation since that will probably amount to some form of donation rather than to the giving of security.[21] That is why

contract. It the debtor fails, then the third person in the relationship, the creditor can turn to the cautioner for relief' (para 801 at 417).

[19] 2003 (6) SA 646 (SCA) para 30 at 661F. Section 6 of the General Law Amendment Act 50 of 1956, as amended, provides that no contract of suretyship is valid unless the 'terms' thereof are embodied in a written document signed by or on behalf of the surety. In *Sapirstein & others v Anglo African Shipping Co (SA) Ltd* 1978 (4) SA 1 (A) at 12B–C the former Appellate Division held that the 'terms' of the contract of suretyship were the identity of the creditor, the identity of the debtor, the identity of the surety, and the nature and the amount of the principal debt. In Scotland an earlier provision expressly relating to the form of cautionary obligations was replaced in 1995 by a general rule that gratuitous unilateral obligations are required to be constituted in writing signed by the grantor or on his behalf. See Eden and Pretorius, note 16 supra, 339–40.

[20] See L Kähler 'Decision-making about Suretyships under Empirical Uncertainty – How Consequences of Decisions about Suretyships Might Influence the Law' (2005) 3 *European Review of Private Law* 333 for an excellent discussion of the various considerations that come into play when making the decision to undertake the liability of another's debts. This article also contains a valuable discussion of the uncertainty that will prevail if courts have to decide on the unfairness of a suretyship. Heine and Janal, note 13 supra, point out: '[F]amily suretyships may be more rational than one might think. While empirical data may show that a large number of family suretyships are motivated by an emotional bond between debtor and surety and also show the characteristics of a financial overextension of the surety, a majority of these contracts may also be highly rational and efficient. . . . [S]o-called family suretyships often assume the form of a gift. In such cases, by definition, the surety does not expect any remuneration for his or her effort' (at 22).

[21] In *Carrim v Omar* 2001 (4) SA 691 (W) at 714 Stegmann J criticised *Caney*'s definition (note 18 supra) and maintained that the surety's obligation is not that the principal debtor will perform but rather that he the surety is or will be liable for the debt, *ab initio*. It is submitted that very few sureties actually contemplate that they will be liable to pay. The surety contemplates or expects that the principal debtor will pay or perform his obligation, and only if the principal debtor is in default that he as surety will be liable to pay. If the surety were so insistent on paying, why not simply make a donation? See also C Forsyth and M du Plessis 'Suretyship, Guarantee and Islamic Banking' (2002) 119 *SALJ* 671; S Scott and E Dirix 'To Have your Cake and Eat it' (2004) 15 *Stell LR* 333 and *Caney*, note 18 supra, 29 n 10. Lotz also criticises *Caney*'s definition and says that while it can be accepted that it will, at the time

the surety's undertaking is that the principal debtor will perform and that failing that, he the surety will perform. The surety has one obligation only: to perform or pay in the debtor's place should the debtor fail to perform.[22]

17.4 THE PRINCIPAL OBLIGATION

The ordinary suretyship is usually in respect of a particular debt or obligation.[23] It is accessory to the transaction that creates the obligation of

> of contracting, be in the mind of both the creditor and the surety that the principal debtor will perform, it seems futile to say that the surety's primary undertaking is that the principal debtor will perform as that 'primary undertaking' clearly does not create a primary (or any) obligation between the creditor and the surety. Furthermore, if such a primary obligation were indeed created, a creditor would probably have to call on a surety to perform in terms of the primary obligation (i.e., call on the surety to persuade the principal debtor to perform) before enforcing the secondary obligation and that is not the law (J G Lotz rev J J Henning 'Suretyship' *The Law of South Africa*, note 9 supra, vol 26 para 191).

[22] *Caney*, note 18 supra, 29 n 19. In *Carrim v Omar*, supra, Stegmann J disagreed with the definition given by *Caney* (note 18 supra) and stated: 'In light of these considerations, I am respectfully, but firmly, of the view that Caney's definition of the contract of suretyship as comprising a primary undertaking by the surety that the principal debtor will perform his obligation, and only a secondary obligation that if the principal debtor defaults, the surety will indemnify the creditor, cannot be supported. The authorities establish clearly enough that by the contract of suretyship, the surety accedes to the obligation of the principal debtor in the sense that, without disturbing the primary liability of the principal debtor, the surety gives a conditional undertaking that if the principal debtor should fail to perform his obligation, the surety will perform it in his place, if appropriate, or will otherwise indemnify the creditor. Such other indemnification will generally take the form of the payment of such damages as the creditor may have suffered in consequence of the principal debtor's breach of contract. It is not a prerequisite of a contract of suretyship that the intending surety should primarily undertake that the principal debtor will perform his obligation to the creditor' (para 57).

[23] The debt or obligation may be created by contract or may arise out of delict or in any manner in which a person may become bound as a debtor to another (*Caney*, note 18 supra, 39). In *Sydney Road Holdings (Pty) Ltd v Simon* 1981 (3) SA 104 (D) 107 Leon J remarked: 'There is no rule of law that damages flowing from a breach of contract by the principal debtor cannot be recovered from a surety. Whether damages can be claimed depends solely and exclusively on what the surety undertook to do: the construction of his undertaking. Where, e.g., a surety bound himself not merely for the due payment of the purchase price but also for the due and proper performance of "all the obligations" of the principal debtor under an agreement it was held that this covered a claim for damages against the principal debtor where the plaintiff had terminated the contract on the principal debtor's breach'. This position appears to be the same in Scotland although the closest example in practice to the surety *ex delicto* is the fidelity guarantee granted on behalf of a bank employee (Eden and Pretorius, note 16 supra, 340). In South Africa it is not essential that the principal obligation exists at the time when the suretyship contract is entered into. A suretyship may be contracted with reference to a principal obligation which is to come into existence in the future (*Trust Bank of Africa Ltd v Frysch* 1977 (3) SA 562 (A) 585; *Television & Electrical Distributors (Pty) Ltd v Coetzer* 1962 (1) SA 747 (T) 749; *Inter-Union Finance Ltd v Franskraalstrand (Edms) Bpk* 1965 (4) SA 180 (W) 187–188). In *Frysch* it was furthermore held that it is not necessary for the suretyship

the principal debtor.[24] The surety's undertaking may be for a limited or an unlimited amount.[25] In Scotland they have an interesting approach to instances where the cautionary obligation is stated to be limited to a certain sum: it may either be a guarantee for a limited part of the debt, or it may be a guarantee for the entire debt subject to a limit to the amount of the cautioner's liability.[26] Although the nature and amount of the principal debt must be recorded in the deed of suretyship, it has been said that the actual amount of the principal debt need not be stated where the surety undertakes unlimited liability which may or may not include liability for a future debt.[27]

contract to indicate whether it precedes or follows the principal contract (585). Where the only principal obligation guaranteed by the suretyship is one to come into existence in the future, the liability of the surety under his guarantee does not arise until the principal obligation has been contracted. It is also not essential that the principal debtor be in existence at the time when the suretyship contract is entered into (*United Dominions Corporation (SA) Ltd v Rokebrand* 1963 (4) SA 411 (T) 413).

[24] *Caney*, note 18 supra, describes the accessory nature of a suretyship as follows: 'The fact that the surety's obligation is an accessory obligation is often invested with an air of mystery that apparently justifies without further explanation many aspects of suretyship. In fact the concept is relatively straightforward. It means simply that for there to be a valid suretyship, between surety and creditor, there has to be a valid principal obligation, between the debtor and the creditor. The suretyship is said to be accessory to the transaction which creates the obligation of the principal debtor. Put another way, every suretyship is conditional upon the existence of a principal obligation' (at 29–30). In Scotland it is also recognised that the cautionary obligations are accessory in nature: 'Cautionary obligations are accessory in nature, which means that there must always be a principal obligation to which the cautionary obligation relates. The principal obligation need not be in existence at the time that caution is undertaken, provided it is then in contemplation. A further consequence of the accessory nature of caution is that there are necessarily three parties concerned: the creditor, the debtor and the cautioner' (Eden and Clark, note 17 supra, para 835).

[25] *Milne NO v Cook & others* 1956 (3) SA 317 (N); *FJ Hawkes & Co v Nagel* 1957 (3) SA 126 (W); *Nedbank Ltd v Wizard Holdings (Pty) Ltd & others* 2010 (5) SA 523 (GSJ) and N J Grové *Die Formaliteitsvereiste by borgstelling* unpublished LLM dissertation, University of Pretoria (1984) at 95. In the Netherlands a contract of suretyship will only be valid if the maximum amount of the surety's potential liability is expressly stated in the contract (JWH Blomkwist *Borgtocht* B78 in *Monografieën Nieuw BW* (1998) 2e at 45).

[26] Eden and Clark, note 17 supra, para 913. If the guarantee is construed as covering the entire debt subject to a limit on the cautioner's liability, the creditor is entitled to take any dividends to which he is entitled in the event of bankruptcy, plus the benefit of any security he may hold in respect of the debt. If there is a shortfall the creditor may hold the cautioner liable for the balance up to the stated amount. If, however, the cautioner is liable only for a limited amount of the debt, then he is entitled to share in any dividends payable to the creditor. In South African law there is authority for the view that both the creditor and the surety are entitled to prove a claim against the insolvent estate of the principal debtor (*Proksch v Die Meester & andere* 1969 (4) SA 567(A) at 586). It is submitted that to allow both the creditor and the surety to prove a claim in respect of the same debt would amount to a duplication of liability of the principal debtor's insolvent estate. See *Caney*, note 18 supra, 168ff for a discussion in this regard.

[27] *First Consolidated Holdings (Pty) Ltd v Bissett & others* 1978 (4) 491 (W) at 496; Grové, note 25 supra, 95ff; *Caney*, note 18 supra, 70. There is no clear authority in Scotland as to whether

The duration of the surety's liability depends upon the terms of the deed of suretyship.[28] Some suretyships are intended to cover a single transaction only, while others called 'continuing suretyships or guarantees', are framed to apply to many different transactions which need not be identified separately.[29] In the case of a single credit transaction the surety's liability extends only to one credit or transaction agreed upon.[30] In the case of a continuing suretyship, the surety's liability extends to a series of credits and transactions.[31] These transactions may relate to some future debt to be incurred or to an existing debt already incurred by the principal debtor. Although it is true, generally speaking, that a surety under a continuous suretyship has the right to unilaterally bring about the termination of the contract of suretyship by giving due and reasonable notice to the creditor, this right is subject to the terms of the deed of suretyship itself.[32] Where the termination

there is a presumption on the limitation to future debts and each case turns on the particular words used, interpreted in the light of the circumstances under which the obligation was given (Eden and Clark, note 17 supra, para 912).

[28] See in general: *Glenn Brothers v Commercial General Agency Co Ltd* 1905 TS 737 741; *Swart v Cape Fabrix (Pty) Ltd* 1979 (1) SA 195 (A) 202; *List v Jungers* 1979 (3) SA 106 (A) 118; *Sydney Road Holdings (Pty) Ltd v Simon* 1981 (3) SA 104 (D) 107; Eden and Clark, note 17 supra, para 912.

[29] In *SA General Electric Co (Pty) Ltd v Sharfman* 1981 (1) SA 592 (W) Boshoff JP described the liability of a surety under a continuing suretyship thus: '[I]n the case of a continuing guarantee the [surety's] liability endures until the credits and transactions contemplated by the parties, and covered by the guarantee, have been exhausted or until the guarantee itself has been revoked. Generally speaking, a surety under a continuing guarantee has, apart from an express or clearly inferential provision to the contrary in his contract, a right to bring about a termination of such a continuing guarantee. Any such notice obviously only relates to amounts advanced to or becoming due by the principal debtor after the notice; the surety's liability in relation to any amount due at the time of the giving of the notice would remain unaffected . . .' (at 595). See also Eden and Pretorius, note 16 supra, at 345, and J T Pretorius 'Continuing Suretyships' (1988) 10 *Modern Business Law* 85.

[30] The contract of suretyship may be extinguished either by causes which are peculiar to it and which do not affect the principal contract, or else it may be discharged by causes which bring about the extinction of the principal contract. In the former, the circumstances connected to the establishment of the *vinculum juris* between the creditor and the surety are the important elements, and these determine, as in the case of other contracts, whether or not the suretyship has come to an end. In the latter, the facts relating to the principal contract are all-important, and, if they are such to enable it to be extinguished, the suretyship contract also expires (*SA General Electric Co (Pty) Ltd v Sharfman* 1981 (1) SA 592 (W) at 595; J W Wessels *The Law of Contract* 2e by A A Roberts (Butterworth 1951) vol II para 4218).

[31] The position is the same in Scotland. Eden and Clark, note 17 supra, point out that a 'guarantee may be either continuing or limited in its extent. A continuing guarantee results in the cautioner being liable, subject to other limits contained in the guarantee, for the amount which is ultimately outstanding by the debtor. Where a guarantee is limited, it applies only to a particular transaction or set of transactions, and so once any balance due in respect of these has been met by the debtor, the cautioner is released from liability. He will not be affected by subsequent dealings by the debtor with the creditor' (para 914).

[32] *Kalil v Standard Bank of South Africa Ltd* 1967 (4) SA 550 (A) 555–6; *Diners Club South Africa (Pty) Ltd v Durban Engineering (Pty) Ltd* 1980 (3) SA 53 (A); *Jenkins & Co v TN Price* (1903) 24

of a continuing suretyship is within the exclusive discretion of the creditor, the surety's position may be rather precarious, especially if the obligations undertaken by the surety are of the widest possible nature as regarding the principal debtor's indebtedness or the obligations for which the surety undertakes liability as well as in regard to the duration of the suretyship.[33] Where the termination of a continuing suretyship is within the exclusive discretion of the creditor, the surety's right to unilaterally terminate liability in respect of future liabilities would be severely restricted or even removed.[34] The surety's position may then be rather precarious, especially in cases where there is no limit on the surety's potential liability and the exact nature of the indebtedness is not properly defined.

17.5 CONTRACT LAW AND THE CONSTITUTION

It has been said that the law of suretyship is simply a backwater off the broad river of the law of contract.[35] In recent years there has been quite an 'endeav-

---

NLR 112 115; *St Patricks Mansions (Pty) Ltd v Grange Restaurant (Pty) Ltd* 1949 (4) SA 57 (W) 71. See also *Caney*, note 18 supra, 87ff; *Wessels*, note 30 supra, paras 4290–1.

[33] Where, e.g., the contract contains a provision that the suretyship shall 'remain in full force . . . until the creditor/s shall have agreed in writing to cancel' (*Neuhoff v New York Timbers Ltd* 1981 (4) SA 666 (T) at 676).

[34] In *Oceanair (Natal) (Pty) Ltd v Sher* 1980 (1) SA 317 (D) Howard J made the following remark in this regard: 'I am of the opinion that, properly construed, the stipulation that the suretyship shall remain in force until the creditor agrees in writing to cancel it effectively removes the right of the individual surety to terminate his liability by notice or by concluding an oral agreement . . . [purporting to cancel the suretyship contract]. The stipulation is valid and enforceable, and affords a sufficient basis for holding that the oral agreement is invalid and evidence of it is accordingly irrelevant and inadmissible' (at 324). *SA General Electric Co (Pty) Ltd v Sharfman* 1981 (1) SA 592 (W) is an example of where the creditor sought to preclude the surety from unilaterally withdrawing his suretyship. Apart from the fact that the suretyship contained a provision that no purported withdrawal shall be effective unless the creditor consents thereto in writing, the surety undertook the liability that the suretyship 'shall remain in force as a continuing security . . . notwithstanding [his] death . . .' (596). The court held that the fact that the suretyship contract contained a clause precluding the surety from withdrawing his suretyship without the consent of the creditor did not preclude his executors from so doing in the absence of an express provision limiting this power of the executors (597–8). In such a case the suretyship shall cease to operate in respect of any debts incurred by the principal debtor after notice had been given. By giving a guarantee for future liabilities, a surety undertakes an obligation which is transmitted to his estate on his death. This obligation is transmitted on his death unless before that event he terminates his obligation by proper notice, where the right to do so is not excluded by the terms of the suretyship (*Caney*, note 18 supra, 110–15; *Kalil v Standard Bank of South Africa Ltd* 1967 (4) SA 550 (A) at 557). In theory it would thus be possible for a surety to undertake liability under a contract of continuous suretyship which may limit the powers of the executors of his estate to terminate the suretyship in respect of future liabilities not yet incurred by the principal debtor. It is submitted that such an undertaking would make it almost impossible to wind up the surety's deceased estate.

[35] C F Forsyth and J T Pretorius *Caney's The Law of Suretyship in South Africa* 5e (Juta 1992) v.

our' to reform the law of contract and it is quite difficult to predict what direction this 'reform' is going to take.[36] The law of suretyship is bearing the brunt of that 'reform'.[37]

The perception that a contract is constituted by agreement infers the recognition of individual autonomy as a philosophical foundation.[38] One of the cornerstones of the contractual theory is the so-called *pacta sunt servanda* principle and sanctity of contract.[39] This principle requires exact enforcement of contractual obligations created in circumstances which are consistent with freedom of contract and consensuality. Courts in the pre-constitutional era held the concept of *pacta sunt servanda* in high regard as a profoundly moral principle and regarded sanctity of contract almost as a universal truth.[40] Nearly ninety years ago, in *Wells v South African Alumenite Company*,[41] Innes CJ remarked the following with regard to a particular undertaking in a contract of sale:

'Now these words are as wide and general as they could well be . . . No doubt the condition is hard and onerous; but if people sign such conditions they must, in the absence of fraud, be held to them. Public policy so demands. "[If] there is one thing which is more than another public policy requires it is that men of full age and competent understanding shall have the utmost liberty of contracting, and that their contracts, when entered freely and voluntarily shall be held sacred and

---

[36] F Brand and D Brodie 'Good Faith in Contract Law' in Zimmermann, Visser and Reid, note 16 supra, 94 at 106ff; F D J Brand 'The Role of Good Faith, Equity and Fairness in the South African Law of Contract: The Influence of the Common Law and the Constitution' (2009) 126 *SALJ* 71 at 73ff; and I M Rautenbach 'Constitution and Contract: The Application of the Bill of Rights to Contractual Clauses and their Enforcement – Reasonableness as Hard Law' 2011 *Annual Banking Law Update* 31 at 34ff .

[37] An examination of the cases will reveal that there is usually some form of suretyship or guarantee involved. See, e.g., *Slip Knot Investments 777 (Pty) Ltd v Project Law Prop (Pty) Ltd & another* (case 36018/2009 dated 1 April 2011 (SGHC)); *Ribeiro & another v Slip Knot Investments 777 (Pty) Ltd* 2011 (1) SA 575 (SCA); *African Dawn Properties Finance 2 (Pty) Ltd v Dream Travel Tours CC & others* 2011 (3) SA 511 (SCA).

[38] S van der Merwe, L F van Huyssteen, M F B Reinecke and G F Lubbe *Contract General Principles* 3e (Juta 2007) 11.

[39] The literature on the *pacta sunt servanda* principle is limitless. See, in general, E Kahn *Contract and Mercantile Law A Source Book* 2e by E Kahn (general editor), C Lewis and C Visser (Juta 1988) vol I 31ff ; van der Merwe et al, note 38 supra, 11ff; and D Moseneke 'Transformative Constitutionalism: Its Implications for the Law of Contract' (2009) 20 *Stell LR* 1 at 9ff.

[40] *Roffey v Catterall, Edwards and Goudré (Pty) Ltd* 1977 (4) SA 494 (N) where Didcott J remarked at 493: 'Contracts valid in form are *prima facie* enforceable in South African law, and effect will be given to them unless grounds for their avoidance are proved. This is no less so when their enforcement is resisted because they are said to clash with public policy than when other answers to them are raised'. See also *Magna Alloys and Research (SA) (Pty) Ltd v Ellis* 1984 (4) SA 874 (A) at 893, and C Visser 'The Principle *Pacta Servanda Sunt* in Roman and Roman-Dutch Law, with Specific Reference to Contracts in Restraint of Trade' (1984) 101 *SALJ* 641.

[41] 1927 AD 69 at 72–73.

shall be enforced by courts of justice." (Per Jessel MR in *Printing & Numerical Registering Company v Sampson* . . .'.[42]

The fact that an obligation is recognised by law necessarily implies that contracting parties, when exercising their private autonomies, are subject to the values of society.[43] Although there had been a vast amount of legal development and writing[44] in this field since the decision in *Wells*, the ques-

---

[42] *Printing & Numerical Registering Company v Sampson* (1875) LR 19 Eq 462 at 465. Kahn, note 39 supra, makes the following observation in this regard: 'When one deals with the subject of sanctity of contract, it is almost a matter of legal etiquette to cite the celebrated, though time-worn, dictum of Sir George Jessel MR. It was probably a piece of conscious hyperbole; and it is a mixture of truism, incompleteness, error and question-begging. In civil law the very essence of a contract *is* the free meeting of the minds of the parties wishing to make a contract . . . But in every legal system at all times limitations have been imposed on the liberty concluding commercial contracts where the general interest has been regarded as taking a priority over the freedom of action of the individual . . . Never has there been a society organized on the basis of a complete delegation of contract-making to individuals, analogous to private legislation. In human affairs competition is imperfect and man's capacity to control his relations with his fellow man by accord is confined' (at 31).

[43] Van der Merwe et al, note 38 supra, 11. See also G Lubbe 'Taking Fundamental Rights Seriously: The Bill of Rights and its Implications for the Development of Contract Law' (2004) 121 *SALJ* 359.

[44] Much has been written on the concept of good faith in contracts and it is not possible within the confines of this discussion to outline even the scope of this vast subject. See Brand and Brodie, note 36 supra, 94ff and Brand, note 36 supra, 7ff for an excellent discussion in this regard. One of the main instruments employed by the courts to transport abstract values of fairness and equity into our substantive contract law, was the defence of 'bad faith' — the *exceptio doli*. It was at one time possible to argue on good authority that the *exceptio doli generalis* was available to assist a surety to resist certain claims by the creditor (J T Pretorius 'The Future of the Law of Suretyship' in M Kidd and S Hoctoer (eds) *Stella Iuris: Celebrating 100 Years of Teaching Law in Pietermaritzburg* (Juta 2010) 149 at 152ff; P van Warmelo 'Exceptio doli' 1981 *De Jure* 202 at 207ff). This defence was believed to have existed to protect a surety when a creditor sought to use the suretyship for a purpose never envisaged by the parties at the time they originally made their contract. The clearest example of a proper use of this defence was when the creditor sought to hold the surety liable for some subsequent and extraneous debt which, although arguably within the terms of a widely phrased suretyship, the parties never intended to secure. Zimmermann points out that the South African courts had over many years used the *exceptio doli* to introduce various equitable doctrines, mostly originating from English law, but unknown to Roman Dutch law — such as fictional fulfillment of conditions, rectification and estoppel into our contract law (Reinhard Zimmermann 'Good Faith and Equity' in Zimmermann and D Visser, note 17 supra, 217 at 221ff). In *Bank of Lisbon and South Africa Ltd v De Ornelas & another* 1988 (3) SA 580 (A), however, the then appellate division held that the *exceptio* never formed part of the modern South African law. The *Bank of Lisbon* decision has been the subject of severe criticism and discussion. See C Lewis 'Demise of the Exceptio Doli: Is there Another Route to Contractual Equity?' (1990) 107 *SALJ* 26; S W J van der Merwe, G F Lubbe and L F van Huyssteen 'The Exceptio Doli Generalis: Requiescat in Pace – Vivat Aequitas' (1989) 106 *SALJ* 235; M A Lambiris 'The Exceptio Doli Generalis: An Obituary' (1988) 105 *SALJ* 644; L Hawthorne and Ph J Thomas 'The Exceptio Doli' (1989) 22 *De Jure* 143; R Zimmermann 'The Law of Obligations:

tion and the debate as to whether the Constitution applies to contracts[45] and the proper place of the doctrine of *pacta sunt servanda* came to a head in the Constitutional Court in *Barkhuizen v Napier*.[46] This matter dealt with the validity of a time bar for the institution of action in a short-term insurance contract. Ngcobo J had no difficulty in acknowledging and confirming that the Constitution should be applicable to contracts:

'Ordinarily constitutional challenges to contractual terms will give rise to the question of whether the disputed provision is contrary to public policy. Public policy represents the legal convictions of the community; it represents those values that are held most dear by the society. Determining the content of public policy was once fraught with difficulties. That is no longer the case. Since the

Character and Influence of the Civilian Tradition' (1992) 3 *Stell LR* 5; *Caney*, note 18 supra, 210ff; C F C van der Walt 'Die Huidige Posisie in die Suid-Afrikaanse Reg met betrekking tot Onbillike Kontraksbedinge' (1986) 103 *SALJ* 646 and Brand, note 36 supra, 73ff. See, however, *Eerste Nasionale Bank van Suidelike Afrika Bpk v Saayman NO* 1997 (4) SA 302 (HCA) 323 where Olivier JA, in the minority judgment, suggested that the criticism may well be misplaced. However, it is suggested that in this case we see a clash between, on the one hand, different (and perhaps conflicting) principles: between the legal certainty (vital for successful commerce) enhanced by holding parties to their bargains however unconscionable they might be, and, on the other hand, equity or justice enhanced by, exceptionally, releasing parties from such bargains. In the commonplace circumstances of today's commercial world where creditors require prospective debtors to provide sureties on the terms which they (the creditors) dictate, to hold sureties in all circumstances to the terms dictated to them by the creditors creates a potential for conflict. In *Brisley v Drotsky* 2002 (4) SA 1 (SCA) the majority of the court remarked that Olivier JA's statement in *Saayman* was based on dubious grounds (at 14). See also Brand, note 36 supra, 78ff for a good discussion of the influence of Olivier JA's minority judgment in *Saayman*. Zimmermann argues that the 'substantive' content of the *exceptio doli* had been absorbed into the requirement of good faith underlying the operation of all consensual contracts. Although the author concedes that no comprehensive analysis has yet appeared of how the principle of good faith operates and what its functions are, he nevertheless argues that it could well be that good faith may become a general principle enabling courts to alter the agreement of parties merely because they consider it reasonable to do so; good faith may give courts general power to refuse to enforce contractual obligations which they consider harsh or inequitable. It is perhaps true that the concepts of freedom of contract and sanctity of contract (*pacta sunt servanda*) have, in the course of this century, increasingly come under attack as a result of, amongst others, rampant inflation, monopolistic practices giving rise to unequal bargaining power, and the large-scale use of standard form contracts. The heyday of extreme individualism was short-lived all over the world and we are witnessing a transition from freedom of contract to social responsibility. However, the perception that the problem of unfair contract terms will have to be tackled in a more fundamental and formal manner has been gaining ground (at 256–7). See also L Hawthorne 'The End of Bona Fides' (2003) 15 *SA Merc LJ* 271; L Hawthorne 'Closing the Open Norms in the Law of Contract' (2004) 67 *THRHR* 294; C-J Pretorius 'Individualism, Collectivism and the Limits of Good Faith' (2003) 66 *THRHR* 638; J Lewis 'Fairness in South African Contract Law' (2003) 120 *SALJ* 330.

[45] The discussion whether the Constitution should apply to contractual relations has generated a substantial amount of literature, on which see Chapters 12 and 13 supra.

[46] 2007 (5) SA 323 (CC).

advent of our constitutional democracy, public policy is now deeply rooted in our Constitution and the values that underlie it.'[47]

The judge remarked that '[w]hile it is necessary to recognise the doctrine of *pacta sunt servanda*, courts should be able to decline the enforcement of a time-limitation clause if it would result in unfairness or would be unreasonable'.[48] His lordship also stressed that:

'On the one hand public policy, as informed by the Constitution, requires in general that parties should comply with contractual obligations that have been freely and voluntarily undertaken. This consideration is expressed in the maxim *pacta sunt servanda*, which, as the Supreme Court of Appeal has repeatedly noted, gives effect to the central constitutional values of freedom and dignity. Self-autonomy, or the ability to regulate one's own affairs, even to one's own detriment, is the very essence of freedom and a vital part of dignity. The extent to which the contract was freely and voluntarily concluded is clearly a vital factor as it will determine the weight that should be afforded to the values of freedom and dignity.'[49]

---

[47] Para 28. Lubbe, note 43 supra, gives the following warning that comes with the recognition of constitutional values: 'The elaboration of the implications of the constitutional right to dignity in the contractual context will not be a simple matter. A balance will have to be struck between an individual's capacity for self-determination by means of contract and the need to override this when it results in "obscene excesses". An incremental development on a case-by-case basis with reference to the notion of public policy is well suited to this end, provided that sufficient cognisance is taken of variables relevant to the evaluation in each given case and that particular regard is had to the relative interests of the parties in respect of each transaction. The courts would also do well to move beyond the bland and abstract considerations implicit in the general principles of contract law in order to have regard to the economic and social ends that are addressed by the various specific contracts recognized in our law. Due regard will also have to be given to the implications of the principle of reciprocity as an expression of what a party seeks to achieve by the conclusion of a synallagmatic contract, as well as to the distinction between so-called discrete and relational contracts. It might also be necessary to differentiate contracts concluded between commercial parties from contracts concluded by individuals in respect of the basic needs of human existence . . . e.g. in relation to housing, education and health. This becomes especially problematic in so far as these needs are served by contracts concluded with commercially oriented entities, under which intrinsically human needs become commercial commodities . . .' (at 422–3).

[48] Para 70. In his minority judgment, Sachs J said the following with regard to the doctrine of *pacta sunt servanda*: 'The doctrine of sanctity of contract and the maxim *pacta sunt servanda* have through judicial and textbook repetition come to appear axiomatic, indeed mesmeric, to many in the legal world. Their virtue, if applied in an unlimited way, is not self-evident, and their reach, if not their essence, has come to be severely restricted in open and democratic societies. This has happened over several decades through the overlapping effects of consumer protection struggles, scholarly critiques, legislative interventions and creative judicial reasoning. The jurisprudential pedestal on which it once imperiously stood has been singularly narrowed in the great majority of democratic societies' (para 141).

[49] Para 57 (footnotes omitted). Ngcobo J also recognised that '[p]*acta sunt servanda* is a profoundly moral principle, on which the coherence of any society relies. It is also a universally recognised legal principle. But the general rule that agreements must be honoured cannot apply to immoral agreements which violate public policy. [Our] courts have recognised

Brand maintains that the values of 'dignity' and 'freedom' have a con-founding capacity to pull in several directions at the same time and that they may fulfil very different roles. He says that by their very nature these values are simply too vague to provide a decisive answer in deciding cases. He claims that he does not believe that we need to find a specific constitutional value, expressly referred to in the Constitution, to underpin every rule of contract law. He affirms that there is nothing in the approach formulated by the Supreme Court of Appeal with regard to the roles of good faith, reasonableness and fairness in our contract law that is in conflict with the constitutional value system.[50] He seems to have some 'reservations' with the following statement of Ngcobo J where the judge had the following to say on the role of good faith in contracts:

> 'As the law currently stands, good faith is not a self-standing rule, but an underly-ing value that is given expression through existing rules of law. In this instance, good faith is given effect to by the existing common-law rule that contractual clauses that are impossible to comply with should not be enforced. To put it dif-ferently: good faith . . . has a creative, a controlling and a legitimating or explana-tory function. It is not, however, the only value or principle that underlies the law of contracts. Whether, under the Constitution, this limited role for good faith is appropriate and whether the maxim *lex non cogit ad impossibilia* alone is sufficient to give effect to the value of good faith are, fortunately, not questions that need be answered on the facts of this case and I refrain from doing so.'[51]

---

this and our Constitution re-enforces it. Furthermore, the application of *pacta sunt servanda* often raises the question whether a purported agreement or pact is indeed a real one, in other words whether true consensus was reached. Therefore the relevance of power imbalances between contracting parties and the question whether true consensus could for that matter ever be reached, have often been emphasised' (para 87).

[50] Brand, note 36 supra, 86. It is quite interesting to note that Calitz argues that in the light of the constitutional right to dignity, freedom of association, freedom of forced labour, freedom of movement, freedom to choose a trade and the right to fair labour practices (which could all be potentially limited by a restraint of trade agreement) the common law rules regulating restraint agreements in employment contracts should be amended to reflect these values. She maintains that the courts could develop the common law applicable to restraint agreements in terms of section 8(3) of the Constitution. This would entail testing the common law rules pertaining to reasonableness of the restraint directly against section 22 and the other relevant rights in the Constitution. She argues that in the alternative the courts could develop the common law through the prism of public policy in terms of section 39(2) to reflect the values of the Constitution without directly testing the law of contract against a specific constitutional right. Should courts develop the common law test for reasonableness in terms of section 39(2), freedom to trade should – in the light of the value of freedom to work and the unequal bargaining position of employees – enjoy primacy instead of *pacta sunt servanda*. See K Calitz 'Restraint of Trade Agreements in Employment Contracts: Time for *Pacta Sunt Servanda* to Bow Out?' (2011) 22 *Stell LR* 50 at 69.

[51] Para 82. It is interesting to note that Kerr submits that the *Barkhuizen* case could be read to support a defence of unfair conduct on the part of the plaintiff at the time the action was brought which could amount to the defence of the *exceptio doli* in modern form (A J Kerr

In the decision of *Bredenkamp & others v Standard Bank of South Africa Ltd*[52] the Supreme Court of Appeal dealt with the right of a banker to close its client's bank accounts. The bank relied on an express contractual provision that allowed it to close its client's accounts with reasonable notice. The bank provided no reasons for the cancellations other than stating that it was done to protect the interests of the bank.[53] The client argued that the express cancellation clause was contrary to public policy since the decision to cancel a contract should be preceded by a hearing and should be based on rational or reasonable grounds. The client thus contended that the bank's decision to suspend the accounts was procedurally and substantially unfair.[54] The finding of the court was that an express cancellation clause, just like an implied cancellation clause, entitles a party unilaterally to cancel a contract without cause by giving reasonable notice. The termination did not offend any identifiable constitutional value and was not otherwise contrary to any other public policy consideration.[55]

The client accepted that the common law rule and the express terms of the contract were fair and reasonable and therefore not in conflict with any constitutional values. Their complaint was limited to the exercise of the admittedly 'fair' and valid contractual right. Their argument proceeded on the basis that the *Barkhuizen* decision stands as authority for the proposition that fairness is a core value of the Bill of Rights and that it is therefore a broad requirement of our law generally. The argument was that this would mean that any conduct (including legislation) which is unfair would be in conflict with the Constitution and, accordingly, void.[56] Harms DP said that he would be surprised if that were indeed what the court in *Barkhuizen* decided, and then sought to summarise his view on what was decided in the *Barkhuizen* case:

'The Defence of Unfair Conduct on the Part of the Plaintiff at the Time Action is Brought: The *exception doli generalis* and the *replication doli* in Modern Law' (2008) 125 *SALJ* 241 at 243–4 and 247. See also G Glover 'Lazarus in the Constitutional Court: An Exhumation of the *exception doli generalis?*' (2007) 124 *SALJ* 449 who argues that although the majority of the court in *Barkhuizen* did not use the terminology, the defence they describe would perform, in substance, exactly the same function as that once performed by the *exceptio doli generalis* and its counterpart, the *replicatio doli generalis* (at 455). The use of the 'fairness' concept led to two conflicting judgments in the provincial courts: *Breedenkamp v Standard Bank of South Africa Ltd* 2009 (5) SA 304 (GSJ) and *Breedenkamp v Standard Bank of South Africa Ltd* 2009 (6) SA 277 (GSJ). These decisions are discussed by M Nortje 'Unfair Contract Terms – Effect of Constitution' (2010) 74 *THRHR* 517 and I M Rautenbach 'Cancellation Clauses in Bank-customer Contracts and the Bill of Rights' 2010 *Tydskrif vir die Suid-Afrikaanse Reg* 637.

[52] 2010 (4) SA 468 (SCA).
[53] Later, in its answering affidavits, the bank contended that providing the banking services could affect the bank's reputation negatively and would entail business risks the bank did not wish to run because the United States Department of Treasury's Office of Foreign Control listed the client on a sanction list as special designated foreigners. See paras 12–18.
[54] Para 61.
[55] Para 64.
[56] Para 27.

'[A]s I understand the [*Barkhuizen*] judgment, if a contract is *prima facie* contrary to constitutional values, questions of enforcement would not arise. However, enforcement of a *prima facie* innocent contract may implicate an identified constitutional value. If the value is unjustifiably affected, the term will not be enforced. An example would be where a lease provides for the right to sublease with the consent of the landlord. Such a term is *prima facie* innocent. Should the landlord attempt to use it to prevent the property being sublet in circumstances amounting to discrimination under the equality clause, the term will not be enforced. . . . [I]f the value is subject to limitation, such as the right of access to courts or to practise a trade or profession, and was 'reasonably' limited within the meaning of section 36 [of the Bill of Rights], the court must assess at the time of enforcement whether the limitation is still fair and reasonable in the circumstances.'[57]

Harms DP also pointed out that our courts have always been fully prepared to reassess public policy and declare contracts invalid on that ground. Determining whether or not an agreement was contrary to public policy requires a balancing of competing values. That contractual promises should be kept is but one of the values.[58] Reasonable people, irrespective of any philosophical or political bent, might disagree whether any particular value judgment was 'correct', in the sense of 'more acceptable'.[59] The judge also said:

'Others have spoken more eloquently about the interaction between the Constitution and the common law, more particularly the law of contract, but I shall attempt to state the basics that have become trite but may not always have

---

[57] Paras 47–8. Rautenbach, note 36 supra, is of the opinion that although the Supreme Court of Appeal's account of the *Barkhuizen* decision is correct, it was somewhat more articulate in certain respects than the Constitutional Court (at 37ff). He concludes that the Supreme Court of Appeal's affirmation of the rule that reasonableness or fairness is not a general over-arching requirement for contracts and their enforcement may have a limited effect since reasonableness will in future play a role as part of a public-policy investigation within the context of the limitation of rights in contractual relations. The taking into account of the factors referred to in section 36(1)(a) to (e) of the Constitution could greatly assist the application of a reasonableness criterion in the law of contract (at 45).

[58] It is also interesting to note that Harms DP denied that *pactum sunt servanda* was a 'holy cow' (para 37). The court also dealt with Kerr's view that the *Barkhuizen* case could be read to support a defence of unfair conduct on the part of the plaintiff at the time the action was brought which could amount to the defence of the *exception doli* in modern form (see note 51 supra). The court denied that this is the case and pointed out that the majority of the court in *Bank of Lisbon*, using a historical analysis, found that the *exceptio* had not been part of our law. It was part of the Roman law of procedure and never a substantive rule, and was used to alleviate the strictness of contracts that were not based on *bona fides*. Since all contracts in our law are considered to be *bonae fidei*, the *exceptio* had no purpose in modern law. The majority also pointed out that a party is bound by a contract provided the contract is valid and untainted and that a party could not raise the *exceptio* merely because one party has exercised a right conferred by the contract (para 33).

[59] Para 38.

been observed. The common law derives its force from the Constitution and is only "valid" to the extent that it complies or is congruent with the Constitution. Every rule has to pass constitutional muster. Public policy and the *boni mores* are now deeply rooted in the Constitution and its underlying values. This does not mean that public policy values cannot be found elsewhere. A constitutional principle that tends to be overlooked when generalized resort to constitutional values is made is the principle of legality. Making rules of law discretionary or subject to value judgments may be destructive of the rule of law.'[60]

The debate on the proper role of the *pacta sunt servanda* principle, the role of the Constitution in contract, the role of good faith and fairness in contracts and sanctity of contract is an extremely important and complex one and will no doubt have a decisive impact on the future of the law of suretyship.[61] It is predicted that the debate on all these issues is far from over and that hindsight might prove them still in their infancy.[62]

17.6 THE 'REGULATION' OF 'UNFAIR SURETYSHIPS'

It is against this backdrop that we can now return to the law of suretyship. It has been pointed out that suretyships are burdensome.[63] With the rejec-

---

[60]　Para 39.
[61]　If one throws into the mixture the problems relating to misrepresentation, mistake, *error* and the so-called *caveat subscriptor* rule, it may indeed turn out to be a very interesting debate or debacle. See, e.g., C-J Pretorius 'Mistake and Suretyship: Avoiding the Spectre of *Brink v Humphries & Jewell (Pty) Ltd*' 2009 *Obiter* 763; *Hartley v Pyramid Freight (Pty) Ltd* 2007 (2) SA 599 (SCA) and the incisive review of this decision by J Barnard-Naudé 'The Decision in *Hartley v Pyramid Freight (Pty) Ltd*: Justice Miscarried?' (2007) 18 *Stell L R* 497 at 506ff and *Slip Knot v Du Toit* 2011(4) SA 72 (SCA).
[62]　D Bhana and M Pieterse 'Towards a Reconciliation of Contract Law and Constitutional Values: *Brisley* and *Afrox* Revisited' (2005) 122 *SALJ* 865 at 872ff; Brand, note 36 supra, 73ff; Brand &Brodie, note 36 supra, at 106ff; Zimmermann, note 44 supra, 221ff; L Hawthorne 'The Principle of Equality in the Law of Contract' (1995) 58 *THRHR* 157; Lewis, note 44 supra; T Naudé 'Unfair Contract Terms Legislation: The Implications of Why We Need it for its Formulation and Applications' (2006) 17 *Stell LR* 361 (an excellent article that contains a wealth of information and references); P J Sutherland 'Ensuring Contractual Fairness in Consumer Contracts after *Barkhuizen v Napier* 2007 5 SA 323 (CC)' Part I (2008) 19 *Stell LR* 390; Part II (2009) 20 *Stell LR* 50 and S Woolman 'The Amazing Vanishing Bill of Rights'(2007) 124 *SALJ* 762.
[63]　*Jans v Nedcor Bank Ltd* 2003 (6) SA 646 (SCA) para 30 at 661F. In this decision the court held that the interruption of prescription against the principal debtor also interrupts prescription against the surety. The court pointed out that '[s]ureties do not assume the obligations of others against their wills, but with their free consent. Once having done so they cannot expect to be entitled simply to disabuse their minds of the fortunes of the principal debtor's liability and then require the law to protect them against their ignorance. If prescription in favour of the principal debtor is delayed or interrupted without their knowledge, they generally have themselves to blame' (at 661F–J, para 30). In *Eley (formally Memmel) v Lynn & Main Inc* 2008 (2) SA 150 (SCA) the Supreme Court of Appeal confirmed that a claim against a surety who bound herself as surety in respect of a debt which was confirmed and reinforced

tion of the *exceptio doli generalis* as a possible defence of last resort for a surety who undertakes an intolerable burden, the surety's lot may even have become more precarious, especially in instances where the surety undertakes liability for an 'unlimited' amount. It is an economic reality today that the terms of the vast majority of deeds of suretyship are dictated to sureties by large financial institutions.[64] These deeds of suretyship are drafted with all the skilled legal advice available and, inevitably, favour the creditor in almost every respect. [65] In the light of the inherent potential inequities and disastrous consequences that may flow from standing surety for somebody else's debt, it is hardly surprising to find that throughout the ages there have been many attempts to lighten the burden of the surety.[66]

---

by a judgment against the principal debtor, prescribed after 30 years as contemplated by s 11(*a*)(ii) of the Prescription Act 68 of 1969. It is suggested that this rule could be quite harsh.

[64] The use of the so-called standard-form contract compounds the problems in this regard. See the minority judgment of Sachs J in *Barkhuizen* paras 122–4. See, however, Brand's, note 36 supra, comments in this regard at 87ff and D Hutchison and C-J Pretorius (eds) *The Law of Contract in South Africa* (Oxford University Press 2009) 24ff.

[65] Some of these contracts are extremely complicated and often very difficult to understand, especially where laypersons are involved. The decision in *Davids en andere v ABSA Bank Bpk* 2005 (3) SA 361 (C) is a good example. Here the court found that the sureties were not liable because of their justifiable mistake in believing that they were signing limited suretyships, whereas they were actually signing unlimited suretyships. In the final analysis the decision really turned on the particular facts presented to the court: we have sureties who testified that they and their spouses were present when one bank official orally conveyed to them that they were signing for R50,000 only; a bank official who did not take part in the negotiations between the parties and who was responsible for obtaining the signatures of the sureties on the document and who did not remember the specific incident four years later and who could merely testify as to what banking practice is, etc. Again, the format of the deed of suretyship also played an important role in determining whether the document induced the mistake on the part of the signatories: the first page of the document contained 1,255 words but only five sentences. The first sentence contained 370 words and the last sentence 584 words. Fourie J said that even though the sureties did not read the documents, the question may be asked whether the sureties would have understood the documents even if they had read them (at 371D-H). What is important though is the observation by the court that the bank official did not explain the contents of the contract to the sureties and that public interest demands that a complicated document of this nature has to be explained to the signatory, especially where the signing thereof could have such drastic consequences (at 371F-H, para 24). This view may have very important consequences. What about creditors who are not financial institutions, and how much 'explanation' would be required? See in this regard, for example, *Yerkey v Jones* (1939) 63 CLR 649; *Garcia v National Bank of Australia Ltd* (1998) 155 ALR 614; C Bacchi 'Do Women Need Equal Treatment or Different Treatment?' (1992) 8 *Australian Journal of Law and Society* 80; M Neave 'From Difference to Sameness-Law and Women's Work' (1992) *Melbourne University Law Review* 768; M Kaye 'Equity's Treatment of Sexually Transmitted Debt' (1997) 5 *Feminist Legal Studies* 35; M Oldham 'Neither a Lender nor a Borrower be: The Life of O'Brien' (1995) 7 *Child and Family Law Quarterly* 104; T Wright 'The Special Wives' Equity and the Struggle for Woman's Equality' (2006) 31 *Alternative Law Journal* 66 and J Pascoe 'Women Who Guarantee Company Debts: wife or Director?' (2003) 8 *Deakin Law Review* 13.

[66] The various exceptions and benefits, such as the benefit of excussion, the benefit of division

The South African law does not differentiate between different 'types' of suretyships and it does not matter in principle whether the surety undertakes liability for a close relative, his marital partner,[67] his business or even for some stranger and even against the express wishes of the stranger.[68] It is, however, true that in a significant number of foreign jurisdictions it is acknowledged that suretyships can be part of, and cause, wider social prob-

amongst co-sureties, the benefit of cession of actions, etc, that were made available to a surety since Roman times are good examples of attempts to lighten the burden of a surety. In practice most sureties usually renounce these benefits. See *Caney*, note 18 supra, at 16ff for a discussion of the history of these benefits. Women were given special protection from the normal consequences of suretyship. See E Kahn 'Farewell *Senatusconsultum Velleianum* and *Authentica si qua mulier*' (1971) 88 *SALJ* 364 and H van den Bergh 'Roman Women: Sometimes Equal and Sometimes Not' 2006 (12–2) *Fundamina* 113 for a discussion of the history of the protection afforded to women. Zimmermann, note 17 supra, points out that it has been argued that the intention of the legislation was to prevent the husband from selling land that the wife obtained in her dowry without her permission (at 148). He submits, however, that the legislation 'dealt with situations where the woman acted in the interest of somebody else; this third party was the "true" debtor, who was to be ultimately responsible for the debt incurred. Thus, the woman could easily be tempted to think of her own obligation as a mere formality which she would never be required to fulfill. Emotionally inclined to rush to somebody else's help when required to do so, acting with undue confidence in this other person's ability and readiness to honour his promise, unable, especially, to withstand the importunacy of their husbands and friends, and generally prone to be influenced by unscrupulous or well-meant but unsound advice . . . women tend to be somewhat frivolous, over-optimistic and reckless of their own interest. The danger therefore existed that they would all too readily bind themselves for others (*pro aliis fieri*), and it was this specific danger that the Senate set out to combat'.

[67] Instances where the surety undertakes liability for a marital partner have become known as 'sexually transmitted debt' and are the subject of extensive legal writing: J A Scutt 'Cash or Kind: Violence and Sexually Transmitted Debt' in A Sev'er (ed) *A Cross-Cultural Exploration of Wife Abuse: Problems and Prospects* (Mellen 1997) 145 at 152ff; B Fehlberg 'Money and Marriage: Sexually Transmitted Debt in England' (1997) 11 *International Journal of Law, Policy and the Family* 320 at 323ff; B Fehlberg *Sexually Transmitted Debt: Surety Experience and English Law* (Clarendon Press, 1997). G Gretton 'Sexually Transmitted Debt' 1999 *Tydskrif vir die Suid-Afrikaanse Reg* 419 points out at 431: 'The doctrine, we are told, applies just as much to men as to woman. But this is absurd: it is a mere figleaf. Everyone knows what is going on. Of course the doctrine is sexist. The case law is studded with remarks about how ordinary woman are incapable of managing their affairs. This is a matter of judicial knowledge. Even if a woman says that she understands a document and that she wants to sign it, it makes little difference. Woman will (it must be understood) say nothing, and what they say must not be taken seriously'. In Austria it is known as 'emotionally transmitted debt' and it reflects more on family relationships than marital relationships (W Faber 'Austria' in Ciacchi and Weatherill, note 10 supra, 45 at 52).

[68] The National Credit Act 34 of 2005 may in certain circumstances provide some protection to sureties. See P Stoop and M Kelly-Louw 'The National Credit Act regarding Suretyships and Reckless Lending' (2011) 14 *Potchefstroom Electronic Law Journal* 67 at 83ff for a discussion of the relevant provisions of the Act. A surety who stands surety against the express instructions of the principal debtor will probably be entitled to have a right of recourse against the principal debtor on the basis of the *negotiorum gestio* (*Caney*, note 18 supra, 31). See, however, N R Whitty and D van Zyl 'Unauthorized Management of Affairs (*Negotiorum Gestio*)' in Zimmermann, Visser and Reid, note 16 supra, 366 at 392ff.

lems. The scale of the loss suffered by the surety may be severe and in some extreme cases it may result in the loss of the family home. Entering into an unwise suretyship may be a mistake and can have disastrous or even ruinous consequences.[69] That is perhaps why in some of the European jurisdictions a distinction is drawn between, *inter alia*, 'consumer' and 'commercial' sure-tyships, and even 'professional' and 'non-professional' suretyships.[70] This sort of 'classification' has led to a mammoth research project by Ciacchi and Weatherill into the legal systems of the European Union in trying to find a solution for what they call 'unfair' suretyships.[71] The authors agree that:

> 'However, despite [the wide variety of suretyships], the binding thread is the accept-ance by a consumer of an obligation to cover debts in the event that they are left unmet by the principal debtor. The consumer then steps in to compensate the lender/creditor. The typical case is where the benefit is conferred by the consumer on a relative or friend or even employer in circumstances where there is no likely commercial gain in prospect for the guarantor, but rather a real risk of long-term and heavy loss. It is precisely the absence of "arm length" bargaining and cool appraisal of costs and benefits that typifies the consumer or non-commercial suretyship . . . Most prominent among the range of reasons that dictate concern of the law to inter-vene in suretyships is the anxiety that "unfairness" contaminates the agreement.'[72]

The challenge for the law is to find a feasible test for the unfairness. Cases where there has been some misrepresentation of the nature of the arrangement

[69] S Weatherill and A C Ciacchi 'Remarks from a Comparative and EU Perspective' in Ciacchi and Weatherill, note 10 supra, 27 at 28 remark that 'suretyships can be part of, and cause, wider social problems. The scale of loss suffered may be relatively severe. In extreme cases it may result in loss of the family home. Entry into an unwise suretyship may be a mistake that is simply catastrophic in its consequences. It cannot be ignored that social welfare concerns are part of the reason for exercising legal supervision of suretyship agreements. So the legal rules that are relevant are broad and not at all confined to contract law'. See also M Habersack and R Zimmermann 'Legal Change in a Codified System: Recent Developments in German Suretyship Law' (1999) 3 *EdinLR* 272 at 281ff.

[70] Weatherill and Ciacchi, note 10 supra, 27 state that suretyships 'take a number of different forms and shapes, and attract diverse legal responses. There is no "typical" suretyship. This is true in the commercial sphere and it is true in the non-commercial or consumer sphere. However, no clear demarcation between commercial and consumer suretyships exists, either in EU law or in a "common core" of the Member States' contract laws. Suretyships undertaken by consumers for commercial debts are very frequent: some (relatively few) legal systems bring them under the umbrella of consumer law; others (the majority) do not'.

[71] Ciacchi and Weatherill, note 10 supra. See also A C Ciacchi 'Non-Legislative Harmonisation: Protection from Unfair Suretyships' in S Vogenauer and S Weatherill (eds) *The Harmonisation of European Contract Law* (Hart 2006) 197 who argues: 'The whole discussion on unfair suretyships gravitates to the fundamental question of personal autonomy and freedom of contract. When someone is asked by both a beloved family member and a bank employee to sign a standard form of guarantee, her or his substantive self-determination is heavily limited. This limitation concerns both core aspects of freedom of contract: the freedom to enter of not to enter into the agreement, and the content of the latter' (at 203).

[72] Weatherill and Ciacchi, note 10 supra, 27.

between the parties are easier. We can look at the developments in Scotland as an example, and in particular at attempts to introduce a much greater degree of protection for cautioners who placed excessive trust in their principal debtors. Prior to the case of *Smith v Bank of Scotland*[73] the rule was that whilst misrepresentation on the part of the creditor would release a cautioner, the misrepresentation of the debtor, a third party to the contract, did not permit a cautioner to escape his liabilities.[74] A creditor was under an obligation to answer fully any questions asked by the cautioner and not to mislead them, but he was entitled to assume that the cautioner had made his own enquiries about the nature of the obligation he was undertaking.[75] Furthermore, the courts have always shown extreme reluctance to operate the doctrine of essential error in the context of documents that have been signed.[76] In *Smith* the House of Lords was asked to consider the position of a wife who had granted a standard security over her share of the matrimonial home to enable her husband to borrow money for his business, and who averred that she had been induced to sign as a result of the misrepresentation by her husband. It seems clear that the action would have failed under Scots law, but three years earlier in England,[77] the House of Lords had extended protection to sureties in this situation through the doctrine of constructive notice.[78] In *Smith* the House of Lords was of the view that the law in Scotland should adopt a rule

---

[73] 1997 SLT 1061. See also Eden and Pretorius, note 16 supra, 363ff.

[74] *Young v Clydesdale Bank* (1889) 17 R 231. This is still the position in South Africa. In the recent decision in *Slip Knot v Du Toit*, note 61, supra Malan JA confirmed the legal position as set out in *National and Overseas Distributors Corporation (Pty) Ltd v Potato Board* 1958 (2) SA 473 (A) where it was said: 'Our law allows a party to set up his own mistake in certain circumstances in order to escape liability under a contract into which he has entered. But where the other party has not made any misrepresentation and has not appreciated at the time of acceptance that his offer was being accepted under a misapprehension, the scope for a defence of unilateral mistake is very narrow, if it exists at all. At least the mistake (*error*) would have to be reasonable (*justus*) and it would have to be pleaded' (at 479G-H). Malan JA held that contracting party is generally not bound to inform the other party of the terms of the proposed agreement. He must do so, however, where there are terms that could not reasonably have been expected in the contract (para 12).

[75] *Royal Bank of Scotland v Greenshields* 1914 SC 259.

[76] E.g. *Royal Bank of Scotland v Purvis* 1990 SLT 262.

[77] *Barclay's Bank v O'Brien* [1994] AC 180.

[78] Broadly, where the creditor is aware that the transaction is not to the advantage of the surety, and that there is a substantial risk that the debtor has engaged in undue influence or misrepresentation, he is ascribed with knowledge of the wrong, which are sufficient grounds to release the surety. See in this regard *Barclays Bank plc v O'Brien* [1994] 1 AC 180; *Royal Bank of Scotland plc v Etridge (No 2)* [2001] 4 All ER 449; B Fehlberg 'The Husband, the Bank, the Wife and her Signature' (1994) 57 *MLR* 467 and 'The Husband, the Bank, the Wife and her Signature – the Sequel' (1996) 59 *MLR* 675; P Giliker '*Barclays Bank v O'Brien* Revisited: What a Difference Five Years Can Make' (1999) *MLR* 609; D Morris 'Wives are Told: Don't Blame the Bank, Sue Your Solicitor' (1999) 7 *Feminist Legal Studies* 193, 'Surety Wives in the House of Lords' (2003) 11 *Feminist Legal Studies* 57 and P O'Hagan 'Legal Advice and Undue Influence: Advice for Lawyers' (1996) 47 *Northern Ireland Legal Quarterly* 74.

to similar effect, but instead of using the doctrine of constructive notice, the rather wider concept of good faith was called upon. The precise content of the rule is still being worked out[79] but broadly, the requirement that the creditor should act in good faith means that where he would reasonably suspect that as a result of an intimate relationship with the debtor, the cautioner's participation might be flawed, he should advise the cautioner to take independent advice. If he does not do so, and an actionable wrong has been committed by the debtor on the cautioner, the cautioner will be released.

The requirement of obtaining independent legal advice may be an admirable one. In Scotland the Banking Code[80] previously specified that banks should recommend that the person 'gets independent legal advice to make sure that they understand their commitment and the possible consequences of their decision'.[81] It has, however, been pointed out that

'[i]ndependent advice cannot be expected to prevent vulnerable transactors from entering surety agreements where they are pressured to do so either by physical threats or by threats of economically and emotionally harmful abandonment. A vulnerable transactor might fully understand her position and the proposed

---

[79] *Braithwaite v Bank of Scotland* 1999 SLT 25; *Royal Bank of Scotland v Clark* 2000 SLT (Sh Ct) 101; *Ahmed v Clydesdale Bank* 2000; *Forsyth v Royal Bank of Scotland* 2000 SLT 1295; *Broadway v Clydesdale Bank (No 1)* 2000 GWD 19–763; *Royal Bank of Scotland v Wilson* 2001 SLT (Sh Ct) 2 and 2004 SC 153. There have been other developments in relation to the defence on the grounds of public policy, a defence which has not so far been raised in Scotland in the context of caution. See also Eden and Pretorius, note 16 supra, 364; Brand and Brodie, note 36 supra, 98ff; S Eden 'Cautionary Tales – the Continued Development of *Smith v Bank of Scotland*' (2003) 7 *EdinLR* 107 and 'More Cautionary Tales' (2004) 8 *EdinLR* 276. Forte, note 17 supra, points out at 101: '[W]e now face a simple choice of action. We can bury our heads in the sand and hope that good faith will go away, which it will not, or we can acknowledge its operation and, as Scots law has done in recent years with the principle of unjustified enrichment, make a start on a systematic analysis and statement of its application'.

[80] As quoted by Smith, note 10 supra, at 502. Smith also points out that the Scottish Solicitors Rules require that any person who undertakes a personal obligation in support of another debt to consult with an independent solicitor other than the one dealing with the obligation itself (Smith at 503).

[81] According to the Council of Mortgage Lenders' website (*http://www.cml.org.uk/cml/policy/issues/111*) the latest version of the 'Mortgage code' will require the lender to 'encourage them to take independent legal advice to make sure that they understand their commitment and the potential consequences of their decision'. In terms of the South African Banking Code the banks also undertake to 'encourage the surety to take independent legal advice to make sure that they understand the commitment and the potential consequences of such a decision. All the documents the surety will be asked to sign will contain this recommendation as a clear and prominent notice'. The banks also undertake that they will advise and caution the surety that by giving the *suretyship* or other *security* they may become liable instead of, or as well as, the client; advise the surety whether it is a limited (and the maximum value) or unlimited *suretyship* and tell them about the implications of an unlimited *suretyship*; and inform the parties of the implications of *suretyships* in terms of their periods of validity, the potential amount/s of indebtedness, the nature of the debt covered and the cancellation or termination process (clause 5.2).

transaction, recognize that it runs against her best interests, and still rationally choose to comply because of the coercive alternative. Similarly, the propensity to unreflective self-sacrifice may not yield the corporative deliberation that an independent advisor should try to provide.'[82]

One of the main problems is to find a proper balance between the interests of the creditor and that of the surety.[83] If sureties can escape liability simply on the basis that they have entered into unfair contracts creditors will be reluctant to grant credit without adequate security and may even insist on other forms of security.[84] This may in turn have serious consequences for the economy as a whole. It is true that the interests of potential creditors must also be protected. The same should apply to lenders as well. That is why there has been legislative intervention in the area of lending practices. But the wisdom of allowing an individual with little commercial experience to stand surety for an unlimited amount for an indeterminate time must also be questioned. The wisdom of allowing any individual to stand surety for an unlimited amount for an indeterminate time and an indeterminable cause of indebtedness is equally questionable.[85] But it has been pointed out that any

---

[82] M Trebilcock and S Elliot 'The Scope and Limits of Legal Paternalism' in P Benson (ed) *The Theory of Contract Law: New Essays* (Cambridge University Press 2001) 45 at 83. See also Bhana and Pieterse, note 62 supra, 868ff; O Gerstenberg 'Private Law and the New European Constitutional Settlement' (2004) 10 *European Law Journal* 766 at 784ff.

[83] See Kähler, note 20 supra, for a discussion of the factors that must be taken into account when trying to balance the interests of the parties to a loan agreement.

[84] M Kenny 'Standing Surety in Europe: Common Core or Tower of Babel?' (2007) 70 *MLR* 175 makes this point at 182: 'While the law must intervene to avoid the proliferation of disproportionate or excessive, "unfair" guarantees, it is equally necessary to protect the creditor against fraud through the transfer of assets between family members. Were suretyships too easily avoided, financial institutions would simply abandon the market, and/or increase the interest payable to compensate the risk of default, or turn to other, even less protective vehicles such as demand guarantees. Alternately, banks might simply revert to insisting on secured credit. Moreover, the poverty law paradox is that, whilst over-indebtedness is a growing problem, the effect of securing higher standards of surety protection might be to isolate the poorest in society even more comprehensively from any access to credit. In this topsy-turvy world of suretyships, the creditor is placed in an invidious position: logically, the fact that a security has been asked for should put the surety on notice that the creditor has doubts about the principal debtor's financial position; yet, instead, responsibility for both the surety's 'unwise' agreement and the principal debtor's wrongdoing is effectively attributed to the creditor. Moreover, if the creditor responds by withdrawing from the market, he can be charged with socially divisive behaviour'. See also R Zimmermann 'Contract Law Reform: The German Experience' in Vogenauer and Weatherill, note 71 supra, 71 at 81ff.

[85] In the Netherlands a contract of suretyship will be valid only if the maximum amount of the surety's potential liability is expressly stated in the contract (J W H Blomkwist *Borgtocht* B78 in *Monografieën Nieuw BW* 2e (Kluwer 1998) at 45). It is perhaps the magnitude of the cession that convinced the court in *Sasfin v Beukes* 1989 (1) SA 1 (A) that the defendant was 'virtually relegated to a slave, working for the benefit of Sasfin' (at 13H) to declare that the provisions of the deed of cession were so unfair and unreasonable that their enforcement would be

'attempt to address the "fairness" of a contract is controversial on several levels. Most of all, it represents an assault on the notion of freedom of contract in its traditional, formal sense – that parties have autonomy to enter into bargains as they see fit, to fix terms that they choose, and to expect the law to protect and enforce agreements that have been freely entered into. To use the law to alter bargains struck by private parties may, on some accounts, damage commercial confidence in the reliability of the law and thus hamper the operation of the market economy. More politically, such intervention attracts criticism for its challenge to individual freedom. And yet in the consumer sphere in particular, it has been recognized in recent decades that the notions of purity of the model of contractual freedom are not consistent with the reality of some aspects of modern market conditions. Interventionism is widely visible. But it is always contested how deeply it should reach.'[86]

17.7 CONCLUSION

It would be correct to say that in the South African law the notion that a surety's undertaking could in certain circumstances be declared 'unfair' is a topic that has received very little attention.[87] The fact that the Constitution may protect freedom of contract may in future perhaps play some role

---

contrary to public policy. See also Brand and Brodie, note 36 supra, 96ff. Standing surety for an unlimited amount for an indeterminate time reminds one of the famous American decision in *Ultramares Corporation v Touche* (1931) 255 NY 170; 174 NE 441; 74 ALR 1139 where Cardozo J raised his legendary argument against the recognition of liability for negligent misrepresentation: 'If liability for negligence exists, a thoughtless slip or blunder, the failure to detect a theft or forgery beneath the cover of deceptive entries, may expose accountants to a liability in an indeterminate amount for an indeterminate time to an indeterminate class. The hazards of a business conducted on these terms are so extreme as to enkindle doubt whether a flaw may not exist in the implication of a duty that exposes to these consequences'. In *Scott Group Ltd v McFarlane* [1978] 1 NZLR 553 (CA) at 571 Woodhouse J of the New Zealand Court of Appeal remarked with reference to the aforesaid quote from *Ultramares* that: '[s]ince then those last few words have been repeated in some judgments almost as though they reveal a self-evident truth'. But the point is that to stand surety for an unlimited amount for an indeterminate time may indeed turn out to be ruinous. It could place the surety's entire estate, let alone his livelihood, in jeopardy. It is almost like Christopher Marlowe's Faust who sold his soul to the devil in *The Tragical History of Doctor Faustus*. It is submitted that the legislature should at least consider the requirement that the surety's maximum liability should be expressly stated in the contract, especially where one is dealing with a natural person.

86 Weatherill and Ciacchi, note 10 supra, 32–3. See also A C Ciacchi 'Freedom of Contract as Freedom from Unconscionable Contracts' in M Kenny and L F O'Mahony (eds) *Unconscionability in European Private Financial Transactions: Protecting the Vulnerable* (Cambridge University Press 2010) 7 for a discussion of the concept of freedom of contract.

87 See, e.g., H L J van Rensburg *Aspects of Banker Liability: Disclosure and Other Duties of Bankers towards Customers and Sureties* (unpublished LLD thesis, University of South Africa (2001)) at 456ff.

and it may change the direction of the law of suretyship. In Germany[88] the Constitutional Court insisted that freedom of contract only existed where both parties had similar bargaining power so that both parties acted in a self-determined manner. Freedom of contract is limited or even absent where one party to a contract exploits the disadvantaged position of the other party. This would be prominent in instances where the surety undertakes liability for a relative. In such cases the weaker party must be protected by law. Today there is a comprehensive body of case law that clarifies the position with regard to family suretyships.[89] The courts have also developed rules for suretyship contracts for employees for their employers' debts and for shareholders and directors for their companies' debts. Under established court practice the courts look at the disproportionality between the amount guaranteed, and the income and property of the surety. If the amount guaranteed is grossly disproportionate to the income and property of the surety and there is a close relationship between the principal debtor and the surety, the courts recognise a rebuttable presumption of immorality in terms of § 138 paragraph 1 the German Civil Code (BGB).[90] In fact the German courts have worked out an elaborate and rather complicated system to deal with suretyships where close family members are involved, where a spouse is called upon to pay after a divorce, and recognise that even experienced persons can act unreasonably because of love and solidarity.[91] The manifest

---

[88] See Habersack and Zimmermann, note 69 supra, 275ff for a background discussion of the importance of the decision by the Federal Constitutional Court. See also P Rott 'Germany' in Ciacchi and Weatherill, note 10 supra, 253 at 256ff.

[89] Rott, note 88 supra, 258ff. Kähler, note 20 supra, points out at 342 that 'to obtain credit was far easier before the Constitutional Court introduced restrictions in 1993'.

[90] BGB § 138 para 1 declares transactions *contra bonus mores* to be void. See Zimmermann, note 17 supra, 714ff; R Zimmermann and N Jansen 'Quieta movere: Interpretative Change in a Codified System' in P Cane and J Stapleton (eds) *The Law of Obligations: Essays in Celebration of John Fleming* (Clarendon Press 1998) 285 at 295 and Brand, note 36 supra, 88. Heine and Janal, note 13 supra, point out: 'Whereas English law aims to safeguard that a close relation enters the transaction "with her eyes open", the German judicature operates with the presumption that even if the surety is fully informed of the nature of the transaction, his or her emotional bond with the principal debtor will restrict the surety in freely forming his or her intent both regarding the conclusion and the content of the contract' (at 20). Ciacchi, note 71 supra, points out: 'In German law, the norm explicitly applied to unfair suretyship cases is the nullity of immoral contracts . . . However, according to a consolidated German jurisprudence, if there is a "gross imbalance" between the amount of the debt and the surety's financial means, and the surety is a close family member of the debtor who does not have an economic interest in the suretyship, it may be presumed that the bank has taken unfair advantage from the surety's lack of experience of affection for the debtor. In other words: grossly disproportionate family relationships are presumed to be immoral' (at 202).

[91] Rott, note 88 supra, 266ff gives a detailed discussion of the German law and it is not necessary to repeat it here. The author makes the following assessment of the overall protection of a surety in German law: 'Overall, the level is unsatisfactory. The case law on immorality has not decreased the frequency of guarantee contracts in practice. The sheer amount of case law, even of the highest instance court, the BGH is more than telling. However, there appears

disproportionality is the main criterion of the immorality of guarantees, although it is as such insufficient to make the guarantee immoral. It must be accompanied by a close emotional relationship or additional circumstances usually contained within the special circumstances of the conclusion of the contract.[92] Brand points out that the further development of public policy as an instrument in the law of contract will require greater awareness and imagination on the part of practitioners. The use of the concept of 'public policy' may also require greater activism and ingenuity on the part of the judiciary than they have hitherto displayed. Perhaps Brand[93] is correct when he states:

> 'If we have learned anything from what happened in the past in South African courts, it is this: imprecise and nebulous statements about the role of good faith, fairness and equity, which would permit idiosyncratic decision-making on the basis of what a particular judge regards as fair and equitable, are dangerous. They lead to uncertainty and a dramatic increase in often pointless litigation and unnecessary appeals. Palm-tree justice cannot serve as a substitute for the established principles of contract law.'

The question as to whether women, or for that matter, certain 'classes' of sureties should be afforded separate or special protection is one that may still occupy the attention of the courts, the law-makers and even the lawyers for years to come.[94] However, it has been said that

> 'antidotes against unfair suretyships are often developed by the courts, not the legislature. While the motives of these judges may be highly beneficial, they are often forced to act upon an insufficient basis of economic and social facts. The resulting decisions are formally legitimized by the rule of law, but they are not held to be efficient in an economic sense (welfare economics) or legitimized by a social

---

to have been a shift to guarantees involving a fixed amount. These appear, at first glance, less controversial and more appropriate and proportionate. Even then, however, banks included standard terms in their contract under which the fixed maximum could be increased by arrears. As recently as 2002, the BGH held standard terms that allowed an increase beyond the agreed maximum amount to be unfair and therefore invalid. But even the fixed amount guarantees that are now requested have frequently been far beyond the guarantors' financial resources' (at 274–5). See also Habersack and Zimmermann, note 69 supra, 275ff; Brand, note 36 supra, 88–90; A C Ciacchi 'Non-Legislative Harmonisation of Private Law under the European Constitution: The Case of Unfair Suretyships' (2005) 3 *European Review of Private Law* 285 at 297ff and Ciacchi, note 71 supra, at 201ff; Kenny, note 84 supra, 184ff.

[92] Rott, note 88 supra, 266. Heine and Janal, note 13 supra, ask: 'When should a debt be considered blatantly disproportionate with respect to the surety's financial means and prospects? The German courts draw the line of demarcation as follows: the debt is considered blatantly disproportionately if that part of the surety's income which is not subject to distress is insufficient to cover the monthly interest rate. The assessment is based on a forecast of the surety's prospective income made at the conclusion of the contract and based upon the surety's skills, training and family commitments' (at 19–20).

[93] Brand, note 36 supra, at 89–90.

[94] Pretorius, note 44 supra, at 166ff.

contract (constitutional economics). Therefore, legions of legal scholars, philosophers, and social scientists are engaged in the pressing question of how paternalistic actions might be legitimized by the preferences of a society's individuals.'[95]

It is submitted that the legislature should at least consider the requirement that the surety's maximum liability should be expressly stated in the contract of suretyship, especially where one is dealing with a natural person who is standing surety for someone else's indebtedness. Standing surety for an unlimited amount and for an indeterminate time and for an indeterminable indebtedness is immoral and should not be allowed.[96] This may be a small first step in an effort to alleviate some of the harshness in the law of suretyship.

[95] Heine and Janal, note 13 supra, at 25.
[96] A similar requirement may also benefit Scots law. See Eden and Clark, note 17 supra, para 914.

Chapter 18

The Human Right of Property in Land Law: Comparing South Africa and Scotland

David Carey Miller

18.1 INTRODUCTION; COVERAGE, SCOPE

Both versions of the human right of property with which we are concerned encompass a conceptual starting point in a commitment to the principle that property rights should be protected, but the functional substance of both is primarily concerned with exceptions which limit this principle. The limitation part, open to development and potentially contentious, defines the right to property and provides for the issue of possible compensation in any particular case.

The most important subject of the protection of property, in both jurisdictions and universally is, of course, land. This is not only because of its significance as an asset but also, and probably primarily, because the need for control and limitation of rights in land is pervasive in the context of the obvious relationship between people and land in any socio-political state.

The trite point of the significance of land in socio-economic and hence political terms need hardly be urged in South Africa but it is also true in Scotland. The private international law of almost all legal systems applies the *lex situs* rule where the issue concerns land, for the obvious reason that the domestic law must apply to what is the very substance of the nation.

Land reform in South Africa has led, in less than 20 years, to a vast development and literature; in Scotland, by coincidence, in a slightly shorter timescale, there has also been significant development, but, of course, one different in character from that in South Africa. Any attempt to cover the substance of the respective developments and their impact on private law is well beyond the limits of this chapter, which will seek only to substantiate the 'different in kind' point. More specifically, selected aspects of the position in the two jurisdictions will be considered in illustration of the dominant *lex situs* thinking, applying to the exclusion of anything reflecting a relevant development of universal human rights norms.

Following some initial points concerning the comparison, the chapter will attempt a concise description of the controlling approaches to the respective property clauses. This will be followed by comment regarding the notion that the established institution of positive (or acquisitive) prescription is a deprivation of property which should be protected against. Following this, public access to private land will be considered as an illustration of very different policy considerations driving the respective land rights' positions. Here the main focus will be on a Scottish post-devolution land reform measure which seems to reflect a limitation of ownership rights as the human right rather than any notion of the protection of the human right of property. In a final substantive point decisions representing apparent affinity in the common issue of a limitation of rights pending actual determination will be compared to illustrate the different agenda factor.

The chapter will try to provide an answer to one of the central questions posed by this book, namely, how the human right protecting property has impacted on private law in the two jurisdictions. Constraining limits necessarily preclude any systematic comparison. The approach will be a selective coverage of material seen to be relevant, with comment seeking illumination of the position. Of course, as already said, in both states the significant development has been in limitations on the right of property which have been possible because the express protection of property comes subject to differing prescriptions as to permissible inroads into the right.

The chapter will contend that while both systems reflect positions brought about by imposing a re-defined basis of property rights upon a system in which the rights structure has developed historically, the end result between the two is very different.

This will lead to a concluding question. Is it rationally possible to compare the effectiveness of the totally different land reform agendas of Scotland and South Africa over the immediate past period? Can we learn anything from the apparent success of the radical but limited Scottish reforms as compared to the slow progress in South Africa of comprehensive land reform, with far-reaching implications, widely considered to be crucial to future national stability?

It emerges from this comparison that a case can be made for a revised approach to the human right of property. Rather than a human right to the individual exclusive holding of land, a starting point in a human right framed in terms of a general public right to reasonable access to and sharing as a possible limitation against the protection of the right of property is perhaps called for.

18.2 SOME INITIAL POINTS

In the context of a remarkably active post-apartheid era of comparison of South African and Scottish private law, coverage of land law has been conspicuously limited.[1] A possible explanation is the factor of different systems

---

[1] See R Zimmermann, D Visser and K Reid (eds) *Mixed Legal Systems in Comparative Perspective: Property and Obligations in Scotland and South Africa* (Oxford 2004).

of conveyancing[2] which was, especially in Scotland, the dominant discourse in land law until relatively recently. This contribution will contend that comparison from the perspective of the human right of property theme has little to offer compared with the many common law matters in which fruitful comparison is possible.

An obvious and major problem is that we are not comparing 'like with like' because in South Africa the human right of property derives from the specifically controlling domestic constitution with a powerful policy agenda, whereas in Scotland an international convention, the European Convention on Human Rights (ECHR) is directed to broad standards which leave room for considerable variation in domestic policy position provided general criteria of 'process' are met. If the controlling *grundnorms* are different in their respective focus, what prospect is there for sufficient affinity to provide a basis for meaningful comparison?

This point is supported in comments in a Cape High Court decision regarding the use of European Court of Human Rights (EctHR) case law in interpreting the South African Constitution. In *Victoria & Alfred Waterfront v Police Commissioner, W Cape*[3] Desai J, concerned with the public access to private property issue considered below,[4] indicated the need for caution in the use of a decision of the ECtHR[5] as a precedent in a South African case because the ECtHR is 'an international court'. Desai J went on to say: 'When it applies the convention to a concrete case in order to decide whether there has been a violation, it allows a "margin of appreciation" to national authorities. What this amounts to is giving a certain amount of deference or leeway to the decision of the domestic body'.[6]

The fact that ECtHR case law is not infrequently influential in South African Constitutional Court decisions is more to do with the approach of that court[7] than an indication of affinity in any substantive sense. Professors Kenneth Reid and CG van der Merwe, observing that the South African court has drawn on ECtHR jurisprudence, go on to note that, '[i]n one important respect, however, the clauses are utterly unlike'.[8] This is a reference to the pervasive land reform agenda aspect of the South African Constitution which the learned writers go on to identify.

---

[2] See K Reid and C G van der Merwe 'Property Law: Some Themes and Some Variations' in Zimmermann, Visser and Reid *Mixed Legal Systems*, note 1 supra, 645–6.

[3] 2004 (4) SA 444 (C) 450.

[4] See section 18.5, note 69 infra.

[5] *Landvreugd v Netherlands* 36 EHRR 56.

[6] *Victoria & Alfred Waterfront*, note 3 supra, at 450.

[7] S 39(1)(c) of the South African Constitution enjoins courts to consider foreign jurisprudence; see D L Carey Miller 'The Great Trek to Human Rights: the Role of Comparative Law in the Development of Human Rights in Post-reform South Africa' in E Örücü (ed) *Judicial Comparativism in Human Rights Cases* (UKNCCL 2003) 201, 202.

[8] See Reid and van der Merwe, note 2 supra, 648.

But while possible South African/Scottish comparison may seem to lack potential, we should note that the South African/German comparison on this subject works well.[9] That comparison, of course, involves two nation state constitutions rather than one such and a convention interpreted to accommodate a range of different national positions.

A feature in common is that in both systems the new human rights norms came to be superimposed over existing norms, largely common law but also policy-driven statutory provisions (as in prescription, on which more later). But, as indicated in the previous point, the position appears to be one of different outcomes arrived at by distinct means.

On this affinity issue, we may note the pertinent comment of Ackermann J in the leading judicial interpretation of the South African property clause in a decision of the Constitutional Court in 2002, referred to in this contribution, as it is in South African writings, as the 'FNB case'.[10] Following an examination of a range of relevant foreign law the judge commented in some detail:

> 'The formulation of property rights and their institutional framework differ, often widely, from legal system to system. Comparative law cannot, by simplistic transference, determine the proper approach to our property clause that has its own context, formulation and history. Yet the comparative perspective does demonstrate at least two important principles. The first is that there are appropriate circumstances where it is permissible for legislation, in the broader public interest, to deprive persons of property without payment of compensation.
>
> The second is that for the validity of such deprivation, there must be an appropriate relationship between means and ends, between the sacrifice the individual is asked to make and the public purpose this is intended to serve. It is one that is not limited to an enquiry into mere rationality, but is less strict than a full and exacting proportionality examination. . . It matters not whether one labels such an approach an "extended rationality" test or a "restricted proportionality" test. Nor does it matter that the relationship between means and ends is labelled "a reasonably proportional" consequence, or "roughly proportional", or "appropriate and adapted" or whether the consequence is called "reasonable" or "a fair balance between the public interest served and the property interest affected".'[11]

This dictum states a clear position. Its starting point is that the role of comparative law is a limited one in the context of widely differing positions regarding the formulation of property rights within particular institutional

---

[9] This is demonstrated in a highly relevant work; see H Mostert *The Constitutional Protection and Regulation of Property and its Influence on the Reform of Private Law and Landownership in South Africa and Germany* (Springer 2002) esp 30–43.

[10] *First National Bank of SA Limited t/a Wesbank v Commissioner for the South African Revenue Services and Another; First National Bank of SA Limited t/a Wesbank v Minister of Finance* 2002 (4) SA 768 (CC).

[11] At paras 97–8.

frameworks. But in two respects a role for comparative law is recognised. First, by way of confirmation that in principle, in appropriate circumstances, there may be legislation 'in the broader public interest' causing a deprivation of property but without producing an obligation to make compensation for the loss. Secondly, comparative law is seen to have a role in demonstrating that proportionality is a universal prerequisite in the sense that 'there must be an appropriate relationship between means and ends, between the sacrifice the individual is asked to make and the public purpose this is intended to serve'.

The first proposition is uncontroversial because in developed society the ownership of most forms of property is subject to general controls or limits which apply to all owners. The issue of compensation does not arise because all property of the type concerned is affected and there is therefore no relative loss of value. On this basis legislation which, in the perceived public interest, limits an owner's rights in all or particular types or classes of, for example, motor vehicles, firearms or land is not a deprivation of property which warrants compensation.

The second proposition is a radical one because it seems to suggest that there is some universal controlling mechanism regulating the balance factor in the context of deprivations in the public interest which affect property rights. Clearly there is in the European context where there is allegiance to a common constitutional position in the ECtHR. Indeed, Judge Ackerman's second proposition could be taken to define the minimal conformity requirement, with its emphasis on fair process and proportionality with limited regard to substance, which the European jurisprudence has come to recognise.[12]

Beyond a possible prerequisite that balancing be addressed, it is difficult to see how there could be any universal criterion of means and ends balancing the 'sacrifice the individual is asked to make and the public purpose this is intended to serve'. The notion of some universal controlling position that operated to set a bar, let us say, limiting the priority of the public interest in the national constitution, is not tenable. In the following section it will be contended that the South African Constitution itself opts for a balance giving priority to land reform.

18.3 THE PROVISIONS AND THEIR INTERPRETATION

This chapter will not consider in any depth or detail the development of the jurisprudence which defines the respective bases of the protection of property and its limits. The relevant domestic literature does this. Rather, the approach will be to attempt to identify the essential features with a view to the question of scope for comparison which the chapter raises. This

---

[12] See section 18.3.1 infra.

treatment will attempt to present a concise overview of the position arrived at in interpretation of the relevant provisions of the ECHR and the South African Constitution. An unequal position – in terms of significance of human rights to property – between the two jurisdictions means that more needs to be said about South Africa with particular attention to the critical *FNB* case[13] and the question of what it actually says by way of interpretation of the South African position. The more straightforward Scottish position will be dealt with first.

18.3.1 Scotland

The ECHR article 1 of the First Protocol is the basis of the human right of property in the jurisdictions bound by it. Although the text is open to criticism for its incoherence,[14] its interpretation is settled. The provision is taken to involve three distinct elements. The (i) principle protecting the peaceful enjoyment of property is (ii) given effect to on the basis that no one shall be deprived unless this is in the public interest and proceeded with in accordance with the law but (iii) without limiting the state's right to enforce laws necessary to control the use of property in the general interest or for fiscal purposes.[15] Inherent in this structure is the recognition of a critical distinction between the public interest expropriation of particular property subject to compensation and the policy-justified control of the use of certain forms of property which may affect a class of possessors but is 'the same for everyone'.

Going a stage further in terms of controlling specifics, a definitive text adopts the position that the critical issue, whether the interference with property is an expropriation (formal or *de facto*) or a mere control of use, is that it must meet three tests of (i) legal certainty (namely, clarity in the sense of being specific and unambiguous), (ii) being justified by the general or public interest and (iii) achieving reasonable proportionality between means used and ends sought to ensure a fair balance between individual and general interests.[16]

Judge Ackermann's *FNB* case interpretation of the ECtHR's case law as it explains the provisions of article 1 of the First Protocol is as good as any in terms of clarity and, of course, appropriate to the present context because the perspective is a comparative one:

---

[13] Note 10 supra.

[14] See G L Gretton 'The Protection of Property Rights' in A Boyle, C Himsworth, A Loux and H MacQueen (eds) *Human Rights and Scots Law* (Hart 2002) 275: 'the conceptual incoherence in which this aspect of the ECHR is bogged down'.

[15] See e.g. *Sporrong & Lonnroth v Sweden* (1983) 5 EHRR 35; *James v UK* (1986) 8 EHRR 116.

[16] See now *AXA General Insurance Ltd v Lord Advocate* [2011] UKSC 46 paras 20–28 (Lord Hope) and 107–134 (Lord Reed) and generally R Reed and J Murdoch *A Guide to Human Rights Law in Scotland* 3e (Tottel 2012) para 8.21.

'These three sentences have come to be referred to as the first, second and third "rules" respectively. The first rule has come to be regarded as an institutional property guarantee. The second rule, despite the use of the word "deprived" has come to be identified with the state's power to expropriate and the third rule with the state's police power to regulate, or as a deprivation clause. Under the third rule dispossessions without compensation have been held to be lawful in cases where heavy property taxes have been imposed; exchange control impositions have been levied; compulsory contributions to a state pension scheme levied; fines imposed for a criminal offence, and smuggled goods forfeited; and property involved in a criminal act forfeited.'[17]

Probably the most important aspect of the ECHR protection of property regime for present purposes is its focus on 'process fairness' and concomitant neutrality in terms of the substance of limitations which affect rights in land in the separate nation states of Europe. The 'proportionality' requirement operates as an agent demanding only compliance with abstract criteria and leaving states free to give effect to domestic policy in controlling the actual use of land. A continuation of the opinion in the *FNB* case explains this position:

'Under the Convention a proportionality analysis has been developed in order to determine whether a deprivation of property is lawful or not. The regulatory measure must comply with a municipal law (be lawful), be in the public interest and establish a fair balance between the public interest served and the property interest affected. As to what is necessary in the public interest, that is left to the State as they are seen to be the best judges on this, but still there must be a purpose. The states are given a wide margin of appreciation in this regard.'[18]

The last two sentences are significant. On this basis the *lex situs* position is alive and well but does a 'loose' constitutional provision, functioning for an alliance of sovereign states, have any possible utility in the interpretation of an individual state constitution drawn with the particular objective of providing a revised property regime consistent with the reformed state's aspirations?

18.3.2 South Africa

In the last decade of the twentieth century the interim[19] and final[20] constitutions of an internally liberated South Africa were critical aspects of the transition from apartheid to democracy. The final constitution is the blueprint

---

[17] *FNB*, note 10 supra, at para 85.
[18] *FNB*, note 10 supra, at para 86.
[19] Constitution of the Republic of South Africa 200 of 1993.
[20] Constitution of the Republic of South Africa 1996.

for the ongoing reform process.[21] The different legal language of the interim and final formulations reflects an intense debate involving the conflicting aspirations of land reform and the protection of property.[22] In stark terms the position reflected the long-standing claim of the overwhelming majority of the population to a fair share of the land against vested interests established by a ruling minority in a development that commenced when the first European settlers arrived in South Africa in the mid-seventeenth century.[23]

The property clause of the South African Constitution reflects the constitution in general in its radical agenda. The price of the peaceful early 1990s transition could never have been any less than a reforming constitution. Noting the 'empowered' South African Constitution's departure from the American liberal model, Professor Gregory Alexander sees it as 'an ongoing attempt to transform society'.[24] In the first systematic analysis of the 1996 property clause, published in 1997, Professor A J van der Walt noted that it was 'clear from the property clause itself that the property guarantee should not impede land reform' and continued to observe that this was 'stated in so many words in section 25(8)'.[25] But most significant of all is a dictum of Ackermann J in the leading decision on the interpretation of the property clause, already referred to. Although the matter in hand had no connection to land reform, the learned judge commented as follows:

'The subsections which have specifically to be interpreted in the present case must not be construed in isolation, but in the context of the other provisions of section 25 and their historical context, and indeed in the context of the Constitution as a whole. Subsections (4) to (9)[26] all, in one way or another, underline the need for and aim at redressing one of the most enduring legacies of racial discrimination in the past, namely the grossly unequal distribution of land in South Africa. The details of these provisions are not directly relevant to the present case, but ought to be borne in mind whenever section 25 is being construed, because they emphasise that under the 1996 Constitution the protection of property as an individual right is not absolute but subject to societal considerations.'[27]

---

[21] Regarding the drafting of the property clause see C Savage 'Negotiating South Africa's New Constitution: an Overview of the Key Players and Negotiation Process' in P Andrews and S Ellmann (eds) *The Post-Apartheid Constitutions* (Witwatersrand University Press/Ohio University Press 2001) 176–81.

[22] See A J van der Walt *The Constitutional Property Clause* (Juta 1997) 2–3.

[23] See chapter 1 ('The Development of Discriminatory Landholding') in D L Carey Miller with A Pope *Land Title in South Africa* (Juta 2000) 1–42.

[24] G S Alexander *The Global Debate over Constitutional Property* (Chicago University Press 2006) 151.

[25] Van der Walt, note 22 supra, 149.

[26] Referring to s 25 – the property clause.

[27] *FNB*, note 10 supra, para 49.

Alexander makes the point that the property clause 'guarantees property as an individual right but not as an institution'[28] and, as he shows, the potential empowerment of public over private law in fulfilment of the constitutional promise 'to bring about equitable access to all South Africa's natural resources'[29] makes this an inevitable position.

Adopting a passage from Professor van der Walt's work on the property clause, the Constitutional Court opinion in the *FBN* case[30] emphasises the significance of the constitutional mandate for social justice in South Africa.

> 'The preamble to the Constitution indicates that one of the purposes of its adoption was to establish a society based, not only on "democratic values" and "fundamental human rights" but also on "social justice". Moreover the Bill of Rights places positive obligations on the state in regard to various social and economic rights. Van der Walt (1997) aptly explains the tension that exists within section 25: "[T]he meaning of section 25 has to be determined, in each specific case, within an interpretative framework that takes due cognisance of the inevitable tensions which characterize the operation of the property clause. This tension between individual rights and social responsibilities has to be the guiding principle in terms of which the section is analysed, interpreted and applied in every individual case."'[31]

A subsequent reference to Professor van der Walt clarifies beyond any doubt that a consequence of giving effect to the Constitution's social imperatives involves a departure from the ethos of private law concerning property:[32]

> 'When considering the purpose and content of the property clause it is necessary, as van der Walt (1997) puts it – ". . . to move away from a static, typically private-law conceptualist view of the constitution as a guarantee of the status quo to a dynamic, typically public-law view of the constitution as an instrument for social change and transformation under the auspices [and I would add "and control"] of entrenched constitutional values."'[33]
>
> That property should also serve the public good is an idea by no means foreign to pre-constitutional property concepts.'

The South African property clause makes the natural distinction between limitation of use and expropriation; regardless of the terminology applied, the distinction is between, on the one hand, limitations which leave the property with its possessor but in some way curtails the use, enjoyment or exclusivity, and, on the other, expropriation or compulsory purchase.[34] The

---

[28] Alexander, note 24 supra, 160.
[29] Ibid.
[30] *FNB*, note 10 supra, para 50.
[31] Van der Walt, note 22 supra, 15–16.
[32] *FNB*, note 10 supra, para 52.
[33] Van der Walt, note 22 supra, 11.
[34] Van der Walt, note 22 supra, 101. The writer's statement that '"deprivation" is distinguished

FBN decision puts the emphasis upon arbitrariness as the basis for denying the constitutionality of a law of general application that provides for a deprivation of property. A law is arbitrary either because there is not a 'sufficient reason for the particular deprivation in question' or it is 'procedurally unfair'.[35] The latter requirement is to do with the prerequisites of process and form established in administrative law.[36] Meeting the 'sufficient reason' test is more complex and a six-stage test is prescribed in *FBN*.[37] Commentators argue, however, that the primary and key aspect of the court's analysis is in fact the 'arbitrary' factor. Professor Theunis Roux notes 'the way in which the court's test for arbitrary deprivation swallows up the other stages of the constitutional property clause inquiry'.[38] Agreeing, Professor Gregory Alexander sees the essential question as 'whether the challenged statute effects an arbitrary deprivation of property'.[39] These views seem to be supported by the final proposition of the six-point approach – 'always bearing in mind that the enquiry is concerned with "arbitrary"'.[40]

Fixing the threshold in relation to the constitutionality issue at the minimal position of an arbitrary deprivation seems justifiable on the basis of the apparently controlling phrase in section 25(1), 'no law may permit arbitrary deprivation of property', the first and foundational part of the property clause. The other obvious point is that a relatively weak protection of property is consistent with the facilitation of land reform to which the South African Constitution commits itself.[41] But this 'overriding position' point – compelling to the present writer – is weakened by the approach, prevalent but perhaps not prevailing, which presents the general position as to permissible deprivation as separate from the land reform agenda.[42]

18.4 ACQUISITIVE PRESCRIPTION AS A DEPRIVATION?

The English case of *Pye v Graham*[43] was concerned with the question whether the system's 'adverse possession' form of positive (or acquisitive) prescrip-

---

very clearly from the narrower term "expropriation" in constitutional jurisprudence worldwide' was adopted by Ackermann J in *FBN*, note 10 supra, para 57.

[35] *FNB*, note 10 supra, para 100.

[36] See I Currie and J De Waal *The Bill of Rights Handbook* 5e (Juta 2005) 544.

[37] *FNB*, note 10 supra, para 100.

[38] 'The "Arbitrary Deprivation" Vortex: Constitutional Property Law after FBN' in S Woolman and M Bishop (eds) *Constitutional Conversations* (Pretoria University Law Press 2008) 265.

[39] Alexander, note 24 supra, 162.

[40] *FNB*, note 10 supra, para 100.

[41] But see Currie and De Waal, note 36 supra, 542–3, seeing the arbitrary criterion as a relatively rigorous position.

[42] P J Badenhorst, J M Pienaar and H Mostert, *Silberberg and Schoeman's Law of Property* 5e (LexisNexis Butterworth 2006) 521: 'a two-pronged mechanism'.

[43] [2000] 3 WLR 242.

tion could amount to a deprivation.[44] Property development company Pye, over a period, granted to neighbouring farmer Graham grazing rights over unimproved land that it held for possible development. When Pye did not renew the grant, Graham continued to graze his stock regardless. Pye eventually sought to recover possession and the issue arose of Graham's possible acquisition on the basis of adverse possession for more than twelve years under the Limitation Act of 1980. Despite the apparent position of the assertion of no more than a grazing right, the trial court found for Graham on the basis that his position in wanting renewal was consistent with the required intention to possess. The Court of Appeal reversed[45] but the House of Lords[46] restored the original decision. In the Lords it was relevant that Pye's loss on the basis of adverse possession occurred before the coming into force of the Human Rights Act 1998 which fully implemented the Convention.

Pye took the UK government to the ECtHR arguing that there had been deprivation without compensation under the Limitation Act. By a three-to-four majority the court found Pye's loss to be an expropriation, disproportionate in the absence of compensation and, accordingly, a contravention of the right to property.[47] The UK government appealed to the Grand Chamber, which reversed the lower Strasbourg court by ten to seven.[48] How this decision was arrived at is not easy to understand.[49] However, an essential aspect was the majority position that the matter was not a deprivation but a regulation of the use of property, which maintained the balance between public interest and individual right.

In a work of general relevance to the present topic, Professor A J van der Walt considers the *Pye* case in a discussion of the question of acquisitive prescription, viewed from the perspective of the protection of property. A concluding observation, relevant to South Africa can be quoted:[50]

> 'it could be efficient and normatively legitimate to allow destitute, landless and homeless squatters to benefit from prescription practice, particularly if certain doctrinal requirements are introduced to ensure that they concentrate on disused land and document their intent by possessing the land openly and by making non-trivial and permanent improvements on the land.'

This is consistent with recognition that domestic priority should be controlling. It could also be suggested that this idea would contribute to moving

---

[44] For a valuable overview from an English law perspective see E Cooke *Land Law* (Oxford 2006) 212–15.
[45] [2001] 2 WLR 1293.
[46] [2003] 1 AC 419 (HL).
[47] (2006) 43 EHRR 3 para 75.
[48] (2008) 46 EHRR 45.
[49] G L Gretton 'Private Law and Human Rights' (2008) 12 *EdinLR* 109 at 111: 'a great and puzzling change of approach'.
[50] *Property in the Margins* (Hart 2009) 188.

the 'human right' of property, in the land context, towards the community and away from the individual interest – an approach that, it is suggested, has much to commend it.

A difficulty in any general notion that acquisitive prescription is a deprivation of property is the range of different applications of the concept. Even between the mixed systems of South Africa and Scotland, with so much in common in their private law, the respective systems of acquisitive and positive prescription applying to land are very different.[51] In Scotland it was structural until the advent of land registration in 1979; even under registration prescription has a potentially important role where title is not guaranteed. As David Johnston has observed in a comment on *Pye*, in Scotland 'it continues to make sense to insist that prescription serves the public interest'.[52] In South Africa the role of acquisitive prescription is marginal but, arguably, one that has served true human right interests in allowing the acquisition of land on the basis of possession 'as owner' for 30 years against the formal interests of a title holder, absent and frequently unknown. The practice of appointment of a *curator ad litem* to represent the interests of an absent owner[53] supports a perception of acquisitive prescription as a concept concerned with just and fair entitlement to land rights possibly trumping formal ownership.

The perception of positive prescription as a contravention of the human right to property reflects a problem brought about by imposing a re-defined basis of property rights upon a system in which the rights structure has developed historically. There has been no challenge to the role of prescription in Scotland; if one did occur, the structure factor would be a powerful counter-argument. In South Africa, with its revised property rights agenda controlling, a revision of the role and application of prescription would be no more than a technical problem.

18.5 PUBLIC ACCESS TO PRIVATE LAND

The controversial issue of public access to private land exemplifies the difference between the two systems in land rights law and policy. In Scotland Part 1 of the Land Reform (Scotland) Act 2003 ('the Act') provides for a general public right of responsible access to private land for certain limited purposes. This radical land reform measure, in its careful balancing of rights and responsibilities, has all the appearance of being written to be ECHR-

---

[51] See D L Carey Miller 'Three of a Kind?: Positive Prescription in Sri Lanka, South Africa and Scotland' (2008) 19 *Stell LR* 209 at 228: 'diversity of domestic land law systems means diversity of prescription provision'.

[52] See '*J A Pye (Oxford) Limited v United Kingdom*: Deprivation of Property Rights and Prescription' (2006) 10 *EdinLR* 277 at 281; D Johnston *Prescription and Limitation* 2e (W Green 2012) para 16.19.

[53] See D L Carey Miller *The Acquisition and Protection of Ownership* (Juta 1986) 98–9.

compliant. The extensive right introduced in this development has attracted international attention.[54] But in its contrast with what might be contemplated in South Africa, is it another illustration of the inherent domesticity of land rights? The position reflected in a South African decision concerned with public access would seem to support this.

The Scottish legislation provides, first, a right of access to all land and inland waterways for recreational or educational purposes and for any commercial purposes involving an activity that is not inherently profit-driven[55] (for example, access by a paid walking-tour guide) and, secondly, the 'right to cross land'.[56] The recreational, educational or potentially commercial aspect is stated to refer to 'going into, passing over and remaining on it [i.e. the land] for any of those purposes and then leaving it, or any combination of those'.[57] The crossing aspect refers to 'going into it, passing over it and leaving it all for the purpose of getting from one place outside the land to another such place'.[58]

Importantly, the right, in both its aspects, is subject to a general exclusion and a limited category of particular exclusions. The general requirement of 'responsible exercise' applies in every instance of the right's availability. This important limitation of the right has a correlative in the landowner's obligation – broadly stated – to co-operate with the system as managed by the local authority. By reason of its generality, the responsible conduct limit is the most significant qualification of the right. But certain specific limits – for example, providing for dwelling house privacy – are also relevant to the quite complex definition of the right.

The significance of the 'responsible exercise' qualification of the right was recognised in the, thus far, only Court of Session decision on the statutory right of access.[59] The focus on appeal was the issue of a landowner's reciprocal obligation to use and manage the land in a responsible manner but, of course, the court needed to interpret the controlling legislative provisions. In the opinion delivered by Lord Eassie, the critical responsibility factor is explained:[60]

'It is evident from these provisions – and appeared to be recognised by counsel on both sides – that the notion of acting "responsibly" plays an important part in the scheme of the legislation. Thus a person taking access to land has no right of access

---

[54] For a comprehensive treatment see J A Lovett 'Progressive Property In Action: The Land Reform (Scotland) Act 2003' (2011) 89 *Neb L Rev* 739; D L Carey Miller 'Public Access to Private Land in Scotland' [2012] PER 19 (at www.nwu.ac.za/af/webfm_send/58100).

[55] S 1(2)(a) & 1(3)(a)(b)&(c).

[56] S 1(2)(b)

[57] S 1(4)(a)(i)&(ii).

[58] S 1(4)(b).

[59] *Tuley v Highland Council* 2009 SLT 616. For an analysis of the decision see M M Combe 'Access to Land and to Landownership' (2010) 14 *EdinLR*, 106 at 107–9.

[60] *Tuley*, supra note 59, at para 17.

if he is not acting "responsibly" (section 2(1)). An attempt to add some precision to the broad concept of "responsible exercise" is to be found in section 2(3). The access-taker is also presumed, subject to certain qualifications, to be exercising access rights responsibly if those rights are exercised so as not to cause unreasonable interference with the rights of any other person (section 2(2)).'

This authoritative interpretation of the core 'responsible exercise' criterion is significant in confirming that the right is denied to an access-taker not acting responsibly. Presenting the proposition in the negative is an acknowledgement of the inherent position of a circumscribed right.

The first decision on the critical issue of the scope of the right of access, in terms of a tension with the privacy of a landowner's domestic sphere, was in *Gloag v Perth & Kinross Council and the Ramblers' Association.*[61] This matter was concerned with Kinfauns Castle near Perth, the residence of bus tycoon Ann Gloag. In issue was access to 4.45 hectares of land, the enclosed grounds of a mansion house with a floor area of almost 0.5 of a hectare. Sheriff Fletcher took the view that 'the landowner is entitled to sufficient land to be excluded *to ensure*[62] that their enjoyment of the house is not unreasonably disturbed'.[63] In the scheme of the Act, land within the zone of the privacy exclusion is land over which access rights are not exercisable. This is made clear in section 1 which establishes the right: 'land in respect of which access rights are exercisable is all land except that specified in or under section 6 below'.[64]

In view of the ECHR scope for the limitation of land rights in the public or general interest and the margin of appreciation,[65] it seems likely that this far-reaching Scottish provision complies with the Convention. This issue has been addressed in respect of the English access provision:[66]

'The 2000 English Act[67] defines public access to access land fairly widely but imposes strict limits on it. Because the Act explicitly establishes a fair balance between public access rights and the private rights of the landowners it could effectively and successfully deprive landowners, without providing for compensation, of their right to sue in trespass anyone who enters the land without their permission.'

Even though the Scottish legislation goes much further as a limitation of the right of property, the better view is that, because of its balancing of right and responsibility, it also complies with the Convention.

---

[61] 2007 SCLR 530.
[62] Sheriff's emphasis.
[63] *Gloag*, supra note 61, at para 42.
[64] S 1(7).
[65] See, e.g., *James v UK* (1986) 8 EHRR 116.
[66] Van der Walt, note 50 supra, 194–5.
[67] Referring to the Countryside and Rights of Way Act 2000.

The South African *Victoria & Alfred Waterfront* case,[68] already referred to,[69] is a somewhat remote point of comparison. Professor A J van der Walt sees the decision as holding 'that the private owner of premises open to the general public does not have an absolute right to exclude certain persons, even when they make a nuisance of themselves on the premises and do not enter the premises as clients'.[70] This, he says, is an example of judicial efforts, outside eviction law, to restrict a landowner's general right to exclude others.

An *obiter* comment of Desai J points to the particular South African history factor which may put into question the relevance of the decision in terms of the law of Scotland:[71]

'I may add that, in the light of the unfortunate recent history of this country, where millions of people were denied access to towns, cities and other public places, the practice of excluding people from parts of a city, albeit for limited periods, may appear repugnant and not pass constitutional muster.'

18.6 APPARENT AFFINITY FACTOR

Apparent scope for comparison may arise through an accidental factor rather than on the basis of the well understood affinity deriving from a fundamental common position between the systems. This commonality – arguably the most usual foundation for any comparative development – can, of course, be seen in the *ius commune* substance factor developed in an Anglo-American process context which brings the two systems together.

An example of an illusion of affinity is in the position between the Court of Session decision in *Karl Construction Ltd v Palisade Properties plc*[72] and the Constitutional Court decision in *Transvaal Agricultural Union v Minister of Land Affairs*.[73] The point in common here is an interim limitation on proprietary rights which is potentially a deprivation of ownership; the outcomes are different because in the South African case the land reform priority is controlling.

In the *Transvaal Agricultural Union* case the issue was the provision of the Restitution of Land Rights Act 22 of 1994 in terms of which publication of a restitution claim notice had the effect of limiting the landowner's normal rights pending finalisation of the claim. The Transvaal Agricultural Union's claim to direct access to the Constitutional Court failed and the decision was accordingly not definitive but the Court approved in principle the 'legitimate

---

[68] Note 3 supra.
[69] See section 18.2 supra, note 3.
[70] Van der Walt, note 50 supra, 195.
[71] *Victoria & Alfred Waterfront*, note 3 supra, at 450.
[72] 2002 SLT 312.
[73] 1997(2) SA 621 CC (considered in *Land Title in South Africa*, note 23 supra, 561–2).

purpose' of a provision 'designed to protect claimants and maintain the *status quo* pending determination'.[74]

Relevantly in the present context, the Scottish decision involved a comparative factor in that Lord Drummond Young noted Scots law's exceptional position vis-à-vis the ECHR in its readiness to allow the inhibition of property pending the outcome of civil litigation.[75] In a significant statement the learned judge referred to 'the near unanimity of approach found in European and North American legal systems' as 'the clearest possible indication Scots law is seriously out of step with general trends of contemporary legal thought in this area'.[76]

A comparison of these two decisions is only fruitful to the extent of providing an illustration of the obvious point that a given position may reflect particular policy factors not generally replicated and, accordingly, not open to useful inclusion in any comparative survey. The Scottish limitation of property rights in issue in *Karl Construction* was to do with a limitation of the normal right of disposal of assets pending the outcome of litigation which, if successful, would give the party seeking the limitation a creditor's claim against the property of the debtor owner. The Scottish court's view was that the provision in issue was a deprivation of property in its form as a manifest concession in favour of one merely making a claim against another. A comparison of the position as to the protection of a claimant's interest vis-à-vis the assets of the alleged debtor in other European jurisdictions tended to confirm the view that the Scottish provision, in its open-endedness in favour of the creditor, was a deprivation of property under the ECHR. Comparing the South African case outcome with this one is unproductive because a position skewed to favour the land restitution claim was provided for by the interim Constitution.

18.7 CHARACTERISATION OF RESPECTIVE POSITIONS AND CONCLUSION

The position regarding private law and the protection of the human right of property in South Africa and Scotland is too different for any comparative exercise to have primary utility. While there are aspects of common ground – such as the implications of the difference between expropriation and deprivation – the systems differ markedly in their essential features because the *grundnorm* aspects are so different. The substantive policy infusion character of the South African position as against the ECHR's policy-neutral stance, almost as a regulation of process, is a controlling difference.

---

[74] *Transvaal Agricultural Union* (supra) per Chaskalson JP at 633.
[75] See A Steven 'The Progress of Article 1 Protocol 1 in Scotland' (2002) 6 *EdinLR* 396 for a comment on this case.
[76] *Karl Construction*, note 72 supra, at 328.

The South African land reform agenda catalyst has significantly limited the common law position in certain areas of the right of ownership. The protection of property under the South African constitution is inseparable from the constitutionally mandated land reform process in any accurate description of the land rights position. Studies of affinity with foreign systems add to the store of knowledge and may be valuable to the extent that they promote the important process of land reform in South Africa. One need hardly say that the importance of that being achieved should not be subject to distraction.

In Scotland the ECHR factor has seen major reforms making significant inroads into the common law. The short era of explicit protection of property under the Convention has been one of unprecedented limitation of the common law position as to landownership rights. The access reforms commented on in this chapter are a striking inroad because they potentially affect all land. The community and crofting rights to buy, also under the 2003 Land Reform (Scotland) Act, are significant in their impact on particular forms of land right.[77]

There is one thing in common. In both South Africa and Scotland the 'human right of property' is more evident as policy-driven limitation – in favour of society at large – of the landowner's common law position, rather than any notion of the protection of proprietary interests as a human right end.

---

[77] See M M Combe, 'Parts 2 and 3 of the Land Reform (Scotland) Act 2003: A Definitive Answer to the Scottish Land Question?' 2006 Juridical Review 195.

Chapter 19

The Margin of Appreciation Doctrine of the European Court of Human Rights: Protection of Ownership and the Right to a Home

J M Milo

19.1 INTRODUCTION

Human rights in European jurisdictions are orchestrated by supranational as well as national institutions, but national autonomy in their application prevails to the extent that the European Court of Human Rights (ECtHR) may defer to national jurisdictions by way of the margin of appreciation doctrine.[1] In particular it hesitates to intervene in any 'longstanding and complex area of law which regulates private law matters between individuals', and does so only when the national result is so anomalous as to render the legislation unacceptable.[2]

In recent years European jurisdictions have been regarded as open towards the acceptance of human rights standards from international sources.[3] A closer look, however, reveals a more complex pattern of development and the degree of such openness is questionable. The fundamental rights to a home and to property are both at stake in the context of procedures to evict unlawful occupiers. Recently Dutch legislation has reinforced the protection of individual, exclusive ownership of buildings, after a 40-year period in which squatters were protected against unlawful eviction, although the courts and public authorities have mitigated the harsher consequences of the new law. This development runs quite contrary to that observed in South African law, which has evolved from preventing illegal squatting[4] towards preventing illegal eviction.[5]

---

[1] On this topic see J Vande Lanotte and Y Haeck *Handboek EVRM I Algemene beginselen* (Intersentia 2005) 204–25; J Gerards 'Pluralism, Deference and the Margin of Appreciation Doctrine' 2011 *European Law Journal* 80.

[2] *Pye v UK* (2008) 46 EHRR 45 at paras 71 and 83.

[3] Some more than others. See G Brüggemeier, A Ciacchi, and G Comandé *Fundamental Rights and Private Law in the European Union* (Cambridge University Press 2010) vol 1 at 740: 'France and the Netherlands seem to embody the largest openness in relying on international sources (mainly the ECHR) in their case law. . .'.

[4] Prevention of Illegal Squatting Act 52 of 1951.

[5] The Prevention of Illegal Eviction from and Unlawful Occupation of Land Act 19 of 1998.

The margin of appreciation doctrine reveals the centre of gravity of human rights in private law. While 'longstanding and complex' are descriptors that hardly clarify the extent of the 'wide margin' in general terms, the 'narrow margin' as applied to the right to a home offers more guidance. However, this may conflict with the protection of individual ownership, particularly as national levels of protecting the right to a home vary in the extent to which they favour private ownership.

19.2 THE MARGIN OF APPRECIATION DOCTRINE: NATIONAL PRIMACY OF HUMAN RIGHTS

The margin of appreciation doctrine has been developed by the ECtHR in order to 'accommodate its complex role as an international human rights court'.[6] It is indeed a complex role, as Europe is a pluralist legal order without a clear hierarchy between the ECtHR and the highest national courts. Decisions of the ECtHR are not binding on jurisdictions other than those involved in the procedure – there is in other words, no *erga omnes* force. The ECtHR has held that the Convention leaves to the contracting states themselves, in the first place, 'the task of securing the rights and liberties it enshrines'.[7] The consequence is clear: national levels of protection of human rights will prevail, as the ECtHR leaves to the national jurisdiction a certain margin of appreciation, wide or narrow. This margin of appreciation doctrine certainly has positive aspects. It may accommodate cultural diversity,[8] and is generally regarded as useful and flexible.[9] It is certainly a necessary tool for the ECtHR in dealing with the enormous increase in its caseload,[10] and it is probably also necessary if the Court's legitimacy is

---

On this development see A J van der Walt *Property in the Margins* (Hart Publishing 2009) 146–61.

[6] It was applied implicitly in *Case Relating to Certain Aspects of the Laws on the Use of Languages In Education In Belgium* (1979–80) 1 EHRR 252; explicitly in *De Wilde, Ooms and Versyp v Belgium* App nos 2832/66; 2835/66; 2899/66 18 June 1971; and it was refined in *Handyside v UK* (1979–80) 1 EHRR 737. See Vande Lanotte and Haeck *Handboek*, note 1 supra, at 207–9; Gerards 'Pluralism, Deference and the Margin of Appreciation Doctrine', note 1 supra, at 102.

[7] *Handyside v UK*, note 6 supra, at para 48.

[8] Ibid: 'In particular, it is not possible to find in the domestic law of the various Contracting States a uniform European conception of morals. The view taken by their respective laws of the requirements of morals varies from time to time and from place to place, especially in our era which is characterised by a rapid and far-reaching evolution of opinions on the subject. By reason of their direct and continuous contact with the vital forces of their countries, State authorities are in principle in a better position than the international judge to give an opinion on the exact content of these requirements as well as on the "necessity" of a "restriction" or "penalty" intended to meet them'.

[9] Gerards 'Pluralism, Deference and the Margin of Appreciation Doctrine', note 1 supra, at 105.

[10] See E Bates *The Evolution of the European Court of Human Rights* (Oxford University Press 2010) 475ff.

not to be challenged too much. Criticism on supranational human rights is indeed increasing.[11] However, the margin of appreciation technique may further be seen as a device that allows the court to abstain from guidance in human rights, and this may serve to lower the threshold of human rights protection.[12]

The question whether an issue is for the national jurisdiction to decide depends upon the extent of the margin of appreciation offered by the ECtHR. When a wide margin is provided to the national jurisdiction, the review by the ECtHR will be superficial and the national arrangement will pass the test unless that judgment is manifestly without reasonable foundation.[13] When only a narrow margin is offered, the test may be quite substantial.[14]

A number of factors are relevant in determining whether the margin is wide or narrow, as set out explicitly in ECtHR case law:[15] whether the national authority is better placed in assessing how the particular Convention right should be given effect; the importance of protection for the individual; and the object pursued by interference with the Convention right. Consensus or common ground in law between member states is also of

---

[11] Lord Hoffmann 'The Universality of Human Rights' (Judicial Studies Board Annual Lecture, 19 March 2009, available at *http://www.judiciary.gov.uk/Resources/JCO/Documents/ Speeches/Hoffmann_2009_JSB_Annual_Lecture_Universality_of_Human_Rights.pdf*) at 27: 'In practice, the Court has not taken the doctrine of the margin of appreciation nearly far enough. It has been unable to resist the temptation to aggrandise its jurisdiction and to impose uniform rules on Member States. It considers itself the equivalent of the Supreme Court of the United States, laying down a federal law of Europe'. It also is clearly visible in the Dutch situation, e.g. in the discussion in the newspapers and in legal literature. See also Th Baudet 'Het Europese Hof voor de Rechten van de mens vormt een ernstige inbreuk op de Democratie' *NRC Handelsblad* 13 November 2010; idem, 'Brits verzet tegen Europees Hof is terecht' *NRC Handelsblad* 14 February 2011; T Zwart 'Een steviger opstelling tegenover het Europese Hof voor de rechten van de Mens bevordert de rechtsstaat' 2011 *Nederlands Juristenblad* 343; J Gerards 'Waar gaat het debat over het Europees Hof voor de Rechten van de Mens nu eigenlijk over?' 2011 *Nederlands Juristenblad* 518.

[12] E Brems 'Human Rights: Minimum and Maximum Perspectives' (2009) 9 *Human Rights Law Review* 349.

[13] As in *James and Others v UK* (1986) 8 EHRR 123 at para 46.

[14] *McCann v UK* (2008) 47 EHRR 40. The actual application of the margin of appreciation by the ECtHR is somewhat confused: Vande Lanotte and Haeck *Handboek*, note 1 supra, at 207–9; Gerards 'Pluralism, Deference and the Margin of Appreciation Doctrine', note 1 supra, at 106. Even after a wide margin has been recognized, a substantive test still may follow. See *Pla and Puncernau v Andorra* (2006) 42 EHRR 25 at para 46: 'When ruling on disputes of this type, the national authorities and, in particular, the courts of first instance and appeal have a wide margin of appreciation. Accordingly, an issue of interference with private and family life could only arise under the Convention if the national courts' assessment of the facts or domestic law were manifestly unreasonable or arbitrary or blatantly inconsistent with the fundamental principles of the Convention'. A substantive analysis followed, and a violation of arts 14 and 8 was found.

[15] *S and Marper v UK* (2009) 48 EHRR 50 at para 102; *Connors v UK* (2005) 40 EHRR 9 at paras 82–3; Vande Lanotte and Haeck *Handboek*, note 1 supra, at 217–20.

importance. Whenever the right at stake is essential for the effective enjoyment of intimate or key rights, the margin will be narrower,[16] but when the interference concerns social or economic policies applied by the state the margin will be wider.

A lack of consensus between the laws of the contracting states indicates there will probably not be sufficient support for an ECtHR decision[17] and thus indicates a wide margin for the national jurisdiction, whereas clear and uncontested evidence of a continuing international trend may narrow the margin of appreciation.[18] When exactly is there common ground? This criterion would call for comparative law research, but whether this would reveal a common ground or not is not easily predicted. Unanimity is not required; an emerging consensus could suffice.[19]

National jurisdictions may be in a better position to assess the issue at stake, as was held in *Gasus v The Netherlands*,[20] dealing with the privileged secured position of the tax authorities, and in *James and others v UK*,[21] concerning reform of leaseholds. In taxation the national authorities enjoy a wide margin.[22] Reform of leaseholds was deemed to be legislation serving social and economic policies, for which a wide margin should be available:[23]

> 'The Court, finding it natural that the margin of appreciation available to the legislature in implementing social and economic policies should be a wide one, will respect the legislature's judgement as to what is "in the public interest" unless that judgement is manifestly without reasonable foundation.'

National authorities 'by reason of their direct and continuous contact with the vital forces of their countries'[24] may be given a wide margin of appreciation as regards disputes of a purely private law nature. The ECtHR has held

---

[16] *S and Marper v UK*, note 15 supra, at para 102.

[17] *Rasmussen v Denmark* (1985) 7 EHRR 371 at para 40: 'The scope of the margin of appreciation will vary according to the circumstances, the subject-matter and its background; in this respect, one of the relevant factors may be the existence or non-existence of common ground between the laws of the Contracting States'.

[18] *Goodwin v UK* (2002) 35 EHRR 18 at para 85.

[19] *Appleby v UK* (2003) 37 EHRR 38 at para 46. For an illustration of the common ground criterion see *Schalk & Kopf v Austria* (2011) 53 EHRR 20 at para 105 (no consensus on gay marriage yet, so the national margin in determining the right to marry was not exceeded).

[20] (1995) 20 EHRR 403.

[21] (1986) 8 EHRR 123.

[22] *Gasus v The Netherlands* (1995) 20 EHRR 403 at para 60: 'In passing such laws [securing the payment of taxes, JMM] the legislature must be allowed a wide margin of appreciation, especially with regard to the question whether – and if so – to what extent – the tax authorities should be put in a better position to enforce tax debts than ordinary creditors are in to enforce commercial debts'.

[23] *James and others v UK* (1986) 8 EHRR 123 at para 46.

[24] *Connors v UK* (2005) 40 EHRR 9 at para 82.

on several occasions that it is 'not in theory required to settle disputes of a purely private nature'.[25]

In theory, however, other factors may come into play to narrow the national margin in private law. The nature of the affected Convention right is of importance, as well as its significance for the individual and the nature of the activities restricted.[26] As noted above, the margin is narrower when the right at stake is crucial to the individual's effective enjoyment of intimate or key rights.[27] In the realm of private law, on the other hand, property law has been provided with the widest margin possible on the basis of its long tradition and complexity.

19.3 THE WIDEST MARGIN FOR NATIONAL PROPERTY LAW

The case of *Pye v United Kingdom*[28] involved article 1 of the First Protocol. In the Court's reading article 1 contains three rules, of which the first sets out the principle of peaceful enjoyment of possessions. The second rule covers deprivation of possessions, subject to certain conditions, and the third rule recognises that the state may control the use of property in accordance with the general interest. Both the second and the third rules must be understood in the light of the principle of peaceful enjoyment, and thus need to be lawful, have a legitimate aim and be proportionate.[29] Deprivation without compensation is usually disproportionate, although this is not so in case of control of use. The boundary between both types of infringement is not clearly defined, as we will see. The margin of appreciation, relevant to various stages of the reasoning in *Pye*, was considered to be a wide one.

In *Pye* the applicant companies were the owners of land which by agreement had been occupied by the owners of adjacent property, a Mr and Mrs Graham. On the expiry of the agreement the Grahams were instructed to vacate the land. They remained in occupation without permission, however, for a further fifteen years. The Grahams then argued title had been obtained by adverse possession, under the Limitation Act 1980 and the Land Registration Act 1925. These acts in combination provided that Pye was deemed to hold

---

[25] *Pla and Puncernau v Andorra*, note 14 supra, at para 56; the phrase appeared also in *Khurshid Mustafa and Tarzibachi v Sweden* (2011) 52 EHRR 24 at para 33.

[26] *Connors v UK*, note 24 supra, at para 82.

[27] Note 16 supra. See also *McCann v UK*, note 14 supra, at para 50: 'The loss of one's home is a most extreme form of interference with the right to respect for the home. Any person at risk of an interference of this magnitude should in principle be able to have the proportionality of the measure determined by an independent tribunal in the light of the relevant principles under Article 8 of the Convention, notwithstanding that, under domestic law, his right of occupation has come to an end'. Some fundamental rights never leave national states a margin of appreciation: art 2 (right to life), art 3 (prohibition of torture) and art 4 §1 (prohibition of slavery) (Vande Lanotte and Haeck *Handboek*, note 1 supra, at 215).

[28] Note 2 supra.

[29] *Sporrong and Lönnroth v Sweden* (1983) 5 EHRR 35 at para 61.

the land in trust for the occupier, without being entitled to compensation. The court at first instance decided in favour of the Grahams, the Court of Appeal ruled in favour of Pye,[30] and the House of Lords found for the Grahams.[31] Pye appealed to the ECtHR, which in 2005 decided in favour of Pye.[32] The substantive rules on adverse possession under English law were judged to be a disproportionate deprivation of property under article 1 of the First Protocol.[33] The Grand Chamber ultimately took a different stance and stepped away from dealing with adverse possession, even from private law in general.[34]

The arguments used were very formal and technical. The Court did make clear, with some reluctance, that horizontal private law relations fall under the constitutional umbrella of the ECHR. Private law relations do not entail a direct infringement by the Government, but rather an indirect one:[35]

> '[T]he responsibility of the Government in the present case is therefore not direct responsibility for an executive or legislative act aimed at the applicant companies, but is rather their responsibility for legislation which is activated as a result of the inter-actions of private individuals.'

Adverse possession pursues a legitimate aim as it concerns itself with social and economic policies for which a wide margin of appreciation is available.[36] 'This is particularly true,' it was said, 'in cases such as the present one where what is at stake is a longstanding and complex area of law which regulates private law matters with individuals'.[37] Similar reasoning has also been applied in relation to housing law.[38]

---

[30] [2001] Ch 804.

[31] [2003] 1 AC 419.

[32] (2006) 43 EHRR 3.

[33] Raising the issue of whether national rules of acquisitive prescription needed to be adjusted. See case commentary by V Sagaert, R Caterina, G Gretton, O Radley-Gardner and J M Milo in (2007) 15 *European Review of Private Law* 251–308.

[34] (2008) 46 EHRR 45.

[35] (2008) 46 EHRR 45 at para 57. The effect of adverse possession was qualified by the Grand Chamber as a control of use, not a deprivation, unlike in the previous decision ((2006) 43 EHRR 3), making it easier for the Government to meet the test of fair balance. Why was it a control of use? Because the rules on adverse possession were not intended to deprive paper owners of their ownership, but rather to regulate questions of title in a system in which, historically, twelve years' adverse possession was sufficient to extinguish the former owners' right to re-enter to recover possession (para 66).

[36] The court refers to *Jahn and Others v Germany* (2006) 42 EHRR 49 at para 91, and *James and others v UK* (1986) 8 EHRR 123.

[37] *Pye v UK*, note 2 supra, at para 71.

[38] *Immobiliare Saffi v Italy* (2000) 30 EHRR 756 at para 49. In spheres such as housing, which plays a central role in the welfare and economic policies of modern societies, the Court will respect the legislature's judgment as to what is in the general interest unless that judgment is manifestly without reasonable foundation. Reference was made to *Mellacher and Others v Austria* (1990) 12 EHRR 391 at para 45, and *Chassagnou and Others v France* (2000) 29 EHRR 615 (the latter case deals with hunting rights).

The 'common ground' factor was also mentioned, but little guidance was offered on this. On the one hand 'a large number of member States possesses some form of mechanism for transferring title in accordance with principles similar to adverse possession' without compensation; on the other hand it 'is a characteristic of property law that different countries regulate its use and transfer in a variety of ways. The relevant rules reflect social policies against the background of the local conception of the importance and role of property'.[39] There was thus common ground on a general abstract level, but not on a more specific level. The margin was therefore wide.

The margin of appreciation doctrine also interacted with the test of proportionality: the question arose whether a fair balance had been struck between the demands of the general interest and the interest of the individuals concerned.[40] A wide margin was permitted in resolving this as the Court was not in theory required to settle disputes of a private nature.[41] Disproportionality would result only if a domestic court's interpretation of a legal act appeared 'unreasonable, arbitrary or . . . inconsistent . . . with the principles underlying the Convention'.[42] Adverse possession was not disproportionate, according to the majority in *Pye*, because the claim concerned private law norms, which meant that the specific facts of the case – such as the parties' conduct or the enormous loss – could not be of any relevance. The objective rules alone – the reflection of a long-established system – were the focus: acquisition of unassailable rights went hand in hand with a corresponding loss;[43] and limitation periods, if they were to fulfil their purpose, had to apply regardless of the size of the claim.[44] However, a minority in the Grand Chamber thought otherwise,[45] and the controversial nature of adverse possession is illustrated by the variation in outcomes as the case progressed through the domestic courts. Furthermore, in another recent case limitation periods *have* been judged disproportionate in the context of article 1 of the First Protocol, and the facts were in that instance determinative.[46]

19.4 THE RIGHT TO A HOME: NARROW MARGINS

In cases dealing with housing the margin of appreciation offered to national jurisdictions with regard to article 8 of the Convention is much narrower.

---

[39] *Pye v UK*, note 2 supra, at para 74.
[40] *Pye v UK*, note 2 supra, at para 75.
[41] *Pye v UK*, note 2 supra, at paras 75 and 82.
[42] *Pye v UK*, note 2 supra, at para 75.
[43] *Pye v UK*, note 2 supra, at para 83.
[44] *Pye v UK*, note 2 supra, at para 84.
[45] *Pye v UK*, note 2 supra, joint dissenting opinion Rozakis, Bratza, Tsatsa-Nikolovska, Gyuluman and Sikuta.
[46] *Zehentner v Austria* (2011) 52 EHRR 22 at paras 61–64.

The ECtHR has held that the question whether a house is to be regarded as a home is a matter of fact, and not of national law.[47] Any interference with the exercise of rights under article 8 needs to meet the conditions of article 8(2), of which a proportionality requirement is an implicit part. An interference will be considered 'necessary in a democratic society' for a legitimate aim 'if it answers a pressing social need and, in particular, if it is proportionate to the legitimate aim pursued'.[48]

The margin of appreciation in the application of article 8 is in the end substantially narrower than in the case of article 1 of the First Protocol. A margin must be left to the state, as it is 'by reason of . . . direct and continuous contact with the vital forces of their countries . . . in principle better placed than an international court to evaluate local needs and conditions'.[49] As we have seen, when housing rights are at issue in the context of article 1 of the First Protocol, the ECtHR has held that it will respect the legislature's judgment as to what is in the general interest, unless that judgment is manifestly without reasonable foundation.[50] Yet housing rights are analysed differently in the context of article 8, as the rights concerned are 'of central importance to the individual's identity, self-determination, physical and moral integrity, maintenance of relationships with others and a settled and secure place in the community'.[51] The context will be taken into account. Particular weight will be attributed to the individual's membership of a vulnerable minority group,[52] to the extent of the intrusion into the applicant's personal sphere,[53] as well as to the availability of procedural safeguards.[54]

In *McCann v United Kingdom* the procedural aspects in particular were stressed:

> '[T]he loss of one's home is a most extreme form of interference with the right to respect for the home. Any person at risk of an interference of this magnitude should in principle be able to have the proportionality of the measure determined by an independent tribunal in the light of the relevant principles under article 8 of the Convention, notwithstanding that, under domestic law, his right to occupation has come to an end.'[55]

---

[47] *Gillow v UK* (1989) 11 EHRR 33; *Buckley v UK* (1997) 23 EHRR 101; *McCann v UK* (2008) 47 EHRR 40.

[48] *Connors v UK*, note 24 supra, at para 81.

[49] *Connors v UK*, note 24 supra, at para 82. The wording had already appeared in *Handyside v UK*, note 3 supra, at para 48.

[50] *Immobiliare Saffi v Italy* (2000) 30 EHRR 756 at para 49.

[51] *Connors v UK*, note 24 supra, at para 82.

[52] *Connors v UK*, note 24 supra, at para 84; and see previously, without a violation of art 8, *Buckley v UK* (1997) 23 EHRR 101 at para 84.

[53] *Connors v UK*, note 24 supra, at para 82.

[54] *Connors v UK*, note 24 supra, at para 83.

[55] *McCann v UK*, note 14, supra, at para 50; see also *Zehentner v Austria* (2011) 52 EHRR 22 at para 65.

The cases are leading and difficult to misinterpret: there is no margin when, as in the *McCann* case, there is no access to an independent tribunal. As we will see, the *McCann* criterion offered the national Dutch courts a necessary foundation in rejecting eviction procedures after new legislation came into force.

19.5 WIDER MARGINS IN RELATION TO OWNERSHIP RIGHTS?

There are thus two conflicting approaches to the margin of appreciation doctrine in relation to eviction procedures. On the one hand there is a wide margin when protection of property is at issue (article 1 of the First Protocol), but on the other hand there is a narrow margin when the right to housing is concerned (article 8). The conflict is usually between individual ownership as against the key right to housing.[56] While the decisions on article 8 provide substantive guidance, restrict the national margin and offer at least a minimal procedural protection to the individual in her right to a home, the decisions concerning private law ownership protection point in the opposite direction. The notion that regulation of this matter is 'longstanding and complex' coincides with the idea that private law is an area of individual autonomy, and that national property law rules serve the necessary legal certainty. Ownership as the most encompassing property right thus remains unaffected by outside elements of reasonableness and fairness, as emerging in this case from human rights. This is a strong and persistent idea.[57] Van der Walt has forcefully analysed the resistance of traditional ownership reasoning, concluding that the influence of supranational human rights in Europe will probably be limited.[58] The recent developments in Dutch law further underline this point. The Dutch legislator has chosen firmly to protect the interests of individual owners.

19.6 OWNERSHIP AND SQUATTING

19.6.1 *Individual and exclusive ownership*

On 1 October 2010 the Dutch legislator provided the private law owner with protection in criminal law.[59] The owner is now entitled to have a third party

---

[56] Although not always: the owner may be obstructed in her wish to use her own property to live in. See, e.g., *Gillow v UK* (1989) 11 EHRR 33; *Schirmer v Poland* (2005) 40 EHRR 47.

[57] As illustrated by the attention which reasonableness and fairness – or objective good faith – and constitutionalisation receive in the area of European contract law, but not in property law at all (see A S Hartkamp et al *Towards a European Civil Code* 4e (Kluwer Law International 2011).

[58] A J van der Walt *Property in the Margins* (Hart Publishing 2009) 166.

[59] *Staatsblad (Stb)* 2010, 320 and 321 art 138a Sr. He who enters or uses an unused building against the law is liable to prosecution for squatting. Prosecution is the joint responsibility

evicted from his or her home with immediate effect, with the assistance of the public prosecutor, and without prior recourse to the courts. The underlying reasons for this change are apparent in the history of the new legislation and are as follows: the legislation is intended to offer a better and more principled protection for ownership; squatting infringes the right of ownership, and should not be tolerated, as it encourages individuals to take the law into their own hands; infringement of ownership rights is morally wrong and should be prohibited; squatting is a significant problem in the Netherlands and should not be used as a tool to combat housing shortage; finally, squatting causes nuisance, criminal behaviour, and attracts foreign migrants.[60] These justifications raise questions as to their empirical foundations, as to constitutional standards, and as to the relative levels of protection offered to owner and squatter before and after the new legislation. Squatting is not a national problem, but mainly restricted to Amsterdam.[61] However, the housing shortage and unoccupied property are still issues,[62] though to a different degree and in a different context as compared with the late nineteenth century and the first half of the twentieth.[63] The new legislation has enhanced the traditional position of the owner in terms of the civil law found in the Code. Ownership is exclusive and entitles the owner to revindicate from whoever holds it without permission; it is formulated abstractly and

of the public prosecution service and the municipality. The provisions on criminal liability are accompanied by legislation which obliges the municipalities to address the problem of unoccupied houses.

[60] PG (*Parlementaire Geschiedenis*; Parliamentary history) MvA (*Memorie van Antwoord*; explanatory memorandum) EK31560c (Eerste Kamer; first chamber of parliament).

[61] The number of squats was in 2008 very roughly estimated at somewhere between 500 and 1000, of which 200–300 were in Amsterdam (P H Renoo *Onderzoeksrapport Kraken en leegstand* 19 December 2008 (Research report on squatting), available at: *http://www.rijksoverheid. nl/documenten-en-publicaties/kamerstukken/2008/12/19/onderzoeksrapport-kraken-en-leegstand-kam erbrief.html.*) The number of civil eviction procedures is estimated to equal the number of criminal eviction procedures. Criminal evictions are well documented and total 85 from 2004 to 2007 (*Onderzoeksrapport* 64).

[62] For 2008 the Central Bureau of Statistics calculated 400,000 uninhabited houses, amounting to 5.7 per cent of the total number of houses. See *http://www.cbs.nl/nl-NL/menu/themas/ bouwen-wonen/publicaties/artikelen/archief/2009/2009-2758-wm.htm.* 300,000 properties are calculated as unoccupied. Unoccupied office space draws more attention. The amount of property unoccupied comprises 4.5 million square metres of office space; 2 million square metres of shops; 11 million square metres of factory space. The estate agent Jones Lang Lasalle found that the percentage of Amsterdam office space unoccupied was 17.3 per cent, second only to Dublin (23 per cent), above Brussels (11.4 per cent), Berlin (9.3 per cent), London (6.9 per cent) and Paris (5.4 per cent) (*NRC Handelsblad* 21 January 2011, 13). See also *Financieel Dagblad* 22 March 2011, 1.

[63] For the Netherlands see A van der Woud *Koninkrijk vol Sloppen* (Bert Bakker 2010); C Leonard and J Ljungberg 'Population and Living Standards 1870–1914' in S Broadberry and K O'Rourke (eds) *The Cambridge Economic History of Europe* (Cambridge University Press 2010) vol 2, 121–2.

also does not prescribe specific duties.[64] Yet in practice the right to be protected in one's home has come to the fore in the case law – mainly summary procedures – and administrative practice. It has followed the path created after the first seminal decisions of the Dutch Supreme Court (*Hoge Raad*) in the late 1960s and early 1970s that set the standards for owners and users of housing space.

19.6.2 *The obligations of ownership*

Seminal decisions by the *Hoge Raad* in 1969 and more particularly in 1971[65] set important standards in this matter. The latter case concerned an eviction on the basis of article 138 Sr of the Criminal Code, imposing liability upon a person who enters and remains in a building 'used by another' without permission. The Court of Appeal interpreted the wording 'used by another' in a rather abstract way: having the (owner's) power to dispose – *beschikken*. This put the dispossessed owner in a strong position, as ownership entails by definition the power freely to dispose. On final appeal it was held that the owner required to have the building in factual use, as the article aims to protect the right to a home. There was no explicit reference to article 8 ECHR.[66]

There were further developments in civil and criminal eviction cases, and in administrative guidelines for evicting by the municipalities and the public prosecution service. The line of reasoning developed in the case law was that the owner's eviction claim would be rejected if allowing it would result in the property becoming unoccupied. The claim to evict would only be permitted if the owner could prove that there were concrete plans to sell, lease, renovate or demolish and rebuild.[67] In 1993 an owner was allowed to have a

---

[64] Article 5: 1: 'Ownership is the most encompassing right a person can have in a thing.'

[65] HR 16 December 1969, 1971 *Nederlandse Jurisprudentie (NJ)* 43. It was held in very general terms that a criminal act such as entering premises without permission could be in principle be justifiable. This is unremarkable, as an accepted argument in any criminal procedure, except that it was a statement in the context of political squatting. However, see also the conclusion under 1971 NJ 385, at 1158, in which the issue is explored further by the Advocate General Langemeijer. Can a public interest make a crime lawful? In Langemeijer's view this issue should be answered only with the utmost caution, and this conclusion may be reached only if there is no legislative provision directly in point and it is reasonable to accede to private pressure.

[66] 1971 NJ 385. While this decision is itself rather short, the advisory opinion of the advocate general and the comments on the case reveal that social contexts played a role: the individual squatter's position; the general problem of housing shortage. But it is the formal principle of legality that supports a restrictive interpretation. See Conclusie A-G Langemeijer at 1157–8; comments by C Bronkhorst at 1160. The housing conditions for a substantial part of the Dutch population fell far below acceptable standards until well into the twentieth century, see A van der Woud *Koninkrijk vol Sloppen* (Bert Bakker 2010) 161.

[67] E.g. Vzr Rb Zwolle 20 July 2009, *LJN* BJ6136; Vzr Rb 's-Gravenhage 8 January 2010, *LJN* BK8654. Too little activity by the owner over a three-year period made the suggested plans implausible. Rb A'dam 29 October 2009, *LJN* BK6078; 21 January 2010, Rb A'dam *LJN*

building standing empty for a year in order to find a use for the building.[68] The guidelines for the municipality of Amsterdam regarding use of police force following civil or criminal proceedings list the following priorities: first, immediate assistance to evict is given if squatters take over a building that is in use; thereafter assistance is given where the building has been unoccupied but the owner can provide plans for using the building; the lowest priority attaches to requests for eviction where the building is unoccupied and the owner has no plans for it. In terms of the case law use may include letting, renovation or demolition. An explicit option is to undertake substantial anti-squatting measures which involve occupancy.[69] The case law has thus provided a framework for ownership whereby eviction is permissible only by reference to certain conditions. These reflect the general interest in appropriate housing policy, and they also entail that the owner has obligations to fulfil. The new legislation, on the other hand, has moved radically towards the immediate protection of individual ownership through criminal sanctions and unconditional eviction.

19.6.3 Legislative change and the contribution of the courts and the administration

New legislation has provided with immediate effect that squatting is a criminal offence – even if it did not contravene the criminal law at the time when the squat began. Entry is permitted to remove the squatters and their effects.[70] As before, municipalities are obliged to assist in eviction,[71] but at the same time they are bound to act effectively to deal with unoccupied housing.[72]

The response of the district courts in summary proceedings was at first

---

BL1044. In one of the first and farthest-reaching decisions, the Middelburg District Court held that infringement of ownership rights was permissible, considering social-economic circumstances, if the ownership right was used in a socially unacceptable manner: Rb Middelburg 24 December 1980, NJ 1981, 374.

[68] Art 429*sexies* Sr; Stb 1992, 548.

[69] Anti-squatting has become a significant commercial activity. See, e.g., *http://www.depers. nl/economie/526735/De-antikraakbranche-is-nergens-bang-voor.html* and its export to other European countries *http://www.depers.nl/buitenland/294391/Antikraak-verovert-Europa.html*

[70] Art. 551a Sv. Where art 138a Sr is thought to have been contravened, the prosecutor may enter and remove persons and effects.

[71] Municipalities were reluctant to carry out their duties under the new legislation, and there was a widely- held opinion that the interests of owners were sufficiently protected by established judicial practice.

[72] At the level of the municipality. See for Amsterdam: *http://www.oga.amsterdam.nl/bijlagen/06%20beleidsregels%20definitief%20plus%20eisen07042011.pdf*. This and similar regulations compel the owner to do what she or he can to ensure that the property does not lie unocccupied. The ultimate option for the municipality is to introduce a mandatory lessee.

to follow the new national legislation and to deny the squatters relief,[73] but on appeal human rights considerations have prevailed. The Court of Appeal in The Hague ruled explicitly that eviction requires to conform with the article 8 standard laid down in *McCann*. Eviction must be preceded by a court decision.[74] This has caused the public prosecution service to issue new guidelines on eviction procedures.[75] Sufficient notice must be given of eviction to allow at least a week in order that summary procedure may be initiated.[76]

But the substantive as well as the procedural aspects require attention. Eviction is usually enforced by means of summary proceedings, which by their nature require a balancing of the interests of the owner on the one hand, and the squatters on the other. Municipalities are often involved in eviction procedures, particularly if public order issues are raised. In that event police assistance will be provided in accordance with policy guidelines, which set priorities depending on the circumstances of the case. High priority will be given where the building was in use or where crimes were being committed. On the other hand low priority will be given where an owner did not have definite plans for using an unoccupied building, or has not adhered to previous agreements with the municipality concerning use of the building.[77] In these policy guidelines it is possible to discern the criteria previously used by courts in order to determine whether eviction should be allowed.

It remains to be seen whether the criteria developed in the case law obliging the owner to act in the public interest to provide housing will survive

---

[73] Vzr Rb Amsterdam, 22 October 2010, nr 471348/KG ZA 10–1832.

[74] Vzr Gerechtshof Amsterdam 8 November 2010 *LJN* BO3249; Vzr Gerechtshof Den Haag 8 November 2010 *LJN* BO3682. *McCann v UK* (2008) 47 EHRR 40 at para 55. Why was this not included? An important reason might have been that the advice of the Council of State was not taken into account. This normally would include a check on the constitutionality of legislation and any judicial failure to undertake constitutional review (Article 120 Dutch constitution). It did severely critique the Bill. Input by the Council of State should compensate for the lack of constitutional review by judges (Article 120, Dutch Constitution).

[75] See 2010 *Staatscourant* 19500 available *at https://zoek.officielebekendmakingen.nl/stcrt-2010–19500.html?zoekcriteria=%3fzkt%3dUitgebreid%26pst%3dStaatscourant%26vrt%3dontruimin g%26zkd%3dInDeGeheleText%26dpr%3dAnderePeriode%26spd%3d20100811%26epd%3d 20111011%26sdt%3dDatumPublicatie%26ap%3d%26pnr%3d1%26rpp%3d10&resultIndex =6&sorttype=1&sortorder=4*

[76] The Gerechtshof Amsterdam decided likewise in a decision of 1 March 2011, *LJN* BP6209: notice must be given of eviction and this needs also to be made clear in legislation. The policy guidelines allow immediate eviction only in certain circumstances, viz where the squatting occurs in the home of another, where there have been criminal acts, where the situation is dangerous, or where public order demands.

[77] Such agreements have a foundation in the legislation – the *Leegstandswet* or Law on Unoccupation. The policy guidelines of the municipality of Amsterdam may be found at: *http://www.amsterdam.nl/publish/pages/312019/notitiebeleidsuitgangspuntenwetkrakenenleeg-standversieraad_2_.pdf.*

this legislative change. It is also unclear what will happen with evictions when social circumstances deteriorate. The Netherlands Institute for Social Research has signalled a substantial increase in poverty,[78] and it is not just in the Netherlands that inequalities have deepened.[79] The European Commission has placed the fight against poverty at the heart of its economic, employment and social agenda.[80] South African law may provide a model for dealing with such problems in a society concerned with redressing inequalities.

19.6.4 Addressing inequality in the South African context

While Roman-Dutch ownership and the Prevention of Illegal Squatting Act 52 of 1951 provided the legislative framework for eviction before 1998,[81] the perspective changed fundamentally with the new Constitution and the Prevention of Illegal Eviction Act 1998.[82] The seminal case of *Port Elizabeth Municipality v Various Occupiers*[83] shows how the balance between private ownership and the right to a home may be struck. The owner is no longer entitled as of right to evict – ownership also entails social responsibilities: '[T]he land-owner cannot simply say: this is my land, I can do with it what I want, and then send in the bulldozers or sledgehammers'.[84] Eviction is still possible, but only after all relevant circumstances and interests are taken into account.[85] Interestingly, the new constitutional arrangements demand the interests of the squatters to be recognised as a right to property 'not previ-

---

[78] The Sociaal en Cultureel Planbureau; *http://www.scp.nl/dsresource?objectid=27223&type=org*. The threshold level of poverty is set at a monthly income of €930 per month.

[79] J Stiglitz *Freefall* (Penguin 2010) 291; see also, from a political angle, T Judt, *Ill Fares the Land* (Penguin 2010).

[80] See *The European Platform against Poverty and Social Exclusion: A European Framework for Social and Territorial Cohesion* COM(2010) 758 final, available at *http://epp.eurostat. ec.europa.eu/portal/page/portal/income_social_inclusion_living_conditions/documents/tab/Tab/ European%20Platform%20against%20Poverty%20and%20Social%20Exclusion.pdf*

[81] *Port Elizabeth Municipality v Various Occupiers* 2005 (1) SA 217 (CC) per Sachs J at para 10: 'The principles of ownership in the Roman-Dutch law then gave legitimation in an apparently neutral and impartial way to the consequences of manifestly racist and partial laws and policies'.

[82] The Prevention of Illegal Eviction from and Unlawful Occupation of Land Act 19 of 1998. *Port Elizabeth Municipality v Various Occupiers*, note 81 supra, per Sachs J at para 12: 'PIE not only repealed PISA [Prevention of Illegal Squatting Act S2 of 1951] but in a sense inverted it'. On this development see A J van der Walt *Property in the Margins* (Hart Publishing 2009) 146–61.

[83] Note 81 supra.

[84] *Port Elizabeth Municipality v Various Occupiers*, note 81 supra, at para 20.

[85] *Port Elizabeth Municipality v Various Occupiers*, note 81 supra, at para 25. The court is required to evaluate the circumstances on the basis of s 4 (eviction by an owner), or s 6 (eviction by a municipality) of the 1998 Act.

ously recognized by common law'.[86] The traditional private law framework of recognised property rights is thereby opened up[87] and issues of fundamental fairness are considered.[88]

19.7 CONCLUSIONS

The margin of appreciation doctrine preserves a balance between the ECtHR and the national jurisdictions in dealing with human rights. Priority lies with the national jurisdictions. Their margin of appreciation is narrow in relation to human rights of 'central importance to the individual's identity, self-determination, physical and moral integrity, maintenance of relationships with others and a settled and secure place in the community',[89] such as the right to a home. It is, however, wide in areas which deal with social and economic policies, and even more so if these areas are longstanding and complex – like private law, particularly property.

By offering such latitude to national jurisdictions in determining the content of private law, the ECtHR has less fortunately tilted the balance towards the individual autonomy of the private owners. The stance taken by the Dutch legislator shows how easily such a position can be taken even on an area for which it should have had only a narrow margin, as it concerned the right to a home. Other legal sources such as administrative guidelines and court decisions have mitigated the consequences to some extent. But it remains to be seen how this traditional ownership paradigm will respond to further developments in social, political and economic contexts, and to the increased national priority in dealing with human rights. It should be appreciated that even 'longstanding' traditions like ownership can be much more receptive to changing contexts, and respond to the protection of fundamental societal interests, as is illustrated by South African law. The ease with which the traditional and dogmatic ownership paradigm has reappeared on a national level in Europe perhaps indicates the need for stronger signals to remind us that private law also, particularly property law, is subject to constitutional standards of human rights.

---

[86] *Port Elizabeth Municipality v Various Occupiers*, note 81 supra, at para 23.
[87] With or without a formal *numerus clausus* principle, as respectively in The Netherlands and in South Africa. See M J De Waal 'Identifying Real Rights in South African Law: The "Subtraction from Dominium" Test and its Application' in S E Bartels and M J Milo *Contents of Real Rights* (Wolf Legal Publishers 2004) 83–98; C G van der Merwe 'Numerus Clausus and the Developments of New Real Rights in South Africa' in Bartels and Milo *Contents of Real Rights* 99–113.
[88] *Port Elizabeth Municipality v Various Occupiers*, note 81 supra, at paras 30–1.
[89] *Connors v UK*, note 24 supra, at para 82, on art 8.

Chapter 20

Environment and Human Rights: The Right to Water in South Africa and Scotland

Loretta Feris and John Gibson

20.1 INTRODUCTION

'The dictionary describes water as colourless, tasteless and odourless – its most important property being its ability to dissolve other substances. We in South Africa do not see water that way. For us water is a basic human right, water is the origin of all things – the giver of life.'[1]

'Our guiding value is that the Scottish people have an inalienable right to Scotland's water resources. No single generation, and no external body, should be able to take decisions which would pre-empt future generations from their enjoyment of this right, or which would have the effect of imposing unnecessary charges upon future generations for their own Scottish water resources.'[2]

Water remains one of the most vital natural resources on earth, and across the globe countries are concerned about issues such as availability and access to fresh water, the quality thereof, including pollution control and the conservation status of water resources overall. This shared concern is clear from the two quotations above. It is also clear that both South Africa and Scotland view water through the lens of a 'rights discourse'. South Africa sees the right to water in light of the profound place it has in the existence of life, as a basic human right. As such it is viewed as a socio-economic right, which must be guaranteed and safeguarded by the state. As a result private rights to water must inevitably take a back seat. Scotland, on the other hand, emphasises the rights of landowners to use water that occurs naturally on their property and protects such private rights from unwarranted interference, while providing safeguards for the interests of other proprietors and the public. Although both approaches require the integration of the principle of sustainability[3] and the sustainable use of water resources, the

---

[1] K Asmal 'Introduction' to the Department of Water Affairs and Forestry (now the Department of Water Affairs) *White Paper on a National Water Policy for South Africa* (April 1997).

[2] *Building a Hydro Nation – A Consultation*, (Scottish Government 2010), s 1.

[3] The World Commission on Environment and Development (WCED) in *Our Common Future* (1987) (available at *http://www.un-documents.net/wced-ocf.htm*) at 8 defines sustainable development as 'development which meets the needs of the present generation without compromising the ability of future generations to meet their own needs'.

different emphases have important consequences for how water resources are regulated within these countries and how the countries apply the rights discourse to water as a resource. This chapter interrogates the regulation of water as a natural resource in both countries and the application of human rights to water. It looks, in particular, at the relationship between property rights and water rights and the ways in which influences such as availability of water and historical experience shape the present rights discourse.

20.2 WATER IN SOUTH AFRICA

South Africa is an arid country with rainfall which is less than the world average and unevenly distributed across the country. 'With just over 1200Kl of available freshwater for each person each year at the present population of about 42 million, we are on the threshold of the international definition of "water stress"'.[4] This scarcity of water is a subject that features in virtually every policy document on water in South Africa.[5] In essence, South Africa's fresh water resources are in short supply and disproportionately spread. To make matters worse climate change will potentially impact significantly on both the availability and requirements for water in South Africa.[6] Modelling studies have shown that the region will become significantly drier,[7] which will have significant impacts on the economy, especially for sectors such as agriculture and tourism. However, whilst the decreasing quantity of water has been a concern for decades, more recently these concerns have been compounded by water quality issues resulting from water pollution. Water pollution results from numerous activities and includes mining, industrial processes and run-off from agriculture. In recent times reports of the potentially disastrous impacts of acid mine drainage (AMD)[8] featured strongly in the media. It eventually became the subject of an inter-ministerial report,[9] which notes that seepage of polluted mine water is one of the biggest threats to water. It impacts not only the quality of water resources, but also threat-

---

[4] *White Paper on a National Water Policy*, note 1 supra, 14.

[5] See, e.g., Department of Water Affairs and Forestry *National Water Resources Strategy* (2004); Department of Water Affairs and Forestry *Management of the Water Resources of the Republic of South Africa* (1986).

[6] *National Water Resources Strategy*, note 5 supra, 50.

[7] F Engelbrecht 'The Scientific Basis for Climate Change' in P Draper and I Mbirimi (eds) *Climate Change and Trade: The Challenges for Southern Africa* (South African Institute of International Affairs 2010) 136.

[8] AMD is generally associated with so-called hard rock mining, i.e. gold, coal and copper. It is caused when rock containing sulphide minerals and tailings disposal areas is exposed to air and water, resulting in the production of highly acidified water containing elevated concentrations of highly toxic heavy metals.

[9] Report to the Inter-ministerial Committee on Acid Mine Drainage *Mine Water Management in the Witwatersrand Goldfields with Special Emphasis on Acid Mine Drainage* (December 2010).

ens human health, livelihoods, agricultural production, heritage resources and the built environment.

In addition, there are a number of other challenges facing the water sector such as ageing water and waste water infrastructure, a severe lack of skilled human resources in the area of water supply management, and illegal use of water. Water and sanitation pose a particular challenge, with many local governments simply unable to comply with their constitutional duties to provide such services.[10] The Green Drop Report[11] is a monitoring tool by national government to assess the management of waste water treatment facilities on an annual basis. The 2011 report paints a bleak picture, with at least three provinces failing dismally.[12] The Blue Drop Report,[13] on the other hand, is used to monitor water quality and measures the performance of water service authorities across the country. The system rewards (or penalises) a municipality upon evidence of its excellence (or failure). This is done according to the minimum standards or requirements that have been defined.[14] Whilst the system shows overall progress in water quality management, concerns are still raised,[15] and it is clear that numerous challenges remain if South Africa wants to adhere to the constitutional mandate to provide water to all South Africans.

20.3 WATER IN SCOTLAND

In contrast to South Africa, Scotland has an abundance of fresh water.[16] Its rainfall, which varies between 700mm and 1700mm per year, is the highest in the United Kingdom, and the Western Highlands of Scotland are wetter than most other parts of Europe. Scotland contains 70 per cent of the total area of inland surface water in the UK and 90 per cent of its volume; Loch Ness alone has almost twice the capacity of all the standing waters in the whole of England

---

[10] The Constitution of the Republic of South Africa, 1996, places some of the environmental functions within the scope of local governance, and Part B of Schedule 4 specifically relegates the functions of 'water and sanitation services' to local government. This is limited, however, to 'potable water supply systems and domestic waste-water and sewage disposal systems'.

[11] Available from *http://www.ewisa.co.za/misc/BLUE_GREENDROPREPORT/GreenDrop2011. htm* (accessed on 6 June 2012).

[12] These are the Northern Cape, Free State and Limpopo.

[13] Available from *http://www.ewisa.co.za/misc/BLUE_GREENDROPREPORT/BlueDrop2011. htm* (accessed on 6 June 2012).

[14] *Blue Drop Report*, note 13 supra, 3.

[15] L Boyd, R Tomkins and R Heath *South African Water Research Commission Report: Integrated Water Quality Management: A Mindset Change* (WRC Report No TT 450/10, 19 April 2010) available from *http://www.wrc.org.za/Knowledge%20Hub%20Documents/Research%20Reports/ TT%20450–10%20Integrated%20Water%20Resource%20Management.pdf* (accessed on 6 June 2012).

[16] *River Basin Management Plan for the Scotland River Basin District 2009–2015* (Scottish Environment Protection Agency 2009) 6.

and Wales. In addition to supplying drinking water and absorbing sewage, the aquatic environment is important to the Scottish economy, including its fishing and fish farming industries, hydropower generation, tourism and the production of Scotch whisky. The quality of fresh water in Scotland is currently high, and 65 per cent of the surface and groundwater bodies have been assessed as 'good' or better under the classification standards prescribed by European Union legislation.[17] Nevertheless, there remain significant problems in places as a result of human activities.[18] These include pollution and acidification from agriculture, sewage disposal and abandoned mines. Abstraction and impoundment for drinking water, irrigation, hydropower and other purposes create further pressures. In addition, some engineering operations for urban development, flood protection, agriculture and forestry have adverse impacts on water by altering the bed, banks and shores of rivers and lochs. Climate change is also likely to affect rainfall patterns in Scotland, resulting in wetter winters, drier summers and more frequent floods. The challenge for the Scottish government is to manage and reduce these impacts more effectively.

20.4 WATER LAW IN SOUTH AFRICA – THE CREATION OF THE RIPARIAN RIGHTS SYSTEM

Water law in South Africa evolved over time, intrinsically linked to and marked by the country's history of colonial dominance and apartheid. Before colonial rule and in terms of customary law water was part of the 'commons' and was not privately owned.[19] Dutch rule[20] introduced Roman-Dutch law which, while influenced by Roman law that distinguished between state-owned and privately-owned water, favoured the position that water was publicly owned.[21] The state was regarded as *dominus fluminis* and had the right to allocate water. Under British rule[22] the principle of *dominus fluminis* began to struggle for survival under the more liberal British system and individual rights to water were granted, introducing the riparian principle.[23] In the landmark decision of *Retief v Louw*[24] where the upstream owner diverted the whole of the stream's summer flow and thus deprived the downstream

17 Ibid 11.
18 Ibid 18.
19 S Burman *Cape Policies Towards African Law in Cape Tribal Territories 1872–1883* (unpublished DPhil thesis University of Oxford 1973) 412.
20 The Dutch landed in South Africa in 1652 and established a halfway station en route to the East.
21 Ownership was not clear. According to authors such as Voet, it belonged to citizens in common property, whilst van Leeuwen argued that it belonged to the state. H Thompson *Water Law* (Juta 2006) 27.
22 1806 to 1910.
23 D Tewari 'An Analysis of Evolution of Water Rights in South Africa: An Account of Three and a Half Centuries from 1652 AD to Present' (2009) 35(5) *Water SA* (2009) 693 at 698.
24 (1874) 4 Buch 165.

owner of water for drinking purposes and irrigation the Court held that for perennial streams running over several adjoining land parcels, landowners 'have each a common right in the use of water which use, at every stage of its exercise by any one of the proprietors, is limited by a consideration of rights of other proprietors'. This decision was followed by a series of other cases which sounded the death knell for the principle of *dominus fluminis*.[25] The principle of riparian rights was finally codified in the Irrigation Act 32 of 1906 of the Cape Colony, the Irrigation Act 11 of 1908 of the Zuid-Afrikaansce Republiek[26] and the Irrigation Act of 1887 of the Natal Colony, which after the former colonies were constituted as a union in 1910 culminated in the Irrigation and Conservation of Waters Act of 1912. The main purpose of this Act was to promote the development of land – that is, by way of large irrigation projects – and assisted riparian owners to use water from public streams to achieve such development. As such whilst public water could not be owned, riparian owners did have entitlements to public water. A landowner was able to enjoy exclusive and unlimited use and enjoyment of all water rising on his or her land,[27] with the only limitation being interference with the rights of another riparian owner.[28]

The riparian rights system was retained during the apartheid era in the Water Act[29] and was intrinsically linked to land access through a series of legislation aimed at dispossessing black people from land ownership.[30] As such the right to access water mirrored the right to access land and the majority of South Africans were consequently dispossessed of both. However, in light of the pressures of industrialisation during the first half of the twentieth century, the increased demand could not be accommodated by the traditional riparian principle.[31] Much more control over public water thus vested in the Minister of Water Affairs by way of so-called control areas where the control of water was deemed to be in the public interest.

Whilst the state had greater control over water, the Act still distinguished between private and public water. Private water was defined as all water which rises or falls naturally on any land or naturally drains or is led onto one or more pieces of land which are the subject of separate original grants, but is not capable of common use for irrigation purposes.[32] In other words it

---

[25] See *Hough v van der Merwe* (1874), *Vermaak v Palmer* (1875) and *Van Heerden v Wiese* (1880).

[26] The area before 1994 known as the Transvaal occupied by Afrikaners who resisted British colonial rule.

[27] S 23.

[28] S 8.

[29] Act 54 of 1956.

[30] See, for instance, the Native Land Act 27 of 1913, the Development Trust and Land Act 18 of 1936 and the Group Areas Acts 41 of 1950 and 36 of 1966.

[31] Tewari, note 23 supra, 701.

[32] S 1. According to s 5 the words 'which rises . . . naturally on land' were required to be taken to mean that point on land where water rises onto the surface from its sources.

was water which was not flowing or derived from a natural river, or where it derived from a natural river, where such water was not suitable for irrigation purposes on at least two or more pieces of riparian land and thus included, for example: spring water; rain water, surface water and drainage water before it joined a public stream; and public water that was no longer part of a river.[33] The owner of private water had exclusive use and enjoyment of such water on his or her land.[34] Some restrictions to the exercise of ownership applied. Private water could not, for instance, be sold to another person without the authorisation of the Minister of Water Affairs.[35] However, this did not apply to an owner of land situated in the area of a municipality or local authority.[36] An owner of private water was also not allowed to pollute the water.[37]

Public water was defined as any water flowing or found in or derived from the bed of a public stream, whether visible or not.[38] With regards to public water riparian owners were granted an entitlement to the reasonable use of the water for agricultural and urban purposes[39] and such a share in public water was either determined by the water court or could be lawfully acquired from another person.[40]

The major focus of the Water Act was the regulation of water use and the protection of the source from an environmental point of view received scant attention. It regulated pollution based on whether water was used for industrial purposes, urban purposes or other purposes. Major pollution cases were litigated not on the basis of the Act, but on common law principles such as the law of nuisance.[41]

By the end of the apartheid era private rights to water were linked to private property rights and landowners could not only assert ownership over

[33] Thompson, note 21 supra, 73.
[34] S 5(1).
[35] S 5(2).
[36] S 5(3)(c).
[37] S 23.
[38] S 1. This section defined public stream as a natural stream of water which flows in a known and defined channel, whether or not such channel is dry during any period of the year and whether or not its conformation has been changed by artificial means, if the water therein is capable of common use for irrigation on two or more pieces of such land and also on state land which is riparian to such stream, provided that a stream which fulfils the foregoing conditions in part only of its course shall be deemed to be a public stream as regards to that part only.
[39] 'Urban purposes' was defined in s 1 as the use of water in an area under the jurisdiction of a local authority for purposes for which water was ordinarily used by a local authority or by the inhabitants of the area, including use for domestic purposes or for the purposes of water-borne sanitation or for the watering of gardens, the watering or cleaning of streets or for industrial purposes.
[40] S 9(1) read with s 1.
[41] See, for instance, *Rainbow Chicken Farm (Pty) Limited v Mediterranean Woollen Mills (Pty) Limited* 1963 (1) SA 201 (N) and *Regal v African Superslate (Pty) Limited* 1963 (1) SA 102 (A).

so-called private water, they also had entitlements to public water which had the effect of ownership. Private rights to water operated in the context of a system where the majority of South Africans were dispossessed of land ownership through a series of laws enacted between 1913 and 1966.[42] Thus, at the dawn of democracy South Africa's history of water regulation left a legacy in which between 12 and 14 million people were without access to safe water and over 20 million were without adequate sanitation.[43] It also left behind deteriorating water quality as regulation of water pollution was based on a command and control approach combined with poor enforcement.[44] It was abundantly clear that private rights to a common resource set against the political and socio-economic context of South Africa were not in the interest of the majority of South Africans or the environment.

20.5 WATER LAW IN SCOTLAND

Scottish private law relating to water is derived from Roman law, and is similar in effect (although not in origin or detail) to the English common law principles of riparian rights that influenced South African law before the legislation of the nineteenth and twentieth centuries.[45] A distinction is drawn between tidal rivers (where the bed is presumed to belong to the Crown) and non-tidal rivers and streams (where the bed is private property).[46] The status of water that runs in defined channels is also distinguished from the ownership and use of standing water. In non-tidal rivers the proprietors of the adjacent land own the bed up to the *medium filum* (middle of the channel), but the water in its natural state is *res nullius* (ownerless). However, riparian proprietors share a common interest in the use of the water, which gives rise to both rights and obligations. Each proprietor is entitled to take any amount of water from the river for primary purposes (such as drinking by humans and animals) and for ordinary domestic purposes (such as cooking and washing). It does not matter if this adversely affects riparian landowners further downstream by reducing or depleting the water available for them. On the other hand, unless a prescriptive right has been acquired by long usage, a proprietor may only take water for secondary purposes like irrigation or manufacturing if the quantity and quality of the river is substantially undiminished as a result. Consequently, lower riparian owners may prevent

---

[42] Native Land Act 27 of 1913, the Development Trust and Land Act 18 of 1936, and the Group Areas Acts 41 of 1950 and 36 of 1966.

[43] *White Paper on a National Water Policy*, note 1 supra, para 2.2.3.

[44] C Bosman and M Kidd 'Water Pollution' in H Strydom and N King (eds) *Environmental Management in South Africa* 2e (Juta 2009) 630 at 651.

[45] For a discussion of the development of water rights in Scots law, see N Whitty 'Water Law Regimes' in K Reid and R Zimmermann (eds) *A History of Private Law in Scotland* (Oxford University Press 2000) vol 1 420.

[46] *Colquhoun's Trustees v Orr Ewing & Co* (1877) 4 R 344.

secondary uses by an upper proprietor that interfere with their own primary rights.

An inland loch that is completely surrounded by the land of a single owner is treated differently. In this situation, the proprietor arguably owns the water as well as the bed, and may use it as he or she wishes. If, on the other hand, the loch is bordered by land belonging to more than one owner, each proprietor normally owns the adjoining bed out to the middle of the loch, but they have a common interest in the water, which may be used for primary purposes as well as sailing and fishing. Nevertheless, if a loch feeds a river, the water of the loch may not be used in a way that infringes riparian rights over that river.

Surface or standing water that accumulates on land (such as a marsh) is regarded as *pars soli* (part of the soil) and may be appropriated and used without restriction. There is less certainty, however, about the status of groundwater beneath the land. If it flows in a defined channel, it seems reasonable to treat it in the same way as a river, but when it is merely percolating through the soil, it has been held to be *pars soli* in the case of *Crichton v Turnbull*.[47] Brian Clark has argued that this distinction is illogical, and that, by analogy with English law, percolating water should also be considered ownerless until it is abstracted.[48]

Although the traditional principles of private law continue to govern water rights in Scotland, the use of the aquatic environment has necessarily also been subject to statutory regulation, which affects the exercise of those rights. Legislation has been introduced since the middle of the nineteenth century to improve the supply of water and prevent pollution, and new public institutions have been created to implement it. More recently, European Union directives have dictated standards for the quality of drinking water and for environmental protection.

At present, there are two major national bodies responsible for different aspects of water in Scotland. The Scottish Environment Protection Agency (SEPA) was established on 1 April 1996 by the Environment Act 1995.[49] It is a non-departmental public body accountable to the Scottish Parliament through the Scottish Ministers. As a regulatory authority, it is tasked with maintaining and improving all parts of the environment, including land and air as well as water, and in relation to the latter it combines the functions of seven former river purification boards and three islands councils. SEPA has a general duty under section 34 of the 1995 Act to promote the cleanliness or rivers, inland waters and groundwater, and to conserve the water resources of Scotland. It also has responsibility for the national flood warning system.

---

[47] 1946 SC 52.
[48] B Clark 'Water Law in Scotland: the Water Environment and Water Services (Scotland) Act 2003 and the European Convention on Human Rights' (2006) 10(1) *EdinLR* 60 at 63.
[49] S 20.

The public supply of drinking water and the provision of sewerage services are undertaken by Scottish Water, which was created on 1 March 2002 by the Water Industry (Scotland) Act 2002.[50] Scottish Water is a publicly owned company, and replaced three regional water and sewerage authorities. It is required by section 1 of the Water (Scotland) Act 1980 to promote the conservation and effective use of water resources and the provision of adequate water supplies throughout Scotland; it must provide wholesome water wherever it is required for domestic purposes, if it can be supplied at a reasonable cost.[51] The assets of Scottish Water include 113 reservoirs, 45 lochs and 70,000 acres of catchments around reservoirs;[52] however, water resources have not been nationalised, and there remain about 30,000 private water supplies that rely on groundwater.[53] It is also the duty of Scottish Water under section 1 of the Sewerage (Scotland) Act 1968 to provide such public sewers as may be necessary for draining its area of domestic sewage, surface water and trade effluent, and to make provision for dealing with the contents of its sewers by sewage treatment works or other means. Scottish Water's performance is subject to supervision by the Water Industry Commission for Scotland and the Drinking Water Quality Regulator for Scotland.

In practice, however, the role of Scottish Water and SEPA not only depends on national legislation, but is also strongly influenced by European Union law. Thus, the quality of the drinking water supplied by Scottish Water and also private water supplies must comply with the standards of wholesomeness prescribed in the 1998 EU Drinking Water Directive.[54] Regulations have been made by the Scottish Ministers to implement its requirements.[55] Moreover, the 2000 EU Water Framework Directive[56] obliges EU Member States to identify river basin districts, and prepare river basin management plans to ensure that most waters are of 'good status' (defined in terms of environmental objectives and quality standards) by 2015. These requirements apply to surface freshwater and groundwater, in addition to estuaries and coastal waters. This Directive, which had to be implemented by 23 December 2003, was transposed into Scots law by the Water Environment and Water Services (Scotland) Act 2003.

---

[50] S 20.

[51] Water (Scotland) Act 1980, s 6(1). The limits of reasonable connection costs are determined by regulations: Provision of Water and Sewerage Services (Reasonable Cost) Regulations 2011 SSI 2011/119.

[52] *Building a Hydro Nation*, note 2 supra, s 2.1.

[53] *River Basin Management Plan*, note 16 supra, 6.

[54] Council Directive 98/83/EC OJ 1998 L330/32.

[55] Water Supply (Water Quality) (Scotland) Regulations 2001 SSI 2001/207, amended by SSI 2001/238 and 2010/95; Private Water Supplies (Scotland) Regulations 2006 SSI 2006/209, amended by SSI 2010/95.

[56] Directive 2000/60/EC OJ 2000– L327/1.

Cross-border arrangements between Scotland and England were introduced by separate regulations.[57] An important provision in article 11(3)(e) of the Water Framework Directive is a requirement that controls involving prior authorisation must be introduced for the abstraction of fresh surface water and groundwater, and for the impoundment of fresh surface water. Consequently, it has been necessary for Scottish legislation to control the exercise of riparian rights when they involve abstraction or impoundment, and both Scottish Water and private landowners must obtain water use licences from SEPA for these activities.[58]

20.6 THE HUMAN RIGHT TO WATER IN SOUTH AFRICA – IMPLICATIONS FOR PROPERTY RIGHTS

In a post-Constitutional order water regulation in South Africa has changed significantly with a greater emphasis on the environmental protection of the source and providing access to water to those people who had been deprived or had inadequate access for decades. In an effort to achieve this, the doctrine of public trust has been applied, riparian rights abolished and the state appointed as custodian of water resources.

The 1996 Constitution ushered in a new paradigm for the regulation of water, through the inclusion of two rights. Section 27 guarantees every South African the right of access to sufficient water and the state is obliged to take reasonable legislative and other measures within its available resources to achieve the progressive realisation of this right.[59] Section 24(a) guarantees a right to an environment that is not harmful to human health or well-being and to environmental protection for the benefit of present and future generations. Section 24(b) directs the state to take reasonable legislative and other measures to prevent pollution, promote conservation, and secure ecologically sustainable development and use of natural resources while promoting justifiable economic and social development. Together these rights require the state to ensure that water as a resource is conserved and protected and that access to the resource is provided.

A range of legislation was enacted to give effect to sections 27 and 24, including the National Environmental Management Act[60] (hereafter NEMA) which regulates the protection of all environmental sources, including water;

---

57 Water Environment (Water Framework Directive) (Northumbria River Basin District) Regulations 2003 SI 2003/3245; Water Environment (Water Framework Directive) (Solway Tweed River Basin District) Regulations 2004 SI 2004/99.

58 Water Environment (Controlled Activities) (Scotland) Regulations 2011 SSI 2011/209. These regulations replace the Water Environment (Controlled Activities) (Scotland) Regulations 2005 SSI 2005/348.

59 S 27(2).

60 Act 108 of 1998.

the National Water Services Act[61] (hereafter (NWSA) which regulates access to water; and the National Water Act[62] (hereafter NWA) which ensures the protection and conservation of water resources.

Together these different pieces of legislation implement the public trust doctrine in water law. This revives the notion of custodianship over water which was part of indigenous customary law and Roman-Dutch law, but, as argued by van der Schyff and Viljoen 'it is the legislative introduction of a foreign legal doctrine that displays similarities with, but goes beyond customary and common law principles'.[63] The authors observe that the doctrine of public trust as it manifests in water legislation is now a statutory creation. One can argue that in essence the South African version of the public trust doctrine is fundamentally derived from the dictates of the Constitution and particularly from section 24, the environmental right, and is circumscribed by the applicable legislation.

The operation of the public trust doctrine was summarised in the *National Water Resources Strategy*[64] as follows:

'As custodian of the Nation's water resources, the National Government shall ensure that the development, apportionment, management and use of those resources is carried out using the criteria of public interest, sustainability, equity and efficiency of use in a manner which reflects its public trust obligations and the value of water to society while ensuring that basic domestic needs, the requirements of the environment and international obligations are met.'

This is reiterated in section 3 of the NWA, which declares that the National Government, acting through the Minister, is the public trustee of the nation's water resources, and must ensure that water is, *inter alia*, protected, conserved and managed in a sustainable and equitable manner for the benefit of all. Consequently, the NWA does away with the concept of riparian rights or entitlements to private water. Instead, the state is custodian over all water resources and water use is regulated by way of a water use system that includes general authorisations and licenses.[65]

Private rights in water therefore no longer exist and constitutional protection *vis-à-vis* the property clause[66] in the Constitution is not an option. The right to hold rights in property, public or private is not guaranteed. The property clause does not expressly bestow a right to acquire and hold rights in property. Instead, it provides for minimum requirements in respect

---

[61] Act 108 of 1997.
[62] Act 36 of 1998.
[63] E van der Schyff and G Viljoen 'Water and the Public Trust Doctrine – A South African Perspective' (2008) 4(2) *Journal for Transdisciplinary Research in Southern Africa* 339 at 342.
[64] Note 5 supra, A1.
[65] Ch 4 of the NWA.
[66] S 25 of the Constitution.

of deprivations of property rights and expropriation of those rights.[67] The property clause must be read in the broader context of South Africa's history and the post-apartheid goals to ensure access to housing, health care and resources such as food and water and from an environmental perspective, South Africa's commitment to sustainable development. As such the right to property must not only be balanced against the right to equality[68] and the right to access to housing,[69] but also the right to access to water and an environment not harmful to health and well-being. In order to fulfil the constitutional mandate of granting each South African access to sufficient water, the state has subsumed trusteeship over water resources. As custodian of water resources the state has the duty to ensure that water is used sustainably and that it is not polluted. In exercising this duty, the state may, in fact, intrude upon the property rights of land owners.

For example, water and environmental legislation includes stringent efforts to protect water resources from pollution[70] and owners of land are now under a strict obligation to prevent pollution of water sources and to employ clean-up measures where a water source has been polluted. The duty to take remedial or other measures applies not only where the pollution was caused by the property owner, but even where it was caused by another and without the knowledge of the property owner.[71] In fact, the courts have gone further and interpreted the NWA as placing strict requirements on owners of land to employ measures to prevent pollution of water, even when the source of the pollution does not originate on said land.

In *Harmony Gold Mining Co Ltd v Regional Director: Free State, Department of Water Affairs and Forestry*[72] a directive issued in terms of section 19(3) of the NWA was interpreted to include the obligation to take clean-up measures on land belonging to another. The case dealt with acid mine drainage and the appellant, Harmony Gold Mining Company, was one of five gold mining companies with mines in the Klerksdorp-Orkney-Stilfontein-Hartebeesfontein (KOSH) basin of North-West Province.[73] The mines were all linked underground and they utilised a labyrinth of horizontal tunnels by means of which groundwater can pass, downstream, from the northern to the southern mines. When water comes into contact with mined-out reefs it becomes polluted and this polluted water was threatening a water source.[74]

The mines started a process of dewatering to extract water at the highest

---

[67] S 25(2), (3) and (4).

[68] S 9 of the Constitution.

[69] S 26 of the Constitution.

[70] See s 19 of the NWA and s 28 of the NEMA.

[71] S 19(1) and (2) of the NWA and s 28(2) read with s 28(1).

[72] [2006] SCA 65 RSA.

[73] The mines are Stilfontein, Buffelsfontein, Hartebeesfontein, Harmony and Anglogold.

[74] *Harmony Gold Mining Co Ltd v Regional Director: Free State, Department of Water Affairs and Forestry* [2006] SCA 65 RSA para 2.

possible level before it becomes polluted and to prevent the deeper mines becoming flooded. The three shallower mines were designed to extract large volumes of water. Because such volumes were not encountered in the deeper mines, their pumps did not have the capacity to extract volumes as large as those of the defunct mines. Accordingly if the upstream mines were to cease dewatering and their water flowed into the Harmony and Anglogold mines, the latter would be incapable of coping with the increased volume and extensive flooding would occur with resultant risk of large-scale loss of life and certain loss of property.

One of the upstream mines, Buffelsfontein, was placed under provisional liquidation and the provisional liquidators gave notice that Buffelsfontein had no funds to pay for continued pumping; the liquidators requested that all the mines in the KOSH basin joined forces with the Stilfontein, Harmony and Anglogold companies in order to fund and secure the dewatering of the defunct mines.[75] However, no joint arrangement came into being and one of the mine owners, the Anglogold company, applied in the High Court for an order, *inter alia*, compelling the Minister of Water Affairs and Forestry to direct the Stilfontein company and the liquidators of Buffelsfontein to continue the dewatering of the three northern mines.

While the Anglogold application was pending, the Regional Director of Water Affairs: Free State, issued two directives to the appellant and the Anglogold and Stilfontein companies respectively ordering the recipients to 'collect, remove and contain water arising in the KOSH basin at the most appropriate location, treat it to standards as may be prescribed from time to time, and use or discharge it in a legal manner' and also requiring Harmony to provide the Regional Director with a determination of its financial capacity, given the respective surface and underground areas exposed by its operations, to contribute to the cost of dewatering at the three northern mines.[76] This directive was the basis for an application to the High Court to set aside the directive. The application was dismissed and the Judge held that 'inadequate dewatering at the northernmost mines would result in the unremoved water reaching appellant's mine and becoming polluted and the matter therefore fell within the provisions of s 19 of the Act, duly enabling the direction in question'.[77] The basis for the appeal was that a directive under section 19(3) could only be given in the event of a failure to take the measures mentioned in subsection (1), and those measures were confined to measures to be taken by the persons, and on the land, referred to in the latter subsection. Harmony argued that the section did not require of those persons that they take, or pay for, anti-pollution measures on *another's* land such as those

---

[75] Ibid para 4.
[76] Ibid paras 7 and 8.
[77] Ibid para 12.

the supplementary directive required of the appellant.[78] In dismissing the appeal, the Supreme Court of Appeal (SCA) held that:

> 'nothing in the wording of Section 19 (1) and (2) warrants the conclusion that the measures required are intended to be confined to the land of the person obliged to take such measures and . . . the wording is wide enough to include measures on another's land.'[79]

It furthermore held that whilst one may not be responsible for the pollution on someone else's land, a person can be directed to take 'reasonable anti-pollution measures' to prevent groundwater from the defunct mines reaching the active ones. In this respect the Court argued that the constitutional and statutory anti-pollution objectives would be obstructed if the measures required of the persons referred to in section 19 were limited to measures on the land mentioned in that subsection.[80]

In essence the constitutional entrenchment of water rights as a socio-economic right and the accompanying protection of the resource by way of the environmental right has not only curbed the extent to which property owners may exercise private rights to water, but has also placed additional burdens on them so as to ensure the protection of the resource.

20.7 HUMAN RIGHTS AND WATER IN SCOTLAND: IMPLICATIONS FOR PROPERTY RIGHTS

Unlike South Africa, the United Kingdom is a party to the International Covenant on Economic, Social and Cultural Rights, which was adopted by the UN General Assembly in December 1966 and entered into force in January 1976. The Covenant does not expressly provide a right to water, but a right to water and sanitation has now been recognised by the UN General Assembly.[81] It forms part of article 11 of the Covenant. Article 11 recognises 'the right of everyone to an adequate standard of living for himself and his family, including adequate food, clothing and housing, and to the continuous improvement of living conditions'.[82] The word 'including' indicates that the reference to food, housing and clothing is not intended to be exhaustive, and access to water is clearly essential for an adequate standard of living. This interpretation is supported by article 12 which acknowledges 'the right of everyone to the enjoyment of the highest attainable standard of physical and mental health',[83] and the steps to be taken by State Parties in order

[78] Ibid para 15.
[79] Ibid para 32.
[80] Ibid para 33.
[81] UN General Assembly *The Human Right to Water and Sanitation* UN Doc A/64/L63/Rev 1, 26 July 2010.
[82] International Covenant on Economic, Social and Cultural Rights, art 11(1).
[83] Ibid art 12(1).

to achieve this include 'improvements in all aspects of environmental and industrial hygiene'.[84] Unpolluted water is obviously essential for physical health. Although the Covenant is binding on the United Kingdom, it has not been specifically incorporated in domestic law, and the fulfilment of these provisions depends therefore on the legal and administrative measures that have been taken to ensure the availability of a sufficient supply of pure fresh water.

There is no explicit right to water in the ECHR. It could perhaps be argued that the right to life under article 2 implies an entitlement to water on which life depends, but article 2 is primarily concerned with preventing unlawful deprivation of life, and it does not analyse the content of the right to life, which it merely acknowledges in the statement that 'everyone's right to life shall be protected by law'. However, there are two other provisions in the ECHR that are relevant to the environment. Article 8 declares the right to respect for private and family life, which includes a person's home. The right expressed in paragraph (1) of article 8 is not absolute, since it is qualified by the exceptions in paragraph (2), which allow interference if it is supported by law and is necessary, for example on social or economic grounds. This inevitably requires competing interests to be balanced, and the restriction of a right must be proportionate to the importance of the purpose served, and must be applied without discrimination.[85] However, the European Court of Human Rights has repeatedly held that States have a wide 'margin of appreciation' or discretion in determining such questions, and the courts should not substitute their own assessment of the best policy to be adopted. Article 1 of the First Protocol further concerns the right to the peaceful enjoyment of possessions, which can include land and buildings, but is similarly subject to qualifications, and the public interest may justify deprivation of property or restrictions on its use.

While a number of cases have accepted the responsibility of public authorities to prevent nuisances such as noise, atmospheric emissions and smells caused by the activities of third parties that interfered with the enjoyment of private property,[86] there has been little litigation about water. In the English case of *Marcic v Thames Water Utilities Ltd*[87] the House of Lords held that a householder whose land was repeatedly flooded by surface water and effluent from an overloaded public sewer could not succeed in a court action against the water company under the Human Rights Act 1998, because the Water Industry Act 1991[88] provided a statutory scheme for the regulation

---

[84] Ibid art 12(2)(b).
[85] ECHR art 14.
[86] *Baggs v United Kingdom* (1985) 9 EHRR 235; *S v France* (1990) 65 DR 250; *Lopez Ostra v Spain* (1994) 20 EHRR 277; *Guerra v Italy* (1998) 26 EHRR 357; *Hatton v United Kingdom* (2003) EHRR 611.
[87] [2004] AC 42.
[88] S 18.

of sewerage undertakers that was compatible with Convention rights. It was the function of the Director General of Water Services to balance public and private interests when deciding whether to take enforcement action again water companies.

The situation in the *Marcic* case related specifically to sewer flooding, and the House of Lords' decision should not be interpreted as excluding the possibility of direct litigation against Scottish Water or SEPA for breach of human rights. Nevertheless, they enjoy the same margin of discretion, and provided that they take all relevant considerations into account, their decisions should not be reviewable by the courts unless they are wholly unreasonable. However, a theoretical question arises as to whether the statutory requirement to obtain a water use licence from SEPA under the Water Environment (Controlled Activities) (Scotland) Regulations 2011[89] for the abstraction of surface water or groundwater or for the construction of impounding works breaches the human rights of landowners under article 1 of the First Protocol to the ECHR. Arguably, there is no deprivation of property by the mere creation of a licensing system, unless a licence is actually refused or made subject to onerous conditions. Yet, although running water (in contrast to standing water) is not the property of a landowner until it is taken into possession, the right to do so is a form of property, which might thus be restricted by a licence. On the other hand, the imposition of environmental controls implementing European Union directives is likely to be regarded by the courts as justified in the public interest, and there seems little prospect of it giving rise to compensation. The same considerations will probably apply if a water use licence is subsequently varied or revoked, provided that the decision is reasonable.[90] However, it has been argued that SEPA might be liable for a breach of its positive obligation to act consistently with Convention rights, if the grant of a licence to abstract water on one person's of land results in subsidence of someone else's property or deprives lower riparian proprietors of their right to receive the flow.[91]

20.8 CONCLUSION

South Africa has made a constitutional commitment to sustainable development. As such human rights such as the right to access to water and the environmental right have led to a return of the doctrine of public trust. It is thus mandated by the Constitution and legislated in the National Water Act and now forms the framework against which all decisions to allocate water

---

[89] SSI 2011/209.
[90] Clark, note 48 supra, 86–8.
[91] Ibid 89–100. Moreover the Regulations themselves could be liable to challenge as outside the legislative competence of the Scottish Parliament if they breached Convention rights (Scotland Act 1998, s 29(1)).

resources are taken. South Africa's scant water resources and its challenges with regards to water quality leave no room for private rights to water, especially in light of the country's socio-political history. As a result legislation that implements the new constitutional dispensation has not only eliminated property rights in water, but has arguably placed more incursive burdens on owners of land.

In contrast to South Africa, private law still remains the fundamental source of water rights in Scotland. Although legislation has placed restrictions on the exercise of those rights in the interests of public health and environmental protection, the modern stimulus for doing so is largely attributable to European Union law rather than human rights considerations. In a country with abundant water resources, it is understandably difficult to discern an explicit human right to water. Although international conventions by which Scotland (as part of the United Kingdom) is bound to support such a right, the European Convention on Human Rights (ECHR) provides protection from environmental nuisances rather than access to environmental resources. It is paradoxical that the ECHR is more likely to protect the rights of Scottish landowners to exploit the aquatic environment than to enable the public in general to enjoy it.

Index